NON-MONOTONIC REASONING

Formalization of Commonsense Reasoning

ELLIS HORWOOD SERIES IN ARTIFICIAL INTELLIGENCE

Joint Series Editors: Professor JOHN CAMPBELL, Department of Computer Science, University College London, and
Dr JEAN HAYES MICHIE, Research Associate, The Turing Institute, Glasgow

Anderson, J. (editor)	POP-11 COMES OF AGE: The Advancement of an AI Programming Language
Andrew, A.M.	CONTINUOUS HEURISTICS: The Prelinguistic Basis of Intelligence
Attar, A.	KNOWLEDGE ENGINEERING*
Bergadano, F., Giordana, A. & Saitta, L.	MACHINE LEARNING: A General Framework and its Applications
Bläsius, K.H. and Bürckert, H.-J.	DEDUCTION SYSTEMS IN AI
Bramer, M.A. (editor)	COMPUTER GAME PLAYING: Theory and Practice
Campbell, J.A. (editor)	IMPLEMENTATIONS OF PROLOG
Campbell, J.A. and Cuena, J. (editors)	PERSPECTIVES IN ARTIFICIAL INTELLIGENCE, Vols 1 & 2
Campbell, J. A. & Cox, P.	IMPLEMENTATIONS OF PROLOG, Vol. 2*
Carter, D.	INTERPRETING ANAPHORS IN NATURAL LANGUAGE TEXTS
Craig, I.D.	FORMAL SPECIFICATION OF ADVANCED PROBLEM SOLVING ARCHITECTURES
Davies, R. (editor)	INTELLIGENT INFORMATION SYSTEMS: Progress and Prospects
Evans, J.B.	STRUCTURES OF DISCRETE EVENT SIMULATION
Farreny, H.	AI AND EXPERTISE
Forsyth, R. & Rada, R.	MACHINE LEARNING: Applications in Expert Systems and Information Retrieval
Frixione, S.G., Gaglio, S., and Spinelli, G.	REPRESENTING CONCEPTS IN SEMANTIC NETS
Fútó, I. & Gergely, T.	ARTIFICIAL INTELLIGENCE IN SIMULATION
Gabbay, D.M.	PROGRAMMING IN PURE LOGIC*
Gottinger, H.W. & Weimann, H.P.	ARTIFICIAL INTELLIGENCE: A Tool for Industry and Management
Hawley, R. (editor)	ARTIFICIAL INTELLIGENCE PROGRAMMING ENVIRONMENTS
Hayes, J.E. & Michie, D. (editors)	INTELLIGENT SYSTEMS: The Unprecedented Opportunity
Levy, D.N.L. & Beal, D.F. (editors)	HEURISTIC PROGRAMMING IN ARTIFICIAL INTELLIGENCE: The First Computer Olympiad
Lopez de Mántaras, R.	APPROXIMATE REASONING MODELS
Łukaszewicz, W.	NON-MONOTONIC REASONING: Formalization of Commonsense Reasoning
McGraw, K. & Westphal, C.	READINGS IN KNOWLEDGE ACQUISITION: Current Practices and Trends
Mellish, C.	COMPUTER INTERPRETATION OF NATURAL LANGUAGE DESCRIPTIONS
Michie, D.	ON MACHINE INTELLIGENCE, Second Edition
Mortimer, H.	THE LOGIC OF INDUCTION
Mozetic, I.	MACHINE LEARNING OF QUALITATIVE MODELS*
Obermeier, K.K.	NATURAL LANGUAGE PROCESSING TECHNOLOGIES IN ARTIFICIAL INTELLIGENCE
Partridge, D.	ARTIFICIAL INTELLIGENCE: Applications in the Future of Software Engineering
Ramsay, A. & Barrett, R.	AI IN PRACTICE: Examples in POP-11
Ras, Z.W. & Zemankova, M.	INTELLIGENT SYSTEMS: State of the Art and Future Directions
Saint-Dizier, P. & Szpakowicz, S. (editors)	LOGIC AND LOGIC GRAMMARS FOR LANGUAGE PROCESSING
Savory, S.E.	ARTIFICIAL INTELLIGENCE AND EXPERT SYSTEMS
Shanahan, M. & Southwick, R.	SEARCH, INFERENCE AND DEPENDENCIES IN ARTIFICIAL INTELLIGENCE
Spacek, L.	ADVANCED PROGRAMMING IN PROLOG
Sparck Jones, K. & Wilks, Y. (editors)	AUTOMATIC NATURAL LANGUAGE PARSING
Steels, L. & Campbell, J.A. (editors)	PROGRESS IN ARTIFICIAL INTELLIGENCE
Smith, B. & Kelleher, G. (editors)	REASON MAINTENANCE SYSTEMS AND THEIR APPLICATIONS
Torrance, S. (editor)	THE MIND AND THE MACHINE
Turner, R.	LOGICS FOR ARTIFICIAL INTELLIGENCE
Wallace, M.	COMMUNICATING WITH DATABASES IN NATURAL LANGUAGE
Wertz, H.	AUTOMATIC CORRECTION AND IMPROVEMENT OF PROGRAMS
Yazdani, M. (editor)	NEW HORIZONS IN EDUCATIONAL COMPUTING
Yazdani, M. & Narayanan, A. (editors)	ARTIFICIAL INTELLIGENCE: Human Effects
Zeidenberg, M.	NEURAL NETWORKS IN ARTIFICIAL INTELLIGENCE

* *In preparation*

NON-MONOTONIC REASONING
Formalization of Commonsense Reasoning

WITOLD ŁUKASZEWICZ
Institute of Informatics
University of Warsaw

ELLIS HORWOOD
NEW YORK LONDON TORONTO SYDNEY TOKYO SINGAPORE

First published in 1990 by
ELLIS HORWOOD LIMITED
Market Cross House, Cooper Street,
Chichester, West Sussex, PO19 1EB, England
A division of
Simon & Schuster International Group
A Paramount Communications Company

Printed and bound in Great Britain
by Hartnolls, Bodmin, Cornwall

British Library Cataloguing in Publication Data

Łukaszewicz, Witold
Non-monotonic reasoning: formalization of commonsense reasoning. —
(Ellis Horwood series in artificial intelligence)
1. Artificial intelligence. Applications of human reasoning
I. Title
006.3
ISBN 0–13–624446–7

Library of Congress Cataloging-in-Publication Data

Łukaszewicz, Witold
Non-monotonic reasoning: formalization of commonsense reasoning /
Witold Łukaszewicz
p. cm. — (Ellis Horwood series in artificial intelligence)
ISBN 0–13–624446–7
1. Artificial intelligence. 2. Reasoning. 3. Logic. I. Title. II. Series.
Q335.L85 1990
006.3–dc20

90–40206
CIP

Table of contents

Preface

Non-monotonic reasoning can be loosely described as the process of drawing conclusions which may be invalidated by new information. Owing to its close relationship to human common-sense reasoning, non-monotonic inference has become one of the major research topics in the field of artificial intelligence (AI).

I have attempted to achieve two goals in writing this book. One was to explain what non-monotonic reasoning is and how it has been approached in the AI research. The other was to provide a detailed study of the most influential non-monotonic logics. The book is primarily addressed to students and research workers in AI (and related disciplines), but should also be useful to practitioners involved in expert and intelligent knowledge-based systems.

Great care has been taken to make this book totally self-contained. Chapter 1 collects all the background material needed in the following chapters. The reader will find there a summary of set-theoretic notions, a presentation of classical (propositional, first- and second-order) logic, including many-sorted first-order logic and elements of automated theorem proving, and a brief exposition of modal logics.

Chapter 2 presents a general discussion of the subject of non-monotonic reasoning. It contains such topics as the role of non-monotonicity in AI, a typology of non-monotonic inference, and a relation between non-monotonic reasoning and reasoning about action.

The goal of Chapter 3 is to give basic ideas of how non-monotonic reasoning has been dealt with in the AI research. The most important computational systems exhibiting non-monotonic behaviour are surveyed and then the leading formal approaches to non-monotonic inference are briefly presented. After completing this chapter, the reader should possess a representative up-to-date picture of the field.

Chapters 4 to 7 provide a detailed study of the most prominent non-monotonic formalisms. Some of the results stated here are new to the literature, and some known results have been given in a more general form. These chapters are more difficult to read and their understanding demands a certain maturity in symbolic thinking. Extensive discussions and carefully chosen examples have been provided for the novice reader.

Chapter 4 presents a number of non-monotonic logics based on modal languages. The most important formalism of this class is autoepistemic logic, studied in Section 4.3. In Chapter 5 two versions of default logic, a famous non-monotonic system developed by Reiter, are examined. In Chapter 6 several versions of circumscription, which according to many AI researchers is the most important formal contribution to the field of non-monotonic reasoning, are extensively discussed. Finally, in Chapter 7 is presented a variety of logics specially developed for the purpose of formalizing the closed-world assumption. These proposals are closely related to the area of logic programming and the theory of databases.

Although the book is written as to be comprehensible without a teacher, it can be used for a graduate course in non-monotonic reasoning. Such a course should treat Chapters 2 and 3, with sections 2.3 and 3.3 possibly omitted, and elements of Chapters 4–7. The material of the following sections is recommended for a two-semester course:

> 4.1, 4.2 (optional), 4.3.1–4.3.4, 5.1–5.6, 5.10–5.11, 6.1–6.3, 6.5.1–6.5.5, 7.1–7.2, 7.5 (optional), 7.6.

Numerous examples incorporated in the text can be employed as routine exercises to test the understanding of the introduced material.

The stylistic conventions we use are fairly standard. The symbol ▌ designates the end of a theorem, an example or a displayed definition. The symbol ■ indicates the end of a lemma. Expressions which are being defined are put in *italics*. Also variables, formulae, and meta-variables denoting formulae are italicized. I have written 'iff' for 'if and only if', and 'wrt' for 'with respect to'.

Acknowledgements

Barbara Dunin-Kęplicz deserves my special thanks for her constant encouragement and many criticisms. She promptly read various drafts of the manuscript, and her suggestions greatly contributed to the final form of the text.

I would also thank Professor Władysław M. Turski and Jacek Pacholczyk for constructive comments and many valuable discussions. Ewa Madalińska found a counter-example to one of the stated results, which led me to provide its correct version. A special thank you to Andrzej Piesiewicz for preparing drawings.

I am indebted to my Ellis Horwood editor, Sue Horwood, for her encouragement and patience during our cooperation.

My deepest thanks go to my wife, Ala, for her patience and understanding support.

This work was sponsored by Polish Ministry of Education under Project R.P.I.09.

Notation

List of non-monotonic logics discussed in the book

4. CWA LOGICS

5. OTHER FORMALISMS

1

Elements of monotonic logics

This chapter provides the necessary background to follow the material contained in the rest of the book. It begins by summarizing the basic mathematical notions used in the text; the propositional part of classical logic is then outlined. The following two sections are devoted to classical first-order logic. In particular, the resolution method is presented, which underlies automated theorem proving in this formalism. Next, we sketch classical second-order logic, widely used in Chapter 6, concluding by briefly discussing modal logic, which forms a theoretic basis for several non-monotonic systems presented in Chapter 4.

The reader familiar with the material contained in this chapter is asked to examine the notation introduced here, because it will be employed throughout the book.

1.1 BASIC NOTIONS

To fix some terminological and notational conventions, we start with a brief summary of various, mostly set-theoretic, notions used in the book.[†]

A *set* is a collection of objects, called *elements* or *members* of the set. No special assumptions as regards the collections which form sets are made, but care will always be taken to avoid paradoxes.[‡] We write $x \in X$ to indicate that x is a member of X. If $x \in X$, then we also say that x *belongs to* X or X *contains* x. As usual, $x \notin X$ stands for the negation of $x \in X$. The notation $x_1, \ldots, x_n \in X$ is an abbreviation for $x_1 \in X, \ldots, x_n \in X$.

[†] For an easy introduction to set theory, see Vaught (1985). A detailed exposition of the subject can be found in Fraenkel *et al.* (1973).

[‡] As common-sense shows, it is necessary to impose some restrictions on the concept of a set. Suppose, for instance, that X is specified as the set of all sets which are not members of themselves, and consider the question whether or not X is its own member. It is easy to see that the answer 'yes' implies the answer 'no' and vice versa, so that the specification of X leads to a contradiction. This example is known in the philosophical literature as Russell's paradox.

The set whose elements are precisely $x_1, \ldots, x_n$ will be denoted by $\{x_1, \ldots, x_n\}$. In particular, the symbol $\{\ \}$ stands for the *empty set*, i.e. the set with no elements at all. If P(x) is a property determining a set, then this set will be denoted by $\{x: P(x)\}$.† For example, if Z denotes the set of integers, then $\{x: x \in Z \text{ and } x > 2\}$ is the set of all integers greater than 2. (Here $P(x)$ is '$x \in Z$ and $x > 2$'.)

If every member of X is a member of Y, then we say that X is a *subset of* Y (alternatively, Y is a *superset of* X), and we write $X \subseteq Y$. For any objects x and y, including sets, we write $x = y$ iff x and y are identical. The negation for '$x = y$' is written '$x \neq y$'. Two sets are assumed identical iff they have the same members, i.e. for any sets X and Y, $X = Y$ iff $X \subseteq Y$ and $Y \subseteq X$. Note that $\{1, 2\} = \{1, 2, 1\}$. X is said to be a *proper subset of* Y, written $X \subset Y$, iff $X \subseteq Y$ but $X \neq Y$. In other words, X is a proper subset of Y iff every member of X is a member of Y, but Y contains an element which does not belong to X. If X is a set, then the set of all subsets of X is denoted by 2^X. 2^X is called the *power set of* X.

For any sets X and Y, $X \cup Y$ is the *union of* X and Y, i.e. the set of all elements which belong to X or to Y or to both. $X \cap Y$ is the *intersection of* X *and* Y, i.e. the set of all objects which belong to both X and Y. Finally, X–Y denotes the *difference of* X *and* Y, i.e. the set of those elements of X which are not members of Y. If $X \cap Y = \{\ \}$, then we say that X and Y are *disjoint*. A *partition of a set* X is any set of non-empty subsets of X enjoying the following properties: (i) Any two distinct subsets are disjoint; (ii) Every element of X lies in one subset.

If I is a set, then $\bigcup_{i \in I} X_i$ (resp. $\bigcap_{i \in I} X_i$) denotes the *union* (resp. the *intersection*) *of sets* X_i, for $i \in I$, i.e. the set of all elements belonging to at least one of the sets (resp. to each of the sets) X_i, for $i \in I$. If I is the set of all intgers greater than $k - 1$, then we write $\bigcup_{i=k}^{\infty} X_i$ and $\bigcap_{i=k}^{\infty} X_i$ instead of $\bigcup_{i \in I} X_i$ and $\bigcap_{i \in I} X_i$, respectively.

Given any objects $x_1, \ldots, x_n$, $n \geq 0$, we denote by $\langle x_1, \ldots, x_n \rangle$ the *(ordered) n-tuple of* $x_1, \ldots, x_n$.‡ The basic property of n-tuples is that $\langle x_1, \ldots, x_n \rangle = \langle y_1, \ldots, y_n \rangle$ iff $x_i = y_i$, for $1 \leq i \leq n$. 2-tuples, 3-tuples and 4-tuples are called *pairs*, *triples* and *quadruples*, respectively. If the value of n is inessential, or, if it follows from the context, the term 'n-tuple' will be abbreviated to 'tuple'. The symbol $\langle\rangle$ stands for the *empty tuple*. Note that $\langle\rangle$ is the only 0-tuple. Occasionally, tuples will be referred to as *lists*. Also, when it is clear from the context, we shall sometimes write $(x_1, \ldots, x_n)$, or even $x_1, \ldots, x_n$, instead of $\langle x_1, \ldots, x_n \rangle$. Two tuples are said to be *disjoint* iff they have no element in common.

For any non-empty sets $X_1, \ldots, X_n$ $(n \geq 0)$, the *Cartesian product of* $X_1, \ldots, X_n$, written $X_1 x \ldots x X_n$, is the set $\{\langle x_1, \ldots, x_n \rangle : x_1 \in X_1, \ldots, x_n \in X_n\}$. X^n is an abbreviation for $Xx \ldots xX$ (n times). In words, X^n is the set of all n-tuples of elements of X. Note that $X^0 = \{\langle\rangle\}$. We adopt the convention that X^1 is identified with X. This permits us, when convenient, to regard any non-empty set as a Cartesian product.

Let X and Y be non-empty sets and suppose that $f \subseteq XxY$. We say that f is a

† Not every property determines a set. For example, there is no set corresponding to the property P stating 'x has the property P iff x is a set which is not its own member'.

‡ Putting the word 'ordered' in parentheses, we indicate that the phrase 'ordered n-tuple' will be usually abbreviated to 'n-tuple'. We shall often employ this convention in the sequel.

function from X *into* Y (alternatively, a *function defined on* X *with values in* Y), and we write f: X → Y, iff for each element x ∈ X there is a unique y ∈ Y such that ⟨x, y⟩ ∈ f; this unique y is denoted by f(x) or f_x, and is referred to as the *value of* f *at* x (synonymously, the *value assigned to* x *by* f). The set X (resp. Y) is called the *domain* (resp. the *counter-domain*) *of* f. If X is $X_1 x \ldots x X_n$ ($n \geq 1$), then f is said to be an n-*ary function*. (Synonymous expressions are 'a *function of arity* n', 'an n-*place function*' and 'a *function of* n *arguments*'.) We usually write $f(x_1, \ldots, x_n)$ instead of $f(\langle x_1, \ldots, x_n \rangle)$. If $X = \{\langle\rangle\}$, then we say that f is an 0-*ary function*. We adopt the convention that each 0-ary function f is identified with a fixed element of its counter-domain, namely with $f(\langle\rangle)$. If f is a function from X into Y and $Z \subseteq X$, then $f|_z$ is the *restriction of* f *to* Z, i.e. the function g: Z → Y such that g(z) = f(z), for every z ∈ Z. In this book, the terms *function*, *mapping*, *transformation*, *operation*, *operator* and *assignment* are regarded as synonyms.

Functions defined on positive (or non-negative) integers are called (*infinite*) *sequences*. Functions specified on a set $\{i, i + 1, \ldots, i + k\}$, where i and k are non-negative integers, are called (*finite*) *sequences*. If f is a sequence and n is in the domain of f, then f(n) is usually written f_n, and the sequence is denoted by $f_1, f_2, \ldots$ $(f_0, f_1, \ldots; f_i, f_{i+1}, \ldots f_{i+k})$.

Let f: X → Y. The *range of* f, written f(X), is the set of all elements f(x), where x ∈ X. We say that f is *surjective* (or a *function from* X *onto* Y) iff f(X) = Y. For instance, if X is the set of integers, then the function f given by f(x) = 2x is surjective, provided that Y is the set of even integers. On the other hand, f is not surjective if Y = X. We say that f is *injective* (or *one-to-one*) iff f(x) = f(x′) implies x = x′. For example, if X and Y are the sets of integers, then the function f given by f(x) = 2x is injective, whereas the function g specified by $g(x) = x^2$ is not. If f is injective, then f^{-1} denotes the *inverse of* f, i.e. the function from f(X) into X such that $f^{-1}(y) = x$ iff f(x) = y. For instance, if X and Y are the sets of integers and f is given by f(x) = 2x, then f^{-1} is the function from even integers into integers such that $f^{-1}(y) = y/2$. A function which is both surjective and injective is said to be *bijective*. If f: X → Y and g: Y → Z, then the *superposition of* f *and* g, written f ∘ g or fg, is the function from X into Z such that f ∘ g(x) = f(g(x)), for all x ∈ X. For instance, if X, Y and Z are the sets of integers, f(x) = 2x and $g(x) = x^2$, then $f \circ g(x) = 2x^2$, whereas $g \circ f(x) = 4x^2$.

A set X is said to be *equinumerous* (or *equipotent*) *with a set* Y, written X ~ Y, iff there is a bijective function f: X → Y. If f: X → Y is bijective, then f^{-1}: Y → X is also bijective, so that X ~ Y iff Y ~ X. For example, if X is the set of positive integers and Y is the set of even positive integers, then X ~ Y, since f(x) = 2x is a bijective function from X onto Y. On the other hand, Y ~ X, because the inverse of f, namely $f^{-1}(x) = x/2$, is a bijective function from Y onto X. If X ~ Y, then we also say that there is *one-to-one correspondence between* X *and* Y.

To any set X, there is uniquely assigned an abstract entity, called the *cardinal number of* X, in such a way that two sets, X and Y, are assigned the same cardinal number iff X ~ Y. The cardinal number of X is also called the *power of* X, and is denoted by card(X). The power of a finite set is just the number of its elements. In particular, card({ }) = 0. Any set equinumerous with the set of non-negative integers is said to be *denumerable* and its cardinal number is denoted by $\aleph_0$. Any set equinumerous with the set of all subsets of a denumerable set has the cardinal number $\mathfrak{c}$ and is said to have the power of the *continuum*. If X is equinumerous with a subset of Y, then we write card(X) ≤ card(Y); card(X) < card(Y) stands for card(X) ≤ card(Y) and card(X) ≠ card(Y). According to Cantor's theorem, for any set X, card(X) < card(2^X), and hence $\aleph_0 < \mathfrak{c}$. The Schröder–Bernstein theorem states that if card(X) $\leq$ card(Y) and card(Y) $\leq$ card(X), then card(X) = card(Y). A set is said to be *countable* if it is either finite or denumerable.

We write $f: X \rightarrow_p Y$ to indicate that f is a *partial function from* X *into* Y, i.e. a function from Z into Y, where $Z \subseteq X$. The set Z is called the *domain of* f and we assume that f is undefined for arguments from X–Z.

Unless the context dictates otherwise, the symbols 1 and 0 stand for the truth-values *truth* and *falsity*, respectively. If $X_1, \ldots, X_n$ are non-empty sets ($n \geq 0$), then any function $R: X_1 x \ldots x X_n \rightarrow \{0, 1\}$ is called an n-*ary* (or n-*place*) *relation on* $X_1 x \ldots X_n$. If R is a relation on $X_1 x X_2$, then we often say that R is a relation between elements from X_1 and those from X_2. 2-ary and 1-ary relations are called *binary relations* and *properties*, respectively. We say that objects $x_1 \in X_1, \ldots, x_n \in X_n$ are in a relation $R: X_1 x \ldots x X_n \rightarrow \{0, 1\}$, written $R(x_1, \ldots, x_n)$, iff $R(x_1, \ldots, x_n) = 1$. If R is a binary relation, then $x_1 R x_2$ is an alternative notation for $R(x_1, x_2)$. For example, if X is the set of reals, then the function $R: X^2 \rightarrow \{0, 1\}$ such that $R(x, y) = 1$ iff x is less than y defines a binary relation on X^2, usually denoted by $<$. Reals x and y are said to be in the relation $<$, written $x < y$, iff x is less than y. If R is an n-ary relation on X^n then we shall often say that R is an n-ary relation on X. Observe that we admit 0-*ary* (or 0-*place*) *relations*, regarded as 0-ary functions from $\{\langle\rangle\}$ into $\{0, 1\}$. According to our previous convention, 0-ary relations are just truth values. Relations will be often referred to as *predicates*.

Suppose that $X_1, \ldots, X_n$, where $n \geq 1$, are non-empty sets. Any relation $R: X_1 x \ldots x X_n \rightarrow \{0, 1\}$ uniquely determines a subset $\phi(R)$ of $X_1 x \ldots x X_n$ given by $\phi(R) = \{\langle x_1, \ldots, x_n\rangle : R(x_1, \ldots, x_n)\}$. On the other hand, for any subset S of $X_1 x \ldots x X_n$, there is exactly one relation $R: X_1 x \ldots x X_n \rightarrow \{0, 1\}$, given by $R(x_1, \ldots, x_n)$ iff $\langle x_1, \ldots, x_n\rangle \in S$, such that $S = \phi(R)$. It follows, therefore, that **relations of positive arity may be always identified with subsets of Cartesian products**. This is what we shall often do in the sequel.

A binary relation R on a set X is *reflexive* iff xRx, for all $x \in X$. R is *symmetric* iff xRy implies yRx. R is *transitive* iff xRy and yRz imply xRz. Finally, R is an *equivalence relation* iff it is reflexive, symmetric and transitive. An example of an equivalence relation is the relation R on the set of all triangles such that xRy iff x and y have the same area. If R is an equivalence relation on X and $x \in X$, then we denote by $|x|$ the set $\{y: y \in X \text{ and } xRy\}$. $|x|$ is called the *equivalence class of* R *generated by* x. It is easy to see that the following conditions hold: (i) $x \in |x|$; (ii) $|x| = |y|$ iff xRy; (iii) $|x| \neq |y|$ implies $|x| \cap |y| = \{\ \}$. Thus, for every equivalence relation R on X, the set of all equivalence classes of R specifies a partition of X.

A binary relation R is said to be *antisymmetric* iff xRy and yRx imply $x = y$. R is said to be a *partial order* iff it is reflexive, transitive and antisymmetric. An example of a partial order is the relation $\subseteq$ on the set of all subsets of a fixed set X. If R is a partial order on a set X, then an element $a \in X$ is said to be the *greatest* (resp. the *least*) *wrt* R iff xRa (resp. aRx), for any $x \in X$. An element $a \in X$ is called *maximal* (resp. *minimal*) *wrt* R iff there is no element $x \in X$ such that *a*R*x* (resp. xRa) and $x \neq a$. For any partial order R, there is at most one greatest element wrt R and at most one least element wrt R. However, R may give rise to many maximal and many minimal elements.

A binary relation R which is reflexive and transitive is called a *pre-order*. An example of a pre-order is the relation $\leq$ on a fixed set of human beings such that $x \leq y$ iff x is not older than y. Note that $\leq$ is neither an equivalence relation nor a partial order. If R is a pre-order on a set X, then the greatest (least) element wrt R is specified as before. It also makes sense to speak about elements which are maximal or minimal wrt R, but the previously given definition requires a modification. Specifically, an element $a \in X$ is *maximal* (resp. *minimal*) *wrt* R iff there is no element $x \in X$ such that aR^*x (resp. xR^*a), where xR^*y iff xRy but not yRx. Pre-orders will play an important role in Chapter 6.

A binary relation R, specified on X, is said to be *asymmetric* iff there are no elements $x, y \in X$ such that xRy and yRx. If R is asymmetric and transitive, then it is called a *strict partial order*. An example of a strict partial order is the relation $\subset$ on the set of all subsets of a fixed set X.

We shall distinguish between sets and *classes*, which also are collections of objects. The notion of a class is more general than that of a set, since every set is a class but not vice versa. Classes which are not sets are said to be *proper*. Roughly speaking, a proper class is a well-defined collection of objects which, if allowed to be a set, would become ill-defined. A typical example is the collection X consisting of all sets which are not members of themselves. Obviously, it makes perfect sense to speak about X, provided, of course, that we restrict ourselves to well-defined sets. This indicates that X must not be referred to as a set (see footnote ‡ on page 21).† In conclusion, X is a (proper) class, but not a set.

Important examples of proper classes are collections of all tuples $\langle x_1, \ldots, x_n \rangle$, where some of $x_1, \ldots, x_n$ are arbitrary sets.‡ Suppose, for instance, that Y is the collection of all pairs $\langle X, n \rangle$, where X is a set and n is a natural number. To see why Y must not be regarded as a set, assume that it is a set. Then 2^Y is also a set, and thus, for any $Z \in 2^Y$, $\langle Z, 1 \rangle \in Y$. It follows, therefore, that $2^Y x \{1\} \subseteq Y$, and so, since $\text{card}(2^Y x \{1\}) = \text{card}(2^Y)$, $\text{card}(2^Y) \leq \text{card}(Y)$. On the other hand, by Cantor's theorem, $\text{card}(Y) \leq \text{card}(2^Y)$ and $\text{card}(Y) \neq \text{card}(2^Y)$. A contradiction with Schröder–Bernstein's theorem.

We assume the reader's familiarity with basic intuitions underlying the notion of an *algorithm*. The formal definition of this concept belongs to recursion theory and is beyond the scope of this book.§ Roughly speaking, an algorithm is an effective procedure whose essential purpose is to solve a particular problem (or all problems from a given class). The term 'procedure' is to be understood here as a computational schema, usually representing a class of computations, which can be governed by a machine. A procedure is said to be effective if all the computations it represents are finite. A well-known example of an algorithm is the Euclidean algorithm for calculating the greatest common divisor of two positive integers. Another example is the algorithm of the sieve of Eratosthenes for obtaining all the primes in a given segment of the natural numbers. A problem which can be solved algorithmically, i.e. by means of an algorithm, is said to be *decidable;* otherwise, *undecidable*. The terms 'an *effective procedure*' and 'an *effective method*' will be used as synonyms for an algorithm.

A function $f: X \to Y$ is said to be (*effectively*) *computable* iff there is an algorithm

---

† Strictly speaking, if X is viewed as a set, then the assumption that we limit ourselves to well-specified sets is no longer valid and, consequently, the specification of X becomes ill-defined.

‡ Actually, all proper classes considered in this book are of this type.

§ The formal specification of an algorithm requires introducing an abstract computational model (machine). A number of such models, giving rise to apparently different but actually equivalent concepts of an algorithm, have been proposed in the literature. The reader interested in the subject is referred to Mendelson (1979, Chapter 5).

which calculates f(x) given an arbitrary element x of X. For instance, the function which assigns to each pair of positive integers their greatest common divisor is computable, since it can be calculated by means of the Euclidean algorithm.

A partial function $f: X \to_p Y$ is said to be *computable* iff there is an algorithm which takes an element x of X, determines whether x is in the domain of f, and, if so, computes f(x).

Let $X \subseteq Y$. We say that X is a *computable subset of* Y iff there is an effective procedure which takes an arbitrary element $y \in Y$ and determines whether or not y is a member of X. Clearly, the set of the prime numbers is a computable subset of the set of positive integers, since the algorithm of Eratosthenes provides an effective method for deciding whether a given positive integer is a prime number. If the set Y can be deduced from the context, the phrase 'X is a computable subset of Y' will be often abbreviated to 'X is computable'. For instance, when we say that a set X of integers is computable, we mean that X is a computable subset of the set of (all) integers. Occasionally, the phrase 'X is computable' will be used in a different sense than it is specified here. In such a case, the precise meaning of the phrase will be explicitly explained.

We say that X is a *partially computable subset of* Y iff there is a procedure Π, not necessarily effective, which takes an arbitrary element $y \in Y$ as input and behaves as follows. If $y \in X$, then Π terminates and reports that y is an element of X. If $y \in Y - X$, then Π either terminates (stating that y is not a member of X) or loops forever. The notion of partial computability is weaker than that of computability since any computable subset of any set is a partially computable subset of this set, but not necessarily vice versa. If the set Y is clear from the context, the phrase 'X is a partially computable subset of Y' will be abbreviated to 'X is partially computable'.

A set X is said to be *recursively enumerable* iff there is a computable function f from the set of non-negative integers onto X. In other words, a set is recursively enumerable if there is an effective method, namely the algorithm computing the function f, which can be used to generate all members of X. If X is recursively enumerable and Y is any superset of X, then X is a partially computable subset of Y. To see this, assume that f is the computable function from the set of non-negative integers onto X, F is the algorithm computing f, and consider the following procedure Π:

```
read(y); {y∈Y}
success := 0; i := −1;
repeat
   i := i + 1; if F(i) = y then success := 1
until success = 1;
write('y is a member of X').
```

It is easy to see that Π terminates, stating that y is a member of X, precisely if $y \in X$.

1.2 CLASSICAL PROPOSITIONAL LOGIC

This section introduces basic concepts of the classical propositional logic. By necessity our discussion is brief, so that the reader wishing a more detailed exposition is referred to the broad literature on the subject. Personally, I recommend Mendelson (1979). See also Church (1956) and van Dalen (1980).

1.2.1 Language of propositional logic

Modern classical logic is a formal system originally developed to deal with logical arguments in mathematics. The propositional part of this system is concerned with arguments constructable using *proposition constants* and *sentential connectives*. The proposition constants are names standing for declarative sentences. The connectives are constructors allowing to form composite sentences out of the simpler ones.

An *alphabet of (classical) propositional logic* consists of *primitive symbols* from the following pairwise disjoint classes:

(i) A countable set of *proposition constants*;
(ii) one *truth-constant: 'True'*;
(iii) *sentential connectives*: '$\supset$' (*implication*) and '$\neg$' (*negation*);
(iv) punctuation marks: '(' and ')'.

The classes (ii)–(iv) are fixed, whereas the class (i) varies from an alphabet into an alphabet and, in particular, may be empty. We always assume that the set of proposition constants is computable.[†] Proposition constants will be normally denoted by the lower case letters, p, q and r, possibly with subscripts and/or primes. When convenient, we shall also denote them by everyday English sentences such as *'sun-is-shining'*, *'John-is-tall'*, etc.

Definition 1.1 The set of *formulae over an alphabet* AL is the smallest set satisfying the following conditions.[‡]

(i) *True* and every proposition constant from AL is a formula.
(ii) If A and B are formulae, then so are $(\neg A)$ and $(A \supset B)$.

∎

The set of all formulae over an alphabet AL is called the *propositional language over* AL, and is denoted by L_{AL}. We shall often assume that the alphabet is fixed and then we shall write L instead of L_{AL}. It is easy to see that the restriction to alphabets with computable sets of proposition constants assures the computability of any propositional language: for any alphabet AL (with a computable set of proposition constants), it is possible to construct an effective procedure for deciding whether or not a given expression (i.e. a sequence of symbols) is a formula over AL.[§]

We use the upper case letters A, B, C and D, with or without subscripts and primes, as syntactic variables ranging over formulae. Formulae of the form $(\neg A)$ and $(A \supset B)$ are to be read 'not A' and 'if A, then B', respectively. $(\neg A)$ is called the *negation of A*. $(A \supset B)$ is called the *implication* with the *antecedent A* and the *consequent B*.

We introduce additional sentential connectives: '$\vee$' (*disjunction*), '$\wedge$' (*conjunction*) and '$\equiv$' (*equivalence*), by the following definitions (the symbol '$=_{\mathrm{DF}}$' is to be read

[†] Strictly speaking, we make the following three assumptions: (i) There is a fixed set S consisting of all possible symbols; (ii) All primitive symbols of any alphabet are chosen from S; (iii) For any alphabet AL, the set of its proposition constants is a computable subset of S, i.e. there is an effective procedure for deciding whether or not a given symbol $s \in S$ is a proposition constant of AL.

[‡] Formulae of propositional logic are sometimes called *propositions* or *statement forms*.

[§] The existence of such a procedure is essential if logical languages are to be useful for the purpose of communication. For, however vague the concept of communication may be, we must at least postulate the ability to effectively device whether a given expression is admitted to communicate some information.

'stands for'):

$$(A \vee B) =_{DF} ((\neg A) \supset B)$$
$$(A \wedge B) =_{DF} (\neg((\neg A) \vee (\neg B)))$$
$$(A \equiv B) =_{DF} ((A \supset B) \wedge (B \supset A))$$

Formulae of the form $(A \vee B)$, $(A \wedge B)$ and $(A \equiv B)$ are to be read 'A or B', 'A and B' and 'A iff B', respectively. $(A \vee B)$ is called the *disjunction of A and B*, which are its *disjuncts*. $(A \wedge B)$ is the *conjunction of A and B*, which are its *conjuncts*. $(A \equiv B)$ is the *equivalence of A and B*.

We introduce the truth-constant '*False*' as an abbreviation for '$\neg$*True*'.

To make formulae easier to comprehend, we adopt two notational conventions. Firstly, the parentheses ( ) will be sometimes replaced by [ ] or { }. Secondly, they will be omitted whenever their omission does not cause any confusion. To minimize the number of parentheses, we introduce the following precedence hierarchy among connectives, with the highest precedence on the left: $\neg$, $\wedge$, $\vee$, $\supset$, $\equiv$. Also, we assume that binary connectives associate to the right and we omit the outer parentheses. Thus, the formula $(((p \wedge q) \vee r) \supset (p \vee r))$ may be rewritten as $p \wedge q \vee r \supset p \vee r$ and the formula $(((p \vee q) \vee False) \wedge (\neg q))$ reduces to $(p \vee q \vee False) \wedge \neg q$.

We write $A = B$ to indicate that A and B are exactly the same formulae.

A is said to be a *subformula of a formula B* iff A is a formula which occurs in B. In particular, for any formula A, A is a subformula of A.

1.2.2 Semantics of propositional logic

The semantics for propositional logic is based on the following notion:

Definition 1.2 An *interpretation for a propositional language* L_{AL} is a function which assigns to each proposition constant of AL an element from $\{0, 1\}$. ▮

Recall that 0 and 1 are meant to represent truth and falsity, respectively. Interpretations then provide truth values for proposition constants.

Definition 1.3 Let m be an interpretation for L and suppose that $A \in L$. The *truth-value of A in* m, written $V^m(A)$, is an element of $\{0, 1\}$, defined by the following recursion on A:

(i) $V^m(True) = 1$;
(ii) $V^m(p) = m(p)$;
(iii) $V^m(\neg B) = 1 - V^m(B)$;
(iv) $V^m(B \supset C) = 1$ iff $V^m(B) = 0$ or $V^m(C) = 1$.

▮

The following truth-conditions easily follow from the definitions of the symbols $\vee$, $\wedge$, $\equiv$ and *False*:

(v) $V^m(B \vee C) = \max(V^m(B), V^m(C))$;
(vi) $V^m(B \wedge C) = \min(V^m(B), V^m(C))$;
(vii) $V^m(B \equiv C) = 1$ iff $V^m(B) = V^m(C)$;
(viii) $V^m(False) = 0$.

Observe that the truth-value of a compound formula is uniquely determined by the truth-values of its components. This principle, called the *Principle of Extensionality* (or *Functionality*), is typical for all systems of classical logic.

We say that A is *true* (resp. *false*) *in* m iff $V^m(A) = 1$ (resp. $V^m(A) = 0$). A is *satisfiable* iff $V^m(A) = 1$, for some interpretation m. A is a *tautology* iff $V^m(A) = 1$, for each interpretation m. If $V^m(A) = 1$, then m is called a *model* of A.

Example 1.4 Let A be of the form $p \vee \neg q \supset p$ (notation: $A = p \vee \neg q \supset p$) and consider two interpretations, m_1 and m_2, such that

$$m_1(p) = m_1(q) = 1; \qquad m_2(p) = m_2(q) = 0$$

A is true in m_1 but false in m_2. Thus, A is satisfiable but not a tautology. The interpretation m_1 is a model of A. ▮

There are various techniques for determining whether a formula is a tautology. The most straightforward one is perhaps that based on the concept of *truth-tables*. We illustrate this method by giving an example.

The truth-table for the formula $(p \supset \neg q) \vee q$ has the following form:

p	q	$\neg q$	$p \supset \neg q$	$(p \supset \neg q) \vee q$
0	0	1	1	1
0	1	0	1	1
1	0	1	1	1
1	1	0	0	1

The table may be viewed as an abbreviation of the following argumentation. Let m be an arbitrary interpretation. If m assigns 0 to both p and q (the first row), then the value of $\neg q$ in m is 1, the value of $p \supset \neg q$ in m is 1 and the value of $(p \supset \neg q) \vee q$ in m is 1. The other rows have a similar meaning and the four rows exhaust all the possible cases. In each case, the value of the formula $(p \supset \neg q) \vee q$ is 1 and hence it is a tautology.

The above technique can be applied to any formula. If the formula contains n different proposition constants, then its truth-table has 2^n rows.

The *validity problem for propositional logic* is the task of determining whether or not a given propositional formula is a tautology. In virtue of the truth-table method, we immediately have:

Theorem 1.5 The validity problem for propositional logic is decidable. ▮

The result of Theorem 1.5 is often expressed by saying that propositional logic is decidable.

We now list a number of tautologies. In the following, A, B and C stand for any formulae.†

(T1) $(A \supset B) \equiv (\neg A \vee B)$

(T2) $(A \equiv B) \equiv ((\neg A \vee B) \wedge (A \vee \neg B))$

(T3) $(\neg(A \wedge B)) \equiv (\neg A \vee \neg B)$ [De Morgan's Laws]

(T4) $(\neg(A \vee B)) \equiv (\neg A \wedge \neg B)$ [De Morgan's Laws]

(T5) $(\neg\neg A) \equiv A$ [Law of Double Negation]

(T6) $(A \vee (B \wedge C)) \equiv ((A \vee B) \wedge (A \vee C))$ [Distributive Laws]

(T7) $(A \wedge (B \vee C)) \equiv ((A \wedge B) \vee (A \wedge C))$ [Distributive Laws]

† Strictly speaking, the expressions given below are schemata, each representing an infinite number of tautologies.

(T8) $(A \wedge B) \equiv (B \wedge A)$ [Commutative Laws]
(T9) $(A \vee B) \equiv (B \vee A)$
(T10) $A \vee \neg A$ [Law of Excluded Middle]
(T11) $A \supset A$ [Reflexive Law of Implication]
(T12) $((A \equiv B) \wedge (B \equiv C)) \supset (A \equiv C)$ [Transitive Law of Equivalence]
(T13) $(A \supset B) \equiv (\neg B \supset \neg A)$ [Law of Contraposition]
(T14) $\neg(A \wedge \neg A)$ [Law of Contradiction]
(T15) $False \supset A$
(T16) $(A \supset False) \equiv \neg A$
(T17) $A \supset True$
(T18) $(True \supset A) \equiv A$

Formulae A and B are said to be (*logically*) *equivalent*, written $A \Leftrightarrow B$, iff both of them yield the same truth-value in any interpretation, or, alternatively, iff they have exactly the same models.† The following theorem lists three important properties of equivalent formulae:

Theorem 1.6

(i) $A \Leftrightarrow B$ iff $A \equiv B$ is a tautology;
(ii) $A \Leftrightarrow B$ and $B \Leftrightarrow C$ imply $A \Leftrightarrow C$; (Transitivity of Equivalent Relation)
(iii) If B is a subformula of A, A' is the result of replacing one or more occurrences of B in A by C, and $B \Leftrightarrow C$, then $A \Leftrightarrow A'$. (Replacement Theorem)

∎

The Replacement Theorem, together with the principle of the transitivity of the equivalence relation, are often used in showing that formulae from a given class can be transformed into equivalent formulae enjoying desired syntactic properties. We illustrate this by proving an important theorem.

We write $\bigwedge_{i=1}^{n} A_i$ and $\bigvee_{i=1}^{n} A_i$, $n \geq 1$, as abbreviations for $A_1 \wedge \cdots \wedge A_n$ and $A_1 \vee \cdots \vee A_n$, respectively. An *atomic formula* is either a proposition constant or a truth-constant. A formula B is said to be in *conjunctive normal form* iff $B = \bigwedge_{i=1}^{n} \left[\bigvee_{j=1}^{m(i)} B_{ij} \right]$, where B_{ij} is either an atomic formula or the negation of an atomic formula. A formula B is said to be a *conjunctive normal form of a formula* A iff B is in conjunctive normal form and $A \Leftrightarrow B$.

Theorem 1.7 Every formula A can be effectively transformed into its conjunctive normal form.

Proof The transformation proceeds in three basic steps.

Step 1. *Eliminate* $\supset$ *and* $\equiv$. Replace in A

$(B \supset C)$ by $(\neg B \vee C)$
$(B \equiv C)$ by $((\neg B \vee C) \wedge (B \vee (B \vee \neg C))$

until the resulting formula contains $\vee$, $\wedge$ and $\neg$ as its only connectives.

† The symbols $\equiv$ and $\Leftrightarrow$ should not be confused. The former is a connective which may occur in formulae; the latter is a meta-language symbol which is used to speak *about* formulae.

Step 2. *Move $\neg$ inward.* In the formula obtained in Step 1, replace

$$\begin{array}{lll} \neg(B \vee C) & \text{by} & \neg B \wedge \neg C \\ \neg(B \wedge C) & \text{by} & \neg B \vee \neg C \\ \neg\neg B & \text{by} & B \end{array}$$

until all occurrences of $\neg$ immediately precede atomic formulae.

Step 3. *Distribute $\wedge$ over $\vee$.* In the formula constructed in Step 2, replace as long as possible

$$\begin{array}{lll} (B \wedge C) \vee D & \text{by} & (B \vee D) \wedge (C \vee D) \\ B \vee (C \wedge D) & \text{by} & (B \vee C) \wedge (B \vee D) \end{array}$$

and denote the resulting formula by A'.

Performing the above algorithm, we construct a sequence of formulae, $A_0, A_1, \ldots, A_n$, such that $A_0 = A$, $A_n = A'$, A' is in conjunctive normal form, and, for each i ($0 \leq i < n$), A_{i+1} is the result of replacing a subformula of A_i by an equivalent subformula. Thus, by the replacement theorem, $A_i \Leftrightarrow A_{i+1}$, for each $0 \leq i < n$, and hence, by the transitivity of the equivalence relation, $A_0 \Leftrightarrow A_n$. Therefore, A' is a conjunctive normal form of A. ∎

As an example, consider the formula $A = r \vee \neg(p \supset q)$. We first eliminate $\supset$ and obtain $r \vee \neg(\neg p \vee q)$. Next, moving the negation inward, we get $r \vee (p \wedge \neg q)$. Finally, distributing $\wedge$ over $\vee$, we obtain $(r \vee p) \wedge (r \vee \neg q)$. This is the desired conjunctive normal form of A.

1.2.3 Propositional theories

One of the central concepts of propositional logic is that of a *propositional theory*. Such a theory is just a collection of formulae over a propositional language, and is meant to provide a description of a particular world (domain, reality, state of affairs, etc.).

Definition 1.8 A *propositional theory* is a pair $T = \langle L, S \rangle$, where L is a propositional language and S is a computable set of formulae from L. The elements of S are called the *axioms* (or the *premisses*) of T. If S is empty, then T is called a *propositional calculus*.† ∎

Throughout this section, the phrase 'propositional theory' will be abbreviated to 'theory'. Theories will be denoted by the upper case letter T, possibly with subscripts and primes. A theory $\langle L, S \rangle$ is said to be *over* L.

Usually, theories will be identified with sets of their axioms. In such the case, we assume that the language of a theory T consists of all the formulae constructable using proposition constants occurring in the axioms of T. For instance, when we say that T consists of

$$p \wedge q \supset r \qquad \text{and} \qquad r \supset q$$

then we make the implicit assumption that $T = \langle L, \{p \wedge q \supset r, r \supset q\} \rangle$, where L is the language corresponding to the alphabet with p, q and r as its only proposition constants.

A theory is *finite* (resp. *infinite*) iff the set of its axioms is finite (resp. infinite). If T is

† Notice that if L_1 and L_2 are different languages, then $\langle L_1, \{\ \} \rangle$ and $\langle L_2, \{\ \} \rangle$ are different proposition calculae.

a finite theory all of whose axioms are $A_1, \ldots, A_n$, then T will be often written as $\{A_1, \ldots, A_n\}$ or simply $A_1, \ldots, A_n$. If T is a theory over L_{AL} and $A_1, \ldots, A_n$ are formulae from $L_{AL'}$, then we denote by $T \cup \{A_1, \ldots, A_n\}$, or simply $T, A_1, \ldots, A_n$, the theory $\langle L_{AL \cup AL'}, T \cup \{A_1, \ldots, A_n\}\rangle$. We say that T' is a *subtheory of* T, written $T' \subseteq T$, iff the axioms of T' form a subset of those of T. Observe that with each formula A we may uniquely associate the theory $\langle L(A), \{A\}\rangle$, where $L(A)$ is the language consisting of all formulae constructable using proposition constants occurring in A. In this sense, **formulae may be always viewed as theories**. We shall often make use of this fact in the sequel.

An interpretation m is a *model of a theory* T if all axioms of T are true in m.† A theory may have none, one or many models. A theory which has a model is called *satisfiable*. Otherwise, it is called *unsatisfiable*.

Theorem 1.9 (Compactness Theorem) A theory T has a model iff each finite subtheory of T has a model. ∎

A formula A is said to be a *semantic consequence of a theory* T, written $T \models A$, iff A is true in every model of T. In particular, A is a semantic consequence of a propositional calculus (over L), written $\models A$, iff A is true in every interpretation (for L).‡

If $T \models A$, then we also say that *A logically follows from T, A is entailed by T, or T entails A*.

Example 1.10 Consider the theory T consisting of:

Sunday
Sunday $\supset$ *I-go-fishing*
I-am-tired $\supset \neg$*I-go-fishing*

The reader may easily check that T has one model m given by

m(*Sunday*) = 1; m(*I-go-fishing*) = 1; m(*I-am-tired*) = 0

Therefore, $T \models \neg$*I-am-tired*. ∎

Observe that the symbol $\models$ denotes a binary relation, usually called the *entailment relation for propositional logic*, which holds between a theory T and a formula A iff T entails A.

Theorem 1.11 The entailment relation for propositional logic enjoys the following properties:

(i) $T \models B$ iff $T \cup \{\neg B\}$ is unsatisfiable;
(ii) $T, A \models B$ iff $T \models A \supset B$;
(iii) $\{A_1, \ldots, A_n\} \models B$ iff $\models A_1 \wedge \cdots \wedge A_n \supset B$;
(iv) If $T \subseteq T'$, then $\{A: T \models A\} \subseteq \{A: T' \models A\}$. (Monotonicity)

∎

Assertions (iii) and (iv) deserve special attention. In view of (iii), the problem of determining whether a formula B follows from a theory $\{A_1, \ldots, A_n\}$ reduces to the task of determining whether the formula $A_1 \wedge \cdots \wedge A_n \supset B$ is a tautology. Proposition (iv) expresses the fact that if A follows from a theory T, then, if we add new

† When we say that m is a model of T, we tacitly assume that m is an interpretation for the language of T.
‡ '$\models A$' is then a symbolic notation for the phrase 'A is a tautology'.

axioms to T, A still follows from the extended theory. This property, called the *Principle of Monotonicity*, underlies all logical systems discussed in Chapter 1.

Theories T and T' are said to be *(logically) equivalent*, written $T \Leftrightarrow T'$, iff they have the same models. The most important property concerning equivalent theories is given in the following theorem:

Theorem 1.12 For any theories T and T', $T \Leftrightarrow T'$ iff $\{A: T \models A\} = \{A: T' \models A\}$.

∎

In view of Theorem 1.12, equivalent theories entail exactly the same formulae. Accordingly, such theories are indistinguishable from the standpoint of practical applications.

Theorem 1.13 If $T = \{A_1, \ldots, A_n\}$, then $T \Leftrightarrow \{A_1 \wedge \cdots \wedge A_n\}$. ∎

Theorem 1.13 permits us, when convenient, to identify any finite theory with the conjunction of all its axioms.

Formulae A and B are said to be *equivalent in a theory* T iff they yield the same truth-value in every model for T, or, alternatively, iff T entails the formula $A \equiv B$.

1.2.4 Propositional logic as a deduction system

So far we have been concerned with the relation between formulae and their meaning (truth-values), i.e. we have looked at propositional logic from a semantic perspective. Now we focus on purely syntactic aspects of this formalism, by viewing it as a deduction system.

Definition 1.14 *A deduction system*† for propositional logic is a triple DS $= \langle L, \mathrm{S}, \mathrm{R}\rangle$, where:

(i) L is a propositional language;
(ii) S is a computable subset of L (the elements of S are called logical axioms);
(iii) $\mathrm{R} = \{\mathrm{R}_1, \ldots, \mathrm{R}_n\}$ is a finite set of *inference rules*. Each R_i is a partial function from L^k into L ($k \geq 1$). If $A_1, \ldots, A_k$ are in the domain of R_i, then we say that R_i is *applicable* to $A_1, \ldots, A_k$, and $\mathrm{R}_i(A_1, \ldots, A_k)$ is then called a *direct consequence* of $A_1, \ldots, A_n$ by virtue of R_i. We assume that each R_i is computable, i.e. there is an effective procedure which takes a tuple $A_1, \ldots, A_k$ of formulae from L, determines whether R_i is applicable to it, and, if so, returns $\mathrm{R}_i(A_1, \ldots, A_k)$.

∎

In the remainder of this section, the phrase 'a deduction system for propositional logic' will be abbreviated to 'a deduction system'.

The best-known inference rule is perhaps *modus ponens* (MP), stating that B is a direct consequence of A and $A \supset B$. (Here A and B stand for any formulae from the considered language L.) MP is usually written in the form

$$\frac{A, A \supset B}{B}$$

and may be formally viewed as the partial function from L^2 into L such that: (i) the domain of MP is $\{\langle A, A \supset B\rangle: A, B \in L\}$; (ii) $\mathrm{MP}(\langle A, A \supset B\rangle) = B$. It is easy to see that modus ponens is a computable rule.

† In the logical literature, deduction systems are also called *inferential systems*, *formal theories*, *axiomatic theories* or *axiomatizations*.

An inference rule R_i is said to be *sound* (synonymously, R_i is a *truth-preserving* rule) iff for every interpretation m and every $A_1, \ldots, A_k$ from the domain of R_i, $R_i(A_1, \ldots, A_k)$ is true in m, provided that $A_1, \ldots, A_k$ are true in m. Clearly, MP is a truth-preserving rule since, for any formulae A and B, B is true in any interpretation in which A and $A \supset B$ are true.

A formula A is *provable*† *in* DS $= \langle L, S, R \rangle$ (alternatively, A is a *theorem in* DS) iff there is a sequence $A_1, \ldots, A_m$ of formulae from L such that A is A_m and, for each $1 \leq i \leq m$, either $A_i \in S$ or A_i is a direct consequence of some preceding formulae by virtue of some rule from R. Such a sequence is called a *proof of A in* DS.

Providing the definition of a deductive system DS $= \langle L, S, R \rangle$, we have made two important assumptions. Firstly, the set S of logical axioms is to be a computable subset of L, i.e. there should exist an effective procedure for deciding whether a given formula from L is a logical axiom. Secondly, any inference rule $R_i \in R$ should be computable in the sense that there is an effective procedure which takes a tuple $A_1, \ldots, A_k$ of formulae from L, determines whether the tuple is in the domain of R_i and, if so, computes $R_i(A_1, \ldots, A_k)$. These assumptions assure, provided that we restrict ourselves to computational languages, that the notion of a proof is computable in the following sense: there is an effective procedure which takes a finite sequence $E_1, \ldots, E_n$ of arbitrary linguistic expressions and determines whether or not the sequence is a proof of E_n in DS. The existence of such a procedure is essential, since the notion of the proof, as specified here, has been originally developed for the purpose of formalizing mathematical arguments. Obviously, if a mathematician demonstrates a proof, there should be an effective method of its verification.

The notion of a proof can be generalized as follows. Let DS $= \langle L, S, R \rangle$ be a deduction system and suppose that T is a theory over L. We say that a formula A is *provable from T in* DS, written $T \vdash_{DS} A$, iff there is a sequence $A_1, \ldots, A_m$ of formulae from L such that A is A_m and, for each $1 \leq i \leq m$, either $A_i \in S \cup T$ or A_i is a direct consequence of some preceding formulae by virtue of some rule from R. Such a sequence is called a *proof of A from T in* DS. If $T \vdash_{DS} A$, then we also say that A is a *syntactic consequence of T in* DS, or A is a *theorem of T in* DS. We write $\vdash_{DS} A$ as an abbreviation for $\{\ \} \vdash_{DS} A$. (Thus, $\vdash_{DS} A$ is a symbolic notation for 'A is a theorem in DS'.)

Defining the notion of a theory, we have assumed that the set of axioms of any theory is a computable subset of its language. This assures, provided that all other computability requirements are fulfilled, that the generalized notion of a proof is computable. In other words, for any theory T and any deduction system DS, there is an effective procedure for deciding whether a given sequence of arbitrary linguistic expressions forms a proof from T in DS.

A deduction system DS is said to be *sound* iff $\vdash_{DS} A$ implies that A is a tautology. To guarantee the soundness, which is clearly the desired property, it suffices to impose two additional requirements on a deduction system. Firstly, all its logical axioms should be tautologies.‡ Secondly, all its inference rules should be sound.

We are principally interested in those sound deduction systems which are also *complete*, i.e. allow to prove every tautology. A number of such systems have been proposed in the literature. The most common is perhaps the following.

† The terms 'derivable' and 'inferable' will be regarded as synonyms for 'provable'.
‡ This explains the term 'logical axiom'.

Definition 1.15 Let L be a propositional language. We denote by PL(L) the deduction system $\langle L, \mathrm{S}, \mathrm{R}\rangle$ given by

(i) S consists of the following axioms (A, B and C stand for any formulae of L):

(A1) *True*
(A2) $A \supset (B \supset A)$
(A3) $(A \supset (B \supset C)) \supset ((A \supset B) \supset (A \supset C))$
(A4) $(\neg B \supset \neg A) \supset ((\neg B \supset A) \supset B)$

(ii) R contains modus ponens as the only inference rule.

▮

Note that (A2)–(A4) are axiom schemata, each representing an infinite number of axioms. It is easily seen that S is a computable subset of L.

We shall normally assume that the language L is fixed and the symbol $\vdash_{\mathrm{PL(L)}}$ will be simply written as $\vdash$. If $T \vdash A$, then we say that A is *provable from T in propositional logic*. Similarly, if $\vdash A$, then we say that A is *provable in propositional logic* or, alternatively, A is a *theorem in propositional logic*. We write $T \nvdash A$ and $\nvdash A$ as the negations for $T \vdash A$ and $\vdash A$, respectively.

The binary relation denoted by the symbol $\vdash$, i.e. the relation which holds between a theory T and a formula A iff $T \vdash A$, is called the *provability relation of (classical) propositional logic*. The binary relation corresponding to the symbol $\nvdash$ is referred to as the *unprovability relation of (classical) propositional logic*.

We denote by Th the *provability operator of (classical) propositional logic*, i.e. the operator which assigns to each theory T the set Th(T) of all formulae provable from T in propositional logic. Symbolically, $\mathrm{Th}(T) = \{A\colon T \vdash A\}$.

Theorem 1.16 The operator Th enjoys the following properties:

(i) $T \subseteq \mathrm{Th}(T)$;
(ii) $\mathrm{Th}(T) = \mathrm{Th}(\mathrm{Th}(T))$; (Idempotence)
(iii) If $T \subseteq T'$, then $\mathrm{Th}(T) \subseteq \mathrm{Th}(T')$. (Monotonicity)

▮

Observe that (iii) is a syntactic counterpart of the Principle of Monotonicity expressed in Theorem 1.11 (iv).

The syntax and the semantics of propositional logic are connected by the following fundamental result:

Theorem 1.17

(i) If $T \vdash A$, then $T \models A$; (Soundness Theorem)
(ii) If $T \models A$, then $T \vdash A$. (Completeness Theorem)

▮

Corollary 1.18 $\vdash A$ iff $\models A$. ▮

A theory T over L is said to be *consistent* iff there is a formula $A \in L$ such that $T \nvdash A$. The notion of consistency is a syntactic counterpart of that of satisfiability:

Theorem 1.19 T is consistent iff it is satisfiable. ▮

The following result corresponds to Theorem 1.11 (ii)–(iii):

Theorem 1.20 (Deduction Theorem)

(i) $T, A \vdash B$ iff $T \vdash A \supset B$;
(ii) $\{A_1, \ldots, A_n\} \vdash B$ iff $\vdash A_1 \wedge \cdots \wedge A_n \supset B$.
∎

We also have the following counterpart of the Compactness Theorem:

Theorem 1.21 T is consistent iff each finite subtheory of T is consistent. ∎

1.3 CLASSICAL FIRST-ORDER LOGIC

Classical first-order logic, known also as *lower predicate logic* and *first-order predicate logic*, is the most fundamental of all logical systems. Its language is sufficiently rich to symbolize the majority of arguments occurring both in mathematics and in non-mathematical applications. This section introduces those elements of classical first-order logic, which will be used in the subsequent chapters. For a more comprehensive treatise of the subject, the reader is recommended to consult Mendelson (1979), Shoenfield (1967) or van Dalen (1980).

1.3.1 Language of first-order logic

An *alphabet of (classical) first-order logic* consists of primitive symbols from the following pairwise disjoint classes:

(i) A denumerable set V of *individual variables*: $\{x_1, x_2, \ldots\}$;
(ii) One truth-constant: *'True'*;
(iii) Sentential connectives: '$\neg$' and '$\supset$';
(iv) *One quantifier;* '$\forall$' (*universal quantifier*);
(v) Punctuation marks: '(', ',' and ')';
(vi) A countable set **P** of *predicate constants*; to each $P \in \mathbf{P}$, there is uniquely assigned a non-negative integer, called the *arity of P*;
(vii) A distinguished 2-ary predicate constant: '$=$' (*equality*);
(viii) A countable set **F** of *function constants*; to each $f \in \mathbf{F}$, there is uniquely assigned a non-negative integer, called the *arity of f*.

The classes (i)–(v) are fixed and their members must be present in any alphabet. The other classes may vary and, in particular, the set of function constants may be empty. We assume, however, that any alphabet includes at least one predicate constant of positive arity. The sets **P** and **F** are required to be computable in the sense that there is an effective procedure Π_P (resp. Π_F) which takes an arbitrary symbol s, determines whether $s \in \mathbf{P}$ (resp. whether $s \in \mathbf{F}$), and, if so, returns the arity of s.

0-ary predicate constants are called *proposition constants*; 0-ary function constants are called *individual* (or *object*) *constants*.

We introduce special symbols (possibly with subscripts and/or primes): x, y, u and z for individual variables; P, Q and R for predicate constants of positive arity; p, q and r for proposition constants; f, g and h for function constants of positive arity; and a, b and c for individual constants. Predicate and function constants will be also denoted by everyday English expressions.

Every alphabet of first-order logic uniquely determines three classes of expressions: *terms*, *atomic formulae* and *formulae*.

Definition 1.22 Let AL be an alphabet of first-order logic.
The set TM_{AL} of *terms over* AL is the smallest set such that: (i) All individual variables and all individual constants from AL are members of TM_{AL}; (ii) If $\alpha_1, \ldots, \alpha_n \in TM_{AL}$ $(n \geq 1)$ and f is an n-ary function constant from AL, then $f(\alpha_1, \ldots, \alpha_n) \in TM_{AL}$.

The set $AFORM_{AL}$ of *atomic formulae over* AL is the smallest set such that: (i) *'True'* and all proposition constants from AL belong to $AFORM_{AL}$; (ii) If $\alpha_1, \ldots, \alpha_n \in TM_{AL}$ $(n \geq 1)$ and P is an n-ary predicate constant from AL, then $P(\alpha_1, \ldots, \alpha_n) \in AFORM_{AL}$; (iii) If $\alpha_1, \alpha_2 \in TM_{AL}$, then $(\alpha_1 = \alpha_2) \in AFORM_{AL}$, provided that AL contains the symbol '='.

The set L_{AL} of *formulae over* AL is the smallest set such that: (i) If $A \in AFORM_{AL}$, then $A \in L_{AL}$; (ii) If $A, B \in L_{AL}$ and x is a variable, then $(\neg A) \in L_{AL}$, $(A \supset B) \in L_{AL}$ and $(\forall x(A)) \in L_{AL}$. ▮

The set L_{AL} is called the first-order language over AL.[†] We shall often assume that AL is fixed and then L_{AL} will be abbreviated to L. It is easily seen that the restriction to alphabets with computable sets of predicate and function constants guarantees the computability of any first-order language.

L_{AL} is said to be a *first-order language with equality* iff '=' $\in$ AL; otherwise, L_{AL} is said to be a *first-order language without equality*.

We use the letters A, B, C and D (resp. α, β and γ), possibly with subscripts and/or primes, as syntactic variables ranging over formulae (resp. terms).

Formulae of the form $(\neg A)$ and $(A \supset B)$ have the same meaning as in propositional logic. A formula of the form $(\forall x(A))$ is to be read 'for every element x, A is true'. We say that the occurrence of x in $\forall x$ is *universally quantified*, A is called *the scope of* $\forall x$ in $(\forall x(A))$, and every occurrence of x in A is said to be *bound by* $\forall x$ *in* $(\forall x(A))$.

The truth-constant *False* and the connectives $\wedge$, $\vee$ and $\equiv$ are defined as in propositional logic. Additionally, we introduce the symbol '$\exists$' (*existential quantifier*) by the following definition.

$$(\exists x(A)) =_{DF} (\neg(\forall x(\neg(A))))$$

A formula of the form $(\exists x(A))$ is to be read 'for some element x, A is true'. The occurrence of x in $\exists x$ is said to be *existentially quantified*, A is called the *scope of* $\exists x$ in $(\exists x(A))$, and every occurrence of x in A is said to be *bound by* $\exists x$ *in* $(\exists x(A))$.

To gain clarity, we shall sometimes replace the parentheses ( ) by [ ] or { }. We adopt the conventions made in section 1.2 as to omission of parentheses. Additionally, we assume that quantifiers $\forall$ and $\exists$ rank in strength as $\neg$, i.e. they apply to the smallest possible scope. Thus, $\forall x P(x) \supset Q(x)$ stands for $((\forall x(P(x))) \supset Q(x))$, and $\forall x\, \exists y P(x, y)$ stands for $(\forall x(\exists y(P(x, y))))$. The expressions '$\forall x_1 \ldots x_n$' and '$\exists x_1 \ldots x_n$', $(n \geq 1)$ are abbreviations for '$\forall x_1 \ldots \forall x_n$' and '$\exists x_1 \ldots \exists x_n$', respectively. A formula of the form $\neg(\alpha_1 = \alpha_2)$ will usually be written as $\alpha_1 \neq \alpha_2$.

We introduce another important convention to minimize the number of parentheses. Specifically, we write '$Q_1 x_1 \ldots Q_n x_n .$', where $Q_1 \ldots Q_n \in \{\forall, \exists\}$, to indicate that all occurrences of $x_1, \ldots, x_n$ following the symbol '.' are bound by $Q_1 x_1, \ldots, Q_n x_n$. According to this convention, $\forall x . P(x) \supset Q(x)$ stands for $\forall x[P(x) \supset Q(x)]$, $\forall x\, \exists y . P(x) \wedge Q(y)$ stands for $\forall x\, \exists y[P(x) \wedge Q(y)]$ and $\forall xy . P(x) \supset Q(x, y)$ is an abbreviation for $\forall xy[P(x) \supset Q(x, y)]$.

[†] Notice that any first-order language includes as a proper subset a class of formulae of propositional logic.

An occurrence of a variable is said to be *free* in a formula A iff it is neither quantified nor bound in A. For instance, in the formula $P(x) \vee Q(x)$, both the occurrences of x are free; in $P(x) \supset \forall x Q(x)$, the first occurrence of x is free, whereas the second and the third are not. A variable x is said to be *free* in A iff x has a free occurrence in A. We write $A(x_1 \ldots x_n)$ to indicate that some of free variables of A are among $x_1, \ldots, x_n$. The notation $A(x_1, \ldots, x_n)$ neither presupposes that all the variables $x_1, \ldots, x_n$ are free in A nor that $x_1, \ldots, x_n$ are the only free variables in A. For any formula $A(x_1, \ldots, x_n)$, we write $A(\alpha_1, \ldots, \alpha_n)$ to denote the result of (simultaneously) substituting in A the terms $\alpha_1, \ldots, \alpha_n$ for all free occurrences of $x_1, \ldots, x_n$, respectively. A formula containing no free variables is said to be *closed*; otherwise, *open*. Closed formulae are also called *sentences*. A formula (term) is said to be *ground* iff it contains no variables at all.

We say that a term α is *free for x in A* iff no free occurrences of x in A lie in the scope of any quantifier of the form $\forall y$ or $\exists y$, where y is a variable in α. For example, the term y is free for x in $P(x)$, but is not free for x in $\exists y P(x, y)$; the term $f(z)$ is free for x in $\forall x . P(x) \wedge Q(y)$, but is not free for x in $\forall z . P(x, a) \vee P(z, a)$. It is worth noting that any ground term is free for any variable in any formula.

Let A be a formula all of whose free variables (in order of their first occurrences) are $x_1, \ldots, x_n$ ($n \geq 0$). The *universal closure of A*, written $\forall A$, is the formula $\forall x_1 \ldots x_n . A$. The *existential closure of A*, written $\exists A$, is the formula $\exists x_1 \ldots x_n . A$. Note that if A is closed, then $\forall A = \exists A = A$.

A is said to be a *subformula of B* iff A occurs in B.

Definition 1.23 Let L_{AL} be a first-order language with equality. The *set of equality axioms for L_{AL}* consists of the following sentences:

(E1) $\forall x . x = x$ (Reflexivity)
(E2) $\forall xy . x = y \supset y = x$ (Symmetry)
(E3) $\forall xyz . x = y \wedge y = z \supset x = z$ (Transitivity)
(E4) $\forall x_1 \ldots x_n y_1 \ldots y_n [x_1 = y_1 \wedge \cdots \wedge x_n = y_n \wedge P(x_1, \ldots, x_n) \supset P(y_1, \ldots, y_n)]$, for each n-ary ($n \geqslant 1$) predicate constant $P \in AL$
(E5) $\forall x_1 \ldots x_n y_1 \ldots y_n [x_1 = y_1 \wedge \cdots \wedge x_n = y_n \supset f(x_1, \ldots, x_n) = f(y_1, \ldots, y_n)]$, for each n-ary ($n \geqslant 1$) function constant $f \in AL$.

∎

The axioms (E4) and (E5) are called the *substitutivity axioms of equality*.

1.3.2 Semantics of first-order logic

The semantics of first-order logic is based on the following concept:

Definition 1.24 A *frame for a first-order language L_{AL}* is a pair $M = \langle D, m \rangle$, where:

(i) D is a non-empty set, called the *domain* (*universe*) of M;
(ii) m is a function which assigns to each n-ary ($n \geq 0$) predicate constant from AL, different from '=', an n-ary relation on D, to the constant '=', if present in AL, the identity relation on D, and to each n-ary ($n \geq 0$) function constant from AL, an n-ary function from D^n into D.

∎

Recall that 0-ary relations on D and 0-ary functions from D^0 into D are identified with truth-values and elements of D, respectively. Thus, for any frame $M = \langle D, m \rangle$ for

L_{AL}, m assigns to each proposition constant in AL, an element from $\{0, 1\}$, and to each individual constant in AL, an element from D.

Given a frame $M = \langle D, m \rangle$ for L_{AL}, we write $|M|$ to denote the domain of M. If K is a predicate or function constant in AL, then $M|K|$ stands for $m(K)$.

We use the phrase 'M is a *first-order frame*' ('M is a *frame for first-order logic*') to indicate that M is a frame for some first-order language L.

For a first-order frame M, we denote by As(M) the set of *assignments over* M, i.e. the set of all functions from the set of variables into $|M|$. If $a \in As(M)$ and x is a variable, then we write $[a]_x$ to denote the set of those assignments over M which differ from 'a' at most on x. Formally, $[a]_x = \{a' : a' \in As(M) \text{ and } a'(y) = a(y), \text{ for every } y \neq x\}$.

Definition 1.25 Let M be a first-order frame for L_{AL}.

The *value* $V_a^M(\alpha)$ *of a term* $\alpha \in TM_{AL}$ *in* M *wrt* $a \in As(M)$ is an element from $|M|$ defined by the following recursion on α:

(i) $V_a^M(x) = a(x)$;
(ii) $V_a^M(a) = M|a|$;
(iii) $V_a^M(f(\alpha_1, \ldots, \alpha_n)) = M|f|(V_a^M(\alpha_1), \ldots, V_a^M(\alpha_n))$.

The *truth-value* $V_a^M(A)$ *of a formula* $A \in L_{AL}$ *in* M *wrt* $a \in As(M)$ is an element of $\{0, 1\}$ defined as follows:

(i) $V_a^M(True) = 1$;
(ii) $V_a^M(p) = M|p|$;
(iii) $V_a^M(P(\alpha_1, \ldots, \alpha_n)) = M|P|(V_a^M(\alpha_1), \ldots, V_a^M(\alpha_n))$;
(iv) $V_a^M(\alpha = \beta) = 1$ iff $V_a^M(\alpha) = V_a^M(\beta)$;
(v) $V_a^M(B \supset C) = 1$ iff $V_a^M(B) = 0$ or $V_a^M(C) = 1$;
(vi) $V_a^M(\neg B) = 1 - V_a^M(B)$;
(vii) $V_a^M(\forall x B) = 1$ iff $V_{a'}^M(B) = 1$, for every $a' \in [a]_x$.

■

The following truth-conditions easily follow from the definitions of the symbols $\wedge$, $\vee$, $\equiv$, *False* and $\exists$:

(viii) $V_a^M(B \wedge C) = \min(V_a^M(B), V_a^M(C))$;
(ix) $V_a^M(B \vee C) = \max(V_a^M(B), V_a^M(C))$;
(x) $V_a^M(B \equiv C) = 1$ iff $V_a^M(B) = V_a^M(C)$;
(xi) $V_a^M(False) = 0$;
(xii) $V_a^M(\exists x B) = 1$ iff $V_{a'}^M(B) = 1$, for some $a' \in [a]_x$.

A formula A is said to be *satisfied in a frame* M *by an assignment* $a \in As(M)$ iff $V_a^M(A) = 1$. *A is satifiable* iff $V_a^M(A) = 1$, for some frame M and some $a \in As(M)$; otherwise A is called *unsatisfiable*. A is *true in* M iff $V_a^M(A) = 1$, for any $a \in As(M)$. If A is true in M, then M is called a *model of A*. A is (*logically*) *valid* iff A is true in every frame M.

Example 1.26 Let $A = P(x, f(x)) \supset \forall y P(x, y)$ and consider the frame M such that $|M|$ is the set of postive integers, $M|P|$ is the relation $\leq$, and $M|f|$ is the successor function. A is satisfied in M by $a \in As(M)$ iff $a(x) = 1$. Thus, A is satisfiable but not valid. ■

The following theorem lists basic results concerning the notions of truth, satisfiability and validity:

Theorem 1.27

(i) A is true in M iff $\forall A$ is true in M;
(ii) A is valid iff $\forall A$ is valid;
(iii) A is satisfiable iff $\exists A$ is satisfiable;
(iv) A is valid iff $\neg A$ is unsatisfiable.
∎

The validity problem of first-order logic is the task of determining whether or not an arbitrarily given first-order formula is valid.

Theorem 1.28 (Church 1936) The validity problem of first-order logic is undecidable. ∎

The above result can be alternatively stated that, in general, the set of valid formulae (over a first-order language L) is not a computable subset of L. However, this set is recursively enumerable and hence we have:

Theorem 1.29 The set of valid formulae over a first-order language L is a partially computable subset of L. ∎

In view of Theorem 1.29, there exists a procedure Π which takes an arbitrary formula $A \in L$ and determines that A is valid, provided that this is indeed the case. Otherwise, i.e. if A is not valid, Π either terminates (and reports the invalidity of A) or loops forever.†

The result of Theorem 1.29 is often expressed by saying that first-order logic is *semi-decidable* or *partially decidable*.

An *instance of a propositional formula A* is any formula obtainable from A by uniformly substituting formulae for proposition constants occurring in A. It is easy to see that any instance of a tautology is valid.

We now list a number of schemata representing valid formulae of practical importance:

(V1) $\forall xA \supset \exists xA$
(V2) $\forall xA(x) \supset A(\alpha)$, if α is free for x in $A(x)$
(V3) $A(\alpha) \supset \exists xA(x)$, if α is free for x in $A(x)$
(V4) $\exists x\, \forall yA \supset \forall y\, \exists xA$
(V5) $\forall xyA \equiv \forall yxA$
(V6) $\exists xyA \equiv \exists yxA$
(V7) $\forall xA \equiv \neg\exists x \neg A$
(V8) $\exists xA \equiv \neg\forall x \neg A$
(V9) $\forall x(A \supset B) \supset (\forall xA \supset \forall xB)$
(V10) $\forall xA \wedge \forall xB \equiv \forall x(A \wedge B)$
(V11) $\forall xA \vee \forall xB \supset \forall x(A \vee B)$
(V12) $\exists xA \vee \exists xB \equiv \exists x(A \vee B)$
(V13) $\exists x(A \wedge B) \supset \exists xA \wedge \exists xB$

The following schemata represent valid formulae, provided that A contains no free occurrences of x:

(V14) $\forall xA \equiv A$

† Actually, a number of such procedures have been proposed in the literature. One of the most efficient will be presented in the next section.

(V15) $\exists x A \equiv A$
(V16) $\exists x B \vee A \equiv \exists x(B \vee A)$
(V17) $A \vee \exists x B \equiv \exists x(A \vee B)$
(V18) $\forall x B \vee A \equiv \forall x(B \vee A)$
(V19) $A \vee \forall x B \equiv \forall x(A \vee B)$
(V20) $\exists x B \wedge A \equiv \exists x(B \wedge A)$
(V21) $A \wedge \exists x B \equiv \exists x(A \wedge B)$
(V22) $\forall x B \wedge A \equiv \forall x(B \wedge A)$
(V23) $A \wedge \forall x B \equiv \forall x(A \wedge B)$

Formulae A and B are said to be *(logically) equivalent*, written $A \Leftrightarrow B$, iff they yield the same truth-value for any frame M and any assignment $a \in As(M)$. The following theorem, which corresponds closely to Theorem 1.6, lists basic properties of equivalent formulae.

Theorem 1.30

(i) $A \Leftrightarrow B$ iff $A \equiv B$ is valid;
(ii) $A \Leftrightarrow B$ and $B \Leftrightarrow C$ imply $A \Leftrightarrow C$; (Transitivity of Equivalence)
(iii) If B is a subformula of A, A' is the result of replacing one or more occurrences of B in A by C, and $B \Leftrightarrow C$, then $A \Leftrightarrow A'$. (Replacement Theorem)

▮

We say that B *is an immediate variant of* A iff $A = Qx_iC(x_i)$ and $B = Qx_jC(x_j)$, where $Q \in \{\forall, \exists\}$, and $C(x_i)$ has no free occurrences of x_j. We say that B is a *variant of* A iff B is the result of replacing one or more subformulae of A by their immediate variants. For example, $\forall x.P(x) \wedge Q(x)$ is an immediate variant of $\forall z.P(z) \wedge Q(z)$. Thus, $\exists y[R(y) \supset \forall z.P(z) \wedge Q(z)]$ is a variant of $\exists y[R(y) \supset \forall x.P(x) \wedge Q(x)]$.

Theorem 1.31 (Variant Theorem) If B is a variant of A, then $A \Leftrightarrow B$. ▮

A formula A is said to be in *prenex conjunctive normal form* iff it is of the form

$$Q_1x_1 \ldots Q_nx_n\left[\bigwedge_{i=1}^{m}\bigvee_{j=1}^{k(i)} A_{ij}\right], \qquad \text{where}$$

(i) For each $1 \leq i \leq n$, $Q_i \in \{\forall, \exists\}$; (ii) $x_1, \ldots, x_n$ are distinct variables occurring in $\bigwedge_{i=1}^{m}\bigvee_{j=1}^{k(i)} A_{ij}$; (iii) Each A_{ij} is either an atomic formula or the negation of an atomic formula. The part '$Q_1x_1 \ldots Q_nx_n$', which may be empty, is called the *prefix of* A; the part $\bigwedge_{i=1}^{m}\bigvee_{j=1}^{k(i)} A_{ij}$ is called the *matrix of* A. We say that B is a *prenex conjunctive normal form of* A iff B is in prenex conjunctive normal form and $A \Leftrightarrow B$.

Theorem 1.32 Every formula A can be effectively transformed into its prenex conjunctive normal form.

Proof We construct a formula A' in prenex conjunctive normal form by successively replacing subformulae of A by their equivalents. Thus, by Theorem 1.30 (ii)–(iii), $A' \Leftrightarrow A$. The construction proceeds in six steps.

Step 1 *Eliminate redundant quantifiers*. Eliminate in A any quantifier $\forall x$ or $\exists x$ whose scope does not contain x. Denote the resulting formula by A_1. (In view of (V14)–(V15), $A_1 \Leftrightarrow A$.)

Step 2 *Rename variables.* Take the leftmost subformula of A_1 of the form $\forall x B(x)$ or $\exists x B(x)$ such that x occurs in some other part of A_1, and replace it by $\forall y B(y)$ or $\exists y B(y)$, respectively, where y is a new variable. Repeat this process until all quantified variables are different and no variable is both bound and free. Denote the resulting formula by A_2. (A_2 is a variant of A_1 and hence $A_1 \Leftrightarrow A_2$.)

Step 3 *Eliminate* $\supset$ *and* $\equiv$. Replace in A_2.

$$\begin{array}{lll} (B \supset C) & \text{by} & (\neg B \vee C) \\ (B \equiv C) & \text{by} & ((\neg B \vee C) \wedge (B \vee \neg C)) \end{array}$$

until the resulting formula, A_3, contains $\vee$, $\wedge$ *and* $\neg$ as its only connectives.

Step 4 *Move* $\neg$ *inward.* Replace in A_3.

$$\begin{array}{lll} \neg\forall x B & \text{by} & \exists x \neg B \\ \neg\exists x B & \text{by} & \forall x \neg B \\ \neg(B \vee C) & \text{by} & \neg B \wedge \neg C \\ \neg(B \wedge C) & \text{by} & \neg B \vee \neg C \\ \neg\neg B & \text{by} & B \end{array}$$

until each occurrence of $\neg$ immediately precedes an atomic formula. Denote the resulting formula by A_4.

Step 5 *Move quantifiers to the left.* Replace in A_4

$$\begin{array}{lll} \exists x B \vee C & \text{by} & \exists x(B \vee C) \\ C \vee \exists x B & \text{by} & \exists x(C \vee B) \\ \forall x B \vee C & \text{by} & \forall x(B \vee C) \\ C \vee \forall x B & \text{by} & \forall x(C \vee B) \\ \exists x B \wedge C & \text{by} & \exists x(B \wedge C) \\ C \wedge \exists x B & \text{by} & \exists x(C \wedge B) \\ \forall x B \wedge C & \text{by} & \forall x(B \wedge C) \\ C \wedge \forall x B & \text{by} & \forall x(C \wedge B) \end{array}$$

until all quantifiers are on the left. Denote the resulting formula by A_5. Observe that, by Step 2, C has no occurrences of x and hence $A_5 \Leftrightarrow A_4$.

Step 6 *Distribute* $\wedge$ *over* $\vee$. Replace in A_5 as long as possible

$$\begin{array}{lll} (B \wedge C) \vee D & \text{by} & (B \vee D) \wedge (C \vee D) \\ B \vee (C \wedge D) & \text{by} & (B \vee C) \wedge (B \vee D) \end{array}$$

Denote the resulting formula by A'. This is the desired prenex conjunctive normal form of A. ▮

We illustrate the above construction by giving an example. Consider the formula

$$A = P(x, y) \supset [\exists x . Q(x) \wedge \exists z(x = y)]$$

Successively performing Steps 1–6, we have:

$$\begin{aligned} A_1 &= P(x, y) \supset [\exists x . Q(x) \wedge x = y] \\ A_2 &= P(x, y) \supset [\exists v . Q(v) \wedge v = y] \\ A_3 &= \neg P(x, y) \vee [\exists v . Q(v) \wedge v = y] \\ A_4 &= A_3 \end{aligned}$$

$$A_5 = \exists v[\neg P(x, y) \vee (Q(v) \wedge v = y)]$$
$$A' = \exists v[(\neg P(x, y) \vee Q(v)) \wedge (\neg P(x, y) \vee v = y)]$$

A' is the prenex conjunctive normal form of A.

A formula A is said to be in *prenex normal form* iff it is of the form $Q_1x_1 \ldots Q_nx_nB$ ($n \geq 0$), where (i) For each $1 \leq i \leq n$, $Q_i \in \{\forall, \exists\}$; (ii) $x_1, \ldots, x_n$ are distinct variables occurring in B; (iii) B contains no quantifiers. As before, '$Q_1x_1 \ldots Q_nx_n$' is called the *prefix of A* and B is called the *matrix of A*. Note that prenex conjunctive normal form is a special case of prenex normal form. It follows, therefore, that any formula may be effectively transformed into its equivalent in prenex normal form.

1.3.3 First-order theories

A *first-order theory* is a pair $T = \langle L, S \rangle$, where L is a first-order language and S is a computable set of sentences (i.e. closed formulae) from L. The elements of S are called the *axioms* (or *premisses*) *of T*. If $S = \{\ \}$, then T is called the *predicate calculus over L*.

In the remainder of this section, the phrase 'first-order theory' will be abbreviated to 'theory'. Theories will be denoted by the letter T, possibly with subscripts and primes. A theory $\langle L, S \rangle$ is said to be *over L*. If L is a language with equality, then $\langle L, S \rangle$ is called a *theory with equality;* otherwise, it is called a *theory without equality*.

Theories will be usually identified with sets of their axioms. In such a case, we adopt the convention that the language of a theory T consists of all formulae constructable using predicate and function constants occurring in the axioms of T.

A theory is *finite* (resp. *infinite*) iff the set of its axioms is finite (resp. infinite). If T is a theory over L_{AL} and $A_1, \ldots, A_n$ are sentences in $L_{AL'}$, then we write $T \cup \{A_1, \ldots, A_n\}$, or simply $T, A_1, \ldots, A_n$, to denote the theory $\langle L_{AL \cup AL'}, T \cup \{A_1, \ldots, A_n\} \rangle$. T is said to be a *subtheory of T'*, written $T \subseteq T'$, iff each axiom of T is also an axiom of T'. Notice that with any sentence A, we may uniquely associate the theory $\langle L(A), \{A\} \rangle$, where $L(A)$ is the language consisting of all formulae constructable from function and predicate constants occurring in A. **Thus, sentences may always be regarded as first-order theories.**

A frame M is a *model of a theory T* iff all axioms of T are true in M. A theory is said to be *satisfiable* iff it has a model; otherwise, it is said to be *unsatisfiable*.

Theorem 1.33 (Compactness Theorem) A theory T has a model iff each finite subtheory of T has a model. ▮

A formula A is a *semantic consequence of a theory T*, written $T \models A$, iff A is true in every model of T.† In particular, A is a semantic consequence of the predicate calculus (over L), written $\models A$, iff A is true in every frame (for L).‡ ▮

If $T \models A$, then we also say that A (*logically*) *follows from T*, *A is entailed by T*, or *T entails A*.

Example 1.34 Let T consist of the following axioms:

Bird(*Tweety*)
$\forall x.$*Bird*(x) $\supset$ *Flies*(x)
$\forall x.$*Flies*(x) $\supset$ *Has-Wings*(x)

† The notation $T \models A$ was given a somewhat different meaning in the previous section, where T was a propositional theory. Possible confusions will be always avoided by the context.
‡ '$\models A$' is then a symbolic notation for the phrase 'a sentence A is valid'.

The reader may easily check that the formulae *Flies*(*Tweety*) and *Has-Wings*(*Tweety*) are true in every model of T. Thus, $T \models$ *Flies*(*Tweety*) and $T \models$ *Has-Wings*(*Tweety*). ▮

The symbol $\models$, as specified in this section, denotes a binary relation, called the *entailment relation of (classical) first-order logic*, which holds between a theory T and a formula A iff $T \models A$.

The following theorem is a counterpart of Theorem 1.11:

Theorem 1.35 The entailment relation of first-order logic enjoys the following properties:

(i) $T \models B$ iff the theory $T \cup \{\neg \forall B\}$ is unsatisfiable;
(ii) $T, A \models B$ iff $T \models A \supset B$;[†]
(iii) $\{A_1, \ldots, A_n\} \models B$ iff $\models A_1 \wedge \cdots \wedge A_n \supset B$;
(iv) If $T \subseteq T'$, then $\{A: T \models A\} \subseteq \{A: T' \models A\}$. (Monotonicity)

▮

In view of (iii), the problem of determining whether a formula B follows from a theory $\{A_1, \ldots, A_n\}$ reduces to the task of determining whether the formula $A_1 \wedge \cdots \wedge A_n \supset B$ is valid. Assertion (iv) expresses the Principle of Monotonicity for first-order logic.

Theories T and T' are (*logically*) *equivalent*, written $T \Leftrightarrow T'$, iff they have the same models. The most important property of equivalent theories is that they entail the same formulae:

Theorem 1.36 $T \Leftrightarrow T'$ iff $\{A: T \models A\} = \{A: T' \models A\}$. ▮

We also have the following counterpart of Theorem 1.13:

Theorem 1.37 If $T = \{A_1, \ldots, A_n\}$, then $T \Leftrightarrow \{A_1 \wedge \cdots \wedge A_n\}$. ▮

Formulae A and B are said to be *equivalent in a theory* T iff they yield the same truth-value in every model M of T, and every a $\in$ As(M).

Let T be a theory over a first-order language L with equality. The *set of equality axioms for* T is just the set of equality axioms for L (see Definition 1.23).

Example 1.38 Let T consist of:

$$Elephant(Joe)$$
$$\forall x . Elephant(x) \supset Elephant(father(x))$$
$$Joe = Clyde$$

The set of equality axioms for T consists of (E1)–(E3) (see Definition 1.23), together with

$$\forall xy[x = y \wedge Elephant(x) \supset Elephant(y)]$$
$$\forall xy[x = y \supset father(x) = father(y)]$$

▮

The following notion will play an important role in Chapters 6 and 7:

Definition 1.39 A sentence is said to be *universal* iff its prenex normal form contains no existential quantifiers. A theory is said to be *universal* iff all of its axioms are universal. ▮

[†] Note that the symbol $\models$ denotes a relation between theories and formulae. Thus, when we write $T, A \models B$, we implicitly assume that A is a sentence.

The following theorem states one of the most important results of first-order logic:

Theorem 1.40 (Skolem–Löwenheim Theorem)

(i) Any satisfiable first-order theory without equality has a model with a denumerable domain.
(ii) Any first-order theory with equality has a model with a countable (i.e. finite or denumerable) domain.

∎

1.3.4 First-order logic as a deduction system

A *deduction system for first-order logic* is defined as that for propositional logic (Definition 1.14), except that L is now a first-order language. If $\langle L, \mathrm{S}, \mathrm{R}\rangle$ is a deduction system for first-order logic and $\mathrm{R_i} \in \mathrm{R}$, then $\mathrm{R_i}$ is said to be *sound* (alternatively, $\mathrm{R_i}$ is a *truth-preserving rule*) iff for every frame M and every formulae $A_1, \ldots, A_k$ from the domain of $\mathrm{R_i}$, $\mathrm{R_i}(A_1, \ldots, A_k)$ is true in M, provided that all $A_1, \ldots, A_k$ are true in M.

The notion of a proof is specified as in section 1.2.4. We write $T \vdash_{\mathrm{DS}} A$ to indicate that A is provable from T in DS; $\vdash_{\mathrm{DS}} A$ is an abbreviation for $\{\ \} \vdash_{\mathrm{DS}} A$.

The computability requirements imposed on deduction systems guarantee, provided that we restrict ourselves to computable first-order languages and computable theories, that the notion of a proof is computable.

A deduction system $\mathrm{DS} = \langle L, \mathrm{S}, \mathrm{R}\rangle$ is said to be *sound* iff $\vdash_{\mathrm{DS}} A$ implies that A is valid. DS is said to be *complete* iff every valid formula from L is provable in DS.

The following deduction system for first-order logic is both sound and complete.

Definition 1.41 Let L be a first-order language. We denote by $\mathrm{FOL}(L)$ the deduction system $\langle L, \mathrm{S}, \mathrm{R}\rangle$ given by:

(i) S consists of the following axioms (A, B and C are any formulae from L):

(A1) *True*
(A2) $A \supset (B \supset A)$
(A3) $(A \supset (B \supset C)) \supset ((A \supset B) \supset (A \supset C))$
(A4) $(\neg B \supset \neg A) \supset ((\neg B \supset A) \supset B)$
(A5) $\forall x A(x) \supset A(\alpha)$, where α is any term free for x in $A(x)$
(A6) $\forall x(A \supset B) \supset (A \supset \forall x B)$, where A contains no free occurrences of x

If L is a language with equality, then S additionally contains the equality axioms for L (see Definition 1.23).

(ii) R consists of the following inference rules:

(MP) B is a direct consequence of A and $A \supset B$;
(GEN) $\forall x A$ is a direct consequence of A.

∎

It is easy to see that $\mathrm{FOL}(L)$ satisfies the computability requirements imposed on deduction systems. (GEN) is called the *rule of generalization*.

We shall normally assume that L is fixed, and $\vdash_{\mathrm{FOL(L)}}$ will be abbreviated to $\vdash$. If $T \vdash A$, then we say that A is *provable from T in first-order logic*. If $\vdash A$, then we say that A is *provable in first-order logic*, or, alternatively, A is a *theorem in first-order logic*. We write $T \nvdash A$ and $\nvdash A$ as the negations for $T \vdash A$ and $\vdash A$, respectively.[†]

The binary relation denoted by the symbol $\vdash$ (resp. $\nvdash$), is called the *provability* (resp. *unprovability*) *relation of classical first-order logic*.

We denote by Th the *provability operator of* (*classical*) *first-order logic*, i.e. the operator which assigns to each first-order theory T the set $\mathrm{Th}(T)$ of all sentences provable from T in first-order logic.[‡]

The operator Th, as specified here, enjoys the basic properties of the provability operator of propositional logic, listed in Theorem 1.16. In particular, for any theories T and T', $T \subseteq T'$ implies $\mathrm{Th}(T) \subseteq \mathrm{Th}(T')$.

The syntax and semantics of first-order logic are connected by the following theorem:

Theorem 1.42
(i) If $T \vdash A$, then $T \models A$; (Soundness Theorem)
(ii) If $T \models A$, then $T \vdash A$. (Completeness Theorem)
∎

Corollary 1.43 $\vdash A$ iff $\models A$. ∎
A theory T over L is said to be *consistent* iff there is a formula $A \in L$ such that $T \nvdash A$. As in the case of propositional logic, the notion of consistency is a syntactic counterpart of that of satisfiability:

Theorem 1.44 T is consistent iff T is satisfiable. ∎
We also have:

Theorem 1.45 (Deduction Theorem)

(i) $T, A \vdash B$ iff $T \vdash A \supset B$;[§]
(ii) $\{A_1, \ldots, A_n\} \vdash B$ iff $\vdash A_1 \wedge \cdots \wedge A_n \supset B$.
∎

Theorem 1.46 T is consistent iff each finite subtheory of T is consistent. ∎

1.3.5 Many-sorted first-order logic

Many-sorted first-order logic differs from ordinary first-order logic in that it employs several types (sorts) of variables – each type associated with a particular subdomain of objects. Also, function and predicate constants are sorted in the sense that their arguments are limited to terms of appropriate types. For instance, using many-sorted logic, we might introduce a binary predicate constant *Teaches* with the intention that its first argument is restricted to the type *Teacher* and its second argument is an object of the type *Student*.

From the technical point of view, many-sorted logics are an expendable luxury, because they are reducible to ordinary logic. However, they often allow the naturalness

[†] The symbols $\vdash$ and $\nvdash$ were given different meanings in the previous section, where they were associated with propositional logic. Possible confusions will be always avoided by the context. (The same remark applies to the symbol Th, which will be specified later.)
[‡] Note that $\mathrm{Th}(T)$ refers to a set of sentences rather than a set of formulae.
[§] Note that the symbol $\vdash$ denotes a relation between theories and formulae. Thus, when we write $T, A \vdash \mathrm{B}$, we implicitly assume that A is a sentence.

of a representation to increase and hence have been employed in many practical applications.

Let k be a positive integer and suppose that $t_1, \ldots, t_k$ are distinct objects, referred to as *basic types*. We define the *set of types based on* $t_1, \ldots, t_k$, written $TP(t_1, \ldots, t_k)$, to be the smallest set satisfying:

(i) $t_i \in TP(t_1, \ldots, t_k)$, for each $1 \leq i \leq k$;
(ii) For any tuple $t = \langle t_{i1}, \ldots, t_{in} \rangle$, where $n \geq 0$ and $t_{i1}, \ldots, t_{in}$ are elements of $\{t_1, \ldots, t_k\}$ (not necessarily distinct), $t \in TP(t_1, \ldots, t_k)$.

Types serve the purpose of classification: basic types are used to classify variables (and, more generally, terms), whereas those of the form $\langle t_{i1}, \ldots, t_{in} \rangle$ provide a classification of predicate and function constants. Specifically, a predicate constant of a type $\langle t_{i1}, \ldots, t_{in} \rangle$ $(n \geq 0)$ represents an n-ary predicate constant with the first argument of the type $t_{i1}, \ldots,$ and the n-th of the type t_{in}. Predicate constants of the type $\langle \rangle$ are just proposition constants. A function constant of a type $\langle t_i, t_{i1}, \ldots, t_{in} \rangle$ $(n \geq 0)$ represents an n-ary function constant which takes terms of the types $t_{i1}, \ldots, t_{in}$ as its arguments and whose value is a term of the type t_i. Function constants of a type $\langle t_i \rangle$ are called *individual constants of a type* t_i.

An *alphabet of* k*-sorted (first-order) logic with* $t_1, \ldots, t_k$ *as basic types* consists of primitive symbols from the following pairwise disjoint categories:

(i) k denumerable sets $V^1, \ldots, V^k$. Elements of V^i $(1 \leq i \leq k)$ are called *individual variables of type* t_i, and we denote them by $x_1^i, x_2^i, \ldots$;
(ii) One truth-constant: *'True'*;
(iii) Sentential connectives: '$\neg$' and '$\supset$';
(iv) One quantifier: '$\forall$';
(v) Punctuation marks: '(', ',' and ')';
(vi) A countable set **P** of *predicate constants*; to each $P \in \mathbf{P}$, there is uniquely assigned a type $\langle t_{i1}, \ldots, t_{in} \rangle \in TP(t_1, \ldots, t_k)$, called the *type of P*;
(vii) A binary predicate constant: '=' it is assumed that the arguments of '=' are of arbitrary types;
(viii) A countable set **F** of function constants; to each $f \in \mathbf{F}$, there is uniquely assigned a non-empty type $\langle t_i, t_{i1}, \ldots, t_{in} \rangle \in TP(t_1, \ldots, t_k)$, called the *type of f*.

The classes (i)–(v) are fixed, whereas the other ones may vary from one alphabet into another. The set of function constants may be empty. We assume that any alphabet contains at least one predicate constant of positive arity, i.e. either an element of **P**, with a type different from $\langle \rangle$, or the constant '='. The sets **P** and **F** are required to be computable in the sense that there is an effective procedure Π_P (resp. Π_F) which takes an arbitrary symbol s, determines whether $s \in \mathbf{P}$ (resp. whether $s \in \mathbf{F}$), and, if so, returns the type of s.

Definition 1.47 Let AL be an alphabet of k-sorted logic with $t_1, \ldots, t_k$ as basic types.

The set TM_{AL}^i of *terms of type* t_i *over* AL $(1 \leq i \leq k)$ is the smallest set such that: (i) all individual variables of type t_i and all individual constants of type t_i are members of TM_{AL}^i; (ii) if f is a function constant of type $\langle t_i, t_{i1}, \ldots, t_{in} \rangle$ and $\alpha_1, \ldots, \alpha_n$ are terms of types $t_{i1}, \ldots, t_{in}$, respectively, then $f(\alpha_1, \ldots, \alpha_n) \in TM_{AL}^i$.

The set $AFORM_{AL}$ of *atomic formulae over* AL is the smallest set such that: (i) *'True'* and all proposition constants from AL are elements of $AFORM_{AL}$; (ii) if P is a predicate constant of type $\langle t_{i1}, \ldots, t_{in} \rangle$ $(n > 0)$ and $\alpha_1, \ldots, \alpha_n$ are terms of types

$t_{i1}, \ldots, t_{in}$, respectively, then $P(\alpha_1, \ldots, \alpha_n) \in AFORM_{AL}$; (iii) If α and β are terms of arbitrary types, then $(\alpha = \beta) \in AFORM_{AL}$, provided that '=' $\in$ AL.

The set L_{AL} of *formulae over* AL is the smallest set such that: (i) if $A \in AFORM_{AL}$, then $A \in L_{AL}$; (ii) if $A, B \in L_{AL}$ and x is an individual variable of any type, then $(\neg A) \in L_{AL}$, $(A \supset B) \in L_{AL}$ and $(\forall x(A)) \in L_{AL}$. ∎

The set L_{AL}, which will be often abbreviated to L, is called the k-*sorted* (*first-order*) *language over* AL. The restriction to alphabets with computable sets of predicate and function constants assures the computability of any k-sorted language.

A k-sorted language L_{AL} is said to be the *language with* (resp. *without*) *equality* iff '=' $\in$ AL (resp. '=' $\notin$ AL).

The truth-constant *False*, the logical connectives $\wedge$, $\vee$, $\equiv$ and the existential quantifier $\exists$ are defined as usual.

All terminological and notational conventions of section 1.3.1 carry over many-sorted logic.

Example 1.48 Assume that the following facts are true:

(F1) Bill, Tom and Mary are students;
(F2) John and Sue are the only teachers;
(F3) All teachers teach Mary;
(F4) Some students are taught by Sue.

We introduce two basic types: *Teacher* and *Student* (abbreviated to t and s, respectively); one binary predicate constant of type $\langle t, s\rangle$: *Teaches*; three individual constants of type s: *Bill*, *Tom* and *Mary*; and two individual constants of type t: *John* and *Sue*. Then (F1)–(F4) can be represented by:

(A1) $\exists x^s y^s z^s . (x^s = Bill) \wedge (y^s = Tom) \wedge (z^s = Mary)$
(A2) $\forall x^t . (x^t = John) \vee (x^t = Sue)$
(A3) $\forall x^t Teaches(x^t, Mary)$
(A4) $\exists x^s Teaches(Sue, x^s)$
∎

We now proceed to the semantics for many-sorted logic.

Definition 1.49 Let AL be an alphabet for k-sorted logic with $t_1, \ldots, t_k$ as basic types. A *frame for* L_{AL} is a tuple $M = \langle D_1, \ldots, D_k, m\rangle$, where:

(i) $D_1, \ldots, D_k$ are non-empty sets, called the *subdomains of* M; $\bigcup_{i=1}^{k} D_i$ is called the *domain of* M;
(ii) m is a function which assigns to each predicate constant of type $\langle t_{i1}, \ldots, t_{in}\rangle$ $(n \geq 0)$ from AL, different from '=', a relation on $D_{i1} x \ldots x D_{in}$, to the constant '=', if present in AL, the identity relation on $\bigcup_{i=1}^{k} D_i$, and to each function constant of type $\langle t_i, t_{i1}, \ldots, t_{in}\rangle$ $(n \geq 1)$, a function from $D_{i1} x \ldots x D_{in}$ into D_i.
∎

Let $M = \langle D_1, \ldots, D_k, m\rangle$ be a frame for a k-sorted first-order language L_{AL}, where AL is an alphabet with $t_1, \ldots, t_k$ as basic types. We write $|M|_i$ to denote the set D_i. If K is a predicate or function constant from AL, then $M|K|$ stands for $m(K)$. By As(M) we denote the *set of assignments over* M, i.e. the set of all functions $a: \bigcup_{i=1}^{k} V^i \rightarrow \bigcup_{i=1}^{k} |M|_i$ such that $a(x^i) \in |M|_i$, for every variable x^i of type t_i. If $a \in As(M)$ and x^i is a variable of type t_i, then $[a]_{x^i}$ denotes the set of those assignments over M which differ from 'a' at most on x^i.

Definition 1.50 Let M be a frame for L_{AL}, where AL is an alphabet for k-sorted logic with $t_1, \ldots, t_k$ as basic types. The *value* $V_a^M(\alpha)$ *of a term* α *of type* t_1 *in* M *wrt* $a \in As(M)$ is an element of $|M|_i$ defined as follows:

(i) $V_a^M(x^i) = a(x^i)$;
(ii) $V_a^M(a) = M|a|$, where a is an individual constant;
(iii) $V_a^M(f(\alpha_1, \ldots, \alpha_n)) = M|f|(V_a^M(\alpha_1), \ldots, V_a^M(\alpha_n))$.

The *truth-value* $V_a^M(A)$ *of a formula* $A \in L_{AL}$ *in* M *wrt* $a \in As(M)$ is an element of $\{0, 1\}$ specified by:

(i) $V_a^M(True) = 1$;
(ii) $V_a^M(p) = M|p|$, where p is a proposition constant;
(iii) $V_a^M(P(\alpha_1, \ldots, \alpha_n)) = M|P|(V_a^M(\alpha_1), \ldots, V_a^M(\alpha_n))$;
(iv) $V_a^M(\alpha = \beta) = 1$ iff $V_a^M(\alpha) = V_a^M(\beta)$;
(v) $V_a^M(B \supset C) = 1$ iff $V_a^M(B) = 0$ or $V_a^M(C) = 1$;
(vi) $V_a^M(\neg B) = 1 - V_a^M(B)$;
(vii) $V_a^M(\forall x^i B) = 1$ iff $V_{a'}^M(B) = 1$, for every $a' \in [a]_{x^i}$.

▮

The notions '*A is satisfied in* M *by* $a \in As(M)$', '*A* is *satisfiable* (*unsatisfiable*)', '*A* is *true in* M', '*A* is *valid*' and '*A* and *B* are *equivalent*' are defined as in section 1.3.2. Theorem 1.30 holds for many-sorted logic. We may also speak about a *theory of k-sorted logic*, viewed as a pair $\langle L, S \rangle$, where L is a k-sorted language and S is a computable set of sentences from S. As usual, M is a *model of a theory T* iff all sentences from S are true in M. A theory which has a model is said to be *satisfiable*. Two theories which have exactly the same models are said to be *equivalent*. We write $T \models A$ to indicate that A is true in every model of T. The results stated in Theorems 1.33, 1.35, 1.36, 1.37 and 1.40 generalize into many-sorted logic.

It is possible to construct a sound and complete deduction system for many-sorted logic, but we omit the details here.

For more information about many-sorted logic, the reader should consult Feferman (1974) and Kreisel & Krivine (1967).

1.4 RESOLUTION METHOD

As remarked in the previous section, the validity problem for first-order logic is undecidable. That is, there is no algorithm for deciding whether or not an arbitrarily given first-order formula is valid. The problem is, however, semi-decidable in the sense that there exists a procedure which confirms the validity of any valid formula, but which runs forever for some invalid formulae. One of such procedures, called the *resolution method*, is outlined in this section. Its efficiency makes it especially well suited to automation on a computer.†

† The resolution method is usually studied in the context of a more general subject, known in the AI literature as *automated theorem proving* (see Chang & Lee, 1973; Loveland 1978).

Before providing the description of the resolution method, we make two important remarks. Firstly, since $\{A_1, \ldots, A_n\} \models A$ iff $A_1 \wedge \cdots \wedge A_n \supset A$ is valid, any procedure capable of confirming the validity of first-order formulae may be used to demonstrate that a given formula is entailed by a given finite first-order theory. Secondly, since a formula is valid iff its negation is unsatisfiable, one way of showing the validity of a formula A is to show the unsatisfiability of $\neg A$. This is the approach taken by the resolution method, which as a matter of fact detects unsatisfiable formulae.† Thus, to demonstrate the validity of a formula A, we apply the resolution method to $\neg A$. If $\neg A$ is unsatisfiable (i.e. A is valid), the procedure will detect it and stop. Otherwise, if $\neg A$ is satisfiable (i.e. A is invalid), the computation process may fail to terminate.

1.4.1 Clausal form

The resolution method applies only to formulae of a special form, called the *clausal form*. To introduce this notion, we need some preliminary terminology.

Literals are atomic formulae (*positive literals*) or their negations (*negative literals*). We use the letter l, with or without subscripts and primes, to denote literals. The symbol $|l|$ stands for the atomic formula of a literal l. For instance, $|P(x, b)| = P(x, b)$; $|\neg Q(f(x))| = Q(f(x))$. We write $\neg l$ to denote the *complement of* l, i.e. the literal $\neg P(\alpha_1, \ldots, \alpha_n)$ if $l = P(\alpha_1, \ldots, \alpha_n)$, and $P(\alpha_1, \ldots, \alpha_n)$ if $l = \neg P(\alpha_1, \ldots, \alpha_n)$.

A *clause* is a formula C of the form $l_1 \vee \cdots \vee l_n$ $(n \geq 0)$, where $l_1, \ldots, l_n$ are literals. If $n = 0$, then C is called the *empty clause*, written $\square$.

A formula is said to be in the *clausal form* iff it is of the form

$$\forall C_1 \wedge \cdots \wedge \forall C_n \qquad (n \geq 1) \tag{1.4.1}$$

where $C_1, \ldots, C_n$ are clauses. A theory is said to be in the clausal form iff all its axioms are in the clausal form. Recall that a sentence is said to be universal iff its prenex normal form contains no existential quantifiers. It is easy to see that by transforming such a sentence into its prenex conjunctive normal form (see Theorem 1.32), we obtain a sentence of the form

$$\forall[C_1 \wedge \cdots C_n] \tag{1.4.2}$$

where $C_1, \ldots, C_n$ are clauses. Since any formula is equivalent to its prenex conjunctive normal form, and since (1.4.2) is equivalent to (1.4.1), we have the following result:

Theorem 1.51

(i) Any universal sentence can be effectively transformed into an equivalent sentence in the clausal form.

(ii) For any universal theory T, there exists a theory T' in the clausal form such that $T \Leftrightarrow T'$.

∎

Theorem 1.51 need not hold for non-universal sentences (theories). However, it can be shown that any formula A can be effectively transformed into a sentence A' in the clausal form such that A is satisfiable iff A' is satisfiable. Also, for any theory T, there exists a theory T' in the clausal form such that T is satisfiable iff T' is satisfiable. The details follow.

† Procedures confirming the validity of a formula by demonstrating the unsatisfiability of its negation are usually called *refutation procedures*.

Definition 1.52 Let A be a formula. A *clausal form of A* is any formula obtained from A by the following construction:

Step 0 *Take the existential closure of A.* Put $A_1 = \exists A$.

Steps 1–4 Apply to A_1 Steps 1–4 from the construction specified in the proof of Theorem 1.32. Denote the resulting formula by A_2.

Step 5 *Move quantifiers to the right.* Replace in A_2 as long as possible (Q denotes $\forall$ or $\exists$; $\diamond$ stands for $\vee$ or $\wedge$)

$$\mathrm{Q}x(B \diamond C) \quad \text{by} \quad \begin{cases} B \diamond (\mathrm{Q}xC) & \text{if } x \text{ is not free in } B \\ (\mathrm{Q}xB) \diamond C & \text{if } x \text{ is not free in } C \end{cases}$$

Denote the resulting formula by A_3.

Step 6 *Eliminate existential quantifiers.* Start with A_3 and repeat the following process (for successively obtained formulae) until all existential quantifiers are eliminated:

> Take any subformula of the form $\exists yB(y)$. Suppose that $x_1, \ldots, x_n$ ($n \geq 0$) are all distinct free variables of $\exists yB(y)$ which are universally quantified to the left of $\exists yB(y)$. If $n = 0$, then replace $\exists yB(y)$ by $B(a)$, where a is a new individual constant. If $n > 0$, then replace $\exists yB(y)$ by $B(f(x_1, \ldots, x_n))$, where f is any new n-ary function constant.

Denote the resulting formula by A_4. The process described above is called *Skolemization*. The introduced symbols are called *Skolem functions*.

Step 7 *Delete quantifiers.* Delete all quantifiers from A_4. Denote the resulting formula by A_5.

Step 8 *Distribute $\wedge$ over $\vee$.* Replace in A_5 as long as possible

$$\begin{array}{lcl} (B \wedge C) \vee D & \text{by} & (B \vee D) \wedge (C \vee D) \\ B \vee (C \wedge D) & \text{by} & (B \vee C) \wedge (B \vee D) \end{array}$$

Denote the resulting formula by A_6.

Step 9 *Eliminate 'True' and 'False'.* A_6 is of the form $C_1 \wedge \cdots \wedge C_n$, where $C_1, \ldots, C_n$ are clauses. Delete any C_i one of whose literals is *True* or $\neg$*False*. From the remaining clauses delete all literals of the form *False* or $\neg$*True*. Denote the resulting formula by A_7.

Step 10 *Add universal quantifiers.* A_7 is of the form $C_1 \wedge \cdots \wedge C_n$, where $C_1, \ldots, C_n$ are clauses. Put $A_8 = \forall C_1 \wedge \cdots \wedge \forall C_n$. This is the desired clausal form of A. ∎

To illustrate the above construction, we consider a simple example. Let $A = P(a, v) \supset \forall x\, \exists y\, \forall u\, \exists z[P(x, y) \wedge Q(u, z)]$.

$$\begin{aligned} A_1 &= \exists v\{P(a, v) \supset \forall x\, \exists y\, \forall u\, \exists z[P(x, y) \wedge Q(u, z)]\} \\ A_2 &= \exists v\{\neg P(a, v) \vee \forall x\, \exists y\, \forall u\, \exists z[P(x, y) \wedge Q(u, z)]\} \\ A_3 &= \exists v \neg P(a, v) \vee [\forall x\, \exists yP(x, y) \wedge \forall u\, \exists zQ(u, z)] \\ A_4 &= \neg P(a, b) \vee [\forall xP(x, f(x)) \wedge \forall uQ(u, g(u))] \end{aligned}$$

(b, f and g are Skolem functions)

$$A_5 = \neg P(a, b) \vee [P(x, f(x)) \wedge Q(u, g(u))]$$
$$A_6 = [\neg P(a, b) \vee P(x, f(x))] \wedge [\neg P(a, b) \vee Q(u, g(u))]$$
$$A_7 = A_6$$
$$A_8 = [\forall x . \neg P(a, b) \vee P(x, f(x))] \wedge [\forall u . \neg P(a, b) \vee Q(u, g(u))]$$

A_8 is a clausal form of A.

Theorem 1.53 If B is a clausal form of a formula A, then B is satisfiable iff A is satisfiable. ▮

Corollary 1.54 Any formula A may be effectively transformed into a formula B in the clausal form such that A is satisfiable iff B is satisfiable. ▮

Corollary 1.54 leads to the following important observation: **as long as we are only interested in satisfiability of formulae, we may always assume that the formulae under consideration are in the clausal form.**

In passing, it is worth remarking that Step 5 in the described construction is optional and might be omitted. Its motivation is purely technical: to minimize the number of arguments in the introduced Skolem functions. (This, in turn, allows us to reduce the complexity of the resolution method.) To see the benefit of Step 5, consider the formula $\forall xy \, \exists z[P(x, x) \vee P(y, z)]$. The reader may easily check that applying the procedure with and without Step 5, we respectively obtain

$$\forall xy[P(x, x) \vee P(y, f(y))] \quad \text{and}$$
$$\forall xy[P(x, x) \vee P(y, f(x, y))]$$

where f is the introduced Skolem function.

Recall that any sentence may be identified with the theory containing the sentence as its only axiom. Furthermore, any theory of the form $\{A_1 \wedge \cdots \wedge A_n\}$ is equivalent to $\{A_1, \ldots, A_n\}$. It follows, therefore, that any sentence of the form (1.4.1) may be identified with the theory $\{\forall C_1, \ldots, \forall C_n\}$. This observation underlies what is called the *clausal notation* for sentences in the clausal form. According to this notation, a sentence (1.4.1) is written as

$$\{C_1, \ldots, C_n\} \tag{1.4.3}$$

where all variables occurring in $C_1, \ldots, C_n$ are implicitly universally quantified. We shall refer to (1.4.3) as the *set of clauses corresponding to* (1.4.1).

If A is a formula, not necessarily in the clausal form, then we write CLAUSES(A) to denote the set of clauses corresponding to an arbitrarily chosen clausal form of A.†

A *clausal form of a theory* T is any theory obtained from T by replacing all its axioms by their clausal forms. Note that if T is defined over a first-order language L_{AL}, then a clausal form of T is a theory over the language $L_{AL \cup F}$, where F is the set of the introduced Skolem functions.

Theorem 1.55 If T' is a clausal form of T, then T' is satisfiable iff T is satisfiable. ▮

Let T be a theory in the clausal form. By the *set of clauses corresponding to* T we mean the union of the sets of clauses corresponding to the axioms of T. If T is any theory, not necessarily in the clausal form, then we write CLAUSES(T) to denote the set of clauses corresponding to an arbitrarily chosen clausal form of T.

---

† The phrase 'arbitrarily chosen' is to be understood here in the following sense: whenever the notation CLAUSES(A) is used, the reader is permitted to freely choose a clausal form of A.

A set CL of clauses is said to be *satisfiable* (resp. *unsatisfiable*) iff the theory $\{\forall C : C \in \mathrm{CL}\}$ is satisfiable (resp. unsatisfiable).

The following theorem is a simple consequence of Theorems 1.35 (i), 1.53 and 1.55:

Theorem 1.56

(i) A is satisfiable iff CLAUSES(A) is satisfiable;
(ii) T is satisfiable iff CLAUSES(T) is satisfiable;
(iii) $T \models B$ iff CLAUSES(T) $\cup$ *CLAUSES*($\neg\forall B$) is unsatisfiable.

▮

1.4.2 Resolution rule

We now present a powerful inference rule, called the *resolution rule* (Robinson 1965), which forms the basis for the resolution method. To fix some ideas, we begin by specifying a restricted version of the rule, called the *ground resolution rule*. Recall that a formula is said to be *ground* iff it contains no variables. The ground resolution rule can be used to show the unsatisfiability of a set of ground clauses. The *ground resolution rule* is the following inference rule: For any two ground clauses C_1, C_2, and any ground literal l, $C_1 \vee C_2$ is a direct consequence of $C_1 \vee l$ and $C_2 \vee \neg l$. This can be symbolically written as

$$\frac{C_1 \vee l,\ C_2 \vee \neg l}{C_1 \vee C_2} \tag{1.4.4}$$

Notice that if $C_1 = C_2 = \square$, then (1.4.4) reduces to

$$\frac{l, \neg l}{\square}$$

It is easily checked that the ground resolution rule is sound, i.e. $C_1 \vee C_2$ is true in every frame in which $C_1 \vee l$ and $C_2 \vee \neg l$ are true. $C_1 \vee C_2$ is called the *ground resolvent of* $C_1 \vee l$ *and* $C_2 \vee \neg l$.

Let CL be a set of ground clauses. A *ground refutation from* CL is a sequence $C_1, \ldots, C_n$ of ground clauses such that $C_n = \square$ and, for each $1 \leq i \leq n$, either $C_i \in \mathrm{CL}$ or C_i is a ground resolvent of C_j and C_k, where $j, k < i$.

Theorem 1.57 A set CL of ground clauses is unsatisfiable iff there is a ground refutation from CL. ▮

Example 1.58 Consider the theory T consisting of:

(1) *Bird(Tweety)*
(2) *Bird(Tweety)* $\supset$ *Flies(Tweety)*
(3) $\neg$*Has-Wings(Tweety)* $\supset$ $\neg$*Flies(Tweety)*

and the sentence

(4) *Has-Wings(Tweety)*

Our purpose is to show that $T \models (4)$. By Theorem 1.35 (iii), it suffices to demonstrate that $(1) \wedge (2) \wedge (3) \supset (4)$ is valid, which, in turn, amounts to proving that $\neg[(1) \wedge (2) \wedge (3) \supset (4)]$ is unsatisfiable. First, we transform the last sentence into the clausal form. Performing the construction described in Definition 1.52, we get

$$[Bird(Tweety)] \wedge [\neg Bird(Tweety) \vee Flies(Tweety)] \wedge$$
$$\wedge [Has\text{-}Wings(Tweety) \vee \neg Flies(Tweety)] \wedge [\neg Has\text{-}Wings(Tweety)]$$

The set of clauses corresponding to this sentence consists of:

(5) *Bird(Tweety)*
(6) $\neg Bird(Tweety) \vee Flies(Tweety)$
(7) $Has\text{-}Wings(Tweety) \vee \neg Flies\ (Tweety)$
(8) $\neg Has\text{-}Wings(Tweety)$

In view of Theorem 1.56 (i) and 1.57, it remains to show that there is a ground refutation from {(5)–(8)}. One of such refutations is given below.

(9)	*Flies(Tweety)*	from (5) and (6)
(10)	$\neg Flies(Tweety)$	from (7) and (8)
(11)	□	from (9) and (10)

∎

To present the resolution rule in its general form, we need some preliminary terminology.

A *substitution* (*of terms for variables*) is any set, possibly empty, of the form $\{x_1 \leftarrow \alpha_1, \ldots, x_n \leftarrow \alpha_n\}$, where $x_1, \ldots, x_n$ are distinct variables and each α_i is a term different from x_i. An expression '$x_i \leftarrow \alpha_i$' may be read 'α_i replaces x_i'. The substitution corresponding to the empty set is called the *empty substitution*, and we denote it by ε.

A *simple expression* is either a literal or a term. Given a simple expression E and a substitution $\vartheta = \{x_1 \leftarrow \alpha_1, \ldots, x_n \leftarrow \alpha_n\}$, we write $E\vartheta$ to denote the expression obtained from E by simultaneously replacing each occurrence of x_i $(1 \leq i \leq n)$ by α_i. For instance, if $E = P(x, f(y), z)$ and $\vartheta = \{x \leftarrow f(y), y \leftarrow g(b)\}$, then $E\vartheta = P(f(y), f(g(b)), z)$. Observe that $E\varepsilon = E$, for any simple expression E.

Let $\vartheta = \{x_1 \leftarrow \alpha_1, \ldots, x_n \leftarrow \alpha_n\}$ and $\tau = \{y_1 \leftarrow \beta_1, \ldots, y_m \leftarrow \beta_m\}$ be substitutions. The *composition* $\vartheta\tau$ *of* ϑ *and* τ is the substitution obtained from the set

$$\{x_1 \leftarrow \alpha_1\tau, \ldots, x_n \leftarrow \alpha_n\tau, y_1 \leftarrow \beta_1, \ldots, y_m \leftarrow \beta_m\}$$

by deleting any element $x_i \leftarrow \alpha_i\tau$ for which $x_i = \alpha_i\tau$ and deleting any element $y_i \leftarrow \beta$ such that $y_i \in \{x_1, \ldots, x_n\}$. For example, if $\vartheta = \{x \leftarrow g(y), y \leftarrow z\}$ and $\tau = \{x \leftarrow a, y \leftarrow b, z \leftarrow y\}$, then $\vartheta\tau = \{x \leftarrow g(b), y \leftarrow y, x \leftarrow a, y \leftarrow b, z \leftarrow y\} - \{y \leftarrow y, x \leftarrow a, y \leftarrow b\} = \{x \leftarrow g(b), z \leftarrow y\}$.

Given a non-empty set $\text{EX} = \{E_1, \ldots, E_n\}$ of simple expressions, a *unifier* ϑ *of* EX is any substitution for which $E_1\vartheta = \cdots = E_n\vartheta$. If EX has a unifier, then we say that EX is *unifiable*. For instance, if $\text{EX} = \{P(a, y), P(x, f(b))\}$, then the substitution $\vartheta = \{x \leftarrow a, y \leftarrow f(b)\}$ is a unifier of EX. The set $\{P(a), P(b)\}$ is not unifiable.

A unifier ϑ of EX is called a *most general unifier of* EX iff for each unifier τ of EX there is a substitution λ such that $\tau = \vartheta\lambda$. It can be shown that any unifiable set of simple expressions has at least one most general unifier. As an example, consider $\text{EX} = \{P(x), P(y)\}$. Each of the following substitutions is a unifier of EX: $\vartheta_1 = \{x \leftarrow y\}$; $\vartheta_2 = \{y \leftarrow x\}$; $\vartheta_3 = \{x \leftarrow a, y \leftarrow a\}$; $\vartheta_4 = \{x \leftarrow f(b), y \leftarrow f(b)\}$. ϑ_1 and ϑ_2 are the only most general unifiers of EX. Notice that $\vartheta_3 = \vartheta_1\{y \leftarrow a\} = \vartheta_2\{x \leftarrow a\}$ and $\vartheta_4 = \vartheta_1\{y \leftarrow f(b)\} = \vartheta_2\{x \leftarrow f(b)\}$.

Let E be a simple expression. E_1 is a *subexpression of* E iff E_1 is any simple expression occurring in E. For instance, the subexpressions of $P(x, f(y, b))$ are $P(x, f(y, b))$, x, $f(y, b)$, y and b.

If EX $= \{E_1, \ldots, E_n\}$ is a set of simple expressions, then the *disagreement set of* EX is a set $\{E'_1, \ldots, E'_n\}$ specified as follows. We regard each of the expressions $E_1, \ldots, E_n$ as a string of symbols and locate the leftmost position at which not all expressions from EX have the same symbol. Then, for each $1 \leq i \leq n$, we put E'_i to be the subexpression of E_i beginning at this position. For example, the disagreement set of $\{P(x, f(a)), P(x, c), P(f(y), d)\}$ is $\{x, x, f(y)\} = \{x, f(y)\}$.

The application of the resolution rule requires the ability of solving the following *unification problem*: Given a finite set EX of simple expressions, determine whether or not EX is unifiable, and, if so, return a most general unifier of EX.

Theorem 1.59 (Robinson 1965) There is an algorithm, called the *unification algorithm*, which solves the unification problem ▮

Actually, a number of unification algorithms have been proposed. The following is perhaps the most straightforward.

UNIFICATION ALGORITHM

Let EX $= \{E_1, \ldots, E_n\}$ be a set of simple expressions. To find a most general unifier (if it exists) of EX, perform the following steps:

Step 1 Put $k := 0$; $\vartheta_0 := \varepsilon$; go to Step 2.

Step 2 If $E_1\vartheta_k = \cdots = E_n\vartheta_k$, then stop; ϑ_k is a most general unifier of EX. Otherwise, construct the disagreement set D_k of $\{E_1\vartheta_k, \ldots, E_n\vartheta_k\}$ and go to Step 3.

Step 3 If D_k contains a variable x and a term α, then put $k := k + 1$; $\vartheta_k = \vartheta_{k-1}\{x \leftarrow \alpha\}$ and go to Step 2. Otherwise, report that EX is not unifiable and stop. ▮

A little reflection will convince the reader that the above algorithm always terminates. Observe also its non-determinism due to the free choice of x and α in Step 3.

Example 1.60 Let EX $= \{Q(x, f(b)), Q(a, f(y))\}$.

(i) $k := 0$; $\vartheta_0 := \varepsilon$.
(ii) $D_0 := \{x, a\}$.
(iii) $k := 1$; $\vartheta_1 := \{x \leftarrow a\}$.
(iv) $D_1 := \{b, y\}$.
(v) $k := 2$; $\vartheta_2 := \{x \leftarrow a; y \leftarrow b\}$.
(vi) ϑ_2 is a most general unifier of EX.

Suppose now that EX $= \{Q(x, x), Q(a, b)\}$

(i) $k := 0$; $\vartheta_0 := \varepsilon$.
(ii) $D_0 := \{x, a\}$.
(iii) $k := 1$; $\vartheta_1 := \{x \leftarrow a\}$.
(iv) $D_1 = \{a, b\}$. EX is not unifiable.

▮

If $C = l_1 \vee \cdots \vee l_n$ and ϑ is a substitution, then $C\vartheta$ stands for $l_1\vartheta \vee \cdots \vee l_n\vartheta$. Note that $l_1\vartheta \vee \cdots \vee l_n\vartheta$ can be sometimes written in an equivalent form with less than n literals. This happens if ϑ is a unifier of two or more literals of C. For instance, if $C = P(x) \vee Q(b, y) \vee Q(z, y)$ and $\vartheta = \{x \leftarrow a, z \leftarrow b\}$, then $C\vartheta = P(a) \vee Q(b, y) \vee Q(b, y) \Leftrightarrow P(a) \vee Q(b, y)$.

Let C be a clause and suppose that V is the set of all variables occurring in C. A *renaming substitution for* C is any substitution $\{x_1 \leftarrow y_1, \ldots, x_n \leftarrow y_n\}$ $(n \geq 0)$ satisfying the following conditions: (i) $\{x_1, \ldots, x_n\} \subseteq V$; (ii) $y_1, \ldots, y_n$ are distinct variables; (iii) $(V - \{x_1, \ldots, x_n\}) \cap \{y_1, \ldots, y_n\} = \{\ \}$. Notice that ε is a renaming substitution for any clause. A clause C_1 is said to be a *variant of* C iff $C_1 = C\vartheta$, where ϑ *is a renaming substitution for* C. For example, $C_1 = P(x, y) \vee Q(z)$ is a variant of $C = P(x, z) \vee Q(u)$, because $C_1 = C\{z \leftarrow y, u \leftarrow z\}$ and $\{z \leftarrow y, u \leftarrow z\}$ is a renaming substitution for C. Since ε is a renaming substitution for any clause, any clause is a variant of itself. If C_1 is a variant of C and $C_1 \neq C$, then we say that C_1 *obtains from C by renaming variables.*

We write $l_1, \ldots, l_n \in C$ to indicate that literals $l_1, \ldots, l_n$ occur in C. If $l_1 \ldots l_n \in C$, then we write $C - \{l_1, \ldots, l_n\}$ to denote the clause obtained from C by deleting $l_1, \ldots, l_n$.

Definition 1.61 Let C_1 and C_2 be clauses such that no variable is common to both C_1 and C_2. Let $l_1, \ldots, l_n \in C_1$ $(n > 0)$ and let $l'_n, \ldots, l'_k \in C_2$ $(k > 0)$. Assume further that $l_1, \ldots, l_n$ are all positive and $l'_1, \ldots, l'_k$ are all negative, or vice versa. If ϑ is a most general unifier of $\{|l_1|, \ldots, |l_n|, |l'_1|, \ldots, |l'_k|\}$, then the clause

$$[C_1\vartheta - \{l_1\vartheta, \ldots, l_n\vartheta\}] \vee [C_2\vartheta - \{l'_1\vartheta, \ldots, l'_k\vartheta\}]$$

is called a *binary resolvent of* C_1 *and* C_2. ∎

Example 1.62 Let

$$C_1 = P(x) \vee P(y) \vee Q(b)$$
$$C_2 = R(a) \vee \neg P(f(a))$$

We take $l_1 = P(x)$, $l_2 = P(y)$ and $l'_1 = \neg P(f(a))$. Since $\vartheta = \{x \leftarrow f(a), y \leftarrow f(a)\}$ is a most general unifier of $\{|l_1|, |l_2|, |l'_1|\}$, the clause $Q(b) \vee R(a)$ is a binary resolvent of C_1 and C_2. ∎

Definition 1.63 *A resolvent of clauses* C_1 *and* C_2, written RES(C_1, C_2), is any binary resolvent of a variant of C_1 and a variant of C_2.† ∎

We now are ready to provide the definition of the resolution rule.

Definition 1.64 The *resolution rule* is the following inference rule: For any clauses C_1 and C_2, RES(C_1, C_2) is a direct consequence of C_1 and C_2. ∎

Let CL be a set of clauses. A *refutation from* CL is a sequence $C_1, \ldots, C_n$ of clauses such that $C_n = \square$ and, for each $1 \leq i \leq n$, either $C_i \in$ CL or C_i is a resolvent of C_j and C_k, where $j, k < i$.

Definition 1.65 Let CL be a set of clauses. We write EQ(CL) to denote the *set of equality clauses for* CL, i.e. the set consisting of the following clauses:

(EC1) $x = x$

(EC2) $x \neq y \vee y = x$

(EC3) $x \neq y \vee y \neq z \vee x = z$

(EC4) $x_1 \neq y_1 \vee \cdots \vee x_n \neq y_n \vee \neg P(x_1, \ldots, x_n) \vee P(y_1, \ldots, y_n)$, for each n-ary $(n > 0)$ predicate constant P occurring in CL

(EC5) $x_1 \neq y_1 \vee \cdots \vee x_n \neq y_n \vee f(x_1, \ldots, x_n) = f(y_1, \ldots, y_n)$, for each n-ary $(n > 0)$ function constant f occurring in CL.

∎

† Since any clause is its own variant, a binary resolvent of C_1 and C_2 is a resolvent of C_1 and C_2.

Note that the equality clauses for CL are just the clauses corresponding to the equality axioms for the language over the alphabet consisting of predicate and function constants occurring in CL (compare Definition 1.23).

We adopt the following notational convention. For any set CL of clauses,

$$\mathrm{CL} \cup [\mathrm{EQ(CL)}] = \begin{cases} \mathrm{CL} & \text{if `$=$' does not occur in CL} \\ \mathrm{CL} \cup \mathrm{EQ(CL)} & \text{otherwise} \end{cases}$$

Theorem 1.66 A set CL of clauses is unsatisfiable iff there is a refutation from $\mathrm{CL} \cup [\mathrm{EQ(CL)}]$. ▮

Example 1.67 Let CL consist of the following clauses:

(1) $\neg P(y, a) \vee \neg P(y, x) \vee \neg P(x, y)$
(2) $P(y, f(y)) \vee P(y, a)$
(3) $P(f(y), y) \vee P(y, a)$

We show that CL is unsatisfiable by demonstrating that □ can be derived from CL by repeatedly applying the resolution rule. First, we try to resolve (1) and (2). To assure that the causes have no variable in common, we replace (2) by one of its variants, say

(2′) $P(y_1, f(y_1)) \vee P(y_1, a)$

We take the literals $l_1 = \neg P(y, a)$, $l_2 = \neg P(y, x)$, $l_3 = \neg P(x, y)$ from (1) and $l'_1 = P(y_1, a)$ from (2′). Since $\vartheta = \{x \leftarrow a, y \leftarrow a, y_1 \leftarrow a\}$ is a most general unifier of $\{|l_1|, |l_2|, |l_3|, |l'_1|\}$, the clause

(4) $P(a, f(a))$

is a binary resolvent of (1) and (2′), and hence a resolvent of (1) and (2). Now, we try to resolve (1) and (3). First, we replace (3) by one of its variants, say

(3′) $P(f(y_2), y_2) \vee P(y_2, a)$

We take l_1, l_2, l_3 as before and $l'_1 = P(y_2, a)$ from (3′). Since $\vartheta = \{x \leftarrow a, y \leftarrow a, y_2 \leftarrow a\}$ is a most general unifier of $\{|l_1|, |l_2|, |l_3|, |l'_1|\}$, we conclude that

(5) $P(f(a), a)$

is a binary resolvent of (1) and (3′), and thus a resolvent of (1) and (3). The next step is to resolve (1) and (4). We take $l_1 = \neg P(x, y)$ from (1) and $l'_1 = P(a, f(a))$ from (4). Since $\vartheta = \{x \leftarrow a, y \leftarrow f(a)\}$ is a most general unifier of $\{|l_1|, |l'_1|\}$, we get $\neg P(f(a), a) \vee \neg P(f(a), a)$, i.e.

(6) $\neg P(f(a), a)$

Finally, from (5) and (6), we obtain (with the empty substitution)

(7) □

In summary, the sequence (1), (2), (3), (4), (5), (6), (7) is a refutation from CL. Thus, CL is unsatisfiable. ▮

The refutation from Example 1.67 can be represented by the *refutation tree* given in Fig. 1.1.

In general, a *refutation tree* for a set CL of clauses is a binary 'upward oriented' tree

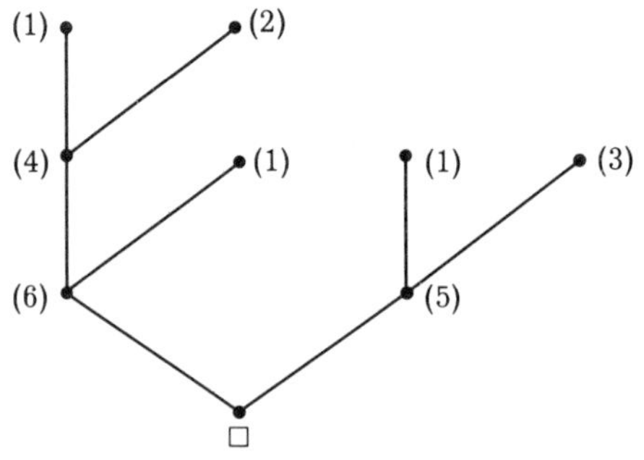

Fig. 1.1 – Refutation tree. (Example 1.67.)

D satisfying the following conditions:

(i) All nodes of D are labelled by clauses;
(ii) Each leaf node of D is labelled by a clause from CL;
(iii) The root node of D is labelled by □;
(iv) If C labels a non-leaf node, then C is a resolvent of the clauses which label the successors of n.

Recall that $T \models A$ iff CLAUSES(T) ∪ CLAUSES($\neg\forall A$) is unsatisfiable (Theorem 1.56 (iii)). This motivates the following definition:

Definition 1.68 A *resolution proof of a formula A from a theory T* is any refutation from

$$\text{CLAUSES}(T) \cup \text{CLAUSES}(\neg\forall A) \cup [\text{EQ}(\text{CLAUSES}(T) \cup \text{CLAUSES}(\neg\forall A))]$$

∎

The following result is a simple corollary of Theorem 1.66:

Theorem 1.69 $T \models A$ iff there is a resolution proof of A from T. ∎

1.4.3 Linear resolution

Automatic reasoning with the resolution rule requires a strategy of choosing clauses to be resolved. The most straightforward approach, called the *basic resolution method*, amounts to systematically generating all possible resolvents. More specifically, to test the unsatisfiability of a finite set CL of clauses, one starts by trying to construct the resolvents of all pairs of clauses from CL. This continues until either the empty clause is derived or no new resolvent can be generated. In the former case, the procedure terminates and reports the unsatisfiability of CL; in the latter, the generated clauses are added to CL and the process is repeated for the enlarged set of clauses.

In spite of its simplicity, the basic resolution method is too ineffective to be of practical use. Fortunately, it can be substantially improved by putting various constraints on the clauses which are to be resolved at a given point of time. One such refinement, called the *linear resolution method* (Loveland 1970; Luckham 1970), is sketched below.

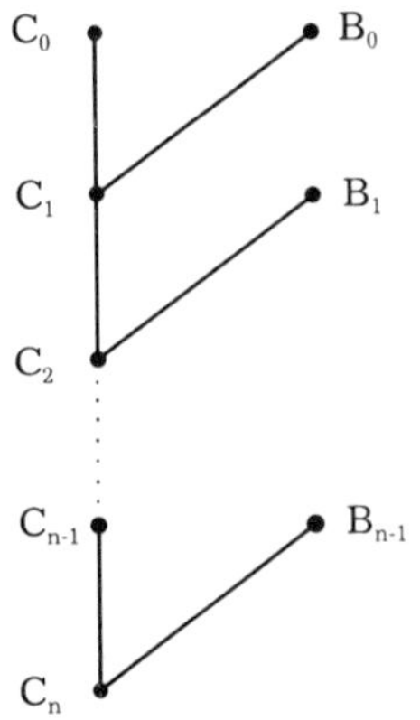

Fig. 1.2 – Linear refutation.

A *linear refutation from a set of clauses* CL has the form of Fig. 1.2, where

(i) $C_0 \in \mathrm{CL}$; (C_0 is called the *top clause of the refutation*);
(ii) for $0 \leq i < n$, $B_i \in \mathrm{CL}$ or B_i is C_j, for some $j < i$;
(iii) for $1 \leq i \leq n$, C_i is a resolvent of C_{i-1} and B_{i-1};
(iv) $C_n = \square$.

Observe that in a linear refutation a new resolvent is always constructed from the preceding one.

Theorem 1.70 A set CL of clauses is unsatisfiable iff there is a linear refutation from $\mathrm{CL} \cup [\mathrm{EQ(CL)}]$. ▮

One problem with constructing a linear refutation is to choose the top clause. The following theorem provides some clues in this direction.

Theorem 1.71 Let CL be an unsatisfiable set of clauses and suppose that $\mathrm{CL}' \subseteq \mathrm{CL}$. If the set $\mathrm{CL} - \mathrm{CL}'$ is satisfiable, then there is a linear refutation from $\mathrm{CL} \cup [\mathrm{EQ(CL)}]$ with a clause $C \in \mathrm{CL}'$ as the top clause. ▮

Definition 1.72 A *linear resolution proof of a formula A from a theory T* is any linear refutation from

$$\mathrm{CLAUSES}(T) \cup \mathrm{CLAUSES}(\neg\forall A) \cup [\mathrm{EQ}(\mathrm{CLAUSES}(T) \cup \mathrm{CLAUSES}(\neg\forall A))]$$

with a clause from $\mathrm{CLAUSES}(\neg\forall A)$ as the top clause. ▮

The next result easily follows from Theorems 1.56 (iii) and 1.71:

Theorem 1.73 If T is satisfiable, then $T \models A$ iff there is a linear resolution proof of A from T.† ▮

† The requirement that T is satisfiable is not so restrictive as it may appear. In practice, theories are meant to represent particular domains of applications. Each such a theory is satisfiable since the domain it represents is one of its models.

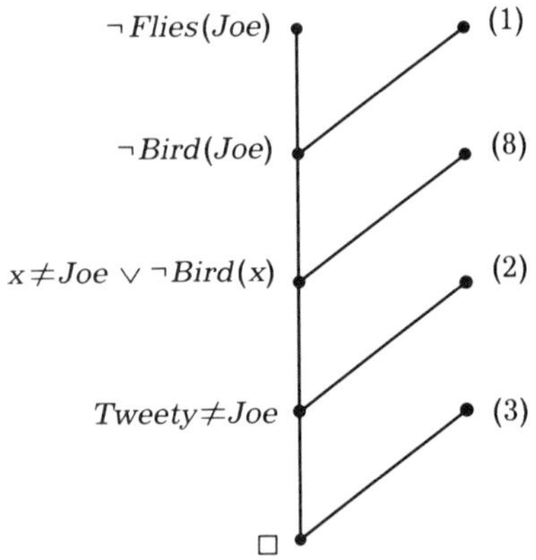

Fig. 1.3 – Linear resolution proof. (Example 1.74.)

Example 1.74 Let T consist of the following axioms:

$\forall x . Bird(x) \supset Flies(x)$
$Bird(Tweety)$
$Tweety = Joe$

We show that $T \models A$, where $A = Flies(Joe)$.

$\text{CLAUSES}(T) = \{(1), (2), (3)\}$, where

(1) $\neg Bird(x) \vee Flies(x)$
(2) $Bird(Tweety)$
(3) $Tweety = Joe$

$\text{CLAUSES}(\neg\forall A) = \{(4)\}$, where (4) $\neg Flies(Joe)$

$\text{EQ}(\text{CLAUSES}(T) \cup \text{CLAUSES}(\neg\forall A)) = \{(5), (6), (7), (8), (9)\}$, where

(5) $x = x$
(6) $x \neq y \vee y = x$
(7) $x \neq y \vee y \neq z \vee x = z$
(8) $x \neq y \vee \neg Bird(x) \vee Bird(y)$
(9) $x \neq y \vee \neg Flies(x) \vee Flies(y)$

A linear resolution proof of A from T is given in Fig. 1.3. ∎

1.5 CLASSICAL SECOND-ORDER LOGIC

Unlike first-order logic, where all variables range over individuals, second-order logic admits, in addition, variables ranging over relations and functions specified over individuals. This section provides a brief exposition of classical second-order logic. The familiarity with the material introduced here is essential to follow Chapter 6.

1.5.1 Language of second-order logic

An *alphabet of* (*classical*) *second-order logic* consists of primitive symbols from the following pairwise disjoint classes:

(i) A denumerable set of n-ary (for each $n \geq 0$) *function variables*: $\{\phi_1^n, \phi_2^n, \ldots\}$; 0-ary function variables are called *individual variables*, and we denote them by $x_1, x_2 \ldots$.
(ii) A denumerable set of n-ary (for each $n \geq 0$) *predicate variables*: $\{\Phi_1^n, \Phi_2^n, \ldots\}$; 0-ary predicate variables are called *proposition variables*.
(iii) One truth-constant: *'True'*.
(iv) Sentential connectives: '$\neg$' and '$\supset$'.
(v) One quantifier: '$\forall$'.
(vi) Punctuation marks: '(', ',' and ')'.
(vii) A countable set **P** of *predicate constants*; to each $P \in \mathbf{P}$ there is uniquely assigned a non-negative integer, called the *arity of P*.
(viii A distinguished 2-ary predicate constant: '='.
(ix) A countable set **F** of *function constants*; to each $f \in \mathbf{F}$, there is uniquely assigned a non-negative integer, called the *arity of f*.

The classes (i)–(vi) and (viii) are fixed, whereas the others may vary, and, in particular, may be empty. The sets **P** and **F** are assumed to be computable.

0-ary predicate constants are called *proposition constants*; 0-ary function constants are called *individual* (or *object*) *constants*.

Every alphabet AL uniquely determines three classes of expressions: *terms* (TM_{AL}), *atomic formulae* ($AFORM_{AL}$) and *formulae* (L_{AL}). These are specified as in classical first-order logic with equality (compare Definition 1.22) with the following additions:

The definition of the set of terms over AL is extended by: (iii) If $\alpha_1, \ldots, \alpha_n \in TM_{AL}$ ($n \geq 1$) and ϕ_i^n is an n-ary function variable, then $\phi_i^n(\alpha_1, \ldots, \alpha_n) \in TM_{AL}$.

The definition of the set of atomic formulae over AL is augmented by: (iv) Each proposition variable is an atomic formula over AL; (v) If $\alpha_1, \ldots, \alpha_n \in TM_{AL}$ ($n \geq 1$) and Φ_i^n is an n-ary predicate variable, then $\Phi_i^n(\alpha_1, \ldots, \alpha_n) \in AFORM_{AL}$.

Finally, the clause (ii) in the definition of the set of formulae over AL should be replaced by (ii′) If $A, B \in L_{AL}$ and X is any variable, then $(\neg A) \in L_{AL}$, $(A \supset B) \in L_{AL}$ and $(\forall X(A)) \in L_{AL}$.

The set L_{AL}, as specified here, is called the *second-order language over* AL. As usual, we typically assume that AL is fixed, and then L_{AL} will be abbreviated to L. The restriction to alphabets with computable sets of predicate and function constants assures the computability of any second-order language.

Recall that any alphabet of second-order logic is supposed to contain the symbol '='. Thus, we do not distinguish between second-order languages with and without equality.

We employ the notational conventions introduced in section 1.3.1 as regards denoting individual variables, individual constants, n-ary ($n \geq 1$) predicate constants, n-ary ($n \geq 1$) function constants, formulae and terms. In addition, we assume that the letters ϕ, ϕ and ψ, possibly subscripted or primed, denote n-ary ($n \geq 1$) function variables, whereas the letters Φ and Ψ refer to n-ary ($n \geq 0$) predicate variables. The symbol X, possibly with subscripts and primes, will be used to denote an arbitrary variable. The logical connectives $\wedge$, $\vee$ and $\equiv$, the existential quantifier $\exists$, and the truth-constant *False* are introduced by the usual definitions.

The definitions of *'universally (existentially) quantified occurrence of a variable'*, *'bound occurrence of a variable'*, *'free occurrence of a variable'*, *'free variable'* and *'scope'* carry over from first-order logic, except that now they apply to all kinds of variables. A *closed formula* (or *a sentence*) is any formula containing no free variables. A formula which is not closed is said to be *open*.

We adopt the conventions made in section 1.3.1 as to omission of parentheses. In particular, we write '$Q_1X_1 \ldots Q_nX_n.$', where $Q_1, \ldots, Q_n \in \{\forall, \exists\}$, to indicate that all occurrences of $X_1, \ldots, X_n$ following the symbol '.' are bound by $Q_1X_1, \ldots, Q_nX_n$. The expressions '$\forall X_1 \ldots X_n$' and '$\exists X_1 \ldots X_n$' are abbreviations for '$\forall X_1 \ldots \forall X_n$' and '$\exists X_1 \ldots \exists X_n$', respectively. As usual, '$\alpha \neq \beta$' stands for $\neg(\alpha = \beta)$.

Example 1.75
Terms: x, $f(a, y)$, $\phi(x, \phi(b, z))$
Atomic formulae: $P(\phi(a), a)$, $\Psi(b, x, \phi(x))$
Formulae: $\forall x \Psi(x)$, $\forall x\, \exists \Phi . \neg\Phi(x) \vee \Psi(x)$, $\forall x \Phi . \Phi(a) \supset \Phi'(x) \wedge \Psi(y)$
∎

The notion '*α is free for x in A*' is specified precisely as in first-order logic. A formula A is said to be a *subformula of B* iff A occurs in B.

1.5.2 Semantics of second-order logic

We now turn to the semantics of second-order logic.

Definition 1.76 A *frame for a second-order language* L_{AL} is a pair $M = \langle D, m \rangle$, where D and m are specified as in Definition 1.24. That is, D is a non-empty set, the *domain* (or *universe*) of M, and m is a function which assigns to each n-ary ($n \geq 0$) predicate constant in AL, different from '=', an n-ary relation on D, to the constant '=', the identity relation on D, and to each n-ary ($n \geq 0$) function constant in AL, an n-ary function from D^n into D. ∎

As usual, given a frame $M = \langle D, m \rangle$ for L_{AL}, we write $|M|$ to denote the domain of M; $M|K|$ stands for $m(K)$, where K is any predicate or function constant in AL.

We say that M is a *second-order frame* (alternatively, a *frame for second-order logic*) iff M is a frame for some second-order language L.†

Let M be a second-order frame. An *assignment over* M is any function which assigns to every n-ary ($n \geq 0$) function variable an n-ary function from $|M|^n$ into $|M|$, and to each n-ary ($n \geq 0$) predicate variable an n-ary relation on $|M|$. (Recall that individual variables are identified with 0-ary function variables.) The set of all assignments over M will be denoted by As(M). If $a \in As(M)$ and X is any variable, then we write $[a]_X$ to denote the set of those assignments over M which differ from 'a' at most at X.

Definition 1.77 Let M be a second-order frame for L_{AL}.

The *value* $V^M_a(\alpha)$ *of a term* $\alpha \in TM_{AL}$ *in* M *wrt* $a \in As(M)$ is an element of $|M|$ defined as follows:

(i) $V^M_a(x) = a(x)$, where x is an individual variable;
(ii) $V^M_a(a) = M|a|$;
(iii) $V^M_a(f(\alpha_1, \ldots, \alpha_n)) = M|f|(V^M_a(\alpha_1), \ldots, V^M_a(\alpha_n))$;
(iv) $V^M_a(\phi(\alpha_1, \ldots, \alpha_n)) = a(\phi)(V^M_a(\alpha_1), \ldots, V^M_a(\alpha_n))$.

† Observe that every second-order frame can be viewed as a first-order frame and vice-versa. Accordingly, the phrases 'a second-order frame' and 'a first-order frame' do not serve to distinguish between different objects, but rather between different logics.

The *truth-value* $V_a^M(A)$ *of a formula A in* M *wrt* $a \in As(M)$ is an element of $\{0, 1\}$ specified as follows:

(i) $V_a^M(True) = 1$;
(ii) $V_a^M(p) = M|p|$;
(iii) $V_a^M(P(\alpha_1, \ldots, \alpha_n)) = M|P|(V_a^M(\alpha_1), \ldots, V_a^M(\alpha_n))$;
(iv) $V_a^M(\alpha = \beta) = 1$ iff $V_a^M(\alpha) = V_a^M(\beta)$;
(v) $V_a^M(\Phi) = a(\Phi)$, where Φ is any proposition variable;
(vi) $V_a^M(\Phi(\alpha_1, \ldots, \alpha_n)) = a(\Phi)(V_a^M(\alpha_1), \ldots, V_a^M(\alpha_n))$, where Φ is any n-ary ($n > 0$) predicate variable;
(vii) $V_a^M(B \supset C) = 1$ iff $V_a^M(B) = 0$ or $V_a^M(C) = 1$;
(viii) $V_a^M(\neg B) = 1 - V_a^M(B)$;
(ix) $V_a^M(\forall X B) = 1$ iff $V_{a'}^M(B) = 1$, for every $a' \in [a]_x$.
▮

The truth-conditions for the symbols $\wedge$, $\vee$, $\equiv$, *False*, and $\exists$ can be easily deduced from their definitions.

A formula A is said to be *satisfied in a frame M by an assignment* $a \in As(M)$ iff $V_a^M(A) = 1$. A is satisfiable iff $V_a^M(A) = 1$, for some frame M and some $a \in As(M)$; otherwise, A is said to be *unsatisfiable*. A is *true in* M iff $V_a^M(A) = 1$, for any $a \in As(M)$. If A is true in M, then we say that M is a *model of A*. A is *valid* iff A is true in every frame M.

Example 1.78 Let $A = \forall\Phi\, \exists\Psi\, \forall xy[\Phi(x, y) \equiv \Psi(y, x)]$.
Intuitively, A states that every binary relation has a converse. We show that A is valid. Assume to the contrary that this is not the case, i.e. $V_a^M(A) = 0$, for some frame M and some $a \in As(M)$. Thus, there is $a' \in [a]_\Phi$ such that

$$V_{a'}^M(\exists\Psi\, \forall xy[\Phi(x, y) \equiv \Psi(y, x)]) = 0.$$

Suppose that $a'(\Phi) = R$ and let a'' be the assignment over M which is identical with a', except that $a''(\Psi)$ is the converse of R. Clearly,

$$V_{a''}^M(\forall xy[\Phi(x, y) \equiv \Psi(y, x)]) = 1$$

and hence $V_{a'}^M(\exists\Psi\, \forall xy[\Phi(x, y) \equiv \Psi(y, x)]) = 1$. A contradiction. ▮

Consider the schema

$$(\alpha = \beta) \equiv (\forall\Phi[\Phi(\alpha) \equiv \Phi(\beta)]) \tag{1.5.1}$$

where α and β stand for any terms. This schema represents Leibnitz's *Principle of the Identity of Indiscernibles*, according to which any two objects enjoying exactly the same properties are identical. It is easy to see that any instance of (1.5.1) is valid. Thus, in second-order logic the constant '$=$' need not be taken as a primitive symbol, but may be introduced by the following definition:

$$\alpha = \beta =_{DF} \forall\Phi[\Phi(\alpha) \equiv \Phi(\beta)].$$

The validity problem for second-order logic is the task of determining whether or not an arbitrarily given second-order formula is valid. Because the class of valid second-order formulae contains the valid formulae of first-order logic, and because the validity problem for first-order logic is undecidable, we immediately have:

Theorem 1.79 The validity problem for second-order logic is undecidable. ▮

In view of Theorem 1.79, we must not just hope to construct an algorithm to decide whether or not a given second-order formula is valid. What is worse, in contrast to first-order logic, it is even impossible to provide a procedure which could be used to confirm the validity of an arbitrarily given second-order valid formula. This latter result is stated below.

Theorem 1.80 Let L be a language of second-order logic. In general, the set of valid formulae over L is not a partially computable subset of L.† ∎

Formulae A and B are said to be *(logically) equivalent*, written $A \Leftrightarrow B$, iff they yield the same truth-value for any frame M and any $a \in As(M)$. Theorem 1.30 generalizes into second-order logic.

1.5.3 Second-order theories

A *second-order theory* is a pair $T = \langle L, S \rangle$, where L is a second-order language and S is a computable set of sentences from L. As usual, the sentences of S are called the *axioms (premisses)* of T. If $S = \{ \}$, then T is called the *second-order predicate calculus over L*.

All of the terminological, notational and other conventions introduced earlier for first-order theories can be imported to second-order theories. In particular, second-order theories will usually be identified with sets of their axioms, which allows us, if we wish, to regard any second-order sentence as a second-order theory.

In the remainder of this section, the phrase 'second-order theory' will be abbreviated to 'theory'.

As usual, a frame in which all the axioms of a theory T are true is called a *model of T*. T is said to be *satisfiable* iff it has a model; otherwise, we say that T is *unsatisfiable*.

A formula A is a *semantic consequence of a theory T* (*A follows from T*, *T entails A*, or *A is entailed by T*), written $T \models A$, iff A is true in every model of T. In particular, A is a semantic consequence of the second-order predicate calculus (over L), written $\models A$, iff A is true in every frame for L.‡

The symbol $\models$, as specified here, denotes a binary relation, called the *entailment relation of classical second-order logic*.

The entailment relation of second-order logic enjoys the properties listed in Theorem 1.35.

Theories T and T' are *(logically) equivalent*, written $T \Leftrightarrow T'$, iff they have the same models.

Theorems 1.36 and 1.37 generalize into second-order logic.

As usual, formulae A and B are said to be *equivalent in a theory* T iff they yield the same truth-value in every model M of T and every $a \in As(M)$.

1.5.4 Deduction systems for second-order logic

Following the course adopted in the previous sections, we now turn our attention to deduction systems for second-order logic. Unfortunately, no such a system is really interesting. The details are these.

† Although the problem of confirming the validity of an arbitrarily given second-order valid formula is undecidable, there is an important restricted class of valid second-order formulae, known in the literature as the *class of secondarily valid formulae*, for which the problem is decidable. The precise definition of this class requires a more general notion of a frame and is beyond the scope of this book. The interested reader is referred to Church (1956) and Rogers (1971).

‡ The notations $T \models A$ and $\models A$ were given different meanings in the previous sections. Possible confusions will be always avoided by the context.

A *deduction system for second-order logic* is specified in the obvious way (see Definition 1.14), except that L is now a second-order language. As usual, given a deduction system DS $= \langle L, \mathrm{S}, \mathrm{R}\rangle$, we say that A is *provable in* DS iff there is a sequence $A_1, \ldots, A_n$ of formulae from L such that $A_n = A$ and, for each $1 \leq i \leq n$, either $A_i \in \mathrm{S}$ or A_i is a direct consequence of some preceding formulae of the sequence by virtue of some rule from R. DS is said to be *sound* iff every formula provable in DS is valid; it is said to be *complete* iff every valid formula of L is provable in DS.

The following theorem states one of the most important results concerning second-order logic:

Theorem 1.81 (Gödel) There is no complete deduction system for second-order logic. ▮

As we remarked earlier, there is an important restricted class of second-order valid formulae, namely, the class of secondarily valid formulae. It is possible to construct a deduction system for second-order logic, which is sound and complete with respect to this class, i.e. a system DS $= \langle L, \mathrm{S}, \mathrm{R}\rangle$ such that A is provable in DS iff A is a secondarily valid formula of L. See Church (1956) and Rogers (1971) for details.

1.5.5 Predicate and function expressions

In first-order logic, it is possible to substitute terms for individual variables. In second-order logic, we may, in addition, substitute predicate expressions for predicate variables and function expressions for function variables.

An n-ary *predicate expression* U is any expression of the form

$$\lambda x_1 \ldots x_n A(x_1, \ldots, x_n) \qquad (n \geq 0)$$

where $x_1, \ldots, x_n$ are individual variables and $A(x_1, \ldots, x_n)$ is any formula of first- or second-order logic. In the former case, U is called a *first-order predicate expression*; in the latter a *second-order predicate expression*. An occurrence of a variable X is said to be *free in* U iff $X \notin \{x_1, \ldots, x_n\}$ and the occurrence is free in $A(x_1, \ldots, x_n)$. Any individual variable which has a free occurrence in U is called a *parameter in* U. If no parameters occur in U, then U is called a *predicate expression without parameters*; otherwise, U is said to be a *predicate expression with parameters*.

The following are predicate expressions:

$$U_1 = \lambda x P(x); \qquad U_2 = \lambda xy[\Phi(x) \vee Q(y)]; \qquad U_3 = \lambda x Q(x, y).$$

U_1 and U_2 are predicate expressions without parameters. U_3 is a predicate expression with y as a parameter.

An n-ary predicate expression U is meant to represent an n-ary predicate (i.e. an n-ary relation), which will be referred to as the *extension of* U.

Definition 1.82 Let U be a predicate expression of the form $\lambda x_1 \ldots x_n A(x_1, \ldots, x_n)$. The *extension* $\mathrm{E}^{\mathrm{M}}_{\mathrm{a}}(U)$ *of* U *in a frame* M *wrt* $\mathrm{a} \in \mathrm{As}(\mathrm{M})$ is the n-ary relation R on $|\mathrm{M}|$ given by

$$\langle \mathrm{d}_1, \ldots, \mathrm{d}_n\rangle \in \mathrm{R} \qquad \text{iff } \mathrm{V}^{\mathrm{M}}_{\mathrm{a}(x_1/\mathrm{d}_1, \ldots x_n/\mathrm{d}_n)}(A) = 1$$

where $\mathrm{a}(x_1/\mathrm{d}_1, \ldots x_n/\mathrm{d}_n)$ is the assignment over M which is identical to 'a', except perhaps on the variables $x_1, \ldots, x_n$; here it assigns $\mathrm{d}_1, \ldots \mathrm{d}_n$, respectively. ▮

Notice that, for any n-ary predicate constant P, $\mathrm{E}^{\mathrm{M}}_{\mathrm{a}}(\lambda x_1 \ldots x_n P(x_1, \ldots, x_n)) =$

$\mathrm{M}|P|$, so that P may be identified with $\lambda x_1 \ldots x_n P(x_1, \ldots, x_n)$. Similarly, for any n-ary predicate variable Φ, $\mathrm{E}^{\mathrm{M}}_{\mathrm{a}}(\lambda x_1, \ldots, x_n \Phi(x_1, \ldots, x_n)) = \mathrm{a}(\Phi)$. Thus, Φ may be identified with $\lambda x_1 \ldots x_n \Phi(x_1, \ldots, x_n)$.

A predicate expression $\lambda x_1 \ldots x_n A(x_1, \ldots, x_n)$ will often be written as $\lambda \bar{x} A(\bar{x})$, where $\bar{x}$ is meant to represent the n-tuple $(x_1, \ldots, x_n)$.

Let U be a predicate expression of the form $\lambda \bar{x} A(\bar{x})$, where $\bar{x} = (x_1, \ldots, x_n)$, and suppose that $\bar{\alpha} = (\alpha_1, \ldots, \alpha_n)$ is an n-tuple of terms. The *application of* U to $\bar{\alpha}$, written $U(\bar{\alpha})$, is the formula $A(\bar{\alpha})$. The application is said to be *correct* iff each α_i, $1 \leq i \leq n$, is free for x_i in $A(\bar{x})$.

For instance, if $U = \lambda xy P(x, y)$ and $\bar{\alpha} = (z, f(b))$, then $U(\bar{\alpha}) = P(z, f(b))$. If $U = \lambda xy\, \exists z P(x, y, z)$ and $\bar{\alpha} = (z, f(a))$, then $U(\bar{\alpha}) = \exists z P(z, f(a), z)$. The first of these applications is correct, whereas the second is not.

A *substitution of predicate expressions for predicate variables* is a set $\{\Phi_1 \leftarrow U_1, \ldots, \Phi_n \leftarrow U_n\}$ $(n \geq 0)$, where $\Phi_1, \ldots, \Phi_n$ are distinct predicate variables, $U_1, \ldots, U_n$ are predicate expressions and, for each $1 \leq i \leq n$, U_i and Φ_i have the same arity.

Definition 1.83 The *application of a substitution* $\vartheta = \{\Phi_1 \leftarrow U_1, \ldots, \Phi_n \leftarrow U_n\}$ *to a formula* A is the formula, written $A\vartheta$, obtained from A by the following construction:

(i) Replace each free occurrence of Φ_i, $1 \leq i \leq n$, in A by $\{U_i\}$.
(ii) In the expression resulting from (i), which in general is not a formula, successively replace each part of the form $\{U_i\}(\bar{\alpha})$ by the application of U_i to $\bar{\alpha}$.

The application of ϑ *to* A is said to be *proper* iff all the applications (of predicate expressions to terms) performed in (i) are correct, and no free occurrence of any variable in any of $U_1, \ldots, U_n$ becomes bound in $A\vartheta$; otherwise, the application of ϑ *to* A is called *improper*. ▮

We say that *B obtains from A by the substitution of* $U_1, \ldots, U_n$ for $\Phi_1, \ldots, \Phi_n$ iff B is the application of $\{\Phi_1 \leftarrow U_1, \ldots, \Phi_n \leftarrow U_n\}$ to A. Similarly, the phrase '*B obtains from A by the proper* (resp. *improper*) *substitution of* $U_1, \ldots, U_n$ *for* $\Phi_1, \ldots, \Phi_n$' is a synonym for '*B is a proper* (resp. *improper*) *application of* $\{\Phi_1 \leftarrow U_1, \ldots, \Phi_n \leftarrow U_n\}$ to A'.

Example 1.84 Let $A = \forall x \Phi(x) \supset \forall x \Phi(b)$, $\vartheta = \{\Phi \leftarrow \lambda y P(x, y)\}$
Applying ϑ to A, we first get

$$\forall x \{\lambda y P(x, y)\}(x) \supset \forall x \{\lambda y P(x, y)\}(b)$$

and then

$$\forall x P(x, x) \supset \forall x P(x, b).$$

Thus, $A\vartheta = \forall x P(x, x) \supset \forall x P(x, b)$. The application of ϑ *to* A is improper because the free occurrence of x in $\lambda y P(x, y)$ becomes bound in $A\vartheta$.

Suppose now that $A' = \forall x \Phi(x) \supset \Phi(y)$ and let $\vartheta' = \{\Phi \leftarrow \lambda x\, \exists y Q(x, y)\}$. Applying ϑ' to A', we first obtain

$$\forall x \{\lambda x\, \exists y Q(x, y)\}(x) \supset \{\lambda x\, \exists y Q(x, y)\}(y)$$

and then

$$A'\vartheta' = \forall x\, \exists y Q(x, y) \supset \exists y Q(y, y)$$

The application of ϑ' to A is improper because the application of $\lambda x\, \exists y Q(x, y)$ to y is not correct (y is not free for x in $\exists y Q(x, y)$).

Finally, let $A'' = \forall xy . \Phi(x, y) \vee \Psi(x, y)$, $\vartheta'' = \{\Phi \leftarrow \lambda xy P(x, y), \Psi \leftarrow \lambda uv Q(u, v)\}$. Applying ϑ'' to A'', we first have

$$\forall xy . \{\lambda xy P(x, y)\}(x, y) \vee \{\lambda uv Q(u, v)\}(x, y)$$

and then

$$A''\vartheta'' = \forall xy . P(x, y) \vee Q(x, y).$$

The application of ϑ'' to A'' is proper. ▮

Theorem 1.85 For any substitution $\vartheta = \{\Phi_1 \leftarrow U_1, \ldots, \Phi_n \leftarrow U_n\}$ and any formula A, the formula

$$\forall \Phi_1 \ldots \Phi_n A \supset A\vartheta$$

is valid, provided that the application of ϑ *to* A is proper. ▮

Theorem 1.85 need not hold if the application of ϑ to A is improper. To see this, consider the formula A and the substitution ϑ from Example 1.84. It is easily checked that the formula $\forall \Phi A$ is valid, whereas the formula $A\vartheta$ is not. Thus, the formula $\forall \Phi A \supset A\vartheta$ is invalid. Consider now the formula A' and the substitution ϑ' from Example 1.84. Again, $\forall \Phi A'$ is valid, whereas $A'\vartheta'$ is not. Thus, the formula $\forall \Phi A' \supset A'\vartheta'$ is invalid.

Theorem 1.85 immediately implies the following result:

Corollary 1.86 For any substitution $\vartheta = \{\Phi_1 \leftarrow U_1, \ldots, \Phi_n \leftarrow U_n\}$ and any sentence of the form $\forall \Phi \ldots \Phi_n A$,

$$\forall \Phi_1 \ldots \Phi_n A \models A\vartheta$$

provided that the application of ϑ to A is proper. ▮

Corollary 1.86 will be intensively used in Chapter 6.

An n-ary *function expression* F is any expression of the form

$$\lambda x_1 \ldots x_n \alpha(x_1, \ldots, x_n) \qquad (n \geq 0)$$

where $x_1, \ldots, x_n$ are individual variables and $\alpha(x_1, \ldots, x_n)$ is a term. (The notation $\alpha(x_1, \ldots, x_n)$ serves to indicate that some individual variables occurring in α are among $x_1, \ldots, x_n$. This neither presupposes that all of $x_1, \ldots, x_n$ occur in α nor that α contains no other individual variables.) An occurrence of an individual variable x is said to be *free in* F iff $x \notin \{x_1, \ldots, x_n\}$ and x occurs in α.

The following are function expressions:

$$F_1 = \lambda x f(x); \qquad F_2 = \lambda xy f(g(x), y); \qquad F_3 = \lambda x \phi(x, y).$$

A function expression F is meant to represent an n-ary function, which we shall refer to as the *extension of* F.

Definition 1.87 Let F be an n-ary function expression of the form $\lambda x_1 \ldots x_n \alpha(x_1, \ldots, x_n)$. *The extension* $E^M_a(F)$ *of* F *in a frame* M *wrt* $a \in As(M)$ is the function f from $|M|^n$ into $|M|$ given by

$$f(d_1, \ldots, d_n) = V^M_{a(x_1/d_1, \ldots, x_n/d_n)}(\alpha)$$

where $a(x_1/d_1, \ldots, x_n/d_n)$ is specified as in Definition 1.82. ▮

Notice that, for any n-ary function constant f, $E_a^M(\lambda x_1 \ldots x_n f(x_1, \ldots, x_n)) = M|f|$, so that f may be identified with $\lambda x_1 \ldots x_n f(x_1, \ldots, x_n)$. Similarly, for any n-ary function variable ϕ, $E_a^M(\lambda x_1 \ldots x_n \phi(x_1, \ldots, x_n)) = a(\phi)$ and hence ϕ may be identified with $\lambda x_1 \ldots x_n \phi(x_1, \ldots, x_n)$.

A function expression $\lambda x_1 \ldots x_n \alpha(x_1, \ldots, x_n)$ will be often written as $\lambda\bar{x}\alpha(\bar{x})$, where $\bar{x}$ is meant to represent the tuple $(x_1, \ldots, x_n)$.

Let F be a function expression of the form $\lambda\bar{x}\alpha(\bar{x})$, where $\bar{x} = (x_1, \ldots, x_n)$ and suppose that $\bar{\beta} = (\beta_1, \ldots, \beta_n)$ is an n-tuple of terms. The *application of F to $\bar{\beta}$*, written $F(\bar{\beta})$, is the term $\alpha(\beta_1, \ldots, \beta_n)$. For example, if $F = \lambda xy\phi(f(x), g(y))$ and $\bar{\beta} = (a, f(a))$, then $F(\bar{\beta}) = \phi(f(a), g(f(a)))$.

A *substitution of function expressions for function variables is a set* $\vartheta = \{\phi_1 \leftarrow F_1, \ldots, \phi_n \leftarrow F_n\}$ $(n \geq 0)$, where $\phi_1, \ldots, \phi_n$ are distinct function variables, $F_1, \ldots, F_n$ are function expressions and, for each $1 \leq i \leq n$, F_i and ϕ_i are of the same arity.

Definition 1.88 The *application of a substitution* $\vartheta = \{\phi_1 \leftarrow F_1, \ldots, \phi_n \leftarrow F_n\}$ *to a formula A* is the formula, written $A\vartheta$, obtained by the following construction:

(i) Replace each free occurrence of ϕ_i, $1 \leq i \leq n$, in A by $\{F_i\}$.
(ii) In the expression resulting from (i), which in general is not a formula, successively replace each part of the form $\{F_i\}(\bar{\beta})$ by the application of F_i to $\bar{\beta}$.

The application of ϑ *to A* is said to be *proper* iff no free occurrence of any individual variable in any of $F_1, \ldots, F_n$ becomes bound in $A\vartheta$; otherwise, the application of ϑ *to A* is called *improper.* ∎

We say that *B obtains from A by the substitution of* $F_1, \ldots, F_n$ for $\phi_1, \ldots, \phi_n$ iff B is the application of $\{\phi_1 \leftarrow F_1, \ldots, \phi_n \leftarrow F_n\}$ to A. The phrase '*B obtains from A by the proper* (resp. *improper*) *substitution of* $F_1, \ldots, F_n$ *for* $\phi_1, \ldots, \phi_n$' is a synonym for '*B is a proper* (resp. *improper*) *application of* $\{\phi_1 \leftarrow F_1, \ldots, \phi_n \leftarrow F_n\}$ *to A.*'

Example 1.89 Let $A = \forall y[P(y) \supset Q(\phi(y))] \supset \forall yz[P(z) \supset Q(\phi(z))]$ and suppose that $\vartheta = \{\phi \leftarrow \lambda xg(y, x)\}$. Applying ϑ *to A*, we first obtain

$$\forall y[P(y) \supset Q(\{\lambda xg(y, x)\}(y))] \supset \forall yz[P(z) \supset Q(\{\lambda xg(y, x)\}(z))]$$

and then

$$A\vartheta = \forall y[P(y) \supset Q(g(y,y))] \supset \forall yz[P(z) \supset Q(g(y, z))].$$

The application of ϑ *to A* is improper because the free occurrence of y in $\lambda xg(y, x)$ becomes bound in $A\vartheta$.

Consider now $A' = \forall z\,.\,\Phi(\phi(z)) \supset P(\phi(z))$, $\vartheta' = \{\phi \leftarrow \lambda xf(x, y)\}$. Applying ϑ' to A', we first obtain

$$\forall z\,.\,\Phi(\{\lambda xf(x, y)\}(z)) \supset P(\{\lambda xf(x, y)\}(z))$$

and then

$$A'\vartheta' = \forall z\,.\,\Phi(f(z, y)) \supset P(f(z, y)).$$

The application of ϑ' to A' is proper. ∎

Theorem 1.90 For any substitution $\vartheta = \{\phi_1 \leftarrow F_1, \ldots, \phi_n \leftarrow F_n\}$ and any formula A, the formula

$$\forall \phi_1 \ldots \phi_n A \supset A\vartheta$$

is valid, provided that the application of ϑ to A is proper. ∎

Theorem 1.90 need not hold if we admit improper applications. Consider, for instance, the formula A and the substitution ϑ from Example 1.89. It is easily seen that the formula $\forall \phi A$ is valid but the formula $A\vartheta$ is not. Thus, the formula $\forall \phi A \supset A\vartheta$ is invalid.

Corollary 1.91 For any substitution $\vartheta = \{\phi_1 \leftarrow F_1, \ldots, \phi_n \leftarrow F_n\}$ and any sentence of the form $\forall \phi_1 \ldots \phi_n A$,

$$\forall \phi_1 \ldots \phi_n A \models A\vartheta$$

provided that the application of ϑ to A is proper. ∎

1.6 MODAL LOGIC

Modal logic has been developed to formalize arguments involving the notions of necessity and possibility. A necessary proposition is a true proposition which could not be false. A possible proposition is the one which may happen to be true. This distinction is often expressed using the concept of 'possible world': necessary propositions are those which are true in all possible worlds, whereas possible propositions are those which are true in at least one possible world.

This section provides a short survey of the basic systems of propositional and first-order modal logic. For a more detailed treatment of the subject, consult Hughes & Cresswell (1972) and Chellas (1980).

The material included in this section will be employed in Chapter 4.

1.6.1 Modal propositional logic

An *alphabet of modal propositional logic* obtains from that of classical propositional logic by the addition of two *modal operators*: M (the *possibility operator*) and L (the *necessity operator*).

Definition 1.92 Let AL be an alphabet of modal propositional logic. The set L_{AL} of *formulae over* AL is the smallest set such that:

(i) *'True'* and all proposition constants from AL are members of L_{AL}.
(ii) If A and B are elements of L_{AL}, then so are $(A \supset B)$, $(\neg A)$, $(\mathrm{L}A)$ and $(\mathrm{M}A)$.

∎

The set L_{AL} is called the *modal propositional language over* AL. As usual, L_{AL} will be often abbreviated to L.

The symbols *False*, $\vee$, $\wedge$ and $\equiv$ are introduced in the ordinary way and have the usual meanings. Formulae of the form $(\mathrm{L}A)$ and $(\mathrm{M}A)$ are to be read 'It is necessary that A' and 'It is possible that A', respectively.

In fact, there is no need to take both of the modal operators as primitive symbols, because each of them can be defined by means of the other. Taking the necessity operator as primitive, we may introduce the possibility operator by

$$(\mathrm{M}A) =_{\mathrm{DF}} \neg(\mathrm{L}\neg A).$$

Similarly, the necessity operator may be defined by

$$(\mathrm{L}A) =_{\mathrm{DF}} \neg(\mathrm{M}\neg A).$$

We adopt the conventions made in section 1.2 as to writing formulae. In addition, we assume that the modal operators bind as tight as the negation sign. Thus, the formula $\mathrm{M}p \supset \mathrm{L}q \vee r$ stands for $((\mathrm{M}p) \supset ((\mathrm{L}q) \vee r))$. The formula $\mathrm{LMLL}p$ is an abbreviation for $(\mathrm{L}(\mathrm{M}(\mathrm{L}(\mathrm{L}p))))$.

We now turn to the semantics of modal propositional logic.†

Definition 1.93 A *frame for a modal propositional language* L_{AL} is a triple $\mathrm{M} = \langle \mathrm{W}, \mathrm{R}, \mathrm{m} \rangle$, where:

(i) W is a non-empty set, called the *set of possible worlds*;
(ii) R is a binary relation on W, called the *accessibility relation*;
(iii) m is a function which assigns to each pair consisting of a proposition constant from AL and an element $\mathrm{w} \in \mathrm{W}$, an element from $\{0, 1\}$.

∎

Possible worlds are abstract objects and their precise meaning could be hardly provided. Intuitively, we are to view them as possible states of affairs, situations, scenarios, etc. Since a proposition may have different truth-values in different states of affairs, the function m assigns the truth-values not to proposition constants alone, but to pairs consisting of a proposition constant and a possible world. The value $\mathrm{m}(p, \mathrm{w})$ is to be thought of as the truth-value of p in w. The accessibility relation is meant to capture the intuition that some things may be possible from the standpoint of one world and impossible from the standpoint of another. If wRw_1, then we say that w_1 is *accessible* (*conceivable*, *visible*) from w. The intention is that the worlds accessible from w are those which are to be considered as possible from the perspective of w.

Definition 1.94 The *truth-value* $\mathrm{V}^{\mathrm{M}}_{\mathrm{w}}(A)$ *of a formula A in a frame* M *wrt* $\mathrm{w} \in \mathrm{W}$ is an element of $\{0, 1\}$ given by the following recursion on A:

(1) $\mathrm{V}^{\mathrm{M}}_{\mathrm{w}}(p) = \mathrm{m}(p, \mathrm{w})$;
(ii) $\mathrm{V}^{\mathrm{M}}_{\mathrm{w}}(\neg B) = 1 - \mathrm{V}^{\mathrm{M}}_{\mathrm{w}}(B)$;
(iii) $\mathrm{V}^{\mathrm{M}}_{\mathrm{w}}(B \supset C) = 1$ iff $\mathrm{V}^{\mathrm{M}}_{\mathrm{w}}(B) = 0$ or $\mathrm{V}^{\mathrm{M}}_{\mathrm{w}}(C) = 1$;
(iv) $\mathrm{V}^{\mathrm{M}}_{\mathrm{w}}(\mathrm{L}B) = 1$ iff $\mathrm{V}^{\mathrm{M}}_{\mathrm{w}'}(B) = 1$, for every $\mathrm{w}' \in \mathrm{W}$ such that wRw';
(v) $\mathrm{V}^{\mathrm{M}}_{\mathrm{w}}(\mathrm{M}B) = 1$ iff $\mathrm{V}^{\mathrm{M}}_{\mathrm{w}'}(B) = 1$, for some $\mathrm{w}' \in \mathrm{W}$ such that wRw'.

∎

Observe that $\mathrm{V}^{\mathrm{M}}_{\mathrm{w}}(\mathrm{L}A)$ and $\mathrm{V}^{\mathrm{M}}_{\mathrm{w}}(\mathrm{M}A)$ are not functions of $\mathrm{V}^{\mathrm{M}}_{\mathrm{w}}(A)$, but depend also on the truth-values of A in words which are accessible from w. Thus, unlike classical logic, modal logic does not obey the Principle of Functionality.

A formula A is said to be *true in a frame* $\mathrm{M} = \langle \mathrm{W}, \mathrm{R}, \mathrm{m} \rangle$ iff $\mathrm{V}^{\mathrm{M}}_{\mathrm{w}}(A) = 1$, for every $\mathrm{w} \in \mathrm{W}$. If A is true in M, then M is called a *model of A*.

Imposing various restrictions on the accessibility relation, we obtain different *systems of modal propositional logic*. Here, we shall be interested in three such systems: T, S4 and S5.

† The semantics we present here is known as Kripke *semantics* or the *possible-world semantics*.

Let $M = \langle W, R, m \rangle$ be a frame. We say that M is a T-*frame* iff R is reflexive. M is called an S4-*frame* iff R is reflexive and transitive. Finally, M is said to be an S5-*frame* iff R is reflexive, transitive and symmetric (i.e. an equivalence relation).

We say that a formula $A \in L$ is X-*valid*, $X \in \{T, S4, S5\}$, iff A is true in every X-frame for L. Obviously, any T-valid formula is also S4-valid and S5-valid. Similarly, any S4-valid formula is S5-valid. The converse, however, is not generally true. That is, there are S5-valid formulae which are neither S4-valid or T-valid. Also, there are S4-valid formulae which are not T-valid.

Example 1.95 We show that every instance of the schema $LA \supset A$ is T-valid (and hence S4-valid and S5-valid). Assume to the contrary that this is not the case. Thus, there is a formula A, a T-frame $M = \langle W, R, m \rangle$, and $w \in W$ such that $V_w^M(LA \supset A) = 0$. It follows, therefore, that $V_w^M(LA) = 1$ and $V_w^M(A) = 0$. Because M is a T-frame, R is reflexive, so that $V_w^M(LA) = 1$ implies $V_w^M(A) = 1$, a contradiction.

Consider now the schema $LA \supset LLA$. We prove that every instance of this schema is S4-valid (and hence S5-valid). Again, assume to the contrary that for some formula A, some S4-frame $M = \langle W, R, M \rangle$ and some $w \in W$, $V_w^M(LA \supset LLA) = 0$. Thus,

$$V_w^M(LA) = 1 \tag{1.6.1}$$

and $V_w^M(LLA) = 0$. Since $V_w^M(LLA) = 0$, there must be $w' \in W$ such that wRw' and $V_{w'}^M(LA) = 0$. But $V_{w'}^M(LA) = 0$ implies the existence of $w'' \in W$ such that $w'Rw''$ and

$$V_{w''}^M(A) = 0. \tag{1.6.2}$$

Since M is an S4-frame, R is transitive. Thus, wRw' and $w'Rw''$ imply wRw''. Given this and (1.6.1), we immediately conclude that $V_{w''}^M(A) = 1$, a contradiction with (1.6.2).

In general, instances of the schema $LA \supset LLA$ are not T-valid. To see this, consider $Lp \supset LLp$ and take the T-frame $M = \langle W, R, m \rangle$, where

$$W = \{w_1, w_2, w_3\};$$
$$R = \{\langle w_1, w_2 \rangle, \langle w_2, w_3 \rangle\} \cup \{\langle w_i, w_i \rangle : 1 \leq i \leq 3\};$$
$$m(p, w_1) = 1;\ m(p, w_2) = 1;\ m(p, w_3) = 0.$$

It is easily checked that $V_{w_1}^M(Lp \supset LLp) = 0$. ∎

The validity problem for T (resp. S4, S5) modal propositional logic is the following task: Given an arbitrary formula A of modal propositional logic, determine whether or not A is T-valid (resp. S4-valid, S5-valid).

Theorem 1.96 For any $X \in \{T, S4, S5\}$, the validity problem for X modal propositional logic is decidable. ∎

In view of Theorem 1.96, it is possible to construct algorithms for deciding whether or not a given formula of modal propositional logic is T-valid, S4-valid or S5-valid. We shall not provide such algorithms here, but merely refer the interested reader to Hughes & Cresswell (1972, pp. 82–122).

We may speak about a *theory of modal propositional logic*, regarded as a pair $T = \langle L, S \rangle$, where L is a modal propositional language, and S, called the set of *axioms of T*, is a computable subset of L. As usual, unless specified otherwise, modal propositional theories will be identified with sets of their axioms.

Let T be a theory. A frame M is called an X-*model of T*, where $X \in \{T, S4, S5\}$, iff M is an X-frame and all axioms of T are true in M. A theory which has an X-model is said to be X-*satisfiable*; otherwise, it is X-*unsatisfiable*. T is said to X-*entail* a formula A

written $T \models_X A$, iff A is true in every X-model of T. As usual, $\models_X A$ stands for $\{\ \} \models_X A$. The relation denoted by $\models_X$ is called the *entailment relation of* X *modal propositional logic*.

A deduction system for modal propositional logic is specified in the ordinary way. We also have the usual definition that A is provable from T in DS; $\vdash_{DS} A$ is an abbreviation for $\{\ \} \vdash A$.

Definition 1.97 Let L be a language of modal propositional logic and suppose that $X \in \{T, S4, S5\}$. We denote by $MPL(L, X)$ the deduction system $\langle L, S_X, R \rangle$ given by

(i) S_T consists of the following axioms:

(A1) *True*
(A2) $A \supset (B \supset A)$
(A3) $(A \supset (B \supset C)) \supset ((A \supset B) \supset (A \supset C))$
(A4) $(\neg B \supset \neg A) \supset ((\neg B \supset A) \supset B)$
(A5) $LA \supset A$
(A6) $L(A \supset B) \supset (LA \supset LB)$

S_{S4} obtains from S_T by the addition of
(A7) $LA \supset LLA$

S_{S5} obtains from S_{S4} by the addition of

(A8) $MA \supset LMA$.

(ii) R consists of the following inference rules:

(MP) B is a direct consequence of A and $A \supset B$;
(NEC) LA is a direct consequence of A.

∎

(NEC) is called the *rule of necessitation*.

As usual, we normally assume that the language under consideration is fixed, and the symbol $\vdash_{MPL(L,X)}$ will be abbreviated to $\vdash_X$. If $T \vdash_X A$, then we say that A is *provable from* T *in* X *modal propositional logic*. If $\vdash_X A$, then A is said to be a *theorem of* X *modal propositional logic*. We write $T \nvdash_X A$ and $\nvdash_X A$ as the negations for $T \vdash_X A$ and $\vdash_X A$, respectively.

We denote by $Th_X(T)$ the *provability operator of* X *modal propositional logic*: $Th_X(T) = \{A: T \vdash_X A\}$.

Theorem 1.98 For any $X \in \{T, S4, S5\}$,

(i) If $T \vdash_X A$, then $T \models_X A$ (Soundness Theorem)
(ii) If $T \models_X A$, then $T \vdash_X A$ (Completeness Theorem)

∎

Corollary 1.99 For any $X \in \{T, S4, S5\}$, $\models_X A$ iff $\vdash_X A$. ∎

Let $X \in \{T, S4, S5\}$. A theory T over L is said to be X-*consistent* iff there is a formula $A \in L$ such that $T \nvdash_X A$.

Theorem 1.100 T is X-consistent iff T is X-satisfiable. ∎

We conclude this section by an important remark. In the logical literature the notions of modal entailment and modal provability are often understood in the following stronger sense. We say that a theory T *strongly* X-*entails a formula* A, written $T \models^s_X A$, iff for each X-frame $M = \langle W, R, m\rangle$ and each $w \in W$, if $V^M_w(B) = 1$, for each $B \in T$, then $V^M_w(A) = 1$. A is said to be *strongly* X-*provable from* T, written $T \vdash^s_X A$, iff there are formulae $B_1, \ldots, B_n \in T$ such that $\vdash_X B_1 \wedge \cdots \wedge B_n \supset A$. It is easy to see that $T \models^s_X A$ implies $T \models_X A$ and $T \vdash^s_X A$ implies $T \vdash_X A$. The converse, however, is not always true. For instance, for any $X \in \{T, S4, S5\}$, $\{p\} \vdash_X Lp$ and $\{p\} \models_X Lp$, but neither $\{p\} \vdash^s_X Lp$ nor $\{p\} \models^s_X Lp$. It can be shown that the notions of strong entailment and strong provability are related as follows: For any $X \in \{T, S4, S5\}$, $T \models^s_X A$ iff $T \vdash^s_X A$.

1.6.2 Modal first-order logic

An *alphabet of modal first-order logic* obtains from that of classical first-order logic by the addition of the operators 'L' and 'M'.

Let AL be an alphabet of modal first-order logic. The *set of terms over* AL and the *set of atomic formulae over* AL are defined as in the classical first-order logic. The *set* L_{AL} *of formulae over* AL is the smallest set such that: (i) All atomic formulae over AL are elements of L_{AL}; (ii) If x is a variable and $A, B \in L_{AL}$, then $(\neg A)$, $(A \supset B)$, $(\forall x(A))$, (LA) and (MA) are members of L_{AL}.

L_{AL} is called the *modal first-order language over* AL and, as usual, we shall often write L instead of L_{AL}.

The semantics of modal first-order logic is based on the following notion:

Definition 1.101 A *frame for a modal first-order language* L_{AL} is a quadruple $M = \langle D, W, R, m\rangle$, where

(i) D is a non-empty set, called the *domain of* M;
(ii) W is a non-empty set of 'possible worlds';
(iii) R is a binary relation of 'accessibility' on W;
(iv) m is a function which assigns to each pair consisting of an n-ary predicate constant ($n \geq 0$), different from '=', and an element w of W, an n-ary relation on D, to the constant '=', if present in AL, the identity relation on D, and to each n-ary function constant ($n \geq 0$), a function from D^n into D.

∎

Given a frame $M = \langle D, W, R, m\rangle$, we write $|M|$ to denote the domain of M. If K is a predicate (resp. function constant), then $M|K, w|$ (resp. $M|K|$) stands for $m(K, w)$ (resp. $m(K)$).

An assignment over a frame M is specified in the usual way. As before, the set of all assignments over M will be denoted by As(M). The symbol $[a]_x$ stands for the set of all assignments over M which are identical to 'a', except perhaps on the variable x.

Definition 1.102 Let M be a frame for L_{AL}.

The *value* $V^M_a(\alpha)$ *of a term* α *in* M *wrt* $a \in As(M)$ is specified as in the classical first-order logic (see Definition 1.25).

The *truth-value* $V^M_{a,w}(A)$ *of a formula* $A \in L_{AL}$ in M *wrt* $a \in As(M)$ *and* $w \in W$ is an element of $\{0, 1\}$ defined as follows:

(i) $V^M_{a,w}(True) = 1$;
(ii) $V^M_{a,w}(P^0) = M|P^0, w|$;
(iii) $V^M_{a,w}(P^n(\alpha_1, \ldots, \alpha_n)) = M|P^n, w|(V^M_a(\alpha_1), \ldots, V^M_a(\alpha_n))$;

(iv) $V^M_{a,w}(\alpha = \beta) = 1$ iff $V^M_a(\alpha) = V^M_a(\beta)$;
(v) $V^M_{a,w}(B \supset C) = 1$ iff $V^M_{a,w}(B) = 0$ or $V^M_{a,w}(C) = 1$;
(vi) $V^M_{a,w}(\neg B) = 1 - V^M_{a,w}(B)$;
(vii) $V^M_{a,w}(\forall x B) = 1$ iff $V^M_{a',w}(B) = 1$, for every $a' \in [a]_x$;
(viii) $V^M_{a,w}((LB) = 1$ iff $V^M_{a,w'}(B) = 1$, for every $w' \in W$ such that wRw';
(ix) $V^M_{a,w}(MB) = 1$ iff $V^M_{a,w'}(B) = 1$, for some $w' \in W$ such that wRw'.

∎

The truth-conditions for the symbols *False*, $\wedge$, $\vee$, $\equiv$ and $\exists$ easily follow from their definitions.

A formula A is said to be *true in* M iff $V^M_{a,w}(A) = 1$, for any $a \in As(M)$ and any $w \in W$. If A is true in M, then we say that M is a *model of A*.

A frame $M = \langle D, W, R, m \rangle$ is said to be a T-*frame* iff R is reflexive. If, in addition, R is transitive, then M is called an S4-*frame*. Finally, if R is an equivalence relation, then M is said to be an S5-*frame*. A formula A is said to be X-*valid*, where $X \in \{T, S4, S5\}$, iff A is true in every X-frame.

Example 1.103 We show that every instance of the schema $\forall x(LA) \supset L(\forall x A)$ is T-valid (and hence S4-valid and S5-valid).†

Assume to the contrary that there is a formula A, a frame $M = \langle D, W, R, m \rangle$, $a \in As(M)$ and $w \in W$ such that $V^M_{a,w}(\forall x(LA) \supset L(\forall x A)) = 0$. Thus, $V^M_{a,w}(\forall x(LA)) = 1$ and $V^M_{a,w}(L(\forall x A)) = 0$. Since $V^M_{a,w}(L(\forall x A)) = 0$, there must be $w' \in W$ and $a' \in [a]_x$ such that wRw' and

$$V^M_{a',w'}(A) = 0. \tag{1.6.3}$$

On the other hand, since $V^M_{a,w}(\forall x(LA)) = 1$, we have $V^M_{a',w}(LA) = 1$, and hence (because wRw') $V^M_{a',w'}(A) = 1$. This contradicts (1.6.3).

Note that we have not used the fact that R is reflexive. It follows, therefore, that every instance of $\forall x(LA) \supset L(\forall x A)$ is true in every frame. ∎

The validity problem for X modal first-order logic ($X \in \{T, S4\ S5\}$) is the task of determining whether or not an arbitrarily given formula of modal first-order logic is X-valid.

Theorem 1.104 For any $X \in \{T, S4, S5\}$, the validity problem of X modal first-order logic is undecidable. ∎

In view of Theorem 1.104, there is no algorithm for deciding whether or not an arbitrarily given formula of modal first-order logic is T-valid (resp. S4-valid, S5-valid). However, as in the case of classical first-order logic, it is possible to construct a procedure Π_T (resp. Π_{S4}, Π_{S5}) which, when supplied with a modal first-order formula A, terminates and reports that A is T-valid (resp. S4-valid, S5-valid), provided that this is indeed the case. Otherwise, i.e. if A is not T-valid (resp. not S4-valid, not S5-valid), then the procedure may never terminate. (See Morgan (1976) for details.)

A *theory of modal first-order logic* is a pair $T = \langle L, S \rangle$, where L is a modal first-order language, and S, the set of *axioms of T*, is a computable set of sentences from L. As in the case of modal propositional logic, we may speak about T-*models*, S4-*models* and S5-*models* of a theory T. If T has an X-model, where $X \in \{T, S4, S5\}$, then T is said to be X-*satisfiable*; otherwise, X-*unsatisfiable*.

The notion 'T X-*entails* A', written $T \models_X A$, is defined as in the case of modal

† The schema $\forall x(LA) \supset L(\forall x A)$ is known in the literature as Barcan's schema.

propositional logic, except that the frames, the theories and the formulae under consideration are now those of modal first-order logic.

Definition 1.105 Let L be a modal first-order language and suppose that $X \in \{T, S4, S5\}$. We denote by MFOL(L, X) the deduction system $\langle L, S_X, R \rangle$ given by

(i) S_T consists of the following axioms:

(A1) *True*
(A2) $A \supset (B \supset A)$
(A3) $(A \supset (B \supset C)) \supset ((A \supset B) \supset (A \supset C))$
(A4) $(\neg B \supset \neg A) \supset ((\neg B \supset A) \supset B)$
(A5) $\forall x A(x) \supset A(\alpha)$, where α is any term free for x in $A(x)$
(A6) $\forall x(A \supset B) \supset (A \supset \forall x B)$, where A contains no free occurrences of x
(A7) $LA \supset A$
(A8) $L(A \supset B) \supset (LA \supset LB)$
(A9) $\forall x(LA) \supset L(\forall x A)$

S_{S4} obtains from S_T by the addition of

(A10) $LA \supset LLA$

S_{S5} obtains from S_{S4} by the addition of

(A11) $MA \supset LMA$

If L is a language with equality, then S_T, S_{S4}, and S_{S5} additionally contain the equality axioms for L.

(ii) R consists of the following inference rules:

(MP) B is a direct consequence of A and $A \supset B$;
(GEN) $\forall x A$ is a direct consequence of A;
(NEC) LA is a direct consequence of A.

∎

As usual, we assume that the language under consideration is fixed, and we shall write $\vdash_X$ instead of $\vdash_{MFOL(L,X)}$.† If $T \vdash_X A$, then we say that A is *provable from T in* X *modal first-order logic*. If $\vdash_X A$, then we say that *A is a theorem of* X modal first-order logic.

$Th_X(T)$ stands for the *provability operator of the* X *modal first-order logic*: $Th_X(T) = \{A: A \text{ is a sentence and } T \vdash_X A\}$.

The next theorem shows that the deduction system provided in Definition 1.105 is both sound and complete:

Theorem 1.106 For any $X \in \{T, S4, S5\}$,

(i) If $T \vdash_X A$, then $T \models_X A$ (Soundness Theorem)
(ii) If $T \models_X A$, then $T \vdash_X A$ (Completeness Theorem)

∎

Corollary 1.107 For any $X \in \{T, S4, S5\}$, $\models_X A$ iff $\vdash_X A$. ∎

Let $X \in \{T, S4, S5\}$. A modal first-order theory T over L is said to be X-*consistent* iff there is a formula $A \in L$ such that $T \nvdash_X A$.

---

† It will be always clear from the context whether the symbol $\vdash_X$ refers to the propositional or to the first-order part of modal logic. (The same remark applies to the symbol Th_X).

Theorem 1.108 T is X-consistent iff T is X-satisfiable. ∎

The notions *'T strongly* X-*entails A'* and *'A is strongly* X-*provable from T'*, introduced in section 1.6.1, can be easily generalized into first-order modal logic. We omit the details here, because these concepts will not be used in the sequel.

This completes our basic presentation of monotonic logics. A few additional results concerning the discussed formalisms will be given when they are directly needed. Also, in Chapter 4, we provide a brief survey of monotonic logics not presented here, namely, propositional *intuitionistic logic* and propositional 3-*valued logic*.

2

Foundations of non-monotonic reasoning

This chapter is devoted to a general discussion of the subject of non-monotonic reasoning. In section 2.1 we define this type of inference, illustrate its close relationship to human common-sense reasoning and sketch its role in artificial intelligence. We also say a little about those trends in modern formal logic that are of some importance to non-monotonic inference. In section 2.2 we compare non-monotonic reasoning with reasoning about action. The latter kind of inference, which is essentially monotonic, involves two famous problems, called the *frame problem* and the *problem of qualification*, that inspired much of early theoretical research on non-monotonic inference. Finally, in section 2.3, we provide a typology of non-monotonic reasoning.

2.1 NON-MONOTONIC REASONING

Traditional deductive logics are always *monotonic*: adding new premisses (axioms) will never invalidate old conclusions (theorems), or, equivalently, the set of conclusions increases monotonically with the set of premisses. Formally, a logic is monotonic iff its provability relation, $\vdash$, enjoys the following property: For any sets of premisses S and S′

$$\mathrm{S} \subseteq \mathrm{S}' \quad \text{implies} \quad \{A : \mathrm{S} \vdash A\} \subseteq \{A : \mathrm{S}' \vdash A\}.$$

Recently, there has been a good deal of interest in logical systems violating the property of monotonicity. They have been primarily studied in the context of human common-sense reasoning.

What characterizes human reasoning is its ability to deal with incomplete information. In everyday life we are constantly faced with situations where not all relevant evidence is known. In fact, apart from the most trivial cases, there are always gaps in our knowledge. Yet, we are not paralysed by our partial ignorance. In order to act, we must be able to draw conclusions even if the available evidence is insufficient to guarantee their correctness. Obviously, such conclusions are risky and may be invalidated in the light of new, more accurate, information.

To illustrate this, suppose that on a Saturday evening I must urgently contact John. The only established fact is:

On Saturday evenings John usually visists his club (2.1.1)

Given this evidence, there are good chances, but only chances, that John is at the club. In fact, I can imagine many different places where he might actually be. But I will never act unless I am prepared to be guided by conclusions that are merely plausible. Thus, instead of sitting and analysing all the possible scenarios – a hopeless task – the only rational behaviour is to assume

John is at the club (2.1.2)

and try to contact him there.

Suppose further that going to the club, I meet Bill, a friend of John. What he tells me is rather unexpected:

Yesterday John had a car accident (2.1.3)

This drastically changes the situation. Given only (2.1.1), it was plausible to assume (2.1.2). Unfortunately, (2.1.2) is no longer plausible given additionally (2.1.3). Going to the club seems now a waste of my time. Rather I should try to contact John in a hospital.

This example brings us directly to the kind of reasoning we shall be interested in. Following the AI terminology, we shall refer to it as *non-monotonic reasoning*. The term was originally proposed by Minsky (1975).

Definition 2.1 By non-monotonic reasoning we understand the drawing of conclusions which may be invalidated in the light of new information. A logical system is called non-monotonic iff its provability relation violates the property of monotonicity. ∎

This is an informal and a very general definition. Viewing non-monotonicity as an abstract syntactic property, it says nothing about the form of non-monotonic inference. We shall return to this point later, but first we must say a little more about common-sense reasoning.

Unlike formal logical reasoning, whose underlying concept is that of *truth*, common-sense inference is grounded on the concept of *rationality*. We cannot expect that our everyday conclusions will always be true. This is simply impossible. Yet, we do not jump to conclusions at random. To minimize the risk of mistaken results, we employ our knowledge and experience before deciding that a conclusion is to be accepted. And although many real-life inferences turn out to be wrong, we always demand them to be rational. The availability of a rational justification is the most fundamental requirement for any conclusion accepted in common-sense reasoning.

Rationality is a vague concept and its precise definition can hardly be expected. Here we remark only that contrasted with the notion of truth it enjoys two specific properties. First, it is *agent-dependent*: different agents may be of different opinions as to what is rational in a given situation. Second, it is *purpose dependent*: the acceptance of a proposition as a rational conclusion depends on the purpose it is to be used for. For instance, given cursory evidence, I may well assume that Bill is honest and lend him £50. But I would be more cautious, and try to conduct a thorough investigation, if I was to consider him as my business partner.

To emphasize the subjective nature of common-sense conclusions, they are usually called *beliefs* in the AI literature.

Referring to common-sense conclusions as beliefs is somewhat misleading. According to the classical meaning, the term 'belief' denotes a fact believed as true. Of course, such a fact may turn out to be false. But this is relatively rare and, more importantly, we are always surprised to learn that our belief is wrong. This cannot be generally said about common-sense inferences. In practice, we often accept conclusions whose truth is *a priori* problematic. A typical example: Suppose that Bill is accused of having committed a crime. Facts are generally against him, so that his guilt is quite probable. Yet, unless there is enough evidence to prove him guilty, the only acceptable position is to assume his innocence.

At this point we must try to answer two fundamental questions:

(1) What really are common-sense conclusions (beliefs)?
(2) What techniques do we use when reaching them?

The first of these questions is given a detailed analysis in Perlis (1987b). In particular, he provides the following informal definition capturing a very wide class of beliefs.[†]

Definition 2.2 A proposition p is believed by an agent g, i.e. g views p as a rational conclusion, if g is prepared to use p as if it were true. ▮

Perlis gives a number of examples illustrating his definition. The following, borrowed from Winograd (1980), will suffice for our purposes.

Assume that I am planning to make a trip by car. To begin with, I must decide where my car actually is. Given no better evidence, it is highly probable that it still is where I last parked it. According to Perlis's definition, the acceptance of this statement as a belief depends upon whether I am prepared to act as if it were true, or not. That is, if I choose to ignore all the circumstances under which the statement could be false and *base my actions* on the assumption that it is true, then although I cannot be sure that the car is indeed in the expected place, I believe that it is there. On the other hand, even if I am almost certain that this statement is true, but at the same time I try to improve my chances by checking whether a bus will pass by, in the case the car is missing, then I do not regard the statement as my belief, but rather as a very likely contingency.

We neither suggest that Perlis's definition is the only possible one, nor that it captures all common-sense inferences. It has been reproduced here because it is certainly worthy of careful consideration. However, since the precise specification of beliefs is not crucial for our discussion, the reader who finds Perlis's definition questionable, is advised to view beliefs as primitive objects.

We now turn our attention to the question of how beliefs are reached. In this context, the most important observation is that human conclusions are often based on both the presence and the absence of information. To illustrate this, consider my reason for believing

(A) John is at his club

[†] These are called *use-beliefs* in Perlis's terminology.

given

(1) It is a Saturday evening
(2) On Saturday evenings John usually visits his club.

Clearly, in virtue of (2), (1) provides some evidence supporting (A). It might then seem that my inference is based upon the rule:

(R) From (1), infer (A).

This, however, cannot be the case. I must not accept (R) and at the same time be prepared to reject (A) in the light of new information; for instance, if I learn that John had a car accident yesterday. The kind of reasoning involved here is more complex. To model it correctly, the application of (R) must be restricted. The rule should be blocked in any situation where its use would be intuitively unacceptable. In other words, given (1), I am prepared to conclude (A) unless there is some evidence making this inferrence irrational. This means that my reasoning is not grounded on (R), but rather on the *ignorance-dependent* rule:

(R′) From (1), in the absence of evidence to suspect otherwise, infer (A).

There is a very close connection between ignorance-dependency and non-monotonicity of common-sense reasoning. On the one hand, since new evidence decreases our ignorance, any ignorance-dependent belief is subject to invalidation by new information. On the other hand, since each ignorance-independent conclusion continues to hold when our knowledge increases, any non-monotonic inference must indeed necessarily refer to the absence of some information.

We now are in a position to be more specific as regards the form of non-monotonic reasoning. Our previous discussion suggests the following informal definition:

Definition 2.3 By a *non-monotonic inference pattern* (a *non-monotnic rule*) we understand the following reasoning schema:

Given information A, in the absence of evidence B, infer a conclusion C.

The intuition, of course, is that A supports the conclusion while the lack of B assures its rationality. ∎

Two remarks about this definition are in order. First, in practical applications, B is often identified with contradictory evidence. That is, many naturally occurring non-monotonic rules are of the form:

Given A, in the absence of evidence to the contrary, infer C.

Second, it should be made clear that this definition does not pretend to be formal. Obviously, it leaves unanswered two fundamental questions. How are non-monotonic rules to be represented? Under which criteria is a piece of information to be considered as given (known)? Unfortunately, answering those questions is a non-trivial task, so that they must be ignored at the moment.†

There are at least two different problems involved in non-monotonic inference. They might be called the *problem of formalization* and the *problem of beliefs revision*.

† In fact, all non-monotonic formalisms studied in this book may be viewed as answers to those very questions.

The former amounts to determining how our knowledge is to be formalized. This includes both specifying how this knowledge is to be represented and defining the set of conclusions (beliefs) derivable from such a representation. The belief-revision problem is that of updating the current model of the world when new evidence invalidates some currently accepted beliefs.

Most frequently, the necessity of updates manifests itself in explicit contradiction. For example, I must not keep believing that John is at his club, if I learn that actually he is at his office. Sometimes, however, the need to revise beliefs arises although new evidence could be consistently accepted. This may happen if a current belief is grounded on the absence of the information just learned. For instance, learning that John had a car accident yesterday makes me retract the belief that he is at the club. Clearly, no direct contradiction is involved here. After all, if the accident were not serious, he could be at the club.

The complexity of the update problem is further increased by the fact that beliefs rarely exist in isolation. Typically, most of them depend on both the presence and the absence of some others. This means that an explicit invalidation of a single belief may trigger off a long chain of necessary updates; both retractions and additions![†] In consequence, if the modelled world is complex, the task of its efficient reorganization can be very hard.

In contrast to many non-standard forms of inference currently employed in AI, non-monotonic reasoning has been rarely studied by logicians. However, formal logic has addressed some issues that are obviously relevant to the field of non-monotonic reasoning. The most important investigations here are those concerning inconsistent information.

Until the last three decades, inconsistent evidence has been given little attention in modern logic. Much of traditional thought is based on the assumption that contradictions cannot exist in any real world. Accordingly, they have been uniformly treated as irrational and unacceptable. In particular, the problem of reasoning from inconsistent information has been dismissed as trivial.[‡]

The recognition that the classical view can be changed is a relatively recent phenomenon. Two research areas worthy of special mention here are *hypothetical* and *counterfactual reasoning* (Rescher 1964, 1976; Lewis 1973; Gardenfors 1978) and *paraconsistent logics* (Anderson & Belnap 1975; Studia Logica 1984).

Both hypothetical and counterfactual reasoning are directed towards the following problem: What would hold in a hypothetical world differing from the actual one in that some specific facts (hypotheses) are true in it? The crucial supposition is that those assumed hypotheses may contradict the actual world, so that the formalization of this type of inference is heavily influenced by the ability to restore consistency. Technically, the task of specifying the hypothetical world can be viewed as the previously discussed belief-revision problem.

Contrasted with hypotheticals and counterfactuals, where inference is virtually performed after eliminating inconsistency, the paraconsistent logics adopt a more radical approach. The point of view they take is that reasoning from contradictory information need not lead to triviality.[§] More specifically, a logic is called

[†] Notice that each retraction may validate some currently invalid belief. This may happen if such a belief depends on the absence of the one just rejected.

[‡] See Priest & Routley (1984).

[§] A set of sentences is called trivial if it includes all sentences of the considered language.

paraconsistent if, for some sentences A and B, $\{A, \neg A\} \nvdash B$. A number of paraconsistent formalisms, the best known being *relevance logics*, can be found in the philosophical literature.† So far these formalisms have been studied in the context of various scientific theories such as the naive set theory, early quantum mechanics or Hegel's dialectic. However, it is clear that the issues addressed by paraconsistent logics are highly relevant to non-monotonic inference. In particular, these logics can be considered as a theoretical basis for the update problem.

Although non-monotonic reasoing has been rather ignored in formal logic, it has had to be studied by AI researchers. The progress of such areas of application as computational vision, planning, the theory of diagnosis, natural language understanding or expert systems clearly depends on the ability to deal with non-monotonic inferences.‡ In fact, as Winograd (1980) points out, many early AI systems employed various non-monotonic mechanisms. Unfortunately, those *ad hoc* tools have worked for the simplest cases only. Since they lacked theoretical foundations, their behaviour in more complex situations was unclear.

The first attempts towards formal non-monotonic systems were made by McCarthy & Hayes (1969) and Sandewall (1972). McCarthy & Hayes give some hints of how non-monotonic inference can be formalized by means of modal operators interpreted as 'consistent' and 'normally'. However, they say nothing of how these modalities are to be specified to capture their intended interpretations. Sandewall represents non-monotonic rules by employing a special 'UNLESS' operator. The intention is that UNLESS(A) holds iff A is not classically provable from axioms. This system, which will be briefly discussed later, seems now to be of historical value only.

In the last ten years a number of more sophisticated formal approaches to the subject of non-monotonic reasoning have been proposed. These will be briefly surveyed in the next chapter and then discussed in the rest of this book.

We conclude this section by remarking that the AI literature offers an alternative class of logic-based systems dealing with incomplete information. This relatively wide class includes formalisms employing various numerical, typically probabilistic, methods. The underlying notion of such systems is that of truth. However, since reasoning from incomplete information involves uncertainty, this type of inference cannot be properly handled in the framework of the standard truth values. Accordingly, to each proposition there is assigned a *generalized truth-value*, frequently a real number from the interval [0, 1], interpreted as a measure of the proposition's credibility.§

2.2 Non-monotonic inference and reasoning about action

Imagine a robot whose environment is a world of blocks. Its task is to transform the world to achieve some desired goal. Much of its time the robot collects facts and makes

† See Studia Logica (1984).

‡ It is not my intention to provide a detailed analysis of this matter here. The importance of non-monotonic inference in natural language understanding has been discussed in Mercer & Reiter (1982), Ascher (1984), Joschi *et al.* (1984), Dunin-Kęplicz & Łukaszewicz (1986), Perrault (1986), Saint-Dizier (1988), Appelt & Konolige (1989). Fischler & Firschein (1984) analyse non-monotonic reasoning in the context of computational vision. Connections between non-monotonic inference and the theory of diagnosis have been discussed by many researchers (see, for example, Poole 1986, Reiter 1987a).

§ The quantitative approach to the problem of incomplete information is beyond the scope of this book. A paper of Prade (1988) provides a good introduction to the subject.

ordinary monotonic inferences about the world. Sometimes, however, it changes the current state of the world by performing an action. Clearly, this may make some of a previously true proposition false. For example, painting a red block green invalidates the proposition that the block is red. This leads to the following two observations:

(1) Each action forces the robot to revise the set of its current beliefs about the world.
(2) This set changes non-monotonically with respect to time.

Can we say that our robot reasons non-monotonically? Certain authors argue that the question should be answered positively. Reinfrank (1985), for example, generalizes the notion of non-monotonic inference by explicitly distinguishing between non-monotonic reasoning and the non-monotonic inference process. He says that a system reasons non-monotonically if the set of its current beliefs grows non-monotonically during problem solving. Respectively, he considers an inferential process as non-monotonic if the acquisition of a new observed information may invalidate beliefs established by previous inferences.

Despite some attractiveness, Reinfrank's generalization seems to miss the point. As long as the robot employs ordinary inference methods, it is simply misleading to say that it reasons non-monotonically. At best, one can say that the robot manifests a specific form of non-monotonic behaviour, typical for any system dealing with a changing world. Such a system, in contrast to really non-monotonic systems, may be forced to retrack some of its previous beliefs not because they turn out to be wrong, but simply because they are no longer true in a new state of the world. That the same proposition may have different truth-values in different states of a world, in particular, that a true sentence may become false when the world changes, is an old logical phenomenon. In fact, it is this observation that underlies temporal reasoning.

Although reasoning about action, at least in its standard form, should be viewed as monotonic, it involves two famous problems that inspired much of early theoretic research on non-monotonic inference. They are called the *frame problem* and the *problem of qualification*.†

Put briefly, the frame problem is the problem of representing which properties persist and which properties change when actions are performed. Typically, performing an action affects only a few aspects of the considered world. For instance, when a block is painted, all its properties except colour, as well as all properties of other objects, remain unchanged. To represent those invariant aspects of the world explicitly, a large number of specific axioms, called *frame axioms*, must be provided. All these axioms can be naturally replaced by a single non-monotonic rule stating 'All aspects of the world remain invariant except for those explicitly changed'.

The qualification problem concerns the observation that the success of an action may depend on a large number of qualifications. For instance, if a robot is planning to put a block A on the top of a block B, B should have a clear top, A must not be too heavy, the robot's arm must not be broken, etc. Even for relatively simple worlds, a number of qualifications assigned to an action may be very large. What is worse, in more realistic worlds, the satisfiability of most of those qualifications will be simply unknown. Planning a trip by car, I may know sufficiently enough to believe that the trip will succeed. Yet, I can always imagine circumstances making my trip impossible.

---

† For a detailed discussion of these problems the reader should consult Hayes (1973). Brown (1987) provides a number of recent contributions to the subject. See also Ginsberg & Smith (1988, 1988b).

Again, the qualification problem can be naturally solved in the framework of non-monotonic reasoning. All we need is the rule stating 'In the absence of evidence to the contrary, assume that an action succeeds.'

2.3 Typology of non-monotonic reasoning

Several types of non-monotonic reasoning can be identified in the literature. They may be classified according to the criteria they accept in explaining derivable conclusions.

The presented classification is based on the observation (Moore 1983) that one should distinguish between incomplete information and incomplete representation of complete information. To illustrate this distinction, consider the following pair of non-monotonic rules:

(1) In the absence of evidence to the contrary, assume that a bird can fly.
(2) Unless your name is on a list of winners, assume that you are a loser (Gabbay & Sergot 1986).

The first rule deals with genuinely incomplete information. If all we know about Tweety is that she is a bird, we may conclude, at least tentatively, that she is a flier. This conclusion is plausible but not watertight; it can be invalidated given better evidence.

The second rule is quite different. It is based on the observation that lists of winners are complete, so that they implicitly contain evidence about losers. This means that the rule does not refer to incomplete information but to incomplete representation of virtually complete knowledge. In consequence, the rule is logically valid: if it is true that a list of winners is complete, and it is true that your name is not on the list, then it must be true that you are a loser. This conclusion cannot be invalidated by providing better evidence because no such evidence is available. At the moment of announcing the list, our knowledge about the actual state of affairs is complete and cannot be extended by a new piece of information. Nevertheless, the rule is non-monotonic. It cannot be properly formalized in any logical system enjoying the property of monotonicity. This is because the rule refers to the absence of some evidence and thus depends on the context within which it operates. It may happen that embedding the rule in a greater context makes some previously inferable conclusions underivable. For instance, given

(1) The list of winners consists of Tom and Bill

the rule allows us to infer that John is a loser. However, if (1) is replaced by

(2) The list of winners consists of Tom, Bill and John

this conclusion is no longer derivable.

Our discussion suggests a distinction between two basic types of non-monotonic inference. Following Moore (1983), we shall call them *default reasoning* and *autoepistemic reasoning*.

By default reasoning we understand the drawing of a rational conclusion, from less than conclusive information, in the absence of evidence making this inference implausible. What typifies default reasoning is its *defeasibility*: Any conclusion derived by default can be invalidated by providing new evidence.

By autoepistemic reasoning we mean reaching a conclusion, from incomplete representation of (hopefully) complete information, under the assumption that since our information is complete, we would know if the conclusion were false. Purely autoepistemic reasoning is not defeasible; its conclusions cannot be invalidated by providing new evidence. However, it is non-monotonic because conclusions derivable by employing any autoepistemic rule change non-monotonically with respect to the contexts in which the rule is embedded.

The autoepistemic reasoning is based on the assumption that we have complete knowledge about some aspect of the world. This assumption can be supported by two different kinds of mechanisms: explicit conventions and our subjective opinions. Accordingly, the autoepistemic reasoning can be further divided into two types.

The example about winners and losers illustrates what might be called *explicit autoepistemic reasoning*. If you are not on a winning list, you may conclude that you are a loser because there is an explicit convention that lists of winners are always complete. Another example of this type of inference is the rule stating 'The meeting will be on Wednesday unless another decision is explicitly made' (Doyle 1979).

Autoepistemic inferences based on subjective opinions represent *subjective autoepistemic reasoning*. Consider my reason to believe that my friend Tom is not a great poet. As a matter of fact, nobody has ever told me that he is not. However, since I believe I know the outstanding poets of my country, I believe that I would know if Tom were one of them. It is exactly the lack of this information that supports my conclusion. Another example of this type is the rule: 'In the absence of evidence to the contrary, assume that you have no elder brother' (Moore 1983).

At least four different types of default reasoning can be identified. The example about birds illustrates *prototypical reasoning*. A characteristic feature of prototypical inferences is that they are always supported by statistical observations. Consider my belief that Tweety flies given that she is a bird. Clearly, it is supported by the observation that almost all birds fly, the majority of birds fly or the typical bird is a flier.

Although prototypical reasoning is based on statistical information, its representation requires no probabilistic numbers. In fact, a number that could be assigned to the proposition 'The typical bird flies' is neither obtainable nor important to support the conclusion that Tweety is a flier. We simply know that the number is high enough to make this inference plausible (provided, of course, that no additional information is available).

A second category of default inferences typifies situations where mistaken results would lead to disastrous consequences. In such a case, we are often prepared to accept a conclusion even if probabilities are against it. A classical example of this kind of inference is the previously mentioned rule stating 'In the absence of evidence to the contrary, assume that the accused is innocent.' We call this *no-risk reasoning*.†

Sometimes, where no good supporting evidence can be found, and yet some decision is to be reached, we jump to a conclusion which for some reason is the best guess to make. Assume, for instance, that there are two shopping centres in a small town where I live. One of them, but I do not know which, is open on Sundays. Now, if it is Sunday and I want to shop, the best guess to make is to assume that the centre that is open is the one nearest to my home. This type of inference might be called *the-best-guess reasoning*.

A little reflection should convince the reader that all the types of inference we have analysed so far share a common property: probabilistic measures that might be assigned to various propositions are either unnecessary (prototypical reasoning) or

† I am indebted to Professor W. M. Turski for suggesting this terminology.

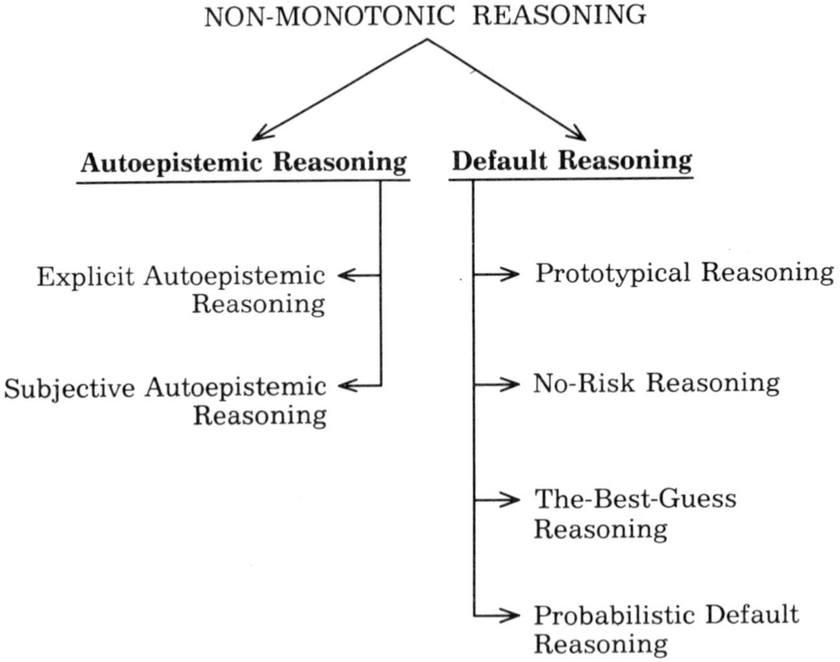

Fig. 2.1 – Typology of non-monotonic reasoning

Table 2.1 – How people explain their conclusions.

TYPE OF REASONING	EXPLANATION OF A CONCLUSION A
Subjective autoepistemic reasoning	According to my subjective opinion, I would know if A were false. Because I lack this information, A must be true.
Explicit autoepistemic reasoning	According to some explicit convention, I would know if A were false. Because I lack this information, A must be true.
Prototypical reasoning	A describes a typical situation. Thus, there are good chances that A holds.
No-risk reasoning	If I accepted $\neg A$, and this turned out to be false, the consequences would be fatal. So, if I am to choose between A and $\neg A$, I must accept A.
The-best-guess reasoning	In view of available evidence, A is the best guess to make.
Probabilistic default reasoning	Assuming that probabilistic values are sufficiently high, it is reasonable to infer A.

irrelevant (both the forms of autoepistemic reasoning, no-risk reasoning, the-best-guess reasoning). However, there are situations where probabilistic values are crucial in reaching rational conclusions. The following example is from Cohen (1987).

'An airplane has crashed in dense jungle. Searchers superimpose a grid on a map of the area and calculate, for each square in the grid, the probability that the plane crashed in that square. They search the high-probability areas first.'

There is an important difference between the prototypical reasoning and the inference pattern underlying this example. In prototypical reasoning there is no need for probabilistic values because we know, *a priori*, that they are sufficiently high. Here, we know that it is rational to start by searching high-probability areas, but we have no information as to which they are. Thus, to formalize this type of inference, probabilistic information must be explicitly embedded in the reasoning process. For the purpose of the present text, this kind of inference will be called *probabilistic default reasoning*.

It should be stressed that the currently existing non-monotonic formalisms cannot handle this type of reasoning. This is because they are always grounded on some kind of traditional logic and thus are not suited to represent probabilistic information.

The discussion is summarized in Fig. 2.1 and Table 2.1. It is not claimed that this typology of non-monotonic reasoning is complete. However, it is sufficiently representative to illustrate a large variety of factors supporting common-sense inferences.

We conclude this section by observing that many non-monotonic rules can be associated with more than one type of non-monotonic inference. Consider, for example, the rule 'In the absence of evidence to the contrary, assume that a boat can be used to cross a river', and the question 'Can this boat be used to cross a river?' Three different explanations can be given to the answer 'yes':

(1) I would know if something were wrong with the boat. Thus, the boat can be used to cross the river (subjective autoepistemic reasoning).

(2) A typical boat can be used to cross a river. Thus, the chances are good that this boat can be used to cross the river (prototypical reasoning).

(3) I would like to cross the river. So, the best guess to make is to assume that this boat can be used to perform the task (the best-guess reasoning).

3

Approaches to non-monotonic reasoning

The aim of this chapter is to provide the reader with basic ideas on how non-monotonic inference has been approached in AI research. First, the most important computational approaches to the subject are briefly presented. The behaviour of these practical systems clearly demonstrates the need for theoretical research on non-monotonic reasoning. The major formal approaches to the field are sketched in section 3.2. Finally, certain objections to formalizing non-monotonic inference that have been raised in the AI literature are discussed.

3.1 COMPUTATIONAL APPROACHES TO NON-MONOTONIC REASONING

As mentioned before, non-monotonic inference has been given both practical and theoretical considerations in AI research. The most influential computational approaches to the subject are discussed below.

3.1.1 MICRO-PLANNER

One of the first practical systems with non-monotonic properties was MICRO-PLANNER – a programming language for representing and manipulating knowledge (Sussman *et al.* 1971). In MICRO-PLANNER, the reality is viewed as a pair consisting of a *data base* and a *program*. The data base is a set of simple facts, represented by atomic sentences, about the modelled world. The program is a collection of subroutines, called *theorems*, which operate on the data base.

MICRO-PLANNER admits three types of subroutines, called *consequent*, *antecedent* and *erasing*. The subroutines of the first kind are to be viewed as specialized inference rules. A simple example of a consequent subroutine is given below.

(THCONSEQUENT(*Mammal* ?*x*) (3.1.1)
  (THGOAL *Dog*(?*x*)))

This subroutine is a procedural representation of the fact 'All dogs are mammals'. Accordingly, it is to be interpreted as 'To prove that an object, say x, is a mammal, try to prove that it is a dog'. The sentence 'x is a dog' may be inferred either by inspecting the data base or by employing some other subroutine. An important remark to make here is that (3.1.1) is logically weaker than the fact it represents. For example, the subroutine cannot be used to infer that a non-mammal is not a dog.

The next example illustrates more sophisticated properties of the MICRO-PLANNER formalism.

```
(THCONSEQUENT(Flies ?x)                                   (3.1.2)
  (THOR(THGOAL(Bird ?x))
       (THGOAL(Plane ?x)))
  (THASSERT(Flies ?x)))
```

Roughly corresponding to the fact 'Both planes and birds are fliers', this subroutine, if it succeeds, extends the data base. Procedurally, the subroutine says something like 'To prove that x flies, first try to prove that x is a bird. If that fails, try to show that x is a plane. If the proposition *Flies*(x) has been proved, add it to the data base'.[†]

To deal with non-monotonic reasoning, MICRO-PLANNER employs a special operator, called THNOT, which is a procedural analogon of negation. To prove a goal of the form THNOT(A), the system attempts to find a proof of A. If this fails, THNOT(A) has succeeded; otherwise THNOT(A) has failed. Under this interpretation, the THNOT primitive provides a natural basis for non-monotonic inferences. For example, the rule 'A person is to be considered innocent unless she/he can be proved guilty' can be represented by

```
(THCONSEQUENT(Innocent ?x)                                (3.1.3)
  (THAND(THGOAL(Person ?x))
        (THGOAL(THNOT(Guilty ?x)))))
```

To manipulate the data base – in particular, to handle the belief-revision problem – MICRO-PLANNER employs antecedent and erasing subroutines. They are activated by explicit changes in the data base and, in consequence, lead to other changes. A simple pair of such subroutines is given below.

```
(THANTECEDENT(Innocent ?x)                                (3.1.4)
  (THERASE (Suspect ?x)))

(THERASING(Penguin ?x)                                    (3.1.5)
  (THGOAL(Bird ?x))
  (THASSERT(Flies ?x)))
```

Subroutine (3.1.4) states: 'Whenever a proposition of the form *Innocent*(x) enters the data base, the proposition *Suspect*(x), if it exists, is to be removed from it'. Subroutine (3.1.5) states: 'Whenever a proposition of the form *Penguin* (x) is removed from the data base, try to show that x is a bird. If that succeeds, add to the data base the proposition *Flies* (x)'.

From Knowledge Representation perspective, MICRO-PLANNER belongs to the

---

[†] It is worth noting that THOR operator is weaker than the usual '$\vee$' connective. THOR(A B) may fail even if $A \vee B$ logically follows from the data base. For example, this happens if neither A nor B is provable, but A can be proved given $\neg B$.

class of procedural representation schemes. What typifies this kind of system is the lack of a general inference mechanism. Instead, a user is provided with a set of programming tools and is made responsible for specifying each inference scheme. The advantage of this approach is that specialized inference rules are computationally more efficient than the general ones. Unfortunately, there is a price to pay for it. The weakness of the procedural schemes is the lack of formal semantics. Consequently, the behaviour of such a system may be difficult to predict in more complex situations. See Hayes (1977) for a detailed discussion on this point.

3.1.2 Network- and frame-based systems

Both the theory of semantic networks (Quillian 1968; Woods 1975) and frames (Minsky 1975; Hayes 1979) have influenced the construction of computational systems with non-monotonic properties (see, for example, Rumelhart & Norman 1973; Hendrix 1975; Bobrow & Winograd 1977; Goldstein & Roberts 1977; Fahlman 1979; Brachman 1979). In spite of many surface dissimilarities, all these inferential systems share two common properties:

(1) They combine deductive structure of standard logic with non-standard reasoning facilities.

(2) The non-monotonic behaviour of those systems follows from their ability to deal consistently with inconsistent information. This, in turn, is achieved on the implementational level by a uniform mechanism: preferring certain types of inferences.

A number of different preferability criteria have been used in network- and frame-based systems. Some of them are discussed below.

Figure 3.1 (a) represents a simple semantic network consisting of *nodes* and *links*. 'Joe', 'Clyde', 'Red', 'Grey' and 'Large' are *constant nodes* interpreted as real or abstract individuals. 'Elephant' is a *predicate node* denoting the set of all elephants. The network includes two kinds of propositions. First, there are atomic propositions: 'Joe is red-coloured' and 'Clyde is an elephant'. They are represented by *constant–constant* and *constant–predicate* links, respectively. Second, there are two universal propositions: 'All elephants are grey-coloured' and 'All elephants are large-sized', expressed by *predicate–constant* links. This network corresponds naturally to the first-order theory given in Fig. 3.1 (b).

(a)

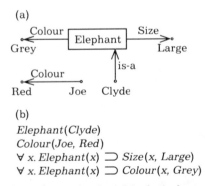

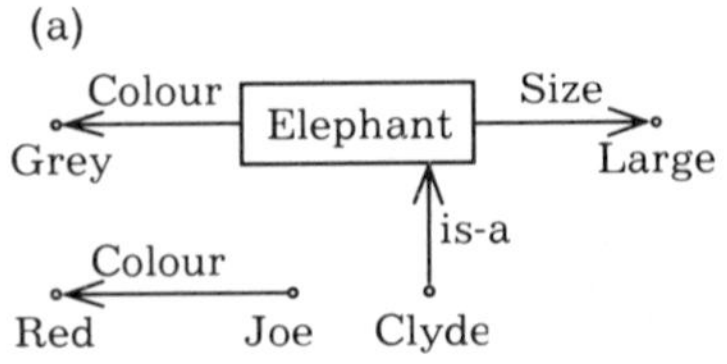

(b)

Elephant(*Clyde*)
Colour(*Joe, Red*)
$\forall x.\, Elephant(x) \supset Size(x, Large)$
$\forall x.\, Elephant(x) \supset Colour(x, Grey)$

Fig. 3.1 – Semantic network and its logical representation.

Drawing conclusions in semantic networks amounts to following links and finding paths between pairs of nodes. For example, in the network of Fig. 3.1 (a), the path from 'Clyde' via 'Elephant' to 'Large' can be regarded as the proof that Clyde is large-sized. Obviously, the inference mechanism employed here is a graphical realization of standard rules: modus ponens and the rule of universal instantiation.†

An important property of many network-based computational systems is that they prefer some kind of links when trying to find a proof. This permits them to handle contradictory information in a consistent way and, in consequence, forces a non-monotonic behaviour of such systems. Assume, for example, that a network-based system prefers constant–constant links and consider the network of Fig. 3.2. This network extends the previous one by including a new proposition, 'Clyde is not large-sized', represented by the negation constant–constant link:

Clyde ╫╫→ Large

The key point is that the system preferring constant–constant links will never learn that this network is inconsistent. Asked whether Clyde is large, the system will find the proof that Clyde is not large (Clyde ╫╫→ Large), and answer 'No' without even trying to find the proof that Clyde is Large (Clyde ⟶ Elephant ⟶ Large).

A major weakness of this kind of system is that its behaviour does not result from a careful development but is an effect of implementational decisions. What is worse, since most network-based systems have been developed to handle consistent collections of data and make ordinary inferences, their implementational details are often not fully specified. In consequence, if such an under-specified system is embedded in a complex inconsistent context, its behaviour may be difficult to predict. Consider, for example, the network of Fig. 3.3. If all we know about the system using the network is that it prefers constant–constant links, its answer to the question 'Is Clyde grey?' is unclear.

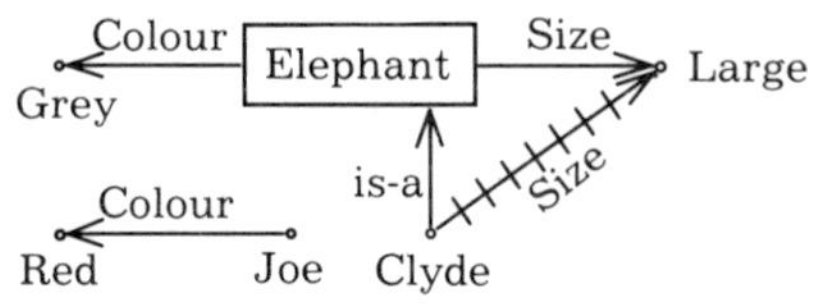

Fig. 3.2 – Contradictory semantic network.

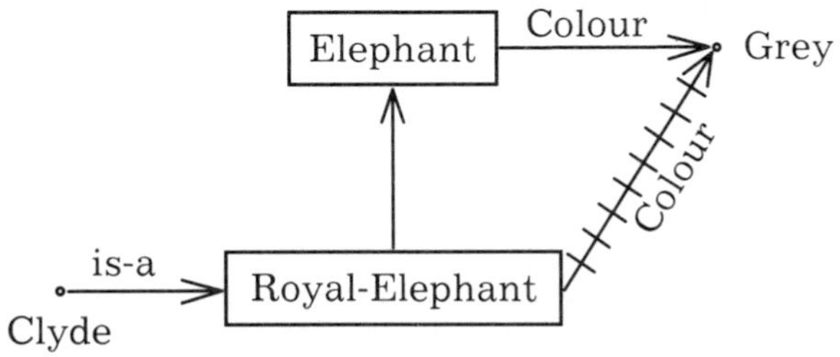

Fig. 3.3 – Another contradictory semantic network.

† The rule of universal instantiation leads from $\forall x A$ to A', where A' obtains from A by proper substitution of some term for x.

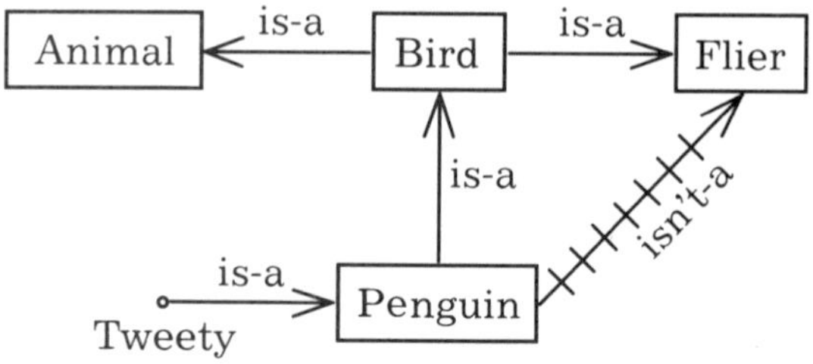

Fig. 3.4 – Inheritance hierarchy with exceptions.

Recently, there have been many attempts to construct network-based systems directly aimed at non-monotonic reasoning. All of them are centred around a specific class of semantic networks, called *inheritance hierarchies with exceptions*.

In its simplest form (see Fig. 3.4) an inheritance hierarchy with exceptions (an *inheritance hierarchy*, for short) consists of constant and predicate nodes, together with two types of links: *assertion links* (*is-a links*) and *negation links* (*isn't-a links*).† An important assumption is that these links do not represent facts but cancellable defaults.‡ For example, the hierarchy of Fig. 3.4 contains the following information: Typically, Tweety is a penguin', 'Typically, penguins are birds', 'Typically, penguins are non-fliers', etc. Because of this interpretation, the hierarchy is not contradictory. It is, however, ambiguous in that it gives rise to two alternative sets of beliefs about Tweety:

$$\{Penguin(Tweety), Bird(Tweety), Animal(Tweety), Flier(Tweety)\}$$
$$\{Penguin(Tweety), Bird(Tweety), Animal(Tweety), \neg Flier(Tweety)\}$$

The task of a computational system dealing with the hierarchy is to resolve this ambiguity by choosing one of those sets.

One of the first systems intended to systematically handle inheritance hierarchies with exceptions was NETL (Fahlman 1979; Fahlman *et al.* 1981). Formally, NETL is a parallel machine with a separate processor assigned to each node of the hierarchy. The computational process amounts to passing 'markers' between adjacent processors, which closely corresponds to following the links. To resolve ambiguities, NETL uses the *shortest path strategy*. Given two conflicting inferences, it prefers that with shorter derivation. For example, operating with the hierarchy of Fig. 3.4, NETL will conjecture that Tweety is not a flier. This is because the proof of that proposition:

Tweety ⟶ Penguin ⧻⧻⟶ Flier

is shorter than that of 'Tweety is a flier':

Tweety ⟶ Penguin ⟶ Bird ⟶ Flier

In spite of its computational effectiveness and conceptual clarity, the NETL system has a serious drawback. As noted by many researchers (Fahlman *et al.* 1981; Etherington 1982, Touretzky 1982; Reiter & Criscuolo 1983), the shortest path

† The discussion here includes only two of many types of links employed by various inheritance hierarchy systems.
‡ Certain approaches to inheritance hierarchies distinguish between facts and defaults.

heuristics can lead to intuitively unsound conclusions. This observation has prompted the development of more sophisticated systems handling inheritance hierarchies with exceptions. It is impossible to discuss all these proposals here. The interested reader is referred to a large body of the literature on the subject (Etherington 1983, 1988; Etherington & Reiter 1983; Touretzky 1984, 1986; Cottrell 1985; Shastri & Feldman 1985; Froidevaux 1986; Touretzky *et al.* 1987; Thomason and Horty 1989).

As mentioned before, there is another group of computational systems employing a 'preference' mechanism to model non-monotonic inferences. These are various representation schemes influenced by the notion of a *frame*. A frame is a data structure for representing a portion of knowledge such as a stereotypical situation (e.g. going into a birthday party), a class of objects (e.g. a prototypical bird) or an individual object (e.g. a real bird named Tweety). A frame contains named *slots* for carrying specific knowledge. For example, a frame describing a prototypical elephant might have slots called *colour*, *owner*, *name* and *elephant-head*, together with additional information about types of values that can be filled into them. A particular elephant is now to be represented by an *instance* of the elephant frame, obtained by filling in the slots (or some of them) with appropriate values. This is illustrated in Fig. 3.5.

Frame-based systems view a knowledge base as a collection of frames, typically structured into an ordinary taxonomy. This organization allows the system to avoid multiple specification of properties that are common to different frames. For example, linking the elephant frame with that of the typical mammal, the elephant Clyde will inherit all the properties that are specific for mammals.

ELEPHANT		ELEPHANT-1	
colour:	grey	colour:	grey
owner:	a person	owner:	unknown
name:	a name	name:	Clyde
elephant-head:	frame-33	elephant-head:	frame-33 instantiated for Clyde

Fig. 3.5 – *Elephant* frame and its instance representing an elephant named Clyde.

Frames have come in a variety of forms and have been used in many different ways. Yet, as Hayes (1979) points out, except for minor aspects, they can be easily understood in terms of standard logic. One of these exceptional details is the concept of a *default value*, i.e. of a value that is to be used as a slot filler in the absence of evidence to the contrary. For example, the elephant frame might have an additional slot, called size, with the default value large.

To deal with default values, frame-based systems employ the general rule that conflicts are to be solved by preferring subclasses over superclasses. Consider, for example, the structure of frames given in Fig. 3.6 and assume that Tweety is known to be a bird. Asked whether Tweety is a flier, a frame-based system will use the default value associated with the bird frame and answer 'Yes'. Yet, if there is additional information that Tweety is a penguin, the system will use the default value assigned to the penguin frame and answer 'No'. On the other hand, if Joe is known to be a canary, it will be inferred that he is a flier unless the contrary is explicitly given.

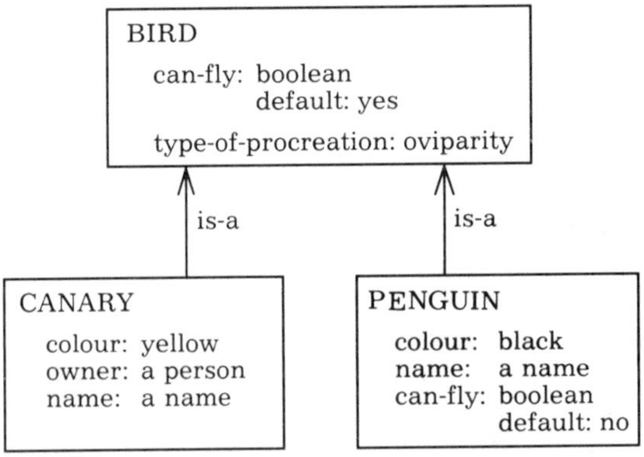

Fig. 3.6 – Structure of frames.

3.1.3 Systems employing meta-level reasoning facilities

Another group of systems worthy of mention here are knowledge representation schemes combining formal logic with meta-level capabilities. Typically, such a system takes some logic formalism as a basis and extends it by offering a direct access to its own meta-language, for both representing meta-facts and carrying deductions. This integration of reasoning and meta-reasoning provides a powerful mechanism allowing a number of complex representation phenomena to be incorporated, including non-monotonic inference.

The approach of extending a logic formalism with meta-level facilities has been proposed by Weyrauch in the FOL system (Aiello & Weyrauch 1975; Weyrauch 1980, 1982) and later employed in the OMEGA representation scheme (Hewitt *et al.* 1980; Attardi & Simi 1981, 1984). Bowen & Kowalski (1982) show how to incorporate this idea into logic programming systems.† It is not my intention to provide a detailed presentation of these proposals. Rather, I want to give the reader a general idea about which meta-level mechanisms are needed and how they are to be used for modelling non-monotonic inferences. While doing this, I shall use an approach loosely corresponding to that of the FOL system.

Let us begin by observing that non-monotonic rules can be viewed as meta-language sentences. Consider: 'If Tweety is a bird, then she flies unless the contrary can be proved.' This is obviously a meta-language sentence stating something like 'If you have a collection of object-language facts and from these facts you can prove (at the object level) the proposition *Bird*(*Tweety*), and you cannot prove (at the object level) the proposition ¬*Flies*(*Tweety*), then you have proven (at the metal level!) the object-level proposition *Flies*(*Tweety*)'. Note the mechanism involved here. We start with an object-level theory, escape at the meta-level and extend the theory by inspecting its meta-level features.

How can this mechanism be incorporated into a computational system? Obviously, there are two properties which such a system must possess. First, it should be able to explicitly refer to the object-level theories it deals with. Second, it must be equipped

† Here we limit our attention to the systems exhibiting non-monotonic behaviour. For various uses of meta-knowledge in AI systems the reader should consult Aiello & Levi (1984). See also Silver (1986).

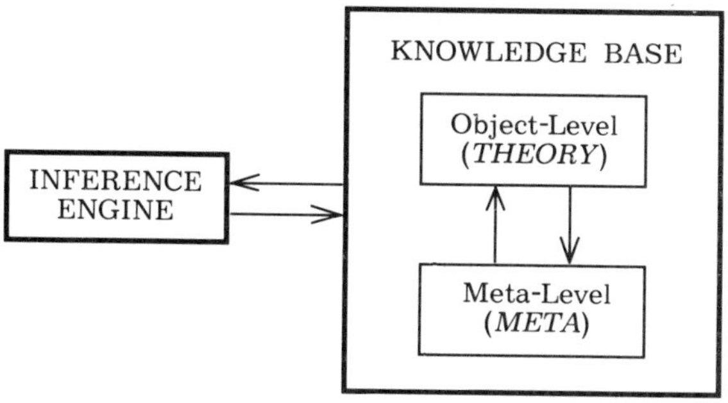

Fig. 3.7 – Possible organization of a theory/meta-theory system.

with facilities to decide what is derivable from those theories. Figure 3.7 illustrates a possible organization of this kind of system.

The system consists of a *knowledge base* and *inference engine*. The knowledge base splits into two separate parts, called $THEORY$ and $META$, both being first-order theories. The former, based on an object-level language $L(T)$, represents knowledge about the modelled world. The latter, formulated in a suitable meta-language $L(M)$, expresses a portion of meta-knowledge. The inference engine can be thought of as an ordinary first-order theorem prover. It is responsible for making standard inferences from both $THEORY$ and $META$.

To represent meta-knowledge, we must name lingustic expressions of L(T) by means of terms of $L(M)$. This can be technically done in many different ways. Here we simply assume that 'E' denotes a term of $L(M)$ naming an expression E of $L(T)$. For example

$$\text{`}\forall x\,.\,Penguin(x) \supset Bird(x)\text{'}$$

stands for a term of $L(M)$ which names the object-level formula

$$\forall x\,.\,Penguin(x) \supset Bird(x).$$

To express the notion of provability (at $THEORY$ level), the meta-language $L(M)$ contains a special unary predicate symbol $THEOREM$. If 'A' is a term of $L(M)$ naming a formula A of $L(T)$, then $THEOREM(\text{`}A\text{'})$ is assumed to hold (at meta-level, of course) iff A can be proved from $THEORY$. To capture this interpretation, the system is equipped with the following inference rules, called *reflexion principles*, allowing communication between $THEORY$ and $META$:

$$\text{(R1)}\quad \frac{THEORY \vdash A}{META \vdash THEOREM(\text{`}A\text{'})} \qquad\qquad \text{(R2)}\quad \frac{META \vdash THEOREM(\text{`}A\text{'})}{THEORY \vdash A}$$

It should be noted that the reflexion principles do not provide the complete description of the predicate $THEOREM$. This is because they force no relation between $\neg THEOREM$ and the notion of unprovability at the object level. Since this relation is crucial as regards non-monotonic inferences, we shall assume that the system is supplied with the rule:

$$\text{(R3)}\quad \frac{THEORY \nvdash A}{META \vdash \neg THEOREM(\text{`}A\text{'})}$$

There are, of course, technical problems in trying to implement (R3). Due to undecidability of first-order logic, the complete implementation of the rule is simply impossible. Thus, unless we are dealing with a decidable subset of first-order logic, we shall be forced to accept some incomplete, implementation-dependent version of (R3); for example:

$$\text{(R3}'\text{)} \quad \frac{\text{The attempt to establish } THEORY \vdash A \text{ fails finitely}}{META \vdash \neg THEOREM(\text{`}A\text{'})}$$

To see how this system can be used to handle non-monotonic reasoning, consider the following knowledge base:

THEORY: (T1) *Bird*(*Tweety*)
(T2) *Yellow*(*Tweety*)

META: (MT1) *THEOREM*('*Bird*(*Tweety*)') ∧ ¬*THEOREM*('¬*Flies*(*Tweety*)') ⊃ *THEOREM*('*Flies*(*Tweety*)')

Given this knowledge base, we expect the system to infer that *Tweety* is a flier. This can be achieved as follows.

The system starts by focusing its attention on *THEORY* and tries to prove *Flies*(*Tweety*) directly from (T1)–(T2). This fails, but the system knows that the formula may be still provable in *META*. So it switches to *META* and looks for a proof of *THEOREM*('*Flies*(*Tweety*)'). It then finds that this proof depends on its ability to show (in *META*):

$$THEOREM(\text{`}Bird(Tweety)\text{'}) \wedge \neg THEOREM(\text{`}\neg Flies(Tweety)\text{'}) \qquad (3.1.6)$$

So the system switches back to *THEORY* and tries to prove *Bird*(*Tweety*) and ¬*Flies*(*Tweety*). Since the first proof succeeds and the second fails, the system concludes, in view of (R1) and (R3), that (3.1.6) and, in consequence, *THEOREM*('*Flies*(*Tweety*)') holds in *META*. Thus, by (R2), *Flies*(*Tweety*) holds in *THEORY*.

The success of this type of system depends heavily upon its control facilities. Especially, the application of (R3), or rather of its computational version, must be carefully coordinated. The rule must not be used unless its consequence is explicitly needed as a step in some meta-proof. Otherwise, the behaviour of the system may be difficult to control. To see this, reconsider the previous example and imagine the following scenario. The system starts by trying to prove *Flies*(*Tweety*) from *THEORY*. When this fails, it applies (R3) and concludes that ¬*THEOREM*('*Flies*(*Tweety*)') holds in *META*. Next, just as before, it finds that *THEOREM*('*Flies*(*Tweety*)') is also provable in *META*. So its final conclusion is that the data base is inconsistent.

We conclude with two remarks. First, combining knowledge and meta-knowledge provides a very powerful and general mechanism, useful in many AI applications. In particular, this mechanism can be used to handle non-monotonic inference. Second, the integration of knowledge and meta-knowledge can be achieved in many different ways. Here we have only attempted to demonstrate basic ideas of how meta-devices can be used in modelling non-monotonic reasoning. The presented system is very simple and has been chosen for the purpose of illustration only. It is non-monotonic because of its ability to directly refer to unprovability (the rule R3). For more sophisticated systems employing a similar mechanism the reader should consult Bowen & Kowalski (1982) and Attardi & Simi (1984):[†]

3.1.4 Truth maintenance systems

An important class of computational systems exhibiting non-monotonic behaviour are *Truth Maintenance Systems*, also called *Belief Revision Systems* or *Reason Maintenance Systems* (Doyle 1979; London 1978; Thompson 1979; McAllester 1980; Goodwin 1982; Martins 1983; McDermott 1983; Martins & Shapiro 1984; Williams 1984; de Kleer 1986a, 1986b, 1986c; van Marcke 1986; Dixon & de Kleer 1989; Dressler 1989). Unlike all the previously discussed systems, which have been primarily developed to represent knowledge and make inferences, the task of truth maintenance systems is to record and maintain beliefs.

A truth maintenance system (TMS) is always designed to cooperate with an external problem solver. The problem solver includes all domain knowledge and inference procedures. It makes inferences and takes actions until some desired goal is reached. An important point is that the conclusions it draws need not be logically valid; typically most of them are merely beliefs. The TMS is a package of procedures which manipulate a special data base. This data base keeps track of all inferences performed by the problem solver so far. In particular, it contains information about what the problem solver currently believes. When a new inference is made (by the problem solver), it is immediately communicated to the data base and the control passes to the TMS. The task of the TMS is to determine the new set of current beliefs for the problem solver. In doing this, the TMS never employs reasoning mechanisms of the problem solver – its behaviour is completely determined by the content of the data base.

Although truth maintenance systems have been organized in a variety of ways, they all adopt much of Doyle's original proposal (Doyle 1979). A brief outline of this TMS follows.

The TMS manipulates a data base consisting of *nodes*. These are complex data structures which represent potential beliefs of the problem solver cooperating with the TMS. Each node is always in one of two states, called *in* and *out*, depending on whether the belief it represents is in, or out of, the set of current beliefs. It should be stressed that if a node n, representing a belief f, is in the state *out*, this is not to be interpreted that $\neg f$ is currently believed. It may even happen that there is no node corresponding to $\neg f$.

A node includes a *statement* and a set of *justifications*. The statement, assigned to the node by the problem solver, is a name of a potential belief represented by the node. For example, a node might have the name *Flies-Tweety*. Justifications, always constructed by the problem solver, represent conditions which must be satisfied to keep the node in the state *in*. The simplest and most frequently used type of justification is *support-list (SL) justification*. It consists of an ordered pair of lists, called *inlist* and *outlist*, both containing (pointers to) nodes. An SL justification is *valid* iff each of the nodes of its inlist is *in* and each of the nodes of its outlist is *out*. A node is believed, i.e. *in*, iff it has at least one valid justification. This may seem circular, but in practice there are always nodes whose state can be specified without reference to the states of other nodes.

[†] Both Bowen & Kowalski (1982) and Attardi & Simi (1984) consider systems which completely amalgamate object- and meta-language.

To illustrate the introduced concepts, consider the following data base.

Node	Statement	Justifications
1	*Bird-Tweety*	SL(()())
2	*Non-Flier-Tweety*	none
3	*Aeroplane-Tweety*	none
4	*Flies-Tweety*	SL((3)(2)); SL((1)(2))

This data base consists of four nodes. The first, representing the belief that Tweety is a bird, is justified by SL(()()). The justification with the empty inlist and the empty outlist is called the *premiss justification*. Each node including this justification is called a *premiss node*. Since the premiss justification is always valid, premiss nodes are always *in*. The nodes 2 and 3 have no justifications at all. In particular, they have no valid justifications, so that they are *out*. Finally, the node 4 has two justifications: SL((3)(2)) and SL((1)(2)). The former, representing the rule 'If Tweety is an aeroplane, then she flies unless the contrary is believed' is invalid (the node 3 is *out*). The latter, 'If Tweety is a bird, then she flies unless she is believed a non-flier' is valid (1 is *in*, 2 is *out*). So the node 4 is *in*. In conclusion, the nodes 1 and 4 are *in*; 2 and 3 are *out*.

To see how the TMS works, consider the following scenario. Assume that Mr Smith was killed and a problem solver tries to find the murderer. According to some of its rules, it decides that Tom will be considered first. So, it starts by constructing two nodes, named *Guilty-Tom* and *Innocent-Tom*, both unjustified.† As remarked, unjustified nodes are always *out*, so at this point the problem solver remains agnostic about Tom's guilt.‡ Next, by inspecting its own data base of facts, different from that manipulated by the TMS, the problem solver finds that Tom has motives to commit the murder. This results in constructing a new node, *Has-Motives-Tom*, justified by the premiss justification SL(()()). As a premiss node it will be always *in*. The current picture of the TMS's data base is the following:

Node	Statement	Justifications	State
1	*Guilty-Tom*	none	*out*
2	*Innocent-Tom*	none	*out*
3	*Has-Motives-Tom*	SL(()())	*in*

Subsequently, the problem solver finds the rule 'Anyone who has motives and is not believed innocent is suspected'. Since the rule is actually applicable to Tom – to determine this, the problem solver inspects the TMS's data base – Tom is considered suspected. This inference leads to constructing a new node, marked *in* by the TMS:

4	*Suspect-Tom*	SL((3)(2))	*in*

Afterwards, again by inspecting its own data base, the problem solver learns that an alibi can be established for Tom:

5	*Has-Alibi-Tom*	(SL(()())	*in*

Finally, by applying the rule 'Anyone with an alibi is innocent', the problem solver concludes that Tom is innocent. Since the node *Innocent-Tom* is already in the data

† In fact, nodes are created by the TMS. The task of the problem solver is to supply them with statements and justifications.

‡ More precisely, after constructing the nodes, control passes to the TMS. It marks both them *out* and returns control to the problem solver.

base, no new node is created. Instead, the existing node is supplied with a new justification

2 *Innocent-Tom* SL((5)())

and control proceeds to the TMS.

So far the TMS's job has been straightforward and has amounted, in the most complex case, to evaluating a state of a new node in terms of states of currently existing nodes. At this point, however, the TMS is faced with much more complex situation. On one hand, since the node 5 is *in*, the node 2 should be also *in*. On the other hand, since 4 is *in*, 2 must be *out*. To resolve this conflict, the TMS uses a special procedure, called *truth maintenance*.

The truth maintenance procedure is responsible for updating the current set of beliefs when a new justification is added to (retracted from) an already existing node. In spite of certain technical problems involved, the procedure is relatively straightforward. We shall not discuss it here, but simply illustrate its use in the presented example (see Doyle 1979 for details).

The procedure starts with the node whose justification set has been changed, the node 2, and looks for nodes which are dependent on it. These are 4 and 5. Next, the justifications of 2, 4 and 5 are examined. Since 5 is a premiss node, it must be *in*. This forces 2 to be *in* too. In consequence, the justification of 4, i.e. SL((3)(2)), becomes invalid and so, 4 is marked *out*. The current state of the data base is the following:

Node	Statement	Justifications	State
1	*Guilty-Tom*	none	*out*
2	*Innocent-Tom*	SL((5)())	*in*
3	*Has-Motives-Tom*	SL(()())	*in*
4	*Suspect-Tom*	SL((3)(2))	*out*
5	*Has-Alibi-Tom*	SL(()())	*in*

Given this data base, the problem solver eliminates Tom from its list of potential murderers and clears the data base. Next, it decides to consider Bill. For a long time, the cooperation between the problem solver and the TMS proceeds as before. Suppose that the current state of the data base is the following:

Node	Statement	Justifications	State
1	*Guilty-Bill*	none	*out*
2	*Innocent-Bill*	none	*out*
3	*Has-Motives-Bill*	SL(()())	*in*
4	*Suspect-Bill*	SL((3)(2))	*in*
5	*Has-Alibi-Bill*	SL(()())	*in*

At this point, the behaviour of the problem solver changes. Instead of concluding that Bill is innocent, by applying the rule 'Anyone with an alibi is innocent', it finds another rule stating 'A person must not be considered suspected if she/he has an alibi'. Trying to use the new rule, the problem solver finds out that it contradicts the current state of the data base (note that the nodes 4 and 5 are both *in*). This observation is recorded as a special *contradiction node*:

6 CONTRADICTION SL((4, 5)())

and control passes to the TMS. If 6 were an ordinary node, it would be marked *in* (since both 4 and 5 are *in*) and control would be returned to the problem solver.

Contradiction nodes, however, convey a special meaning: the TMS forces them to be *out*.

When, according to the current state of the data base, a contradiction node should be assigned *in*, the TMS invokes a special procedure, called *dependency-directed backtracking*. Its task is to update the current state of beliefs to restore consistency.† This is technically done by removing (from the current set of beliefs) at least one *assumption* which contributes to the contradiction.‡ In our example, there is only one assumption

4 *Suspect-Bill* SL((3)(2)) *in*

and indeed, removing it, i.e. making it *out*, restores consistency.

To remove the chosen assumption, the procedure invalidates its justification by providing a new valid justification for one of the nodes of its outlist. In our example, 4 will be removed by adding a new valid justification to 2. This new justification refers to a special new node, created by the procedure, but we omit details here. The final (approximate) picture of the data base is given below.

Node	Statement	Justifications	State
1	*Guilty-Bill*	none	*out*
2	*Innocent-Bill*	⟨a certain valid justification⟩	*in*
3	*Has-Motives-Bill*	SL(()())	*in*
4	*Suspect-Bill*	SL((3)(2))	*out*
5	*Has-Alibi-Bill*	SL(()())	*in*
6	CONTRADICTION	SL((4, 5)())	*out*

In virtue of this data base, Bill must be removed from the list of potential murderers and the problem solver will eventually continue its work.

In summary, Doyle's TMS is a general-purpose system for handling beliefs. Apart from keeping beliefs resulting from non-monotonic inferences, it can be also used in the context of monotonic reasoning about dynamically changing worlds. The TMS provides two basic mechanisms: truth maintenance and dependency-directed backtracking. While both serve to update the current set of beliefs, they are used in different situations. The former is invoked when a new justification is added to (subtracted from) an already existing node. The latter is employed when the set of current beliefs forces a contradiction node to be *in*.

Certain limitations of Doyle's original proposal have given rise to the development of more efficient systems.§ One of the most interesting truth maintenance systems currently available, called ATMS (an assumption-based TMS), has been constructed by de Kleer (1986a, b,c). This system is too complex for a detailed description to be given here. Its basic characteristics are sketched below.

Like traditional truth maintenance systems, the ATMS is designed to cooperate with a problem solver. It is assumed that the problem solver's work consists of two basic activities: deriving conclusions and introducing hypotheses. Each inference is

† It should be made clear that the notion of contradiction involved here has little to do with logical contradiction. The problem solver may choose any set of beliefs and report its inconsistency by constructing an appropriate contradiction node. Whether or not this set is logically inconsistent plays no role here. Contradictory nodes should be always viewed as a general mechanism which allow some combinations of beliefs to be ruled out.

‡ An assumption is a node whose valid justification has a non-empty outlist.

§ A detailed analysis of weaknesses of Doyle's TMS can be found in de Kleer (1986a).

communicated to the ATMS's data base as a *justification*. The important point is that ATMS's justifications represent monotonic inferences only, so that they never refer to what is disbelieved.† Introducing a hypothesis amounts to assuming an unsupported (from logical point of view) proposition. Typically, most of these hypotheses will turn out incorrect and will be withdrawn. However, at the point they are introduced, they are likely guesses that are needed for problem solving to proceed. Each decision to introduce a hypothesis is communicated to the data base as an *assumption* (*node*).‡ It should be stressed that creating this node does not automatically imply that the assumed proposition is currently believed.

Essentially, an assumption is neither believed nor disbelieved. The general idea is that assumptions, combined with the justifications, form a basis from which all beliefs can be monotonically derived. Sets of assumptions are called *environments*. An environment can be intuitively viewed as a potential way of action of the problem solver. Each environment defines a *context*: the set of nodes (beliefs) monotonically derivable (via justifications) from the assumptions included in the environment. Intuitively, contexts represent potential sets of beliefs of the problem solver. One of them, namely that corresponding to the set of all currently accepted assumptions, is to be regarded as the problem solver's current context.

Unlike traditional truth maintenance systems, the ATMS never knows the current context. Instead, it is able to specify the content of any possible context. Of course, the problem solver knows the set of its currently accepted assumptions (its current environment), so that, in practice, it will always ask about the current context.

A crucial issue of the ATMS is the organization of the data base it manipulates. In traditional truth maintenance systems each node has an associated state (*in* or *out*). The set of all nodes being *in* defines the current context for the problem solver. In contrast, ATMS's nodes have no states assigned to them. Instead, with each node there is associated a *label* which (almost) explicitly represents the contexts under which the node holds.§ In other words, while the data base of a conventional TMS represents one context at a time, the ATMS's data base can be viewed as describing all potential contexts simultaneously.

In conclusion, the ATMS offers a new kind of truth maintenance mechanism. By keeping track of all potential contexts, it avoids most of limitations typical of traditional truth maintenance systems. In particular, it almost never employs any form of backtracking, so that problem solving with the ATMS is generallly very efficient. The system is particularly well-suited for tasks where many solutions are to be found and for those involving work with multiple contradictory assumptions. The major drawback of the ATMS is that it is very sensitive to erroneous data. Therefore, its interface with the problem solver must be carefully developed (see de Kleer 1986c).

In passing, it is worth remarking that the subject of truth maintenance systems has been also approached from the theoretic perspective. The interested reader may consult Brown (1985), Brown *et al.* (1986, 1987), Doyle (1980, 1983a, 1983b), Ginsberg (1988), Goodwin (1987).

This completes the presentation of computational approaches to non-monotonic reasoning. The discussion has been somewhat sketchy but a separate book would be

† Although ATMS's justifications are always monotonic, non-monotonic justifications can be easily encoded into the system. See de Kleer (1986b) for details.

‡ Notice that the notion of an assumption employed here differs from that used in Doyle's TMS.

§ In traditional truth maintenance systems this information is implicitly given by means of justifications.

required to cover the subject in detail. It is hoped that two important points have been illustrated. First, many of practical approaches to non-monotonic inference are based on intuitions rather than formal precision. Second, problematic behaviour of those, often under-specified, systems clearly demonstrates the need for theoretic research on non-monotonic reasoning.

3.2 FORMAL APPROACHES TO NON-MONOTONIC REASONING

This section provides a brief survey of formal approaches to the subject of non-monotonic inference. The most important ones will be thoroughly studied in the following chapters.

3.2.1 Sandewall's formalism

The first attempt to systematically formalize non-monotonic inference was made by Sandewall (1972). His system, originally proposed as a solution to the frame problem, extends the language of ordinary first-order logic by introducing a proposition-forming 'UNLESS' operator. Corresponding roughly to MICRO-PLANNER's 'THNOT', UNLESS is meant to represent classical first-order unprovability. If T is a theory and A is a sentence, then UNLESS(A) is assumed to be derivable (in the system) from T iff A cannot be derived from T using classical inference rules. More formally,

$$\mathrm{T} \mathrel{|\!\sim} \mathrm{UNLESS(A)} \quad \text{iff} \quad T \nvdash A$$

where $\mathrel{|\!\sim}$ and $\nvdash$ denote the provability relation of Sandewall's system and unprovability relation of classical first-order logic, respectively.

As an example, consider the theory T given by

$$\forall x.\,Bird(x) \wedge \mathrm{UNLESS}(\neg Flies(x)) \supset Flies(x)$$
$$Bird(Tweety).$$

The first axiom represents the rule 'A bird flies unless the contrary can be proved'. Since $T \nvdash \neg Flies(Tweety)$, we have $T \mathrel{|\!\sim} \mathrm{UNLESS}(\neg Flies(Tweety))$. In consequence, assuming that the relation $\mathrel{|\!\sim}$ is closed under ordinary inference rules, we obtain $T \mathrel{|\!\sim} Flies(Tweety)$.†

Sandewall's formalism has some undesirable properties, so that its usefulness is rather doubtful. First, it may well happen that both A and UNLESS(A) are inferable. For example, given

$$A$$
$$A \wedge \mathrm{UNLESS}(B) \supset C$$

one can easily infer both C and UNLESS(C). Second, the system is too strong to deal properly with conflicting non-monotonic rules. Consider (Reiter & Criscuolo 1983):

$$Quaker(Nixon) \wedge Republican(Nixon)$$
$$\forall x.\,Quaker(x) \wedge \mathrm{UNLESS}(\neg Pacifist(x)) \supset Pacifist(x)$$
$$\forall x.\,Republican(x) \wedge \mathrm{UNLESS}(Pacifist(x)) \supset \neg Pacifist(x)$$

† Sandewall is not precise while specifying his system. He neither gives formation rules for UNLESS operator nor provides formal definition of the provability relation $\mathrel{|\!\sim}$. However, since his system admits all the classical inferences, the relation $\mathrel{|\!\sim}$ is obviously closed under ordinary inference rules.

Given this theory, there are reasons to believe that Nixon is a pacifist and there are reasons to believe that he is not. Perhaps the best policy would be to remain agnostic about his pacifism. The point, of course, is that *Pacifist*(*Nixon*) and $\neg$*Pacifist*(*Nixon*) must not be accepted simultaneously. Yet, under Sandewall's interpretation of UNLESS operator, the theory is inconsistent. This is because both UNLESS(*Pacifist*(*Nixon*)) and UNLESS($\neg$*Pacifist*(*Nixon*)) are inferable.

To avoid these difficulties, UNLESS operator should be redefined. Clearly, UNLESS(A) must not mean that A is classically unprovable, but rather that A is unprovable in the system. This suggests the following rule:

$$\text{From not } (T \mid\!\sim A) \qquad \text{infer} \qquad T \mid\!\sim \text{UNLESS}(A)$$

i.e. if A cannot be derived (in the system) from T, then UNLESS(A) is derivable (in the system) from T. Although intuitively plausible, this rule is circular and hence ill-formed. Because 'derivable' means 'derivable from axioms by repeated application of inference rules', the rule refers to itself. It is this difficulty that has given rise to the development of more sophisticated non-monotonic formalisms – especially early versions of *modal non-monotonic logics*.

3.2.2 Modal non-monotonic logics

The term 'modal non-monotonic logic' refers to a family of non-monotonic formalisms employing modal operators to represent the notions of 'consistency' and/or 'belief' in the object language. These logics interpret the rule 'In the absence of evidence to the contrary, infer A' as 'If A can be consistently believed, then infer it' or 'If $\neg A$ is disbelieved, then infer A'.

The language of modal non-monotonic logics obtains from that of classical logic by the addition of a modal operator 'M', interpreted as 'It is consistent to believe'. Usually, a dual modal operator 'L', with the intended interpretation 'It is believed' or 'It is non-monotonically provable', is introduced as an abbreviation for '$\neg$M$\neg$'.

In modal non-monotonic logics, non-monotonic rules are always represented in the object language. For example, the rule about birds can be expressed by

$$\forall x\,.\,Bird(x) \wedge \mathrm{M}Flies(x) \supset Flies(x). \tag{3.2.1}$$

Given that Tweety is a bird, and nothing more, it is consistent to believe that she flies, so that (3.2.1) should allow us to infer this proposition. However, if we learn that Tweety is a penguin, and we already know that penguins do not fly, it is inconsistent to believe that Tweety flies and hence the conclusion should be blocked.

Of course, to achieve such an effect, it is necessary to capture the intended meaning of the 'M' operator. This problem is usually solved by means of fixed-point constructions and its different solutions lead to different modal non-monotonic logics.

A number of the most interesting modal non-monotonic logics will be studied in Chapter 4.

3.2.3 Default logic

Default logic was originally introduced in Reiter (1980a). Like modal non-monotonic logics, it refers to the notion of 'consistency' while interpreting non-monotonic rules. In contrast, however, these rules are represented not as formulae of the object language, but as meta-language expressions, called *defaults*.

The rule about birds can be expressed by the following default

$$\frac{Bird(x)\colon Flies(x)}{Flies(x)}$$

with the intended interpretation: 'For each individual x, if x is a bird and it is consistent to believe that x flies, then it may be believed that x flies.'

In default logic, common-sense knowledge is represented as a *default theory*, viewed as a pair $T = \langle W, D \rangle$, where W is a set of first-order sentences, the *axioms of T*, and D is a set of defaults. The axioms are meant to contain the whole information known to be true. The defaults extend this information by supporting plausible conclusions. The set of beliefs about the world represented by a default theory T is called an *extension of T*, and is defined by a fixed-point construction. A detailed presentation of two versions of default logic will be given in Chapter 5.

3.2.4 Circumscription

The term 'circumscription', introduced by McCarthy (1980), refers to a class of non-monotonic formalisms centred around the following idea: the objects that can be shown to satisfy a certain predicate are all the objects satisfying it. For instance, to circumscribe the predicate 'Green' is to assume that any object which cannot be proved green is not green.

Unlike modal non-monotonic logics and default logic, circumscription admits first-order representation of non-monotonic rules. To achieve this, McCarthy (1984) introduces a special predicate constant Ab, standing for 'abnormal', with intuitive interpretation that the abnormal objects are those violating the rule. Given this interpretation, the 'Bird' rule can be represented by the sentence

$$\forall x\ Bird(x) \wedge \neg Ab(x) \supset Flies(x) \qquad (3.2.2)$$

stating that all normal birds fly.

Clearly, by applying deductive structure of classical logic, it is impossible to use (3.2.2) to infer that a particular bird flies. This is because standard logic offers no way to conclude that the bird is normal. But circumscription does. All we have to do is to circumscribe the property of being abnormal. Circumscribing this property, we infer that any bird that cannot be proved abnormal is normal and, consequently, that it flies.

Circumscription can be naturally viewed as a form of minimization – to circumscribe a predicate is to minimize its extension.† In contrast to other formalisms capturing this type of minimization, see 3.2.5 below, circumscription enjoys the following features:

(1) It is always the task of the user to specify predicates whose extensions are to be minimized.
(2) Common to all versions of circumscription is the existence of a *circumscription axiom* (*circumscription schema*), which is implicitly added to the representation of the modelled world.
(3) All individuals of the domain, not only those referable by ground terms, take part in the process of minimization.

'Circumscriptive' formalisms will be studied in Chapter 6.

† By the extension of a predicate P we mean here the set of objects (tuples of objects) satisfying P.

3.2.5 Reasoning under the closed world assumption

Sometimes it is appropriate to assume that all relevant information is available. For example, a robot operating within a simple world of blocks can be often supplied with the complete description of its environment.

To deal efficiently with completely specified worlds, Reiter (1978) introduced a non-monotonic rule, called the *closed world assumption* (henceforward CWA). It states that for any n-ary relation symbol R and any n-tuple of ground terms $\alpha_1, \ldots, \alpha_n$ one may assume $\neg R(\alpha_1, \ldots, \alpha_n)$ unless the contrary can be classically proved.

If the CWA is in force, there is no need to represent the whole relevant information. Only *positive information*, i.e. the facts stating what is true, should be kept in the data base. The *negative facts*, specifying what is false, will be inferred implicitly. Since typically they vastly outnumber the positive facts, employing the CWA greatly simplifies the resulting representation.

From the formal point of view, the CWA can be added to any first-order representation. In practice, however, the use of the rule should be restricted to the cases where one assumes the total knowledge about a world. Otherwise, i.e. where one remains agnostic with respect to some aspects, the application of the CWA is clearly inappropriate.†

There are a number of systems that have been constructed for the purpose of formalizing the CWA. Like circumscription, they are directed at minimizing extensions of predicates. In contrast, however, the minimization captured by these systems is relatively weak in that it is restricted to nameable (by ground terms) individuals.

Various formalizations of the CWA will be presented in Chapter 7.

3.2.6 Poole's approach to non-monotonic reasoning

In Poole (1984) we are presented with a very simple non-monotonic formalism, close in spirit to default logic. Under Poole's approach, our knowledge is to be represented as a pair $\langle F, \Delta \rangle$, where F is a consistent set of first-order sentences and Δ is a set of *hypotheses*. The members of F express facts known to be true. The hypotheses represent non-monotonic rules. Formally, a hypothesis is any expression of the form

$$(x_1, \ldots, x_n) \text{ ASSUME } A(x_1, \ldots, x_n)$$

where A is a first-order formula whose free variables are precisely $x_1, \ldots, x_n$. We are to read this as 'For all individuals $x_1, \ldots, x_n$, represented by ground terms $\alpha_1, \ldots, \alpha_n$, if $A(\alpha_1, \ldots, \alpha_n)$ can be consistently assumed, then assume it'. The sentence $A(\alpha_1, \ldots, \alpha_n)$ is called an *instance* of the hypothesis.

Given a pair $\langle F, \Delta \rangle$, we are permitted to build ordinary first-order theories of the form $F \cup D$, called *theories for* $\langle F, \Delta \rangle$, where D is any set of instances of members of Δ such that $F \cup D$ is consistent. A sentence A is said to be *explainable in* $\langle F, \Delta \rangle$ iff there is a theory $F \cup D$ for $\langle F, \Delta \rangle$ such that $F \cup D \vdash A$. $F \cup D$ is said to be the *theory that explains* A. A set S of sentences is explainable in $\langle F, \Delta \rangle$ iff there is a theory for $\langle F, \Delta \rangle$ that explains all members of S.

To illustrate the introduced notions, consider the pair $\langle F, \Delta \rangle$, where F consists of

$$Republican(Nixon) \wedge Quaker(Nixon)$$

† This remark concerns Reiter's original formulation of the CWA. As we shall see in Chapter 7, there are less restrictive versions of the rule, which may be properly applied to genuinely incomplete knowledge.

and Δ contains

$$(x)\ \text{ASSUME}\ \mathit{Republican}(x) \supset \neg \mathit{Pacifist}(x)$$
$$(x)\ \text{ASSUME}\ \mathit{Quaker}(x) \supset \mathit{Pacifist}(x)$$

$\langle F, \Delta \rangle$ gives rise to two theories: $F \cup D_1$ and $F \cup D_2$, where

$$D_1 = \{\mathit{Republican}(\mathit{Nixon}) \supset \neg \mathit{Pacifist}(\mathit{Nixon})\}$$
$$D_2 = \{\mathit{Quaker}(\mathit{Nixon}) \supset \mathit{Pacifist}(\mathit{Nixon})\}$$

$F \cup D_1$ explains $\neg \mathit{Pacifist}(\mathit{Nixon})$; $F \cup D_2$ explains $\mathit{Pacifist}(\mathit{Nixon})$. (Observe that $F \cup D_1 \cup D_2$ is inconsistent and hence not a theory.)

In Poole's logic, any set of sentences explainable in $\langle F, \Delta \rangle$ may be viewed as the set of beliefs about the world represented by $\langle F, \Delta \rangle$. Thus, in the example above, we are allowed to believe that Nixon is a pacifist, and we are allowed to believe that he is not. However, we are not permitted to accept both these conclusions simultaneously, because there is no theory that explains $\{\mathit{Pacifist}(\mathit{Nixon}), \neg \mathit{Pacifist}(\mathit{Nixon})\}$.

For more information about Poole's formalism, the reader is referred to Poole (1984, 1985, 1987, 1988).

3.2.7 Model-theoretic approach to non-monotonic reasoning

Shoham (1988) approaches the problem of formalizing non-monotonic inference from a different perspective. Instead of characterizing this type of reasoning syntactically, he bases non-monotonicity on a modified notion of semantic entailment. The value of Shoham's formalization is that it provides a uniform semantic framework sufficiently general to capture many existing non-monotonic logics.

Suppose given that Tweety is a bird, we conclude that she flies. Then, *ipso facto*, we decide to reject all states of affairs where Tweety is not a flier, or, equivalently, we decide to prefer those where she is. It is this observation that underlies Shoham's approach.

Let L be a language of some monotonic logic. We put no constraints on the logic, except that it is equipped with model-theoretic semantics. That is, we assume that it makes sense to speak about the truth-values of formulae from L in frames (interpretations, modal frames or similar objects). By a theory we mean any computable set of sentences from L. As usual, a frame M is said to be a model of T iff all sentences of T are true in M. We assume from this point on that L has been fixed.

Shoham identifies non-monotonic logics with pairs $\langle L, \sqsubset \rangle$, where $\sqsubset$ is a strict partial order specified on frames for L. $M_1 \sqsubset M_2$ is to be read as 'M_2 is *preferred over* M_1'. Given a theory T, we say that M is a $\sqsubset$*-preferred model of* T iff M is a model of T and there is no other model M′ of T such that $M \sqsubset M'$. We say that T $\sqsubset$*-preferentially entails* a sentence A, written $T \models_{\sqsubset} A$, iff A is true in all $\sqsubset$-preferred models of T. The sentences $\sqsubset$-preferentially entailed by T are to be viewed as those which non-monotonically follow from T in the logic $\langle L, \sqsubset \rangle$.

An example may help to illustrate this. Suppose that we are dealing with classical first-order logic and consider the theory T given by

$$\mathit{Bird}(\mathit{Tweety})$$
$$\forall x . \mathit{Bird}(x) \wedge \neg \mathit{Ab}(x) \supset \mathit{Flies}(x)$$

Our intention is to prefer those models of T in which Ab has a minimal extension. Thus, we put

$$M_1 \sqsubset M_2 \text{ iff } |M_1| = |M_2| \quad \text{and} \quad M_2|Ab| \subset M_1|Ab|.$$

Clearly, if M is a $\sqsubset$-preferred model of T, then $M|Ab| = \{\ \}$. So, $T \models_{\sqsubset} Flies(Tweety)$. Suppose now that T' obtains from T by the addition of $\neg Flies(Tweety)$. If M is a $\sqsubset$-preferred model of T', then $M|Ab| = \{M|Tweety|\}$. Thus, $T' \not\models_{\sqsubset} Flies(Tweety)$.

Shoham illustrates his construction by providing strict partial orders corresponding to circumscription, a version of default logic, a version of modal non-monotonic logic and a few other existing non-monotonic formalisms. The idea of preferential models has been further developed by Sandewall (1989), Makinson (1989), Geffner (1989), Brown & Shoham (1989).

This completes our short exposition of formal approaches to non-monotonic reasoning. For other proposals, see Łukaszewicz (1987), Delgrande (1988), Ginsberg (1988) and Lin & Shoham (1989). A paper of Lifschitz (1989a) provides a list of 'benchmark' problems for formal non-monotonic reasoning.

3.3 OBJECTIONS TO NON-MONOTONIC FORMALISMS

A number of objections to non-monotonic formalisms have been raised in the AI literature. Some of them are presented below.

The first criticism of formalizing non-monotonic inference was made by Kramosil (1975). Inspired by Sandewall's UNLESS operator, he considered systems employing inference rules of the form:

$$\text{From } \vdash A_1, \ldots, \vdash A_n, \nvdash B_1, \ldots, \nvdash B_m, \text{ infer } \vdash C \qquad (3.3.1)$$

where $A_1, \ldots, A_n$, $B_1, \ldots, B_m$ and C (n, m ≥ 0) are all first-order sentences, and '$\vdash$' and '$\nvdash$' denote the relations of first-order provability and unprovability, respectively.

The first thing to notice here is that (3.3.1) is a strange rule. It says: 'If $A_1, \ldots, A_n$ are all first-order provable and none of $B_1, \ldots, B_m$ is first-order provable, then infer that C is first-order provable.' The key point is that first-order provability is a well-defined notion, so that it makes little sense to force first-order provability of C simply by employing a rule like (3.3.1). Assume, for example, that we are prepared to infer that Tweety flies on the basis that she is a bird and we have no proof that she is a non-flier. Obviously, we do not try to conclude that the proposition *Flies*(*Tweety*) is first-order provable.

To summarize Kramosil's results we need the following terminology. For the sake of simplicity, Kramosil's original presentation is reformulated here.

We assume that all considered concepts are specified over a fixed first-order language L.

Let r be a rule of the form (3.3.1). We say that *r* is a *non-monotonic rule* iff m $\geq$ 1. r is said to be a *truth-preserving rule* iff for each (first-order) frame M the following holds: If $A_1, \ldots, A_n$ are true in M and $B_1, \ldots, B_m$ are false in M, then C is true in M.

A *theory* is a pair $T = (\text{AX}, \text{R})$, where AX is a set of first-order sentences, called *axioms of T*, and R is a set of non-monotonic truth-preserving rules.

Let $S \subseteq L$ be a set of sentences and suppose that r is a non-monotonic rule. We say that S is *closed under* r iff the following holds: If $A_1, \ldots, A_n \in S$ and $B_1, \ldots, B_m \notin S$, then

$C \in S$. S is said to be *closed under a set of non-monotonic rules* R iff S is closed under r, for each $r \in R$.

We are now in a position to define the set of theorems derivable from a given theory, called an *extension* of the theory. Kramosil's definition is equivalent to the following.

Let $T = (AX, R)$ be a theory. The *extension of T* is the smallest set S of sentences satisfying:

(E1) $S = Th(S)$, where $Th(X) = \{A : X \vdash A\}$;
(E2) $AX \subseteq S$;
(E3) S is closed under R.

It is worth noting that Kramosil's definition of an extension corresponds closely to that of the set of theorems provable in ordinary monotonic logics. It is well known that this set can be defined as the smallest set including axioms and closed under (ordinary) inference rules.

The following theorem holds:

Theorem 3.1 (Kramosil 1975) Let $T = (AX, R)$ be a theory. Then either T lacks an extension or the set Th(AX) is the extension of T. ▮

In view of Theorem 3.1, Kramosil claims that he has shown that non-monotonic rules are either meaningless or useless.

Kramosil's interpretation of Theorem 3.1 is obviously too pessimistic. In fact, it is his formalization of non-monotonic rules that makes them either meaningless or useless. More precisely, his definition of an extension does not capture the intentended interpretation of non-monotonic rules. To illustrate this, consider the theory consisting of the axiom

Bird(*Tao*)

and the rule

From $\vdash$ *Bird*(*Tao*) and $\nvdash \neg$*Flies*(*Tao*), infer $\vdash$ *Flies*(*Tao*)

Since both $\vdash$ *Bird*(*Tao*) and $\nvdash \neg$*Flies*(*Tao*) hold, we intuitively feel that the theory should have the extension

S = Th({*Bird*(*Tao*), *Flies*(*Tao*)})

However, under Kramosil's formalization, the theory lacks an extension. This is because there are two minimal sets of formulae satisfying (E1)–(E3):

S = Th({*Bird*(*Tao*), *Flies*(*Tao*)})
S′ = Th({*Bird*(*Tao*), ¬*Flies*(*Tao*)}).

Kramosil's mistake is that he tries to formalize non-monotonic inferences by employing techniques which are appropriate while formalizing ordinary monotonic reasoning. When this fails, he does not consider these techniques inappropriate. Instead, he claims that non-monotonic inference cannot be correctly formalized.

As a matter of fact, Kramosil provides another result which, according to him, supports his claim. This result is based on a notion of 'formal proof' in systems using non-monotonic rules. Again, however, the definition he provides has little to do with non-monotonic inference. Consequently, his second result is also useless (see Kramosil 1975, for details).

In conclusion, Kramosil's paper does not show that non-monotonic rules cannot be properly formalized. It merely shows that this task cannot be achieved by employing techniques that are typically used when formalizing ordinary monotonic inference.

Another criticism of formalizing non-monotonic reasoning is based on the observation that non-monotonicity hides the monotonic inference process. For example, if I conclude that Tweety flies because there is no proof to the contrary, then, in fact, I start by trying to monotonically prove that Tweety is not a flier and jump to my conclusion just when this latter proof fails. Of course, there is a technical difficulty involved here: due to undecidability of first-order logic, the problem of determining whether a first-order proof fails is, in general, computationally ineffective. Accordingly, many AI researchers, for example Kowalski (1979), Israel (1980), Winograd (1980), consider the formal study of non-monotonic inference as a pure intellectual exercise. The problem, they argue, is not to formalize this type of reasoning, but rather to computationally coordinate the underlying monotonic process involved. Since programs modelling non-monotonic inference will be limited by lack of resources, the real question is the following: When does it make sense to stop trying to prove a proposition and act as if it were unprovable?

Obviously, this is an important question. However, as McDermott (1982) correctly stated, 'it seems like a waste of our resources to implement programs for default reasoning without giving any thought to what conclusions they ought to come to.' To illustrate this, reconsider the example about quakers and republicans.

Suppose that we have the following pair of rules

(R1) If there is no proof to the contrary, assume that a quaker is a pacifist
(R2) If there is no proof to the contrary, assume that a republican is not a pacifist

together with the fact

(F) Nixon is both a quaker and a republican.

Given this information, there are reasons to believe that Nixon is a pacifist and there are reasons to believe that he is not. It may be also reasonable to remain agnostic about his pacifism. What is then the set of theorems non-monotonically derivable from (R1)–(R2), (F)? This question must be answered before a program dealing with non-monotonic inferences is written. Otherwise the value of the program will be very problematic.

Certain objections to non-monotonic formalisms have been raised by AI researchers concerned with quantitative reasoning. Ginsberg (1985), for example, suggests that implementations of common-sense inference should be probabilistic. However, his paper amounts to presenting a quantitative approach which partially overcomes the usual difficulty of all probabilistic reasoning methods: 'How are the initial probabilities to be obtained?' The real problem, i.e. whether probabilistic techniques are appropriate for the purpose of formalizing common-sense reasoning, has been left untouched.

Cheeseman (1985) argues that while non-monotonic formalisms may be suitable for dealing with incomplete representation of complete information (autoepistemic reasoning), they are inappropriate in genuinely less than conclusive situations (default reasoning). His main claim is that Bayesian probability theory is sufficient for all uncertain inference in AI.

By inspecting the typology of non-monotonic reasoning (section 2.3), the reader may be convinced that Cheeseman's claim is at least arguable. In fact, only a small part of uncertain inference is explicitly influenced by probabilistic information. Apart from probabilistic default reasoning, explicit probabilistic measures are either unnecessary (prototypical reasoning) or even irrelevant (no-risk reasoning, the best-guess reasoning).

The lack of a general correlation between viewing a proposition as a rational conclusion and its credibility, i.e. the probabilistic measure of an entity's belief in that proposition, is not surprising. This only shows that the task of handling incomplete information cannot be reduced to that of measuring uncertainty. The real problem that must be necessarily solved is *how is this uncertainty to be managed?* As we observed, there are many external factors to consider while managing uncertainty. There is no *a priori* reason to assert that probabilistic evidence is generally of greater importance than, for example, a subjective guess or the risk of reaching a mistaken decision. In fact, it is the real situation that makes one of those factors more relevant than the others.

If we agree with this point of view, then the probabilistic and the non-monotonic approaches should not be considered as mutually exclusive, but rather as complementary. Although both deal with uncertain information, they operate on different levels. While probabilistic methods can be useful to measure uncertainty, the non-monotonic formalisms provide a general framework to manage it.

4

Modal non-monotonic logics

As remarked earlier, the term 'modal non-monotonic logic' is reserved for non-monotonic formalisms introducing the notion of 'consistency' and/or 'belief' into the object language. This is achieved by employing a modal operator 'M', interpreted 'It is consistent to believe'.

Consider the non-monotonic rule stating 'In the absence of evidence to the contrary, assume that an elephant is grey.' In the framework of modal non-monotonic logic, this rule can be represented by the object-language sentence

$$\forall x . Elephant(x) \wedge \mathrm{M}Grey(x) \supset Grey(x) \tag{4.0.1}$$

with the intended reading 'For any individual x, if x is an elephant and it is consistent to believe that x is grey, then assume that x is grey'. Now, if all we know about Clyde is that he is an elephant, then it is consistent to believe that he is grey and, consequently, (4.0.1) will allow us to derive this proposition. On the other hand, if we learn that Clyde is an albino elephant and we know that albino elephants are not grey, then it is inconsistent to assume that Clyde is grey and so this proposition will not be derivable using (4.0.1).

The major problem in constructing modal non-monotonic logic is to capture the intended interpretation of the 'M' operator. A number of solutions to this problem, leading to different versions of modal non-monotonic logic, have been proposed in the AI literature. The most important ones will be discussed in this chapter.

First, the earliest version of modal non-monotonic logic due to McDermott & Doyle (1980) is presented. Next, a group of stronger logics developed by McDermott (1982) is discussed. Some weaknesses of McDermott and Doyle's systems led Moore (1983) to construct an alternative modal non-monotonic logic. This very important formalism, called *autoepistemic logic*, is studied in section 4.3. Finally, two versions of modal non-monotonic logic based on more exotic foundations are briefly discussed:

Gabbay's (1982) system grounded on intuitionistic logic and Turner's (1984) proposal employing Kleene's three-valued logic.

4.1 MODAL NON-MONOTONIC LOGIC OF McDERMOTT AND DOYLE

The first attempt to construct a modal non-monotonic logic was made by McDermott & Doyle (1980). The language they use is that of the modal first-order logic. A formula of the form 'MA' is to be read 'It is consistent to believe A' or 'A may be consistently believed'. Formulae of the form 'LA' are interpreted as 'A is non-monotonically provable', or, better, 'A is believed'. In McDermott and Doyle's system, 'M' is viewed as the primary operator, whereas 'L' is defined as an abbreviation for '$\neg M \neg$'.

The objects we shall be primarily interested in are *theories* – computable sets of sentences over the language under consideration – interpreted as sets of premisses about the modelled world. In what follows, we write L_T to denote the language of a theory T. As usual, unless stated otherwise, we assume that L_T consists of the formulae constructable using predicate and function constants occurring in T.

In this section the symbols 'Th' and '$\vdash$' ('$\nvdash$') refer to the provability operator and the provability (unprovability) relation of the classical first-order logic. To make these symbols applicable to modal languages, we assume that MA and LA are formally treated as atomic formulae.

The central concept of the modal non-monotonic logic is that of an *extension of a theory* T. Intuitively, such an extension is to be viewed as the set of beliefs one may hold, given T as the set of his initial premisses.†

There are three conditions to be expected of an extension S of a theory T:

(1) S should be deductively closed: $S = Th(S)$;
(2) S ought to include the premisses: $T \subseteq S$;
(3) S should contain any sentence of the form MA, provided that $S \nvdash \neg A$.‡

This motivates the following definition:

Definition 4.1 Let T be a theory. A set of sentences $S \subseteq L_T$ is an *extension of* T iff

$$S = Th(T \cup \{MA: A \text{ is a sentence of } L_T \text{ and } \neg A \notin S\})$$

∎

Sentences of the form MA will be called *assumptions*.

Definition 4.1 specifies the notion of an extension in a non-constructive way. To simplify our subsequent discussion, we provide a partial constructive characterization of this concept.

Let T be a theory and suppose that $\lambda = \{A_i: i = 0, 1, \ldots\}$ is an enumeration of all sentences from L_T. By $S(T, \lambda)$ we denote the set§

$$S(T, \lambda) = Th\left(\bigcup_{i=0}^{\infty} S_i\right), \text{ where}$$

---

† In McDermott & Doyle's original terminology, an extension of a theory T is called a fixed point of T.

‡ Note that in view of (1), (3) can be replaced by: 'S should contain any sentence of the form MA, provided that $\neg A \notin S$'.

§ This construction is due to Davis (1980).

$S_0 = T$, and for $i \geq 0$

$$S_{i+1}\begin{cases} L_T & \text{– if for some } B \in L_T,\ MB \in S_i \text{ and } S_i \vdash \neg B \\ S_i \cup \{MA_i & \text{– otherwise, if } S_i \nvdash \neg A_i \\ S_i & \text{– otherwise} \end{cases}$$

Theorem 4.2 For any T and λ, if $S(T, \lambda)$ is consistent, then it is an extension of T.

Proof Assume that $S(T, \lambda)$ is consistent. To prove that $S(T, \lambda)$ is an extension of T, it suffices to show that

$$\bigcup_{i=0}^{\infty} S_i = T \cup \{MA: A \text{ is a sentence and } \bigcup_{i=0}^{\infty} S_i \nvdash \neg A\}$$

Denote the right hand side of this equation by RHS.

Assume first that $B \in \bigcup_{i=0}^{\infty} S_i$. If $B \in S_0$, then clearly $B \in \text{RHS}$. Otherwise, B is of the form MA, for some sentence A. We show that $B \in \text{RHS}$ by proving that $\bigcup_{i=0}^{\infty} S_i \nvdash \neg A$. Assume to the contrary that this is not the case. Thus, since $S_0 \subseteq S_2 \subseteq \ldots$, $S_j \vdash \neg A$, for some $j \geq 0$. On the other hand, because $MA \in \bigcup_{i=0}^{\infty} S_i$, $MA \in S_k$, for some $k \geq 0$. Put $m = \max(j, k)$ and consider the set S_{m+1}. By the construction, $S_{m+1} = L_T$, and so $S(T, \lambda) = L_T$. A contradiction.

Assume now that $B \in \text{RHS}$. If $B \in T$, then trivially $B \in \bigcup_{i=0}^{\infty} S_i$. Otherwise, $B = MA$, for some sentence A such that $\bigcup_{i=0}^{\infty} S_i \nvdash \neg A$. Let $A = A_j$ in the enumeration λ. Consider the set S_{j+1}. Since $\bigcup_{i=0}^{\infty} S_i \nvdash \neg A$, $S_j \nvdash \neg A$. So, by the construction, $MA \in S_{j+1} \subseteq \bigcup_{i=0}^{\infty} S_i$.

∎

Let $\lambda = \{A_i: i = 0, 1, \ldots\}$ be any enumeration of all sentences of L_T. λ is called *admissible* if it satisfies the property that if A_i is a subformula of A_j, then $i \leq j$.

Example 4.3 Let $T = \{Mp \supset p\}$, where p is a proposition constant. Let $\lambda = \{A_i: i = 0, 1, \ldots\}$ be any admissible enumeration of sentences of L_T. (Note that we are dealing with a propositional theory, so that any formula of L_T is a sentence.) It is easily checked that $S(T, \lambda)$ is consistent and includes Mp and thus p. So, by Theorem 4.2, T has at least one extension which contains Mp and p. It can be shown, but we ignore the proof here, that T has exactly one extension. ∎

Example 4.4 Let $T = \{Mp \supset \neg q; Mq \supset \neg p\}$, where p and q are proposition constants. Let λ_1 be any admissible enumeration of sentences of L_T such that $A_0 = p$. It is easily checked that $S(T, \lambda_1)$ is consistent. Clearly, $Mp \in S(T, \lambda_1)$ and $Mq \notin S(T, \lambda_1)$. Similarly, take any admissible enumeration λ_2 such that $A_0 = q$. $S(T, \lambda_2)$ is consistent, $Mq \in S(T, \lambda_2)$ and $Mp \notin S(T, \lambda_2)$. Thus, T has at least two extensions. One of them includes Mp and $\neg q$; the other contains Mq and $\neg p$. It can be shown that T has exactly two extensions. ∎

Theorem 4.5 Let T consist of the following axioms:

$\forall x . f(x) \neq a$

$\forall xy . f(x) = f(y) \supset x = y$

$\forall x . MP(x) \supset [P(x) \wedge \forall y . x \neq y \supset \neg P(y)]$

Let Terms $= \{a, f(a), f(f(a)), \ldots)$. For $\alpha \in$ Terms, let λ_α be any admissible enumeration of sentences of L_T such that $A_0 = P(\alpha)$. It is readily verified that

(i) $S(T, \lambda_\alpha)$ is consistent, for all $\alpha \in$ Terms;
(ii) for any $\alpha_1, \alpha_2 \in$ Terms, $\alpha_1 \neq \alpha_2$ implies $S(T, \lambda_{\alpha_1}) \neq S(T, \lambda_{\alpha_2})$.

This means that T has infinitely many extensions. ∎

Unfortunately, there are theories lacking extensions.

Example 4.6 Let $T = \{Mp \supset \neg p\}$. T has no extension. To show this, assume to the contrary that S is an extension of T and consider two cases:

(i) $\neg p \notin S$. Then $Mp \in S$ and thus, $\neg p \in S$. A contradiction.
(ii) $\neg p \in S$. Then $\neg p$ can be classically proved from $T \cup \{MA\colon A$ is a sentence from L_T and $\neg A \notin S\}$. Clearly, this cannot be the case unless $Mp \in \{MA\colon A$ is a sentence from L_T and $\neg A \notin S\}$. Thus, $\neg p \notin S$. A contradiction. ∎

The next theorem shows that extensions are (set inclusion-) minimal.

Theorem 4.7 (McDermott & Doyle 1980) Let T be a theory. If S_1 and S_2 are extensions of T and $S_1 \subseteq S_2$, then $S_1 = S_2$.

Proof Assume that $S_1 \subseteq S_2$. Thus, $\{MA\colon A$ is a sentence from L_T and $\neg A \notin S_2\} \subseteq \{MA\colon A$ is a sentence from L_T and $\neg A \notin S_1\}$. So, since S_1 and S_2 are extensions, we have $S_2 \subseteq S_1$. ∎

Corollary 4.8 (McDermott & Doyle 1980) If L_T is an extension of T, then it is the only extension of T. ∎

Corollary 4.9 L_T is an extension of T iff T is inconsistent. ∎

So far we have not answered the fundamental question: what is the set of theorems non-monotonically derivable from a theory T? If T has a unique extension S, it is natural to identify the set of theorems of T with S. The problem, however, is that a theory may have several extensions or none at all. McDermott and Doyle resolve this difficulty as follows.

Let T be a theory. By $\mathrm{EXT}(T)$ we denote the set of all extensions of T.

Definition 4.10 (McDermott & Doyle 1980) Let T be a theory. The *set of theorems non-monotonically derivable from* T, denoted by $\mathrm{TH}(T)$, is given by

$$\mathrm{TH}(T) = \begin{cases} \bigcap \{S\colon S \in \mathrm{EXT}(T)\} & \text{if } \mathrm{EXT}(T) \neq \{\ \} \\ L_T & \text{otherwise} \end{cases}$$

∎

In words, the set of theorems derivable from a theory T is the intersection of all extensions of T, or the whole language if T has no extension.

Example 4.11 Reconsider the theory $T = \{Mp \supset \neg q;\ Mq \supset \neg p\}$ from Example 4.4. T has two extensions. One of them includes Mp but not Mq; the other includes Mq but not Mp. Thus:

$$Mp \vee Mq \in \mathrm{TH}(T); \quad \neg p \vee \neg q \in \mathrm{TH}(T); \quad Mp \notin \mathrm{TH}(T);$$
$$Mq \notin \mathrm{TH}(T); \quad \neg p \notin \mathrm{TH}(T); \quad \neg q \notin \mathrm{TH}(T). \quad ∎$$

We say that a theory T is *non-monotonically inconsistent* (*consistent*) iff

$\mathrm{TH}(T) = L_T$ ($\mathrm{TH}(T) \neq L_T$). Notice that a theory is non-monotonically inconsistent if it is classically inconsistent or it has no extension.

McDermott & Doyle's logic has a number of unusual properties. The most striking result is the following.

Theorem 4.12 (McDermott & Doyle 1980) A subtheory of a non-monotonically consistent theory may be non-monotonically inconsistent.

Proof Consider the theory $T = \{\mathrm{M}p \supset \neg p; \neg p\}$. T is clasically consistent. Moreover, T has a consistent extension (to show this, take any admissible enumeration of all the sentences of L_T and apply Theorem 4.2). So, T is non-monotonically consistent. However, its subtheory $\{\mathrm{M}p \supset \neg p\}$ has no extension and hence is inconsistent. ∎

McDermott and Doyle provide what they call *model theory* or *semantics* of their logic. Unfortunately, this semantics has very little to do with the usual meaning of the word and so we omit it here.

McDermott and Doyle's non-monotonic logic is too weak to capture the intended meaning of modal operators. A few examples will help to illustrate this.

Example 4.13 Let $T = \{\mathrm{M}p, \neg p\}$. This theory amounts to simultaneously saying that p is false and p is consistent with everything believed. It is difficult to imagine the situation where both these assertions could be consistently accepted. In McDermott and Doyle's logic, however, T has a consistent extension. To show this, consider the following construction.

Let $\lambda = \{A_i: \mathrm{i} = 0, 1, \ldots\}$ be any admissible enumeration of all sentences of L_T. We define a sequence of sets of formulae of L_T, $S_0 \subseteq S_1 \subseteq \ldots$, by

$$S_0 = T, \text{ and for } i \geq 0$$

$$S_{i+1} = \begin{cases} S_i \cup \{\mathrm{M}A_i\} & \text{if } S_i \nvdash \neg A_i \\ S_i & \text{otherwise} \end{cases}.$$

It is routine to check that $\bigcup_{i=0}^{\infty} S_i$ is consistent and

$$\bigcup_{i=0}^{\infty} S_i = T \cup \left\{\mathrm{M}A: A \text{ is a sentence from } L_T \text{ and } \bigcup_{i=0}^{\infty} S_i \nvdash \neg A\right\}.$$

Thus, the set $\mathrm{Th}\left(\bigcup_{i=0}^{\infty}\right)$ is a consistent extension of T.

It is interesting to note that the existence of this extension cannot be proved by applying Theorem 4.2 (observe that $S(T, \lambda) = L_T$, for any enumeration λ). This invalidates a result of Davis (1980) who claims that A is non-monotonically derivable from a theory T, i.e. $A \in \mathrm{TH}(T)$, iff $A \in S(T, \lambda)$, for each enumeration λ. ∎

Example 4.14 Let $T = \{\neg \mathrm{M}p\}$. This theory asserts that p is inconsistent with everything believed and so, implicitly, suggests that $\neg p$ is believed. Nothing unusual seems to be hidden here. However, in McDermott and Doyle's logic, T is non-monotonically inconsistent. The reason is that although $\neg \mathrm{M}p$ follows from T, $\neg p$ does not. This forces $\mathrm{M}p$ to be assumed and, consequently, T has no extension. ∎

Example 4.15 Let $T = \{\mathrm{M}(p \wedge q), \neg p\}$. Intuitively, it is difficult to simultaneously accept that p is false and $p \wedge q$ can be consistently believed. However, in McDermott and Doyle's logic, T is consistent. The theory has one consistent extension including $\mathrm{M}(p \wedge q)$, but not $\mathrm{M}p$. The existence of this extension can be easily verified by applying Theorem 4.2. ▮

This completes our presentation of McDermott and Doyle's non-monotonic logic. A number of other results concerning this formalism, including a proof procedure for non-monotonic propositional theories, can be found in their original paper.

4.2 MODAL NON-MONOTONIC LOGICS OF McDERMOTT

The weaknesses of McDermott and Doyle's formalism (see Examples 4.13, 4.14 and 4.15) led McDermott (1982) to develop a group of stronger non-monotonic logics. He retains all the ideas of the earlier system with one exception: the new formalisms are based on modal deductive structure.

According to McDermott, there are three modal systems worth considering as appropriate bases of non-monotonic logic. These are T, S4 and S5. Recall that T obtains from the classical logic by the addition of the schemata

(A1) $\mathrm{L}A \supset A$
(A2) $\mathrm{L}(A \supset B) \supset (\mathrm{L}A \supset \mathrm{L}B)$
(A3) $\forall x(\mathrm{L}A) \supset \mathrm{L}(\forall x A)$

and the rule of inference

$$\frac{A}{\mathrm{L}A} \quad \text{(NEC)}$$

S4 is obtained by the addition of

(A4) $\mathrm{L}A \supset \mathrm{LL}A$

to T. S5 obtains by adding

(A5) $\mathrm{M}A \supset \mathrm{LM}A$

to S4.

In this section the symbols 'Th_{X}' and '$\vdash_{\mathrm{X}}$' ('$\nvdash_{\mathrm{X}}$') denote the provability operator and the provability (unprovability) relation of X modal first-order logic, respectively, where $\mathrm{X} \in \{\mathrm{T}, \mathrm{S4}, \mathrm{S5}\}$.

Definition 4.16 (McDermott 1982) Let T be a theory. A set of sentences $\mathrm{S} \subseteq L_{\mathrm{T}}$ is called an X-*extension of T* iff

$$\mathrm{S} = \mathrm{Th}_{\mathrm{X}}(T \cup \{\mathrm{M}A\colon A \text{ is a sentence from } L_{\mathrm{T}} \text{ and } \neg A \notin \mathrm{S}\}).$$

▮

Recall that a theory T is X-*consistent* iff $T \nvdash_{\mathrm{X}} A$, for some formula A. Otherwise, T is called X-*inconsistent*.

The notion of an X-extension may be given the following constructive characterization.

Let T be a theory and suppose that $\lambda = \{A_i\colon i = 0, 1, \ldots\}$ is an enumeration of all sentences of L_T. By $S_X(T, \lambda)$ we denote the set

$$S_X(T, \lambda) = Th_X\left(\bigcup_{i=0}^{\infty} S_i\right)$$

where

$$S_0 = T, \text{ and for } i \geq 0$$

$$S_{i+1} = \begin{cases} S_i \cup \{MA_i\} & \text{if } S_i \nvdash_X \neg A_i \\ S_i & \text{otherwise} \end{cases}.$$

There are two differences between this construction and that from the previous section. First, the classical deductive structure has been replaced by the modal one. Second, the definition of S_{i+1} has been simplified. Notice, however, that this simplification is inessential: by (NEC) and the equivalence $MB \equiv \neg L \neg B$, $MB \in S_i$ and $S_i \vdash \neg B$ imply that S_i is X-inconsistent, for any $X \in \{T, S4, S5\}$.

Theorem 4.17 For any theory T and any enumeration λ, if $S_X(T, \lambda)$ is X-consistent, then it is an X-extension of T.

Proof Similar to the proof of Theorem 4.2. ∎

By X-EXT(T) we denote the set of all X-extensions of T.

Definition 4.18 (McDermott 1982) Let T be a theory. The *set of X-theorems non-monotonically derivable from* T, denoted by $TH_X(T)$, is defined by

$$TH_X(T) = \begin{cases} \bigcap \{S : S \in X\text{-EXT}(T)\} & \text{if } X\text{-EXT}(T) \neq \{\ \} \\ L_T & \text{otherwise} \end{cases}$$

∎

The modal versions of non-monotonic logic retain many properties of McDermott and Doyle's first proposal.

Theorem 4.19 If S_1 and S_2 are X-extensions of a theory T and $S_1 \subseteq S_2$, then $S_1 = S_2$.

Proof Similar to the proof of Theorem 4.7. ∎

Corollary 4.20 If L_T is an X-extension of T, then it is the only X-extension of T. ∎

Theorem 4.21 L_T is an X-extension of T iff T is X-inconsistent.

Proof Straightforward. ∎

Corollary 4.22 If T is X-consistent and T has an X-extension, then $TH_X(T)$ is X-consistent.

Proof By Corollary 4.20 and Theorem 4.21. ∎

In the following, we shall often state without the proof that certain (propositional) formulae are theorems of the modal system T, S4 or S5. To verify such statements, the reader may use proof procedures from Hughes & Cresswell (1972, pp. 82–122).

Example 4.23 Let $T = \{Mp \supset p\}$. T has one T-extension and one S4-extension, both including Mp and p. Their existence can be shown by taking any admissible enumeration λ with $A_0 = p$ and applying Theorem 4.17. Thus, $p \in TH_T(T)$ and $p \in TH_{S4}(T)$. As regards the S5 version of non-monotonic logic, the situation is more complex. As will soon be clear, T has more than one S5 extension. In particular, there is a consistent S5-extension of T containing $\neg p$, so that $p \notin \mathrm{TH}_{S5}(T)$. This contradicts our intuitions and suggests that there may be fundamental problems with basing non-monotonic logic on the S5 system. ▮

Example 4.24 Let $T = \{\mathrm{M}p \supset \neg p\}$. As we saw (Example 4.6), T has no extension in McDermott and Doyle's system. Roughly speaking, this is due to the following unsolvable conflict. If Mp is not in an extension, there is no way to infer $\neg p$ and so, Mp must be in the extension. On the other hand, if Mp is in an extension, $\neg p$ becomes inferable and thus, Mp must not enter the extension.

In the modal versions of non-monotonic logic, the conflict no longer occurs since $T \vdash_{(T,S4,S5)} \neg p$ and so, Mp is never forced to enter an extension. (We write $T \vdash_{(T,S4,S5)} A$ to indicate that $T \vdash_X A$, for any $X \in \{T, S4, S5\}$.) Consequently, T has extensions in any of the considered modal versions of non-monotonic logic. ▮

Basing non-monotonic logic on the modal logic allows us to avoid some peculiarities of McDermott and Doyle's formalization (see Examples 4.13, 4.14 and 4.15).

Example 4.25 Let $T = \{\mathrm{M}p, \neg p\}$. Since $\{\neg p\} \vdash_{(T,S4,S5)} \mathrm{L}\neg p$ and $\vdash_{(T,S4,S5)} \mathrm{L}\neg p \equiv \neg \mathrm{M}p$, then $T \vdash_{(T,S4,S5)} \neg \mathrm{M}p$. Thus, T is (T-, S4-, S5-) inconsistent and so, $\mathrm{TH}_X(T) = L_T$, for any $X \in \{T, S4, S5\}$. This is intuitively sound. ▮

Example 4.26 Let $T = \{\neg \mathrm{M}p\}$. In McDermott and Doyle's system, T lacks an extension. The reason is that $\neg p$ does not follow from T and so, Mp must be assumed, contradicting T. This is no longer true in McDermott's logics because $\vdash_{(T,S4,S5)} \neg \mathrm{M}p \supset \neg p$. Thus, $T \vdash_{(T,S4,S5)} \neg p$, and hence M$p$ is never forced to enter an extension. In consequence, T has extensions in all of the considered modal versions of non-monotonic logic. ▮

Example 4.27 Let $T = \{\mathrm{M}(p \wedge q), \neg p\}$.
Since $\vdash_{(T,S4,S5)} \mathrm{M}(p \wedge q) \supset \mathrm{M}p$, T is (T-, S4-, S5-) inconsistent (by the argument used in Example 4.25). Thus, for any $X \in \{T, S4, S5\}$, $\mathrm{TH}_X(T) = L_T$. This agrees with our intuition. ▮

We now proceed to a detailed investigation of the S5 version of non-monotonic logic. We need some preliminary results.

It is interesting to notice that the classical Deduction Theorem is not generally valid in modal logic. For instance, $\{p\} \vdash_{(T,S4,S5)} \mathrm{L}p$, but $\nvdash_{(T,S4,S5)} p \supset \mathrm{L}p$. However, for S4 and S5 modal systems, the following weaker version of the theorem holds:

Theorem 4.28 (Weak Deduction Theorem) Let T be a theory and let A be a sentence. If $T \cup \{A\} \vdash_{(S4,S5)} B$, then $T \vdash_{(S4,S5)} \mathrm{L}A \supset B$.

Proof Let $A_0, \ldots, A_n$ ($n \geq 0$) be an (S4-, S5-) proof of B from $T \cup \{A\}$. It suffices to show that $T \vdash_{(S4,S5)} \mathrm{L}A \supset A_i$, for all $i \leq n$. This is proved by induction on i, just like in a typical proof of Deduction Theorem for classical first-order logic (see, for example, Mendelson 1979). The only new case to consider is: A_i is obtained by applying the (NEC) rule, i.e. $A_i = \mathrm{L}A_j$, for some $j < i$.

By induction hypothesis, $T \vdash_{(S4,S5)} \mathrm{L}A \supset A_j$ and so, $T \vdash_{(S4,S5)} \mathrm{L}(\mathrm{L}A \supset A_j)$, by (NEC). Thus, since $\vdash_{(S4,S5)} \mathrm{L}(\mathrm{L}A \supset A_j) \supset (\mathrm{LL}A \supset \mathrm{L}A_j)$ and $\vdash_{(S4,S5)} \mathrm{L}A \supset \mathrm{LL}A$, we have $T \vdash_{(S4,S5)} \mathrm{L}A \supset \mathrm{L}A_j$, by propositional logic. But $\mathrm{L}A_j = A_i$ and so, $T \vdash_{(S4,S5)} \mathrm{L}A \supset A_i$. ▮

Theorem 4.29 Let T be a theory. For each sentence $A \in L_T$, if $T \nvdash_{S5} \neg A$, then $T \cup \{MA\}$ is S5-consistent.

Proof Assume to the contrary that $T \nvdash_{S5} \neg A$ and $T \cup \{MA\}$ is S5-inconsistent. Thus, $T \cup \{MA\} \vdash_{S5} L \neg A$, and so

$$T \vdash_{S5} LMA \supset L \neg A \tag{4.2.1}$$

by Theorem 4.28. On the other hand,

$$\vdash_{S5} MA \supset LMA. \tag{4.2.2}$$

From (4.2.1) and (4.2.2), $T \vdash_{S5} MA \supset L \neg A$ and thus, since $\vdash_{S5} MA \equiv \neg L \neg A$, we have $T \vdash_{S5} \neg L \neg A \supset L \neg A$. Consequently, $T \vdash_{S5} L \neg A$ and so, $T \vdash_{S5} \neg A$, by modulus ponens and axiom schema (A1). A contradiction. ∎

We are now in a position to provide a general characterization of S5 non-monotonic logic.

Theorem 4.30 Let T be a theory and suppose that $\lambda = \{A_i : i = 0, 1, \ldots\}$ is any enumeration of all sentences of L_T. Then the set $S_{S5}(T, \lambda)$ is an S5-extension of T.

Proof If T is S5-inconsistent, then $S_{S5}(T, \lambda) = L_T$ and the theorem clearly holds. Assume, therefore, that T is S5-consistent. Thus, by the construction of $S_{S5}(T, \lambda)$ and Theorem 4.29, $S_{S5}(T, \lambda)$ is S5-consistent. So, $S_{S5}(T, \lambda)$ is an S5-extension of T, by Theorem 4.17. ∎

Corollary 4.31 Every theory has an S5-extension. ∎

Corollary 4.32 If T is S5-consistent, then $TH_{S5}(T)$ is S5-consistent.

Proof By Corollary 4.22 ∎

Example 4.23 (continued) Reconsider the theory $T = \{Mp \supset p\}$. Let λ_1 be any enumeration with $A_0 = p$. Since $T \nvdash_{S5} \neg p$, $Mp \in S_{S5}(T, \lambda_1)$. Thus, by Theorem 4.30, there is an S5-extension of T including Mp (and hence p). Now, let λ_2 be any enumeration with $A_0 = \neg p$. Since, $T \nvdash_{S5} p$, there is an S5-extension of T, namely $S_{S5}(T, \lambda_2)$, containing $M \neg p$. Clearly, each S5-extension of T includes $L(Mp \supset p)$. So, since $\vdash_{S5} L(Mp \supset p) \wedge M \neg p \supset \neg p$, the S5-extension $S_{S5}(T, \lambda_2)$ contains $\neg p$. ∎

The existence of extensions is a nice property of the S5 version of non-monotonic logic. Unfortunately, as we have already seen, S5-extensions may contain intuitively unacceptable sentences. This is not a specific property of the examples we have discussed. In fact, any sentence which can be S5-consistently added to a theory T is a member of some S5-extension of T.

Theorem 4.33 Let T be a theory and suppose that $T \cup \{A\}$ is S5-consistent. Then there is an S5-extension of T including A.

Proof Let λ be any enumeration of all the sentences of L_T with $A_0 = LA$. Since $T \cup \{A\}$ is S5-consistent, $T \cup \{LA\}$ is also S5-consistent and hence, $T \nvdash_{S5} \neg LA$. Thus, $MLA \in S_{S5}(T, \lambda)$. But $\vdash_{S5} MLA \supset A$ and so, because $S_{S5}(T, \lambda)$ is deductively closed, $A \in S_{S5}(T, \lambda)$. Therefore, by Theorem 4.30, there is an S5-extension of T including A. ∎

The main result concerning S5-non-monotonic logic is provided by the following theorem:

Theorem 4.34 (McDermott 1982) For any theory T, $TH_{S5}(T) = Th_{S5}(T)$.

Proof Obviously $Th_{S5}(T) \subseteq TH_{S5}(T)$.

To show that $TH_{S5}(T) \subseteq Th_{S5}(T)$, assume on the contrary that $A \in TH_{S5}(T)$ and $A \notin Th_{S5}(T)$. Consider two cases.
(1) $\neg A \in Th_{S5}(T)$. Then, since $Th_{S5}(T) \subseteq TH_{S5}(T)$ and $A \in TH_{S5}(T)$, $TH_{S5}(T)$ is S5-inconsistent. On the other hand, $A \notin Th_{S5}(T)$ implies that $Th_{S5}(T)$ is S5-consistent and so, by Corollary 4.32, $TH_{S5}(T)$ is S5-consistent. A contradiction.
(2) $\neg A \notin Th_{S5}(T)$. Then, $L\neg A \notin Th_{S5}(T)$ and thus $T \cup \{ML\neg A\}$ is S5-consistent, by Theorem 4.29. Hence, by Theorem 4.33, there is an S5-extension of T, say S, such that $ML\neg A \in S$. So, since $S = Th_{S5}(S)$ and $\vdash_{S5} ML\neg A \supset \neg A$, we have $\neg A \in S$. Since T is S5-consistent, S is also S5-consistent. Thus, $A \notin S$ and so, $A \notin TH_{S5}(T)$. A contradiction. ∎

In view of this result, S5-non-monotonic logic collapses to a monotonic S5 modal system. For this reason McDermott falls back to S4 and T versions of non-monotonic logic. Unfortunately, these versions have their own peculiarities. In particular, as we shall see, neither T- nor S4-extensions are assured to exist.

As remarked in the previous section, McDermott and Doyle's non-monotonic logic lacks satisfactory semantics. This weakness is partially rectified in McDermott's systems, where extensions are given Kripke-style semantic characterization. The details follow.†

The semantics provided by McDermott is based on possible-world semantics for standard first-order modal logic (see section 1.6.2). We begin with some preliminary notions.

Let $M = \langle D, W, R, m \rangle$ be a frame for modal first-order language L. We say that a sentence $A \in L$ is *satisfiable in* M *by* $w \in W$, written $M \models_w A$ iff $V_w^M(A) = 1$. (Notice that an assignment to variables is irrelevant here because A is a sentence.) A is said to be *satisfiable in* M iff $M \models_w A$, for some $w \in W$. We write $M \models A$ to indicate that A is *true in* M, i.e. $M \models_w A$, for all $w \in W$. We write ASSUMPT(M) to denote the set of all assumptions, i.e. sentences of the form MA, which are true in M.

Definition 4.35 (McDermott 1982) Let M be a (T-, S4-, S5-) model of a theory T. We say that M is a (T-, S4- S5-) *non-committal model of* T iff, for every sentence $A \in L_T$, $M \models MA$ whenever A is satisfiable in some (T, S4, S5-) model of $T \cup$ ASSUMPT(M). ∎

Intuitively, a model M is non-committal if it assures the truth of any assumption MA unless $\neg A$ is true in every model of $T \cup$ ASSUMPT(M).

Example 4.36 Let $T = \{Mp \supset p\}$. Assume that L_T is a sentential language including p as its only proposition constant. Let M be the model of T such that $W = \{w_1\}$, $R = \{\langle w_1, w_1 \rangle\}$ and $m(p, w_1) = 1$. M is an S4-non-committal model of T. To show this, take any S4-model M_1 of $T \cup$ ASSUMPT(M). Since $Mp \in$ ASSUMPT(M), we have $M_1 \models Mp$ and so, $M_1 \models p$ (because $Mp \supset p$ is in T). Thus, since p is the only proposition constant in L_T, any formula which is satisfiable in M_1 is true in M_1. So, because M_1 is a model of $T \cup$ ASSUMPT(M) and M is a model of T, any formula which is satisfiable in M_1 must be true in M. In consequence, M is an S4-non-committal model of T. The same argument can be used to show that M is also a (T-, S5-) non-committal model of T.

† For the sake of simplicity, we slightly change McDermott's original presentation.

Now, let M_2 be the S4-model of T such that $W = \{w_1\}$, $R = \{\langle w_1, w_1\rangle\}$ and $m(p, w_1) = 0$. M_2 is not an S4-non-committal model of T. To see this, consider the S4-modal frame M_3 such that:

$$W = \{w_1, w_2\}; \qquad R = \{\langle w_1, w_1\rangle, \langle w_2, w_2\rangle, \langle w_1, w_2\rangle\};$$
$$m(p, w_1) = 1; \qquad m(p, w_2) = 0$$

It is easily verified that M_3 is an S4-model of $T \cup \text{ASSUMPT}(M_2)$ and $M_3 \models_{w_1} p$. Thus, if M_2 were an S4-non-committal model of T, Mp would be true in M_2. Since Mp is not true in M_2, M_2 is not an S4-non-committal model of T. The same argument shows that M_2 is not a T-non-committal model of T. The reader may check that M_2 is an S5-non-committal model of T. ▮

Non-committal models characterize extensions:

Theorem 4.37 (McDermott 1982) M is a (T-, S4-, S5-) model of a (T-, S4-, S5-) extension of T iff M is a (T-, S4-, S5-) non-committal model of T.

Proof Through this proof we omit prefixes (T-, S4-, S5-).

Assume first that M is a model of an extension S. Let M′ be a model of $T \cup \text{ASSUMPT}(M)$ such that $V_w^{M'}(A) = 1$, for some sentence $A \in L_T$. So, by Soundness Theorem for modal logic (Theorem 1.106), $T \cup \text{ASSUMPT}(M) \nvdash \neg A$. Thus, since S is an extension and M is a model of S, $MA \in S$ and, consequently, $M \models MA$. So, M is non-committal.

Assume now that M is a non-committal model of T. To show that M is a model of an extension of T, it suffices to prove that $\text{Th}(T \cup \text{ASSUMPT}(M))$ is an extension of T, i.e.

$$\text{Th}(T \cup \text{ASSUMPT}(M)) = \\ \text{Th}(T \cup \{MA\text{: } A \text{ is closed and } \neg A \notin \text{Th}(T \cup \text{ASSUMPT}(M))\})$$

Obviously, this will be proved if we show

$$\text{ASSUMPT}(M) = \{MA\text{: } A \text{ is closed and } \neg A \notin \text{Th}(T \cup \text{ASSUMPT}(M))\}$$

which is left to the reader as an exercise. ▮

Corollary 4.38 For any $X \in \{T, S4, S5\}$, $A \in \text{TH}_X(T)$ iff A is true in all X-non-committal models of T. ▮

Example 4.39 We use these results to show that the theory $T = \{LMp \supset \neg p\}$ has neither a T- nor an S4-extension. We first show the following: if M is a (T-, S4-) non-committal model of T, then Mp is true in M. Let W_M and R_M be the set of possible worlds and the accessibility relation of M, respectively. Assume that $w_0 \notin W_M$. Consider a (T-, S4-) modal frame M_1 satisfying:

$$W_{M_1} = W_M \cup \{w_0\}; \qquad R_{M_1} = R_M \cup \{(w_0, w)\text{: } w \in W_M\}; \qquad m(p, w_0) = 1.$$

It is easily checked that M_1 is a (T-, S4-) model of $T \cup \text{ASSUMPT}(M)$. Thus, since M is non-committal and $M_1 \models_{w_0} p$, Mp is true in M.

Given this result, it is easily verified that T has no (T-, S4-) non-committal models. Indeed, assume that M is such a model. Since $M \models Mp$, then $M \models LMp$. But M is a model of T. Thus, $M \models \neg p$. A contradiction.

Now, in view of Corollary 4.38, $\text{TH}_{(T,S4)}$ is (T-, S4-) inconsistent. But T is (T-, S4-) consistent. So, by Corollary 4.22, T lacks a (T-, S4-) extension. ▮

The problem with this semantics is that it provides no satisfactory meaning of formulae of the form MA. This is discussed in Turner (1984):

'... I believe that there is an even more fundamental problem with McDermott's approach. What is the intended interpretation of the operator M? ... According to the semantic clause, MA is true at a world w, just in case A is true at some world accessible to w. But what are we to intuitively understand by "accessible" here? ... If possible worlds are "complete states of affairs", no two distinct worlds can be considered "consistent" in any obvious sense. It really is quite difficult to grasp what intuitions McDermott is appealing to. Perhaps there are not meant to be any, and all of McDermott's semantics is no more than a formal device to define precisely the nature of non-monotonic reasoning. But, if so, this is indefensible. Any semantic theory worthy of its name must capture some underlying intuitions which relate in some way to our primitive understanding of the constructs of the language.'

Not denying all this, we think that McDermott's proposal can be partially defended if taken at its real value – not as a semantics of non-monotonic logic, but rather as a semantic characterization of extensions, specified in terms of restrictions on standard Kripke models. True, such a characterization does not provide a satisfactory meaning of the operator M, and so may be uninteresting to philosophers. However, it does provide us with an alternative view of extensions, which are not easy to comprehend.

Obviously, McDermott's non-monotonic logics are much more interesting than McDermott and Doyle's earlier developments. However, they are not free of their own problems.

First, the collapse of non-monotonic S5 into monotonic S5 forced McDermott to base non-monotonic logic on weaker modal systems. This is unjustified in the context of his own claim that the characteristic axiom of S5, i.e. M$A \supset$ LMA, should be considered valid in any non-monotonic logic based on the concept of 'consistency' (McDermott 1982, p. 35).

Second, although non-monotonic T and S4 avoid the collapse, they raise doubts about their consistency. McDermott offers no proof that the theory $T = \{\ \}$ is (T-, S4-) consistent in the framework of first-order non-monotonic logic. Clearly, such proofs are crucial if first-order non-monotonic T and S4 are to be viewed seriously.[†]

This completes our basic presentation of McDermott's modal non-monotonic logics. We shall return to these formalisms, as well as to McDermott and Doyle's earlier proposal, in section 4.3.7.

4.3 AUTOEPISTEMIC LOGIC

One of the most interesting contributions to the subject of non-monotonic reasoning is *autoepistemic logic*. This formalism was developed by Robert Moore (1983; 1984) to be a reconstruction of McDermott and Doyle's earlier proposals.

4.3.1 Preliminaries

Moore starts his presentation by analysing what kind of inference modal non-monotonic logic is intended to model. In contrast to McDermott and Doyle, who

[†] Actually, McDermott shows the consistency of this theory for propositional S4. A similar argument allows to conclude its consistency in sentential T (see McDermott 1982, pp. 45–50).

claim that their formalisms model default reasoning, he argues convincingly that the logic deals with autoepistemic reasoning. To illustrate this, consider the sentence

$$\forall x . Child(x) \wedge \mathrm{M} Has\text{-}Parents(x) \supset Has\text{-}Parents(x). \tag{4.3.1}$$

If M is interpreted as 'It is consistent to believe', the sentence has the following reading: 'For each x, if x is a child and it is consistent to believe that x has parents, then x has parents'. Since the proposition that x has parents can be consistently believed if and only if its negation is not believed, what the sentence really says is that the only children that have no parents are the ones that are believed not to have. Read in this way, (4.3.1) should not be considered as a form of default reasoning. We cannot accept the reading simply because the typical child has parents. To accept it, we must believe that we know all the instances of children that have no parents. Clearly, then, (4.3.1) represents autoepistemic inference.

Although Moore is right in claiming that modal non-monotonic logic models autoepistemic reasoning, it is not inappropriate to use it for the purpose of formalizing default reasoning. Obviously, the real difference between these types of inference manifests itself on the philosophical level only. From the technical point of view, both autoepistemic reasoning and default reasoning should be considered as the drawing of conclusions in the absence of some specific information. In fact, if we are prepared to infer that Joe has parents, simply because there is no evidence to the contrary, it is technically unimportant whether this conclusion is based on the observation that the typical child has parents or on our subjective opinion that we know all the instances of children who have no parents.

4.3.2 Semantic considerations

The language of autoepistemic logic is that of modal logic, i.e. the classical language supplied with the operators 'M' and 'L'. In autoepistemic logic, 'L' (read 'It is believed') is taken as the primitive operator, whereas 'M' (read 'It is consistent to believe') is an abbreviation for '$\neg \mathrm{L} \neg$'.

Following Moore, we restrict our attention to propositional autoepistemic logic. However, its first-order counterpart is easily obtainable, provided that no open formulae occur within the scope of modal operators (more on this generalization in section 4.3.8).

The objects we shall be primarily interested in are sets of formulae, selected from the language under consideration L, referred to as *belief sets*. Intuitively, such a set is to be viewed as the total collection of beliefs of an agent reasoning about his own beliefs.†

Our first task is to provide a model-theoretic semantics for autoepistemic logic. We proceed in the usual way, first specifying the notion of an interpretation and then defining the truth-value of a formula in such an interpretation.

In classical propositional logic, the truth-value of a formula entirely depends on the truth-values of the proposition constants it includes. Accordingly, classical propositional interpretations are identified with assignments of truth-values to proposition constants. In autoepistemic logic this simple schema does not work, because there is no systematic connection between the truth of a formula A and formulae of the form $\mathrm{M}A$ and $\mathrm{L}A$. Surely, if $\mathrm{L}A$ is to be interpreted as 'A is believed', the

† To make this chapter terminologically uniform, I sometimes change Moore's original terminology. In particular, belief sets are called by him *autoepistemic theories*.

truth-value of LA depends upon whether A is indeed believed. Similarly, the value of MA depends on whether A is consistent with what is believed. To capture this intuition, modalized formulae must be evaluated with respect to a belief set. Accordingly, such a set should be included in any autoepistemic interpretation.

Definition 4.40 An *autoepistemic interpretation* (*AE interpretation*) *for L* is a pair $V = \langle m, S \rangle$, where m is an assignment of truth-values to proposition constants occurring in L and $S \subseteq L$ is a belief set. Such an interpretation will be usually referred to as an *autoepistemic interpretation of S*. ▮

Intuitively, an AE interpretation $\langle m, S \rangle$ may be considered as a description of a particular world, together with an agent situated in it: m specifies what is actually true in the world, whereas S determines what the agent actually believes.

Definition 4.41 Let $V = \langle m, S \rangle$ be an AE interpretation. The *value of a formula A in* V, denoted by V(A), is a truth-value specified by the following rules:

(1) $V(p) = m(p)$, if p is a proposition constant;
(2) $V(\neg B) = 1$ iff $V(B) = 0$;
(3) $V(B \supset C) = 1$ iff $V(B) = 0$ or $V(C) = 1$;
(4) $V(LB) = 1$ iff $B \in S$.†

▮

Definition 4.42 Let $V = \langle m, S \rangle$ be an AE interpretation of S and suppose that X is a set of formulae. V is an *autoepistemic model* (*AE model*) of X iff $V(A) = 1$, for each $A \in X$. We shall write $X \models_S A$ to indicate that a formula A is true in every AE interpretation of S which is an AE model of X. ▮

Example 4.43 Consider an AE interpretation $V = \langle m, S \rangle$, where $m(p) = m(q) = 1$ and $S = \{p, Lp, Lq\}$. We have: $V(p) = V(q) = 1$, $V(Lp) = 1$, $V(Lq) = 0$. Thus, V is not an AE model of S. However, V is an AE model of $\{q, p, Lp\}$. ▮

With this semantics in mind, we are now in a position to consider the notion of inference in autoepistemic logic. The question we are concerned with is the following: what beliefs an ideally rational agent should accept on the basis of an initial set of his premisses? To be in accord with our earlier terminology, we refer to sets of premisses as (*autoepistemic*) *theories*. Similarly, a belief set of an ideally rational agent, whose initial set of premisses is T, will be called an *extension* of T.‡ As usual, we shall write L_T to denote the language of a theory T.

Moore argues that there are two semantic constraints that have to be put on a belief set S of an ideally rational agent reasoning on the basis of a set of premisses T. First, S should be *sound* with respect to T: the truth of the premisses must guarantee the truth of the beliefs. Second, S ought to be *semantically complete*: it must include every formula that the agent is semantically justified to conclude on the basis that all his beliefs are true.

Definition 4.44 A belief set S is *sound with respect to a theory T* iff every AE interpretation of S which is an AE model of T is also an AE model of S. ▮

This notion of soundness indeed captures its intended meaning. Let $V = \langle m, S \rangle$ be an AE interpretation, where m describes what is true in the actual world and S is a belief

† Since MB is regarded as an abbreviation for $\neg L \neg B$, we immediately have: $V(MB) = 1$ iff $\neg B \notin S$.
‡ A *stable expansion* in Moore's original terminology.

set of an agent situated in the world. If all the beliefs of S are true in every AE interpretation in which all the premisses of T are true, then all the beliefs of S must be true in V, provided that all the premisses are true in V. Thus, the truth of the agent's premisses in the actual world guarantees the truth of his beliefs in the world.

Definition 4.45 A belief set S is *semantically complete* iff S contains any formula A, provided that A is true in every AE interpretation of S which is an AE model of S. ∎

If a formula A is true in every AE model of an agent's belief set, then, no matter what the actual world looks like, A must be true in it, provided that all the agent's beliefs are true. Thus, the agent is semantically justified in concluding A and so, he should include it into his belief set.

Our discussion motivates the following definition.

Definition 4.46 A belief set $S \subseteq L_T$ is an AE *extension of T* iff
(1) S is sound with respect to T;
(2) S is semantically complete;
(3) $T \subseteq S$.
∎

As we shall see, the notion of an AE extension can be given a number of alternative characterizations. The following is due to Konolige (1988).

Theorem 4.47 A set S is an AE extension of T iff

$$S = \{A \in L_T\colon T \models_S A\}$$

Proof Assume first that S is an AE extension of T. Since S is sound with respect to T, we immediately have $S \subseteq \{A \in L_T\colon T \models_S A\}$. By semantic completeness of S, we infer that $\{A \in L_T\colon S \models_S A\} \subseteq S$. Since $T \subseteq S$, every AE interpretation of S which is an AE model of S is also an AE model of T. Thus, $\{A \in L_T\colon T \models_S A\} \subseteq \{A \in L_T\colon S \models_S A\}$ and so, $\{A \in L_T\colon T \models_S A\} \subseteq S$. In conclusion, $S = \{A \in L_T\colon T \models_S A\}$.

Assume now that $S = \{A \in L_T\colon T \models_S A\}$. $S \subseteq \{A \in L_T\colon T \models_S A\}$ implies that every AE interpretation of S which is an AE model of T is also an AE model of S. Hence S is sound with respect to T. Obviously, $T \models_S A$, for each $A \in T$. So, $\{A \in L_T\colon T \models_S A\} \subseteq S$ implies that $T \subseteq S$. Finally, let A be true in every AE interpretation of S which is an AE model of S. Then, since S is sound with respect to T, A must be true in every AE interpretation of S which is an AE model of T, i.e. $T \models_S A$. Thus $A \in S$, by $\{A \in L_T\colon T \models_S A\} \subseteq S$ and so, S is semantically complete. In conclusion, S is sound with respect to T, $T \subseteq S$ and S is semantically complete. Therefore, S is an AE extension of T. ∎

Neither Definition 4.46 nor Theorem 4.47 provide a convenient method of finding AE extensions. However, the theorem can be used to show that a particular theory lacks an AE extension.

Example 4.48 Let $T = \{Lp\}$. T has no AE extension. To show this, assume that S is an AE extension of T, i.e. $S = \{A\colon T \models_S A\}$, and consider two cases:
(1) $p \notin S$. Then there is no AE interpretation of S which is an AE model of $\{Lp\}$. Thus $\{Lp\} \models_S A$, for any $A \in L_T$, and so, $S = L_T$. This contradicts $p \notin S$.
(2) $p \in S$. Consider the AE interpretation $V = \langle m, S \rangle$, where $m(p) = 0$. Clearly, $V(Lp) = 1$ and $V(p) = 0$. So it cannot be that $\{Lp\} \models_S p$ and thus, $p \notin S$. A contradiction.
∎

4.3.3 Syntactic characterization of AE extensions

Having specified the notion of an extension semantically, we now proceed to give its syntactic characterization. In what follows, 'Th' and '$\vdash$' ('$\nvdash$') denote the provability operator and the provability (unprovability) relation of classical propositional logic, respectively.

Notice that any language of propositional modal logic (with L as its primitive modal operator) may be viewed as a language of standard propositional logic, provided that all formulae of the form LA are treated as proposition constants. This justifies the following notions.

A *propositional interpretation for* L is any function mp from $\{p: p$ is a proposition constant of $L\} \cup \{\mathrm{L}A: A \in L\} \rightarrow \{0, 1\}$.

By $\mathrm{V}^{\mathrm{mp}}(A)$ we denote the *value of* A in mp. This is defined by the usual rules for propositional logic, together with the rule:

$$\mathrm{V}^{\mathrm{mp}}(\mathrm{L}A) = \mathrm{mp}(\mathrm{L}A).$$

A propositional interpretation mp is called a *propositional model of* T iff $\mathrm{V}^{\mathrm{mp}}(A) = 1$, for each $A \in T$. We write $T \models A$ to point out that a formula A is true in every propositional model of T.

The following facts will be used in many arguments:

Theorem 4.49 For each $T \subseteq L_{\mathrm{T}}$ and each $A \in L_{\mathrm{T}}$:

(1) $T \vdash A$ iff $T \models A$;
(2) T is consistent iff there exists a propositional model of T;
(3) If all formulae of T are true in an AE interpretation V and $T \vdash A$, then A is true in V.

Proof (1) follows from soundness and completeness of standard propositional logic. (2) is an immediate consequence of (1). (3) follows from (1) and the following fact: for each $A \in L_{\mathrm{T}}$ and each AE interpretation $\mathrm{V} = \langle \mathrm{m}, \mathrm{S} \rangle$, $\mathrm{V}(A) = \mathrm{V}^{\mathrm{mp}}(A)$, where mp is a propositional interpretation for L_{T} such that:

$$\mathrm{mp}(p) = \mathrm{m}(p), \text{ for each proposition constant } p \in L_{\mathrm{T}};$$
$$\mathrm{mp}(\mathrm{L}B) = \mathrm{V}(\mathrm{L}B), \text{ for each } B \in L_{\mathrm{T}}.$$

∎

Definition 4.50 A belief set S is *stable* iff it satisfies the following conditions:

(ST1) $\mathrm{S} = \mathrm{Th}(\mathrm{S})$;
(ST2) If $A \in \mathrm{S}$, then $\mathrm{L}A \in \mathrm{S}$;
(ST3) If $A \notin \mathrm{S}$, then $\neg \mathrm{L}A \in \mathrm{S}$ (equivalently, $\mathrm{M}\neg A \in \mathrm{S}$).

∎

The notion of a stable belief set was introduced in Stalnaker (1980). Such a set may be considered as a syntactic description of a belief state of an ideally rational agent reflecting upon his beliefs. (ST1) assures that the agent is able to perform all ordinary inferences, whereas (ST2) and (ST3) guarantee that he is perfectly aware of both what he believes and what he disbelieves.

Theorem 4.51 Every stable belief set S enjoys the following properties:

(ST4) If $LA \in S$, then $A \in S$;
(ST5) If $\neg LA \in S$, then $A \notin S$, provided that S is consistent;
(ST6) $LA \vee B \in S$ iff $A \in S$ or $B \in S$;
(ST7) $\neg LA \vee B \in S$ iff $A \notin S$ or $B \in S$;
(ST8) $\neg LA \vee LB_1 \vee \cdots \vee LB_k \vee C \in S$ iff $A \notin S$ or some of $B_i \in S$ $(1 \leq i \leq k)$ or $C \in S$.

Proof Left to the reader as an easy exercise. (ST6) and (ST7) were first observed by Halpern & Moses (1984). ∎

Stable belief sets play a crucial role in AE logic. To investigate their properties, we need the following preliminary terminology.

A formula has a *modal depth* k $(k \geq 0)$ iff its modal operators are nested to a depth of k. For instance, the modal depth of $L(Mp \supset LMp)$ is 3. The modal depth of A will be denoted by m-depth(A).

If L is a language, then we write $L(k)$ to denote those formulae from L whose modal depth is at most k. If $S \subseteq L$, then S_k stands for $S \cap L(k)$. S_k is then the set of all formulae of S whose modal depth is k or less.

A is an *objective formulae*, if m-depth$(A) = 0$. Objective formulae are then those containing no modal operators.

If $S \subseteq L$, then we write **LS** to denote the set $\{LA: A \in S\}$. $\neg\mathbf{L}\bar{\mathbf{S}}$ and $\neg\mathbf{L}\bar{\mathbf{S}}_k$ stand for the sets $\{\neg LA: A \in L - S\}$ and $\{\neg LA: A \in L(k) - S_k\}$, respectively.

We say that a formula A is in *normal form* iff $A = \bigwedge_{i=1}^{n} C_i$, where each C_i is a disjunction (possibly degenerate) of the form

$$A_1^i \vee LA_2^i \vee \cdots \vee LA_k^i \vee \neg LA_{k+1}^i \vee \cdots \vee \neg LA_{k+r}^i$$

with A_1^i objective.

We shall need the following fact:

Theorem 4.52 For any formula A, there is a formula A' such that A' is in normal form, $\vdash A \equiv A'$, and m-depth$(A) =$ m-depth(A').†

Proof Without loss of generality we may assume that A does not contain the operator M (otherwise, replace every MB by $\neg L \neg B$). As we know from Chapter 1 (see Theorem 1.7), every formula of classical propositional logic may be transformed into its equivalent of the form $\bigwedge_{i=1}^{n} C_i$, where all C_i's are disjunctions of proposition constants and/or their negations. Thus, regarding all subformulae of A of the form LB as proposition constants, we infer that A can be transformed into A' such that $\vdash A \equiv A'$ and $A' = \bigwedge_{i=1}^{n} C_i$, where each C_i is of the form

$$A_1^i \vee LA_2^i \vee \cdots \vee LA_k^i \vee \neg LA_{k+1}^i \vee \cdots \vee \neg LA_{k+r}^i$$

with A_i objective. Obviously, m-depth $(A') =$ m-depth(A). ∎

† A' will be referred to as a normal form of A.

Corollary 4.53 Let S be a set of formulae such that $S = Th(S)$ and suppose that A' is a normal form of A. Then:

(1) $A \in S$ iff $A' \in S$.
(2) $A \in S_i$ iff $A' \in S_i$, for all $i \geq 0$.

▮

Stable belief sets have a number of interesting properties. We begin by showing that each such a set is entirely determined by its objective formulae. More precisely:

Theorem 4.54 (Moore 1983) Two stable belief sets containing the same objective formulae are identical.

Proof Let $S \subseteq L$ and $S' \subseteq L$ be stable belief sets such that $S_0 = S'_0$. If $S = L$, then $S_0 = L(0)$. Thus, $S'_0 = L(0)$ and so, $S' = L$. Similarly, if $S' = L$, then $S = L$. Therefore, we may assume that S and S′ are both consistent.

Lemma 4.54.1 For all $i \geq 0$, $S_i = S'_i$.

Proof Induction on i. Trivially, $S_0 = S'_0$. Assume that $S_i = S'_i$, for all $i \leq l$.

We first show that $A \in S_{l+1}$ implies $A \in S'_{l+1}$. By virtue of Corollary 4.53, we may assume that $A = \bigwedge_{i=1}^{n} C_i$, where each C_i is of the form

$$A_1^i \vee LA_2^i \vee \cdots \vee LA_k^i \vee \neg LA_{k+1}^i \vee \cdots \vee \neg LA_{k+r}^i$$

with A_1^i objective. Clearly, m-depth$(C_i) \leq l + 1$ $(i = 1, \ldots, n)$.

For each C_i consider three cases.

Case 1 $LA_j^i \in S$, for some $2 \leq j \leq k$.
Then, by the stability condition (ST4), $A_j^i \in S$. Since m-depth$(C_i) \leq l + 1$, m-depth$(A_j^i) \leq l$. So, $A_j^i \in S_l$ and thus, $A_j^i \in S'_l \subseteq S'$, by induction hypothesis. Consequently, $LA_j^i \in S'$, by (ST2). But C_i is a tautological consequence of LA_j^i and thus $C_i \in S'$.

Case 2 $\neg LA_j^i \in S$, for some $k + 1 \leq j \leq k + r$.
Then, since S is consistent, $A_j^i \notin S$, by (ST5). But m-depth$(A_j^i) \leq l$. So, $A_j^i \notin S_l$. By induction hypothesis, we therefore infer that $A_j^i \notin S'_l$. Thus, since m-depth$(A_j^i) \leq l$, $A_j^i \notin S'$ and so, $\neg LA_j^i \in S'$, by (ST3). But C_i is a tautological consequence of $\neg LA_j^i$ and hence, $C_i \in S'$.

Case 3 Neither of the previous cases holds.
By (ST2) and (ST3), either $LA \in S$ or $\neg LA \in S$, for each $A \in L$. So, if neither of $LA_2^i, \ldots, LA_k^i, \neg LA_{k+1}^i, \ldots, \neg LA_{k+r}^i$ is in S, S must contain $\neg LA_2^i, \ldots, \neg LA_k^i$, $LA_{k+1}^i, \ldots, LA_{k+r}^i$. But A_1^i is a tautological consequence of these formulae and C_i, so that $A_1^i \in S$. Therefore, since A_1^i is objective, $A_1^i \in S'$. So, because C_i is a tautological consequence of A_1^i, $C_i \in S'$.

We have shown that all C_i's are in S'. This obviously implies that $A \in S'$ and so, since m-depth$(A) \leq l + 1$, we conclude that $A \in S'_{l+1}$.

The same argument can be used to show that $A \in S'_{l+1}$ implies $A \in S_{l+1}$. ■

Given the lemma, the proof of the theorem is straightforward. ▮

The next theorem shows that no stable belief set can be consistently extended to another such a set.

Theorem 4.55 If $S \subseteq L$ and $S' \subseteq L$ are consistent stable belief sets and $S \subseteq S'$, then $S = S'$.

Proof Assume to the contrary that $S \neq S'$. Thus, since $S \subseteq S'$, there is a formula $A \in L$ such that $A \in S'$ and $A \notin S$. By (ST3), $A \notin S$ implies $\neg LA \in S$ and hence, $\neg LA \in S'$. By (ST2), $A \in S'$ implies $LA \in S'$. So S' is inconsistent. A contradiction. ∎

The next theorem provides an explicit construction of a stable belief set out of its objective formulae.

Theorem 4.56 (Marek 1985) Let $X_0 \subseteq L(0)$ be a deductively closed set of objective formulae, i.e. $[Th(X_0)]_0 = X_0$, and suppose that

$$Z(X_0) = \bigcup_{i=0}^{\infty} S^i, \text{ where}$$

$$S^0 = X_0, \text{ and for } i = 0, 1, \ldots$$
$$S^{i+1} = [Th(S^i \cup \{LA: A \in S^i\} \cup \{\neg LA: A \in L(i) - S^i\})]_{i+1}.$$

Then:

(1) $Z(X_0)$ is consistent iff X_0 is consistent;
(2) $Z(X_0)$ is a stable belief set such that $[Z(X_0)]_0 = X_0$.

Proof

(1) Obviously, the consistency of $Z(X_0)$ implies the consistency of X_0. For the implication from right to left, assume that X_0 is consistent. Then, there is an interpretation m for $L(0)$, i.e. a truth-assignment to all the proposition constants of $L(0)$, under which all the formulae of X_0 are true. We extend m to a propositional interpretation mp for L:

$$mp(p) = m(p), \text{ for each proposition constant } p \in L$$
$$mp(LA) = 1 \text{ iff } LA \in Z(X_0).$$

It is easily verified that mp is well-defined and mp is a propositional model for $Z(X_0)$. Thus, by Theorem 4.49 (2), $Z(X_0)$ is consistent.

(2) We first show that $Z(X_0)$ is stable. (ST1) is straightforward. For the proof of (ST2), take any $A \in Z(X_0)$. Then $A \in S^m$, where $m = \text{m-depth}(A)$ and so, by the construction, $LA \in S^{m+1} \subseteq Z(X_0)$. To show (ST3), assume that $A \notin Z(X_0)$. Then $A \notin S^m$, where $m = \text{m-depth}(A)$. Thus, by the construction (notice that $S^i \subseteq L(i)$, for each $i \geq 0$), $\neg LA \in S^{m+1} \subseteq Z(X_0)$.

We now show that $X_0 = [Z(X_0)]_0$. Obviously, $X_0 \subseteq [Z(X_0)]_0$. To prove that $[Z(X_0)]_0 \subseteq X_0$, assume to the contrary that there is a formula $A \in [Z(X_0)]_0$ such that $A \notin X_0$. Then, since X_0 is deductively closed, there is, by completeness of standard propositional logic, a truth-assignment m to all proposition constants of L under which all formulae in X_0 are true and A is false. m can be extended to a propositional interpretation mp for L in which all formulae of $Z(X_0)$ are true (see the proof of (1)). So, A is true in mp. Since A is objective, its true-value is entirely determined by the truth-values assigned to proposition constants of L. Moreover, mp extends m, i.e. $mp(p) = m(p)$, for each proposition constant p of L. Therefore, since A is true in mp, A is true in m. A contradiction. ∎

Corollary 4.57 For any deductively closed set of objective formulae X_0, there is a unique stable belief set S such that $X_0 = S_0$. If X_0 is consistent, S is also consistent.

Proof Take $S = Z(X_0)$. ∎

The next theorem shows that any stable belief set is sound with respect to its objective formulae.

Theorem 4.58 (Moore 1983) If S is a stable belief set, then any AE interpretation of S in which all the formulae of S_0 are true is an AE model of S.

Proof Let $V = \langle m, S\rangle$ be an AE interpretation of S in which all the formulae of S_0 are true. Clearly, S must be consistent. Take any formula $A \in S$. We may assume that A is in normal form, i.e. $A = \bigwedge_{i=1}^{n} C_i$, where each C_i is of the form

$$A_1^i \vee LA_2^i \vee \cdots \vee LA_k^i \vee \neg LA_{k+1}^i \vee \cdots \vee \neg LA_{k+r}^i$$

with A_1^i objective. For each C_i consider two cases:

(1) At least one of $LA_2^i, \ldots, LA_k^i, \neg LA_{k+1}^i, \ldots, \neg LA_{k+r}^i$ is in S.
Then, since S is consistent and V is an AE interpretation of S, we conclude, by (ST4) and (ST5), that at least one of these formulae is true in V. But each of them entails C_i and so, C_i is true in V, by Theorem 4.49 (3).
(2) None of $LA_2^i, \ldots, LA_k^i, \neg LA_{k+1}^i, \ldots, \neg LA_{k+r}^i$ is in S.
Then, by the same argument as in the proof of Theorem 4.54 (Case 3), we infer that $A_1^i \in S$. Thus, since this formula is objective, it is true in V. But C_i is a tautological consequence of A_1^i and so, C_i is true in V, by Theorem 4.49 (3).

We have shown that all C_i are true in V. Because $A = \bigwedge_{i=1}^{n} C_i$, we therefore conclude that A is true in V. But A was chosen arbitrarily. So, V is an AE model of S. ∎

Given this result, we are now ready to show that stability is a syntactic counterpart of semantic completeness.

Theorem 4.59 (Moore 1983) A belief set is stable iff it is semantically complete.

Proof

(⇒) Assume that S is stable. We show that S is semantically complete by proving that if $A \notin S$, then A is false in some AE interpretation of S which is an AE model of S. Again, we may assume that $A = \bigwedge_{i=1}^{n} C_i$ where each C_i is of the form

$$A_1^i \vee LA_2^i \vee \cdots \vee LA_k^i \vee \neg LA_{k+1}^i \vee \cdots \vee \neg LA_{k+r}^i$$

with A_1^i objective. Since S is stable and $A \notin S$, at least one of $C_1, \ldots, C_n$ is not in S. Suppose that $C_i \notin S$. So, by (ST1), none of the disjuncts of C_i is in S.

> **Lemma 4.59.1** There is an AE interpretation V of S which is a model of S such that all the disjuncts of C_i are false in V.
>
> **Proof** Consider A_1^i. Since S is stable and $A_1^i \notin S$, A_1^i cannot be proved from S_0. Thus, by completeness of classical propositional logic, there is a truth-assignment to proposition constants, say m, in which all the formulae of S_0 are true and A_1^i is false (recall that A_1^i is objective). Let $V = \langle m, S\rangle$. Trivially, $V(A_1^i) = 0$ and $V(B) = 1$, for each $B \in S_0$. So, by Theorem 4.58, V is an AE model of S in which A_1^i is false.
>
> Consider now the other disjuncts of C_i. Given that none of them is in S, it is

easily verified, by (ST2) and (ST3), that all of them are false in any AE interpretation of S. In particular, they are all false in V. ■

Given the lemma, we immediately infer that A is false in V.

($\Leftarrow$) Assume that S is semantically complete. We show that S is stable by proving the conditions (ST1)–(ST3).

(ST1) Let $A_1, \ldots, A_n \in \mathrm{S}$ and $\{A_1, \ldots, A_n\} \vdash B$. Since all A_i's are true in all AE models of S, B must be also true in any such a model (by Theorem 4.49 (3)). So, by semantic completeness of S, $B \in \mathrm{S}$.

(ST3)–(ST3) Let $A \in \mathrm{S}$ (resp. $A \notin \mathrm{S}$). Then LA (resp. $\neg$LA) is true in any AE interpretation of S which is a model of S. So, by semantic completeness of S, L$A \in \mathrm{S}$ (resp. $\neg LA \in \mathrm{S}$). ■

Theorem 4.59 provides a partial syntactic characterization of AE extensions. To make this characterization complete, we need a syntactic counterpart of the notion of soundness.

Definition 4.60 A belief set S is *grounded in a theory T* iff $\mathrm{S} \subseteq \mathrm{Th}(T \cup \mathbf{L}\mathrm{S} \cup \neg\mathbf{L}\bar{\mathrm{S}})$. ■

Notice that groundedness guarantees that the only beliefs of an agent are his initial premisses and the propositions required by the stability conditions.

Theorem 4.61 (Moore 1983) A belief set $\mathrm{S} \subseteq L_{\mathrm{T}}$ is grounded in T iff it is sound with respect to T.

Proof

($\Rightarrow$) Assume that S is gounded in T. We show that S is sound with respect to T by taking any AE interpretation V of S in which all the formulae of T are true and showing that V is an AE model of S.

If $A \in T$, then trivially $\mathrm{V}(A) = 1$. If A is of the form LB (resp. $\neg$LB) and $B \in \mathrm{S}$ (resp. $B \notin \mathrm{S}$), then $\mathrm{V}(A) = 1$, by Definition 4.41. Thus, all the formulae of the set X, where $\mathrm{X} = T \cup \mathbf{L}\mathrm{S} \cup \neg\bar{\mathbf{L}}\mathrm{S}$, are true in V and so, all the formulae of Th(X) must be true in V, by Theorem 4.49 (3). But $\mathrm{S} \subseteq \mathrm{Th(X)}$ because S is grounded in T. Thus, all the formulae of S are true in V.

($\Leftarrow$) Assume that S is sound with respect to T. We prove that S is grounded in T by taking any $A \in \mathrm{S}$ and showing that $A \in \mathrm{Th(X)}$, where X is as before.

In view of Theorem 4.49 (1), it suffices to prove that A is true in every propositional model for X. Let mp be such a model. Take $\mathrm{V} = \langle \mathrm{m}, \mathrm{S} \rangle$, where $\mathrm{m}(p) = \mathrm{mp}(p)$, for each proposition constant $p \in L_{\mathrm{T}}$.

Lemma 4.61.1 For each $C \in L_{\mathrm{T}}$, $\mathrm{V}(C) = \mathrm{V}^{\mathrm{mp}}(C)$.

Proof Straightforward induction on C. ■

Since mp is a propositional model for X and $T \subseteq \mathrm{X}$, $\mathrm{V}^{\mathrm{mp}}(C) = 1$, for each $C \in T$. Thus, by Lemma 4.61.1, $\mathrm{V}(C) = 1$, for each $C \in T$. So, since S is sound with respect to T, every formula of S is true in V. In particular, $\mathrm{V}(A) = 1$. Hence, $\mathrm{V}^{\mathrm{mp}}(A) = 1$, by Lemma 4.61.1. ■

Combining Theorems 4.59 and 4.61, we immediately obtain:

Theorem 4.62 A belief set S is an AE extension of T iff

(1) S is grounded in T;

(2) S is stable;
(3) $T \subseteq$ S.

▮

Corollary 4.63 No consistent AE extension properly includes other AE extension.

Proof By Theorems 4.55 and 4.62. ▮

Corollary 4.64 A set S is an AE extension of T iff

$$\mathrm{S} = \mathrm{Th}(T \cup \mathbf{L}\mathrm{S} \cup \neg \mathbf{L}\bar{\mathrm{S}}).^{\dagger}$$

Proof By Theorem 4.62 and Definition 4.60 ▮

Corollary 4.65 A set S is an AE extension of T iff

$$\mathrm{S} = \{A\colon T \cup \mathbf{L}\mathrm{S} \cup \neg \mathbf{L}\bar{\mathrm{S}} \models A\}.$$

Proof By Corollary 4.64 and Theorem 4.49 (1). ▮

Corollary 4.65 provides another semantic characterization of AE extensions. In contrast to that from Theorem 4.47, the new characterization is based on the classical validity relation '$\vdash$'. However, since '$\models$' is stronger than '$\models_{\mathrm{S}}$' ($T \models A$ implies $T \models_{\mathrm{S}} A$, but not vice versa), autoepistemic models of T have to be replaced by propositional models of $T \cup \mathbf{L}\mathrm{S} \cup \neg \mathbf{L}\bar{\mathrm{S}}$. It is not difficult to see why this works. The key point is that if mp is a propositional model of $T \cup \mathbf{L}\mathrm{S} \cup \neg \mathbf{L}\bar{\mathrm{S}}$, then mp(L$A$) = 1 iff $A \in$ S. This means that $T \models_{\mathrm{S}} A$ iff $T \cup \mathbf{L}\mathrm{S} \cup \neg \mathbf{L}\bar{\mathrm{S}} \models A$, so that $\{A\colon T \models_{\mathrm{S}} A\} = \{A\colon T \cup \mathbf{L}\mathrm{S} \cup \neg \mathbf{L}\bar{\mathrm{S}} \models A\}$.

Theorem 4.66 Any stable set S is the unique AE extension of S_0.

Proof Since each stable set is uniquely determined by its objective formulae, S is the unique stable set including S_0. Thus, in view of Theorem 5.56, S = Z(S_0). Inspecting the construction of Z(S_0), it is easily seen that Z(S_0), and hence S, is grounded in S_0. Therefore, by Theorem 4.62, S is the unique AE extension of S_0. ▮

A theory may have none (Example 4.48), one or several extensions.

Example 4.67 Let $T = \{\mathrm{M}p \supset p\}$. Assume that S is an AE extension of T. Since S must be grounded in T, $\mathrm{S}_0 = [\mathrm{Th}(\{\ \})]_0$ or $\mathrm{S}_0 = [\mathrm{Th}(\{p\})]_0$ (notice that L_{T} is not grounded in T). Thus, by Corollary 4.57, the only cadidates for AE extensions of T are S1 = Z($[\mathrm{Th}(\{\ \})]_0$) and S2 = Z($[\mathrm{Th}(\{p\})]_0$). Since S1 does not include T, it is not an AE extension of T. S2 is an AE extension of T: it is grounded in T, stable and contains $\mathrm{M}p \supset p$. ▮

Example 4.68 Let $T = \{\mathrm{M}p \supset \neg q;\ \mathrm{M}q \supset \neg p\}$. Since each AE extension of T must be grounded in T, the only candidates are:

$$\mathrm{S1} = \mathrm{Z}([\mathrm{Th}(\{\neg p\})]_0);$$
$$\mathrm{S2} = \mathrm{Z}([\mathrm{Th}(\{\neg q\})]_0);$$
$$S3 = \mathrm{Z}([\mathrm{Th}(\{\ \})]_0).$$

The reader may check that S1 and S2 are AE extensions of T. S3 is not an AE extension of T since T is not a subset of S3. ▮

There still remains the problem of specifying what is to be regarded as the set of theorems of a theory T, especially if T has none or several AE extensions. We could

† Observe that this can be equivalently stated as $\mathrm{S} = \mathrm{Th}(T \cup \{\mathrm{L}A\colon A \in \mathrm{S}\} \cup \{\mathrm{M}A\colon \neg A \notin \mathrm{S}\})$.

define this set in the manner of McDermott and Doyle, but Moore offers a different solution. Because AE extensions express complete belief sets, it is natural to view each such an extension as an alternative set of derivable theorems. This proposal may seem strange at first sight, but since it represents the point of view of a reasoning agent, it is in accord with the general philosophy of autoepistemic logic. As Moore points out, McDermott and Doyle's solution, although also reasonable, has a diffferent interpretation. It represents what an outside observer would know about the agent's beliefs, given only his set of premisses.

4.3.4 Possible-world semantics for autoepistemic logic

The semantics we have described in section 4.3.2 is sufficiently general to be applied to arbitrary belief sets. However, since autoepistemic logic has been designed to model the behaviour of ideally rational agents, it is primarily concerned with stable belief sets. It turns out that these sets can be semantically characterized by Kripke-style modal frames. Our subsequent presentation closely follows Moore (1984).

Modal frames we shall be interested in are S5 propositional frames in which every world is accessible from every world. These will be referred to as *complete* S5-*frames*.

Definition 4.69 A *complete* S5-*frame for* L is a pair $\langle \mathrm{W}, \mathrm{m}\rangle$, where W is a set of 'possible worlds' and m is a function which assigns to each pair, consisting of a proposition constant from L and an element of W, an element of $\{0, 1\}$.† ▮

Notice that we make no assumption that the set of possible worlds is non-empty. There is exactly one complete S5-frame corresponding to this set. It will be called the *empty frame* and denoted by $\mathrm{M}_{\perp}$.

The *value of a formula A in* $\mathrm{M} = \langle \mathrm{W}, \mathrm{m}\rangle$ *with respect to* $\mathrm{w} \in \mathrm{W}$, denoted by $\mathrm{V}^{\mathrm{M}}_{\mathrm{w}}(A)$, is specified in the usual way (see Chapter 1, Definition 1.94), taking into account the specific character of the accessibility relation. Thus, formulae of the form $\mathrm{L}A$ and $\mathrm{M}A$ are evaluated by the following rules:

$$\mathrm{V}^{\mathrm{M}}_{\mathrm{w}}(\mathrm{L}A) = 1 \quad \text{iff} \quad \mathrm{V}^{\mathrm{M}}_{\mathrm{w}'}(A) = 1, \text{ for all } \mathrm{w}' \in \mathrm{W}$$
$$\mathrm{V}^{\mathrm{M}}_{\mathrm{w}}(\mathrm{M}A) = 1 \quad \text{iff} \quad \mathrm{V}^{\mathrm{M}}_{\mathrm{w}'}(A) = 1, \text{ for some } \mathrm{w}' \in \mathrm{W}.$$

As usual, A is *true* in $\mathrm{M} = \langle \mathrm{W}, \mathrm{m}\rangle$, written $\mathrm{M} \models A$, iff $\mathrm{V}^{\mathrm{M}}_{\mathrm{w}}(A) = 1$, for all $\mathrm{w} \in \mathrm{W}$. Obviously, $\mathrm{M}_{\perp} \models A$, for each $A \in L$.

The key result is the following theorem:

Theorem 4.70 (Moore 1984)‡ A set of formulae $\mathrm{S} \subseteq L$ is stable iff S is the set of all formulae which are true in some complete S5-frame.

Proof The proof of the 'if part' of the theorem is left to the reader as an easy exercise. For the proof in the opposite direction, assume that S is stable. If $\mathrm{S} = L$, then all formulae of S are true in $\mathrm{M}_{\perp}$. So assume that S is consistent and consider the set $\mathscr{M}$ of all truth-assignments to proposition constants occurring in L in which all the formulae of S_0 are true. This is a non-empty set since S is consistent. Let M be a complete S5 frame in which each of these assignments specifies a possible world. More precisely, $\mathrm{M} = \langle \mathrm{W}, \mathrm{m}\rangle$, where $\mathrm{W} = \mathscr{M}$ and $\mathrm{m}(p, \mu) = \mu(p)$, for any proposition constant p and

† Since it is assumed that every world is accessible from every world, a complete S5-frame need not include the accessibility relation.

‡ This result was independently reported in Halpern & Moses (1984).

any $\mu \in \mathcal{M}$. Obviously, the set of all objective formulae which are true in M is exactly S_0. In view of the 'if-part' of this theorem, the set of all formulae which are true in M is stable. Call this set S′. By Theorem 4.54, S′ = S because S and S′ are stable sets containing the same objective formulae. Thus, S is the set of all formulae which are true in M. ▮

Corollary 4.71 If $S \subseteq L$ is a stable belief set, then $S = Th_{S5}(S)$.

Proof Since $L = Th_{S5}(L)$, we may assume that S is consistent. So, by Theorem 4.70, there is a complete S5 frame M, $M \neq M_{\perp}$, such that S is the set of all formulae which are true in M. Each complete S5-frame, different from $M_{\perp}$, is a modal S5 frame. Moreover, the set $Th_{S5}(S)$ is the set of all formulae which are true in every modal S5-frame of S (see Theorem 1.98, Chapter 1). So, if $A \in Th_{S5}(S)$, A must be true in M and thus, $Th_{S5}(S) \subseteq S$. Trivially, $S \subseteq Th_{S5}(S)$. Thus, $S = Th_{S5}(S)$. ▮

In virtue of Theorem 4.70, any AE interpretation of a stable belief set may be naturally viewed as a pair consisting of a truth-assignment to proposition constants (to specify what is true in a world) and a complete S5-frame (to determine a stable belief set of an agent situated in the world).

Definition 4.72 A *possible-world AE interpretation for L* is a pair $PV = \langle m_{PV}, M \rangle$, where m_{PV} is an assignment of truth-values to proposition constants of L and M is a complete S5 frame for L. We say that PV is a *possible-world interpretation of* S, if S is the set of all formulae which are true in M. ▮

To evaluate formulae in possible-world AE interpretations, we proceed as in the case of ordinary AE interpretations (see Definition 4.41), taking into account that belief sets are now determined by complete S5-frames.

Definition 4.73 Let $PV = \langle m_{PV}, M \rangle$ be a possible-world AE interpretation. The *value of A in* PV, written $PV(A)$, is a truth-value defined by the following rules:

(1) $PV(p) = m_{PV}(p)$ if p is a proposition constant;
(2) $PV(\neg B) = 1$ iff $PV(B) = 0$;
(3) $PV(B \supset C) = 1$ iff $PV(B) = 0$ or $PV(C) = 1$;
(4) $PV(LB) = 1$ iff $M \models LB$ (equivalently, iff $M \models B$.[†]

▮

Observe that a formula is true in $PV = \langle m_{PV}, M \rangle$ iff it is true according to standard rules of propositional logic, where proposition constants are evaluated by means of m_{PV} and formulae of the form LA are evaluated in M.

Definition 4.74 A possible-world AE interpretation of $S \subseteq L$ in which all the formulae of $X \subseteq L$ are true is called a *possible-world AE model of* X. ▮

In virtue of Theorem 4.70, it is clear that for each stable belief set S, there is a natural correspondence between AE interpretations of S and possible-world AE interpretations of S. Thus, by Definition 4.44 and Theorem 4.58, we immediately obtain the following result:

Theorem 4.75 If S is a stable belief set, then:

(1) S is sound with respect to T iff every possible-world AE interpretation of S in which all the formulae of T are true is a possible-world AE model of S.

[†] Notice that formulae of the form MB are evaluated by the rule: $PV(MB) = 1$ iff it is not the case that $M \models \neg B$.

(2) Any possible-world AE interpretation of S in which all the formulae of S_0 are true is a possible-world AE model of S.

∎

Following Moore (1984), we shall identify a possible world w of a complete S5-frame with a set U consisting of proposition constants and their negations. It is assumed that $p \in U$ if p is true in w and $\neg p \in U$ if p is false in w. For instance, the set $\{p, \neg q\}$ represents the world in which p is true and q is false.† Similarly, any truth-assignment m to proposition constants may be identified with such a set U. It is assumed that $p \in U$ if $m(p) = 1$ and $\neg p \in U$ if $m(p) = 0$. Under this interpretation, the set $\{p, \neg q\}$ represents the assignment m such that $m(p) = 1$ and $m(q) = 0$.

Example 4.76 Assume that p and q are the only proposition constants occurring in L. Consider the stable set $S \subseteq L$ determined by the complete S5-frame M consisting of exactly two worlds: $w = \{p, q\}$ and $w' = \{\neg p, \neg q\}$. Let $PV = \langle m_{PV}, M \rangle$, where $m_{PV} = \{p, \neg q\}$. We have:

$$PV(Mp) = 1; \qquad PV(\neg p \vee q) = 0; \qquad PV(Mp \supset (\neg p \vee q)) = 0.$$

Since $Mp \supset (\neg p \vee q) \in S$ (notice that this formula is true in M), PV is not a possible-world AE model of S. ∎

Definition 4.77 Let $PV = \langle m_{PV}, M \rangle$ be a possible-world AE interpretation. We say that m_{PV} is *compatible with* M iff m_{PV} is one of the worlds of M. ∎

Example 4.78 Let $PV = \langle m_{PV}, M \rangle$ be the possible-world AE interpretation from Example 4.76. m_{PV} is not compatible with M. Consider now the interpretation $PV' = \langle m'_{PV'}, M' \rangle$, where $m'_{PV'} = \{p, \neg q\}$; $M' = \{\{p, q\}, \{p, \neg q\}, \{\neg p, \neg q\}\}$. Clearly, $m'_{PV'}$ is compatible with M'. ∎

Theorem 4.79 (Moore 1984) Let $PV = \langle m_{PV}, M \rangle$ be a possible-world AE interpretation of $S \subseteq L$. Then:

(1) If m_{PV} is compatible with M, then PV is a possible-world AE model of S;
(2) If PV is a possible-world AE model of S, then m_{PV} is compatible with M, provided that there are only finitely many proposition constants occurring in L.

Proof (1) Assume that m_{PV} is compatible with M, i.e. $m_{PV} = w$, for some world w of M. Given this, it is easily verified (by induction on A) that $PV(A) = V^M_w(A)$, for each $A \in L$. Thus, since $M \models A$ implies $M^M_w(A) = 1$, $M \models A$ implies $PV(A) = 1$. So, PV is a possible-world AE model of S.

(2) Suppose that m_{PV} is not compatible with M. Then, for every world $w \in W$, there is a proposition constant, p_w, which is true in w (i.e. $p_w \in w$) and false in m_{PV} (i.e. $p_w \notin m_{PV}$), or vice versa. Let q_w be p_w if $p_w \in w$, and $\neg p_w$ otherwise. Since L includes a finite number of proposition constants, there are finitely many different worlds in M. In consequence, there are finitely many different q_w's. Let A be their disjunction. Clearly, A is true in M and A is false in PV. So, PV is not a possible-world AE model of S. ∎

Without the assumption that L includes finitely many proposition constants, (2) is no longer true. To show this, assume that there are infinitely many proposition constants in the language: $p_1, p_2, \ldots$, and suppose that $\mathcal{M}$ is the set of all truth-assignments to them. Consider the possible-world AE interpretation PV given by:

$$m_{PV} = \{p_1, p_2, \ldots\}; \qquad M = \mathcal{M} - \{m_{PV}\}.$$

† Note that under this convention, complete S5-frames may be identified with sets of their possible worlds.

Surely, m_{PV} is not compatible with M. However, as the reader may check, PV is a possible-world AE model for the set of formulae which are true in M. (Hint: show that the only objective formulae true in M are objective propositional tautologies and apply Theorem 4.75 (2).)

The possible-world semantics provides a convenient method for finding AE extensions of theories including finitely many proposition constants.

Example 4.80 Let $T = \{M(p \wedge q), \neg p\}$. We first show that L_T is an AE extension of T. Notice that $PV(M(p \wedge q)) = 0$, for any possible-world AE interpretation $PV = \langle m_{PV}, M_{\perp} \rangle$. This means that there is no possible-world AE interpretation of L_T in which the formulae of T are true. In consequence, by Theorem 4.75 (1), L_T is sound with respect to T. Thus, since L_T is stable and includes T, L_T is an AE extension of T.

To show that T lacks a consistent AE extension, assume to the contrary that S is such an AE extension. Since each AE extension is stable, there must be a complete S5 frame M such that S is the set of all formulae which are true in M. In particular, since each AE extension includes premisses, both $M(p \wedge q)$ and $\neg p$ must be true in M. This is possible only if M is the empty frame. But then, S is inconsistent. A contradiction. ▮

Example 4.81 Let $T = \{Mp \supset Lp\}$ and suppose that p is the only proposition constant of L_T. There are four different complete S5-frames which can be constructed over such a language and so there are four stable belief sets which should be considered as candidates for AE extensions of T:

(1) $S = L_T$. This set corresponds to the empty frame. It is easily checked that L_T is not an AE extension of T.

(2) Let S be the belief set specified by the complete S5 frame M which contains $\{p\}$ as its unique world. M gives rise to two possible-world AE interpretations of S:

$$PV = \{\{p\}, \{\{p\}\}\} \qquad \text{and} \qquad PV' = \{\{\neg p\}, \{\{p\}\}\}.$$

Since $\{\neg p\}$ is not compatible with $\{\{p\}\}$, PV′ is not a possible-world AE model of S, by Theorem 4.79. On the other hand, $Lp \supset Mp$ is true in PV′. So, in view of Theorem 4.75 (1), we infer that S is not sound with respect to T and consequently, S is not an AE extension of T.

(3) Let $S = \{A: M \models A\}$, where M is a complete S5 frame with $\{\neg p\}$ as its unique world. The only possible-world AE interpretations of S are

$$PV = \{\{p\}, \{\{\neg p\}\}\} \qquad \text{and} \qquad PV' = \{\{\neg p\}, \{\{\neg p\}\}\}.$$

It is seen immediately that $Mp \supset Lp$ is true in PV but PV is not a possible-world AE model of S. Thus, by the same argument as before, S is not an AE extension of T.

(4) Finally, let $S = \{A: M \models A\}$, where M contains exactly two worlds: $\{p\}$ and $\{\neg p\}$. Clearly, $Mp \supset Lp \notin S$ and so, S is no AE extension of T.

Since every complete S5-frame based on the language including p as its only proposition constant is equivalent to one of those we have considered, we conclude that T lacks an AE extension. ▮

Example 4.82 Let $T = \{Mp \supset q; M\neg q \supset \neg q\}$ and assume that p and q are the only proposition constants of L_T. Let S be the stable set determined by the complete

S5-frame M consisting of two worlds: $\{p, q\}$ and $\{\neg p, q\}$. By exhaustive enumeration, the reader may check that there are two possible-world AE interpretations of S in which $\mathrm{M}p \supset q$ and $\mathrm{M}\neg q \supset \neg q$ are both true:

$$\mathrm{PV} = \{\{p, q\}, \{\{p, q\}, \{\neg p, q\}\}\}; \qquad \mathrm{PV}' = \{\{\neg p, q\}, \{\{p, q\}, \{\neg p, q\}\}\}.$$

Since both $\{p, q\}$ and $\{\neg p, q\}$ are compatible with M, we infer that PV and PV′ are both possible-world AE models of S. Thus S is sound with respect to T. Since S is also stable and contains the premisses (notice that $\mathrm{M} \models \mathrm{M}p \supset q$ and $\mathrm{M} \models \mathrm{M}\neg q \supset \neg q$), S is an AE extension of T.

We leave it to the reader to show that S is the only AE extension of T. ∎

Example 4.83 Let $T = \{\mathrm{L}p \supset p\}$ and suppose that p is the only proposition constant of L_{T}. Like in Example 4.81, there are four cases to consider.

(1) $\mathrm{S} = L_{\mathrm{T}}$. It is easily checked that S is not an AE extension of T.

(2) Let $\mathrm{S1} = \{A: \mathrm{M1} \models A\}$, where M1 contains $\{p\}$ as its unique world. There is one possible-world AE interpretation of S1 in which $\mathrm{L}p \supset p$ is true. This is $\mathrm{PV} = \{\{p\}, \{\{p\}\}\}$. Since $\{p\}$ is compatible with M1, we infer that PV is a possible-world AE model of S1 and so S1 is sound with respect to T. Moreover, S1 is stable and includes $\mathrm{L}p \supset p$. Thus S1 is an AE extension of T.

(3) Let $\mathrm{S2} = \{A: \mathrm{M2} \models A\}$, where M2 contains two worlds: $\{p\}$ and $\{\neg p\}$. There are two possible-world AE interpretations of S2 in which $\mathrm{L}p \supset p$ is true:

$$\mathrm{PV} = \{\{p\}, \{\{p\}, \{\neg p\}\}\} \qquad \text{and} \qquad \mathrm{PV}' = \{\{\neg p\}, \{\{p\}, \{\neg p\}\}\}$$

Using the same argument as before, we easily infer that S2 is an AE extension of T.

(4) Let $\mathrm{S3} = \{A: \mathrm{M3} \models A\}$, where $\mathrm{M3} = \{\{\neg p\}\}$. There are two possible-world AE interpretations of S3 in which $\mathrm{L}p \supset p$ is true:

$$\mathrm{PV} = \{\{p\}, \{\{\neg p\}\}\} \qquad \text{and} \qquad \mathrm{PV}' = \{\{\neg p\}, \{\{\neg p\}\}\}$$

Since $\{p\}$ is not compatible with M3, S3 is not sound with respect to T. Consequently, S3 is not an AE extension of T.

In conclusion, $T = \{\mathrm{L}p \supset p\}$ has two AE extensions:

$$\mathrm{S1} = \{A: \mathrm{M1} \models A\}, \text{ where } \mathrm{M1} = \{\{p\}\} \quad \text{and}$$
$$\mathrm{S2} = \{A: \mathrm{M2} \models A\}, \text{ where } \mathrm{M2} = \{\{p\}, \{\neg p\}\}$$

$\mathrm{S1}_0 = [\mathrm{Th}(\{p\})]_0$; $\mathrm{S2}_0 = [\mathrm{Th}(\{\ \})]_0$; S1 contains p and $\mathrm{L}p$; S2 includes $\mathrm{M}p$ and $\mathrm{M}\neg p$. ∎

The possible-world semantics offers another semantic characterization of AE extensions. In the following, $\mathrm{X} \models_{\mathrm{PV}} A$ states that a formula A is true in every possible-world AE model of X. If $\mathrm{S} \subseteq L$, then we write $\mathbf{LS}_0$ and $\neg\mathbf{L}\bar{\mathrm{S}}_0$ to denote the sets $\{\mathrm{L}A: A \in \mathrm{S}_0\}$ and $\{\neg\mathrm{L}A: A \in L(0) - \mathrm{S}_0\}$, respectively.

Theorem 4.84† A set S is an AE extension of T iff

$$\mathrm{S} = \{A: T \cup \mathbf{LS}_0 \cup \neg\mathbf{L}\bar{\mathrm{S}}_0 \models_{\mathrm{PV}} A\} \tag{4.3.2}$$

† This result, in a slightly different but equivalent form, was given by Konolige (1988, Propositions 2.7 and 3.3).

Proof We first prove the following:

Lemma 4.84.1 If S is stable, then for each $A \in L$

$$T \models_S A \text{ iff } T \cup \mathbf{L}S_0 \cup \neg\mathbf{L}\bar{S}_0 \models_{PV} A$$

Proof If $\langle m_{PV}, M\rangle$ is a possible-world AE model of $T \cup \mathbf{L}S_0 \cup \neg\mathbf{L}\bar{S}_0$, then the set of objective formulae which are true in M is precisely S_0. Thus, since S is stable, the set of all formulae which are true in M is S. Given this, it is easily verified that $T \models_S A$ iff $T \cup \mathbf{L}S_0 \cup \neg\mathbf{L}\bar{S}_0 \models_{PV} A$. ■

We proceed to the theorem. Its 'only-if' part is an immediate consequence of Theorem 4.47 and Lemma 4.84.1. For the proof in the opposite direction, assume that S satisfies (4.3.2). Clearly, S = Th(S) and so, $S_0 = [\mathrm{Th}(S_0)]_0$. Hence, by Corollary 4.57, there is a unique stable set, say S′, such that $S_0 = S'_0$. Therefore, by Lemma 3.84.1, (4.3.2) implies

$$S = \{A \colon T \models_{S'} A\}. \tag{4.3.3}$$

We prove that S is an AE extension of T by showing that S = S′ and invoking Theorem 4.47.

Let T' be the set of formulae in T, where each LA is replaced by *True* if $A \in S'$, and by *False* if $A \notin S'$. It is easily checked that for each AE interpretation V of S′, V is a model of T iff V is a model of T'. Hence, by (4.3.3), we have

$$S = \{A \colon T' \models_{S'} A\}. \tag{4.3.4}$$

All formulae in T' are objective and $\mathrm{Th}(T') = S_0$ (by (4.3.4)). Moreover, $S_0 = S'_0$. Therefore (4.3.4) implies

$$S = \{A \colon S'_0 \models_{S'} A\}. \tag{4.3.5}$$

By Theorem 4.66, we know that the unique stable set including X as its objective part is an AE extension of X. So S′ is an AE extension of S'_0 and thus, by Theorem 4.47, the right hand side of (4.3.5) is S′. In conclusion, S = S′. ▮

The modal system K45 is the system S5 without the axiom schema L$A \supset A$. The appropriate Kripke frames for K45 are those in which the accessibility relation is transitive and *Euclidean* (wRw′ and wRw″ imply w′Rw″). As usual, the symbol $\vdash_{K45}$ stands for the K45 provability relation.

There is an interesting relationship between autoepistemic logic and K45 modal logic. To present it, we need the following concept. We say that a formula A is *strongly* K45-*provable* from a theory T, written $T \vdash^{s}_{K45} A$, iff there are formulae $A_1, \ldots, A_n \in T$ such that $\vdash_{K45} A_1 \wedge \cdots \wedge A_n \supset A$. It should be noted that strong K45-provability and K45-provability are different concepts. Although $T \vdash^{s}_{K45}$ implies $T \vdash_{K45} A$, the converse need not be true. For instance, $\{p\} \vdash_{K45} \mathrm{L}p$. However, since $p \supset \mathrm{L}p$ is not a theorem of K45, Lp is not strongly K45-provable from $\{p\}$.

It can be shown (see Konolige 1988) that the strong K45-provability relation is precisely the syntactic counterpart of the relation $\models_{PV}$. More specifically:

Theorem 4.85 (Konolige 1988) For any $T \subseteq L_T$ and any $A \in L_T$:

$$T \models_{PV} A \qquad \text{iff} \qquad T \vdash^{s}_{K45} A.$$

▮

We write $\mathrm{Th}^{s}_{K45}(T)$ to denote the set $\{A: T \vdash^{s}_{K45} A\}$.

In virtue of Theorem 4.85, we have the following proof-theoretic analog of Theorem 4.84:

Theorem 4.86 (Konoligie 1988) A set S is an AE extension of T iff $S = \mathrm{Th}^{s}_{K45}(T \cup \mathbf{LS}_0 \cup \neg\mathbf{L}\bar{S}_0)$. ∎

For convenience we summarize various characterizations of AE extensions:

Theorem 4.87 The following conditions are equivalent:

(1) S is an AE extension of T;
(2) $T \subseteq S$, S is semantically complete and S is sound with respect to T;
(3) $T \subseteq S$, S is stable and S is grounded in T;
(4) $S = \{A: T \models_S A\}$;
(5) $S = \{A: T \cup \mathbf{LS} \cup \neg\mathbf{L}\bar{S} \models A\}$;
(6) $S = \mathrm{Th}(T \cup \mathbf{LS} \cup \neg\mathbf{L}\bar{S})$;
(7) $S = \{A: T \cup \mathbf{LS}_0 \cup \neg\mathbf{L}\bar{S}_0 \models_{PV} A\}$;
(8) $S = \mathrm{Th}^{s}_{K45}(T \cup \mathbf{LS}_0 \cup \neg\mathbf{L}\bar{S}_0)$.

∎

4.3.5 Reduction theorem

An important result concerning autoepistemic logic is that nesting of modal operators gives no additional power to the language: all types of inference expressible in the logic may be represented by premisses whose modal depth is at most 1. To present this result, originally developed in Konolige (1988), we employ the possible-world semantics. We proceed in two steps, first specifying a semantic notion of autoepistemic equivalence, strong enough to assure that two autoepistemically equivalent theories have exactly the same AE extensions, and then showing that for each theory $T \subseteq L_T$, there exists its autoepistemic equivalent $T' \subseteq L_T(1)$.

For any formula A, $\mathrm{MOD}_{AE}(A)$ stands for the class of all possible-world AE models of $\{A\}$. Similarly, for any theory T, $\mathrm{MOD}_{AE}(T)$ is the class of all possible-world AE models of T.

Definition 4.88 Formulae A and B are *autoepistemically equivalent* (*AE equivalent*), written $A \equiv_a B$, iff $\mathrm{MOD}_{AE}(A) = \mathrm{MOD}_{AE}(B)$. Theories T and T' are AE equivalent, $T \equiv_a T'$, iff $\mathrm{MOD}_{AE}(T) = \mathrm{MOD}_{AE}(T')$. ∎

Notice that formulae A and B are AE equivalent iff $\mathrm{PV}(A) = \mathrm{PV}(B)$, for each possible-world AE interpretation PV.

Theorem 4.89 The following AE equivalences hold:

(AE1) $\mathrm{L}(A \wedge B) \equiv_a \mathrm{L}A \wedge \mathrm{L}B$
(AE2) $\mathrm{LL}A \equiv_a \mathrm{L}A$
(AE3) $(\mathrm{L}\neg\mathrm{L}A \equiv_a \neg\mathrm{L}A \vee \mathrm{L}\mathit{False}$
(AE4) $\mathrm{L}(\mathrm{L}A \vee B) \equiv_a \mathrm{L}A \vee \mathrm{L}B$
(AE5) $\mathrm{L}(\neg\mathrm{L}A \vee B) \equiv_a \neg\mathrm{L}A \vee \mathrm{L}\mathit{False} \vee \mathrm{L}B$.

Proof Take any $\mathrm{PV} = \langle m_{PV}, M\rangle$. Assume first that $M = M_{\perp}$. Then, for each formula A, $\mathrm{PV}(\mathrm{L}A) = 1$ and $\mathrm{PV}(\neg\mathrm{L}A) = 0$. Thus, for each $A \equiv_a B$ from (AE1)–(AE5), $\mathrm{PV}(A) = \mathrm{PV}(B) = 1$. Assume now that $M \neq M_{\perp}$. Then, for each $A \equiv_a B$ from

(AE1)–(AE5). PV(A) = PV(B) iff $A \equiv B$ is true in M. It is easily checked that each instance of these schemata is a theorem of S5. Moreover, since $M \neq M_\perp$, M is an S5 modal frame. So, it must be the case that all instances of (AE1)–(AE5) are true in M. ∎

If $T \subseteq L$ and $T' \subseteq L$ are AE equivalent, then for each $X \subseteq L$, $\{A: T \cup X \models_{PV} A\} = \{A: T' \cup X \models_{PV} A\}$. Therefore, in view of Theorem 4.84, we immediately obtain:

Theorem 4.90 For any theories T and T', $T \equiv_a T'$ implies that T and T' have exactly the same AE extensions. ∎

We say that theories T and T' are K45-equivalent, written $T \equiv_{K45} T'$, iff $Th^s_{K45}(T) = Th^s_{K45}(T')$. Similarly, formulae A and B are K45-equivalent, $A \equiv_{K45} B$, iff $\{A\} \equiv_{K45} \{B\}$. It is easily verified that $A \equiv_{K45} B$ iff $\vdash_{K45} A \equiv B$.

In view of Theorem 4.85, we immediately have:

Theorem 4.91

(1) $T \equiv_a T'$ iff $T \equiv_{K45} T'$;
(2) $A \equiv_a B$ iff $A \equiv_{K45} B$ iff $\vdash_{K45} A \equiv B$.

∎

We now show that each formula $A \in L$ is reducible to its autoepistemic equivalent of modal depth at most 1.

Theorem 4.92 (Reduction Theorem, Konolige 1988) For each $A \in L$, there exists $B \in L(1)$ such that $A \equiv_a B$.

Proof We show by induction on the modal depth of A that there is an effective procedure transforming A into its AE equivalent $B \in L(1)$. If m-depth(A) ≤ 1, this is trivially true, since we may put $B = A$. Assume, therefore, that m-depth(A) = k (k $\geq$ 2) and suppose that we know how to transform any formula whose m-depth is less than k into its AE equivalent of m-depth at most 1. By propositional equivalences (see Theorem 4.52), A may be replaced by $A_1 = \bigwedge_{i=1}^{n} C_i$, where each C_i is of the form

$$D^i_1 \vee LD^i_2 \vee \cdots \vee LD^i_k \vee \neg LD^i_{k+1} \vee \cdots \vee \neg LD^i_{k+r}$$

with D^i_1 objective. To prove the theorem it suffices to show that for each $1 \leq i \leq n$, C_i may be transformed into its AE equivalent whose m-depth is at most 1. Take any C_i. By Theorem 4.52, m-depth(A) = k implies m-depth (A_1) = k, and thus, m-depth(C_i) $\leq$ k. Hence, for each $2 \leq j \leq k + r$, m-depth (D^i_j) < k. By induction hypothesis, we may therefore assume that each D^i_j ($2 \leq j \leq k + r$) is replaced by its AE equivalent of modal depth at most 1. Given this, the proof will be completed if we show:

Lemma 4.92.1 Each formula of the form LB, where $B \in L(1)$, can be constructively transformed into a formula $C \in L(1)$ such that $LB \equiv_a C$.

Proof By Theorems 4.52 and 4.89 (AE1), LB may be replaced by $\bigwedge_{i=1}^{n} LC_i$, where each C_i is of the form

$$D^i_1 \vee LD^i_2 \vee \cdots \vee LD^i_k \vee \neg LD^i_{k+1} \vee \cdots \vee \neg LD^i_{k+r}$$

with D^i_1 objective. Since $B \in L(1)$, each D^i_j ($1 \le i \le n, 2 \le j \le k + r$) must be also objective. By Theorem 4.89 (AE2)–(AE5), it is easily seen that each LC_i is AE equivalent to

$$E_i = LD^i_1 \vee LD^i_2 \vee \cdots \vee LD^i_k \vee \neg LD^i_{k+1} \vee \cdots \vee \neg LD^i_{k+r} \vee L\mathit{False}$$

Put $C = \bigwedge_{n=1}^{n} E_i$. Obviously, $LB \equiv_a C$ and $C \in L(1)$. ■

▮

Example 4.93 Let $A = L(Lp \vee \neg L(p \vee Lq)) \supset r$. We reduce A to its AE equivalent from $L(1)$. By propositional logic, A may be replaced by $A_1 = \neg L(Lp \vee \neg L(p \vee Lq)) \vee r$. Applying (AE4), A_1 is transformed to $A_2 = \neg(Lp \vee L\neg L(p \vee Lq)) \vee r$. By (AE3), this is reduced to $A_3 = \neg(Lp \vee \neg L(p \vee Lq) \vee L\mathit{False}) \vee r$. Finally, in view of (AE4), A_3 may be replaced by $A_4 = \neg(Lp \vee \neg(Lp \vee Lq) \vee L\mathit{False}) \vee r$. ▮

Theorem 4.94 For each theory T, there exists a theory T' such that $T \equiv_a T'$ and all formulae of T' have modal depth at most 1.

Proof By Theorem 4.92. ▮

Definition 4.95 We say that a formula A is in AE *normal form* iff A is a disjunction

$$\neg LA \vee LB_1 \vee \cdots \vee LB_k \vee C,$$

where $A, B_1, \ldots, B_k$ and C are all objective. Any of the disjuncts, except for C, may be absent. ▮

Corollary 4.96 (Konolige 1988) Each theory T is AE equivalent to a theory T' in which each formula is in AE normal form.

Proof By Theorems 4.52, 4.89 (AE1), 4.94 and the propositional equivalence: $A \equiv A \vee \mathit{False}$. (Note that (AE1) implies $\neg LA \vee \ldots \vee \neg LA_n \equiv_a \neg L(A_1 \wedge \ldots \wedge A_n)$.) ▮

4.3.6 Minimal, strongly grounded and superstrongly grounded AE extensions

To assure that AE extensions exclude unjustified beliefs, they are required to be grounded: the only beliefs an agent is justified to accept are those forced by his initial set of premisses and the stability conditions. This guarantees that all the agent's beliefs are true, provided that his premisses are true.

In spite of its conceptual clarity, Moore's notion of groundedness is too weak to exclude 'self-grounded' beliefs, i.e. beliefs about the external world which are solely justified by the fact that they have been adopted as beliefs. Consider, for instance, the theory $T = \{Lp \supset p\}$. Intuitively, given $Lp \supset p$ as the only premiss, there are no objective reasons to believe in p. However, as we saw in Example 4.83, T has an AE extension including p. This is because $Lp \supset p$ allows an agent to justify p simply by choosing to believe in it. In other words, he may first decide to assume p and then justify the belief by using the premiss $Lp \supset p$.

If we agree that the agent is justified to believe in any proposition which must be true, provided that his premisses are true, we must accept self-grounded beliefs. However, since they are intuitively problematic, we may wish to construct a version of autoepistemic logic in which self-grounded beliefs are disallowed.

The simplest way to exclude self-grounded beliefs is to minimize what an agent believes about his world.

Definition 4.97 (Konolige 1988) An AE extension S of T is *minimal for* T iff there is no stable set X containing T such that $X_0 \subset T_0$. ▮

Example 4.98 Let $T = \{Lp \supset p\}$. T has two AE extensions, S and S′, where $S_0 = [Th(\{p\})]_0$ and $S'_0 = [Th(\{\ \})]_0$. Obviously, only S′ is minimal for T. ▮

Example 4.99 Let $T = \{\neg Lp \supset q, \neg Lq \supset p\}$. T has two AE extensions, S and S′, where $S_0 = [Th(\{p\})]_0$ and $S'_0 = [Th(\{q\})]_0$. Both S and S′ are minimal for T. ▮

Minimal AE extensions can be given the following characterization:

Theorem 4.100 (Konolige 1988) A set S is a minimal AE extension of T iff $S = \{A: T \cup \mathbf{L}T \cup \neg\mathbf{L}\bar{S}_0 \models_{PV} A\}$.

Proof See Konolige (1988, Proposition 2.8). ▮

Corollary 4.101 A set S is a minimal AE extension of T iff $S = Th^{s}_{K45}(T \cup \mathbf{L}T \cup \neg\mathbf{L}\bar{S}_0)$.

Proof By Theorems 4.85 and 4.100. ▮

Corollary 4.102 If $T \equiv_a T'$, then T and T' have exactly the same minimal AE extensions.

Proof Use Theorem 4.100. ▮

The following notion will be useful in section 5.9:

Definition 4.103 A stable set S is *minimal for a theory* T iff $T \subseteq S$ and there is no other stable set S′ containing T such that $S'_0 \subset S_0$. ▮

In view of Definitions 4.97 and 4.103, we immediately have:

Corollary 4.104 Every minimal AE extension of T is a minimal stable set for T. ▮

The converse of this corollary is not always true. Consider, for instance, the theory $T = \{Lp\}$. As we know (Example 4.48), T has no AE extension. However, the stable set S, with $[Th(\{p\})]_0$ as its objective part, is a minimal stable set for T.

If a minimal stable set for T is an AE extension of T, then it must be a minimal AE extension, because every AE extension is a stable set. Thus, we have:

Corollary 4.105 If a minimal stable set for T is an AE extension of T, then it is a minimal AE extension of T. ▮

Since minimal AE extensions exclude self-grounded beliefs, they appear ideal candidates for belief sets of perfectly rational agents. Unfortunately, it turns out that a minimal AE extension may still contain unwanted beliefs.

Example 4.106 (Konolige 1988) Let $T = \{\neg Lp \supset q; Lp \supset p\}$. T has two AE extensions, S and S′, whose objective parts are $[Th(\{q\})]_0$ and $[Th(\{p\})]_0$, respectively. Although both S and S′ are minimal for T, only S is intuitively plausible.

It is obvious how S comes into existence: assuming $\neg Lp$, q is derived from $\neg Lp \supset q$. S′ is more difficult to analyse. At first sight, p seems self-grounded. But recall that S′ is minimal for T, so that it excludes this type of beliefs. This means that there must be a derivation of p which does not rely on assuming Lp. Indeed: Since $\neg Lp \supset q$ is a premiss, we are allowed to accept $L(\neg Lp \supset q)$, or, equivalently, $L(Lp \vee q)$. Now, $L(Lp \vee q)$ is AE equivalent to $Lp \vee Lq$ (Theorem 4.89 (AE4)) which, in turn, can be written as $\neg Lq \supset Lp$. From this, assuming $\neg Lq$, we infer Lp. In consequence, by $Lp \supset p$, we arrive at p. ∎

What is intuitively strange in the last derivation is that Lp is inferred before p is. It is as if an agent concludes 'I believe in p' without believing in p itself. This closely resembles the mechanism of arriving at self-grounded beliefs. The only difference is that, there, Lp is assumed, rather than inferred.

It is possible to further strengthen the notion of an AE extension. We want to assure that if an objective formula A is in an extension, then there is a derivation of A which does not rely on LA. Following Konolige (1988), we shall call such extensions *strongly grounded.*

The notion of a strongly grounded AE extension is conceptually complex. To fix some ideas, reconsider the previous theory $\{\neg Lp \supset q;\ Lp \supset p\}$. As we saw, the premiss $\neg Lp \supset q$ can be used in two different ways. Firstly, it may be employed to directly derive q. Secondly, it can be used as a derivation step, allowing to infer Lp (via $L(\neg Lp \supset q) \equiv_a \neg Lq \supset Lp$). Notice that it is this second usage that leads to a derivation in which Lp precedes p.

Suppose that T is a theory all of whose premisses are in AE normal form

$$\neg LA \vee LB_1 \vee \cdots \vee LB_n \vee C \qquad \text{(equivalently,}$$
$$LA \wedge \neg LB_1 \wedge \ldots \wedge \neg LB \supset C)$$

Recall that $A, B_1, \ldots, B_n, C$ are all objective and at least C must be present. We want every modalized premiss of T, i.e. a premiss in which at least one of $A, B_1, \ldots, B_n$ is present, to be used only for a derivation of C. This guarantees, for every objective formula B, that LB will never be derived without having derived B first.

How can we verify, given an AE extension S of a theory T (in AE normal form), that all its modalized premisses have been used in the desired way? The answer is based on the observation that if this is indeed the case, then each premiss whose objective part is not in S is redundant. More specifically, let T' be the theory obtained from T by excluding all premisses whose objective parts are not in S. If every one of the premisses of T has been used only for a derivation of its objective part, then it must be the case that S is a minimal AE extension of T'. Moreover, if S is a minimal AE extension of T', we have the guarantee that all the premisses of T have been used in this way. The assumption that S is minimal for T' is necessary to prevent self-grounded beliefs.

Our discussion motivates the following definition:

Theorem 4.107 (Konolige 1988) Let T be a theory in AE normal form and suppose that S is an AE extension of T. Let T' be the set of formulae from T whose objective parts are in S. We say that S is a *strongly grounded* AE extension of T iff

$$S = \{A\colon T' \cup \mathbf{L}T' \cup \neg \mathbf{L}\bar{S}_0 \models_{PV} A\}$$

i.e. iff S is a minimal AE extension of T'. ∎

Example 4.106 (continued) It is easily seen that S is a minimal AE extension of $\{\neg Lp \supset q\}$. Hence S is a strongly grounded AE extension of T. S′ is not a minimal AE extension of $\{Lp \supset p\}$, so that S′ is not a strongly grounded AE extension of T. ∎

Theorem 4.108 (Konolige 1988) If S is a strongly grounded AE extension of T, then S is a minimal AE extension of T.

Proof We know that

$$S = \{A\colon T' \cup \mathbf{L}T' \cup \neg \mathbf{L}\bar{S}_0 \models_{PV} A\}. \tag{4.3.6}$$

Since S is an AE extension of T, both T and $\mathbf{L}T$ are in S. Hence (4.3.6) can be replaced by

$$S = \{A: T' \cup T \cup \mathbf{L}T' \cup \mathbf{L}T \cup \neg\mathbf{L}\bar{S}_0 \models_{PV} A\}. \quad (4.3.7)$$

Recall that $T' \subseteq T$ and so $\mathbf{L}T' \subseteq \mathbf{L}T$. Therefore, for any possible-world AE interpretation PV, PV is a model of $T \cup \mathbf{L}T \cup \neg\mathbf{L}\bar{S}_0$ iff PV is a model of $T' \cup T \cup \mathbf{L}T' \cup \mathbf{L}T \cup \neg\mathbf{L}\bar{S}_0$. This allows us to replace (4.3.7) by

$$S = \{A: T \cup \mathbf{L}T \cup \neg\mathbf{L}\bar{S}_0 \models_{PV} A\}$$

and so, S is a minimal AE extension of T, by Theorem 4.100. ▮

Strongly grounded AE extensions have a curious property. As we know, two AE equivalent theories have exactly the same AE extensions and the same minimal AE extensions. This is not generally true for strongly grounded AE extensions. Moreover, as the next example shows, even propositionally equivalent theories may have different strongly grounded AE extensions.

Example 4.109 (Konolige 1988) Consider the theories:

$$T = \{p, \mathrm{L}p \vee \mathit{False}\}; \qquad T1 = \{\neg\mathrm{L}p \vee p, \mathrm{L}p \vee \mathit{False}\}.^{\dagger}$$

It is easily checked that T and $T1$ have exactly the same propositional models, so that they are propositionally equivalent (and hence AE equivalent). They both have one AE extension S, where $S_0 = [\mathrm{Th}(\{p\})]_0$. S is minimal for T and for $T1$. Since S is a minimal AE extension of $\{p\}$, it is a strongly grounded AE extension of T. However, S is not a strongly grounded AE extension of $T1$, because it is not a minimal AE extension of $\{\neg\mathrm{L}p \vee p\}$ (see Example 4.98). ▮

It turns out that strongly grounded AE extensions may still contain intuitively problematic beliefs. The following example is from Marek & Truszczynski (1989).

Example 4.110 Let $T = \{\mathrm{L}p \supset p, \neg\mathrm{L}p \supset p\}$.

Given these premisses, there is no reason to believe in p (note that $\neg\mathrm{L}p \supset p$ is to be read as 'If p is not believed, then it is true'). However, T has one AE extension, with $[\mathrm{Th}(\{p\})]_0$ as its objective part, which is strongly grounded. This is because p is a logical consequence of T (observe that T classically entails $\mathrm{L}p \vee \neg\mathrm{L}p \supset p$ which, in turn, entails p).

In conclusion, neither $\mathrm{L}p \supset p$ nor $\neg\mathrm{L}p \supset p$ give rise to belief p. However, p must be believed as their logical consequence. ▮

As this example shows, the definition of a strongly grounded AE extension allows for interactions of premisses which may result in unintuitive conclusions. The simplest way to break such interactions is to regard modalized premisses as inference rules. More specifically, given a premiss

$$\neg\mathrm{L}A \vee \mathrm{L}B_1 \vee \cdots \vee \mathrm{L}B_n \vee C$$

or, equivalently

$$\mathrm{L}A \wedge \neg\mathrm{L}B_1 \wedge \cdots \wedge \neg\mathrm{L}B_n \supset C$$

we would like to view it as the rule saying 'If A is believed and none of $B_1, \ldots, B_n$ is believed, then C is to be believed.'

† $\mathrm{L}p \vee \mathit{False}$ is propositionally equivalent to $\mathrm{L}p$. However, since we want all the premisses to be in AE normal form, *False* cannot be omitted.

Definition 4.111 Let $D = \mathrm{L}A \wedge \neg\mathrm{L}B_1 \wedge \cdots \wedge \neg\mathrm{L}B_n \supset C$ (equivalently, $D = \neg\mathrm{L}A \vee \mathrm{L}B_1 \vee \cdots \vee \mathrm{L}B_n \vee C$) and let S be a deductively closed set of formulae. D is said to be *applicable wrt* S iff $A \in \mathrm{S}$ and $B_1, \ldots, B_n \notin \mathrm{S}$; otherwise, D is said to be *inapplicable wrt* S.† ∎

Suppose that we are given a theory T (in AE normal form) and let S be an AE extension of T. How can we check that all (modalized) premisses of T have been used as inference rules? A little reflexion should convince the reader that if this is indeed the case, then each premiss which is inapplicable wrt S is redundant. More precisely, let T'' obtain from T by deleting all premisses which are inapplicable wrt S. If all the premisses from T have been used as inference rules, S must be a minimal AE extension of T''. Conversely, if S is a minimal AE extension of T'', then all the premisses of T had to be used in this way. The requirement that S is a minimal AE extension of T'' serves to exclude self-grounded beliefs.

Our considerations lead to the following definition:

Definition 4.112 Let T be a theory in AE normal form and suppose that S is an AE extension of T. Let T'' be the theory obtained from T by deleting all modalized premisses which are inapplicable wrt S. S is said to be a *superstrongly grounded* AE extension of T iff

$$\mathrm{S} = \{A\colon T'' \cup \mathbf{L}T'' \cup \neg\mathbf{L}\bar{\mathrm{S}}_0 \models_{\mathbf{PV}} A\}$$

i.e. iff S is a minimal AE extension of T''.‡ ∎

Example 4.110 (continued) S is not a superstrongly grounded AE extension of T, because S is not a minimal AE extension of $\{\mathrm{L}p \supset p\}$. ∎

Theorem 4.113 Every superstrongly grounded AE extension of T is a strongly grounded AE extension of T.

Proof Left to the reader as an exercise. (Compare the proof of Theorem 4.108.) ∎

Superstrongly grounded AE extensions will play an important role in comparing autoepistemic logic with default logic in Chapter 5.

4.3.7 A comparison of autoepistemic logic to non-monotonic logics of McDermott and Doyle

We now compare autoepistemic logic with McDermott and Doyle's non-monotonic logics. In the following, we generally assume that all the discussed formalisms are based on the propositional language.§

Autoepistemic logic is similar to McDermott and Doyle's first formalization in that they are both based on classical foundations. The crucial difference concerns the notion of an extension. In autoepistemic logic, S is an extension of T iff $\mathrm{S} = \mathrm{Th}(T \cup \{\mathrm{L}A\colon A \in \mathrm{S}\} \cup \{\neg\mathrm{L}A\colon A \notin \mathrm{S}\})$; in McDermott and Doyle's logic, S is assumed to satisfy the equation $\mathrm{S} = \mathrm{Th}(T \cup \{\mathrm{M}A\colon \neg A \notin \mathrm{S}\})$ or, equivalently, $\mathrm{S} = \mathrm{Th}(T \cup \{\neg\mathrm{L}A\colon A \notin \mathrm{S}\})$.

The lack of '$\{\mathrm{L}A\colon A \in \mathrm{S}\}$' in McDermott and Doyle's definition has a consequence

† Notice that if D is applicable wrt S and $D \in \mathrm{S}$, then $C \in \mathrm{S}$.

‡ The term 'supergounded AE extension' is from Marek & Truszczynski (1989).

§ The subsequent discussion is influenced by Moore (1983).

that their logic admits extensions which include A but exclude LA. In other words, under the intended interpretation of 'L', the logic models the behaviour of an agent who is always aware of his disbeliefs but may remain agnostic as to what he believes.

This explains some weaknesses of McDermott and Doyle's first logic. For instance, contrary to our intuitions, the theory $T = \{\mathrm{M}p, \neg p\}$ has a consistent extension in their formalism (Example 4.13). The reason, of course, is that there is no way to conclude Lp from p and so, Mp and $\neg p$ may coexist in a consistent environment. In autoepistemic logic this is impossible and thus, L_T is the only AE extension of T.

A similar example is provided by the theory $T = \{\mathrm{M}(p \wedge q), \neg p\}$. Again, contrary to what one might expect, T has a consistent extension in McDermott and Doyle's logic. (Example 4.15.) The reason is exactly as before: the lack of any mechanism allowing to derive LA from A.

The relation between autoepistemic logic and McDermott's modal non-monotonic formalisms is more complex. The latter modify the original non-monotonic logic in two ways. First, the classical deductive structure is augmented by the modal inference rule $\frac{A}{\mathrm{L}A}$ (NEC). Second, each theory contains as premisses the axioms of one of the modal systems T, S4 or S5.

Let $\mathrm{Th}_{\mathrm{Nec}}$ stand for the provability operator of classical logic augmented by the NEC rule. We say that a set $\mathrm{S} \in L_T$ is an N-*extension of* T iff $\mathrm{S} = \mathrm{Th}_{\mathrm{Nec}}(T \cup \neg\mathbf{L}\bar{\mathrm{S}})$. (Recall that $\neg\mathbf{L}\bar{\mathrm{S}}$ denotes the set $\{\neg \mathrm{L}A \colon A \in L_T - \mathrm{S}\}$.)

The first of McDermott's modifications brings his logic close to autoepistemic logic. In particular:

Theorem 4.114 If S is an N-extension of T, then S is an AE extension of T.

Proof Assume that S satisfies $\mathrm{S} = \mathrm{Th}_{\mathrm{Nec}}(T \cup \neg\mathbf{L}\bar{\mathrm{S}})$. It is immediately seen that S is stable, and so $\mathbf{LS} \subseteq \mathrm{S}$. Therefore, S must enjoy

$$\mathrm{S} = \mathrm{Th}_{\mathrm{Nec}}(T \cup \mathbf{LS} \cup \neg\mathbf{L}\bar{\mathrm{S}}).$$

To prove that S is an AE extension of T, it suffices to show that $A \in \mathrm{Th}_{\mathrm{Nec}}(T \cup \mathbf{LS} \cup \neg\mathbf{L}\bar{\mathrm{S}})$ implies $A \in \mathrm{Th}(T \cup \mathbf{LS} \cup \neg\mathbf{L}\bar{\mathrm{S}})$. Let $A_0, \ldots, A_k = A$ be a proof (perhaps with NEC) of A from $T \cup \mathbf{LS} \cup \neg\mathbf{L}\bar{\mathrm{S}}$. By straightforward induction on i, one verifies that for each $0 \le i \le k$, $A_i \in \mathrm{Th}(T \cup \mathbf{LS} \cup \neg\mathbf{L}\bar{\mathrm{S}})$. Hence, since $A_k = A$, we conclude that $A \in \mathrm{Th}(T \cup \mathbf{LS} \cup \neg\mathbf{L}\bar{\mathrm{S}})$. ∎

The converse to Theorem 4.114 does not hold. Employing $\frac{A}{\mathrm{L}A}$ as an inference rule, instead of adding $\{\mathrm{L}A \colon A \in \mathrm{S}\}$ to the specification of S, disallows justification of A by assuming LA first. Accordingly, N-extensions never contain self-grounded beliefs, so that they restrict the class of AE extensions. To illustrate this, consider the theory $T = \{\mathrm{L}p \supset p\}$. As we know, T has two AE extensions, S and S′, whose objective parts are $[\mathrm{Th}(\{\ \})]_0$ and $[\mathrm{Th}(\{p\})]_0$, respectively. However, only S is an N-extension of T; S′ is not an N-extension of T, because NEC gives no way to justify p.[†]

We now proceed to McDermott's second modification: the addition of axioms of various modal systems. He considers the following axioms (recall that we limit

[†] One may suspect, therefore, but we have no proof, that each N-extension is a minimal AE extension.

ourselves to the propositional case):

(A1) $\mathrm{L}A \supset A$
(A2) $\mathrm{L}(A \supset B) \supset (\mathrm{L}A \supset \mathrm{L}B)$
(A3) $\mathrm{L}A \supset \mathrm{LL}A$
(A4) $\neg\mathrm{L}A \supset \mathrm{L}\neg\mathrm{L}A$ (equivalently, $\mathrm{M}A \supset \mathrm{LM}A$)

Axioms (A2)–(A4) describe a belief state of an ideally rational agent; in fact, they are just the stability conditions, (ST1)–(ST3), expressed in the object language. (A2) says that the agent's beliefs are closed under modus ponens, whereas (A3) and (A4) state that whenever he believes (disbelieves) in a proposition, he believes that he believes (disbelieves) in it. Surely, any ideally rational agent will accept (A2)–(A4) as valid principles, and thus he may well add them to the list of his premisses.

In autoepistemic logic, the addition of (A2)—(A4) as extra premisses has no influence on what will be inferable – they are precisely the axioms of the modal system K45 , and, as we know, K45-equivalent theories have exactly the same AE extensions (Theorems 4.90 and 4.91). This is not true for McDermott's logics; if it were, all his formalisms would be equivalent. It follows, therefore, that S5 version of non-monotonic logic is better motivated than those based on the systems T or S4.

The problem with all these logics is that they contain the schema $\mathrm{L}A \supset A$, (A1), which says that whatever an agent believes is true. Obviously, this is not the case, even for an ideally rational agent. What is worse, if the agent *a priori* assumes that all his beliefs are always true, the assumption allows hims to justify whatever he wishes to believe. This beautifully manifests itself in autoepistemic logic, where the addition of $\mathrm{L}A \supset A$ as a premiss schema may sanction any belief. The key result is the following:

Theorem 4.115 If $\{\mathrm{L}A \supset A\colon A \in L_{\mathrm{T}}\} \subseteq T$, then every stable set containing T is an AE extension of T.

Proof Assume that S is a stable set including T. It suffices to prove that S is grounded in T, i.e.

$$\mathrm{S} \subseteq \mathrm{Th}(T \cup \mathbf{L}\mathrm{S} \cup \neg\mathbf{L}\bar{\mathrm{S}}). \tag{4.3.8}$$

Denote the right-hand side of (4.3.8) by RHS. Assume that $B \in \mathrm{S}$. Then $\mathrm{L}B \in \mathbf{L}\mathrm{S}$ and so, $\mathrm{L}B \in \mathrm{RHS}$. Therefore, since $\mathrm{L}B \supset B \in \mathrm{RHS}$ and RHS is closed under Th, $B \in \mathrm{RHS}$. ∎

Corollary 4.116 If $\{\mathrm{L}A \supset A\colon A \in L_{\mathrm{T}}\} \subseteq T$, then L_{T} is an AE extension of T. ∎

Corollary 4.117 Let $\{\mathrm{L}A \supset A\colon A \in L_{\mathrm{T}}\} \subseteq T$. For any $B \in L_{\mathrm{T}}$, there is an AE extension of T containing B. If there is a consistent stable set including $T \cup \{B\}$, then there is a consistent AE extension of T containing B. ∎

Corollary 4.118 If $\{\mathrm{L}A \supset A\colon A \in L_{\mathrm{T}}\} \subseteq T$, then $\mathrm{Th}_{\mathrm{S5}}(T)$ is the intersection of all AE extensions of T.

Proof Follows from Theorems 1.98, 4.70, 4.115 and the following obvious fact: A formula A is true in every S5 modal frame in which all formulae of T are true iff A is true in every complete S5 frame of this property. ∎

Given these results, it is clear that the axiom schema $\mathrm{L}A \supset A$ may justify any belief in autoepistemic logic. If the schema is adopted, every theory T has generally a great number of different AE extensions, including L_{T}, whose intersection is precisely the set of theorems monotonically S5-provable from T.

As we know, this is not generally true for McDermott's (T-, S4-) non-monotonic logics – roughly, because their extensions restrict the class of AE extensions. However, as we also know, the analog of Corollary 4.118 holds for his S5 non-monotonic logic – because if $LA \supset A$ and $\neg LA \supset L\neg LA$ (the characteristic axiom of S5) are mixed together, N- and AE extensions become almost equivalent concepts:

Theorem 4.119 Let $\{LA \supset A: A \in L_T\} \cup \{\neg LA \supset L\neg LA: A \in L_T\} \subseteq T$. For any consistent set $S \subseteq L_T$, S is an N-extension of T iff S is an AE extension of T.

Proof (⇒) By Theorem 4.114.
(⇐) Assume that S is an AE extension of T, i.e.

$$S = Th(T \cup \mathbf{LS} \cup \neg\mathbf{L}\bar{S}). \tag{4.3.9}$$

We have to show that

$$S = Th_{Nec}(T \cup \neg\mathbf{L}\bar{S}). \tag{4.3.10}$$

Denote the right-hand sides of (4.3.9) and (4.3.10) by RHS1 and RHS2, respectively.

To show the right to left inclusion of (4.3.10), assume that $A \in$ RHS2. Let $A_0, \ldots, A_k = A$ be proof (perhaps with NEC) of A from $T \cup \neg\mathbf{L}\bar{S}$. It is readily checked, by induction on i, that $A_i \in$ RHS1, for each $0 \leq i \leq k$. Hence, since $A_k = A$ and RHS1 = S, we have $A \in S$.

For the proof of the converse inclusion, assume that $A \in S$. Thus, by (4.3.9), $LA \in S$ and so, since S is consistent, $\neg LA \notin S$. Hence $\neg L\neg LA \in \neg\mathbf{L}\bar{S}$ and, consequently, $\neg L\neg LA \in$ RHS2. Given this, and $\{LA \supset A, \neg LA \supset L\neg LA\} \subseteq T \subseteq$ RHS2, it is easily verified, by propositional logic alone, that $A \in$ RHS2. ∎

The collapse of non-monotonic S5 into monotonic S5 forces McDermott to abandon this system. To restore non-montonicity, he suggests rejecting the characteristic axiom of S5 and base non-monotonic logic on the systems T or S4. This solution is ill-motivated. As is clear from our discussion, the appropriate basis for non-monotonic logic is the system K45. An interesting question is whether K45 non-monotonic logic is just autoepistemic logic restricted to minimal AE extensions.

4.3.8 Conclusions

Autoepistemic logic is one of the most important contributions to the subject of non-monotonic reasoning. It is much more interesting, clearer and better motivated than McDermott and Doyle's earlier developments.

The major advantage of autoepistemic logic is its natural semantics, relatively simple when compared with model theories of many other non-monotonic formalisms. It should be stressed that unlike McDermott's semantic characterization of extensions, Moore's semantics capture the intended interpretation of the modalities involved.

Autoepistemic logic is based on the following two assumptions:

(1) All the beliefs of an agent are true, provided that his premisses are (soundness).
(2) The set of beliefs contains every proposition that the agent is semantically justified to infer on the basis that all his beliefs are true (semantic completeness).

The problem is that not every set of premisses gives rise to a belief set satisfying these assumptions and this is exactly the reason why there are theories lacking AE extensions. This may even happen for naturally appearing theories. An example of this kind is the theory $T = \{Lp\}$, stating that p is believed by an agent. Since the agent believes p, p must be in his belief set (by semantic completeness). However, given that p is believed, there is no guarantee that p is true. In consequence, there is no appropriate belief set corresponding to the theory T.

Autoepistemic logic was originally constructed for the propositional language. However, as Konolige (1988) has shown, the formalism can be easily extended into the first-order language, provided that no open formula lies in the scope of modal operators. More specifically, Konolige considers the first-order modal language, where the usual formatting rule specifying formulae of the form LA is replaced by

If A is a closed formula, then LA is a formula.

All the results of this section hold for such a restricted first-order autoepistemic logic, provided, of course, that various propositional notions are replacec by their first-order counterparts.

We hope to have provided a relatively detailed description of autoepistemic logic. A few other results concerning this formalism, in particular, a syntactic characterization of theories possessing AE extensions, can be found in a paper of Marek & Truszczynski (1988). See also Konolige (1989) and Morris (1989). For a decision procedure for autoepistemic logic, consult Niemelä (1988).

4.4 OTHER BASES FOR MODAL NON-MONOTONIC LOGIC

In this section we briefly present two versions of modal non-monotonic logic based on different foundations. We start with Gabbay's proposal based on intuitionistic logic and then sketch Turner's system employing Kleene's three-valued logic.

4.4.1 Intuitionistic basis for modal non-monotonic logic

Inspired by significant weaknesses of McDermott and Doyle's first non-monotonic formalism, Gabbay (1982) suggests reconstructing it in terms of intuitionistic inference. Before discussing this proposal, the reader is provided with a brief introduction to monotonic intuitionistic logic.

The intuitionistic logic is a result of certain philosophical considerations on the foundations of mathematics, known as *intuitionism*. Intuitionists' point of view on the nature of basic logical and set-theoretical concepts differs from that of most mathematicians. One of the differences concerns the interpretation of logical constants.

Classically, the meaning of a logical constant is a rule specifying the truth-conditions for a formula containing the constant as its primary connective. For instance, the meaning of the implication is the rule stating that any formula of the form $A \supset B$ is true iff A is false or B is true.

Intuitionism is heavily influenced by the assumption that a formula is true iff it has a proof. Accordingly, intuitionistic meaning of a logical constant is best understood when viewed as a specification of what is to count as aproof of a formula with the constant as its main connective.† For instance, the intuitionistic meaning of the implication is the statement that to prove a formula of the form $A \supset B$ is to find a

† This interpretation was originally proposed by Heyting (1930).

method by which any (intuitionistic) proof of A can be transformed into (intuitionistic) proof of B. In other words, the intuitionist accepts a formula $A \supset B$ iff a proof of B can be constructively deduced from a proof of A. The negation is closely related to the implication. To intuitionistically prove a formula $\neg A$ is to show $A \supset False$. That is, $\neg A$ is accepted by the intuitionist if the acceptance of A allows a contradiction to be constructively derived. Under this interpretation of implication and negation, it should be clear that the formula $A \supset \neg(\neg A)$ is intuitionistically acceptable, whereas the formula $\neg(\neg A) \supset A$ is not.

To intuitionistically prove a disjunction is to prove one of its disjuncts. Accordingly, $A \vee B$ is accepted by the intuitionist iff at least one of A, B is provable and there is a constructive method allowing determination as to which of them it is. The latter requirement forces the intuitionist to reject the law of excluded middle: $A \vee \neg A$.

Finally, to intuitionistically prove a conjunction is to have proofs of both its conjuncts.

The detailed presentation of intuitionism is beyond the scope of this book.[†] We focus not on intuitionism itself but on *intuitionistic logic* – a deduction system intended to formalize basic ideas of intuitionism. We limit our attention to the propositional case.[‡]

The language of (propositional) intuitionistic logic is the usual propositional language with $\neg$, $\supset$, $\vee$ and $\wedge$ as sentential connectives.[§] Like classical logic, intuitionistic logic may be defined as a deduction system. The following specification is due to Heyting (1930).

Definition 4.120 Let L be a propositional language. By $\mathrm{I}(L)$ we denote the deduction system $\langle L, \mathrm{S}, \mathrm{R}\rangle$, where

(i) S consists of the following axioms (A, B and C stand for any formulae from L):

(1) $A \supset (A \wedge A)$
(2) $(A \wedge B) \supset (B \wedge A)$
(3) $(A \supset B) \supset ((A \wedge C) \supset (B \wedge C))$
(4) $((A \supset B) \wedge (B \supset C)) \supset (A \supset C)$
(5) $B \supset (A \supset B)$
(6) $(A \wedge (A \supset B)) \supset B$
(7) $A \supset (A \vee B)$
(8) $(A \vee B) \supset (B \vee A)$
(9) $((A \supset C) \wedge (B \supset C)) \supset ((A \vee B) \supset C)$
(10) $\neg A \supset (A \supset B)$
(11) $((A \supset B) \wedge (A \supset \neg B)) \supset \neg B$.

(ii) R contains modus ponens as its only rule.

∎

[†] The best introductions to intuitionism are Heyting (1956) and Dummett (1977).

[‡] It should be made clear that intuitionistic logic reflects foundations of intuitionism from the standpoint of the classical mathematician. Many results concerning this formalism, especially those obtained by non-constructive methods, are unacceptable for the real intuitionist.

[§] In intuitionistic logic neither disjunction nor conjunction can be defined by means of negation and implication; both $\vee$ and $\wedge$ must be taken as primitive connectives.

All ordinary notions of classical logic carry over to intuitionistic logic. So, we may speak about intuitionistic proofs, theorems, theories, etc. We normally assume that the language L is fixed and we write $\vdash_I$ instead of $\vdash_{I(L)}$. Th_I stands for the intuitionistic provability operator, i.e. $\mathrm{Th}_I(T) = \{A: T \vdash_I A\}$.

We state a few facts concerning this axiomatization. For proofs the reader may consult Rasiowa & Sikorski (1970).

Theorem 4.121 For any theory T, $\mathrm{Th}_I(T) \subset \mathrm{Th}(T)$, where Th is the provability operator of classical propositional logic. ∎

Theorem 4.122 The addition of the schema $A \vee \neg A$ to (1)–(11) leads to classical propositional logic. ∎

Theorem 4.123 For every theory T and formula A:

(1) $A \in \mathrm{Th}(T)$ iff $\neg\neg A \in \mathrm{Th}_I(T)$
(2) $\neg A \in \mathrm{Th}(T)$ iff $\neg A \in \mathrm{Th}_I(T)$.

∎

The logical literature offers a few semantics for intuitionistic logic. The most common is perhaps that of Kripke (1965).†

Kripke's semantics is best illustrated in terms of acquiring knowledge. Consider a flow of time $(\mathrm{U}, \leq)$, where U is a set of moments of time and $\leq$ is a pre-order on U, i.e. a transitive and reflexive relation on U, interpreted as the earlier–later relation. To each $\mathrm{t} \in \mathrm{U}$ and each proposition constant p, there is assigned a truth-value $\mathrm{m}(\mathrm{t}, p)$. $\mathrm{m}(\mathrm{t}, p)$ is not interpreted as 'p is true at t'; it is interpreted as 'p is *established* (*known*) at t'. An important assumption is that if $\mathrm{t} \leq \mathrm{t}'$ and $\mathrm{m}(\mathrm{t}, p) = 1$, then $\mathrm{m}(\mathrm{t}', p) = 1$ – once p is established, it will never be lost.

Proposition constants represent unit facts which can be used to establish complex statements. Accordingly, the notion of 'being established' is extended to the whole language. A formula of the form $A \vee B$ (resp. $A \wedge B$) is viewed as established at t iff A is established at t or (resp. and) B enjoys this property. $A \supset B$ is established at t iff for any $\mathrm{t}' \in \mathrm{U}$, if $\mathrm{t} \leq \mathrm{t}'$ nd A is established at t', then B is also established. Finally, $\neg A$ is established at t, iff there is no $\mathrm{t}' \in \mathrm{U}$ such that $\mathrm{t} \leq \mathrm{t}'$ and A is established at t'. Given these rules and the mentioned constraint on m, it is readily seen that no piece of established information will be ever discarded; as time proceeds, more and more knowledge is acquired.

All this is formalized below.

Definition 4.124 An *intuitionistic frame for* L is a triple $\mathrm{M} = \langle \mathrm{U}, \leq, \mathrm{m} \rangle$, where

(i) U is a non-empty set of 'moments of time';
(ii) $\leq$ is a reflexive and transitive relation on U;
(iii) m is a function which to each $\mathrm{t} \in \mathrm{U}$ and each proposition constant from L assigns an element of $\{0, 1\}$; if $\mathrm{t} \leq \mathrm{t}'$ and $\mathrm{m}(\mathrm{t}, p) = 1$, then $\mathrm{m}(\mathrm{t}', p) = 1$.

∎

In the following, $\mathrm{t} \geq \mathrm{t}'$ stands for $\mathrm{t}' \leq \mathrm{t}$.

We employ the notation $\mathrm{t} \models_{\mathrm{M}} A$ to indicate that A is *established at* t *in* M. This is defined by the following rules:

(1) $\mathrm{t} \models_{\mathrm{M}} p$ iff $\mathrm{m}(\mathrm{t}, p) = 1$, where p is a proposition constant in L;

† I slightly change Kripke's original presentation here.

(2) $t \models_M A \vee B$ iff $t \models_M A$ or $t \models_M B$;
(3) $t \models_M A \wedge B$ iff $t \models_M A$ and $t \models_M B$;
(4) $t \models_M A \supset B$ iff $t' \models_M B$ whenever $t' \models_M A$, for each $t' \geq t$;
(5) $t \models_M \neg A$ iff there is no $t' \geq t$ such that $t' \models_M A$.
∎

We write $t \not\models_M A$ as the negation of $t \models_M A$.

Definition 4.125 We say that A is *true* in $M = \langle U, \leq, m\rangle$ iff $t \models_M A$, for all $t \in U$. A theory T is said to be *established at* t *in* M, written $t \models_M T$, iff $t \models_M A$, for all $A \in T$. T is *satisfiable* iff $t \models_M T$, for some M, t. Theories T and T' are *intuitionistically equivalent* iff, for each frame $M = \langle U, \leq, m\rangle$ and each $t \in U$, $t \models_M T$ iff $t \models_M T'$. Formulae A and A' are intuitionistically equivalent iff the theories $\{A\}$ and $\{A'\}$ enjoy this property. A formula A is *intuitionistically entailed by a theory* T, written $T \models_I A$, iff, for each $M = \langle U, \leq, t\rangle$ and each $t \in U$, $t \models_M A$ whenever $t \models_M T$. Finally, we say that A is *intuitionistically valid*, and we write $\models_I A$, iff A is entailed by $T = \{\ \}$, or, equivalently, iff A is true in every intuitionistic frame M. ∎

The following result is due to Kripke:

Theorem 4.126 For any T and A:

(1) $\vdash_I A$ iff $\models_I A$
(2) $T \vdash_I A$ iff $t \models_I A$.
∎

Example 4.127 Consider the frame $M = \langle U, \leq, m\rangle$, where $U = \{a, b\}$, $a \leq b$, $m(a, p) = 0$ and $m(b, p) = 1$. Since $a \not\models_M \neg p$ and $a \not\models_M p$, $a \not\models_M p \vee \neg p$. This shows that $p \vee \neg p$ is not intuitionistically valid. ∎

Example 4.128 Define $A \equiv B$ as the usual abbreviation for $(A \supset B) \wedge (B \supset A)$ and consider the schema $A \vee B \equiv \neg A \supset B$. This clasically valid schema is intuitionistically invalid. To show this, put $A = p$, $B = \neg p$ and take the frame from Example 4.127. Since $a \not\models_M p \vee \neg p$ and $a \models_M \neg p \supset \neg p$, we have $a \not\models_M (p \vee \neg p) \equiv (\neg p \supset \neg p)$. ∎

We are now ready to present Gabbay's non-monotonic logic. He starts by extending Kripke's semantics for intuitionistic logic to the propositional modal language including M as its only modal operator. We shall refer to this language as $L^{(M)}$.† According to Gabbay, a formula of the form MA is to be read 'It is consistent to assume at this stage that A is true.' Thus, MA may be considered as established now if it is possible that A will be established in the future.‡

Let $A \in L^{(M)}$. The relation $t \models_M A$ (A is established at t in M) is defined by the rules (1)–(5) above and

(6) $t \models_M MA$ iff $t' \models_M A$, for some $t' \geq t$.

Gabbay ignores the operator L and we shall not try to introduce it to the language. The reader may easily verify that the usual definition of L as an abbreviation for $\neg M \neg$

† In fact, due to the free choice of proposition constants, $L^{(M)}$ refers to a family of languages.
‡ Of course, the possibility of establishing A in the future does not mean that this will be the case. Notice that since $\leq$ need not be a linear ordering in U, an intuitionistic frame generally admits many different scenarios of acquiring knowledge.

leads to the following rule:

$$\mathrm{t} \models_{\mathrm{M}} \mathrm{L}A \text{ iff for each } \mathrm{t}' \geq \mathrm{t} \text{ there is } \mathrm{t}'' \geq \mathrm{t}' \text{ such that } \mathrm{t}'' \models_{\mathrm{M}} A.$$

All the semantic notions from Definition 4.125 carry over to Gabbay's extension of intuitionistic logic (G-logic, for short). To indicate that these concepts concern the extended system, they will be prefixed by 'G'. So, we may say that a formula A is G-*true in* M; A is G-*satisfiable*; T and T' (resp. A and A') are G-*equivalent*, A is G- entailed by T (notation $T \models_{\mathrm{G}} A$); A is G-*valid*.

Example 4.129 We show that for each $A \in L^{(\mathrm{M})}$, the formula $\mathrm{M}A \vee \neg A$ is G-valid. Take any frame $\mathrm{M} = \langle \mathrm{U}, \leq, \mathrm{m} \rangle$ and let $\mathrm{t} \in \mathrm{U}$. Consider two cases:

(1) $\mathrm{t}' \models_{\mathrm{M}} A$, for some $\mathrm{t}' \geq \mathrm{t}$. Then, $\mathrm{t} \models_{\mathrm{M}} \mathrm{M}A$, and so, $\mathrm{t} \models_{\mathrm{M}} \mathrm{M}A \vee \neg A$.
(2) $\mathrm{t}' \not\models_{\mathrm{M}} A$, for all $\mathrm{t}' \geq \mathrm{t}$. Then $\mathrm{t} \models_{\mathrm{M}} \neg A$, and thus, $\mathrm{t} \models_{\mathrm{M}} \mathrm{M}A \vee \neg A$.

Since M and t were chosen arbitrarily, we conclude that $\mathrm{M}A \vee \neg A$ is G-valid. ∎

The reader may easily check that the following schemata are G-valid:

(G1) $\neg \mathrm{M}A \equiv \neg A$
(G2) $(\mathrm{M}A \supset B) \equiv \neg A \vee B$
(G3) $(\mathrm{M}A \supset A) \equiv \neg A \vee A$
(G4) $(\mathrm{M}A \supset \neg A) \equiv \neg A$
(G5) $\mathrm{M}(A \wedge B) \supset \mathrm{M}A \wedge \mathrm{M}B$.

Although G-logic is only a basis for Gabbay's non-monotonic formalism, it is strong enough to solve the problems typical for McDermott and Doyle's first non-monotonic logic (Examples 4.13, 4.14 and 4.15).

Example 4.130 Let $T = \{\mathrm{M}p, \neg p\}$. In conformity with our intuition, T is unsatisfiable in G-logic by (G1). ∎

Example 4.131 Let $T = \{\neg \mathrm{M}p\}$. In G-logic, T is equivalent to $\{\neg p\}$ by (G1). This agrees with our expectations. ∎

Example 4.132 Let $T = \{\mathrm{M}(p \wedge q), \neg p\}$. By (G1) and (G5), T is unsatisfiable in G-logic. This is intuitively sound. ∎

Gabbay provides an axiomatization for G-logic but we omit it here.

We now proceed to present Gabbay's non-monotonic logic. In contrast to the non-monotonic logics we have studied so far, Gabbay's proposal is not based on the notion of an extension. Instead, he introduces the following concept:

Definition 4.133 (Gabbay 1982) We say that a formula B *non-monotonically follows from a formula* A, and we write $A \mathrel{|\!\sim}_{\mathrm{G}} B$, iff there exists a finite sequence of formulae $C_0 = A, C_1, \ldots, C_n = B$ and a set EA of formulae

$$\begin{array}{ccc} \mathrm{M}D^1_1, & \ldots, & \mathrm{M}D^1_{\mathrm{k}(1)} \\ \vdots & & \vdots \\ \mathrm{M}D^{\mathrm{n}}_1, & \ldots, & \mathrm{M}D^{\mathrm{n}}_{\mathrm{k}(\mathrm{n})} \end{array}$$

called *extra assumptions*, such that:

(1) $\left\{C_{\mathrm{i}-1} \wedge \bigwedge_{\mathrm{j}=1}^{\mathrm{k}(\mathrm{i})} \mathrm{M}D^{\mathrm{i}}_{\mathrm{j}}\right\} \models_{\mathrm{G}} C_{\mathrm{i}}$, for all $1 \leq \mathrm{i} \leq \mathrm{n}$, $1 \leq \mathrm{j} \leq \mathrm{k}(\mathrm{i})$;

(2) If $\{A\}$ is G-satisfiable, then EA $\cup \{A\}$ is G-satisfiable.

The sequence $C_0, C_1, \ldots, C_n$ is called a *non-monotonic proof of B from A*. ▮

Condition (2), actually omitted in Gabbay's original definition, restricts extra assumptions of a non-monotonic proof to those not leading to G-unsatisfiability. If this restriction is ignored, the notion of a non-monotonic proof becomes very problematic. For instance, any formula will non-monotonically follow from any formula of the form $\neg A$ (we may take MA as an extra assumption and then, since $t \not\models_M \neg A \wedge MA$ (for all M, t), we have $\{\neg A \wedge MA\} \models_G B$, for every formula B).

Example 4.134 Let $A = Mp \supset p$. Since $\{(Mp \supset p) \wedge Mp\} \models_G p$ and $\{(Mp \supset p) \wedge Mp\}$ is G-satisfiable, the sequence $C_0 = Mp \supset p, C_1 = p$ is a non-monotonic proof of p from A. The set of extra assumptions used in this proof is EA $= \{M\, p\}$.

Similarly, since $\{(Mp \supset p) \wedge M\neg p\} \models_G \neg p$ and $\{(Mp \supset p) \wedge M\neg p\}$ is G-satisfiable, the sequence $C'_0 = Mp \supset p, C'_1 = \neg p$ is a non-monotonic proof of $\neg p$ from A. For this proof, E$A = \{M\neg p\}$.

In conclusion, $A \mid\!\sim_G p$ and $A \mid\!\sim_G \neg p$. ▮

This example shows that Gabbay's system is problematic as regards its application to formalizing common-sense reasoning. That a formula and its negation may be non-monotonically derivable from a particular sentence is neither surprising nor leads to real difficulties. We may, as Gabbay puts it, take any alternative and go on from there. The problem, however, is that if we choose to infer $\neg p$ from $Mp \supset p$, our choice will be intuitively unsound. Remember that from common-sense perspective, the intended interpretation of $Mp \supset p$ is 'p is to be considered true as default'.

The concept '*B non-monotonically follows from a formula A*' can be trivially generalized to '*B non-monotonically follows from a theory T*':

Definition 4.135 A formula B *non-monotonically follows from a theory T*, written $T \mid\!\sim_G B$, iff $A \mid\!\sim_G B$, where $A = A_1 \wedge \cdots \wedge A_n$, and $A_i \in T$, for each $1 \leq i \leq n$. ▮

Example 4.136 Let $T = \{Mp \supset p, p \wedge Mq \supset q\}$.
Take $A = (Mp \supset p) \wedge (p \wedge Mq \supset q)$. Since $\{A \wedge Mp\} \models_G A \wedge p$, $\{A \wedge p \wedge Mq\} \models_G q$, and the set $\{A\} \cup \{Mp, Mq\}$ is G-satisfiable, the sequence $C_0 = A$, $C_1 = A \wedge p$, $C_2 = q$ is a non-monotonic proof of q from A. (EA $= \{Mp, Mq\}$.) Thus, $T \mid\!\sim_G q$. ▮

For some further results concerning G-logic, the reader is referred to Clarke (1988).

We conclude this section by remarking that Gabbay offers a sketch of another non-monotonic system employing intuitionistic logic as a basis. This system does not belong to the class of modal non-monotonic logics since it is specified over a non-modal language. (See Gabbay 1982 for details.)

4.4.2 3-Valued basis for modal non-monotonic logic

Another approach to the problem of formalizing non-monotonic logic has been proposed by Turner (1984). His system, related to that of Gabbay, is based on Kleene's 3-valued logic.

In contrast to the classical view, where each formula is either true or false, 3-valued logics admit a third truth-value. This value may be interpreted differently in different logics, but generally represents a state between truth and falsehood.[†]

[†] A detailed survey of three-valued logics can be found in Haack (1974, 1978). For an introduction to the subject the reader may consult Turner (1984).

In Kleene's 3-valued logic (Kleene 1952), a formula may be *true* (1), *false* (0) or *undecided* (u). Intuitively, a formula is to be assigned the value u if its classical truth-value is unknown. This interpretation leads to the following truth-tables for sentential connectives:

$\neg$A	
1	0
u	u
0	1

A $\wedge$ B	1	u	0
1	1	u	0
u	u	u	0
0	0	0	0

A $\vee$ B	1	u	0
1	1	1	1
u	1	u	u
0	1	u	0

A $\supset$ B	1	u	0
1	1	u	0
u	1	u	u
0	1	1	1

A $\equiv$ B	1	u	0
1	1	u	0
u	u	u	u
0	0	u	1

Kleene's logic (K-*logic*, for short) is specified over the classical language L. To simplify our discussion, only the propositional part of L will be considered. We omit the axiomatization of Kleene's logic and directly proceed to its semantics.

Definition 4.137 A *partial interpretation* for L is a function m which assigns to each proposition constant from L an element of $\{0, 1, u\}$. ∎

The *value of a formula A in an interpretation* m, denoted by $V^m(A)$, is an element of $\{0, u, 1\}$ specified as follows:

(1) $V^m(p) = m(p)$, for each proposition constant p
(2) $V^m(\neg A) = \neg V^m(A)$
(3) $V^m(A \wedge B) = V^m(A) \wedge V^m(B)$
(4) $V^m(A \vee B) = V^m(A) \vee V^m(B)$
(5) $V^m(A \supset B) = V^m(A) \supset V^m(B)$
(6) $V^m(A \equiv B) = V^m(A) \equiv V^m(B)$

where $\neg$, $\wedge$, $\vee$, $\supset$ and $\equiv$ are evaluated according to the truth-tables above.

We say that A is K-*valid* iff $V^m(A) = 1$, for each partial interpretation m.

It is interesting to notice that the law of excluded middle fails in K-logic, i.e. the schema $A \vee \neg A$ is not K-valid.

The set of truth-values $\{1, u, 0\}$ has a natural partial ordering, $\leq$, given by: $1 \leq 1$, $u \leq u$, $0 \leq 0$, $u \leq 0$, $u \leq 1$. Pictorially:

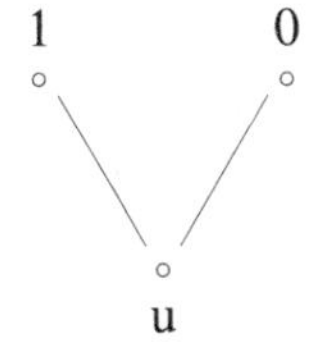

Intuitively, $i \leq j$ iff i provides less (or equal) information than j.

Definition 4.138 Let m and m′ be partial interpretations for L. We say that m′ *extends* m, written $m \leq m'$, iff $m(p) \leq m'(p)$, for each proposition constant $p \in L$. ∎

Theorem 4.139 For each $A \in L$, if $m \leq m'$, then $V^{m}(A) \leq V^{m'}(A)$.

Proof Straightforward induction on A. ▮

Given this result, the statement 'm_1 extends m_2' has a natural interpretation: m_1 provides more (or equal) information about the current state of affairs than m_2.

We now pass to Turner's non-monotonic logic. In his original presentation, the system is specified over a first-order modal language, including M as its only modal operator. Here, we shall limit our attention to the propositional part of the language, denoted by $L^{(M)}$. A formula of the form MA is to be read as 'A is plausible'.

Turner's proposal is conceptually based on the following two assumptions:

(1) Non-monotonic inferences are necessary and appropriate in these situations only when our knowledge about the actual world is incomplete.
(2) Any non-monotonically derived conclusion must be *plausible* with respect to our partial state of information.

In Turner's system, incomplete states of information are represented by partial interpretations of K-logic. To capture the idea of 'plausible conclusion', he introduces a binary relation, $\sqsubseteq$, operating between such interpretations. $m_1 \sqsubseteq m_2$ is to be read 'm_2 plausibly extends m_1'. The intention is that A is plausible relative to a state of knowledge represented by m iff A is true in some interpretation which plausibly extends m.

It should be stressed that the plausibility relation $\sqsubseteq$ is a primitive concept. Just like the accessibility relation employed in modal logic, it is not subject to the precise definition. The best we may expect is to impose certain properties on this relation, reflected by our understanding of the word 'plausible'.

Definition 4.140 (Turner 1984) Let $\sqsubseteq$ be a binary relation specified on a set F of partial interpretations of K-logic. We say that $\sqsubseteq$ *is a plausibility relation* iff

(1) $m \sqsubseteq m'$ implies $m \leq m'$
(2) $m \sqsubseteq m$
(3) $m \sqsubseteq m'$ and $m' \sqsubseteq m''$ implies $m \sqsubseteq m''$

for all m, m′, m″ in F. ▮

Turner's non-monotonic logic is based on the following semantic concept:

Definition 4.141 (Turner 1984) A *model structure for* $L^{(M)}$ is a system $M = \langle F, \sqsubseteq \rangle$, where F is the set of all partial interpretations for $L^{(M)}$ and $\sqsubseteq$ is a plausibility relation on F. ▮

It is interesting to observe that the notion of a model structure restricts the concept of Kripke's intuitionistic frame. More specifically, each model structure $\langle F, \sqsubseteq \rangle$ can be viewed as an intuitionistic frame $\langle F, \sqsubseteq, m \rangle$, where for every $m' \in F$, $m(m', p) = 1$ iff $m'(p) = 1$. We leave it to the reader to check that $\langle F, \sqsubseteq, m \rangle$ is an intuitionistic frame, provided that $\langle F, \sqsubseteq \rangle$ is a model structure.

Definition 4.142 (Turner 1984) Let $M = \langle F, \sqsubseteq \rangle$ be a model structure for $L^{(M)}$. By $V^{M}_{m}(A)$ we denote the *value of a formula A in* M *wrt* $m \in F$. This is an element of $\{1, u, 0\}$, defined by the following rules:

(1) $V^{M}_{m}(p) = m(p)$, for each proposition constant $p \in L^{(M)}$
(2) $V^{M}_{m}(A \vee B) = V^{M}_{m}(A) \vee V^{M}_{m}(B)$

(3) $V_m^M(A \wedge B) = V_m^M(A) \wedge V_m^M(B)$
(4) $V_m^M(\neg A) = \neg V_m^M(A)$
(5) $V_m^M(A \supset B) = V_m^M(A) \supset V_m^M(B)$
(6) $V_m^M(A \equiv B) = V_m^M(A) \equiv V_m^M(B)$
(7) $$V_m^M(MA) = \begin{cases} 1 & \text{if } V_{m'}^M(A) = 1, \text{ for some } m' \in F \text{ such that } m \sqsubseteq m' \\ 0 & \text{if } V_{m'}^M(A) = 0, \text{ for each } m' \in F \text{ such that } m \sqsubseteq m' \\ u & \text{otherwise} \end{cases}$$

where $\vee$, $\wedge$, $\neg$, $\supset$ and $\equiv$ are connectives of Kleene's logic. ∎

The rules (1)–(6) are exactly the evaluation rules for K-logic. (7) provides the semantics for the operator M. According to the rule, M*A* is true wrt a partial interpretation m iff *A* is true wrt some interpretation which plausibly extends m; M*A* is false wrt m iff *A* is false wrt all interpretations with this property.

Turner's generalization of K-logic will be referred to as T-logic.

Corollary 4.143 Let $A \in L$, i.e. *A* involves no occurrences of the operator M, and suppose that $M = \langle F, \sqsubseteq \rangle$ is a model structure. Then, for all m, m′ in F, $m \sqsubseteq m'$ implies $V_m^M(A) \leq V_{m'}^M(A)$.

Proof By Theorem 4.139. ∎

This result does not generalize to the language $L^{(M)}$.

Example 4.144 Assume that *p* is the only proposition constant of $L^{(M)}$ and consider the model structure $M = \langle F, \sqsubseteq \rangle$ defined by:

$$F = \{m_1, m_2, m_3\}, \text{ where } m_1(p) = u;\ m_2(p) = 0;\ m_3(p) = 1;$$
$$\sqsubseteq = \{\langle m_1, m_2 \rangle, \langle m_1, m_3 \rangle\} \cup \{\langle m_i, m_i \rangle : i = 1, 2, 3\}.$$

Take $A = Mp$. Clearly, $V_{m_1}^M(A) = 1$ and $V_{m_2}^M(A) = 0$. ∎

The semantic notions specified in Definition 4.125 carry over into T-logic. In particular, we say that a formula *A* is *true in* $M = \langle F, \sqsubseteq \rangle$ iff $V_m^M(A) = 1$, for each $m \in F$. A theory *T* is T-*satisfied in* M *by* m, written $m \models_M T$ iff $V_m^M(A) = 1$, for each $A \in T$. *T* is T-*satisfiable* iff $m \models_M T$, for some $M = \langle F, \sqsubseteq \rangle$ and some $m \in F$. A formula *A* is T-*entailed by T*, written $T \models_T A$, iff $m \models_M A$ whenever $m \models_M T$, for every $M = \langle F, \sqsubseteq \rangle$ and every $m \in F$. If $T \models_T A$, we also say that *A* T-*follows* from *T*.

Turner advocates T-logic as a basis for non-monotonic logic. However, just like G-logic, it is strong enough to avoid the typical problems of McDermott and Doyle's logic.

Example 4.145 Let $T = \{\neg Mp\}$. In accord with our intuition, $T \models_T \neg p$. To show this, take any model structure $M = \langle F, \sqsubseteq \rangle$ and assume that $V_m^M(\neg Mp) = 1$, for some $m \in F$. Then, $V_m^M(Mp) = 0$ and so, $V_{m'}^M(p) = 0$, for each m′ such that $m \sqsubseteq m'$. In particular, $V_m^M(p) = 0$ since $m \sqsubseteq m$. Thus, $V_m^M(\neg p) = 1$. ∎

Example 4.146 Let $T = \{Mp, \neg p\}$. In agreement with our expectations, *T* is T-unsatisfiable and hence, any formula T-follows from *T*. To see this, assume to the contrary that $V_m^M(Mp) = 1$ and $V_m^M(\neg p) = 1$, for some $M = \langle F, \sqsubseteq \rangle$ and some $m \in F$. $V_m^M(Mp) = 1$ implies $V_{m'}^M(p) = 1$, for some m′ such that $m \sqsubseteq m'$. $V_m^M(\neg p) = 1$ implies (by Corollary 4.143) that $V_m^M(p) = 0$, for all m′ such that $m \sqsubseteq m'$. A contradiction. ∎

The same argument can be used to show the unsatisfiability of the theory $\{MA, \neg A\}$, provided that *A* involves no occurrences of the operator M. Otherwise, i.e. if *A* includes the operator, $\{MA, \neg A\}$ may be T-satisfiable. Take, for example,

$A = \neg Mp$ and consider the model structure from Example 4.144. It is easily verified that $V^{M}_{m_1}(MA) = 1$ and $V^{M}_{m_1}(\neg A) = 1$.

Turner regards this situation as intuitively correct and I agree with him. Any reader of a different opinion should notice an important point. Any formula without modalities represents a fact about the actual world. Indeed, it is irrational to accept that such a fact is false and simultaneously consider it as plausible. However, if a formula includes modalities, it represents what an agent regards as plausible (implausible) about the world. Since a fact may be plausible with respect to a state of knowledge m and implausible in some extension of m, modalized formulae may change their truth-values when the agent's knowledge increases. If A is such a formula, forcing the unsatisfiability of $\{MA, \neg A\}$ is intuitively unjustified.

Example 4.147 Let $T = \{M(p \wedge q), \neg p\}$. This theory is T-unsatisfiable. More generally, the theory $\{M(A \wedge B), \neg A\}$ is T-unsatisfiable if A includes no occurrences of M. Otherwise, it may be T-satisfiable. ∎

To construct a non-monotonic version of T-logic, Turner suggests employing the 'extra assumption' mechanism of Gabbay.

Replacing the prefix 'G-' by 'T-', everywhere in Definition 4.133, and changing '$\models_G$' into '$\models_T$', we obtain the notion '*B non-monotonically* T-*follows from a formula A*', written $A \mid\!\sim_T B$. This is easily generalized to '*B non-monotonically T-follows from a theory T*, written $T \mid\!\sim_T B$ (compare Definition 4.135).

Example 4.148 Let $T = \{Mp \supset p\}$. In Turner's non-monotonic logic, T behaves exactly like in Gabbay's system, i.e. $T \mid\!\sim_T p$ and $T \mid\!\sim_T \neg p$. We show that $T \mid\!\sim_T \neg p$ by showing that $\{(M_p \supset p) \wedge M\neg p\} \models_T \neg p$ (the reader may easily check that $\{Mp \supset p, M\neg p\}$ is T-satisfiable). Take any model structure $M = \langle F, \sqsubseteq \rangle$ such that $V^{M}_{m}((Mp \supset p) \wedge M\neg p) = 1$, for some $m \in F$, and assume to the contrary that $V^{M}_{m}(\neg p) \neq 1$. Consider two cases.

(1) $V^{M}_{m}(\neg p) = 0$. Then $V^{M}_{m}(p) = 1$ and so, $V^{M}_{m'}(p) = 1$, for any m′ such that $m \sqsubseteq m'$ (by Corollary 4.143). On the other hand, $V^{M}_{m}((Mp \supset p) \wedge M\neg p) = 1$ implies $V^{M}_{m}(M\neg p) = 1$ and thus, $V^{M}_{m'}(p) = 0$, for some m′ such that $m \sqsubseteq m'$. A contradiction.
(2) $V^{M}_{m}(\neg p) = u$. Then, $V^{M}_{m}(p) = u$. $V^{M}_{m}((Mp \supset p) \wedge M\neg p) = 1$ implies $V^{M}_{m}(Mp \supset p) = 1$. Thus, since $V^{M}_{m}(p) = u$, $V^{M}_{m}(Mp) = 0$. So, $V^{M}_{m'}(p) = 0$, for each m′ such that $m \sqsubseteq m'$. In particular, $V^{M}_{m}(p) = 0$ since $m \sqsubseteq m$. A contradiction.
∎

The possibility of deriving $\neg p$ from $Mp \supset p$ shows that Turner's non-monotonic logic suffers exactly the same problems as Gabbay's formalism when viewed as a tool for representing common-sense inferences (see the discussion following Example 4.134).

This exhausts our presentation of modal non-monotonic logics. For other relevant contributions to the subject the reader may consult Levesque (1982), Łukaszewicz (1984a) and Halpern & Moses (1984).

5

Default logic

This chapter is devoted to *default logic* – a non-monotonic formalism introduced by Reiter (1980a). Conceptual simplicity makes Reiter's proposal one of the most interesting formal approaches to the subject of non-monotonic inference.

The major distinction between default logic and modal non-monotonic logics studied in the previous chapter arises from different representation of non-monotonic rules. While in modal non-monotonic logics these rules are expressed by formulae of the object language, in default logic they are represented by special linguistic expressions, referred to as *defaults*.

In default logic the rule sanctioning non-monotonic inferences about birds being able to fly can be expressed by the following default:

$$\frac{Bird(x)\colon Can\text{-}Fly(x)}{Can\text{-}Fly(x)}.$$

This default is intuitively interpreted as 'For every individual x, if x is a bird and it is consistent to believe that x can fly, then it is to be believed that x can fly.' Thus, if all we know about Tweety is that she is a bird, we are permitted to believe that she flies. However, if we learn that Tweety is an ostrich, and we already know that ostriches are not fliers, it is inconsistent to believe that Tweety flies and, in consequence, the application of the default will be blocked.

In default logic, common-sense knowledge about the modelled world is represented as a *default theory*, i.e. a pair consisting of a set of first-order sentences, called the *axioms* of the theory, and a set of defaults. The axioms represent logically valid, but generally incomplete information about the world. The defaults extend this information by sanctioning plausible, although not necessarily true conclusions.

Any set of beliefs one may hold about a world described by a default theory is called an *extension* of the theory. The formal definition of this concept is technically complex.

Intuitively, an extension contains all the sentences which can be derived from axioms either by classical first-order logic or by applying defaults.

The rest of this chapter is organized as follows. After preliminary considerations, the problem of transforming arbitrary default theories into a special class of *closed default theories* is discussed. In section 5.3, the foundations of Reiter's original version of default logic are studied. A formal definition of an extension is introduced and basic properties of default theories are examined. The most pessimistic result is that there are theories lacking extensions. Section 5.4 is devoted to a very important class of *normal default theories*. It is shown that each closed normal default theory has at least one extension. In section 5.5 some representational issues are discussed and a more general class of *semi-normal default theories* is introduced. It is argued that these theories are sufficient to cover all settings which occur in practical applications. Formal properties of semi-normal theories are examined in section 5.6. Sections 5.7 and 5.8 are concerned with semantics and proof theory of default logic, whereas section 5.9 provides a relationship between Reiter's formalism and autoepistemic logic. In section 5.10, an alternative definition of an extension, leading to a different version of default logic, is introduced. The foundations of this system are studied in section 5.11. It turns out that the new version has some nice properties, not guaranteed in Reiter's original proposal. Semantics and proof theory of the alternative default logic are discussed in sections 5.12 and 5.13.

In this chapter, except for section 5.9, the symbols 'Th' and '$\vdash$' ('$\nvdash$') refer to the provability operator and the provability (unprovability) relation of classical first-order logic.

5.1 PRELIMINARIES

As remarked, default logic makes explicit distinction between undeniable facts and non-monotonic rules. The former are expressed by sentences of classical first-order logic. The latter are represented by special linguistic expressions, called defaults.

Definition 5.1 (Reiter 1980a) A *default* is any expression of the form

$$\frac{A(\bar{x})\colon B_1(\bar{x}), \ldots, B_k(\bar{x})}{C(\bar{x})} \tag{5.1.1}$$

where $A(\bar{x})$, $B_1(\bar{x})$, ..., $B_k(\bar{x})$, and $C(\bar{x})$ are first-order formulae whose free variables are among those of $\bar{x} = (x_1, \ldots, x_n)$. $A(\bar{x})$ is called the *prerequisite*, $B_1(\bar{x}), \ldots, B_k(\bar{x})$ the *justifications*, and $C(\bar{x})$ the *consequent* of the default.† ∎

The default (5.1.1) is to be interpreted as 'For all individuals $\bar{x} = (x_1, \ldots, x_n)$, if $A(\bar{x})$ is believed and $B_1(\bar{x}), \ldots, B_k(\bar{x})$ are all consistent with what is believed, then $C(\bar{x})$ is to be believed'.

We now give a number of examples illustrating how various forms of non-monotonic reasoning can be expressed by defaults. The terminology used is that of Chapter 2.

Example 5.2 (Prototypical Reasoning)

Typically, children have parents. (5.1.2)

† In plain text, the default (5.1.1) will be usually written in the form $A(\bar{x})\colon B_1(\bar{x}), \ldots, B_k(\bar{x})/C(\bar{x})$.

(5.1.2) is to be interpreted as the non-monotonic rule stating 'In the absence of evidence to the contrary, assume about any particular child that it has parents.' We represent this by the default:

$$\frac{Child(x) \colon Has\text{-}Parents(x)}{Has\text{-}Parents(x)}.$$

The exceptional cases are stated in the framework of first-order representation:

$\neg Has\text{-}Parents(Joe)$
$\forall x \,.\, Lives\text{-}in\text{-}Orphanage(x) \supset \neg Has\text{-}Parents(x)$
etc.

▮

Example 5.3 (Prototypical Reasoning)

> Typically, if one has a birthday, friends give him/her gifts. (Dunin-Kęplicz 1984)

We represent this by

$$\frac{Birthday(x) \wedge Friend(y, x) \colon Gives\text{-}Gift(y, x)}{Gives\text{-}Gift(y, x)}.$$

▮

Example 5.4 (No-risk Reasoning)

> Assume that the accused is innocent unless you know otherwise. (Bowen & Kowalski 1982)

This rule can be expressed by

$$\frac{Accused(x) \colon Innocent(x)}{Innocent(x)}.$$

▮

Example 5.5 (The Best-Guess Reasoning)

> In the absence of evidence to the contrary, assume that the best solution found so far is the best one.

This non-monotonic rule (McCarthy 1984) can be represented by

$$\frac{Solution\text{-}Found\text{-}So\text{-}Far\text{-}Best(x) \colon Best\text{-}Solution(x)}{Best\text{-}Solution(x)}.$$

▮

Example 5.6 (Explicit Autoepistemic Reasoning)

> The meeting will be on Wednesday unless another decision is explicitly made (Doyle 1979).

We represent this by

$$\frac{\colon Meeting\text{-}at\text{-}Wednesday}{Meeting\text{-}at\text{-}Wednesday}^{\dagger}.$$

▮

† This prerequisite-free default is an abbreviation for *True: Meeting-at-Wednesday/Meeting-at-Wednesday*.

Example 5.7 (Subjective Autoepistemic Reasoning)

> In the absence of evidence to the contrary, assume that you have no elder brother. (Moore 1983)

This can be represented by the following default:

$$\frac{:\neg I\text{-}Have\text{-}Brother}{\neg I\text{-}Have\text{-}Brother}.$$

∎

Default logic considers pairs consisting of a set of first-order sentences and a set of defaults as the primary objects of interest. Such a pair, called a *default theory*, is meant to represent common-sense knowledge about a world.

Definition 5.8 (Reiter 1980a) A default theory is a pair $T = \langle W, D \rangle$, where W is a set of first-order sentences, *axioms of T*, and D is a set of defaults.† ∎

Example 5.9 Assume that our initial knowledge about a world consists of the proposition 'Marco, Carlo and Giuseppe are Italians' and the prototypical fact 'Typically, Italians are Christians'. This information can be represented by the default theory consisting of the axiom

(A1) $Italian(Marco) \wedge Italian(Carlo) \wedge Italian(Giuseppe)$

and the single default

(D1) $\dfrac{Italian(x)\colon Christian(x)}{Christinan(x).}$

Given the above theory, we can infer that each of the three Italians is a Christian.

Suppose now that we learn that Giuseppe is not a Christian. To formalize this, we add the axiom

(A2) $\neg Christian(Giuseppe)$.

Observe that our previous belief about Giuseppe's Christianity has been invalidated.

Assume now that Marco has turned out to be a communist. We formalize this by adding the axiom

(A3) $Communist(Marco)$.

Note that given all the above information, we may still infer that Marco is a Christian.

Depending upon our opinion about communists' Christianity, this problematic conclusion can be blocked in various ways.

If we believe that communists are never Christians, we add the axiom

(A4) $\forall x\,.\,Communist(x) \supset \neg Christian(x)$.

If we want to remain agnostic about the Christian status of communists, we replace

---

† Strictly speaking, a default theory should be specified as a triple $\langle L, W, D \rangle$, where L is a first-order language, W is a set of sentences from L, and D is a set of defaults whose prerequisites, justifications and consequents are formulae of L. When we say that a default theory is a pair $\langle W, D \rangle$, we implicitly assume that the language is fixed.

(D1) by

$$\text{(D2)}\quad \frac{Italian(x)\colon Christian(x) \wedge \neg Communist(x)}{Christian(x)}.$$

Note that given the theory $\langle\{A1, A2, A3\}, \{D2\}\rangle$, we can neither infer that Marco is a Christian nor that he is not.

The third way of blocking the conclusion that Marco is a Christian is to introduce the new default stating 'In the absence of evidence to the contrary, assume that a communist is not a Christian':

$$\text{(D3)}\quad \frac{Communist(x)\colon \neg Christian(x)}{\neg Christian(x)}.$$

The problem with this representation is that there is a conflict between (D1) and (D3) concerning Marco. Although each of these defaults is applicable to him, we cannot apply them both.† This suggests that the theory $\langle\{(A1), (A2), (A3)\}, \{(D1), (D2)\}\rangle$ supports two different sets of beliefs about the modelled world. One of them contains the proposition that Marco is a Christian, the other that he is not. Although such alternative sets of beliefs are sometimes reasonable, this is not the case here. Given that Marco is both an Italian and a communist, we should prefer to believe that he is not a Christian. The reader will check that the desired effect can be obtained by replacing (D1) by (D2), with (D3) unchanged. ∎

A default $A(\bar{x})\colon B_1(\bar{x}), \ldots, B_k(\bar{x})/C(\bar{x})$ is called *open* iff at least one of $A(\bar{x})$, $B_1(\bar{x}), \ldots, B_k(\bar{x})$, $C(\bar{x})$ contains a free variable; otherwise, it is called *closed*. A default theory is said to be *open* iff it contains at least one open default; otherwise, it is said to be *closed*. All the defaults we have considered so far, except for those from Examples 5.6 and 5.7, are open.

It is important to note that free variables in a default are viewed as implicitly universally quantified, with scope to cover the whole default. Accordingly, an open default represents a general schema which can be applied to various tuples of individuals.

An *instance* of an open default is the result of uniformly replacing all free occurrences of variables by ground terms. More specifically, an instance of an open default $A(\bar{x})\colon B_1(\bar{x}), \ldots, B_k(\bar{x})/C(\bar{x})$, where $\bar{x} = (x_1, \ldots, x_n)$, is any closed default of the form $A(\bar{\alpha})\colon B_1(\bar{\alpha}) \ldots B_k(\bar{\alpha})/C(\bar{\alpha})$, where $\bar{\alpha}$ is an n-tuple of ground terms. For example, the closed defaults

$$\frac{Fish(Peggy)\colon Can\text{-}Swim(Peggy)}{Can\text{-}Swim(Peggy)} \quad \text{and}$$

$$\frac{Fish(Cousin(Dick))\colon Can\text{-}Swim(Cousin(Dick))}{Can\text{-}Swim(Cousin(Dick))}$$

are instances of

$$\frac{Fish(x)\colon Can\text{-}Swim(x)}{Can\text{-}Swim(x)}.$$

† The application of (D1) blocks that of (D3) and vice versa.

To complete the specification of default logic, we must define the notion of an extension of a default theory. As we remarked, an extension should include whatever can be inferred from axioms either by ordinary logic or by applying defaults. There are then three conditions which can be reasonably imposed on such an extension E of a default theory $\langle W, D \rangle$:

(i) E should be deductively closed with respect to standard logic: $E = Th(E)$.
(ii) E should contain axioms: $W \subseteq E$.
(iii) E should contain a maximal set of conclusions obtainable by applying defaults from D.[†]

Clause (iii) is imprecise because it says nothing about what the phrase 'a maximal set of conclusions obtainable by applying defaults' means. We shall answer this question in the subsequent sections, but first let us consider a simple example.

Example 5.10 Consider the theory T consisting of the axiom

$$Basket\text{-}Player(Bill)$$

and the defaults

$$\frac{Basket\text{-}Player(x): Tall(x)}{Tall(x)} \qquad \frac{Basket\text{-}Player(x): Nimble(x)}{Nimble(x)}.$$

By the first default, Bill is tall; by the second, he is nimble. Since both these defaults can be applied simultaneously, T gives rise to one extension given by

$$E = Th(\{Basket\text{-}Player(Bill), Tall(Bill), Nimble(Bill)\}).$$

Suppose that T' obtains from T by adding the axiom

$$\neg(Tall(Bill) \wedge Nimble(Bill)).$$

Now the situation is more complex. If we start by invoking the first default, we infer that Bill is tall, but the application of the second default will be blocked. If we choose to invoke the second default first, we conclude that he is nimble, but this makes the first default inapplicable. In other words, we can believe that Bill is either tall or nimble, but not both. In consequence, there are two alternative sets of beliefs supported by T':

$$E_1 = Th(\{Basket\text{-}Player(Bill), \neg(Tall(Bill) \wedge Nimble(Bill)), Tall(Bill)\})$$
$$E_2 = Th(\{Basket\text{-}Player(Bill), \neg(Tall(Bill) \wedge Nimble(Bill)), Nimble(Bill)\}).$$

∎

5.2 OPEN DEFAULTS AND THEIR INSTANCES

Since open defaults represent general inference schemata, which can be applied to various individuals, it is natural to indentify such a default with the set of all its instances. Adopting this point of view, we shall be able to eliminate open defaults in favour of their closed instances and, in consequence, to limit our attention to closed theories only.

† Observe that (i)–(iii) imply that an extension of a theory $\langle W, D \rangle$ is always given by $Th(W \cup X)$, where X is a set of conclusions obtainable by applying defaults from D.

The purpose of this section is to formalize the above idea. This will be done by defining a mapping which to every open default theory T assigns a closed theory CLOSED(T), obtaininable from T by replacing all T's open defaults by sets of their instances.

An instance of an open default has been specified as the result of replacing free occurrences of variables by ground terms. Since these terms are to be intuitively viewed as individuals, the first task is to specify the set of individuals of a default theory. To fix some ideas, let us consider a number of examples.

Example 5.11 Let *T be the theory consisting of*:

$$Bird(Tweety) \wedge Bird(Mick) \wedge Fish(Nelly)$$

$$\frac{Bird(x): Has\text{-}Wings(x)}{Has\text{-}Wings(x)}.$$

Given the information included in *T*, *Tweety*, *Mick* and *Nelly* are the only individuals which can be proved to exist in the world modelled by *T*.† It is then reasonable to identify the set of individuals of T with $\{Tweety, Mick, Nelly\}$. In consequence, the closed theory corresponding to T, i.e. CLOSED(T), is

$$Bird(Tweety) \wedge Bird(Mick) \wedge Fish(Nelly)$$

$$\frac{Bird(Tweety): Has\text{-}Wings(Tweety)}{Has\text{-}Wings(Tweety)}$$

$$\frac{Bird(Mick): Has\text{-}Wings(Mick)}{Has\text{-}Wings(Mick)}$$

$$\frac{Bird(Nelly): Has\text{-}Wings(Nelly)}{Has\text{-}Wings(Nelly)}.$$

Since there is no way to infer that Nelly is a bird, the third default will never be applied. However, there is nothing wrong with it. If Nelly were a bird, the conclusion that she is winged would be plausible. ∎

Example 5.12 Let T consist of:

$$Fish(Bob); \forall x . Fish(x) \supset Fish(father(x))$$

$$\frac{Fish(x): Swims(x)}{Swims(x)}.$$

The set of individuals of T is clearly $\{Bob, father(Bob), father(father(Bob)), \ldots\}$. Thus, CLOSED($T$) contains infinitely many defaults of the form

$$\frac{Fish(Bob): Swims(Bob)}{Swims(Bob)}$$

$$\frac{Fish(father(Bob)): Swims(father(Bob))}{Swims(father(Bob))}$$

† This does not mean, of course, that the world cannot contain other individuals.

$$\frac{Fish(father(father(Bob))): Swims(father(father(Bob)))}{Swims(father(father(Bob)))}$$

etc.

∎

As the above examples show, any ground term constructable from function constants explicitly occurring in a theory should be regarded as its individual. That is, the free variables of open defaults should range at least over these terms.

In simple cases, we may restrict ourselves to explicitly nameable individuls. In general, however, there will also be implicitly specified individuals introduced by existential quantifiers.

Example 5.13 Let T be the theory:

$$\exists x . Butterfly(x)$$

$$\frac{Butterfly(x): Brightly\text{-}Coloured(x)}{Brightly\text{-}Coloured(x)}.$$

T refers to an implicitly defined butterfly introduced via the existential quantifier. Intuitively, we would like to infer that this butterfly is brightly coloured, i.e. we expect the sentence $\exists x . Butterfly(x) \wedge Brightly\text{-}Coloured(x)$ to be in an extension of T. To achieve this, we introduce a new individual constant, say a, to denote the butterfly, and replace the axiom of T by $Butterfly(a)$. Then, since the new theory contains no implicitly defined individuals, we continue as in the previous examples. This leads to the following closed theory:

$$Butterfly(a)$$

$$\frac{Butterfly(a): Brightly\text{-}Coloured(a)}{Brightly\text{-}Coloured(a)}.$$

This theory gives rise to one extension:

$$E = Th(\{Butterfly(a), Brightly\text{-}Coloured(a)\})$$

which contains the desired sentence. ∎

An important remark should be made here. Our intention is to regard extensions of a theory T as those of CLOSED(T). Unfortunately, due to introducing new function constants, extensions of CLOSED (T) may admit formulae meaningless with respect to T. (For instance, *Butterfly*(a) in the previous example.) To reject them, the extensions of T should be identified with those of CLOSED(T), restricted to the language of T.

In view of Example 5.13, all axioms of a default theory should be replaced by their Skolemized counterparts, and any ground term constructable from function constants, including constants introduced by Skolemization, is to be regarded as an individual of the theory. While this resolves the problem of implicitly defined individuals introduced by axioms, there still remain those introduced by defaults.

Example 5.14 Let T consist of:

$$Birthday(Bill)$$

$$\frac{:\exists x.Friend(x, Bill)}{\exists x.Friend(x, Bill)}$$

$$\frac{Birthday(y) \wedge Friend(x, y): Gives\text{-}Gift(x, y)}{Gives\text{-}Gift(x, y)}.$$

T names an individual Bill, and implicitly refers to a friend of Bill (introduced by the first default). We intuitively feel that the sentence $\exists x.Friend(x, Bill) \wedge Gives\text{-}Gift(x, Bill)$ should be in an extension of T. To accommodate this, we introduce a new individual constant, say b, and replace the first default by its *Skolemized form*:

$$\frac{:\exists xFriend(x, Bill)}{Friend(b, Bill)}.\dagger$$

Now we proceed in the usual way, arriving at the following theory:

$$Birthday(Bill)$$

$$\frac{:\exists xFriend(x, Bill)}{Friend(b, Bill)}$$

$$\frac{Birthday(Bill) \wedge Friend(b, Bill): Gives\text{-}Gift(b, Bill)}{Gives\text{-}Gift(b, Bill)}$$

$$\frac{Birthday(Bill) \wedge Friend(Bill, Bill): Gives\text{-}Gift(Bill, Bill)}{Gives\text{-}Gift(Bill, Bill)}$$

$$\frac{Birthday(b) \wedge Friend(Bill, b): Gives\text{-}Gift(Bill, b)}{Gives\text{-}Gift(Bill, b)}$$

$$\frac{Birthday(b) \wedge Friend(b, b): Gives\text{-}Gift(b, b)}{Gives\text{-}Gift(b, b)}.$$

∎

In summary, the set of individuals of a default theory should be identified with the set of ground terms constructable from function constants, including those introduced by Skolemizing axioms and defaults.

Let A be a sentence. A *Skolemized form of A* is any universal sentence obtained from any prenex normal form of A by the process of Skolemization.‡

Definition 5.15 A *Skolemized form of a default*

$$\frac{A(\bar{x}): B_1(\bar{x}), \ldots, B_k(\bar{x})}{C(\bar{x})} \qquad x = (x_1, \ldots, x_n)$$

obtains by replacing $C(\bar{x})$ by any Skolemized form of $\forall C(\bar{x})$ and deleting all quantifiers from the consequent of the resulting default. Any Skolem function constant introduced in Skolemization must be distinct from any constant occurring in $A(\bar{x})$, $B_1(\bar{x}), \ldots, B_k(\bar{x})$. ∎

† Observe that the justification of the default remains unchanged.

‡ Recall that any formula may be effectively transformed into its equivalent in prenex normal form (see the discussion following Theorem 1.32, Chapter 1).

Note that only the consequent of a default is changed in converting the default into its Skolemized form. Observe also that due to the free choice of Skolem functions, a default may have more than one Skolemized form.

Definition 5.16 A *Skolemized form of a default theory* T is any theory obtained by replacing defaults and axioms of T by their Skolemized forms. All the introduced Skolem functions must be different and they must also differ from the constants explicitly occuring in T. ▮

Let $T = \langle W, D \rangle$ be a default theory. By TERMS(T) we denote the set of all ground terms constructable using function constants occurring in W and D.

We now are ready to define the transformation CLOSED.

Definition 5.17 Let T be a default theory. A *closure of* T, written CLOSED(T), is any theory obtained by the following construction.

(i) If T is closed, then put CLOSED(T) = T. Otherwise:
(ii) Replace T by its Skolemized form. Denote the resulting theory by T_1.
(iii) Let T_2 be the theory obtained from T_1 by replacing all its open defaults by the set of their instances over TERMS(T_1). This is the desired closure of T.†

▮

Some remarks about this definition are in order.

(1) An open default may give rise to infinitely many instances. Thus, if T is an open theory, the set of defaults of CLOSED(T) will in general be infinite.
(2) If T is an open theory, the languages of T and CLOSED(T) are usually different due to the introduced Skolem functions.
(3) Our definition differs slightly from that of Reiter (1980a) as regards closed theories. According to Reiter, a closure of a closed theory T is to be viewed as the Skolemized form of T, rather than T itself. By virtue of our subsequent development, this difference is of no practical importance.

Our intention is to eliminate open theories by their closures. This requires us to define extensions of T in terms of CLOSED(T). The simplest approach, actually adopted by Reiter, is to identify extensions of T and CLOSED(T). But, as we have observed, such an identification is problematic. A better solution seems to define extensions of T as those of CLOSED(T) restricted to the language of T.

Definition 5.18 Let T be a default theory over a language L_T.‡ E is an extension of T iff $E = E' \cap L_T$ and E′ is an extension of CLOSED(T). ▮

It is worth noting that an extension of an open theory T never depends upon the introduced Skolem functions occurring in CLOSED(T).

5.3 CLOSED DEFAULT THEORIES

We now move on to provide a formal definition of an extension of a default theory. In view of our previous considerations, we may limit our attention to closed theories only.

† Due to the free choice of Skolem functions in step (ii), a theory may have more than one closure. When we write CLOSED(T), the reader is permitted to choose any closure he or she wishes.
‡ If L_T is not explicitly given (the usual case), then we identify it with the set of formulae constructable from function and predicate constants occurring in the axioms and defaults of T.

Because of its technical complexity, the definition of an extension will be developed step by step. Recall the conditions which can be naturally imposed on an extension E of a theory $\langle W, D \rangle$:

(i) $E = Th(E)$;
(ii) $W \subseteq E$;
(iii) E should contain a maximal set of conclusions obtainable by applying defaults from D.

Our primary task is to formalize clause (iii). To begin, observe that any conclusion derivable by a closed default is just its consequent. Accordingly, the conclusions obtainable by defaults of a closed theory $\langle W, D \rangle$ are nothing else but the consequents of the applicable defaults from D. This suggests the following reformulation of (iii):

(iii′) E should contain the consequent of any applicable default from D.

Although (iii′) is more precise than (iii), there still remains the problem of specifying the formal criterion of default's applicability. Intuitively, we interpret a closed default $A: B_1, \ldots, B_k/C$ as saying 'If A is believed and $B_1, \ldots, B_k$ are all consistent with what is believed, i.e. none of $\neg B_1, \ldots, \neg B_k$ is believed, then C is to be believed'. It is then reasonable to replace (iii′) by

(iii″) If $(A: B_1, \ldots, B_k/C) \in D$, $A \in E$ and $\neg B_1 \notin E, \ldots, \neg B_k \notin E$, then $C \in E$.

The clauses (i), (ii) and (iii″) will be referred to as the *closure conditions*.

Specifying what should be in an extension, the closure conditions say nothing about what should be omitted. In consequence, they admit unsupported beliefs.† In order to eliminate them, we have to add a constraint specifying that the sentences required by the closure conditions are the only ones entering extensions. To achieve this, one may try the following 'definition':

E is an extension of a closed default theory $\langle W, D \rangle$ iff E is the smallest set satisfying the closure conditions.

In spite of its naturalness, this definition is wrong. It suffices to note that we cannot define an extension in this way and at the same time accept more than one extension of a theory.

Since an extension cannot be defined as the smallest set satisfying the closure conditions, it may seem reasonable to replace the word 'smallest' by 'minimal':

E is an extension of a closed default theory $\langle W, D \rangle$ iff E is a minimal set enjoying the closure conditions.

The problem with this definition is that minimal sets satisfying the closure conditions may still contain unsupported beliefs. Consider, for example, the theory

$$T = \langle \{P(a)\}, \{P(a): Q(a)/Q(a)\} \rangle.$$

T gives rise to two minimal sets of sentences satisfying the closure conditions:

$$E_1 = Th(\{P(a), Q(a)\}) \qquad E_2 = Th(\{P(a), \neg Q(a)\}).$$

Obviously, only E_1 is to be viewed as an extension of T.

The source of difficulties in defining an extension lies in the fact that the criterion of

† Observe, for instance, that the set of all sentences satisfies the closure conditions.

defaults' applicability refers not only to what is believed but also to what is not believed. This allows the application of any default to be blocked by starting to believe the negation of one of its justifications. The problem arises when this negation is unsupported and hence should not enter an extension.

To reach the correct definition of an extension, let us first solve the following simpler task:

> Assume that E and Γ(E) denote the same extension of ⟨W, D⟩. How to define Γ(E) by means of E?

A little reflection should convince the reader that a possible solution is to specify Γ(E) as the smallest set enjoying the following properties:

(1) $\Gamma(\mathrm{E}) = \mathrm{Th}(\Gamma(\mathrm{E}))$
(2) $\mathrm{W} \subseteq \Gamma(\mathrm{E})$
(3) If $(A: B_1, \ldots, B_k/C) \in \mathrm{D}$, $A \in \Gamma(\mathrm{E})$ and $\neg B_1 \notin \mathrm{E}, \ldots, \neg B_k \notin \mathrm{E}$, then $C \in \Gamma(\mathrm{E})$.

Although (1)–(3) are very similar to the closure conditions, there is a crucial difference. Given E and Γ(E), we have been able to formally distinguish between beliefs and disbeliefs in specifying the criterion of defaults' applicability. This technical trick is just what we need to provide the appropriate definition of an extension.

Definition 5.19 (Reiter 1980a). Let $T = \langle \mathrm{W}, \mathrm{D} \rangle$ be a closed default theory over a first-order language L. For any set of sentences $\mathrm{S} \subseteq L$, let Γ(S) be the smallest set of sentences from L satisfying the following properties:

(D1) $\Gamma(\mathrm{S}) = \mathrm{Th}(\Gamma(\mathrm{S}))$
(D2) $\mathrm{W} \subseteq \Gamma(\mathrm{S})$
(D3) If $(A: B_1, \ldots, B_k/C) \in \mathrm{D}$, $A \in \Gamma(\mathrm{S})$ and $\neg B_1 \notin \mathrm{S}, \ldots, \neg B_k \notin \mathrm{S}$, then $C \in \Gamma(\mathrm{S})$.

A set of sentences $\mathrm{E} \subseteq L$ is an extension of T iff $\mathrm{E} = \Gamma(\mathrm{E})$, i.e. iff E is a fixed point of the operator Γ. ▮

Example 5.20 Reconsider the theory

$$T = \langle \{P(a)\}, \{P(a): Q(a)/Q(a)\} \rangle.$$

As we have observed, T gives rise to two minimal sets satisfying the closure conditions:

$$\mathrm{E}_1 = \mathrm{Th}(\{P(a), Q(a)\}) \qquad \mathrm{E}_2 = \mathrm{Th}(\{P(a), \neg Q(a)\})$$

Since

$$\Gamma(\mathrm{E}_1) = \mathrm{Th}(\{P(a), Q(a)\}) = \mathrm{E}_1$$
$$\Gamma(\mathrm{E}_2) = \mathrm{Th}(\{P(a)\}) \neq \mathrm{E}_2$$

only E_1 is an extension of T. ▮

Example 5.21 Let T be the theory

$$\langle \{Bird(a) \vee Bird(b)\}, \{: \neg Bird(x)/\neg Bird(x)\} \rangle$$

Note that T is an open theory. The theory CLOSED(T) is

$$\langle \{Bird(a) \vee Bird(b)\}, \{: \neg Bird(a)/\neg Bird(a),\ : \neg Bird(b)/\neg Bird(b)\} \rangle$$

Since T and CLOSED(T) are specified over the same language, the extensions of T are those of CLOSED(T). They are given by

$$E_1 = \mathrm{Th}(\{Bird(a) \vee Bird(b), \neg Bird(a)\})$$
$$E_2 = \mathrm{Th}(\{Bird(a) \vee Bird(b), \neg Bird(b)\})$$

▮

Example 5.22 Let $T = \langle W, D\rangle$, where

$$W = \{Republican(Nixon) \wedge Quaker(Nixon)\}$$

$$D = \left\{\frac{Republican(x): \neg Pacifist(x)}{\neg Pacifist(x)}, \frac{Quaker(x): Pacifist(x)}{Pacifist(x)}\right\}$$

CLOSED(T) = $\langle W, D'\rangle$, where

$$D' = \left\{\frac{Republican(Nixon): \neg Pacifist(Nixon)}{\neg Pacifist(Nixon)}, \frac{Quaker(Nixon): Pacifist(Nixon)}{Pacifist(Nixon)}\right\}$$

CLOSED(T), and hence T, has two extensions:

$$E_1 = \mathrm{Th}(\{Republican(Nixon) \wedge Quaker(Nixon), \neg Pacifist(Nixon)\})$$
$$E_2 = \mathrm{Th}(\{Republican(Nixon) \wedge Quaker(Nixon), Pacifist(Nixon)\}).$$

▮

Example 5.23 Let $T = \langle W, D\rangle$, where $W = \{\ \}$ and

$$D = \left\{\frac{: \exists x Bird(x)}{\exists x Bird(x)}, \frac{Bird(x): Can\text{-}Fly(x)}{Can\text{-}Fly(x)}\right\}$$

CLOSED(T) = $\langle\{\ \}, D'\rangle$, where

$$D' = \left\{\frac{: \exists x Bird(x)}{Bird(a)}, \frac{Bird(a): Can\text{-}Fly(a)}{Can\text{-}Fly(a)}\right\}$$

where a is the introduced Skolem function. This theory has one extension given by

$$E = \mathrm{Th}(\{Bird(a), Can\text{-}Fly(a)\}).$$

Since T and CLOSED(T) are specified over different languages, the unique extension of T is

$$E' = \mathrm{Th}(\{Bird(a), Can\text{-}Fly(a)\}) \cap L_T.$$

Observe that $Bird(a) \notin E'$; $\exists x . Bird(x) \wedge Can\text{-}Fly(x) \in E'$. ▮

Example 5.24 Consider the theory T consisting of the empty set of axioms and one default

$$d = : Bird(Joe)/\neg Bird(Joe)$$

T has no extension. This is because the consequent of d denies its justification. If d is not applied, then there is no way to derive $\neg Bird(Joe)$, so that we are forced to apply it. But if we do this, $\neg Bird(Joe)$ will obtain the status of a belief and d will become inapplicable.

To show formally that T lacks an extension, note that the only candidates are $E_1 = \mathrm{Th}(\{\neg Bird(Joe)\})$ and $E_2 = \mathrm{Th}(\{\ \})$. Since $\Gamma(E_1) = \mathrm{Th}(\{\ \}) \neq E_1$ and $\Gamma(E_2) = \mathrm{Th}(\{\neg Bird(Joe)\}) \neq E_2$, neither E_1 nor E_2 are extensions of T. ▮

The practical usefulness of the above theory is rather doubtful. The next example shows a more interesting theory without an extension.

Example 5.25 Consider the theory $T = \langle W, D \rangle$, where

$$W = \{\neg \textit{Sun-Shining} \wedge \textit{Summer}\}; \qquad D = \{\textit{Summer}: \neg \textit{Rain}/\textit{Sun-Shining}\}$$

We leave it to the reader to formally show that T has no extension. The problem, of course, is that the consequent of the default denies the axiom. So, as before, we are forced to apply the default which, after its application, becomes inapplicable. ▮

The definition of an extension is technically complex. The next theorem provides a more intuitive characterization of this notion.

Theorem 5.26 (Reiter 1980a) If $T = \langle W, D \rangle$ is a closed default theory, then a set E of sentences is an extension of T iff $E = \bigcup_{i=0}^{\infty} E_i$, where

$$E_0 = W, \text{ and for } i \geq 0$$
$$E_{i+1} = Th(E_i) \cup \{C: (A: B_1, \ldots, B_k/C) \in D, \text{ where } E_i \vdash A \text{ and } \neg B_1 \notin E, \ldots, \neg B_k \notin E\}.^{\dagger}$$

Proof Observe first that the following conditions hold:

(D1′) $\bigcup_{i=0}^{\infty} E_i = Th\left(\bigcup_{i=0}^{\infty} E_i\right)$

(D2′) $W \subseteq \bigcup_{i=0}^{\infty} E_i$

(D3′) If $(A: B_1, \ldots, B_k/C) \in D$, $A \in \bigcup_{i=0}^{\infty} E_i$ and $\neg B_1 \notin E, \ldots, \neg B_k \notin E$, then $C \in \bigcup_{i=0}^{\infty} E_i$.

Thus, by the minimality of Γ, we have

$$\Gamma(E) \subseteq \bigcup_{i=0}^{\infty} E_i. \tag{5.3.1}$$

For the proof from left to right, assume that E is an extension of T, i.e.

$$E = \Gamma(E). \tag{5.3.2}$$

By straightforward induction on i, one easily shows that $E_i \subseteq E$, for all $i \geq 0$. Thus, $\bigcup_{i=0}^{\infty} E_i \subseteq E$, and so, by (5.3.1) and (5.3.2), $E = \bigcup_{i=0}^{\infty} E_i$.

For the proof from right to left, assume that $E = \bigcup_{i=0}^{\infty} E_i$. By straightforward induction on i, the reader may readily check that $E_i \subseteq \Gamma(E)$, for all $i \geq 0$. In view of this, $\bigcup_{i=0}^{\infty} E_i \subseteq \Gamma(E)$ and thus, by (5.3.1), $\bigcup_{i=0}^{\infty} E_i = \Gamma(E)$. But $E = \bigcup_{i=0}^{\infty} E_i$. Thus, $E = \Gamma(E)$, and hence E is an extension of T. ▮

Theorem 5.26 implies the following corollaries:

† Note that E_i's are defined by means of E.

Corollary 5.27 A closed default theory $T = \langle W, D \rangle$ has an inconsistent extension iff W is inconsistent. ▮

Corollary 5.28 If a closed default theory has an inconsistent extension, then this is its only extension. ▮

By virtue of Definition 5.18, the above corollaries generalize into open theories.

Theorem 5.29 (Maximality of Extensions, Reiter 1980a) If E and F are extensions of a closed default theory $\langle W, D \rangle$ and $E \subseteq F$, then $E = F$.

Proof Let $(E_0, E_1, \ldots)$ and $(F_0, F_1, \ldots)$ be sequences of sets of sentences defined as in Theorem 5.26 (for E and F, respectively). In view of this thorem,

$$E = \bigcup_{i=0}^{\infty} E_i \quad \text{and} \quad F = \bigcup_{i=0}^{\infty} F_i. \tag{5.3.3}$$

By easy induction on i, the reader may verify that $F_i \subseteq E_i$, for all $i \geq 0$. Thus, by (5.3.3), $F \subseteq E$, and so, $E = F$. ▮

By Definition 5.18, Theorem 5.29 generalizes into open default theories.

Let D be any set of defaults (not necessarily closed). By PREREQUISITES(D), JUSTIFICATIONS(D) and CONSEQUENTS(D) we denote the set of prerequisites, justifications and consequents, respectively, of the defaults from D.

Definition 5.30 Let T be a closed default theory and suppose that E is an extension of T. The set of *generating defaults for* E *wrt* T, written GD(E, T), is defined by

$$\mathrm{GD}(E, T) = \{(A: B_1, \ldots, B_k/C) \in D: A \in E \text{ and } \neg B_1 \notin E, \ldots, \neg B_k \notin E\}.$$

▮

Theorem 5.31 (Reiter 1980a) If E is an extension of a closed default theory $T = \langle W, D \rangle$, then

$$E = \mathrm{Th}(W \cup \mathrm{CONSEQUENTS}(\mathrm{GD}(E, T))).$$

Proof Denote Th(W ∪ CONSEQUENTS(GD(E, T))) by RHS.

In view of Theorem 5.26,

$$E = \bigcup_{i=0}^{\infty} E_i \tag{5.3.4}$$

where $E_0, E_1, \ldots$ are specified as usual. By induction on i, it is easy to show that $E_i \subseteq \mathrm{RHS}$, for all $i \geq 0$. Thus, by (5.3.4), $E \subseteq \mathrm{RHS}$.

To prove that $\mathrm{RHS} \subseteq E$, observe first that it suffices to show that CONSEQUENTS(GD(E, T)) ⊆ E. Let $C \in$ CONSEQUENTS(GD(E, T)). Thus, there is a default $(A: B_1, \ldots, B_k/C) \in D$ such that $A \in E$ and $\neg B_1 \notin E, \ldots, \neg B_k \notin E$. So, by (5.3.4), $A \in E_i$, for some $i \geq 0$, and hence $C \in E_{i+1} \subseteq E$. ▮

5.4 NORMAL DEFAULT THEORIES

The most pessimistic result of the previous section is that there are theories lacking extensions. It is then reasonable to look for a restricted class of theories for which extensions can be proved to exist.

Definition 5.32 (Reiter 1980a) Any default of the form

$$\frac{A(\bar{x}) : B(\bar{x})}{B(\bar{x})}$$

is said to be *normal*. A theory $\langle W, D \rangle$ is said to be *normal* iff every default from D is normal. ▮

Normal defaults are sufficient to cover many practically occurring settings. Reviewing the examples from the previous sections, the reader may be convinced that the majority of defaults we have considered so far are of this form.

Normal default theories have many nice properties. The most important one is given in the next theorem.

Theorem 5.33 (Reiter 1980a) Every closed normal default theory has an extension.

Proof Let $T = \langle W, D \rangle$ be a closed normal default theory. If W is inconsistent, then T has an inconsistent extension by Corollary 5.27. Thus, without loss of generality, we may assume that W is consistent. Define the sequence $E_0, E_1, \ldots$ of sets of sentences by

$E_0 = W$, and for $i \geq 0$
$E_{i+1} = Th(E_i) \cup T_i$, where T_i is a maximal set of sentences satisfying the following conditions:

(1) $E_i \cup T_i$ is consistent
(2) If $B \in T_i$, then there is a default $(A : B/B) \in D$ such that $E_i \vdash A$.

Put $E = \bigcup_{i=0}^{\infty} E_i$. We claim that E is an extension of T. In view of Theorem 5.26, it suffices to show

$$T_i = \{B : (A : B/B) \in D, \text{ where } E_i \vdash A \text{ and } \neg B \notin E\}.$$

Denote by RHS the right hand side of the above equation and assume to the contrary that $T_i \neq$ RHS. Thus, since clearly $T_i \subseteq$ RHS, there must be a sentence $B \in \text{RHS} - T_i$. By the maximality of T_i, the set $E_i \cup T_i \cup \{B\}$ is inconsistent, and so, because $E_i \cup T_i \subseteq E_{i+1} \subseteq E$, $E \cup \{B\}$ is also inconsistent. Therefore, since E is deductively closed, we have $\neg B \in E$. This contradicts $B \in \text{RHS} - T_i$ and thus completes the proof of the theorem. ▮

Unfortunately, Theorem 5.33 does not generalize into open default theories. This may be a surprising result for those familiar with Reiter's original paper (Reiter 1980a), but consider the following example.

Example 5.34 Consider the theory $T = \langle \{\ \}, D \rangle$, where

$$D = \left\{ \frac{r : \exists x P(x)}{\exists x P(x)}, \frac{: r \wedge \neg P(x)}{r \wedge \neg P(x)} \right\} \qquad (r \text{ is a proposition constant})$$

CLOSED$(T) = \langle \{\ \}, D' \rangle$, where

$$D' = \left\{ \frac{r : \exists x P(x)}{P(a)}, \frac{: r \wedge \neg P(a)}{r \wedge \neg P(a)} \right\} \qquad (a \text{ is a Skolem function})$$

To show that CLOSED(T) (and hence T) has no extension, notice that the only candidates are $E_1 = Th(\{\ \})$, $E_2 = Th(\{P(a)\})$ and $E_3 = Th(\{r \wedge \neg P(a)\})$.[†] Since $\Gamma(E_1) = Th(\{r \wedge \neg P(a), P(a)\}) \neq E_1$, $\Gamma(E_2) = Th(\{\ \}) \neq E_2$, and $\Gamma(E_3) = Th(\{P(a), r \wedge \neg P(a)\}) \neq E_3$, none of E_1, E_2 and E_3 is an extension of T. ∎

The obvious reason why Theorem 5.33 fails for open default theories is that the transformation CLOSED does not preserve normality. In view of this, it is natural to modify the transformation by jointly Skolemizing the justification and the consequent of any normal default.[‡] However, a similar effect can be achieved by approaching the problem from the other side. Instead of modifying the transformation CLOSED, we may retain its original formulation and isolate a restricted class of normal theories for which the transformation preserves normality.

Definition 5.35 A default is said to be *C-universal* iff the prenex normal form of its consequent contains no existential quantifiers. A default theory $\langle W, D\rangle$ is *C-universal* iff every default from D is C-universal. ∎

Since the transformation CLOSED preserves normality for C-universal theories, we immediately have:

Corollary 5.36 Any C-universal open normal theory has an extension. ∎

At first sight, restricting the class of normal open theories to the C-universal ones seems less general than the previously mentioned modification of the transformation CLOSED. However, this is not the case. We are compensated by the fact that, if we wish, we may in advance pass from any open normal theory into a C-universal one by jointly Skolemizing justifications and consequents of its defaults.

The next theorem shows that keeping beliefs from distinct extensions can lead to inconsistency:

Theorem 5.37 (Orthogonality of Extensions; Reiter 1980a) If a closed normal default theory $\langle W, D\rangle$ has distinct extensions E and F, then $E \cup F$ is inconsistent.

Proof By Theorem 5.26, $E = \bigcup_{i=0}^{\infty} E_i$ and $F = \bigcup_{i=0}^{\infty} F_i$, where

$$E_0 = F_0 = W, \text{ and for } i \geq 0$$
$$E_{i+1} = Th(E_i) \cup \{B\colon (A\colon B/B) \in D, \text{ where } E_i \vdash A \text{ and } \neg B \notin E\}$$
$$F_{i+1} = Th(F_i) \cup \{B\colon (A\colon B/B) \in D, \text{ where } F_i \vdash A \text{ and } \neg B \notin F\}.$$

Since $E \neq F$ and $E_0 = F_0$, there must be an integer $i \geq 0$ such that $E_i = F_i$ and $E_{i+1} \neq F_{i+1}$. Thus, for some $(A\colon B/B) \in D$, we have

$$(*)\ B \in E_{i+1} \text{ and } B \notin F_{i+1} \qquad \text{or} \qquad (**)\ B \in F_{i+1} \text{ and } B \notin E_{i+1}.$$

Assume first that $(*)$ holds. So, $E_i \vdash A$, and hence $F_i \vdash A$. But if $F_i \vdash A$ and $B \notin F_{i+1}$, then $\neg B \in F$. On the other hand, $B \in E_{i+1} \subseteq E$. Thus, $E \cup F$ is inconsistent.

Assuming that $(**)$ holds, we easily reach the same conclusion by showing that $\neg B \in E$ and $B \in F$. ∎

Corollary 5.38 If E and F are distinct extensions of a C-universal open normal theory, then $E \cup F$ is inconsistent.

[†] By Corollary 5.27, no extension of CLOSED(T) may contain the consequents of both the defaults.

[‡] As a matter of fact, Reiter seems to have such the modification in mind while providing a proof theory for his system.

Proof Straightforward. ▮

It is worth remarking that Theorem 5.37 (and hence Corollary 5.38) may fail to hold for non-normal theories. Nevertheless, even in such a case, beliefs from distinct extensions should not be kept together. To illustrate this, consider the theory $T = \langle W, D \rangle$, where $W = \{\ \}$ and $D = \{: p/\neg r, : r/\neg p\}$. T has two extensions: $E = Th(\{\neg r\})$ and $F = Th(\{\neg p\})$. Obviously, $E \cup F$ is consistent. However, since $\neg r$ is justified by the consistency of p, and $\neg p$ is justified by the consistency of r, $\neg r$ and $\neg p$ should not be regarded as coexisting beliefs.

Definition 5.19 and Theorem 5.26 provide recursive specifications of the notion of an extension. If we limit our attention to normal theories, it is possible to characterize extensions in a non-recursive way. The details follow.[†]

A *belief set* is any set S of sentences such that $S = Th(S)$.

Definition 5.39 Let $d = A: B/B$ be a closed normal default and suppose that S is a belief set. We say that d is *applicable wrt* S iff $S \vdash A$ and $S \nvdash \neg B$. ▮

Example 5.40 The default $d = P(a): R(a)/R(a)$ is applicable wrt $S_1 = Th(\{P(a)\})$, but is inapplicable wrt $S_2 = Th(\{P(b)\})$. ▮

The key observation underlying the new characterization is that any closed normal default can be viewed as a mapping from belief sets into such sets.

Definition 5.41 Let S be a belief set. To each closed normal default $d = A: B/B$ we assign a mapping, denoted by d, given by

$$d(S) = \begin{cases} Th(S \cup \{B\}) & \text{if d is applicable wrt S} \\ S & \text{otherwise.} \end{cases}$$

▮

Intuitively, S and d(S) are to be interpreted as sets of beliefs before and after the application of d, respectively.

Example 5.40 (continued) $d(S_1) = Th(\{P(a), R(a)\})$; $d(S_2) = S_2$. ▮

Definition 5.42 Let S be a belief set and suppose that D is a set of closed normal defaults. We say that S is *stable wrt* D iff $d(S) = S$, for all $d \in D$. ▮

Intuitively, the stability of S wrt D means that S cannot be extended by applying defaults from D.

Although any extension of a closed normal theory $\langle W, D \rangle$ is stable wrt D, the converse does not always hold. Even a minimal stable belief set containing W need not be an extension of $\langle W, D \rangle$. To see this, consider the theory $T = \langle W, D \rangle$, where $W = \{P(a)\}$, $D = \{P(a): R(a)/R(a)\}$. It is easily seen that $S = Th(\{P(a), \neg R(a)\})$ is a minimal stable belief set containing $P(a)$. However, S is not an extension of T.

Recall that $X \subset Y$ stands for $X \subseteq Y$ and $X \neq Y$.

Definition 5.43 Let W be a set of sentences and let D be a set of closed normal defaults. Assume further that S is a belief set. We say that S is *approachable from* W *wrt* D iff, for each belief set S_1 such that $W \subseteq S_1 \subset S$, there is a default $d \in D$ such that $S_1 \subset d(S_1) \subseteq S$. ▮

Intuitively, a belif set S is approachable from W wrt D iff, for any smaller belief set S_1 such that $W \subseteq S_1 \subset S$, there is a default which takes us closer to S.

[†] This characterization corresponds closely to that of Sandewall (1985).

We now are ready to provide the desired characterization of extensions for closed normal default theories.

Theorem 5.44 Let $T = \langle W, D \rangle$ be a closed normal default theory and suppose that E is a belief set. Then E is an extension of T iff

(i) $W \subseteq E$;
(ii) E is stable wrt D;
(iii) E is approachable from W wrt D.

Proof We prove this theorem directly from the definition of an extension. Let $\Gamma(E)$ be the smallest set of sentences such that

(1) $\Gamma(E) = Th(\Gamma(E))$;
(2) $W \subseteq \Gamma(E)$;
(3) If $(A: B/B) \in D$, $A \in \Gamma(E)$ and $\neg B \notin E$, then $B \in \Gamma(E)$.

For the proof from left to right, assume that E is an extension of T. Thus, by Definition 5.19,

$$E = \Gamma(E) \tag{5.4.1}$$

We shall prove that (i)–(iii) hold. (i) is obvious.

Lemma 5.44.1 If $(A: B/B) \in D$, $A \in E$ and $\neg B \notin E$, then $B \in E$.

Proof By (3) and (5.4.1). ■

To prove (ii), take any $d = (A: B/B) \in D$. If d is inapplicable wrt E, then clearly $d(E) = E$. Otherwise, $E \vdash A$ and $E \nvdash \neg B$. Thus, since $E = Th(E)$, we have $A \in E$ and $\neg B \notin E$. Therefore, by Lemma 5.44.1, $B \in E$, and so $d(E) = E$.

To prove (iii), assume on the contrary that E is not approachable from W wrt D. Thus, there is a belief set E_1 such that $W \subseteq E_1 \subset E$ and

$$\text{For all } d \in D,\ d(E_1) = E_1 \text{ or } d(E_1) \nsubseteq E \tag{5.4.2}$$

Lemma 5.44.2 E_1 satisfies (1′)–(3′) below.

(1′) $E_1 = Th(E_1)$;
(2′) $W \subseteq E_1$;
(3′) If $(A: B/B) \in D$, $A \in E_1$ and $\neg B \notin E$, then $B \in E_1$.

Proof (1′) and (2′) are straightforward. To prove (3′), assume that $(A: B/B) \in D$, $A \in E_1$ and $\neg B \notin E$. Thus, since $E_1 = Th(E_1)$ and $E_1 \subset E$, d is applicable wrt E_1. Furthermore, by Lemma 5.44.1, $B \in E$. By (5.4.2), there are two cases to consider.

Case 1. $d(E_1) \nsubseteq E$. Since $E_1 \subset E$, $d(E_1) = Th(E_1 \cup \{B\})$ and $B \in E$, this case is impossible.

Case 2. $d(E_1) = E_1$. Then $E_1 = d(E_1) = Th(E_1 \cup \{B\})$, and so $B \in E_1$.

This completes the proof of (3′), and thus proves the lemma. ■

Since (1′)–(3′) are simply (1)–(3) with $\Gamma(E)$ replaced by E_1, then by the minimality of $\Gamma(E)$, we conclude $\Gamma(E) \subseteq E_1$. Thus, in view of (5.4.1), $E \subseteq E_1$. This contradicts $E_1 \subset E$, and hence proves (iii).

For the proof from right to left, assume that E satisfies (i)–(iii). We have to show

(5.4.1). If W is inconsistent, then, by (i) and Corollaries 5.27 and 5.28, (5.4.1) obviously holds. Assume, therefore, that W is consistent.

Lemma 5.44.3 E is consistent.

Proof Assume that E is inconsistent. Since W is consistent and $W \subseteq E$, there is a maximally consistent set of sentences $X \subset E$ containing W. Clearly $X = Th(X)$. Therefore, since E is approachable from W wrt D, and $X \subset E$, there is a default $d = (A\colon B/B) \in D$ such that $X \subset d(X) \subseteq E$. Thus, $X \not\vdash \neg B$, and hence $X \cup \{B\}$ is consistent. So, since X is a maximally consistent set of sentences, it must be the case that $B \in X$. On the other hand, $X \subset d(X) = Th(X \cup \{B\})$. A contradiction. ■

Lemma 5.44.4 E satisfies (1″)–(3″) below.

(1″) $E = Th(E)$
(2″) $W \subseteq E$
(3″) If $(A\colon B/B) \in D$, $A \in E$ and $\neg B \notin E$, then $B \in E$.

Proof (1″) and (2″) are obvious. To prove (3″), assume that $(A\colon B/B) \in D$, $A \in E$ and $\neg B \notin E$. Thus, since $E = Th(E)$, d is applicable wrt E, and hence $d(E) = Th(E \cup \{B\})$. So, since E is stable wrt D, $d(E) = E$, and thus, $B \in E$. ■

We now proceed to prove (5.4.1). Since (1″)–(3″) are simply (1)–(3) with $\Gamma(E)$ replaced by E, then, by the minimality of Γ, we have $\Gamma(E) \subseteq E$. Thus, to prove (5.4.1), it suffices to show

$$\Gamma(E) \not\subset E. \tag{5.4.3}$$

Assume to the contrary that $\Gamma(E) \subset E$. Thus, since $W \subseteq E$, $\Gamma(E) = Th(\Gamma(E))$, and E is approachable from W wrt D, we have

$$\Gamma(E) \subset d(\Gamma(E)) \subseteq E, \text{ for some } d = (A\colon B/B) \in D. \tag{5.4.4}$$

$\Gamma(E) \subset d(\Gamma(E))$ implies that d is applicable wrt $\Gamma(E)$. So, in particular

$$\Gamma(E) \vdash A \tag{5.4.5}$$
$$d(\Gamma(E)) = Th(\Gamma(E) \cup \{B\}). \tag{5.4.6}$$

By (5.4.4) and (5.4.6), we immediately obtain

$$\Gamma(E) \subset Th(\Gamma(E) \cup \{B\}) \subseteq E \tag{5.4.7}$$

Thus, $B \in E$. This, together with Lemma 5.44.3, implies $\neg B \notin E$. On the other hand, since $\Gamma(E) = Th(\Gamma(E))$, $A \in \Gamma(E)$ by (5.4.5). Therefore, by the definition of Γ, $B \in \Gamma(E)$. A contradiction with (5.4.7). This proves (5.4.3), and hence the right to left part of the theorem. ■

Theorem 5.45 (Semi-Monotonicity; Reiter 1980a) Let D and D_1 be sets of closed normal defaults such that $D_1 \subseteq D$. Let E_1 be an extension of $T_1 = \langle W, D_1 \rangle$ and suppose that $T = \langle W, D \rangle$. Then T has an extension E such that $E_1 \subseteq E$.†

---

† We assume here that the language of a default theory consists of the formulae constructable using predicate and function constants explicitly occurring in the theory.

Proof Consider the theory $T_2 = \langle E_1, D\rangle$. Since T_2 is a closed normal theory, there is a belief set, say E, which is an extension of T_2. Clearly, $E_1 \subseteq E$. Thus, to prove the theorem, it suffices to show that E is an extension of T. We show this by proving that

(1) $W \subseteq E$

(2) E is stable wrt D

(3) E is approachable from W wrt D

and invoking Theorem 5.44. (1) is straightforward. For (2), observe that E is an extension of $\langle E_1, D\rangle$ and apply Theorem 5.44. To prove (3), assume that F is a belief set such that $W \subseteq F \subset E$ and consider two cases.

Case 1. $W \subseteq F \subset E_1$. Since E_1 is an extension of $\langle W, D_1\rangle$, then, by Theorem 5.44, E_1 is approachable from W wrt D_1. Thus, there is a default $d \in D_1 \subseteq D$ such that $F \subset d(F) \subseteq E_1 \subseteq E$.

Case 2. $E_1 \subseteq F \subset E$. Since E is an extension of $\langle E_1, D\rangle$, we similarly show that $F \subset d(F) \subseteq E$, for some $d \in D$.

In view of Cases 1 and 2, it is immediately seen that E is approachable from W wrt D. This proves (3), and therefore completes the proof of Theorem 5.45. ∎

What Theorem 5.45 really says is that any belief derivable from a closed normal default theory T cannot be invalidated by augmenting T by a new set of closed normal defaults. In other words, closed normal default theories are monotonic with respect to defaults.†

Semi-monotonicity is a very desired property as regards proof theory of default theories. It allows us to construct a proof procedure focusing only on those defaults which are relevant to proofs. To see what it means, assume that we are trying to determine whether a sentence A is a member of some extension of a closed normal default theory $T = \langle W, D\rangle$. A natural solution of this task is to start with W and extend it systematically by applying the defaults from D, one at a time, until the extended set, say F, contains A. Although F need not be an extension of T, semi-monotonicity guarantees that F is a subset of such an extension. This makes the above procedure sound despite the fact that not necessarily all defaults of D have been involved in the proof.

Theorem 5.45 easily generalizes into C-universal open normal theories:

Corollary 5.46 Let $T_1 = \langle W, D_1\rangle$ and $T = \langle W, D\rangle$ be C-universal open normal theories and suppose that $D_1 \subseteq D$. If E_1 is an extension of T_1, then T has an extension E such that $E_1 \subseteq E$.

Proof Left to the reader as an easy exercise. ∎

Unfortunately, Theorem 5.45 need not hold for non-normal theories. Consider, for instance, the theory $T = \langle W, D\rangle$, where $W = \{\ \}$ and $D = \{: p/q\}$. T has one extension, namely, $E = Th(\{q\})$. Augmenting T by the new default $:\neg p/\neg p$, we obtain a new theory with one extension F given by $F = Th(\{\neg p\})$. Obviously, $E \not\subseteq F$.

5.5 REPRESENTATIONAL ISSUES

The existence of extensions and semi-monotonicity makes normal theories attractive from the standpoint of knowledge representation. It would then be interesting to know

† Of course, they are non-monotonic with respect to axioms.

to what extent normal defaults are sufficient for the purpose of practical applications. The following discussion is based on Reiter & Criscuolo (1983) and Łukaszewicz (1985).

Viewing various naturally occurring settings, one easily sees that the most common non-monotonic rules are those of the form 'If A, believe B unless you know otherwise'. Since any such a rule readily translates into the normal default $A\colon B/B$, it is not surprising that normal defaults are extremely common in practice. Actually, in his original paper (Reiter 1980a) Reiter has claimed that all naturally occurring non-monotonic rules can be given normal representation. Unfortunately, as it has been observed in Reiter & Criscuolo (1983), the situation is more complex. The crucial observation is that many non-monotonic rules, which in isolation are naturally expressed by normal defaults, must be re-represented when regarded in a wider context. Three examples are sufficient for the purpose of our discussion. All derive from Reiter & Criscuolo (1983).

Example 5.47 Suppose we are given:

> Bill is a high school dropout.
> Typically, high school dropouts are adults.
> Typically, adults are employed.

These common-sense facts are naturally represented by the following normal theory T:

$$\mathrm{W} = \{Dropout(Bill)\}$$

$$\mathrm{D} = \left\{\frac{Dropout(x)\colon Adult(x)}{Adult(x)}, \frac{Adult(x)\colon Employed(x)}{Employed(x)}\right\}.$$

Although intuition suggests that we should remain agnostic about the employment status of Bill, T forces us to believe that he is employed. The problem arises because dropouts are atypical adults as regards the state of employment, so that the transitivity from 'dropout' via 'adult' to 'employed' is intuitively unjustified. There are many ways to block this transitivity. The simplest solution is to replace the second default by the non-normal default

$$\frac{Adult(x)\colon Employed(x) \wedge \neg Dropout(x)}{Employed(x)}$$

which is inapplicable to known dropouts. ▮

Example 5.48 Consider:

> Bill is a 21-year-old.
> All 21-year-olds are adults.
> Typically, adults are married.

This may be expressed by the following theory T:

$$\mathrm{W} = \{21\text{-}Year\text{-}Old(Bill), \forall x\,.\,21\text{-}Year\text{-}Old(x) \supset Adult(x)\}$$

$$\mathrm{D} = \left\{\mathrm{d} = \frac{Adult(x)\colon Married(x)}{Married(x)}\right\}.$$

While Example 5.47 shows that interacting defaults can lead to unintuitive conclusions, this example illustrates that such inferences may also result from interactions among defaults and axioms. Given that Bill is 21 years old, we would not like to infer that he is married. Yet, T forces this conclusion. The problem, of course, is that 21-year-olds are atypical adults with respect to the marital status. To restore the intended interpretation, we must block the transitivity from '21-year-old' via 'adult' to 'married'. This can be easily achieved by replacing d by the non-normal default

$$\frac{Adult(x): Married(x) \wedge \neg 21\text{-}Year\text{-}Old(x)}{Married(x)}.$$

▮

Example 5.49 Consider:

John is an adult full-time student.
Typically, full-time students are not employed.
Typically, adults are employed.

This may be represented by

$$\mathrm{W} = \{Adult(John) \wedge Full\text{-}Time\text{-}Student(John)\}$$

$$\mathrm{D} = \left\{\frac{Full\text{-}Time\text{-}Student(x): \neg Employed(x)}{\neg Employed(x)}, \frac{Adult(x): Employed(x)}{Employed(x)}\right\}.$$

This theory has two extensions, which differ on the employment status of John. One of them, namely that containing *Employed(John)*, is intuitively unacceptable. To eliminate this extension, we may replace the second default by

$$\frac{Adult(x): Employed(x) \wedge \neg Full\text{-}Time\text{-}Student(x)}{Employed(x)}.$$

▮

Observe that all of the above examples describe the following general situation. We are given a non-monotonic rule which, in isolation, is naturally represented by a normal default

$$d = \frac{A(\bar{x}): B(\bar{x})}{B(\bar{x})}.$$

Unfortunately, when the rule is embedded in a context, there are some exceptional circumstances, say $E(\bar{x})$, which make its application unacceptable. To avoid counter-intuitive inferences, the rule must be re-represented. The most natural solution is to replace d by

$$\frac{A(\bar{x}): B(\bar{x}) \wedge \neg E(\bar{x})}{B(\bar{x})}.$$

Definition 5.50 Any default of the form

$$\frac{A(\bar{x}): B(\bar{x}) \wedge C(\bar{x})}{B(\bar{x})}$$

is called *semi-normal*. A default theory is *semi-normal* iff all of its defaults are semi-normal.[†] ▮

[†] Observe that any normal default $A: B/B$ may be identified with the semi-normal default $A: B \wedge True/B$. It follows, therefore, that the class of semi-normal defaults includes normal defaults.

Semi-normal default theories will be discussed in the next section. Here we only remark that they lack some of the nice properties of normal theories. Even a closed semi-normal theory may have no extension. Also, in general, semi-normal theories lack the property of semi-monotonicity.

In the remainder of this section we focus on the following two questions:

(1) Are semi-normal defaults sufficient to cover all naturally occurring practical situations?
(2) To what extent can the effects obtainable by using semi-normal defaults be achieved in the framework of normal representation?

These questions have been addressed in Łukaszewicz (1985). He provides a simple schema which can be used to translate an arbitrary single-justification default into a normal one. Although not generally valid, the schema works for a very wide class of naturally occurring defaults. The details follow.

The proposed translation proceeds in two steps. The first one is to replace any default of the form

$$\mathrm{d} = \frac{A(\bar{x})\colon B(\bar{x})}{C(\bar{x})}$$

by the semi-normal default

$$\mathrm{d}_1 = \frac{A(\bar{x})\colon B(\bar{x}) \wedge C(\bar{x})}{C(\bar{x})}.$$

This step seems to be intuitively incontroversial. The only distinction between d and d_1 arises from different criteria under which they can be applied. Because the criterion of applying d_1 is stronger than that of d, any agent including d into his knowledge base, who does not accept to replace it by d_1, considers the applicability criterion of d_1 too strong. Thus, he must be prepared to apply d when the application of d_1 is explicitly blocked. In other words, he considers it possible to apply d when $B(\bar{x})$ is consistent with what he believes, while $B(\bar{x}) \wedge C(\bar{x})$ is not. But in such a case, applying d contradicts its justification. This means that the agent is irrational and implies that any reasonable agent prepared to include d into his knowledge base should replace it by d_1.

The fact that any single-justification default can be reasonably replaced by its semi-normal translation leads to the following important observation: Any common-sense setting which can be correctly modelled by using single-justification defaults may be expressed by means of semi-normal defaults.†

It should be stressed that a default and its semi-normal translation need not be formally equivalent. To see this, consider the default $\mathrm{d} = :p/\neg p$ and its translation $\mathrm{d}_1 = :p \wedge \neg p/\neg p$. While the theory $\langle\{\ \},\{\mathrm{d}\}\rangle$ lacks an extension, the theory $\langle\{\ \},\{\mathrm{d}_1\}\rangle$ has one extension given by $\mathrm{Th}(\{\ \})$.

The second step of the proposed translation is to replace the semi-normal default

$$\mathrm{d}_1 = \frac{A(\bar{x})\colon B(\bar{x}) \wedge C(\bar{x})}{C(\bar{x})}$$

by the normal default

$$\mathrm{d}_2 = \frac{A(\bar{x})\colon B(\bar{x}) \wedge C(\bar{x})}{B(\bar{x}) \wedge C(\bar{x})}.$$

† See Morris (1988) for a different opinion on this point.

This step is more controversial in that it is possible to find common-sense examples when it does not work. Before giving formal criteria under which the transformation can safely be applied, we begin by observing that it is often the case that the condition 'Typically, if $A(\bar{x})$, then $B(\bar{x})$' holds. Consider a default from Example 5.47:

$$d_1 = \frac{Adult(x) \colon Employed(x) \wedge \neg Dropout(x)}{Employed(x)}.$$

Applying the translation schema, we replace d_1 by

$$d_2 = \frac{Adult(x) \colon Employed(x) \wedge \neg Dropout(x)}{Employed(x) \wedge \neg Dropout(x)}.$$

Note that the only difference between d_1 and d_2 is that the consequent of d_2 is stronger than that of d_1. Applying d_2 for an adult individual, we can infer not only that he is employed but also that he is not a high school dropout. However, since a typical adult is not a high school dropout, this extra conclusion is well-motivated.

The observation that the condition 'Typically, if $A(\bar{x})$, then $B(\bar{x})$' often holds, underlies a method of translating semi-normal defaults into normal ones suggested in Reiter & Criscuolo (1983). They propose to replace a semi-normal default

$$\frac{A(\bar{x}) \colon B(\bar{x}) \wedge C(\bar{x})}{C(\bar{x})}$$

by the pair of normal defaults

$$\frac{A(\bar{x}) \colon B(\bar{x})}{B(\bar{x})} \quad \frac{A(\bar{x}) \wedge B(x) \colon C(\bar{x})}{C(\bar{x})}.$$

According to this method, the default about employed adults

$$\frac{Adult(x) \colon Employed(x) \wedge \neg Dropout(x)}{Employed(x)}$$

is represented by

$$\frac{Adult(x) \colon \neg Dropout(x)}{\neg Dropout(x)} \quad \frac{Adult(x) \wedge \neg Dropout(x) \colon Employed(x)}{Employed(x)}.$$

To compare Reiter and Criscuolo's normal representation with ours, assume that John is an adult. If there is no further information about him, both the representations lead to the conclusion that he is an employed not high school dropout. A difference arises when we additionally know that John is unemployed: Reiter and Criscuolo's representation forces him not to be a high school dropout, while ours remains agnostic on this point.

Even if 'Typically, if $A(\bar{x})$, then $B(\bar{x})$' is unacceptable, our translation schema still works if a weaker condition, namely, 'Typically, if $A(\bar{x})$ and $C(\bar{x})$, then $B(\bar{x})$', is satisfied. To illustrate this, consider a default from Example 5.48:

$$d_1 = \frac{Adult(x) \colon Married\ (x) \wedge \neg 21\text{-}Year\text{-}Old(x)}{Married(x)}.$$

If all we know about John is that he is an adult, we do not assume that he is not 21 years old. However, if we additionally believe him to be married, the conclusion that he is not

21 years old seems to be plausible. In other words, we accept the statement 'Typically, married adults are not 21 years old'. Observe that applying d_1 to John, we start to believe that he is married, and so, it is justified to conclude that he is not 21 years old. The same effect is achieved when d_1 is replaced by

$$\frac{Adult(x): Married(x) \wedge \neg 21\text{-}Year\text{-}Old(x)}{Married(x) \wedge \neg 21\text{-}Year\text{-}Old(x)}.$$

Our discussion can be summarized as follows. If

$$d = \frac{A(\bar{x}): B(\bar{x})}{C(\bar{x})}$$

is any default, then it is always reasonable to replace it by

$$d_1 = \frac{A(\bar{x}): B(\bar{x}) \wedge C(\bar{x})}{C(\bar{x})}.$$

If the condition 'Typically, if $A(\bar{x})$ and $C(\bar{x})$, then $B(\bar{x})$' is acceptable, d_1 can be further replaced by

$$d_2 = \frac{A(\bar{x}): B(\bar{x}) \wedge C(\bar{x})}{B(\bar{x}) \wedge C(\bar{x})}.$$

We conclude by showing that the plausibility of the second step of the proposed schema crucially depends on the fulfilment of the condition 'Typically, if $A(\bar{x})$ and $C(\bar{x})$, then $B(\bar{x})$'. Consider the default (Etherington 1988):

$$d = \frac{Has\text{-}Motive(x): Guilty(x)}{Suspect(x)}.$$

Although it is reasonable to replace this by

$$d_1 = \frac{Has\text{-}Motive(x): Guilty(x) \wedge Suspect(x)}{Suspect(x)}$$

the second step of the translation, i.e. replacing d_1 by

$$d_2 = \frac{Has\text{-}Motive(x): Guilty(x) \wedge Suspect(x)}{Guilty(x) \wedge Suspect(x)}$$

is obviously unjustified.†

5.6 SEMI-NORMAL DEFAULT THEORIES

We stated in the previous section that semi-normal theories lack (in general) two important properties: the existence of extensions and semi-monotonicity. In this section we show these negative results. We also provide a condition which is sufficient to assure the existence of extensions for a subclass of semi-normal theories.

That semi-normal theories lack the property of semi-monotonicity is evidenced by the following example.

† Note that we do not accept the statement 'Typically, if a suspect has a motive, then he/she is to be considered guilty'.

Example 5.51 Let $T = \langle\{R(a)\}, \{R(a): P(a) \wedge Q(a)/Q(a)\}\rangle$. T has one extension: $E = Th(\{R(a), Q(a)\})$. Adding the default $: \neg P(a)/\neg P(a)$, we obtain a new theory with the single extension given by $F = Th(\{R(a), \neg P(a)\})$. Clearly, $E \not\subseteq F$. ∎

The next example illustrates that there are semi-normal theories without extensions.

Example 5.52 (Reiter & Criscuolo 1983) Consider the theory T consisting of the empty set of axioms and the following triple of defaults:

$$d_1 = \frac{: p \wedge \neg q}{\neg q} \qquad d_2 = \frac{: q \wedge \neg r}{\neg r} \qquad d_3 = \frac{: r \wedge \neg p}{\neg p}.$$

The reader can formally check that T has no extension. The reason is that applying any one default forces the application of one of the other two, but applying the latter contradicts the justification of this already applied: if we choose to start by applying d_1, we are forced to apply d_3, but the application of d_3 denies the justification of d_1; if we begin with d_2, we are forced to apply d_1, but the application of d_1 contradicts the justification of d_2. Finally, starting from d_3 leaves d_2 applicable, but applying d_2 denies the justification of d_3. ∎

Inspecting Example 5.52, together with Examples 5.24 and 5.25, we see that there is a uniform characteristic among default theories without extensions. The lack of an extension is always the result of a conflict arising from the requirement to apply a default which cannot be applied. Generally, the application of an 'applicable' default may be impossible for one of the following reasons:

(1) The consequent of the default, together with axioms and the consequents of other defaults already applied, contradicts some of its own justifications (Example 5.24).
(2) The consequent of the default, together with axioms and the consequents of other defaults already applied, denies the justifications of some other default already applied (Example 5.52).
(3) The consequent of the default contradicts some sentence derivable from axioms and the consequents of other defaults already applied (Example 5.25).

If we restrict our attention to semi-normal theories, the situation simplifies in two respects. First, since the consequent of any semi-normal default is a part of its justification, the cases (1) and (3) never occur. Second, once a semi-normal default $A: B \wedge C/B$ has been applied, only the 'non-normal' part of its justification, i.e. C, is potentially refutable by other defaults. These observations led Etherington (1983) to specify a class of semi-normal theories for which extensions can be proved to exist.

A closed default theory is said to be *universal* iff all of its axioms as well as the prerequisites, the justifications and the consequents of all of its defaults are universal sentences. (See Definition 1.39.)

Definition 5.53 (Etherington 1983) Let $T = \langle W, D\rangle$ be a universal closed semi-normal theory. Without loss of generality we may assume that all sentences occurring in T are in clausal form. Let LITERALS denote the set of all literals occurring in these sentences. We define two relations $\leqslant$ and $\ll$, on LITERALSxLITERALS, as follows (the intention is that $A \leqslant B$ or $A \ll B$ if A can serve to infer B):

(1) If $A_1 \vee \cdots \vee A_n \in W$ ($n \geq 1$), then $\neg A_i \leqslant A_j$, for all $A_i \neq A_j$.

(2) Let $(A\colon B \wedge C/B) \in \mathrm{D}$ and suppose that $A_1, \ldots, A_n, B_1, \ldots, B_s$ and $C_1, \ldots, C_t$ are the literals of the clausal forms of A, B and C, respectively. Then

(i) $A_i \lessapprox B_j$, for all $1 \le i \le n$, $1 \le j \le s$.
(ii) $\neg C_i \ll B_j$, for all $1 \le j \le s$ and each $C_i \notin \{B_1, \ldots, B_s\}(1 \le i \le t)$.
(iii) Let $B = B^1 \wedge \cdots \wedge B^m$ $(m \ge 1)$ and suppose that for each $1 \le i \le m$, $B^i = B_{i,1} \vee \cdots \vee B_{i,m_i}$. Then $\neg B_{i,j} \lessapprox B_{i,k}$, provided that $B_{i,j}, B_{i,k} \in \{B_{i,1}, \ldots, B_{i,m_i}\}$ and $B_{i,j} \neq B_{i,k}$.

(3) The relations $\lessapprox$ and $\ll$ are transitive, i.e.

(i) If $A \lessapprox B$ and $B \lessapprox C$, then $A \lessapprox C$.
(ii) If $A \ll B$ and $B \ll C$, then $A \ll C$.
(iii) If $A \ll B$ and $B \lessapprox C$ or $A \lessapprox B$ and $B \ll C$, then $A \ll C$.

∎

A few comments about this definition are in order. As we already remarked, the intention is that $A \lessapprox B$ or $A \ll B$ iff the inference of B may depend on A. The fact that only the non-normal part of a justification of a default is potentially refutable by the consequents of other defaults is emphasized by using the relation $\ll$ in (2) (ii). The relation $\lessapprox$ is auxiliary. It only serves to provide the correct definition of $\ll$. The intuition behind (1) and (2) (iii) is that any disjunction of the form $A_1 \vee \cdots \vee A_n$ is logically equivalent to the implication $\neg A_1 \wedge \cdots \wedge \neg A_{j-1} \wedge \neg A_{j+1} \wedge \cdots \wedge \neg A_n \supset A_j$, for any $1 \le j \le n$.

Definition 5.54 (Etherington 1983) A universal closed semi-normal default theory is *ordered* iff there is no literal A occurring in T such that $A \ll A$. ∎

Example 5.52 (continued) Since $\neg p \ll \neg q$, $\neg q \ll \neg r$ and $\neg r \ll \neg p$, we have $\neg p \ll \neg p$. Thus, T is not ordered. ∎

Example 5.55 (Etherington 1983) Consider the theory $T = \langle \mathrm{W}, \mathrm{D} \rangle$, where $\mathrm{W} = \{\ \}$ and

$$\mathrm{D} = \left\{ \frac{: p \wedge \neg q}{p}, \frac{: q \wedge \neg s}{q}, \frac{: (r \supset s) \wedge \neg p}{r \supset s} \right\}.$$

This theory is also not ordered. Its defaults lead to the following relationships, respectively:

$$\{q \ll p\}; \{s \ll q\}; \{r \lessapprox s, \neg s \lessapprox \neg r, p \ll \neg r, p \ll s\}.$$

Therefore, $p \ll s \ll q \ll p$. ∎

Theorem 5.56 (Etherington 1983) If a universal semi-normal default theory is ordered, then it has an extension.

Proof See Etherington (1983). ∎

We conclude this section with two remarks. Firstly, since only non-normal defaults give rise to '$\ll$' relationships, normal theories are ordered. Thus, for universal theories, Theorem 5.56 implies Theorem 5.33. Secondly, the orderedness is the sufficient but not the necessary condition for the existence of extensions. To see this, reconsider the theory T from Example 5.55. T has one extension given by $\mathrm{E} = \mathrm{Th}(\{q, r \supset s\})$.

5.7 SEMANTIC CHARACTERIZATION OF EXTENSIONS

Specifying default logic, Reiter has provided no semantics for the formalism. However, he has observed that the general idea might be to view defaults of a theory ⟨W, D⟩ as restricting the models of W in such a way that

(1) Any restricted class of models of W is the class of all models of some extension of ⟨W, D⟩.
(2) If E is any extension of ⟨W, D⟩, then there is some such restricted class of models of W which is the class of all models of E.

These intuitions were formalized by Łukaszewicz (1985) for closed normal theories, and generalized by Etherington (1988) for arbitrary closed theories with single-justification defaults. Etherington's formalization, extended to theories with multiple-justification defaults, is discussed below. For the sake of simplicity, we slightly reformulate his original presentation.

Some preliminary terminology. In what follows, the term 'frame' refers to a frame of classical first-order logic. We write $\mathrm{M} \models A$ to indicate that a sentence A is true in a frame M. For any class $\mathfrak{M}$ of frames and any sentence A, we write $\mathfrak{M}(A)$ to denote the class of all frames from $\mathfrak{M}$ in which A is true. Formally, $\mathfrak{M}(A) = \{\mathrm{M}: \mathrm{M} \in \mathfrak{M}$ and $\mathrm{M} \models A\}$. A frame M is said to be a model of a set of sentences S iff $\mathrm{M} \models A$, for each $A \in \mathrm{S}$. A class $\mathfrak{M}$ of frames is called *elementary* iff $\mathfrak{M}$ is the class of all models of some set of sentences S.

Definition 5.57 Let $\mathfrak{M}$ be a class of frames and let U be a set of sentences. The pair $\langle \mathfrak{M}, \mathrm{U} \rangle$ is called *a structure* iff

(i) $\mathfrak{M}$ is elementary;
(ii) For every $A \in \mathrm{U}$, $\mathfrak{M}(A) \neq \{\ \}$.

∎

Intuitively, a structure $\langle \mathfrak{M}, \mathrm{U} \rangle$ is to be interpreted as a class of all models of some set of beliefs and a set of justifications for these beliefs, respectively. Clause (ii) assures that each justification is consistent with the beliefs.

Definition 5.58 Let $\mathfrak{M}$ be an elementary class of frames and let $\mathrm{d} = A: B_1, \ldots, B_k/C$ be a closed default. We say that d is *R-APPLICABLE wrt* $\mathfrak{M}$ iff

(i) $\mathrm{M} \models A$, for all $\mathrm{M} \in \mathfrak{M}$;
(ii) For every B_i $(1 \leq i \leq k)$, there is $\mathrm{M} \in \mathfrak{M}$ such that $\mathrm{M} \models B_i$.

∎

Observe that the notion of R-APPLICABILITY can be viewed as a semantic counterpart of Reiter's applicability criterion (hence the prefix 'R'). If $\mathfrak{M}$ is interpreted as the class of all models of a set of beliefs, then a default is R-APPLICABLE wrt $\mathfrak{M}$ iff its prerequisite is believed and all of its justifications are consistent with what is believed.

Any pair $\langle \mathfrak{M}, \mathrm{U} \rangle$, where $\mathfrak{M}$ is *any* class of frames and U is *any* set of sentences will be called a *frames-sentences pair*, *FS-pair*, for short. Obviously, any structure is a FS-pair, but not necessarily vice versa.

Definition 5.59 To each closed default $\mathrm{d} = A: B_1, \ldots, B_k/C$ we assign a mapping, denoted by d^{R}, from FS-pairs into FS-pairs given by

$$d^R(\langle \mathfrak{M}, U\rangle) = \begin{cases} \langle \mathfrak{M}(C), U \cup \{B_1, \ldots, B_k\}\rangle & \text{if } \langle \mathfrak{M}, U\rangle \text{ is a structure and d is R-APPLICABLE wrt } \mathfrak{M} \\ \langle \mathfrak{M}, U\rangle & \text{if } \langle \mathfrak{M}, U\rangle \text{ is a structure and d is not R-APPLICABLE wrt } \mathfrak{M} \\ \langle \{\ \}, \{False\}\rangle & \text{otherwise.} \end{cases}$$

▮

An important observation is that $d^R(\langle \mathfrak{M}, U\rangle)$ need not be a structure even if $\langle \mathfrak{M}, U\rangle$ is a structure. Consider:

$$d = p\colon q/\neg q; \qquad \mathfrak{M} = \{M\colon M \models p\}; \qquad U = \{\ \}.$$

$\langle \mathfrak{M}, U\rangle$ is a structure and d is R-APPLICABLE wrt $\mathfrak{M}$. Thus, $d^R(\langle \mathfrak{M}, U\rangle) = \langle \mathfrak{M}_1, U_1\rangle$, where $\mathfrak{M}_1 = \{M\colon M \models p \wedge \neg q\}$ and $U_1 = \{q\}$. Since $\mathfrak{M}_1(q) = \{\ \}$, $\langle \mathfrak{M}_1, U_1\rangle$ is not a structure.

Definition 5.60 Let $\langle \mathfrak{M}, U\rangle$ be a structure and let D be a set of closed defaults. We say that $\langle \mathfrak{M}, U\rangle$ is *R-STABLE wrt* D iff $d^R(\langle \mathfrak{M}, U\rangle) = \langle \mathfrak{M}, U\rangle$, for all $d \in D$. ▮

Definition 5.61 Let $\langle \mathfrak{M}, U\rangle$ be a FS-pair and let $\langle d_i\rangle$ be a sequence of closed defaults. By $\langle d_i\rangle^R(\langle \mathfrak{M}, U\rangle)$ we denote a FS-pair given by

$$\langle d_i\rangle^R(\langle \mathfrak{M}, U\rangle) = \begin{cases} \langle \mathfrak{M}, U\rangle & \text{if } \langle d_i\rangle = \langle\rangle \text{ (the empty sequence)} \\ \langle \bigcap \mathfrak{M}_i, \bigcup U_i\rangle & \text{otherwise} \end{cases}$$

where $\langle \mathfrak{M}_0, U_0\rangle = \langle \mathfrak{M}, U\rangle$ and, for $i = 0, 1, \ldots$ [$i = 0, \ldots, N$]

$$\langle \mathfrak{M}_{i+1} U_{i+1}\rangle = d_i^R(\langle \mathfrak{M}_i, U_i\rangle). \quad ▮$$

Note that if $\langle d_i\rangle$ is a finite sequence, i.e. $\langle d_i\rangle = d_0, \ldots, d_N$, then $\langle d_i\rangle^R(\langle \mathfrak{M}, U\rangle) = d_N(d_{N-1}(\ldots d_0(\langle \mathfrak{M}, U\rangle)\ldots))$.

Definition 5.62 Let $\langle \mathfrak{M}, U\rangle$ be a structure, $\mathfrak{N}$ be an elementary class of frames and suppose that $\langle d_i\rangle$ is a sequence of closed defaults. We say that $\langle \mathfrak{M}, U\rangle$ is $\langle d_i\rangle^R$-*ACCESSIBLE from* $\mathfrak{N}$ iff $\langle \mathfrak{M}, U\rangle = \langle d_i\rangle^R(\langle \mathfrak{N}, \{\ \}\rangle)$. We say that $\langle \mathfrak{M}, U\rangle$ is *R-ACCESSIBLE from* $\mathfrak{N}$ *wrt* D iff there is a sequence (possibly empty) $\langle d_i\rangle$ of defaults from D such that $\langle \mathfrak{M}, U\rangle$ is $\langle d_i\rangle^R$-ACCESSIBLE from $\mathfrak{N}$. ▮

We are now ready to provide a semantic characterization of extensions.

Theorem 5.63 Let $T = \langle W, D\rangle$ be a closed default theory and let $\mathfrak{N}$ be the class of all models of W. A class of frames $\mathfrak{M}$ is the class of all models for some extension of T iff there is a structure $\langle \mathfrak{M}, U\rangle$ such that

(1) $\langle \mathfrak{M}, U\rangle$ is R-STABLE wrt D;
(2) $\langle \mathfrak{M}, U\rangle$ is R-ACCESSIBLE from $\mathfrak{N}$ wrt D.

Proof ($\Rightarrow$) Assume first that $\mathfrak{M}$ is the class of all models of E, where E is an extension of T. Let D_1 be the set of generating defaults for E wrt T. Take $U = \text{JUSTIFICATIONS}(D_1)$. Using Definition 5.30, it is easily checked that $\langle \mathfrak{M}, U\rangle$ is a structure. We shall show that $\langle \mathfrak{M}, U\rangle$ satisfies (1) and (2).

To prove (1), take any $d = (A\colon B_1, \ldots, B_k/C) \in D$ and consider two cases.

Case 1. $d \notin D_1$. Then, in view of Definition 5.30, $A \notin E$ or $\neg B_i \in E$, for some $1 \le i \le k$. Thus, since $\mathfrak{M}$ is the class of all models of E, $M \models \neg A$, for some $M \in \mathfrak{M}$, or

$M \models \neg B_i$, for all $M \in \mathfrak{M}$ and some $1 \leq i \leq k$. In consequence, d is not R-APPLICABLE wrt $\mathfrak{M}$ and hence $d^R(\langle \mathfrak{M}, U \rangle) = \langle \mathfrak{M}, U \rangle$.

Case 2. $d \in D_1$. Then $A \in E$ and $\neg B_i \notin E$, for all $1 \leq i \leq k$. So, since $\mathfrak{M}$ is the class of all models of E, $M \models A$, for any $M \in \mathfrak{M}$, and for each $1 \leq i \leq k$, there is $M \in \mathfrak{M}$ such that $M \models B_i$. Thus, d is R-APPLICABLE with respect to $\mathfrak{M}$, and hence, $d^R(\langle \mathfrak{M}, U \rangle) = \langle \mathfrak{M}(C), U \cup \{B_1, \ldots, B_k\} \rangle$. In view of Theorem 5.31, $C \in E$, and thus, $\mathfrak{M}(C) = \mathfrak{M}$. Furthermore, since $U = \text{JUSTIFICATIONS}(D_1)$ and $d \in D_1$, we clearly have $B_1, \ldots, B_k \in U$. Thus, $d^R(\langle \mathfrak{M}, U \rangle) = \langle \mathfrak{M}, U \rangle$.

We now proceed to (2). Let $\langle d_i \rangle$ be any sequence of all defaults from D_1. We define the sequence $\langle d'_i \rangle$ by

> $d'_i = d_j$ where j is the smallest integer such that: (i) d_j is R-APPLICABLE wrt $\mathfrak{M}'$, where $\mathfrak{M}'$ is the first element of the pair $\langle d'_0, \ldots d'_{i-1} \rangle^R(\langle \mathfrak{N}, \{\ \} \rangle)$; (ii) $d_j \notin \{d'_0, \ldots, d'_{i-1}\}$.

Employing Theorems 5.26 and 5.31, the reader may easily check that the sequence $\langle d'_i \rangle$ is well-defined and uses all of $\langle d_i \rangle$. By straightforward induction on k ($k \geq -1$), one readily verifies that $\langle d'_0, \ldots, d'_k \rangle^R(\langle \mathfrak{N}, \{\ \} \rangle) = \langle \mathfrak{M}_{k+1}, U_{k+1} \rangle$, where $\mathfrak{M}_{k+1}$ is the class of all models of $\text{Th}(W \cup \text{CONSEQUENTS}(\{d'_0, \ldots, d'_k\}))$ and $U_{k+1} = \text{JUSTIFICATIONS}(\{d'_0, \ldots, d'_k\})$. Thus, since $\mathfrak{M}$ is the class of all models of E and $U = \text{JUSTIFICATIONS}(D_1)$, we have $\langle d'_i \rangle^R(\langle \mathfrak{N}, \{\ \} \rangle) = \langle \mathfrak{M}, U \rangle$, by Theorem 5.31. This proves (2) and hence completes the proof from left to right in Theorem 5.63.

($\Leftarrow$) Assume now that $\langle \mathfrak{M}, U \rangle$ is a structure satisfying (1) and (2), and suppose that $\mathfrak{M}$ is the class of all models of a set of sentences E. We have to show that E is an extension of T. By (2), $\langle \mathfrak{M}, U \rangle = \langle d_i \rangle^R(\langle \mathfrak{N}, \{\ \} \rangle)$, for some, possibly empty, sequence $\langle d_i \rangle$ of defaults from D. Consider two cases.

Case 1. $D = \{\ \}$. Then $\langle d_i \rangle = \langle \rangle$, so that $\mathfrak{M} = \mathfrak{N}$. On the other hand, $D = \{\ \}$ implies that T has one extension F given by $F = \text{Th}(W)$. Since $\mathfrak{M} = \mathfrak{N}$, and $\mathfrak{N}$, $\mathfrak{M}$ are the classes of all models of W and E, respectively, we conclude that $E = F$. Thus, E is an extension of T.

Case 2. $D \neq \{\ \}$. Let $d \in D$. If $\langle d_i \rangle$ is a finite sequence, i.e. $\langle d_i \rangle = d_0, \ldots, d_N$ ($N \geq -1$), we define the infinite sequence $\langle d'_i \rangle$ by

$$d'_i = d_i \quad \text{if } 0 \leq i \leq N$$
$$d'_i = d \quad \text{if } i > N.$$

By (1), $\langle \mathfrak{M}, U \rangle = \langle d_i \rangle^R(\langle \mathfrak{N}, \{\ \} \rangle)$ implies $\langle \mathfrak{M}, U \rangle = \langle d'_i \rangle^R(\langle \mathfrak{N}, \{\ \} \rangle)$. Thus, without loss of generality, we may assume that $\langle d_i \rangle$ is infinite, and hence

$$\mathfrak{M} = \bigcap_{i=0}^{\infty} \mathfrak{M}_i \text{ and } U = \bigcup_{i=0}^{\infty} U_i, \text{ where } \mathfrak{M}_0 = \mathfrak{N},\ U_0 = \{\ \} \text{ and, for } i \geq 0,$$

$$\langle \mathfrak{M}_{i+1}, U_{i+1} \rangle = d_i^R(\langle \mathfrak{M}_i, U_i \rangle).$$

Let F_i ($i \geq 0$) be the set of sentences which are true in all frames from $\mathfrak{M}_i$. By straightforward induction on i, one easily shows that $\mathfrak{M}_i$ is the class of all models of F_i. Thus, since $\mathfrak{M} = \bigcap_{i=0}^{\infty} \mathfrak{M}_i$, we infer that $\mathfrak{M}$ is the class of all models of $\bigcup_{i=0}^{\infty} F_i$, and hence

$E = \bigcup_{i=0}^{\infty} F_i$. To show that E is an extension of T, define:

$$E_0 = W \text{ and, for } i \geq 0,$$
$$E_{i+1} = Th(E_i) \cup \{C: (A: B_1, \ldots, B_k/C) \in D,\ E_i \vdash A \text{ and } \neg B_1, \ldots, B_k \notin E\}.$$

By simple induction of i, one easily proves that, for all $i \geq 0$, $F_i \subseteq \bigcup_{i=0}^{\infty} E_i$ and $E_i \subseteq E$. Thus, since $E = \bigcup_{i=0}^{\infty} F_i$, we immediately have $E = \bigcup_{i=0}^{\infty} E_i$. So, by Theorem 5.26, E is an extension of T. ▮

Theorem 5.63 can be given a natural pictorial interpretation. More specifically, to each closed theory $\langle W, D \rangle$ we may assign a transition network, whose nodes are FS-pairs and whose arcs are labelled by defaults of D. Any node which is a structure is called *viable*. Otherwise, it is called *contradictory*. This network is specified as follows.

(1) The set of nodes of the network is the smallest set satisfying:

(i) $\langle \mathfrak{N}, \{\ \} \rangle$, where $\mathfrak{N}$ is the class of all models of W, is a node. This is a viable node, called the *root node*.

(ii) If n is a viable node and $d \in D$, then $d^R(n)$ is a node.

(2) From each viable node n, for each $d \in D$, an arc, labelled by d, leads to $d^R(n)$.

Let $N_{\langle W,D \rangle}$ be the network assigned to a closed theory $\langle W, D \rangle$. The nodes of $N_{\langle W,D \rangle}$ all of whose outbound arcs loop back are called *leaves*. Any viable leaf of $N_{\langle W,D \rangle}$ characterizes an extension of $\langle W, D \rangle$, i.e. if $\langle \mathfrak{M}, U \rangle$ is such a leaf, then $\mathfrak{M}$ is the class of all models of some extension of $\langle W, D \rangle$. Moreover, if the network is finite, every extension of $\langle W, D \rangle$ is semantically characterized by some such a viable leaf. If the network has infinitely many nodes, extensions are also characterized by infinite paths, from the root, of different nodes (these are always viable nodes). More specifically, if $\langle \mathfrak{M}_0, U_0 \rangle, \langle \mathfrak{M}_1, U_1 \rangle, \ldots$ is such a path, then $\bigcap_{i=0}^{\infty} \mathfrak{M}_i$ is the class of all models for some extension of $\langle W, D \rangle$.

Example 5.64 Let $T = \langle W, D \rangle$, where $W = \{p, q\}$ and $D = \{d_1 = p: (r \wedge \neg s)/r, d_2 = q: s/s\}$. T leads to the network given in Fig. 5.1. Since the network is finite and has one viable leaf, T has one extension: $E = Th(\{p, q, s\})$. ▮

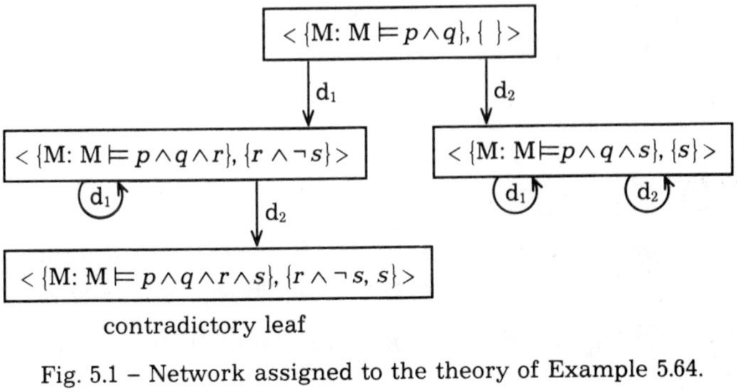

Fig. 5.1 – Network assigned to the theory of Example 5.64.

Example 5.65 Let $T = \langle W, D\rangle$, where $W = \{\ \}$ and $D = \{d_1 = : p/\neg p\}$. T produces the network given in Fig. 5.2. Since this is a finite network without viable leaves, we conclude that T has no extension. ▮

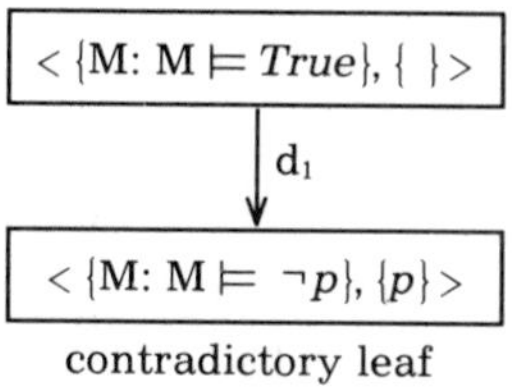

Fig. 5.2 – Network associated with the theory of Example 5.65.

Example 5.66 Let $T = \langle W, D\rangle$, with $W = \{P(a)\}$ and $D = \{d_i : i \geq 1\}$, where $d_1 = P(a): Q_1(a)/Q_1(a)$ and, for $i \geq 1$, $d_{i+1} = Q_i(a): Q_{i+1}(a)/Q_{i+1}(a)$. T leads to the network shown in Fig. 5.3. This network has no leaves. However, there is an infinite path $\langle \mathfrak{M}_0, U_0\rangle, \langle \mathfrak{M}_1, U_1\rangle, \ldots$, from the root, where

$$\langle \mathfrak{M}_0, U_0\rangle = \langle\{M: M \models P(a)\}, \{\ \}\rangle \text{ and, for } i > 0,$$
$$\langle \mathfrak{M}_i, U_i\rangle = \langle\{M: M \models P(a) \wedge Q_1(a) \wedge \cdots \wedge Q_i(a)\}, \{Q_1(a), \ldots, Q_i(a)\}\rangle.$$

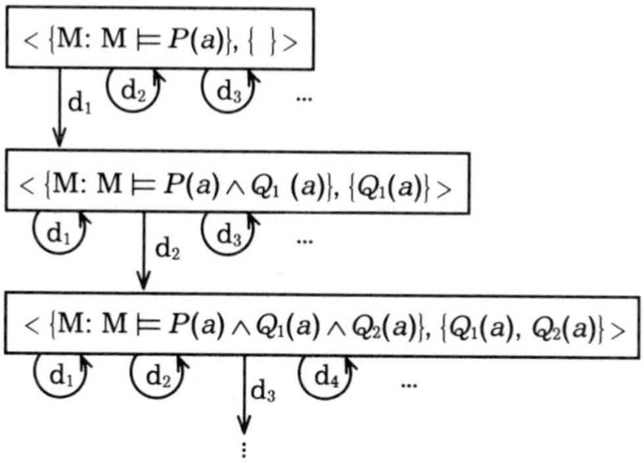

Fig. 5.3 – Network corresponding to the theory of Example 5.66.

Thus, T has one extension: $E = Th(\{P(a), Q_1(a), Q_2(a), \ldots\})$. ▮

Example 5.67 Let $T = \langle W, D\rangle$, where $W = \{p\}$ and

$$D = \{d_1 = p: q/q, \quad d_2 = p: q, \neg q/r\}$$

The network corresponding to T is given in Fig. 5.4. Since the network is finite and has one viable leaf, T has one extension: $E = Th(\{p, q\})$. ▮

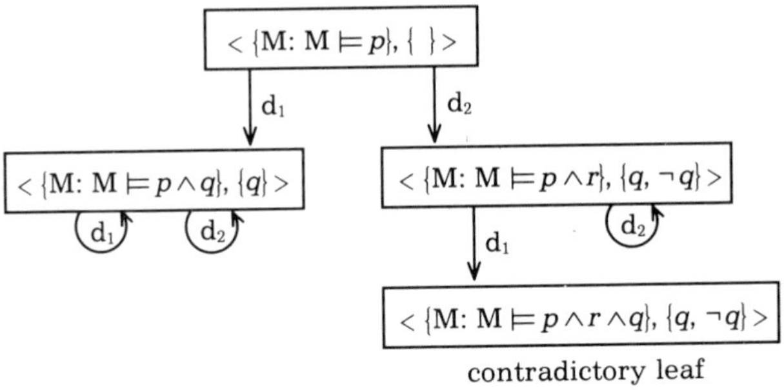

Fig. 5.4 – Network corresponding to the theory of Example 5.67.

5.8 PROOF THEORY FOR CLOSED NORMAL DEFAULT THEORIES

This section is devoted to a proof theory for closed normal default theories. By a proof theory we understand here the following formal task: Given a closed normal default theory T and a sentence C, determine whether there is an extension of T containing C.

If $X = \{A_1, \ldots, A_n\}$ is a finite set of first-order sentences, then we write Cnj(X) to denote the sentence $A_1 \wedge \cdots \wedge A_n$.

Definition 5.68 (Reiter 1980a) Let $T = \langle W, D \rangle$ be a closed normal default theory and let C be a sentence. A finite sequence $D_0, \ldots, D_k$ ($k \geq 0$) of finite subsets of D is called a *default proof of C wrt T* iff

(P1) $W \cup \text{CONSEQUENTS}(D_0) \vdash C$;

(P2) For $1 \leq i \leq k$

$$W \cup \text{CONSEQUENTS}(D_i) \vdash \text{Cnj}(\text{PREREQUISITES}(D_{i-1}));$$

(P3) $D_k = \{\ \}$;

(P4) $W \cup \bigcup_{i=0}^{k} \text{CONSEQUENTS}(D_i)$ is consistent.

▮

Example 5.69 Let $T = \langle W, D \rangle$, where $W = \{P(a)\}$ and

$$D = \left\{ d_1 = \frac{P(a) : Q(a)}{Q(a)},\quad d_2 = \frac{Q(a) : R(a)}{R(a)} \right\}.$$

The sequence $\{d_2\}, \{d_1\}, \{\ \}$ is a default proof of $R(a)$ wrt T. ▮

As it stands, the definition of a default proof seems to be practically useless in that it provides no method of determining the sets D_i. We shall return to this point later, but first we shall show that the notion of a default proof indeed captures its intended meaning. That is, whenever the conditions (P1)–(P4) are satisfied, for some closed normal default theory $T = \langle W, D \rangle$ and some sentence C, then T has an extension E such that $C \in E$. Conversely, if C is a member of some extension of T, then there is a sequence $D_0, \ldots, D_k$ of finite subsets of defaults from D enjoying (P1)–(P4).

Theorem 5.70 (Reiter 1980a) Let T be a closed normal default theory and let C be a sentence. If C has a default proof wrt T, then T has an extension E such that $C \in E$.

Proof We begin by proving an auxiliary lemma.

Lemma 5.70.1 Let $\langle W, D\rangle$ be a closed normal default theory and let $d = (A\colon B/B) \in D$. If $W \vdash A$ and $W \cup \{B\}$ is consistent, then any extension of the theory $\langle W \cup \{B\}, D\rangle$ is also an extension of $\langle W, D\rangle$.

Proof Assume that E is an extension of $\langle W \cup \{B\}, D\rangle$. Then, by Theorem 5.44, (i) $W \cup \{B\} \subseteq E$; (ii) E is stable wrt D; (iii) E is approachable from $W \cup \{B\}$ wrt D. We show that E is an extension of $\langle W, D\rangle$ by proving that

$$W \subseteq E \tag{5.8.1}$$

$$\text{E is stable wrt D} \tag{5.8.2}$$

$$\text{E is approachable from W wrt D} \tag{5.8.3}$$

and invoking Theorem 5.44. (5.8.1) and (5.8.2) are obvious. To show (5.8.3), take any belief set S satisfying $W \subseteq S \subset E$. If $B \notin S$, then clearly $W \subset d(S) \subseteq E$. Otherwise, (5.8.3) immediately follows from (iii). ■

In view of Lemma 5.70.1, we immediately have:

Corollary 5.70.2 Let $\langle W, D\rangle$ be a closed normal default theory and let $D' \subseteq D$. Suppose that $W \cup \text{CONSEQUENTS}(D')$ is consistent and $W \vdash \text{Cnj}(\text{PREREQUISITES}(D'))$. Then any extension of $\langle W \cup \text{CONSEQUENTS}(D'), D\rangle$ is an extension of $\langle W, D\rangle$. ■

We now proceed to the theorem. Assume that $D_0, \ldots, D_k$ is a default proof of C wrt T and consider the theory $T' = \langle W, \bigcup_{i=0}^{k} D_i\rangle$.

Lemma 5.70.3 T' has an extension E' such that $C \in E'$.

Proof By (P2), $W \cup \text{CONSEQUENTS}(D_k) \vdash \text{Cnj}(\text{PREREQUISITES}(D_{k-1}))$. By (P4), $W \cup \text{CONSEQUENTS}(D_{k-1})$ is consistent. Thus, since $D_k = \{\ \}$, any extension of $T'_1 = \langle W \cup \text{CONSEQUENTS}(D_{k-1}), \bigcup_{i=0}^{k} D_i\rangle$ is an extension of T', by Corollary 5.70.2. So, since T'_1 is a closed normal theory, T'_1 has an extension which is an extension of T.

By (P2), $W \cup \text{CONSEQUENTS}(D_{k-1}) \vdash \text{Cnj}(\text{PREREQUISITES}(D_{k-2}))$ and, by (P4), $W \cup \text{CONSEQUENTS}(D_{k-1}) \cup \text{CONSEQUENTS}(D_{k-2})$ is consistent. Thus, by Corollary 5.70.2, the theory

$$T'_2 = \langle W \cup \text{CONSEQUENTS}(D_{k-1}) \cup \text{CONSEQUENTS}(D_{k-2}), \bigcup_{i=0}^{k} D_i\rangle$$

has an extension which is an extension of T'_1 and hence which is an extension of T'.

We proceed in this way, finally arriving at the theory

$$T'_k = \langle W \cup \bigcup_{i=1}^{k} \text{CONSEQUENTS}(D_{k-i}), \bigcup_{i=0}^{k} D_i\rangle$$

which has an extension E' which is also an extension of T'. Obviously, $W \cup \text{CONSEQUENTS}(D_0) \subseteq E'$. Thus, since $W \cup \text{CONSEQUENTS}(D_0) \vdash C$, we infer that $C \in E'$. ■

In view of Lemma 5.70.3, the theory $\langle W, \bigcup_{i=0}^{k} D_i \rangle$ has an extension E′ such that $C \in E'$. Thus, since $\bigcup_{i=0}^{k} D_i \subseteq D$, we conclude, by Theorem 5.45, that the theory $\langle W, D \rangle$ has an extension containing C. This completes the proof of Theorem 5.70. ∎

Let $P_C = D_0, \ldots, D_k$ be a default proof of C wrt T. The *default support of* P_C is given by

$$DS(P_C) = \bigcup_{i=0}^{k} D_i.$$

A default theory $\langle W, D \rangle$ is said to be *consistent* iff W is consistent.

Theorem 5.71 (Reiter 1980a). If E is an extension of a consistent closed normal default theory $T = \langle W, D \rangle$ and $C \in E$, then C has a default proof wrt T.

Proof We start by proving a few auxiliary lemmas.

Lemma 5.71.1 Let $T = \langle W, D \rangle$ be a closed normal default theory and let C' and C'' be sentences. Then $C' \wedge C''$ has a default proof wrt T iff C' and C'' have default proofs $P_{C'}$ and $P_{C''}$ wrt T such that the set $W \cup \text{CONSEQUENTS}(DS(P_{C'})) \cup \text{CONSEQUENTS}(DS(P_{C''}))$ is consistent.

Proof The left-to-right direction immediately follows from the fact that any default proof of $C' \wedge C''$ wrt T is also a default proof of C' wrt T and a default proof of C'' wrt T.

To prove the right-to-left direction, assume that $P_{C'} = D'_0, \ldots, D'_m$ and $P_{C''} = D''_0, \ldots, D''_n$ are default proofs of C' and C'', respectively, and suppose that $n \geq m$. Obviously, $P = D'_0 \cup D''_0, \ldots, D'_m \cup D''_m, D''_{m+1}, \ldots, D''_n$ is a default proof of $C' \wedge C''$ wrt T. ∎

Lemma 5.71.2 Let $T = \langle W, D \rangle$ be a closed normal default theory and let $C_1, \ldots, C_r$ have default proofs $P_{C_1}, \ldots, P_{C_r}$, respectively, wrt T. Assume that $W \cup \text{CONSEQUENTS}\left(\bigcup_{i=1}^{r} DS(P_{C_i})\right)$ is consistent. Then $C_1 \wedge \cdots \wedge C_r$ has a default proof P wrt T such that $DS(P) = \bigcup_{i=1}^{r} DS(P_{C_i})$.

Proof Note that in the proof of the right-to-left direction of Lemma 5.71.1 the default proof P of $C' \wedge C''$ satisfies the property $DS(P) = DS(P_{C'}) \cup DS(P_{C''})$. This immediately implies Lemma 5.71.2. ∎

Lemma 5.71.3 Let P_C be a default proof of C wrt a closed normal default theory $T = \langle W, D \rangle$. Assume further that the sentence $C \supset B$ is valid. Then P_C is also a default proof of B wrt T.

Proof Let $P_C = D_0, \ldots, D_k$. Thus, $W \cup \text{CONSEQUENTS}(D_0) \vdash C$. Since $C \supset B$ is valid, $W \cup \text{CONSEQUENTS}(D_0) \vdash C \supset B$, and hence, by modus ponens, $W \cup \text{CONSEQUENTS}(D_0) \vdash B$. It follows, therefore, that P_C is a default proof of B wrt T. ∎

We now turn to prove Theorem 5.71. By Theorem 5.26, $E = \bigcup_{i=0}^{\infty} E_i$, where

$E_0 = W$ and, for $i \geq 0$,
$E_{i+1} = Th(E_i) \cup \{B\colon (A\colon B/B) \in D, E_i \vdash A \text{ and } \neg B \notin E\}$.

Since $C \in E$, there is an integer $i \geq 0$ such that $C \in E_i$. Now the proof of Theorem 5.71 immediately follows from the next lemma.

Lemma 5.71.4 Let C be any sentence. For all $i \geq 0$, if $C \in E_i$, then there is a default proof P_C of C wrt T such that $DS(P_C) \subseteq GD(E, T)$.†

Proof Induction on i. The case $i = 0$ is trivial. Assume, therefore, that the induction hypothesis holds for all sentences from E_i and suppose that $C \in E_{i+1}$. Consider two cases.

Case 1. $C \in Th(E_i)$. Then there exist $C_1, \ldots, C_n \in E_i$ such that $\{C_1, \ldots, C_n\} \vdash C$. By the induction hypothesis, each C_i has a default proof P_{C_i} such that $DS(P_{C_i}) \subseteq GD(E, T)$. Thus $\bigcup_{i=1}^{n} DS(P_{C_i}) \subseteq GD(E, T)$. By virtue of Theorem 5.31, $E = Th(W \cup \text{CONSEQUENTS}(GD(E, T)))$, and thus, since T is consistent, $W \cup \text{CONSEQUENTS}(GD(E, T))$ is also consistent, by Corollary 5.27. So, $W \cup \text{CONSEQUENTS}\left(\bigcup_{i=1}^{n} DS(P_{C_i})\right)$ is consistent, and so, by Lemma 5.71.2, $C_1 \wedge \cdots \wedge C_n$ has a default proof P such that

$$DS(P) = \bigcup_{i=1}^{n} DS(P_{C_i}) \subseteq GD(E, T) \tag{5.8.4}$$

Since $\{C_1, \ldots, C_n\} \vdash C$, $C_1 \wedge \cdots \wedge C_n \supset C$ is valid. Thus, by Lemma 5.71.3, P is a default proof of C. By (5.8.4), $DS(P) \subseteq GD(E, T)$.

Case 2. C is B, where $(A\colon B/B) \in D$, $E_i \vdash A$ and $\neg B \notin E$. Using the same argument as in Case 1, we show that A has a default proof $P_A = D_0, \ldots, D_k$ such that $DS(P_A) \subseteq GD(E, T)$. Consider the sequence $P_B = \{A\colon B/B\}, D_0, \ldots, D_k$. It is easily verified that P_B is a default proof of B wrt T satisfying $DS(P_B) \subseteq GD(E, T)$. ■

▮

Combining Theorems 5.70 and 5.71, we obtain the following completeness result:

Theorem 5.72 (Reiter 1980a) Let C be a sentence. A consistent closed normal default theory T has an extension containing C iff there is a default proof of C wrt T. ▮

Due to the consistency test (condition P4), the notion of a default proof is not even semi-decidable. That is, there is no procedure which, when supplied with an arbitrary closed normal default theory $T = \langle W, D\rangle$, an arbitrary sentence C and an arbitrary sequence $D_0, \ldots, D_k$ of finite subsets of D, terminates and reports that $D_0, \ldots, D_k$ is a default proof of C wrt T, provided that this is indeed the case. Accordingly, the task of finding such a proof is also not semi-decidable, and, consequently, Theorem 5.72 does not give rise to a procedure which could be used to confirm that a given sentence belongs to an extension of a given closed normal default theory. As Reiter shows, this is not an accidental feature of his approach, but rather a more general phenomenon.

† Recall that $GD(E, T)$ is the set of generating defaults for E wrt T (Definition 5.30).

Theorem 5.73 (Reiter 1980a) Let T be a closed normal default theory over a language L and suppose that EXT(T) is the union of all extensions of T. In general, E is not a partially computable subset of L.

Proof The proof is fairly easy, but refers to the theory of recursive functions and hence will not be given here. The interested reader should consult Reiter (1980a). ▮

In view of Theorem 5.73, any proof procedure for closed normal default theories must necessarily refer to some non-semi-decidable process. It follows, therefore, that any computational approach to such theories must depend on some heuristic component and will sometimes lead to incorrect results.

In the remainder of this section we show how Reiter's proof theory can be combined with a resolution theorem prover for ordinary first-order logic. The forthcoming discussion, which closely follows Reiter (1980a, section 5), presupposes the familiarity with the material of section 1.4.

Reiter suggests the following top-down approach to the task of finding a default proof of a sentence C wrt a closed normal default theory $T = \langle W, D \rangle$. We start by determining a subset D_0 of D such that $W \cup \text{CONSEQUENTS}(D_0) \vdash C$. Next, for $i > 0$, if D_{i-1} has been specified, we try to determine a subset D_i of D such that $W \cup \text{CONSEQUENTS}(D_i) \vdash \text{Cnj}(\text{PREREQUISITES}(D_{i-1}))$. If, for some $k \geq 0$, $D_k = \{\ \}$ and $W \cup \bigcup_{i=0}^{k} \text{CONSEQUENTS}(D_i)$ is consistent, then $D_0, \ldots, D_k$ is a default proof of C wrt T.

At first sight the above approach does not seem to be computationally attractive. Even if we ignore the consistency test, there still remains the problem of determining the sets $D_0, \ldots, D_k$. Fortunately, this problem is not so hard as it might appear. For, if we use a top down theorem prover, then C (resp. $\text{Cnj}(\text{PREREQUISITES}(D_{i-1}))$, $i \geq 1$) will help to find the set D_0 (resp. D_i).[†]

Linear resolution is an example of a top-down theorem prover. Recall that a *linear resolution proof of A from a set of clauses* CL has the form of Fig. 5.5, where

(i) The top clause, C_0, is a clause of $\neg A$;

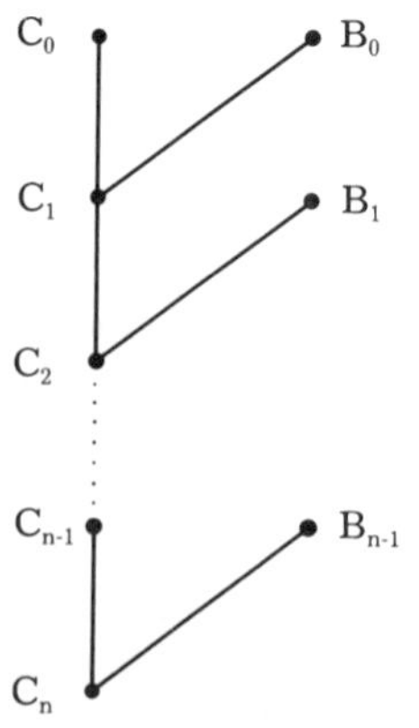

Fig. 5.5 – Linear resolution proof.

[†] Roughly speaking, a top-down theorem prover is the one which starts with the goal to be proved and reasons backwards.

(ii) For $0 \leq i < n$, $B_i \in$ CL or B_i is a clause of $\neg A$ or B_i is C_j, for some $j < i$;
(iii) For $1 \leq i \leq n$, C_i is a resolvent of C_{i-1} and B_{i-1};
(iv) $C_n = \square$.

Our intention is to use linear resolution to determine the set D_0 (resp. $D_i, i \geq 1$) on the basis of the goal sentence C (resp. the sentence Cnj(PREREQUISITES(D_{i-1}))). For this purpose, we need a suitable *clausal form* of a closed normal default theory $T = \langle W, D \rangle$. First of all, we assume that W is a set of clauses. In addition, we require a special clausal representation of the consequents of defaults from D. Let $d = (A: B/B) \in D$ and suppose that $B_1, \ldots, B_n$ are all of the clauses of B. Then the ordered pair $\langle B_i, \{d\} \rangle$, $1 \leq i \leq n$, is said to be a *consequent clause of* d.

Example 5.74 Let $T = \langle W, D \rangle$, where $W = \{P_1(a), P_2(a)\}$ and

$$D = \left\{ d_1 = \frac{P_1(a): Q_1(a)}{Q_1(a)}, d_2 = \frac{P_2(a): Q_2(a)}{Q_2(a)}, \right.$$

$$\left. d_3 = \frac{Q_1(a) \wedge Q_2(a): R(b) \wedge p}{R(b) \wedge p}, d_4 = \frac{: \neg R(b)}{\neg R(b)} \right\}.$$

The consequent clauses are: $\langle Q_1(a), \{d_1\} \rangle$, $\langle Q_2(a), \{d_2\} \rangle$, $\langle R(b), \{d_3\} \rangle$, $\langle p, \{d_3\} \rangle$, $\langle \neg R(b), \{d_4\} \rangle$. ▮

Let $T = \langle W, D \rangle$ be a closed normal default theory, where W is a set of ordinary clauses. We define CLAUSES(T) =

$$\{\langle C, \{d\} \rangle : d \in D \text{ and } \langle C, \{d\} \rangle \text{ is a consequent clause of d}\} \cup \{\langle C, \{\ \} \rangle : C \in W\}$$

A pair $\langle C, D \rangle$, where C is a clause and D is a set of closed normal defaults, will be referred to as an *indexed clause*.

Definition 5.75 (Reiter 1980a) If $\langle C_1, D_1 \rangle$ and $\langle C_2, D_2 \rangle$ are indexed clauses and R is the usual resolvent of C_1 and C_2, then $\langle R, D_1 \cup D_2 \rangle$ is a *resolvent of the indexed clauses* $\langle C_1, D_2 \rangle$ and $\langle C_2, D_2 \rangle$. A *linear resolution proof of a sentence A from a set of indexed clauses* CL is specified precisely as that using non-indexed clauses, except that now all of the clauses of the proof are indexed. More specifically, such a proof has the form of Fig. 5.5, where

(i) $C_0 = \langle C, \{\ \} \rangle$, where C is a clause of $\neg A$;
(ii) For $0 \leq i < n$, $B_i \in$ CL, or $B_i = \langle B, \{\ \} \rangle$, where B is a clause of $\neg A$, or B_i is C_j, for some $j < i$;
(iii) For $1 \leq i \leq n$, C_i is a resolvent of indexed clauses C_{i-1} and B_{i-1};
(iv) $C_n = \langle \square, \{D\} \rangle$, for some set of defaults D.

We say that such a proof *returns* D. ▮

We now return to our original task. Given a closed normal default theory $T = \langle W, D \rangle$ and a sentence C, we try to determine a linear resolution proof of C from the set of indexed clauses CLAUSES(T). If this succeeds, and the proof returns D_0, then clearly $W \cup$ CONSEQUENTS(D_0) $\vdash C$. Having established D_0, we seek, if $D_0 \neq \{\ \}$, a linear resolution proof of Cnj(PREREQUISITES(D_0)) from CLAUSES(T). If L is such a proof, and L returns D_1, then $W \cup$ CONSEQUENTS(D_1) $\vdash$ Cnj(PREREQUISITES(D_0)). We proceed in this top-down fashion until, for some $k \geq 0$, $D_k = \{\ \}$. Then, if the set

$\mathrm{W} \cup \mathrm{CONSEQUENTS}\left(\bigcup_{i=0}^{k} \mathrm{D_i}\right)$ is consistent, the sequence $\mathrm{D}_0, \ldots, \mathrm{D}_k$ is a default proof of C wrt T.

Our discussion motivates the following definition:

Definition 5.76 (Reiter 1980a) Let $T = \langle \mathrm{W}, \mathrm{D} \rangle$ be a closed normal default theory (in causal form). A *top-down default proof of C wrt T* is a sequence $\mathrm{L}_0, \ldots, \mathrm{L}_k$ of linear resolution proofs such that

(i) L_0 is a linear resolution proof of C from CLAUSES(T);
(ii) For $0 \leq i \leq k$, $\mathrm{L_i}$ returns $\mathrm{D_i}$;
(iii) For $1 \leq i \leq k$, $\mathrm{L_i}$ is a linear resolution proof of Cnj(PREREQUISITES(D_{i-1})) from CLAUSES(T);
(iv) $\mathrm{D}_k = \{\ \}$;
(v) $\mathrm{W} \cup \mathrm{CONSEQUENTS}\left(\bigcup_{i=0}^{k} \mathrm{D_i}\right)$ is consistent.

∎

Example 5.74 (continued) T has two extensions:

$$\mathrm{E}_1 = \mathrm{Th}(\mathrm{W} \cup \{Q_1(a), Q_2(a), R(b), p\})$$
$$\mathrm{E}_2 = \mathrm{Th}(\mathrm{W} \cup \{Q_1(a), Q_2(a), \neg R(b)\}).$$

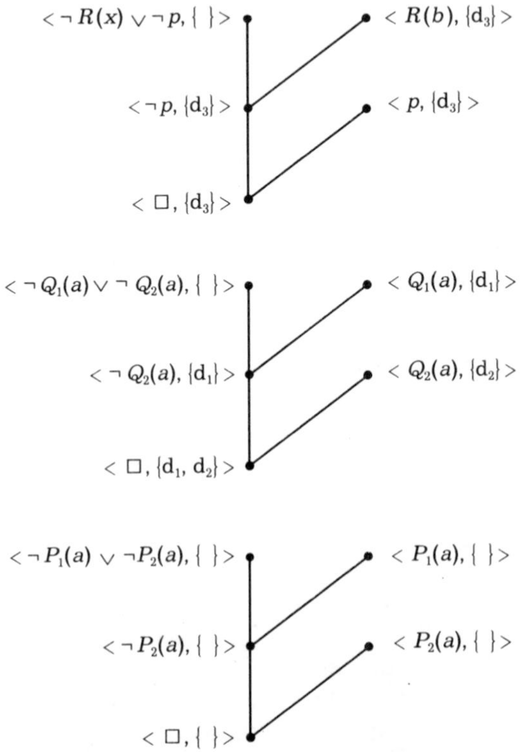

Fig. 5.6 – Top down default proof. (Example 5.74.)

CLAUSES(T) = $\{\langle P_1(a), \{\ \}\rangle, \langle P_2(a), \{\ \}\rangle, \langle Q_1(a), \{d_1\}\rangle, \langle Q_2(a), \{d_2\}\rangle, \langle R(b), \{d_3\}\rangle, \langle p, \{d_3\}\rangle, \langle \neg R(b), \{d_4\}\rangle\}$.

Figure 5.6 represents a top-down default proof of $\exists x R(x) \wedge p$ wrt T. Note that $D_0 = \{d_3\}$, $D_1 = \{d_1, d_2\}$ and $D_3 = \{\ \}$. Since the set W $\cup$ CONSEQUENTS($\{d_1, d_2, d_3\}$) is consistent, this is indeed a top-down default proof. ∎

It is easy to show, using Theorem 1.73 (Chapter 1), that C has a top down default proof wrt a consistent closed normal default theory T (in causal form) iff it has a default proof wrt T. Thus, by Theorem 5.72, we immediately obtain:

Theorem 5.77 (Reiter 1980a) If T is a consistent closed normal default theory (in clausal form) and C is a sentence, then T has an extension containing C iff there is a top down default proof of C wrt T. ∎

The presented proof theory can be generalized into open universal normal default theories. See Reiter (1980a) for details.

5.9 A COMPARISON BETWEEN DEFAULT LOGIC AND AUTOEPISTEMIC LOGIC

In this section we compare default and autoepistemic logics. Since the latter has been introduced on the basis of propositional language, we restrict our attention to the propositional part of default logic. The subsequent presentation presupposes the familiarity with the material contained in section 4.3 (Chapter 4).

In the following, the symbol 'Th' refers to the provability operator of the classical propositional logic over a modal language. We write $[\mathrm{Th}(X)]_0$ to denote the set of objective propositional formulae classically derivable from X.

Definition 5.78 (Konolige 1988) Let d be a *propositional default*, i.e. an expression of the form $A{:}\, B_1, \ldots, B_k/C$, where A, $B_1, \ldots, B_k$ and C are formulae of classical propositional logic. The AE *transform of* d, written $\mathrm{TR_{AE}}(\mathrm{d})$, is the formula of autoepistemic logic given by

$$\neg \mathrm{L}A \vee \mathrm{L}\neg B_1 \vee \cdots \vee \mathrm{L}\neg B_k \vee C.$$

Let T be a *propositional default theory*, i.e. a pair $\langle W, D\rangle$, where W is a set of propositional formulae and D is a set of propositional defaults. The *AE transform of* T, written $\mathrm{TR_{AE}}(T)$, is the theory of autoepistemic logic specified by

$$W \cup \{\mathrm{TR_{AE}}(d) : d \in D\}.$$

∎

The objective part of a stable set S, i.e. S_0, is called the *kernel of* S. Recall that any stable set is uniquely determined by its kernel (Theorem 4.54, Chapter 4).

As we shall see, if E is an extension of a propositional default theory T, then E is the kernel of an AE extension of $\mathrm{TR_{AE}}(T)$.† The converse, however, is not always true. Consider, for instance, the theory $T = \langle\{\ \}, \{p{:}\, True/p\}\rangle$. T has one extension: $E = [\mathrm{Th}(\{\ \})]_0$. $\mathrm{TR_{AE}}(T) = \{\neg \mathrm{L}p \vee \mathrm{L}\neg True \vee p\}$. This theory has two AE extensions, determined by the kernels $[\mathrm{Th}(\{p\})]_0$ and $[\mathrm{Th}(\{\ \})]_0$.

† An extension of a propositional default theory is defined in the usual way (see Definition 5.19), except that it is now restricted to propositional formulae.

Konolige (1988) claims that extensions of a default theory T and the kernels of strongly grounded AE extensions of $\mathrm{TR_{AE}}(T)$ are precisely the same objects. However, as Marek & Truszczynski (1989) have observed, this claim is false. To see this, take $T = \langle\{\ \}, \{p\colon True/p, :\neg p/p\}\rangle$. It is easily checked that T lacks an extension. $\mathrm{TR_{AE}}(T) = \{\neg \mathrm{L}p \vee \mathrm{L}\neg True \vee p, \mathrm{L}p \vee p\}$ has one AE extension, with $[\mathrm{Th}(\{p\})]_0$ as its kernel, which is strongly grounded.

It turns out that the set of extensions of a default theory T is just the set of kernels of superstrongly grounded AE extensions of $\mathrm{TR_{AE}}(T)$. To show this, we need a preliminary result.

Theorem 5.79 (Konolige 1988) Let T be a propositional default theory and suppose that E is an extension of T. Then E is the kernel of a minimal AE extension of $\mathrm{TR_{AE}}(T)$.

Proof Let $T = \langle \mathrm{W}_1\mathrm{D}\rangle$. We begin by proving an auxiliary lemma.

Lemma 5.79.1 E is the kernel of a minimal stable set containing $\mathrm{TR_{AE}}(T)$.

Proof $\mathrm{TR_{AE}}(T) = \mathrm{W} \cup \mathrm{D}'$, where D′ is the set of AE transforms of defaults from D. Clearly, the stable set S whose kernel is E contains W. To show that $\mathrm{D}' \subseteq \mathrm{S}$, take the AE transform $\neg \mathrm{L}A \vee \mathrm{L}\neg B_1 \vee \cdots \vee \mathrm{L}\neg B_k \vee C$ of any default from D and suppose that it is not in S. Then, by Theorem 4.51 (ST8), $A \in \mathrm{S}$, $\neg B_1, \ldots, \neg B_k \notin \mathrm{S}$ and $C \notin \mathrm{S}$. Thus, since S is the stable set whose kernel is E and $A, B_1, \ldots, B_k, C$ are all objective, we conclude that $A \in \mathrm{E}$, $\neg B_1, \ldots, B_k \notin \mathrm{E}$ and $C \notin \mathrm{E}$. But E is an extension of T, and so, $\mathrm{E} = \Gamma(\mathrm{E})$. Therefore, $A \in \Gamma(\mathrm{E})$, $\neg B_1, \ldots, \neg B_k \notin \mathrm{E}$ and $C \notin \Gamma(\mathrm{E})$. A contradiction with the definition of the operator Γ.

To show that S is minimal, assume on the contrary that there is $\mathrm{V} \subset \mathrm{E}$ which is the kernel of a stable set containing $\mathrm{W} \cup \mathrm{D}'$. Consider any member $\neg \mathrm{L}A \vee \mathrm{L}\neg B_1 \vee \cdots \vee \mathrm{L}\neg B_k \vee C$ of D′. Because it is an element of the stable set determined by V, either $A \notin \mathrm{V}$, or $\neg B_i \in \mathrm{V}$ (for some $1 \leq i \leq k$), or $C \in \mathrm{V}$. Thus, since V is deductively closed and $\mathrm{W} \subseteq \mathrm{V}$, we infer that $\Gamma(\mathrm{E}) \subseteq \mathrm{V}$, by the minimality of Γ. In consequence, since $\mathrm{E} = \Gamma(\mathrm{E})$, we conclude that $\mathrm{E} \subseteq \mathrm{V}$. A contradiction with the assumption that $\mathrm{V} \subset \mathrm{E}$. ■

We now proceed to prove the theorem. By Lemma 5.79.1, E is the kernel of a minimal stable set S containing $\mathrm{TR_{AE}}(T)$. Consider the set X given by

$$\mathrm{X} = \{A\colon \mathrm{TR_{AE}}(T) \cup \mathbf{LS} \cup \neg\mathbf{L}\bar{\mathrm{S}} \models A\} \tag{5.9.1}$$

Lemma 5.79.2 X = S.

Proof The following facts are easy to verify:

(1) mp is a propositional model of $\mathrm{TR_{AE}}(T) \cup \mathbf{LS} \cup \neg\mathbf{L}\bar{\mathrm{S}}$ iff mp is a propositional model of $\mathrm{X}_0 \cup \mathbf{LS} \cup \neg\mathbf{L}\bar{\mathrm{S}}$.
(2) $\mathrm{X}_0 = \Gamma(\mathrm{E})$ and hence, since $\Gamma(\mathrm{E}) = \mathrm{E}$ and $\mathrm{E} = \mathrm{S}_0$, $\mathrm{X}_0 = \mathrm{S}_0$.

In view of (1), $\mathrm{X} = \{A\colon \mathrm{X}_0 \cup \mathbf{LS} \cup \neg\mathbf{L}\bar{\mathrm{S}} \models A\}$ and thus, by (2),

$$\mathrm{X} = \{A\colon \mathrm{S}_0 \cup \mathbf{LS} \cup \neg\mathbf{L}\bar{\mathrm{S}} \models A\}. \tag{5.9.2}$$

Since S is stable, it is an AE extension of S_0 (Theorem 4.66), and hence, by Corollary 4.65

$$\mathrm{S} = \{A\colon S_0 \cup \mathbf{LS} \cup \neg\mathbf{L}\bar{\mathrm{S}} \models A\}. \tag{5.9.3}$$

By virtue of (5.9.2) and (5.9.3), we immediately conclude that S = X. ■

By Lemma 5.79.2, the equation (5.9.1) may be rewritten as $\mathrm{S} = \{A\colon \mathrm{TR_{AE}}(T) \cup \mathbf{LS} \cup \neg\mathbf{L}\bar{\mathrm{S}} \models A\}$. Thus, by Corollary 4.65, S is an AE extension of $\mathrm{TR_{AE}}(T)$. Furthermore, since S is minimal for $\mathrm{TR_{AE}}(T)$, it is also a minimal AE extension of $\mathrm{TR_{AE}}(T)$, by Corollary 4.105. ▮

We are now ready to prove the main result of this section.

Theorem 5.80 Let $T = \langle \mathrm{W}, \mathrm{D} \rangle$ be a propositional default theory. E is an extension of T iff it is the kernel of a superstrongly grounded AE extension on $\mathrm{TR_{AE}}(T)$.

Proof ($\Rightarrow$) Assume first that E is an extension of T and suppose that $\mathrm{D}' \subseteq \mathrm{D}$ is the set of generating defaults for E wrt T. Clearly, E is an extension of $T' = \langle \mathrm{W}, \mathrm{D}' \rangle$. Thus, by Theorem 5.79, the theories $\mathrm{TR_{AE}}(T)$ and $\mathrm{TR_{AE}}(T')$ have minimal AE extensions, say S and S′, whose kernel is E. Since AE extensions are uniquely determined by their kernels, S = S′. Thus, by Theorem 4.100,

$$\mathrm{S} = \{A\colon \mathrm{TR_{AE}}(T') \cup \mathbf{L}\mathrm{TR_{AE}}(T') \cup \neg\mathbf{L}\bar{\mathrm{S}}_0 \models_{\mathrm{PV}} A\}.$$

It is easily verified that $\mathrm{TR_{AE}}(T')$ obtains from $\mathrm{TR_{AE}}(T)$ by deleting all modalized axioms which are not applicable wrt S. It follows, therefore, that S is a superstrongly grounded AE extension of $\mathrm{TR_{AE}}(T)$.

($\Leftarrow$) Assume now that E is the kernel of a superstrongly grounded AE extension S of $\mathrm{TR_{AE}}(T)$. Thus,

$$\mathrm{S} = \{A\colon T' \cup \mathbf{L}T' \cup \neg\mathbf{L}\bar{\mathrm{S}}_0 \models_{\mathrm{PV}} A\}$$

where T' obtains from $\mathrm{TR_{AE}}(T)$ by deleting all modalized axioms which are inapplicable wrt S.

Lemma 5.80.1 $\Gamma(\mathrm{S}_0)$ is not a proper subset of S_0.

Proof Assume to the contrary that $\Gamma(\mathrm{S}_0) \subset \mathrm{S}_0$. Let $\mathrm{D}' \subseteq \mathrm{D}$ be the set of those members of D whose AE transforms are in T'. Consider the AE transform $\neg\mathrm{L}A \vee \mathrm{L}\neg B_1 \vee \cdots \vee \mathrm{L}\neg B_k \vee C$ of any default from D′. Since $\neg\mathrm{L}A \vee \mathrm{L}\neg B_1 \vee \cdots \vee \mathrm{L}\neg B_k \vee C$ is applicable wrt S, $A \in \mathrm{S}$, $\neg B_1, \ldots, \neg B_k \notin \mathrm{S}$ and $C \in \mathrm{S}$. So, because $A, \neg B_1, \ldots, \neg B_k$ and C are all objective, $A \in \mathrm{S}_0$, $\neg B_1, \ldots, \neg B_k \notin \mathrm{S}_0$ and $C \in \mathrm{S}_0$, and thus, by the definition of Γ, $C \in \Gamma(\mathrm{S}_0)$ or $A \notin \Gamma(\mathrm{S}_0)$. Let S′ be the stable set whose kernel is $\Gamma(\mathrm{S}_0)$. Clearly, $\mathrm{W} \subseteq \Gamma(\mathrm{S}_0) \subseteq \mathrm{S}'$. Furthermore, since for every AE transform $\neg\mathrm{L}A \vee \mathrm{L}\neg B_1 \vee \cdots \vee \mathrm{L}\neg B_k \vee C$ of any default from D′, $C \in \Gamma(\mathrm{S}_0)$ or $A \notin \Gamma(\mathrm{S}_0)$, all members of D′ belong to S′, by Theorem 4.51 (ST8). Thus, $T' \subseteq \mathrm{S}'$. On the other hand, since S is a superstrongly grounded AE extension of T', it is also a minimal AE extension of T', and hence, by Corollary 4.104, S is a minimal stable set for T'. This, together with $T' \subseteq \mathrm{S}'$, contradicts $\Gamma(\mathrm{S}_0) \subset \mathrm{S}_0$. ■

Lemma 5.80.2 S_0 satisfies the following conditions:

(1) $\mathrm{S}_0 = [\mathrm{Th}(\mathrm{S}_0)]_0$;
(2) $\mathrm{W} \subseteq \mathrm{S}_0$;
(3) For any $(A\colon B_1, \ldots, B_k/C) \in \mathrm{D}$, if $A \in \mathrm{S}_0$ and $\neg B_1, \ldots, \neg B_k \notin \mathrm{S}_0$, then $C \in \mathrm{S}_0$.

Proof (1) and (2) are obvious. To prove (3), assume that $A \in S_0$ and $\neg B_1, \ldots, \neg B_k \notin S_0$. Thus, since $A, B_1, \ldots, B_k$ are all objective, $A \in S$ and $\neg B_1, \ldots, \neg B_k \notin S$. So, $\neg LA \vee L\neg B_1 \vee \cdots \vee L\neg B_k \vee C$ is a member of T' and hence a member of S. But $A \in S$ and $\neg B_1, \ldots, \neg B_k \notin S$ imply $\neg LA \notin S$ and $L\neg B_1, \ldots, L\neg B_k \notin S$, and so, $C \in S$. Since C is objective, we finally conclude that $C \in S_0$. ■

By Lemma 5.80.2, it is clear that $\Gamma(S_0) \subseteq S_0$. Thus, by Lemma 5.80.1, $\Gamma(S_0) = S_0$. So, since $S_0 = E$, E is an extension of T. ▮

For more results concerning relationships between default and autoepistemic logics, see Marek & Truszczynski (1989).

5.10 ALTERNATIVE FORMALIZATION OF DEFAULT LOGIC

In this section we provide an alternative formalization of default logic. The new version, obtained by modifying the criterion of defaults' applicability, has been introduced in Łukaszewicz (1984b). In contrast to Reiter's proposal, it guarantees the existence of extensions and semi-monotonicity.

The new formalization is based on the assumption that it is useless to force the application of a default which all the same cannot be applied. As we observed in section 5.6, the application of an 'applicable' default may be impossible by one of the following reasons:

(1) The consequent of the default, together with axioms and the consequents of other already applied defaults, contradicts some of its own justifications.
(2) The consequent of the default, together with axioms and the consequents of other already applied defaults, denies the justifications of some other already applied default.
(3) The consequent of the default contradicts some sentence derivable from axioms and the consequents of other already applied defaults.

To explicitly block the application of a default when one of the above situations occur, the new formalism employs the following modified criterion of defaults' applicability:

> 'If the prerequisite of a default is believed, [its justifications are consistent with what is believed], and adding its consequent to the set of beliefs neither leads to inconsistency nor contradicts the justifications of this or any other already applied default, then the consequent of the default is to be believed.'†

Before going into technical details, let us see how this modification works in practice.

Example 5.81 (Łukaszewicz 1984b) Assume that the following is true:

> Usually on Sundays I go fishing, except if I wake up late.
> Usually when I am on holiday, I wake up late.

† Note that the part in the brackets is redundant.

This can be represented by the following pair of defaults:

$$d_1 = \frac{\textit{Sunday}: \textit{I-Go-Fishing} \wedge \neg \textit{I-Wake-Up-Late}}{\textit{I-Go-Fishing}}$$

$$d_2 = \frac{\textit{Holidays}: \textit{I-Wake-Up-Late}}{\textit{I-Wake-Up-Late}}.$$

Suppose that it is Sunday and I am on holiday. By d_1, common-sense reasoning allows me to conclude *I-Go-Fishing*, and by d_2, *I-Wake-Up-Late*. Because the first inference assumes the consistency of $\neg$*I-Wake-Up-Late*, one must not apply both the defaults simultaneously. This suggests two extensions, including *I-Go-Fishing* and *I-Wake-Up-Late*, respectively. In Reiter's system, however, there is only one extension: E = Th({*Sunday*, *Holidays*, *I-Wake-Up-Late*}). Thus the proposition *I-Go-Fishing* does not belong to any set of beliefs about the world under consideration.

The extension E comes into existence when the defaults are invoked in the order d_2, d_1. Let us analyse what happens for the reverse order. By d_1 we infer *I-Go-Fishing*. This conclusion, however, is based on the assumption that $\neg$*I-Wake-Up-Late* is consistent with what is believed. Accordingly, since d_2 can be now applied only at the risk of the denial of this assumption, it should be blocked. This would lead to the second extension, namely, Th({*Sunday*, *Holidays*, *I-Go-Fishing*}). In Reiter's formalism, however, the application of d_2 depends only on whether *I-Wake-Up-Late* is consistent with what is believed. This leads to the unsolvable conflict: applying d_2 results in the denial of a prior assumption; blocking it requires an unsupported belief, namely, $\neg$*I-Wake-Up-Late*. In consequence, there is no extension corresponding to the sequence d_1, d_2 in Reiter's system. ▮

Example 5.82 (Łukaszewicz 1984b) Assume that the following is true:

> Usually on Sundays I go fishing, except when I am tired.
> Usually, if I worked hard yesterday, I am tired, except when I woke up late today.
> Usually, if I am on holiday, I wake up late, except when I go fishing.

This can be represented by the following triple of defaults:

$$\frac{\textit{Sunday}: \textit{I-Go-Fishing} \wedge \neg \textit{I-Am-Tired}}{\textit{I-Go-Fishing}}$$

$$\frac{\textit{I-Worked-Hard}: \textit{I-Am-Tired} \wedge \neg \textit{I-Wake-Up-Late}}{\textit{I-Am-Tired}}$$

$$\frac{\textit{Holidays}: \textit{I-Wake-Up-Late} \wedge \neg \textit{I-Go-Fishing}}{\textit{I-Wake-Up-Late}}.$$

Suppose that it is Sunday, I worked hard yesterday and I am on holiday. This theory fits the general pattern of the theory of Example 5.52 and thus has no extension in Reiter's formalism. The reason, as we observed, is that applying any one default forces the application of one of the other two, but applying the latter makes the one already applied inapplicable. All we need to resolve this conflict is the modified criterion of defaults' applicability. According to it, applying any one default makes the other two inapplicable. This immediately results in three extensions:

$E_1 = \mathrm{Th}(\{\mathit{Sunday}, \mathit{I\text{-}Worked\text{-}Hard}, \mathit{Holidays}, \mathit{I\text{-}Go\text{-}Fishing}\})$
$E_2 = \mathrm{Th}(\{\mathit{Sunday}, \mathit{I\text{-}Worked\text{-}Hard}, \mathit{Holidays}, \mathit{I\text{-}Am\text{-}Tired}\})$
$E_3 = \mathrm{Th}(\{\mathit{Sunday}, \mathit{I\text{-}Worked\text{-}Hard}, \mathit{Holidays}, \mathit{I\text{-}Wake\text{-}Up\text{-}Late}\})$.

These extensions seem to agree with our intuitions. Given the information contained in the theory, there are reasons to believe *I-Go-Fishing*, *I-Am-Tired*, or *I-Wake-Up-Late*. But accepting any one of these propositions makes the other two unacceptable. If one, for example, believes that I go fishing, one must not at the same time believe that I am tired or that I woke up late. ▮

We now pass to formalize the above ideas. In contrast to Reiter's criterion, the modified criterion of defaults' applicability refers not only to the default under consideration but to the other defaults too. Accordingly, the new version of default logic is formally more complex than that of Reiter. The formal definition of an extension makes use of a pair of operators. One of them is concerned with beliefs derivable from a given theory. The other keeps track of justifications supporting those beliefs. The details are the following.

In the remainder of this chapter, the symbols 'Th', and '$\vdash$' ('$\nvdash$') refer to the provability operator and the provability (unprovability) relation of classical first-order logic, respectively.

Definition 5.83 (Łukaszewicz 1984b) Let $T = \langle W, D \rangle$ be a closed default theory over a first-order language L. Define the operators Γ_1 and Γ_2, specified on pairs of sets of sentences from L, such that for any pair (S, U), $\Gamma_1(S, U)$ and $\Gamma_2(S, U)$ are the smallest sets of sentences from L satisfying:

(MD1) $\Gamma_1(S, U) = \mathrm{Th}(\Gamma_1(S, U))$;
(MD2) $W \subseteq \Gamma_1(S, U)$;
(MD3) If $(A: B_1, \ldots, B_k/C) \in D$, $A \in \Gamma_1(S, U)$ and, for all $X \in U \cup \{B_1, \ldots, B_k\}$, $S \cup \{C\} \nvdash \neg X$, then
(i) $C \in \Gamma_1(S, U)$;
(ii) $B_1, \ldots, B_k \in \Gamma_2(S, U)$.

A set of sentences $E \subseteq L$ is a *modified extension* (*m-extension*) *of* T *wrt* F iff $E = \Gamma_1(E, F)$ and $F = \Gamma_2(E, F)$. E is an *m-extension of* T iff there is a set F such that E is an m-extension of T wrt F. The set F is called the *set of justifications supporting* E. ▮

Roughly speaking, Γ_1 and Γ_2 correspond to beliefs and justifications supporting these beliefs, respectively. Observe that a sentence is believed iff it is an axiom, or it is monotonically derivable from other beliefs or it is the consequent of an applicable default. On the other hand, a sentence is in the set of justifications supporting beliefs iff it is the justification of an applicable default. A default is applicable iff its prerequisite is believed and adding its consequent to the set of beliefs neither leads to inconsistency nor contradicts the justifications of this or some other already applied default. This is just what we have postulated.

Example 5.84 (Łukaszewicz 1984b) Consider the theory

$$W = \{p\}; \qquad D = \{: r/p, : q/\neg r\}.$$

This theory has two m-extensions: $E_1 = \mathrm{Th}(\{p\})$ and $E_2 = \mathrm{Th}(\{p, \neg r\})$, with respect to $F_1 = \{r\}$ and $F_2 = \{q\}$, respectively. ▮

As follows from Example 5.84, m-extensions need not be maximal sets of beliefs. A non-maximal m-extension is the result of applying a default whose consequent is already believed while one of its justifications blocks the application of some other default. This suggests that the new approach does not model the behaviour of an ideally rational agent. Referring to the previous example, an unwise agent can accept the m-extension E_1. He may simply fail to notice that the consequent of the first default is already believed. A more rational agent will not start his reasoning process by applying this default and, therefore, he will arrive at E_2.

An alternative approach would be to consider the maximal m-extensions only. For those preferring this solution three remarks are in order. Firstly, it seems to be a worse approximation of human reasoning. Secondly, the real problem we are interested in is the following: Given a default theory and a set S of sentences, determine whether all the elements of S can be simultaneously believed or, in other words, whether S is a subset of some m-extension of the theory. It is quite unimportant whether this m-extension is maximal or not. Thirdly, maximal m-extensions may fail to exist. This is illustrated in the following example.

Example 5.85 (Łukaszewicz 1984b) Consider:

$$W = \{\ \}$$
$$D = \{: q_1/\neg r\} \cup \{: q_i/\neg r \wedge \neg q_1 \wedge \cdots \wedge \neg q_{i-1} : i = 2, 3, \ldots\}$$

This theory has infinitely many m-extensions $E_1 \subseteq E_2 \subseteq \cdots$ with respect to $F_1, F_2, \ldots$, respectively, where

$$E_i = Th(\{\neg r \wedge \neg q_1 \wedge \cdots \wedge \neg q_{i-1}\})$$
$$F_i = \{q_i\}.$$

▮

The reader may have the impression that the version of default logic we are advocating here is rather strange. This, however, is not the case. As we shall see in the next section, the new formalization is a natural generalization of Reiter's original proposal.

5.11 BASIC PROPERTIES OF THE NEW FORMALIZATION

In this section we provide a variety of results concerning default theories and their m-extensions. We start by generalizing the notion of an m-extension for open theories.

Definition 5.86 Let T be an open default theory over a language L. E is an *m-extension of* T iff $E = E' \cap L$ and E′ is an m-extension of CLOSED(T).† ▮

The next theorem, corresponding to Theorem 5.26, provides a more intuitive characterization of m-extensions.

Theorem 5.87 (Łukaszewicz 1984b) If $T = \langle W, D\rangle$ is a closed default theory, then E is an m-extension of T wrt F iff

$$E = \bigcup_{i=0}^{\infty} E_i \qquad \text{and} \qquad F = \bigcup_{i=0}^{\infty} F_i$$

† Recall that the justifications of a default remain unchanged while converting it into Skolemized form. Accordingly, E and E′ are supported by the set of justifications.

where

$$E_0 = W; \qquad F_0 = \{\ \}$$

and for $i \geq 0$

$$E_{i+1} = Th(E_i) \cup \{C\colon (A\colon B_1, \ldots, B_k/C) \in D,\ E_i \vdash A,$$
$$\text{and for each } X \in F \cup \{B_1, \ldots, B_k\},\ E \cup \{C\} \nvdash \neg X\}$$
$$F_{i+1} = F_i \cup \{B_1, \ldots, B_k\colon (A\colon B_1, \ldots, B_k/C) \in D,\ E_i \vdash A,$$
$$\text{and for each } X \in F \cup \{B_1, \ldots, B_k\},\ E \cup \{C\} \nvdash \neg X\}.$$

Proof We begin by observing that the following conditions hold:

(MD1′) $\bigcup_{i=0}^{\infty} E_i = Th\left(\bigcup_{i=0}^{\infty} E_i\right)$;

(MD2′) $W \subseteq \bigcup_{i=0}^{\infty} E_i$;

(MD3′) If $(A\colon B_1, \ldots, B_k/C) \in D$, $\bigcup_{i=0}^{\infty} E_i \vdash A$, and for each $X \in F \cup \{B_1, \ldots, B_k\}$, $E \cup \{C\} \nvdash \neg X$, then $C \in \bigcup_{i=0}^{\infty} E_i$ and $B_1, \ldots, B_k \in \bigcup_{i=0}^{\infty} F_i$.

Thus, by the minimality of Γ_1 and Γ_2, we have

$$\Gamma_1(E, F) \subseteq \bigcup_{i=0}^{\infty} E_i \quad \text{and} \quad \Gamma_2(E, F) \subseteq \bigcup_{i=0}^{\infty} F_i. \tag{5.11.1}$$

For the proof from left to right, assume that E is an m-extension of T wrt to F, i.e.

$$E = \Gamma_1(E, F) \quad \text{and} \quad F = \Gamma_2(E, F). \tag{5.11.2}$$

By induction on i, one easily shows that $E_i \subseteq E$ and $F_i \subseteq F$, for all $i \geq 0$. Hence, $\bigcup_{i=0}^{\infty} E_i \subseteq E$ and $\bigcup_{i=0}^{\infty} F_i \subseteq F$. Thus, by (5.11.1) and (5.11.2), $E = \bigcup_{i=0}^{\infty} E_i$ and $F = \bigcup_{i=0}^{\infty} F_i$.

For the proof from right to left, assume that $E = \bigcup_{i=0}^{\infty} E_i$ and $F = \bigcup_{i=0}^{\infty} F_i$. Applying straightforward induction on i, it is easy to show that $E_i \subseteq \Gamma_1(E, F)$ and $F_i \subseteq \Gamma_2(E, F)$. Thus, $\bigcup_{i=0}^{\infty} E_i \subseteq \Gamma_1(E, F)$ and $\bigcup_{i=0}^{\infty} F_i \subseteq \Gamma_2(E, F)$. So, by (5.11.1), $\bigcup_{i=0}^{\infty} E_i = \Gamma_1(E, F)$ and $\bigcup_{i=0}^{\infty} F_i = \Gamma_2(E, F)$. But $E = \bigcup_{i=0}^{\infty} E_i$ and $F = \bigcup_{i=0}^{\infty} F_i$. Therefore, $E = \Gamma_1(E, F)$ and $F = \Gamma_2(E, F)$, i.e. E is an m-extension of T wrt F. ▮

The following corollaries are easy consequences of Theorem 5.87.

Corollary 5.88 A default theory (open or closed) has an inconsistent m-extension iff W is inconsistent. ▮

Corollary 5.89 If a default theory has an inconsistent m-extension, then this is its only m-extension. ▮

Corollary 5.90 The set of justifications for the inconsistent m-extension is the empty set. ▮

Corollary 5.91 If E is an m-extension of a closed default theory T wrt F, then, for every sentence $X \in F$, $E \nvdash \neg X$. ∎

The next theorem guarantees the existence of m-extensions.

Theorem 5.92 (Łukaszewicz 1984b) Every closed default theory has an m-extension.

Proof Let $T = \langle W, D \rangle$ be a closed default theory and suppose that d_0, $d_1, \ldots$ [$d_0, \ldots, d_N$] is a fixed enumeration of all defaults of D. We construct two sequences of sets of sentences $E_0 \subseteq E_1 \subseteq \cdots$ and $F_0 \subseteq F_1 \subseteq \cdots$ as follows.

$$E_0 = W; \qquad F_0 = \{\ \}.$$

Given E_i and F_i, we define three sequences of sets of sentences

$$E_i^0 \subseteq E_i^1 \subseteq \cdots; \qquad F_i^0 \subseteq F_i^1 \subseteq \cdots; \qquad R_i^0 \subseteq R_i^1 \subseteq \cdots$$
$$[E_i^0 \subseteq \cdots \subseteq E_i^N; F_i^0 \subseteq \cdots \subseteq F_i^N; R_i^0 \subseteq \cdots \subseteq R_i^N]$$

by

$$E_i^0 = E_i; \qquad F_i^0 = F_i; \qquad R_i^0 = \{\ \}.$$

Assume that $d_j = A_j: B_{j1}, \ldots, B_{jk}/C_j$.

For $j = 0, 1, \ldots$ [$j = 0, \ldots, N$]:

If $E_i \vdash A_j$ and, for any $X \in F_i^j \cup \{B_{j1}, \ldots, B_{jk}\}$, $E_i^j \cup \{C_j\} \nvdash \neg X$, then

$$E_i^{j+1} = E_i^j \cup \{C_j\}; \quad F_i^{j+1} = F_i^j \cup \{B_{j1}, \ldots, B_{jk}\}; \quad R_i^{j+1} = R_i^j \cup \{C_j\}$$

else

$$E_i^{j+1} = E_i^j; \qquad F_i^{j+1} = F_i^j; \qquad R_i^{j+1} = R_i^j.$$

Put $E_{i+1} = \mathrm{Th}(E_i) \cup \bigcup_j R_i^j$ and $F_{i+1} = F_i \cup \bigcup_j F_i^j$.

Define

$$E = \bigcup_{i=0}^{\infty} E_i \qquad \text{and} \qquad F = \bigcup_{i=0}^{\infty} F_i.$$

We claim that E is an m-extension of T wrt F. By Theorem 5.87 and the above construction, it is clearly sufficient to show that for all $i \geq 1$

$$[A1] \quad \bigcup_j R_i^j = \{C: (A: B_1, \ldots, B_k/C) \in D,\ E_i \vdash A \text{ and for each } X \in F \cup \{B_1, \ldots, B_k\},\ E \cup \{C\} \nvdash \neg X\}$$

$$[A2] \quad \bigcup_j F_i^j = \{B_1, \ldots, B_k: (A: B_1, \ldots, B_k/C) \in D,\ E_i \vdash A \text{ and for each } X \in F \cup \{B_1, \ldots, B_k\},\ E \cup \{C\} \nvdash \neg X\}.$$

It is easily checked that, for each $X \in F$,

$$E \nvdash \neg X \tag{5.11.3}$$

Proof of [A1] Denote the right-hand side of [A1] by RHS[A1].

Assume first that $C \in \bigcup_j R_i^j$. Since $R_i^0 = \{\ \}$, there must be the smallest integer $l \geq 0$ such that $C \in R_i^{l+1}$. Thus there is a default $d_l = A: B_1, \ldots, B_k/C$ such that $E_i \vdash A$ and for each $X \in F_i^l \cup \{B_1, \ldots, B_k\}$, $E_i^l \cup \{C\} \nvdash \neg X$. Note that $\{B_1, \ldots, B_k\} \subseteq F_i^{l+1} \subseteq F$

and $C \in R_i^{l+1} \subseteq E$. So, by (5.11.3), for each $X \in F \cup \{B_1, \ldots, B_k\}$, $E \cup \{C\} \nvdash \neg X$. Thus, since $E_i \vdash A$, we conclude $C \in RHS[A1]$.

Assume now that $C \in RHS[A1]$. Thus there is a default $d_n = (A\colon B_1, \ldots, B_k/C) \in D$ such that $E_i \vdash A$ and, for each $X \in F \cup \{B_1, \ldots, B_k\}$, $E \cup \{C\} \nvdash \neg X$. Hence, since $F_i^n \subseteq F$ and $E_i^n \subseteq E$, we conclude that, for each $X \in F_i^n \cup \{B_1, \ldots, B_k\}$, $E_i^n \cup \{C\} \nvdash \neg X$. So, since $E_i \vdash A$, $C \in R_i^{n+1} \subseteq \bigcup_j R_i^j$. This completes the proof of [A1].

Proof of [A2] Similar to that of [A1]. ▮

Corollary 5.93 Every default theory has an m-extension.

Proof By Theorem 5.92 and Definition 5.86. ▮

Although, as we observed in Example 5.84, m-extensions need not be maximal sets of beliefs, the following weaker result holds.

Theorem 5.94 (Weak Maximality of m-Extensions; Łukaszewicz 1984b) Let $T = \langle W, D\rangle$ be a closed default theory. Let E and E′ be m-extensions of T wrt F and F′, respectively. If $E \subseteq E'$ and $F \subseteq F'$, then $E = E'$ and $F = F'$.

Proof Define:

$$E_0 = W;\ E'_0 = W;\ F_0 = \{\ \};\ F'_0 = \{\ \} \text{ and, for } i \geq 0$$

$$\begin{aligned}
E_{i+1} &= Th(E_i) \cup \{C\colon (A\colon B_1, \ldots, B_k/C) \in D,\ E_i \vdash A,\\
&\qquad \text{and for each } X \in F \cup \{B_1, \ldots, B_k\},\ E \cup \{C\} \nvdash \neg X\}\\
,F_{i+1} &= F_i \cup \{B_1, \ldots, B_k\colon (A\colon B_1, \ldots, B_k/C) \in D,\ E_i \vdash A,\\
&\qquad \text{and for each } X \in F \cup \{B_1, \ldots, B_k\},\ E \cup \{C\} \nvdash \neg X\}\\
E'_{i+1} &= Th(E'_i) \cup \{C\colon (A\colon B_1, \ldots, B_k/C) \in D,\ E'_i \vdash A,\\
&\qquad \text{and for each } X \in F' \cup \{B_1, \ldots, B_k\},\ E' \cup \{C\} \nvdash \neg X\}\\
F'_{i+1} &= F'_i \cup \{B_1, \ldots, B_k\colon (A\colon B_1, \ldots, B_k/C) \in D,\ E'_i \vdash A,\\
&\qquad \text{and for each } X \in F' \cup \{B_1, \ldots, B_k\},\ E' \cup \{C\} \nvdash \neg X\}.
\end{aligned}$$

In view of Theorem 5.87, we have

$$E = \bigcup_{i=0}^{\infty} E_i; \qquad F = \bigcup_{i=0}^{\infty} F_i; \qquad E' = \bigcup_{i=0}^{\infty} E'_i; \qquad F' = \bigcup_{i=0}^{\infty} F'_i.$$

The proof of the theorem immediately follows from the next lemma.

Lemma 5.94.1 If $E \subseteq E'$ and $F \subseteq F'$, then $E'_i \subseteq E_i$ and $F'_i \subseteq F_i$, for all $i \geq 0$..

Proof Straightforward induction on i. ■

▮

We now proceed to investigate the relationship between extensions and m-extensions. The next theorem shows that the notion of m-extension is a natural generalization of that of an extension.

Theorem 5.95 Let $T = \langle W, D\rangle$ be a default theory and suppose that E is an extension of T. Then E is an m-extension of T.

Proof In view of Definitions 5.18 and 5.86, we may clearly assume that T is closed. Define:

$$F = \{B_1, \ldots, B_k\colon (A\colon B_1, \ldots, B_k/C) \in D,\ A \in E \text{ and } \neg B_1, \ldots, \neg B_k \notin E\}$$

We claim that E is an m-extension of T wrt F.

Since E is an extension of T, then $E = \bigcup_{i=0}^{\infty}$, where

$$E_0 = W \text{ and, for } i \geq 0$$
$$E_{i+1} = Th(E_i) \cup \{C: (A: B_1, \ldots, B_k/C) \in D,\ E_i \vdash A \text{ and } \neg B_1, \ldots, \neg B_k \notin E\}.$$

Define:

$$E'_0 = W; \qquad F'_0 = \{\ \}$$

and, for $i \geq 0$

$$E'_{i+1} = Th(E'_i) \cup \{C: (A: B_1, \ldots, B_k/C) \in D,\ E'_i \vdash A, \text{ and for each } X \in F \cup \{B_1, \ldots, B_k\},\ E \cup \{C\} \nvdash \neg X\}$$
$$F'_{i+1} = F'_i \cup \{B_1, \ldots, B_k: (A: B_1, \ldots, B_k/C) \in D,\ E'_i \vdash A, \text{ and for each } X \in F \cup \{B_1, \ldots, B_k\},\ E \cup \{C\} \nvdash \neg X\}.$$

By virtue of Theorem 5.87, it suffices to show

$$[A3]\ E = \bigcup_{i=0}^{\infty} E'_i$$

and

$$[A4]\ F = \bigcup_{i=0}^{\infty} F'_i.$$

Lemma 5.95.1 Let $(A: B_1, \ldots, B_k/C) \in D$. If $C \in E$, then the following conditions are equivalent:

(1) $\neg B_1, \ldots, \neg B_k \notin E$;
(2) For each $X \in F \cup \{B_1, \ldots, B_k\}$, $E \cup \{C\} \nvdash \neg X$.

Proof Straightforward. ■

Since $E = \bigcup_{i=0}^{\infty} E_i$, [A3] follows immediately from the next lemma.

Lemma 5.95.2 For all $i \geq 0$, $E_i = E'_i$.

Proof Induction on i. For the inclusion from right to left apply Lemma 5.95.1. ■

We now proceed to prove [A4]. By induction on i, it is easily verified that, for all $i \geq 0$, $F'_i \subseteq F$. This implies $\bigcup_{i=0}^{\infty} F'_i \subseteq F$.

For the inclusion from left to right, assume $B \in F$. Thus, there is a default $(A: B_1, \ldots, B_k/C) \in D$ such that B is B_i (for some $1 \leq i \leq k$), $A \in E$ and $\neg B_1, \ldots, \neg B_k \notin E$. By [A3], $A \in E$ implies

$$A \in E'_j, \text{ for some } j \geq 0. \tag{5.11.4}$$

Thus, by Lemma 5.95.2, $C \in E_{j+1} \subseteq E$ and so, by Lemma 5.95.1, $\neg B_1, \ldots, \neg B_k \notin E$ implies

$$\text{For each } X \in F \cup \{B_1, \ldots, B_k\},\ E \cup \{C\} \nvdash \neg X. \tag{5.11.5}$$

From (5.11.4) and (5.11.5), we immediately obtain

$$\{B_1, \ldots, B_k\} \subseteq F'_{j+1} \subseteq \bigcup_{i=0}^{\infty} F'_i.$$

Since B is one of $B_1, \ldots, B_k$, we finally conclude $B \in \bigcup_{i=0}^{\infty} F'_i$. ∎

Of course, the converse theorem does not generally hold. However:

Theorem 5.96 Let $T = \langle W, D \rangle$ be a closed normal default theory and suppose that E is an m-extension of T. Then E is an extension of T.

Proof Let E be an m-extension of T wrt F. Define:

$$\begin{aligned} E_0 &= W;\ F_0 = \{\ \} \text{ and, for } i \geq 0 \\ E_{i+1} &= Th(E_i) \cup \{B\colon (A\colon B/B) \in D,\ E_i \vdash A, \\ &\qquad \text{and for each } X \in F \cup \{B\},\ E \cup \{B\} \nvdash \neg X\} \\ F_{i+1} &= F_i \cup \{B\colon (A\colon B/B) \in D,\ E_i \vdash A, \\ &\qquad \text{and for each } X \in F \cup \{B\},\ E \cup \{B\} \nvdash \neg X\}. \end{aligned}$$

Since E is an m-extension of T wrt F, we have

$$E = \bigcup_{i=0}^{\infty} E_i \quad \text{and} \quad F = \bigcup_{i=0}^{\infty} F_i.$$

The key observation is the following lemma.

Lemma 5.96.1 $F \subseteq E$.

Proof Straightforward. ∎

Define:

$$E'_0 = W \text{ and, for } i \geq 0$$

$$E'_{i+1} = Th(E'_i) \cup \{B\colon (A\colon B/B) \in D,\ E'_i \vdash A \text{ and } \neg B \notin E\}.$$

We show that E is an extension of T. In view of Theorem 5.26, it is sufficient to prove $E = \bigcup_{i=0}^{\infty} E'_i$. This immediately follows from $E = \bigcup_{i=0}^{\infty} E_i$ and the following lemma.

Lemma 5.96.2 For all $i \geq 0$, $E_i = E'_i$.

Proof Induction on i. Apply Lemma 5.96.1. ∎

∎

Of course, even for closed normal default theories the notions of an m-extension and an extension are not identical. The formal difference is that while extensions are considered in isolation, each m-extension is always relativized to a set of justifications. Nevertheless, since the purpose of this set is to keep track of sentences which are to be consistent with what is believed, and since justifications of applicable closed normal defaults obtain the status of beliefs, the set of justifications corresponding to an m-extension of a closed normal default theory is redundant.

Theorem 5.96 leads to the following corollary.

Corollary 5.97 Let T be a C-universal open normal default theory. If E is an m-extension of T, then it is also an extension of T. ▮

We now turn to specifying another characterization of m-extensions. It corresponds to the characterization of extensions for closed normal theories specified in Theorem 5.44.

Definition 5.98 Let $\langle S, U \rangle$ be a pair of sets of sentences. We say that $\langle S, U \rangle$ is a *beliefs–justifications pair* (*BJ-pair*, for short), iff

(1) $S = Th(S)$;
(2) For each $X \in U$, $S \nvdash \neg X$.

▮

Intuitively, a BJ-pair $\langle S, U \rangle$ is to be interpreted as a set of beliefs and a set of justifications for those beliefs, respectively. Observe that the definition neither specifies how S and U have been constructed nor depends on the notion of a default theory. All we assume here is that the set of beliefs is deductively closed and each justification is consistent with it.

The next theorem, which follows trivially from Corollary 5.91, shows that characterizing m-extensions, we may limit ourselves to BJ-pairs.

Theorem 5.99 Let T be a closed theory. If E is an m-extension of T wrt F, then $\langle E, F \rangle$ is a BJ-pair. ▮

Definition 5.100 Let $\langle S, U \rangle$ be a BJ-pair. We say that a closed default $A: B_1, \ldots, B_k/C$ is *m-applicable wrt* $\langle S, U \rangle$ iff

(1) $A \in S$;
(2) For each $X \in U \cup \{B_1, \ldots, B_k\}$, $S \cup \{C\} \nvdash \neg X$.

▮

Example 5.101 The default d = (*Summer*: *Sun-shining*/*Sun-shining*) is m-applicable wrt $\langle S_1, U_1 \rangle = \langle Th(\{Summer\}), \{\ \} \rangle$, but is neither m-applicable wrt $\langle S_2, U_2 \rangle = \langle Th(\{Holidays\}), \{I\text{-}go\text{-}fishing\} \rangle$ nor wrt $\langle S_3, U_3 \rangle = \langle Th(\{Summer\}), \{\neg Sun\text{-}shining\} \rangle$. ▮

Closed defaults can be naturally viewed as mappings from BJ-pairs into such pairs. The formal definition is given below.

Definition 5.102 Let $\langle S, U \rangle$ be a BJ-pair. To each closed default d = $A: B_1, \ldots, B_k/C$ we assign a mapping, denoted by d^m, given by

$$d^m(\langle S, U \rangle) = \begin{cases} \langle Th(S \cup \{C\}), U \cup \{B_1, \ldots, B_k\} \rangle & \text{iff d is m-applicable wrt } \langle S, U \rangle \\ \langle S, U \rangle & \text{otherwise.} \end{cases}$$

▮

Applying Definitions 5.98 and 5.100, it is readily checked that $d^m(\langle S, U \rangle)$ is a BJ-pair. Intuitively, $\langle S, U \rangle$ and $d^m(\langle S, U \rangle)$ are to be interpreted as pairs, consisting of a set of beliefs and a set of justifications, before and after applying the default d, respectively.

Example 5.101 (continued)

$$d^m(\langle S_1, U_1\rangle) = \langle Th(\{\mathit{Summer}, \mathit{Sun\text{-}shining}\}), \{\mathit{Sun\text{-}shining}\}\rangle$$
$$d^m(\langle S_2, U_2\rangle) = \langle S_2, U_2\rangle$$
$$d^m(\langle S_3, U_3\rangle) = \langle S_3, U_3\rangle.$$

▮

Definition 5.103 Let $\langle S, U\rangle$ be a BJ-pair and let D be a set of closed defaults. We say that $\langle S, U\rangle$ is *m-stable wrt* D iff $d^m(\langle S, U\rangle) = \langle S, U\rangle$, for all $d \in D$. ▮

We shall use the following notation. If $\langle X, Y\rangle$ and $\langle X', Y'\rangle$ are pairs of sets, then $\langle X, Y\rangle \subseteq \langle X', Y'\rangle$ is the abbreviation for $X \subseteq X'$ and $Y \subseteq Y'$. $\langle X, Y\rangle \subset \langle X', Y'\rangle$ is an abbreviation for $\langle X, Y\rangle \subseteq \langle X', Y'\rangle$ and $\langle X, Y\rangle \neq \langle X', Y'\rangle$.

Definition 5.104 Let W be a set of sentences and let D be a set of closed defaults. We say that a BJ-pair $\langle S, U\rangle$ is *m-approachable from* W *wrt* D iff, for each BJ-pair $\langle S_1, U_1\rangle$ such that $\langle S_1, U_1\rangle \subset \langle S, U\rangle$ and $W \subseteq S_1$, there is a default $d \in D$ such that $\langle S_1, U_1\rangle \subset d^m(\langle S_1, U_1\rangle) \subseteq \langle S, U\rangle$. ▮

The next theorem, corresponding closely to Theorem 5.44, provides the desired characterization of m-extensions of closed default theories.

Theorem 5.105 Let $T = \langle W, D\rangle$ be a closed default theory and suppose that $\langle E, F\rangle$ is a BJ-pair. Then E is an m-extension of T wrt F iff

(1) $W \subseteq E$;
(2) $\langle E, F\rangle$ is m-stable wrt D;
(3) $\langle E, F\rangle$ is m-approachable from W wrt D.

Proof Let $\Gamma_1(E, F)$ and $\Gamma_2(E, F)$ be the smallest sets of sentences satisfying:

(4) $\Gamma_1(E, F) = Th(\Gamma_1(E, F))$;
(5) $W \subseteq \Gamma_1(E, F)$;
(6) If $(A\colon B_1, \ldots, B_k/C) \in D$, $A \in \Gamma_1(E, F)$ and, for each $X \in F \cup \{B_1, \ldots, B_k\}$, $E \cup \{C\} \nvdash \neg X$, then
 (i) $C \in \Gamma_1(E, F)$
 (ii) $B_1, \ldots, B_k \in \Gamma_2(E, F)$.

Assume first that E is an m-extension of T wrt F. Thus, by Definition 5.83,

$$E = \Gamma_1(E, F) \qquad (5.11.6)$$
$$F = \Gamma_2(E, F) \qquad (5.11.7)$$

We have to show that (1)–(3) holds. (1) is obvious.

Lemma 5.105.1 If $(A\colon B_1, \ldots, B_k/C) \in D$, $A \in E$ and, for each $X \in F \cup \{B_1, \ldots, B_k\}$, $E \cup \{C\} \nvdash \neg X$, then $C \in E$ and $B_1, \ldots, B_k \in F$.

Proof Straightforward, by (6), (5.11.6) and (5.11.7). ■

To prove (2), assume that $d = (A\colon B_1, \ldots, B_k/C) \in D$. If d is not m-applicable wrt $\langle E, F\rangle$, then clearly $d^m(\langle E, F\rangle) = \langle E, F\rangle$. Otherwise, $A \in E$ and, for each $X \in F \cup \{B_1, \ldots, B_k\}$, $E \cup \{C\} \nvdash \neg X$. Thus, by Lemma 5.105.1, $C \in E$ and $B_1, \ldots, B_k \in F$. Therefore, $d^m(\langle E, F\rangle) = \langle Th(E \cup \{C\}), F \cup \{B_1, \ldots, B_k\}\rangle = \langle Th(E), F\rangle$. But $\langle E, F\rangle$ is a BJ-pair, so that E is deductively closed. Consequently, $d^m(\langle E, F\rangle) = \langle E, F\rangle$.

To prove (3), assume to the contrary that $\langle E, F\rangle$ is not m-approachable from W wrt D. Thus, there is a BJ-pair $\langle E_1, F_1\rangle$ such that $\langle E_1, F_1\rangle \subset \langle E, F\rangle$, $W \subseteq E_1$ and

For each $d \in D$,
$$d^m(\langle E_1, F_1\rangle) = \langle E_1, F_1\rangle \text{ or } d^m(\langle E_1, F_1\rangle) \nsubseteq \langle E, F\rangle \qquad (5.11.8)$$

Lemma 5.105.2 $\langle E_1, F_1\rangle$ satisfies (4′)–(6′) below.

(4′) $E_1 = Th(E_1)$;
(5′) $W \subseteq E_1$;
(6′) If $(A: B_1, \ldots, B_k/C) \in D$, $A \in E_1$ and, for each $X \in F \cup \{B_1, \ldots, B_k\}$, $E \cup \{C\} \nvdash \neg X$, then $C \in E_1$ and $B_1, \ldots, B_k \in F_1$.

Proof (4′) and (5′) are obvious. For the proof of (6′), use (5.11.8) and apply Lemma 5.105.1. ■

Note that (4′)–(6′) are simply (4)–(6) with $\Gamma_1(E, F)$ and $\Gamma_2(E, F)$ replaced by E_1 and F_1, respectively. Thus, by minimality of Γ_1 and Γ_2, we have $\Gamma_1(E, F) \subseteq E_1$ and $\Gamma_2(E, F) \subseteq F_1$. By (5.11.6) and (5.11.7), we therefore obtain $E \subseteq E_1$ and $F \subseteq F_1$. This contradicts $\langle E_1, F_1\rangle \subset \langle E, F\rangle$ and thus proves (3).

This completes the implication from left to right in Theorem 5.105.

Assume now that $\langle E, F\rangle$ satisfies (1)–(3). To prove that E is an m-extension of T wrt F, we show that

$$E = \Gamma_1(E, F) \qquad \text{and} \qquad F = \Gamma_2(E, F). \qquad (5.11.9)$$

Lemma 5.105.3 E and F satisfy (4″)–(6″) below.

(4″) $E = Th(E)$;
(5″) $W \subseteq E$;
(6″) If $(A: B_1, \ldots, B_k/C) \in D$, $A \in E$ and, for each $X \in F \cup \{B_1, \ldots, B_k)$, $E \cup \{C\} \nvdash \neg X$, then $C \in E$ and $B_1, \ldots, B_k \in F$.

Proof (4″) and (5″) are obvious. For the proof of (6″), use the fact that $\langle E, F\rangle$ is m-stable wrt D. ■

We now proceed to prove (5.11.9). (4″)–(6″) are simply (4)–(6) with $\Gamma_1(E, F)$ and $\Gamma_2(E, F)$ replaced by E and F, respectively. Thus, by minimality of Γ_1 and Γ_2, we conclude $\Gamma_1(E, F) \subseteq E$ and $\Gamma_2(E, F) \subseteq F$. To prove (5.11.9), it suffices therefore to show

$$\langle \Gamma_1(E, F), \Gamma_2(E, F)\rangle \not\subset \langle E, F\rangle. \qquad (5.11.10)$$

Assume to the contrary that this is not the case. It is readily verified that $\langle \Gamma_1(E, F), \Gamma_2(E, F)\rangle$ is a BJ-pair and clearly $W \subseteq \Gamma_1(E, F)$. Thus, by m-approachability of $\langle E, F\rangle$, there is a default $d = (A: B_1, \ldots, B_k/C) \in D$ such that

$$\langle \Gamma_1(E, F), \Gamma_2(E, F)\rangle \subset d^m(\langle \Gamma_1(E, F), \Gamma_2(E, F)\rangle) \subseteq \langle E, F\rangle \qquad (5.11.11)$$

By (5.11.11), d is m-applicable wrt $\langle \Gamma_1(E, F), \Gamma_2(E, F)\rangle$. Thus

$$A \in \Gamma_1(E, F) \qquad (5.11.12)$$

$$d^m(\langle \Gamma_1(E, F), \Gamma_2(E, F)\rangle) = \langle Th(\Gamma_1(E, F) \cup \{C\}), \Gamma_2(E, F) \cup \{B_1 \ldots B_k\}\rangle. \qquad (5.11.13)$$

By (5.11.11) and (5.11.13), we infer

$$\langle \Gamma_1(\mathrm{E, F}), \Gamma_2(\mathrm{E, F})\rangle \subset \langle \mathrm{Th}(\Gamma_1(\mathrm{E, F}) \cup \{C\}), \Gamma_2(\mathrm{E, F}) \cup \{B_1, \ldots, B_k\}\rangle \subseteq \langle \mathrm{E, F}\rangle. \tag{5.11.14}$$

Applying (5.11.14), one easily verifies

$$\text{For each } X \in \mathrm{F} \cup \{B_1, \ldots, B_k\},\ \mathrm{E} \cup \{C\} \nvdash \neg X. \tag{5.11.15}$$

But $A \in \Gamma_1(\mathrm{E, F})$ by (5.11.12). Thus, in view of (5.11.15) and the definition of Γ_1 and Γ_2, $C \in \Gamma_1(\mathrm{E, F})$ and $B_1, \ldots, B_k \in \Gamma_2(\mathrm{E, F})$. By (5.11.14), we therefore infer

$$\langle \Gamma_1(\mathrm{E, F}), \Gamma_2(\mathrm{E, F})\rangle \subset \langle \mathrm{Th}(\Gamma_1(\mathrm{E, F})), \Gamma_2(\mathrm{E, F})\rangle.$$

But $\Gamma_1(\mathrm{E, F})$ is deductively closed, so that we finally conclude $\langle \Gamma_1(\mathrm{E, F}), \Gamma_2(\mathrm{E, F})\rangle \subset \langle \Gamma_1(\mathrm{E, F}), \Gamma_2(\mathrm{E, F})\rangle$. A contradiction. This proves (5.11.9) and, hence, the implication from right to left in Theorem 5.105. ▮

Theorem 5.106 (Semi-Monotonicity; Łukaszewicz 1984b) Let D and D_1 be sets of closed defaults such that $\mathrm{D}_1 \subseteq \mathrm{D}$. Let E_1 be an m-extension of a closed theory $T_1 = \langle \mathrm{W}, \mathrm{D}_1\rangle$ wrt F_1 and let $T = \langle \mathrm{W, D}\rangle$. Then T has an m-extension E wrt F such that $\mathrm{E}_1 \subseteq \mathrm{E}$ and $\mathrm{F}_1 \subseteq \mathrm{F}$.

Proof Let $\mathrm{d}_0, \mathrm{d}_1, \ldots [\mathrm{d}_0, \ldots, \mathrm{d}_N]$ be any fixed enumeration of all defaults from D. We define two sequences of sets of sentences $\mathrm{S}_0 \subseteq \mathrm{S}_1 \subseteq \cdots$ and $\mathrm{U}_0 \subseteq \mathrm{U}_1 \subseteq \cdots$ as follows.

$$\mathrm{S}_0 = \mathrm{E}_1; \qquad \mathrm{U}_0 = \mathrm{F}_1.$$

Given S_i and U_i, we construct two sequences of sentences $\mathrm{S}_i^0 \subseteq \mathrm{S}_i^1 \subseteq \cdots$ and $\mathrm{U}_i^0 \subseteq \mathrm{U}_i^1 \subseteq \cdots [\mathrm{S}_i^0 \subseteq \cdots \subseteq \mathrm{S}_i^N$ and $\mathrm{U}_i^0 \subseteq \cdots \subseteq \mathrm{U}_i^N]$ by

$$\mathrm{S}_i^0 = \mathrm{S}_i; \qquad \mathrm{U}_i^0 = \mathrm{U}_i.$$

Assume that $\mathrm{d}_j = A_j\colon B_{j1}, \ldots B_{jk}/C_j$. For $j = 0, 1 \ldots [j = 0, \ldots N]$: If $\mathrm{S}_i \vdash A_j$ and, for each $X \in \mathrm{U}_i^j \cup \{B_{j1}, \ldots, B_{jk}\}$, $\mathrm{S}_i^j \cup \{C_j\} \nvdash \neg X$, then

$$\mathrm{S}_i^{j+1} = \mathrm{S}_i^j \cup \{C_j\}; \qquad \mathrm{U}_i^{j+1} = \mathrm{U}_i^j \cup \{B_{j1}, \ldots, B_{jk}\}$$

else

$$\mathrm{S}_i^{j+1} = \mathrm{S}_i^j; \qquad \mathrm{U}_i^{j+1} = \mathrm{U}_i^j.$$

Put

$$\mathrm{S}_{i+1} = \mathrm{Th}(\mathrm{S}_i) \cup \bigcup_j \mathrm{S}_i^j; \qquad = \mathrm{U}_{i+1} = \mathrm{U}_i \cup \bigcup_j \mathrm{U}_i^j.$$

Define

$$\mathrm{E} = \bigcup_{i=0}^{\infty} \mathrm{S}_i \qquad \text{and} \qquad \mathrm{F} = \bigcup_{i=0}^{\infty} \mathrm{U}_i.$$

Trivially, $\mathrm{E}_1 \subseteq \mathrm{E}$ and $\mathrm{F}_1 \subseteq \mathrm{F}$. So, to prove the theorem, it suffices to show that E is an m-extension of T wrt F. Define:

$$\mathrm{G}_0 = \mathrm{W};\ \mathrm{V}_0 = \{\ \}\ \text{and, for } i \geq 0$$
$$\mathrm{G}_{i+1} = \mathrm{Th}(\mathrm{G}_i) \cup \{C\colon (A\colon B_1, \ldots, B_k/C) \in \mathrm{D},\ \mathrm{G}_i \vdash A$$
$$\text{and, for each } X \in \mathrm{F} \cup \{B_1, \ldots, B_k\},\ \mathrm{E} \cup \{C\} \nvdash \neg X\}$$

$$V_{i+1} = V_i \cup \{B: (A: B_1, \ldots, B_k/C) \in D,\ B = B_j \text{ (for some } 1 \le j \le k),\ G_i \vdash A \text{ and, for each } X \in F \cup \{B_1, \ldots, B_k\},\ E \cup \{C\} \nvdash \neg X\}.$$

By Theorem 5.87, we have to show

[A5] $E = \bigcup_{i=0}^{\infty} G_i$

[A6] $F = \bigcup_{i=0}^{\infty} V_i$.

Lemma 5.106.1 For all $i \geq 0$, $G_i \subseteq S_i$ and $V_i \subseteq U_i$.

Proof Straightforward induction on i. ■

In view of Lemma 5.106, we conclude

$$\bigcup_{i=0}^{\infty} G_i \subseteq \bigcup_{i=0}^{\infty} S_i = E \quad \text{and} \quad \bigcup_{i=0}^{\infty} V_i \subseteq \bigcup_{i=0}^{\infty} U_i = F$$

which proves the right to left inclusions of [A5] and [A6]. Thus the theorem will be proved if we show

[A7] $E \subseteq \bigcup_{i=0}^{\infty} G_i$

[A8] $F \subseteq \bigcup_{i=0}^{\infty} V_i$.

Lemma 5.106.2 $E_1 \subseteq \bigcup_{i=0}^{\infty} G_i$ and $F_1 \subseteq \bigcup_{i=0}^{\infty} V_i$.

Proof Let $H_0 \subseteq H_1 \subseteq \cdots$ and $W_0 \subseteq W_1 \subseteq \cdots$ be sequences of sets of sentences defined as in Theorem 5.87 for E_1 and F_1 wrt T_1. In view of this theorem

$$E_1 = \bigcup_{i=0}^{\infty} H_i \quad \text{and} \quad F_1 = \bigcup_{i=0}^{\infty} W_i.$$

By induction on i, one readily checks that, for all $i \geq 0$, $H_i \subseteq G_i$ and $W_i \subseteq V_i$. Thus, $\bigcup_{i=0}^{\infty} H_i = E_1 \subseteq \bigcup_{i=0}^{\infty} G_i$ and $\bigcup_{i=0}^{\infty} W_i = F_1 \subseteq \bigcup_{i=0}^{\infty} V_i$. ■

[A7] and [A8] follow immediately from the next lemma.

Lemma 5.106.3 For all $j \geq 0$, $S_j \subseteq \bigcup_{i=0}^{\infty} G_i$ and $U_j \subseteq \bigcup_{i=0}^{\infty} V_i$.

Proof Induction on j. For $j = 0$ apply Lemma 5.106.2. ■

This completes the proof of Theorem 5.106. ■

Corollary 5.107 Let $T_1 = \langle W, D_1 \rangle$ and $T = \langle W, D \rangle$ be open default theories such that $D_1 \subseteq D$ and $L(T_1) \subseteq L(T)$† If E_1 is an m-extension of T_1, then T has an m-extension E such that $E_1 \subseteq E$.

† $L(T)$ and $L(T_1)$ denote the languages of T and T_1, respectively.

Proof Denote by $\bar{D}_1$ and $\bar{D}$ the sets of defaults of CLOSED(T_1) and CLOSED(T), respectively. Obviously, $\bar{D}_1 \subseteq \bar{D}$. By Definition 5.86, $E_1 = E'_1 \cap L(T_1)$, where E'_1 is an m-extension of CLOSED(T_1). Notice that CLOSED(T_1) and CLOSED(T) have the same axioms. Thus, by Theorem 5.106, CLOSED(T) has an m-extension E′ such that $E'_1 \subseteq E'$. Therefore, since $L(T_1) \subseteq L(T)$, we clearly have $E'_1 \cap L(T_1) \subseteq E' \cap L(T)$. So, because $E'_1 \cap L(T_1) = E_1$ and $E' \cap L(T)$ is an m-extension of T (by Definition 5.86), the corollary is proved. ∎

We conclude this section by providing just another characterization of m-extensions. In contrast to that specified in Theorem 5.105, it is both more constructive and intuitively clearer.

Imagine an agent reasoning on the basis of a closed default theory $T = \langle W, D\rangle$. His initial set of beliefs should be identified with Th(W). The set of justifications for those beliefs is clearly the empty set. In other words, the agent's initial BJ-pair is $B_0 = \langle Th(W), \{\ \}\rangle$. At each step the agent chooses a default $d \in D$ and tries to apply it to his current BJ-pair B_i. This leads to constructing a new BJ-pair given by

$$B_{i+1} = d^m(B_i).$$

Let us assume that the agent is able to repeat this process infinitely. It may happen, perhaps after applying infinitely many defaults, that his current BJ-pair is m-stable, i.e. it cannot be extended by continuing the application of defaults from D. As we shall see, each m-stable BJ-pair obtainable by the above process characterizes some m-extension of T. Furthermore, each m-extension of T is characterized by some m-stable BJ-pair resulting from the process. The formal details follow.

Definition 5.108 Let $\langle S, U\rangle$ be a BJ-pair and let $\langle d_i\rangle$ be a sequence of closed defaults. By $\langle d_i\rangle^m(\langle S, U\rangle)$ we denote a BJ-pair given by

$$\langle d_i\rangle^m(\langle S, U\rangle) = \begin{cases} \langle S, U\rangle & \text{if } \langle d_i\rangle \text{ is the empty sequence} \\ \langle \bigcup S_i, \bigcup U_i\rangle & \text{otherwise} \end{cases}$$

where $\langle S_0, U_0\rangle = \langle S, U\rangle$ and, for $i = 0, 1, \ldots$ [$i = 0, \ldots, N$], $\langle S_{i+1}, U_{i+1}\rangle = d_i^m(\langle S_i, U_i\rangle)$.
∎

Observe that if $\langle d_i\rangle = d_0, \ldots, d_N$ is a finite sequence then $\langle d_i\rangle^m(\langle S, U\rangle) = d_N^m(d_{N-1}^m(\ldots(d_0^m(\langle S, U\rangle))\ldots))$.

Definition 5.109 Let $\langle S, U\rangle$ be a BJ-pair, W a set of sentences, and suppose that $\langle d_i\rangle$ is a sequence of closed defaults. We say that $\langle S, U\rangle$ is $\langle d_i\rangle$-*m-accessible from* W iff $\langle S, U\rangle = \langle d_i\rangle^m(\langle Th(W), \{\ \}\rangle)$. We say that $\langle S, U\rangle$ is *m-accessible from* W *wrt a set of closed defaults* D iff there is a sequence of defaults $\langle d_i\rangle$ such that each $d_i \in D$ and $\langle S, U\rangle$ is $\langle d_i\rangle$-m-accessible from W. ∎

Example 5.110 Let

$$W = \{p, q\}; \qquad D = \{d_1 = p\colon r/r,\ d_2 = q\colon s/s\}.$$

The following BJ pairs are m-accessible from W wrt D:

$$\begin{array}{ll} \langle Th(\{p, q\}), \{\ \}\rangle & (\langle d_i\rangle = \langle\rangle) \\ \langle Th(\{p, q, r\}), \{r\}\rangle & (\langle d_i\rangle = d_1) \\ \langle Th(\{p, q, s\}), \{s\}\rangle & (\langle d_i\rangle = d_2) \\ \langle Th(\{p, q, r, s\}), \{r, s\}\rangle & (\langle d_i\rangle = d_1, d_2). \end{array}$$

∎

We now are ready to give the desired characterization of m-extensions.

Theorem 5.111 Let $T = \langle W, D \rangle$ be a closed default theory and let $\langle E, F \rangle$ be a BJ-pair. Then E is an m-extension of T wrt F iff

(1) $\langle E, F \rangle$ is m-stable wrt D;
(2) $\langle E, F \rangle$ is m-accessible from W wrt D.

Proof The theorem follows directly from Theorem 5.105 and the next lemma.

Lemma 5.111.1 $\langle E, F \rangle$ is m-accessible from W wrt D iff

(i) $W \subseteq E$;
(ii) $\langle E, F \rangle$ is m-approachable from W wrt D.

Proof Assume first that $\langle E, F \rangle$ is m-accessible from W wrt D, i.e.

$$\langle E, F \rangle = \langle d_i \rangle^m(\langle Th(W), \{\ \} \rangle). \tag{5.11.16}$$

Clearly, (i) holds. If $\langle d_i \rangle = \langle \rangle$, then (ii) is obvious. Assume, therefore, that $\langle d_i \rangle \neq \langle \rangle$ and take any BJ-pair $\langle E', F' \rangle$ such that $W \subseteq E'$ and $\langle E', F' \rangle \subset \langle E, F \rangle$. By (5.11.16), $\langle E, F \rangle = \langle \bigcup E_i, \bigcup F_i \rangle$, where $\langle E_0, F_0 \rangle = \langle Th(W), \{\ \} \rangle$ and, for $i=0, 1, \ldots$ $[i = 0, \ldots, N]$, $\langle E_{i+1}, F_{i+1} \rangle = d_i^m(\langle E_i, F_i \rangle)$. Thus, $\langle E', F' \rangle \subset \langle \bigcup E_i, \bigcup F_i \rangle$. Hence there is an integer $j \geq 0$ such that

$$\langle E_j, F_j \rangle \subseteq \langle E', F' \rangle \subset \langle E_{j+1}, F_{j+1} \rangle. \tag{5.11.17}$$

It is easily verified that d_j is m-applicable wrt $\langle E', F' \rangle$ and $d_j^m(\langle E', F' \rangle) = \langle E_{j+1}, F_{j+1} \rangle$. So, in view of (5.11.17), $\langle E', F' \rangle \subset d_j^m(\langle E', F' \rangle) \subseteq \langle E, F \rangle$. This proves (ii) and hence completes the implication from left to right in Lemma 5.111.1.

Assume now that (i) and (ii) hold. We show that $\langle E, F \rangle$ is $\langle d_i \rangle$-m-accessible from W for some sequence $\langle d_i \rangle$ of defaults from D. If $E = Th(W)$ and $F = \{\ \}$, then $\langle E, F \rangle$ is $\langle \rangle$-m-accessible from W. Assume, therefore, that $\langle E, F \rangle \neq \langle Th(W), \{\ \} \rangle$. Thus, by (i), $\langle Th(W), \{\ \} \rangle \subset \langle E, F \rangle$, and so, by (ii), there is a default $d \in D$ such that $\langle Th(W), \{\ \} \rangle \subset d^m(\langle Th(W), \{\ \} \rangle) \subseteq \langle E, F \rangle$. Define:

$$E_0 = Th(W); \qquad F_0 = \{\ \}; \qquad d_0 = d$$

Assume that E_i, F_i and d_i are specified.

If $d_i^m(\langle E_i, F_i \rangle) = \langle E, F \rangle$, then put

$$\langle E_{i+1}, F_{i+1} \rangle = \langle E, F \rangle; \qquad d_{i+1} = d_i.$$

Otherwise, $d_i^m(\langle E_i, F_i \rangle) \subset \langle E, F \rangle$. So, by (ii), there is a default $d \in D$ such that $d_i^m(\langle E_i, F_i \rangle) \subset d^m(d_i^m(\langle E_i, F_i \rangle)) \subseteq \langle E, F \rangle$. Put

$$\langle E_{i+1}, F_{i+1} \rangle = d^m(d_i^m(\langle E_i, F_i \rangle)); \qquad d_{i+1} = d.$$

Take $\langle d_i \rangle = d_0, d_1, \ldots$. It is easily checked that $\langle d_i \rangle$ is well-defined and $\langle d_i \rangle^m(\langle Th(W), \{\ \} \rangle) = \langle E, F \rangle$. This completes the right to left implication in Lemma 5.111.1. ■

▮

Theorem 5.111 can be given a pictorial interpretation. More specifically, to each closed default theory $\langle W, D\rangle$ we may assign a transition network, whose nodes are BJ-pairs and whose arcs are labelled by defaults of D, as follows:

(1) The set of nodes of the network is the smallest set such that:
  (i) $\langle Th(W), \{\ \}\rangle$ is a node. This is called the *root node*.
  (ii) If n_i is a node and $d \in D$, then $d^m(n_i)$ is a node.
(2) From each node n_i, for each $d \in D$, an arc, labelled by d, leads to $d^m(n_i)$.

Assume that $N_{\langle W,D\rangle}$ is the network assigned to $\langle W, D\rangle$. Each of its leaves, i.e. a node all of whose outbound arcs loop back, characterizes an m-extension, together with the corresponding set of justifications, of $\langle W, D\rangle$. Furthermore, if $N_{\langle W,D\rangle}$ has finitely many nodes, each m-extension of $\langle W, D\rangle$ is characterized by some such a leaf node. If $N_{\langle W,D\rangle}$ has infinitely many nodes, m-extensions are also characterized by infinite paths, from the root, of different nodes. More precisely, if $\langle E_0, F_0\rangle$, $\langle E_1, F_1\rangle, \ldots$ is such a path, then $\bigcup E_i$ is an m-extension of $\langle W, D\rangle$ wrt $\bigcup F_i$.

Example 5.112 Consider:

$$W = \{p\}; \qquad D = \{d_1 = p: q/q,\ d_2 = q: r/r,\ d_3 = q: \neg r/\neg r\}.$$

This theory leads to the network shown in Fig. 5.7. This is a finite network with two leaves. Accordingly, the theory has two m-extensions:

$$E_1 = Th(\{p, q, r\}) \qquad (\text{wrt } \{q, r\})$$
$$E_2 = Th(\{p, q, \neg r\}) \qquad (\text{wrt } \{q, \neg r\}).$$

∎

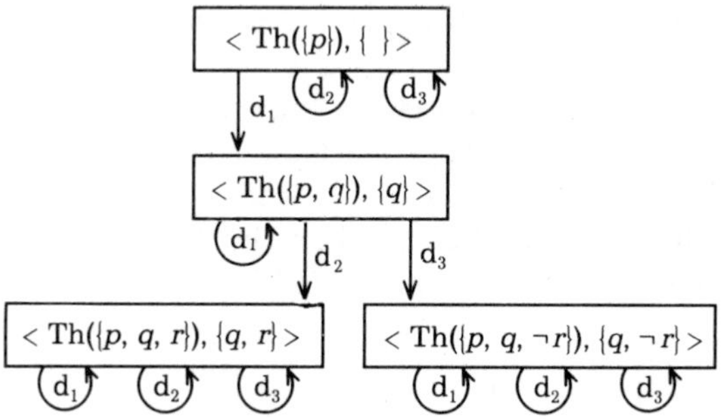

Fig. 5.7 – Network assigned to the theory of Example 5.112.

Example 5.113 Consider:

$$W = \{\ \}; \qquad D = \{d_i : i = 0, 1, \ldots\}$$

where $d_0 = :\neg p/\neg p$, $d_1 = : p/q_1$ and, for $i > 1$, $d_i = q_{i-1}: p/q_i$. This theory produces an infinite network given in Fig. 5.8. The network has one leaf, namely $\langle Th(\{\neg p\}), \{\neg p\}\rangle$, and thus $Th(\{\neg p\})$ is an m-extension of $\langle W, D\rangle$ wrt $\{\neg p\}$. Furthermore, there is an infinite path $\langle E_0, F_0\rangle, \langle E_1, F_1\rangle, \ldots$ from the root given by

$$\langle E_0, F_0\rangle = \langle Th(\{\ \}), \{\ \}\rangle$$
$$\langle E_i, F_i\rangle = \langle Th(\{q_1, \ldots, q_i\}), \{p\}\rangle \quad \text{for } i \geq 1.$$

Therefore, the set $Th(\{q_1, q_2, \ldots\})$ is also an m-extension of $\langle W, D\rangle$ (wrt $\{p\}$). ∎

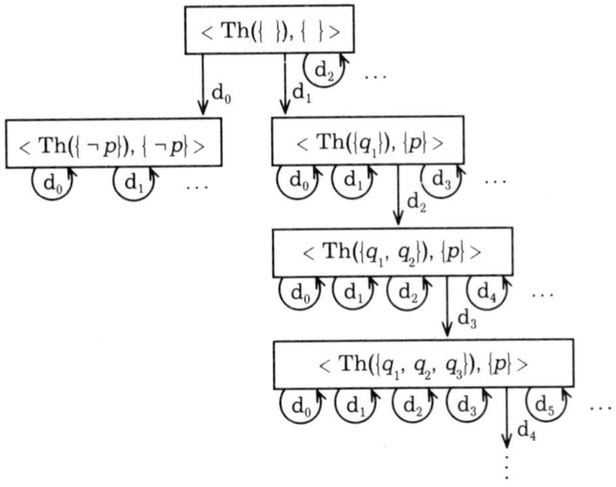

Fig. 5.8 – Network corresponding to the theory of Example 5.113.

5.12 SEMANTIC CHARACTERIZATION OF m-EXTENSIONS

We now provide a model-theoretic characterization of m-extensions of closed default theories. In what follows, the term 'frame' refers to an ordinary frame of classical first-order logic. We write $M \models A$ to indicate that a sentence A is true in a frame M.

Recall that, for any class of frames $\mathfrak{M}$ and any sentence A, we write $\mathfrak{M}(A)$ to denote the class of those members of $\mathfrak{M}$ which are models of A. Recall also that $\mathfrak{M}$ is called *elementary* iff it is the class of all models of some set of sentences S.

Our subsequent discussion is close in spirit to that of section 5.7. That is, we would like to view defaults of a closed default theory $\langle W, D\rangle$ as restricting the models of W in such a way that: (i) Any restricted class of models of W is the class of all models of some m-extension of $\langle W, D\rangle$; (ii) If E is any m-extension of $\langle W, D\rangle$, then there is some such restricted class of models of W which is the class of all models of E.

For convenience we repeat the definition of a structure, introduced in section 5.7.

Let $\mathfrak{M}$ be a class of frames and let U be a set of sentences. The pair $\langle \mathfrak{M}, U\rangle$ is called a *structure* iff (i) $\mathfrak{M}$ is elementary; (ii) For each $A \in U$, $\mathfrak{M}(A) \neq \{\ \}$.

We need the following concepts which are semantic counterparts of concepts introduced in the previous section.

Definition 5.114 Let $\langle \mathfrak{M}, U\rangle$ be a structure and let $d = A\colon B_1, \ldots, B_k/C$ be a closed default. We say that d is *M-APPLICABLE wrt* $\langle \mathfrak{M}, U\rangle$ iff

(1) $M \models A$, for each $M \in \mathfrak{M}$;
(2) For each $X \in U \cup \{B_1, \ldots, B_k\}$, there is $M \in \mathfrak{M}$ such that $M \models C \wedge X$.

∎

Example 5.115 The default $d = p\colon q/q$ is M-APPLICABLE wrt $\langle \mathfrak{M}_1, U_1\rangle = \langle\{M\colon M \models p\}, \{r\}\rangle$, but is not M-applicable wrt $\langle \mathfrak{M}_2, U_2\rangle = \langle\{M\colon M \models p \wedge \neg q\}, \{r\}\rangle$.

∎

As we have seen in the previous section, closed defaults can be viewed as transformations from BJ-pairs into BJ-pairs. They can be also considered as transformations from structures into structures.

Definition 5.116 To each closed default $d = A: B_1, \ldots, B_k/C$ we assign a mapping, denoted by d^M, from structures into structures, given by

$$d^M(\langle \mathfrak{M}, U\rangle) = \begin{cases} \langle \mathfrak{M}(C), U \cup \{B_1, \ldots, B_k\}\rangle & \text{iff d is M-APPLICABLE wrt } \langle \mathfrak{M}, U\rangle \\ \langle \mathfrak{M}, U\rangle & \text{otherwise.} \end{cases}$$

∎

It is easily checked that $d^M(\langle \mathfrak{M}, U\rangle)$ is indeed a structure.

Example 5.115 (continued)

$$d^M(\langle \mathfrak{M}_1, U_1\rangle) = \langle \{M: M \models p \wedge q\}, \{r, q\}\rangle$$
$$d^M(\langle \mathfrak{M}_2, U_2\rangle) = \langle \mathfrak{M}_2, U_2\rangle.$$

∎

Definition 5.117 Let $\langle \mathfrak{M}, U\rangle$ be a structure and let D be a set of closed defaults. We say that $\langle \mathfrak{M}, U\rangle$ is *M-STABLE wrt* D iff $d^M(\langle \mathfrak{M}, U\rangle) = \langle \mathfrak{M}, U\rangle$, for all $d \in D$. ∎

Definition 5.118 Let $\langle \mathfrak{M}, U\rangle$ be a structure and suppose that $\langle d_i\rangle$ is a sequence of closed defaults. By $\langle d_i\rangle^M(\langle \mathfrak{M}, U\rangle)$ we denote the structure given by

$$\langle d_i\rangle^M(\langle \mathfrak{M}, U\rangle) = \begin{cases} \langle \mathfrak{M}, U\rangle & \text{if } \langle d_i\rangle = \langle\rangle \\ \langle \bigcap \mathfrak{M}_i, \bigcup U_i\rangle & \text{otherwise} \end{cases}$$

where $\langle \mathfrak{M}_0, U_0\rangle = \langle \mathfrak{M}, U\rangle$ and, for $i = 0, 1, \ldots$ [$i = 0, \ldots, N$], $\langle \mathfrak{M}_{i+1}, U_{i+1}\rangle = d_i^M(\langle \mathfrak{M}_i, U_i\rangle)$. ∎

Definition 5.119 Let $\langle \mathfrak{M}, U\rangle$ be a structure, $\mathfrak{N}$ be an elementary class of frames, and suppose that $\langle d_i\rangle$ is a sequence of closed defaults. We say that $\langle \mathfrak{M}, U\rangle$ is $\langle d_i\rangle$-*M-ACCESSIBLE from* $\mathfrak{N}$ iff $\langle \mathfrak{M}, U\rangle = \langle d_i\rangle^M(\langle \mathfrak{N}, \{\ \}\rangle)$. We say that $\langle \mathfrak{M}, U\rangle$ is *M-ACCESSIBLE from* $\mathfrak{N}$ *wrt a set of closed defaults* D iff there is a sequence $\langle d_i\rangle$ such that each $d_i \in D$ and $\langle \mathfrak{M}, U\rangle$ is $\langle d_i\rangle$-M-ACCESSIBLE from $\mathfrak{N}$. ∎

We are now in a position to give a model-theoretic characterization of m-extensions. The following theorem is a semantic counterpart of Theorem 5.111.

Theorem 5.120 Let $T = \langle W, D\rangle$ be a closed default theory and suppose that $\mathfrak{N}$ is the class of all models of W. Then a class of frames $\mathfrak{M}$ is the class of all models of some m-extension of T iff there is a structure $\langle \mathfrak{M}, U\rangle$ such that

(1) $\langle \mathfrak{M}, U\rangle$ is M-STABLE wrt D;
(2) $\langle \mathfrak{M}, U\rangle$ is M-ACCESSIBLE from $\mathfrak{N}$ wrt D.

Proof Assume first that $\mathfrak{M}$ is the class of all models of E, where E is an m-extension of T wrt U. Obviously, $\langle \mathfrak{M}, U\rangle$ is a structure. We shall show that $\langle \mathfrak{M}, U\rangle$ satisfies (1)–(2). By Theorem 5.111, we have

$$\langle E, U\rangle \text{ is m-stable wrt D} \tag{5.12.1}$$

$$\langle E, U\rangle \text{ is m-accessible from W wrt D.} \tag{5.12.2}$$

To prove (1), take any $d = (A: B_1, \ldots, B_k/C) \in D$. If d is not M-APPLICABLE wrt $\langle \mathfrak{M}, U\rangle$, then clearly $d^M(\langle \mathfrak{M}, U\rangle) = \langle \mathfrak{M}, U\rangle$. Assume, therefore, that d is

M-APPLICABLE wrt $\langle \mathfrak{M}, \mathrm{U} \rangle$. Thus,

$$d^{M}(\langle \mathfrak{M}, U \rangle) = \langle \mathfrak{M}(C), U \cup \{B_1, \ldots, B_k\} \rangle. \tag{5.12.3}$$

It is easily verified that the M-APPLICABILITY of d wrt $\langle \mathfrak{M}, \mathrm{U} \rangle$ implies the m-applicability of d wrt $\langle \mathrm{E}, \mathrm{U} \rangle$. Therefore, $d^{m}(\langle E, U \rangle) = \langle \mathrm{Th}(E \cup \{C\}), U \cup \{B_1, \ldots, B_k\} \rangle$. So, by (5.12.1), $B_1, \ldots, B_k \in \mathrm{U}$ and $C \in \mathrm{Th(E)}$, and hence $\mathfrak{M} = \mathfrak{M}(C)$. In consequence, by (5.12.3), $d^{M}(\langle \mathfrak{M}, U \rangle) = \langle \mathfrak{M}, U \rangle$.

We now proceed to (2). In view of (5.12.2), there is a sequence $\langle d_i \rangle$ such that

$$\langle E, U \rangle = \langle d_i \rangle^{m}(\langle \mathrm{Th}(W), \{\ \} \rangle). \tag{5.12.4}$$

Lemma 5.120.1 $\langle \mathfrak{M}, U \rangle = \langle d_i \rangle^{M}(\langle \mathfrak{N}, \{\ \} \rangle)$.

Proof If $\langle d_i \rangle = \langle\ \rangle$, the lemma trivially follows from (5.12.4). Otherwise, by (5.12.4),

$$\langle E, U \rangle = \langle \bigcup E_i, \bigcup U_i \rangle \tag{5.12.5}$$

where $\langle E_0, U_0 \rangle = \langle \mathrm{Th}(W), \{\ \} \rangle$ and, for $i \geq 0$, $\langle E_{i+1}, U_{i+1} \rangle = d_i^{m}(\langle E_i, U_i \rangle)$. Let $\mathfrak{N}_i$ be the class of all models of E_i ($i = 0, 1, \ldots$ or $i = 0, \ldots, N$). It is easily verified that

$$\langle \mathfrak{N}_0, U_0 \rangle = \langle \mathfrak{N}, \{\ \} \rangle$$
$$\langle \mathfrak{N}_{i+1}, U_{i+1} \rangle = d_i^{M}(\langle \mathfrak{N}_i, U_i \rangle), \qquad \text{for } i \geq 0$$

and hence

$$\langle d_i \rangle^{M}(\langle \mathfrak{N}, \{\ \} \rangle) = \langle \bigcap \mathfrak{N}_i, \bigcup U_i \rangle. \tag{5.12.6}$$

On the other hand, using (5.12.5), it is routine to check that $U = \bigcup U_i$ and $\mathfrak{M} = \bigcap \mathfrak{N}_i$. This, together with (5.12.6), proves the lemma. ∎

In view of Lemma 5.120.1 $\langle \mathfrak{M}, U \rangle$ is M-ACCESSIBLE from $\mathfrak{N}$ wrt D, which proves (2).

This completes the proof of the implication from left to right in Theorem 5.120.

Assume now that $\langle \mathfrak{M}, U \rangle$ is a structure satisfying (1) and (2) and suppose that $\mathfrak{M}$ is the class of all models of E. We shall show that E is an m-extension of T wrt U. It is easily seen that $\langle E, U \rangle$ is a BJ-pair. So, by Theorem 5.111, it suffices to prove that $\langle E, U \rangle$ satisfies (5.12.1) and (5.12.2).

To verify (5.12.1), take any $d = (A{:}\ B_1, \ldots, B_k/C) \in \mathrm{D}$. Clearly, we may assume that d is m-applicable wrt $\langle E, U \rangle$, and hence

$$d^{m}(\langle E, U \rangle) = \langle \mathrm{Th}(E \cup \{C\}), U \cup \{B_1, \ldots, B_k\} \rangle. \tag{5.12.7}$$

One readily verifies that the m-applicability of d wrt $\langle E, U \rangle$ implies the M-APPLICABILITY of d wrt $\langle \mathfrak{M}, U \rangle$. Thus, $d^{M}(\langle \mathfrak{M}, U \rangle) = \langle \mathfrak{M}(C), U \cup \{B_1, \ldots, B_k\} \rangle$, and so, by (1), $B_1, \ldots, B_k \in \mathrm{U}$ and $\mathfrak{M} = \mathfrak{M}(C)$. Thus, $C \in \mathrm{Th}(E) = E$, and, consequently, $d^{m}(\langle E, U \rangle) = \langle E, U \rangle$, by (5.12.7).

We proceed now to prove (5.12.2). By (2), there is a sequence $\langle d_i \rangle$ of defaults from D satisfying

$$\langle \mathfrak{M}, U \rangle = \langle d_i \rangle^{M}(\langle \mathfrak{N}, \{\ \} \rangle). \tag{5.12.8}$$

Lemma 5.120.2 $\langle E, U \rangle = \langle d_i \rangle^{m}(\langle \mathrm{Th}(W), \{\ \} \rangle)$..

Proof If $\langle d_i \rangle = \langle \, \rangle$, the lemma obviously holds. Otherwise, by (5.12.8)

$$\langle \mathfrak{M}, U \rangle = \langle \bigcap \mathfrak{N}_i, \bigcup U_i \rangle \tag{5.12.9}$$

where $\langle \mathfrak{N}_0, U_0 \rangle = \langle \mathfrak{N}, \{ \, \} \rangle$ and, for $i \geq 0$, $\langle \mathfrak{N}_{i+1}, U_{i+1} \rangle = d_i^M(\langle \mathfrak{N}_i, U_i \rangle)$. Let $E_i = \{A: M \models A, \text{for all } M \in \mathfrak{N}_i\}$ ($i = 0, 1, \ldots$ or $i = 0, \ldots, N$). It is easily checked that

$$\langle E_0, U_0 \rangle = \langle Th(W), \{ \, \} \rangle$$
$$\langle E_{i+1}, U_{i+1} \rangle = d_i^m(\langle E_i, U_i \rangle), \text{ for } i \geq 0$$

from which it follows

$$\langle d_i \rangle^m(\langle Th(W), \{ \, \} \rangle) = \langle \bigcup E_i, \bigcup U_i \rangle. \tag{5.12.10}$$

On the other hand, using (5.12.9), it is easily checked that $U = \bigcup U_i$ and $E = \bigcup E_i$. This, by (5.12.10), proves the lemma. ■

By Lemma 5.120.2, we infer that $\langle E, U \rangle$ is m-accessible from W wrt D. This proves (5.12.2) and hence completes the proof of the implication from right to left in Theorem 5.120. ▮

Like Theorem 5.111, Theorem 5.120 may be given a transition network interpretation. Specifically, to each closed default theory $\langle W, D \rangle$ we assign a network whose nodes are structures and whose arcs are labelled by defaults from D. There is a root node corresponding to $\langle \mathfrak{N}, \{ \, \} \rangle$, where $\mathfrak{N}$ is the class of all models of W. The set of nodes is the smallest set including the root node and closed under the mapping d^M. From a node $\langle \mathfrak{M}, U \rangle$, for each $d \in D$, an arc, labelled d, leads to $d^M(\langle \mathfrak{M}, U \rangle)$.

Each leaf node of the network provides a semantic characterization of an m-extension of $\langle W, D \rangle$. More precisely, if $\langle \mathfrak{M}, U \rangle$ is such a leaf node, then $\mathfrak{M}$ is the class of all models of some m-extension of $\langle W, D \rangle$. Furthermore, if the network has finitely many nodes, then each m-extension of $\langle W, D \rangle$ is semantically characterized by some such a leaf. If the network has infinitely many nodes, m-extensions of $\langle W, D \rangle$ are also characterized by infinite paths, from the root, of different nodes: if $\langle \mathfrak{M}_0, U_0 \rangle, \langle \mathfrak{M}_1, U_1 \rangle, \ldots$ is such a path, then $\bigcap \mathfrak{M}_i$ is the class of all models of some m-extension of $\langle W, D \rangle$.

Example 5.121 Let

$$W = \{p \vee q\}$$
$$D = \{d_1 = :\neg p/\neg p, d_2 = :\neg q/\neg q\}.$$

The network associated with this theory is shown in Fig. 5.9. This is a finite network

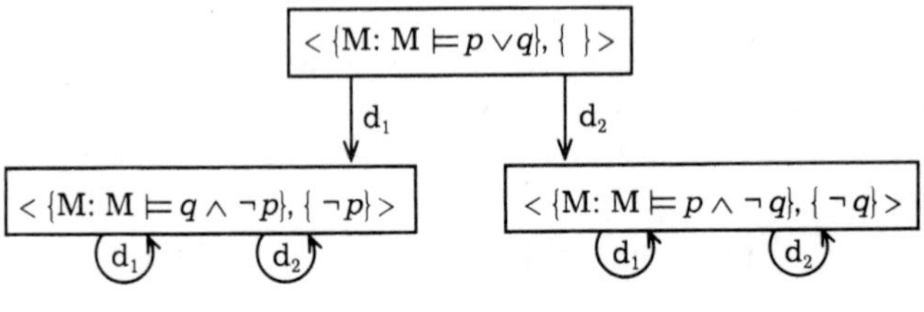

Fig. 5.9 – Network corresponding to the theory of Example 5.121.

with two leaves. Accordingly, the theory has two m-extensions:

$$E_1 = \mathrm{Th}(\{q \wedge \neg p\}) \qquad (\text{wrt } \{\neg p\})$$
$$E_2 = \mathrm{Th}(\{p \wedge \neg q\}) \qquad (\text{wrt } \{\neg q\}).$$

▮

Example 5.122 Consider:

$$W = \{\ \}$$
$$D = \{d_i : i = 1, 2, \ldots\}$$

where $d_1 = : q_1/p_1$ and, for $i \geq 1$, $d_{i+1} = p_i : q_{i+1}/p_{i+1}$. This theory gives rise to the network shown in Fig. 5.10. The network has no leaves. However, there is an infinite path $\langle \mathfrak{M}_0, U_0 \rangle, \langle \mathfrak{M}_1, U_1 \rangle, \ldots$, from the root, where

$$\mathfrak{M}_0 = \{M \models True\};\ U_0 = \{\ \} \text{ and, for } i \geq 1$$
$$\mathfrak{M}_i = \{M : M \models p_1 \wedge \cdots \wedge p_i\};\ U_i = \{q_1, \ldots, q_i\}.$$

Thus, the theory has one m-extension:

$$E_1 = \mathrm{Th}(\{p_1, p_2, \ldots\}) \qquad (\text{wrt } \{q_1, q_2, \ldots\}).$$

▮

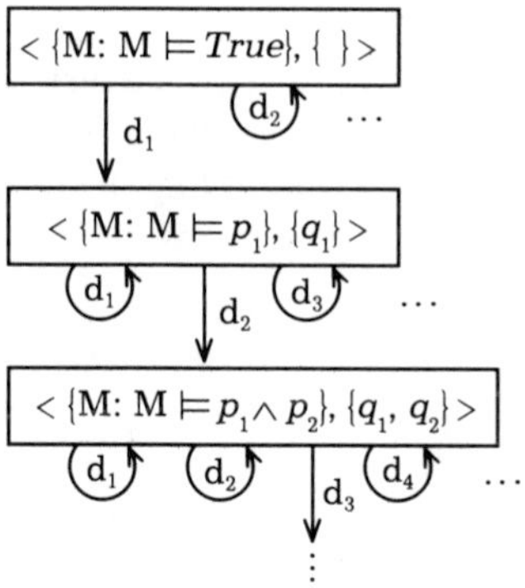

Fig. 5.10 – Network assigned to the theory of Example 5.122.

Example 5.123 Consider the theory $T = \langle W, D \rangle$, where

$$W = \{p, q\}; \qquad D = \{d_1 = p : (r \wedge \neg s)/r,\ d_2 = q : s/s\}.$$

This is the theory from Example 5.64. As we saw (Fig. 5.1), T has one extension given by $\mathrm{Th}(\{p, q, s\})$. According to the semantics given in this section, T gives rise to the network shown in Fig. 5.11. This is a finite network with two leaves. Thus, T has two m-extensions:

$$E_1 = \mathrm{Th}(\{p, q, r\}) \qquad (\text{wrt } \{r \wedge \neg s\})$$
$$E_2 = \mathrm{Th}(\{p, q, s\}) \qquad (\text{wrt } \{s\}).$$

▮

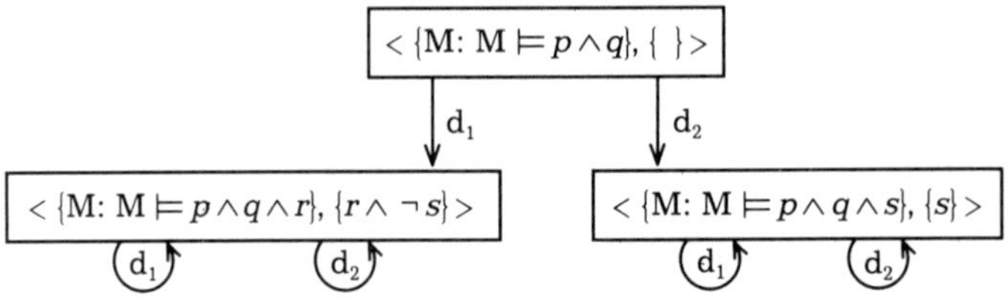

Fig. 5.11 – Network associated with the theory of Example 5.123.

5.13 PROOF THEORY FOR ALTERNATIVE DEFAULT LOGIC

In this section we are concerned with the following problem: Given a closed default theory T and a sentence C, determine whether there is an m-extension of T containing C.

Let $\langle S, U \rangle$ be a BJ-pair. By BELIEFS($\langle S, U \rangle$) we denote the set S.

Definition 5.124 (Łukaszewicz 1984b) Let $T = \langle W, D \rangle$ be a closed default theory and let C be a sentence. A finite sequence $\langle d_i \rangle = d_0, \ldots, d_N$ $(N \geq -1)$, where for each $0 \leq i \leq N$, $d_i \in D$, is a *modified default proof of C wrt T* iff

$$C \in \text{BELIEFS}(\langle d_i \rangle^m(\langle \text{Th}(W), \{\ \} \rangle)).$$

∎

This definition can be given a simple procedural interpretation. To determine whether a sentence C belongs to some m-extension of $\langle W, D \rangle$, we start with the BJ-pair $\langle \text{Th}(W), \{\ \} \rangle$ and extend it by applying defaults from D, one at a time, until the set of beliefs of the resulting BJ-pair contains C. The sequence of successive defaults involved in this process is a modified default proof of C wrt T.

Theorem 5.125 (Łukaszewicz 1984b) Let $T = \langle W, D \rangle$ be a closed default theory. A sentence C has a modified default proof wrt T iff there is an m-extension of T containing C.

Proof (⇒) Assume that $\langle d_i \rangle = d_0, \ldots, d_N$ $(N \geq -1)$ is a modified default proof of C wrt T, i.e.

$$C \in \text{BELIEFS}(\langle d_i \rangle^m(\langle \text{Th}(W), \{\ \} \rangle)). \tag{5.13.1}$$

Let $D' = \{d_j : d_j \in \{d_0, \ldots, d_N\}$ and d_j is m-applicable wrt $\langle d_i \rangle^m(\langle \text{Th}(W), \{\ \} \rangle)\}$. Consider the theory $T' = \langle W, D' \rangle$. Clearly, $\langle d_i \rangle^m(\langle \text{Th}(W), \{\ \} \rangle)$ is m-stable wrt D' and m-accessible from W wrt D'. Thus, by Theorem 5.111, BELIEFS($\langle d_i \rangle^m(\langle \text{Th}(W), \{\ \} \rangle)$) is an m-extension of T'. Since $D' \subseteq D$, then, by Theorem 5.106, BELIEFS($\langle d_i \rangle^m(\langle \text{Th}(W), \{\ \} \rangle)$) $\subseteq$ E, where E is some m-extension of T. This, together with (5.13.1), completes the proof of the left to right direction of the theorem.

(⇐) Assume that E is an m-extension of T and suppose that $C \in E$. In view of Theorem 5.111, there is a sequence $\langle d_i \rangle$ of defaults from D such that $E = \text{BELIEFS}(\langle d_i \rangle^m(\langle \text{Th}(W), \{\ \} \rangle))$. From this and Definition 5.108, it is straightforward to check that

$$E = \bigcup E_j$$

where

$$E_0 = \text{BELIEFS}(\langle\rangle^m(\langle \text{Th}(W), \{\ \}\rangle))$$

and, for $j = 0, 1, \ldots$ [$j = 0, \ldots, N$],

$$E_{j+1} = \text{BELIEFS}(\langle d_0, \ldots, d_j\rangle^m(\langle \text{Th}(W), \{\ \}\rangle)).$$

Thus, since $C \in E$, there is the smallest integer $k \geq -1$ such that $C \in \text{BELIEFS}(\langle d_0, \ldots, d_k\rangle^m(\langle \text{Th}(W), \{\ \}\rangle))$. It is easily seen that $d_0, \ldots, d_k$ is a modified default proof of C wrt T. ▮

The next theorem shows that modified default proofs can be regarded as natural generalizations of default proofs introduced in section 5.8 for normal default theories (see Definition 5.68).

Theorem 5.126 (Łukaszewicz 1984b) Let $T = \langle W, D\rangle$ be a consistent closed default theory. A sentence C has a modified default proof wrt T iff there exists a finite sequence $D_0, \ldots, D_k$ ($k \geq 0$) of finite subsets of D such that

(1) $W \cup \text{CONSEQUENTS}(D_0) \vdash C$;
(2) For $1 \leq i \leq k$, $W \cup \text{CONSEQUENTS}(D_i) \vdash C_{nj}(\text{PREREQUISITES}(D_{i-1}))$;
(3) $D_k = \{\ \}$;
(4) For each $B \in \bigcup_{i=0}^{k} \text{JUSTIFICATIONS}(D_i)$, $W \cup \bigcup_{i=0}^{k} \text{CONSEQUENTS}(D_i) \cup \{B\}$ is consistent.

Proof (outline) Assume first that $d_0, \ldots, d_N$ ($N \geq -1$) is a modified default proof of C wrt T. Let $d'_0, \ldots, d'_M$ ($M \leq N$) obtains from $d_0, \ldots, d_N$ by deleting any default d_j ($1 \leq j \leq N$) such that d_j is not m-applicable wrt $\langle d_0, \ldots, d_{j-1}\rangle^m(\langle \text{Th}(W), \{\ \}\rangle)$. We construct a sequence $D_0, \ldots, D_{M+1}$ of finite subsets of D by

$$D_0 = \{d'_0, \ldots, d'_M\}$$
$$D_j = \{d'_0, \ldots, d'_{M-j}\}, \text{ for } 1 \leq j \leq M$$
$$D_{M+1} = \{\ \}.$$

It is easily checked that $D_0, \ldots, D_{M+1}$ satisfies (1)–(4).

Assume now that $D_0, \ldots, D_k$ satisfies (1)–(4). For $0 \leq j \leq k$, let $d^j_0, \ldots, d^j_{m_j}$ be any sequence of all elements of D_j. Consider the sequence

$$d^{k-1}_0, \ldots, d^{k-1}_{m_{k-1}}, d^{k-2}_0, \ldots, d^0_0, \ldots, d^0_{m_0}.$$

Using (1)–(4), it is routine to show that the above sequence is a modified default proof of C wrt T. ▮

We conclude our presentation of default logic by remarking that this formalism has proved useful in many AI applications such as inheritance hierarchies with exceptions (Etherington & Reiter 1983; Froidevaux 1986), diagnostic reasoning (Poole 1986; Reiter 1987a) and various aspects of natural language processing (Mercer & Reiter 1982; Dunin-Kęplicz 1984; Perrault 1986; Saint-Dizier 1988).

A paper of Kautz & Selman (1989) provides a number of complexity results concerning Reiter's version of default logic.

6

Circumscription

6.1 INTRODUCTION

Circumscription is a powerful non-monotonic formalism created by John McCarthy (1977, 1980), generalized in McCarthy (1984) and independently explored by many AI researchers. It is both the most fascinating and the most controversial of all the formal approaches to non-monotonic reasoning.

To speak about circumscription, we need a preliminary terminology. We distinguish between a predicate, thought of as a particular relation specified over a particular domain, and predicate expressions, including predicate constants and predicate variables, which can be used to denote this relation (see section 1.5.5, Chapter 1). According to the established philosophical tradition, the predicate denoted by an expression U will be called the *extension of U*.† For example, if U is an unary predicate constant *Bird* and we denote by D the universe of all individuals, then the extension of U is a subset of D, intuitively interpreted as the set of all birds. Similarly, if U is of the form $\lambda xy.Likes(x, y) \wedge \neg Likes(y, x)$, then its extension is a subset of D^2 (the set of all pairs $\langle d_1, d_2 \rangle$ such that d_1 likes d_2, but not vice-versa). In general, if U is of the arity n, then its extension is a subset of D^n. Therefore, given a set of predicate expressions of the same arity, the set of their extensions is naturally ordered by the relation of set inclusion.

Circumscription attempts to capture the following idea: the objects (tuples of objects) that can be shown to satisfy a certain predicate are the *only* objects (tuples of objects) enjoying it. More specifically, given a theory T, i.e. a set of axioms, and an n-ary predicate constant P, circumscription of P in T can be viewed as saying that the extension of P is minimal in the sense that it could not be made smaller without

---

† Notice that the term *extension* is used here in a quite different sense than in the previous chapters. In the philosophical literature, the extension of an expression V is also called the *denotation of V*.

contradicting T. Circumscription is thus a form of minimization: to circumscribe a predicate constant is to minimize its extension.[†]

Consider a simple example. Let T consist of the axiom

$$Red(a) \wedge On(a, b). \tag{6.1.1}$$

Circumscribing *Red* in T, we may expect to infer the sentence

$$\forall x . Red(x) \supset x = a$$

stating that a is the only red object. Respectively, the circumscription of *On* in T should allow us to conclude

$$\forall xy . On(x, y) \supset x = a \wedge y = b. \tag{6.1.2}$$

Circumscription can be also used to minimize several predicates simultaneously. For instance, in the previous example, we may wish to jointly circumscribe *Red* and *On*. Performing this circumscription, we may expect to derive the conjunction of (6.1.1) and (6.1.2).

About ten different versions of circumscription are currently offered on the AI market. All of them share the following common characteristics:

(1) Unlike the logics studied in the previous chapters, circumscription allows us to formalize non-monotonic reasoning directly in the language of classical logic.
(2) It is always the task of the user to specify predicates which are to be minimized. Circumscription provides a general method which can be applied to arbitrarily chosen predicates.
(3) Circumscription is based on syntactic manipulations. Given a theory T and a list of predicate constants $P_1, \ldots, P_n$, circumscription of $P_1, \ldots, P_n$ in T amounts to implicitly adding to T a special second-order sentence (a set of first-order formulae, in some versions of circumscription) capturing the desired minimization.

Our goal in this chapter is to survey the most influential circumscriptive logics and to illustrate how they can be used to formalize common-sense inferences. We begin by informally discussing *abnormality formalism* – a general tool for representing non-monotonic rules in the framework of circumscription. In section 6.3, we study one of the first versions of circumscription, known in the AI literature as *predicate circumscription* (McCarthy 1980). Its generalization, namely *formula circumscription* (McCarthy 1984), is briefly presented in section 6.4. In section 6.5, we address *second-order circumscription*, Lifschitz's (1985b) reformulation of formula circumscription. Section 6.6 is devoted to *non-recursive circumscription*, introduced by Mott (1987). In section 6.7, we present a circumscriptive logic directed at the problem of formalizing the *domain closure assumption*. It is known in the AI literature as *domain circumscription* (McCarthy 1977; Etherington & Mercer 1987). Finally, in section 6.8, we discuss *pointwise circumscription*, a very interesting formalism developed by Lifschitz (1988b).

For lack of space, we omit proofs of most of the results provided in this chapter.

The following discussion assumes familiarity with the material contained in section 1.5 (Chapter 1).

[†] Observe that the objects being circumscribed are predicate constants, whereas those being minimized are their extensions. In the sequel, however, we shall not pay much attention to this distinction. In particular, we shall often speak about circumscribing predicates.

6.2 ABNORMALITY FORMALISM

Providing a general mechanism of minimizing arbitrarily chosen predicates, circumscriptive logics leave two fundamental questions unanswered:

(1) How is common-sense knowledge, including non-monotonic rules, to be represented in the framework of circumscription?
(2) Which predicates are to be minimized to assure intuitively acceptable results?

In this section we provide a partial answer to these questions, based on a conception of *abnormality predicates* (Grosof 1984; McCarthy 1984).

To represent a non-monotonic rule admitting exceptions, McCarthy (1984) suggests employing a special predicate constant, *Ab*, standing for *abnormal*. The intention is that abnormal objects are those violating the rule. Under this interpretation, the rule about flying birds can be expressed by the sentence

$$\forall x\,.\,Bird(x) \wedge \neg Ab(x) \supset Flies(x). \qquad (6.2.1)$$

Circumscribing *Ab* in a theory containing (6.2.1), we should be able to derive that any bird flies unless it can be proved abnormal.†

To illustrate the abnormality formalism in detail, let us analyse an example. Suppose that T is a theory consisting of (6.2.1) and

$$Bird(Tweety). \qquad (6.2.2)$$

Given (6.2.1) and (6.2.2) as the only axioms, the minimal possible extension of *Ab* is the empty set. Therefore, circumscription of *Ab* in T should lead to

$$\forall x \neg Ab(x) \qquad (6.2.3)$$

and so to

$$\forall x\,.\,Bird(x) \supset Flies(x) \qquad (6.2.4)$$

and

$$Flies(Tweety). \qquad (6.2.5)$$

To express the fact that Clyde is a non-flying bird, we extend our theory by adding

$$Bird(Clyde) \wedge \neg Flies(Clyde) \wedge Clyde \neq Tweety. \qquad (6.2.6)$$

Observe that (6.2.1) and (6.2.6) imply that Clyde is abnormal, so that he is now the only element of the minimal possible extension of *Ab*. Accordingly, neither (6.2.3) nor (6.2.4) can be inferred by circumscribing *Ab* in $T = \{(6.2.1), (6.2.2), (6.2.6)\}$. However, performing this circumscription, we may expect to derive

$$\forall x\,.\,x \neq Clyde \supset \neg Ab(x) \qquad (6.2.7)$$

and thus

$$\forall x\,.\,Bird(x) \wedge x \neq Clyde \supset Flies(x). \qquad (6.2.8)$$

Suppose now that the theory $\{(6.2.1), (6.2.2), (6.2.6)\}$ is further extended by

$$Ostrich(Joe) \wedge Joe \neq Clyde \wedge Joe \neq Tweety \qquad (6.2.9)$$

$$\forall x\,.\,Ostrich(x) \supset Bird(x). \qquad (6.2.10)$$

† We write 'we should be able' instead of 'we shall be able', because, as we shall see, not all versions of circumscription capture their intended meaning.

Circumscribing Ab in {(6.2.1), (6.2.2), (6.2.6), (6.2.9), (6.2.10)}, we should be able to infer that Joe is normal and, consequently, that he flies. This intuitively problematic conclusion can be blocked in different ways.

If we believe that ostriches never fly, we add the axiom:

$$\forall x . Ostrich(x) \supset \neg Flies(x). \tag{6.2.11}$$

If we want to remain agnostic about the flying abilities of ostriches, we add

$$\forall x . Ostrich(x) \supset Ab(x). \tag{6.2.12}$$

Notice that (6.2.12) does not imply that ostriches are non-fliers, but rather that they are abnormal birds as regards flying. Given (6.2.12), it may still be possible to infer that a particular ostrich flies. However, this conclusion will be never obtained by using (6.2.1).

The third method of blocking the inference that Joe flies is to introduce a new non-monotonic rule stating 'An ostrich cannot fly unless the contrary is proved'. On analogy of (6.2.1), one may try to represent this by

$$\forall x . Ostrich(x) \wedge \neg Ab(x) \supset \neg Flies(x).$$

However, we should take into consideration that being abnormal as a non-flying bird means something quite different from being abnormal as a flying ostrich, so that we must distinguish between the two aspects of abnormality. The proper solution is to introduce a new abnormality predicate constant, say Ab_1, and to represent the rule about ostriches by

$$\forall x . Ostrich(x) \wedge \neg Ab_1(x) \supset \neg Flies(x). \tag{6.2.13}$$

The idea of distinguishing between different kinds of abnormality by using different abnormality predicates is due to Grosof (1984).[†] In McCarthy's original presentation (McCarthy 1984), this distinction is expressed by means of special function constants, called *aspects*. Under this convention, sentences (6.2.1) and (6.2.13) should be rewritten as

$$\forall x . Bird(x) \wedge \neg Ab(aspect_0(x)) \supset Flies(x)$$
$$\forall x . Ostrich(x) \wedge \neg Ab(aspect_1(x)) \supset \neg Flies(x)$$

respectively. The difference between Grosof's and McCarthy's approaches is mainly notational. Personally, I prefer the former.

When we are dealing with several abnormality predicates, they should all be simultaneously minimized. In our example, we must jointly circumscribe Ab and Ab_1 in $T = \{(6.2.1), (6.2.2), (6.2.6), (6.2.9), (6.2.10), (6.2.13)\}$. The problem with this circumscription is that there is a conflict concerning Joe. Given T as the premisses, he may be assumed a normal bird or a normal ostrich, but not both. Accordingly, there are two conflicting minimizations of Ab and Ab_1 in T. One of them allows to infer $\neg Ab(Joe)$ and hence $Flies(Joe)$; the other, $\neg Ab_1(Joe)$ and $\neg Flies(Joe)$.[‡]

In the case of several conflicting minimizations, circumscription takes their 'intersection' as the set of derivable theorems. More precisely, if circumscription of $P_1, \ldots, P_n$ in T gives rise to minimizations $m_1, \ldots, m_k$ and $E_1, \ldots, E_k$ are sets of

[†] At least, for the purpose of circumscription.

[†] Conflicting minimizations closely correspond to alternative extensions in modal non-monotonic and default logics.

formulae 'inferable' by performing $m_1, \ldots, m_k$, respectively, then the set of theorems obtainable by circumscribing $P_1, \ldots, P_n$ in T is $E_1 \cap \cdots \cap E_k$. It follows, therefore, that neither $\neg Ab(Joe)$ nor $\neg Ab_1(Joe)$, and hence neither $Flies(Joe)$ nor $\neg Flies(Joe)$, can be derived by jointly circumscribing Ab and Ab_1 in T. The best we can deduce by performing this circumscription is $\neg Ab(Joe) \vee \neg Ab_1(Joe)$ and hence, $Flies(Joe) \vee \neg Flies(Joe)$.

As our discussion indicates, the conclusions obtainable by circumscribing Ab and Ab_1 in T are too weak. Given that Joe is an ostrich, and no more, we intuitively feel that he should be considered as a non-flier. To get the desired effect, we must block the minimization leading to $\neg Ab(Joe)$. This can be achieved in several different ways. The simplest method is perhaps to add (6.2.12) and to circumscribe Ab, Ab_1 in $T \cup \{(6.2.12)\}$.†

It is worth noting that there are non-monotonic rules requiring many-place abnormality predicates. Consider, for instance, the rule: 'In the absence of evidence to the contrary, assume that x gives y a gift, provided that y has a birthday and x is a friend of y'. The appropriate representation of this rule requires using a binary abnormality predicate:

$$\forall xy\,.\, Birthday(y) \wedge Friend(x, y) \wedge \neg Ab(x, y) \supset Gives\text{-}gift(x, y).$$

Here '$Ab(x, y)$' may be interpreted: 'x behaves abnormally with respect to y in the situation where y has a birthday and x is a friend of y'.

6.3 PREDICATE CIRCUMSCRIPTION

We begin our formal discussion of circumscription by presenting one of its earliest versions, called *predicate circumscription*. It was developed by McCarthy (1980) and thoroughly explored by Etherington *et al.* (1985).

6.3.1 Preliminaries

Let L be a fixed first-order language with equality. The objects under consideration, referred to as (*circumscriptive*) *theories*, are finite sets of sentences stated in L. Since each such a set is logically equivalent to the conjunction of its members, a circumscriptive theory may be always viewed as a single first-order sentence. In the sequel, we shall never distinguish between a theory T and the sentence being the conjunction of all members of T. We write $T(P_1, \ldots, P_n)$ to indicate that some (but not necessarily all) of predicate constants occurring in T are among $P_1, \ldots, P_n$. Notice that this does not imply that each P_i, $1 \leq i \leq n$, occurs in T.

Although predicate circumscription is based on first-order logic, its definition requires using an auxiliary second-order language. In the following, L_2 is a second-order language whose alphabet is that of L, together with an infinite set of n-place predicate variables (for each $n \geq 0$).

We shall intensively make use of predicate expressions and their substitutions for free predicate variables. These notions were discussed in detail in section 1.5.

† As we shall see, there are circumscriptive logics allowing to block unwanted minimizations by establishing relative priorities between circumscribed predicates. Using such a *prioritized circumscription*, it is possible to infer $\neg Flies(Joe)$ by circumscribing Ab, Ab_1 in T, provided that Ab_1 is given a priority over Ab.

The following notation will be useful. Let U and V be n-ary predicate expressions. We write $U \leq V$ as an abbreviation for $\forall \bar{x} . U(\bar{x}) \supset V(\bar{x})$, where $\bar{x} = (x_1, \ldots, x_n)$ is an n-tuple of new individual variables and $\forall \bar{x}$ stands for $\forall x_1, \ldots, x_n$. $U \leq V$ states that the extension of U is a subset (not necessarily proper) of the extension of V.

The relation '$\leq$' can be naturally generalized. Let $\bar{U} = (U_1, \ldots, U_n)$ and $\bar{V} = (V_1, \ldots, V_n)$ be similar tuples of predicate expressions, i.e. U_i and V_i have the same arities, for each $1 \leq i \leq n$. We write $\bar{U} \leq \bar{V}$ to denote the sentence

$$\bigwedge_{i=1}^{n} [U_i \leq V_i] \qquad \text{or, equivalently,} \qquad \bigwedge_{i=1}^{n} [\forall \bar{x} . U_i(\bar{x}) \supset V_i(\bar{x})].$$

$\bar{U} \leq \bar{V}$ states that the extension of each member of $\bar{U}$ is a subset of the extension of the corresponding member of $\bar{V}$.

Let $T(P_1, \ldots, P_n)$ be a theory. We want to express the fact that the extensions of $P_1, \ldots, P_n$ are all minimal with respect to T, i.e. none of them may be made smaller without violating T. A possible way to achieve this is to employ the following sentence of L_2:

$$\forall \Phi_1 \ldots \Phi_n \{[T(\Phi_1, \ldots, \Phi_n) \wedge \bigwedge_{i=1}^{n} [\Phi_i \leq P_i]] \supset \bigwedge_{i=1}^{n} [P_i \leq \Phi_i]\}. \tag{6.3.1}$$

Here $\Phi_1, \ldots, \Phi_n$ are predicate variables with the same arities as $P_1, \ldots, P_n$, respectively. $T(\Phi_1, \ldots, \Phi_n)$ is the sentence obtained from $T(P_1, \ldots, P_n)$ by replacing all occurrences of $P_1, \ldots, P_n$ by $\Phi_1, \ldots, \Phi_n$, respectively. Notice that the presence of $T(\Phi_1, \ldots, \Phi_n)$ in (6.3.1) assures that the extensions of $P_1, \ldots, P_n$ are minimized with respect to T; if this conjunct were absent, (6.3.1) would say that all P_i's have the empty extensions.

After these remarks, we now proceed to provide the formal definition of predicate circumscription. The question we are primarily interested in is: What is the set of theorems derivable by circumscribing $P_1, \ldots, P_n$ in T? The general idea is to identify this set with the set of formulae monotonically derivable from $T \wedge$ (6.3.1). However, since (6.3.1)$\in L_2$, taking this sentence in its original form, would force us to base predicate circumscription on second-order logic. An alternative solution, actually adopted by McCarthy, is to regard (6.3.1) as a set of first-order formulae – those obtainable from (6.3.1) by substituting predicate expressions for universally quantified predicate variables. The formal details follow.

Definition 6.1 (McCarthy 1980) The *circumscription schema of* $P_1, \ldots, P_n$ *in* T, denoted by $CS(T; P_1, \ldots, P_n)$, is the second-order formula

$$[T(\Phi_1, \ldots, \Phi_n) \wedge \bigwedge_{i=1}^{n} [\Phi_i \leq P_i]] \supset \bigwedge_{i=1}^{n} [P_i \leq \Phi_i] \tag{6.3.2}$$

or, equivalently,

$$[T(\Phi_1, \ldots, \Phi_n) \wedge \bigwedge_{i=1}^{n} [\forall \bar{x} . \Phi_i(\bar{x}) \supset P_i(\bar{x})]] \supset \bigwedge_{i=1}^{n} [\forall \bar{x} . P_i(\bar{x}) \supset \Phi_i(\bar{x})]$$

where $\Phi_1, \ldots, \Phi_n$ and $T(\Phi_1, \ldots, \Phi_n)$ are defined as before. ∎

Notice that (6.3.2) results from (6.3.1) by deleting the prefix $\forall \Phi_1 \ldots \Phi_n$.

Example 6.2 Let $T = \{Red(a) \wedge On(a, b)\}$.

$$CS(T; Red) = [\Phi_1(a) \wedge On(a, b) \wedge [\forall x . \Phi_1(x) \supset Red(x)]] \supset \supset [\forall x . Red(x) \supset \Phi_1(x)]$$

$$CS(T; On) = [Red(a) \wedge \Phi_2(a, b) \wedge [\forall xy . \Phi_2(x, y) \supset On(x, y)]] \supset \supset [\forall xy . On(x, y) \supset \Phi_2(x, y)]$$

$$CS(T; Red, On) = [\Phi_1(a) \wedge \Phi_2(a, b) \wedge [\forall x . \Phi_1(x) \supset Red(x)] \wedge \wedge [\forall xy . \Phi_2(x, y) \supset On(x, y)]] \supset [[\forall x . Red(x) \supset \Phi_1(x)] \wedge \wedge [\forall xy . On(x, y) \supset \Phi_2(x, y)]].$$

∎

Consider the circumscription schema (6.3.2). Since T is a first-order theory, any proper substitution of first-order predicate expressions (possibly with parameters) for $\Phi_1, \ldots, \Phi_n$ in (6.3.2) results in a first-order formula. Our intention is to view (6.3.2) as the set of all the formulae obtainable in this way.

Definition 6.3 Let $T(P_1, \ldots, P_n)$ be a theory and suppose that $\overline{CS}(T; P_1, \ldots, P_n)$ is the set of all formulae obtainable from $CS(T; P_1, \ldots, P_n)$ by proper substitutions of first-order predicate expressions for $\Phi_1, \ldots, \Phi_n$. The *predicate circumscription of* $\bar{P} = (P_1, \ldots, P_n)$ *in* T, written $CIRC_{PR}(T; \bar{P})$, is the set of formulae $T \cup \overline{CS}(T; P_1, \ldots, P_n)$. The set of theorems derivable by circumscribing $\bar{P} = (P_1, \ldots, P_n)$ in T is identified with the set of theorems classically derivable from $CIRC_{PR}(T; \bar{P})$.† ∎

In this section, '$\vdash$' is the provability relation of classical first-order logic.

Example 6.2 (continued) We show that the sentence

$$\forall x . Red(x) \supset x = a$$

is derivable by circumscribing *Red* in *T*, i.e.

$$CIRC_{PR}(T; Red) \vdash \forall x . Red(x) \supset x = a. \tag{6.3.3}$$

Substituting the predicate expression $\lambda x . x = a$ for Φ_1 (notation: $\{\Phi_1 \leftarrow \lambda x . x = a\}$), in $CS(T; Red)$, we obtain

$$[(a = a) \wedge On(a, b) \wedge [\forall x . x = a \supset Red(x)]] \supset [\forall x . Red(x) \supset x = a]. \tag{6.3.4}$$

Obviously, the antecedent of (6.3.4) is derivable from T and hence it is also derivable from $CIRC_{PR}(T; Red)$. Therefore, since $(6.3.4) \in CIRC_{PR}(T; Red)$, we have $CIRC_{PR}(T; Red) \vdash (6.3.3)$, by modus ponens.

Substituting $\lambda xy . x = a \wedge y = b$ for Φ_2 in $CS(T; On)$, it is easily verified that $CIRC_{PR}(T; On) \vdash \forall xy . On(x, y) \supset x = a \wedge y = b$.

Finally, taking $\{\Phi_1 \leftarrow \lambda x . x = a\}$ and $\{\Phi_2 \leftarrow \lambda xy . x = a \wedge y = b\}$, the reader may check that $CIRC_{PR}(T; Red, On) \vdash [\forall x . Red(x) \supset x = a] \wedge [\forall xy . On(x, y) \supset x = a \wedge y = b]$.

∎

If one of the predicates being circumscribed in a theory T is the equality predicate, '=', we shall always assume that T contains its equality axioms. This assumption is crucial to assure that all the usual properties of equality hold after circumscription. If

† We adopt the convention that A is clasically derivable from a set of formulae S iff A is classically derivable from the set of sentences $\{\forall B : B \in S\}$; $\forall B$ stands for the universal closure of B.

the equality axioms are omitted, circumscription of the equality predicate may produce unintuitive results and often leads to inconsistency. This is illustrated below.

Example 6.4 We circumscribe '=' in the theory $T=\{P(a)\}$.

$$CS(T; =) = [P(a) \wedge [\forall xy.\Phi(x, y) \supset x = y]] \supset [\forall xy.x = y \supset \Phi(x, y)].$$

Letting $\{\Phi \leftarrow \lambda xy.False\}$ in CS(T; =), we get

$$[P(a) \wedge [\forall xy.False \supset x = y]] \supset [\forall xy.x = y \supset False]$$

which is equivalent to $P(a) \supset \forall xy.x \neq y$. Since $T \vdash P(a)$, we infer $CIRC_{PR}(T; =) \vdash \forall xy.x \neq y$. This means that $CIRC_{PR}(T; =)$ is inconsistent.

We leave it to the reader to show that if T is supplied with its equality axioms (in fact, $\forall x.x = x$ will do), then the above derivation is blocked. ▮

6.3.2 Semantics for predicate circumscription

We now proceed to provide a semantics for predicate circumscription. Recall that we write |M| to denote the domain of a frame M = ⟨D, m⟩. M|K|, where K is a predicate or function constant, stands for m(K).† The set of all assignments over M is denoted by As(M).

Definition 6.5 (McCarthy 1980) Let $T(P_1, \ldots, P_n)$ be a theory, some of whose predicate constants are among $\bar{P} = (P_1, \ldots, P_n)$. A model M of T is a $\bar{P}$-*submodel* of a model N of T, written $M \leq^{\bar{P}} N$, iff

(i) |M| = |N|;
(ii) M|K| ⊆ N|K|, for every predicate constant K in $\bar{P}$;
(iii) M|K| = N|K|, where K is any function constant or any predicate constant not in $\bar{P}$.

M is a $\bar{P}$-*minimal model of* T iff every model of T which is a $\bar{P}$-submodel of M is identical to M. ▮

Theorem 6.6 (Soundness Theorem; McCarthy 1980) If $CIRC_{PR}(T; \bar{P}) \vdash A$, then A is true in every $\bar{P}$-minimal model of T.

Proof Exceptionally, we provide a proof because that given in McCarthy (1980) is very sketchy.

By soundness of classical first-order logic, it suffices to show the following: If $A \in CIRC_{PR}(T; \bar{P})$, then A is true in every $\bar{P}$-minimal model of T. This is trivially true if $A \in T$. Suppose, therefore, that $A \in \overline{CS}(T; \bar{P})$, and assume to the contrary that there is a $\bar{P}$-minimal model of T, say M, such that

$$V_a^M(A) = 0 \tag{6.3.5}$$

for some $a \in As(M)$. Since $A \in \overline{CS}(T; \bar{P})$, (6.3.5) may be rewritten as

$$V_a^M([T(U_1, \ldots, U_n) \wedge \bigwedge_{i=1}^{n} [\forall \bar{x}.U_i(\bar{x}) \supset P_i(\bar{x})]] \supset \bigwedge_{i=1}^{n} [\forall \bar{x}.P_i(\bar{x}) \supset U_i(\bar{x})]) = 0 \tag{6.3.6}$$

† Recall that the set of function constants contains individual constants.

where $T(U_1, \ldots U_n)$ obtains by a proper substitution of first-order predicate expressions $U_1, \ldots U_n$ for $\Phi_1, \ldots, \Phi_n$ in $T(\Phi_1, \ldots, \Phi_n)$. (6.3.3) clearly implies

$$V_a^M(T(U_1, \ldots, U_n)) = 1 \tag{6.3.7}$$

$$V_a^M(\forall \bar{x} . U_i(\bar{x}) \supset P_i(\bar{x})) = 1, \text{ for each } 1 \leq i \leq n \tag{6.3.8}$$

$$V_a^M(\forall \bar{x} . P_j(\bar{x}) \supset U_j(\bar{x})) = 0, \text{ for some } 1 \leq j \leq n. \tag{6.3.9}$$

Assume that $U_i = \lambda x_1 \ldots x_m . A_i(x_1, \ldots, x_m)$. We denote by $|U_i|_a^M$ a subset of $|M|^m$ given by

$$(d_1, \ldots, d_m) \in |U_i|_a^M \quad \text{iff} \quad V^M_{a(x_1/d_1, \ldots, x_m/d_m)}(A) = 1$$

where $a(x_1/d_1, \ldots, x_m/d_m)$ denotes the assignment which is identical to 'a' except perhaps on the variables $x_1, \ldots, x_m$; here it assigns $d_1, \ldots, d_m$, respectively.

Define a frame N as follows:

$|N| = |M|$;
$N|K| = M|K|$, for each (predicate or function) constant K not in $\bar{P}$;
$N|P_i| = |U_i|_a^M$, for $1 \leq i \leq n$.

Given that $T(U_1, \ldots, U_n)$ obtains by a proper substitution of $U_1, \ldots, U_n$ for $\Phi_1, \ldots, \Phi_n$ in $T(\Phi_1, \ldots, \Phi_n)$, the reader may easily verify (by induction on the form of T) that

$$V_a^M(T(U_1, \ldots, U_n)) = V_a^N(T(P_1, \ldots, P_n)).$$

Thus, by (6.3.7), $V_a^N(T(P_1, \ldots, P_n)) = 1$ and so, since T is a sentence, N is a model of T. On the other hand, by (6.3.8), (6.3.9) and the construction of N, it is readily checked that $N \leq^{\bar{P}} M$ and $N \neq M$. This contradicts the assumption that M is a $\bar{P}$-minimal model of T. ∎

The presented semantics is usually called the *minimal model semantics* for predicate circumscription. Unfortunately, as we shall see, the converse of Theorem 6.6 in general does not hold, so that the semantics is incomplete. Instead of showing this directly, we first provide a complete semantics for predicate circumscription, originally developed by Besnard *et al.* (1989).

Definition 6.7 Let L be a first-order language and suppose that M is a frame for L. A subset S of $|M|^n$ is *definable in* M *with respect to* $a \in As(M)$, iff there is a formula $A(x_1, \ldots, x_n) \in L$, called the *formula defining* S, such that

$$(d_1, \ldots, d_n) \in S \quad \text{iff} \quad V^M_{a(x_1/d_1, \ldots, x_n/d_n)}(A) = 1.$$

A tuple $\bar{S} = (S_1, \ldots, S_m)$ of subsets of $|M|^{n(1)}, \ldots, |M|^{n(m)}$, respectively, is *definable in* M *with respect to* $a \in As(M)$, iff every S_i is definable in M with respect to a. $\bar{S}$ is *definable in* M iff $\bar{S}$ is definable in M with respect to some $a \in As(M)$. ∎

We shall write $M <^{\bar{P}} N$ as an abbreviation for $M \leq^{\bar{P}} N$ and $M \neq N$.

Definition 6.8 Let $T(\bar{P})$, where $\bar{P} = (P_1, \ldots, P_n)$, be a theory. A model M of T is a *weakly $\bar{P}$-minimal model of* T iff there is no model N of T such that $N <^{\bar{P}} M$ and $(N|P_1|, \ldots, N|P_n|)$ is definable in M. ∎

Clearly, every $\bar{P}$-minimal model of T is a weakly $\bar{P}$-minimal model of T. As we shall see, the converse generally does not hold.

The next theorem shows that weakly minimal models provide a sound and complete semantics for predicate circumscription.

Theorem 6.9 (Besnard *et al.* 1989) $\mathrm{CIRC}_{\mathrm{PR}}(T; \bar{P}) \vdash A$ iff A is true in every weakly $\bar{P}$-minimal model of T.

Proof It suffices to show the following: A model M of T is a model of $\overline{\mathrm{CS}}(T; \bar{P})$ iff M is a weakly $\bar{P}$-minimal model of T.

($\Rightarrow$) Let M be a model of $T \cup \overline{\mathrm{CS}}(T; \bar{P})$ and assume on the contrary that M is not weakly $\bar{P}$-minimal. Thus, there is a model N of T such that

$$\mathrm{N} <^{\bar{P}} \mathrm{M} \tag{6.3.10}$$

$$(\mathrm{N}|P_1|, \ldots, \mathrm{N}|P_n|) \text{ is definable in M (with respect to some } \mathrm{a1} \in \mathrm{As(M)}). \tag{6.3.11}$$

Let $A_i(\bar{x})$ be the formula defining $\mathrm{N}|P_i|$ in M. Put $U_i = \lambda\bar{x}.A_i(\bar{x})$ and consider $T(U_1, \ldots, U_n)$. We may assume that $T(U_1, \ldots, U_n)$ obtains by a proper substitution of $U_1, \ldots, U_n$ for $\Phi_1, \ldots, \Phi_n$ in $T(\Phi_1, \ldots, \Phi_n)$ since, otherwise, it is always possible to rename variables in $A_1, \ldots, A_n$, eventually changing the assignment a1, in such a way that the substitution is proper and (6.3.10)–(6.3.11) hold. Given this, since M is a model of $\overline{\mathrm{CS}}(T, \bar{P})$, we infer

$$\mathrm{V}^{\mathrm{M}}_{\mathrm{a1}}([T(U_1, \ldots, U_n) \wedge \bigwedge_{i=1}^{n} [\forall\bar{x}.U_i(\bar{x}) \supset P_i(\bar{x})]] \supset \bigwedge_{i=1}^{n} [\forall\bar{x}.P_i(\bar{x}) \supset U_i(\bar{x})]) = 1 \tag{6.3.12}$$

Assume that k(i) is the arity of P_i. We write $\mathrm{a1}(\bar{x}/\bar{\mathrm{d}}_i)$ for $\mathrm{a1}(x_1/\mathrm{d}_1, \ldots, x_{\mathrm{k(i)}}/\mathrm{d}_{\mathrm{k(i)}})$. Employing (6.3.11), one verifies that

$$\mathrm{V}^{\mathrm{M}}_{\mathrm{a1}(\bar{x}/\bar{\mathrm{d}}_i)}(U_i(\bar{x})) = \mathrm{V}^{\mathrm{N}}_{\mathrm{a1}(\bar{x}/\bar{\mathrm{d}}_i)}(P_i(\bar{x})) \tag{6.3.13}$$

for each $1 \le i \le n$ and each $(\mathrm{d}_1, \ldots, \mathrm{d}_{\mathrm{k(i)}}) \in |\mathrm{M}|^{\mathrm{k(i)}}$.

Because $\mathrm{N} <^{\bar{P}} \mathrm{M}$, we have $\mathrm{N}|K| = \mathrm{M}|K|$, for each constant K not in $P_1, \ldots, P_n$. From this and (6.3.13), it is easily checked that $\mathrm{V}^{\mathrm{M}}_{\mathrm{a1}}(T(U_1, \ldots, U_n)) = \mathrm{V}^{\mathrm{N}}_{\mathrm{a1}}(T(P_1, \ldots, P_n))$ and so, since N is a model of $T(P_1, \ldots, P_n)$,

$$\mathrm{V}^{\mathrm{M}}_{\mathrm{a1}}(T(U_1, \ldots, U_n)) = 1. \tag{6.3.14}$$

On the other hand, since $\mathrm{N} <^{\bar{P}} \mathrm{M}$, $\mathrm{V}^{\mathrm{N}}_{\mathrm{a}}(P_i(\bar{x})) = 1$ implies $\mathrm{V}^{\mathrm{M}}_{\mathrm{a}}(P_i(\bar{x})) = 1$, for each $\mathrm{a} \in \mathrm{As(M)}$ and each $1 \le i \le n$. Thus, in view of (6.3.13), $\mathrm{V}^{\mathrm{M}}_{\mathrm{a1}}(\forall\bar{x}.U_i(\bar{x}) \supset P_i(\bar{x})) = 1$, for $1 \le i \le n$. In consequence, by (6.3.12) and (6.3.14), we have $\mathrm{V}^{\mathrm{M}}_{\mathrm{a1}}(\forall\bar{x}.P_i(\bar{x}) \supset U_i(\bar{x})) = 1$, for $1 \le i \le n$, and so, $\mathrm{V}^{\mathrm{M}}_{\mathrm{a1}}(\forall\bar{x}.P_i(\bar{x}) \equiv U_i(\bar{x})) = 1$, for $1 \le i \le n$. Given this, together with (6.3.13), we obtain $\mathrm{N}|P_i| = \mathrm{M}|P_i|$, for $1 \le i \le n$. A contradiction with (6.3.10).

($\Leftarrow$) Similar to the proof of Theorem 6.6.

∎

Our next task is to show that the class of weakly minimal models properly extends that of minimal models. For this purpose, we shall need the following notion.

Definition 6.10 Let T be a theory over a first-order language L. We say that T *admits quantifier elimination* iff for each $A \in L$ there is a quantifier free formula $B \in L$ such that $T \vdash A \equiv B$. ∎

A *simple existential formula* is any formula of the form $\exists x A$, where A is quantifier free. The following result is well-known (see, for example, Shoenfield 1967):

Theorem 6.11 Let $T \subseteq L$ be a first-order theory. If for every simple existential formula $A \in L$ there is a quantifier free formula $B \in L$ such that $T \vdash A \equiv B$, then T admits quantifier elimination. ▮

As a simple consequence of Theorem 6.11, we have:

Corollary 6.12 Let $T \subseteq L$ be a first-order theory. If for every simple existential formula $A \in L$ such that $A = \exists x C$, where C is a conjunction of literals, there is a quantifier free formula $B \in L$ such that $T \vdash A \equiv B$, then T admits quantifier elimination.

Proof By predicate logic and Theorem 6.11. ▮

We are now ready to show that the class of weakly minimal models properly extends the class of minimal models.

Example 6.13† Let L be a first-order language over the alphabet consisting of a one-place predicate constant P, a one-place function constant s, an object constant b, truth constants *True* and *False*, and the equality constant '='. Suppose that T is the theory given by

$$P(b)$$
$$\forall xy.P(x) \wedge [s(x) = y \vee s(y) = x] \supset P(y)$$
$$\forall x.b \neq s(x)$$
$$\forall xyz.[s(x) = z \wedge s(y) = z] \supset x = y$$
$$\forall xyz.[s(x) = y \wedge s(x) = z] \supset z = y$$

Let $\mathbf{N} = \{0, 1, 2, \ldots\}$ and $\mathbf{N}' = \{0', 1', 2', \ldots\}$. Consider a frame M for L such that

$$|\mathrm{M}| = \mathbf{N} \cup \mathbf{N}'; \ \mathrm{M}|b| = 0; \ \mathrm{M}|P| = |\mathrm{M}|;$$
$$\mathrm{M}|s| = \text{the successor function in } \mathbf{N} \text{ and in } \mathbf{N}'.$$

It is immediately seen that M is a model of T. Consider now a frame N for L such that $|\mathrm{N}| = |\mathrm{M}|$, $\mathrm{N}|b| = 0$, $\mathrm{N}|s| = \mathrm{M}|s|$ and $\mathrm{N}|P| = \mathbf{N}$. Clearly, N is also a model of T and $\mathrm{N} <^P \mathrm{M}$. Therefore, M is not a P-minimal model of T. However, M is a weakly P-minimal model of T. To show this, notice first that N is the only model of T, different from M, which is a P-submodel of M. Therefore, if M were not a weakly P-minimal model of T, then $\mathrm{N}|P|$ (i.e. $\mathbf{N}$) would be definable in M. But this is impossible by virtue of the following:

Lemma 6.13.1 If $\mathrm{S} \subseteq |\mathrm{M}|$ is definable in M, then either S or $|\mathrm{M}| - \mathrm{S}$ is finite.

Proof Suppose that $\mathrm{S} \subseteq |\mathrm{M}|$ is definable in M, i.e. there is a formula $A \in L$ and an assignment $\mathrm{a} \in \mathrm{As}(\mathrm{M})$ such that

$$\mathrm{d} \in \mathrm{S} \quad \text{iff} \quad \mathrm{V}^{\mathrm{M}}_{\mathrm{a(x/d)}}(A) = 1.$$

By straightforward induction on the form of A, one verifies that the lemma holds, provided that A is quantifier free. Therefore, to complete the proof, it suffices to show that for each $A \in L$ there is a quantifier free formula B such that for each $\mathrm{d} \in |\mathrm{M}|$, $\mathrm{V}^{\mathrm{M}}_{\mathrm{a(x/d)}}(A) = \mathrm{V}^{\mathrm{M}}_{\mathrm{a(x/d)}}(B)$. This, in turn, will be proved if we show that the theory $T_{\mathrm{M}} = \{A \in L : \mathrm{M} \models A\}$ admits quantifier elimination. Obviously, T_{M} is deductively closed. Thus, by Corollary 6.12, it is enough to show the following: For each $A \in L$ such that $A = \exists x.l_1 \wedge \cdots \wedge l_n$, where $l_1, \ldots, l_n$ are literals, there is a quantifier free formula B such that $(A \equiv B) \in T_{\mathrm{M}}$.

† This example is a slight modification of an example from Besnard *et al.* (1989.

Let $A = \exists x . l_1 \wedge \cdots \wedge l_n$, where $l_1, \ldots, l_n$ are literals. Since $\exists x(C \wedge D)$ is logically equivalent to $(\exists x C) \wedge D$, provided that x has no free occurrences in D, we may assume that each l_j contains x. We shall write $s^0(\alpha)$ for α and $s^{k+1}(\alpha)$ for $s(s^k(\alpha))$, $k \geq 0$, where α is any term.

We begin by the following observations:

(i) Each term, over the alphabet of L, containing x is of the form $s^k(x)$, for some $k \geq 0$.
(ii) If some l_p, $1 \leq p \leq n$, is $P(\alpha)$, then A is equivalent in T_M either to $\exists x . l_1 \wedge \cdots \wedge l_{p-1} \wedge l_{p+1} \wedge \cdots \wedge l_n$ or to *True* (if $n = 1$).
(iii) If some l_p is $\neg P(\alpha)$ then A is equivalent in T_M to *False*.

It follows, therefore, that we may assume that A is of the form

$$\exists x[s^{i1}(x) = \alpha_1 \wedge \cdots \wedge s^{ik}(x) = \alpha_k \wedge s^{j1}(x) \neq \beta_1 \wedge \cdots \wedge s^{jl}(x) \neq \beta_l] \tag{6.3.15}$$

where $\alpha_1, \ldots, \alpha_k, \beta_1, \ldots, \beta_l$ are terms of L and $l + k > 0$.

Notice that the following equivalences hold in T_M:

$$\alpha_i = \alpha_j \equiv s^k(\alpha_i) = s^k(\alpha_j)$$
$$\alpha_i \neq \alpha_j \equiv s^k(\alpha_i) \neq s^k(\alpha_j)$$

for any terms α_i, α_j and any $k \geq 0$. Thus (6.3.15) is equivalent in T_M to

$$\exists x[s^p(x) = \alpha'_1 \wedge \cdots \wedge s^p(x) = \alpha'_k \wedge s^p(x) \neq \beta'_1 \wedge \cdots \wedge s^p(x) \neq \beta'_l] \tag{6.3.16}$$

where $p = \max\{i1, \ldots, ik, j1, \ldots, jl\}$, $\alpha'_j = s^{p-ij}(\alpha_j)$ and $\beta'_m = s^{p-jm}(\beta_m)$. Observe further:

(iv) If some α'_j contains x and α'_j is different from $s^p(x)$, then (6.3.16) is equivalent in T_M to *False*.
(v) If some α'_j contains x and α'_j is $s^p(x)$, then (6.3.16) is equivalent in T_M to a formula obtainable from (6.3.16) by removing the literal $s^p(x) = \alpha'_j$. In particular, if $s^p(x) = \alpha'_j$ is the only literal in (6.3.16), i.e. if $k = 1$ and $l = 0$, then (6.3.16) is equivalent in T_M to *True*.
(vi) If some β'_j contains x and β'_j is $s^p(x)$, then (6.3.16) is equivalent in T_M to *False*.
(vii) If some β'_j contains x and β'_j is different from $s^p(x)$, then (6.3.16) is equivalent in T_M to a formula obtainable from (6.3.16) by removing $s^p(x) \neq \beta'_j$.

In view of (iv)–(vii), we may assume that A is of the form (6.3.16), where none of $\alpha'_1, \ldots, \alpha'_k, \beta'_1, \ldots, \beta'_l$ contains x.

Now, there are three cases to consider:

Case 1 $k > 0$ and $l > 0$. Then (6.3.16) is equivalent in T_M to $\alpha'_1 = \alpha'_2 \wedge \cdots \wedge \alpha'_1 = \alpha'_k \wedge \alpha'_1 \neq \beta'_1 \wedge \cdots \wedge \alpha'_1 \neq \beta'_l$. (Notice that this formula is quantifier-free.)
Case 2 $k = 0$ and $l > 0$. Then (6.3.16) is equivalent in T_M to *True*.
Case 3 $k > 0$ and $l = 0$. Then, since $s^p(x) \neq s^{p-1}(b)$ is equivalent in T_M to *True*, (6.3.16) is equivalent in T_M to

$$\exists x[s^p(x) = \alpha'_1 \wedge \cdots \wedge s^p(x) = \alpha'_k \wedge s^p(x) \neq s^{p-1}(b)].$$

Thus this case reduces to Case 1.

This shows that the theory T_m admits quantifier elimination and so the lemma is proved. ■

▮

This example can be used to show that the minimal semantics for predicate circumscription is incomplete. To this end, consider the formula

$$A = \forall x . P(x) \supset [x = b \vee \exists y . s(y) = x].$$

It is easily checked that A is true in every $\bar{P}$-minimal model of T. However, since A is not true in M, A is not derivable by circumscribing P in T (in view of Theorem 6.9).

6.3.3 Consistency of predicate circumscription

It is reasonable to ask whether predicate circumscription preserves consistency. Unfortunately, as the next example shows, this is not always the case.

Example 6.14 (Etherington *et al.* 1985) Let T consist of:

$$\exists x . P(x) \wedge [\forall y . P(y) \supset x \neq s(y)]$$
$$\forall x . P(x) \supset P(s(x))$$
$$\forall xy . s(x) = s(y) \supset x = y.$$

Let $\mathbf{N} = \{0, 1, 2 \ldots\}$. Consider a frame M, where $|\mathrm{M}| = \mathbf{N}$, $\mathrm{M}|P| = \mathbf{N}$ and $\mathrm{M}|s|$ is the successor function. It is easily seen that M is a model of T, so that T is consistent. However, $\mathrm{CIRC}_{\mathrm{PR}}(T, P)$ is inconsistent: circumscribing P in T and putting $\{\Phi \leftarrow \lambda x[P(x) \wedge \exists y . x = s(y) \wedge P(y)]\}$, one may derive $\forall x . P(x) \supset \exists y[P(y) \wedge x = s(y)]$, which contradicts the first axiom (the reader is asked to perform appropriate calculations). ▮

In view of this example, it is natural to seek classes of theories for which predicate circumscription preserves consistency.

Definition 6.15 (Etherington *et al.* 1985) A theory T is *well-founded with respect to a finite tuple of predicate constants* $\bar{P}$ iff each model of T has a P-submodel which is a $\bar{P}$-minimal model of T. T is *well-founded* iff T is well-founded with respect to every finite tuple of predicate constants $\bar{P}$. ▮

In view of Theorem 6.6, we immediately have:

Theorem 6.16 Assume that a theory T is consistent. If T is well-founded with respect to $\bar{P}$, then $\mathrm{CIRC}_{\mathrm{PR}}(T; \bar{P})$ is consistent. If T is well-founded, then $\mathrm{CIRC}_{\mathrm{PR}}(T; \bar{P})$ is consistent with respect to every finite $\bar{P}$. ▮

While a complete syntactic characterization of well-founded theories is an open problem, the following partial result is known. Recall that a theory is said to be universal iff the prenex normal form of each of its axioms contains no existential quantifier. (Obviously, any finite universal theory is logically equivalent to a sentence of the form $\forall x_1 \ldots x_n . A$, where A is quantifier free.)

Theorem 6.17 (Etherington *et al.* 1985) Universal theories are well-founded with respect to every finite tuple $\bar{P}$ of predicate constants. ▮

Corollary 6.18 If T is a consistent universal theory, then $\mathrm{CIRC}_{\mathrm{PR}}(T; \bar{P})$ is consistent for any finite tuple $\bar{P}$ of predicate constants. ▮

This result was extended by Lifschitz (1986).

Definition 6.19 A theory is *almost universal with respect* to $\bar{P} = (P_1, \ldots, P_n)$ iff it is logically equivalent to a sentence of the form $\forall x_1 \ldots x_n . A$, where no predicate constant $P \in \bar{P}$ has a positive occurrence within A in the scope of quantifiers occurring in A. ▮

Clearly, every universal theory is almost universal with respect to any finite $\bar{P}$.

Theorem 6.20 (Lifschitz 1986)† If a theory T is almost universal with respect to $\bar{P}$, then T is well-founded with respect to $\bar{P}$. ▮

Corollary 6.21 If a theory T is consistent and almost universal with respect to $\bar{P}$, then $\mathrm{CIRC}_{\mathbf{PR}}(T; \bar{P})$ is consistent. ▮

6.3.4 Expressive power of predicate circumscription

We now discuss expressive power of predicate circumscription with respect to well-founded theories. All the results presented below are due to Etherington *et al.* (1985). Since circumscription minimizes circumscribed predicates, one may expect that it never yields a new positive ground instance of such a predicate. For well-founded theories, this is indeed the case.

Theorem 6.22 (Etherington *et al.* 1985) If T is a well-founded theory, $P \in \bar{P}$ is an n-ary predicate constant and $\bar{\alpha}$ is an n-tuple of ground terms, then

$$\mathrm{CIRC}_{\mathbf{PR}}(T; \bar{P}) \vdash P(\bar{\alpha}) \quad \text{iff} \quad T \vdash P(\bar{\alpha}).$$

▮

Before providing the next result, it will be instructive to consider a simple example.

Example 6.23 Let T be the following well-founded theory:

$$Bird(Tweety)$$
$$\forall x . Bird(x) \wedge \neg Ab(x) \supset Flies(x).$$

Circumscribing Ab in T, one may expect to derive $Flies(Tweety)$. Unfortunately, this is impossible. To see why, consider a frame M such that $|\mathrm{M}| = \{\mathrm{TWEETY}\}$, $\mathrm{M}|Bird| = \mathrm{M}|Ab| = \{\mathrm{TWEETY}\}$ and $\mathrm{M}|Flies| = \{\ \}$. It is clear that M is a model of T. The problem, however, is that M is an Ab-minimal model of T (we cannot make $\mathrm{M}|Ab|$ smaller preserving T and $\mathrm{M}|Flies|$). Thus, since $Flies(Tweety)$ is false in M, this formula cannot be derived by circumscribing Ab in T (in view of Theorem 6.6). ▮

Example 6.23 illustrates a more general phenomenon: **neither positive nor negative new ground instances of uncircumscribed predicates can be derived by predicate circumscription with respect to well-founded theories.**

Theorem 6.24 (Etherington *et al.* 1985) If T is a well-founded theory, $P \notin \bar{P}$ is an n-ary predicate constant and $\bar{\alpha}$ is an n-tuple of ground terms, then

(i) $\mathrm{CIRC}_{\mathbf{PR}}(T; \bar{P}) \vdash P(\bar{\alpha})$ iff $T \vdash P(\bar{\alpha})$
(ii) $\mathrm{CIRC}_{\mathbf{PR}}(T; \bar{P}) \vdash \neg P(\bar{\alpha})$ iff $T \vdash \neg P(\bar{\alpha})$.

▮

Combining Theorems 6.22 and 6.24, it is clear that the only new ground literals that

† Actually, Lifschitz proved this theorem for a more general version of circumscription, namely, *second-order circumscription*, where the notion of well-foundedness is slightly reformulated (see section 6.5, Definition 6.44). However, there is no difficulty in modifying his proof for the purpose of predicate circumscription.

can be obtained by applying predicate circumscription to well-founded theories are negative instances of circumscribed predicates. This is indeed a very pessimistic result, showing that predicate circumscription is generally too weak to properly handle non-monotonic rules.

One may be tempted to strengthen predicate circumscription by allowing to circumscribe within a part of a theory, rather than within the theory itself. Technically, this modification amounts to defining the set of theorems derivable by circumscribing $\bar{P} = (P_1, \ldots, P_n)$ in T as the set of formulae monotonically derivable from $T \cup \overline{\mathrm{CS}}(T'; \bar{P})$, where T' is a fixed subset of T. If one adopts such a generalization, which, as a matter of fact, was employed in one example presented by McCarthy (1980), Theorems 6.22 and 6.24 are no longer true. For instance, taking the theory T from Example 6.23 and letting $T' = \{Bird(Tweety)\}$, circumscription of Ab in T will yield

$$[Bird(Tweety) \wedge [\forall x . \Phi(x) \supset Ab(x)]] \supset [\forall x . Ab(x) \supset \Phi(x)].$$

From this, putting $\{\Phi \leftarrow \lambda x . False\}$, we may derive $\neg Ab(Tweety)$ and hence $Flies(Tweety)$.

It is now well-recognized that the above generalization is ill-motivated in two respects (Etherington 1988). Firstly, its semantics is unclear, so that it is difficult to predict what this formalism actually computes. Secondly, one has to be extremely careful to preserve consistency, because replacing $T(\Phi_1, \ldots, \Phi_n)$ by a weaker $T'(\Phi_1, \ldots, \Phi_n)$ generally admits too small extensions of the predicates being minimized. For example, circumscribing P in $\{P(a), Q(a)\}$ and letting $T' = \{Q(a)\}$, allows $\neg P(a)$ to be derived despite the fact that $P(a)$ is actually known.

Another group of limitations of predicate circumscription concerns equality. In particular, this formalism is ill-suited to handle two important forms of closed world reasoning: the *unique names assumption* and the *domain closure assumption.*

The unique names assumption was introduced in the context of databases (Reiter 1980b). It states that any pair of distinct ground terms, not specified as identical, represents different individuals. For instance, given $Bird(Tweety) \wedge Bird(father(Opus))$, the unique names assumption allows us to conclude $Tweety \neq Opus$, $Tweety \neq father(Opus)$, $Opus \neq father(Tweety)$, etc.

A natural way to formalize the unique names assumption is to circumscribe the equality predicate.† Unfortunately, as the next theorem shows, no new information can be obtained by this circumscription.

Theorem 6.25 (Etherington *et al.* 1985) For any theory T and any formula A, $\mathrm{CIRC}_{\mathrm{PR}}(T; =) \vdash A$ iff $T \vdash A$. ∎

Theorem 6.25 is not surprising. It immediately follows from Theorem 6.9 by observing that each model of T is a $(=)$-minimal (and hence a weakly $(=)$-minimal) model of T.

Since circumscription of the equality predicate alone yields nothing new, one might try to capture the unique names assumption by circumscribing a tuple of predicates. The following theorem shows that, for well-founded theories at least, this method fails.

Theorem 6.26 (Etherington *et al.* 1985) If T is a well-founded theory, α and β are ground terms, and $\bar{P}$ is a finite tuple of predicate constants, then

† Recall that circumscribing the equality predicate in a theory T, we always assume that T explicitly includes its equality axioms.

(i) $\text{CIRC}_{\text{PR}}(T; \bar{P}) \vdash \alpha = \beta$ iff $T \vdash \alpha = \beta$
(ii) $\text{CIRC}_{\text{PR}}(T; \bar{P}) \vdash \alpha \neq \beta$ iff $T \vdash \alpha \neq \beta$.

∎

The domain closure assumption, with respect to a theory T, is the assumption that the only individuals to be considered are those forced by the Herbrand universe of T. In the simplest situation, i.e. when T has a finite Herbrand universe $\{c_1, \ldots, c_n\}$, the domain closure assumption can be formalized by employing the *domain closure axiom for T* (Reiter 1980b):

$$\forall x . x = c_1 \lor \cdots \lor x = c_n.$$

It turns out that no such axiom can be derived by predicate circumscription for well-founded theories:

Theorem 6.27 (Etherington *et al.* 1985) If T is a well-founded theory, $\alpha_1, \ldots, \alpha_n$ are ground terms, and $\bar{P}$ is a finite tuple of predicate constants, then

$$\text{CIRC}_{\text{PR}}(T; \bar{P}) \vdash \forall x . x = \alpha_1 \lor \cdots \lor x = \alpha_n$$
$$\text{iff } T \vdash \forall x . x = \alpha_1 \lor \cdots \lor x = \alpha_n.$$

∎

A circumscriptive approach to the domain closure assumption will be discussed in section 6.7.

As follows from our exposition, predicate circumscription is relatively weak. The most pessimistic result is that the formalism is generally incapable to deal with non-monotonic rules (Theorem 6.24). In the next section we shall present a more powerful version of circumscription, strong enough to overcome this difficulty.

Some connections between predicate circumscription and the notion of implicit definition in mathematical logic are studied in Doyle (1985).

6.4 FORMULA CIRCUMSCRIPTION

To eliminate some of the limitations of predicate circumscription, McCarthy (1984) introduced a more powerful circumscriptive logic, called *formula circumscription*. The major strength of the new formalism is its ability to deal properly with non-monotonic rules.

Formula circumscription extends its predecessor in three ways:

(i) The new logic allows us to minimize extensions of arbitrary predicate expressions (without parameters), treating the minimization of predicate constants as a special case.
(ii) The process of minimization is expressed by a special circumscription axiom, viewed as a single second-order sentence, rather than a set of first-order formulae.
(iii) The extensions of arbitrarily chosen predicate constants, also of those not occurring in the minimized expression, may be varied during the minimization.

It is the last of these modifications that gives formula circumscription its power. The employment of a circumscription axiom instead of a circumscription schema provides some additional strength, but is not essential. In section 6.5, we shall present a schema-based variant of formula circumscription which, although slightly weaker, is adequate for many practical applications. Finally, the possibility of circumscribing predicate expressions, rather than predicate constants, does not increase the expressiveness of the new logic. As we shall see, the effect of circumscribing a predicate expression can always be obtained by circumscribing a predicate constant, provided that the extensions of arbitrary predicates are allowed to vary.

In this section, the term *theory* refers to a finite set of first- or second-order sentences. As usual, we shall not distinguish between a theory and the conjunction of its members. The term *predicate expression* will always refer to a first-order predicate expression without parameters. Recall that any n-ary predicate constant P can be identified with the predicate expression $\lambda x_1 \ldots x_n . P(x_1, \ldots, x_n)$. Similarly, any n-ary predicate variable Φ may be identified with $\lambda x_1 \ldots x_n .\ \Phi(x_1, \ldots, x_n)$. (See the discussion following Definition 1.82, Chapter 1.)

Let $T(\bar{P}, \bar{Q})$ be a theory some of whose predicate constants are among $\bar{P} = (P_1, \ldots, P_n)$ and $\bar{Q} = (Q_1, \ldots, Q_m)$. Let U be a predicate expression of the form $\lambda \bar{x} . E(\bar{P}, \bar{x})$, where predicate constants and free individual variables of E are precisely $\bar{P}$ and $\bar{x} = (x_1, \ldots, x_k)$. How can we express that the extension of U is minimal with respect to T, provided that the extensions of $P_1, \ldots, P_n$ are allowed to vary in the process of minimization? A natural solution is to use the sentence

$$\forall \bar{\Phi} \{[T(\bar{\Phi}, \bar{Q}) \wedge [\forall \bar{x} . E(\bar{\Phi}, \bar{x}) \supset E(\bar{P}, \bar{x})]] \supset [\forall \bar{x} . E(\bar{P}, \bar{x}) \supset E(\bar{\Phi}, \bar{x})]\} \tag{6.4.1}$$

where $\bar{\Phi} = (\Phi_1, \ldots, \Phi_n)$ is a tuple of predicate variables with the same arities as $P_1, \ldots, P_n$, respectively, and $T(\bar{\Phi}, \bar{Q})$ (respectively, $E(\bar{\Phi}, \bar{x})$) obtains from $T(\bar{P}, \bar{Q})$ (respectively, $E(\bar{P}, \bar{x})$) by replacing each occurrence of each P_i by Φ_i.

Suppose now that we want to express that the extension of U is minimal with respect to T under the additional assumption that the extensions of $Q_1, \ldots, Q_m$ are also allowed to vary in the process of minimization. A little reflexion should convince the reader that this can be achieved by strengthening (6.4.1) to

$$\forall \bar{\Phi} \bar{\Psi} \{[T(\bar{\Phi}, \bar{\Psi}) \wedge [\forall x . \bar{E}(\bar{\Phi}, \bar{x}) \supset E(\bar{P}, \bar{x})]] \supset [\forall \bar{x} . E(\bar{P}, \bar{x}) \supset E(\bar{\Phi}, \bar{x})]\} \tag{6.4.2}$$

where $\bar{\Psi} = (\Psi_1, \ldots, \Psi_m)$ is a tuple of predicate variables with the same arities as $Q_1, \ldots, Q_m$, respectively, and $T(\bar{\Phi}, \bar{\Psi})$ is the result of replacing each occurrence of each Q_i, in $T(\bar{\Phi}, \bar{Q})$, by Ψ_i.

Definition 6.28 (McCarthy 1984)† Let $T(\bar{P}, \bar{Q})$ be a theory, some of whose predicate constants are among disjoint tuples $\bar{P} = (P_1, \ldots, P_n)$ and $\bar{Q} = (Q_1, \ldots, Q_m)$. Suppose that $E(\bar{P}, \bar{x})$ is a first-order formula whose predicate constants and free individual variables are precisely $P_1, \ldots, P_n$ and $\bar{x} = (x_1, \ldots, x_k)$, respectively. Let U be a predicate expression of the form $\lambda \bar{x} . E(\bar{P}, \bar{x})$. The *formula circumscription of U in $T(\bar{P}, \bar{Q})$ with variable $\bar{Q}$*, denoted $\mathrm{CIRC}_{\mathrm{FC}}(T; U; \bar{Q})$, is the second-order sentence

$$T(\bar{P}, \bar{Q}) \wedge \forall \bar{\Phi} \bar{\Psi} \{[T(\bar{\Phi}, \bar{\Psi}) \wedge [\forall \bar{x} .\ E(\bar{\Phi}, \bar{x}) \supset E(\bar{P}, \bar{x})]] \supset \\ \supset [\forall \bar{x} . E(\bar{P}, \bar{x}) \supset E(\bar{\Phi}, \bar{x})]\} \tag{6.4.3}$$

where $\bar{\Phi}$ and $\bar{\Psi}$ are tuples of predicate variables corresponding to $\bar{P}$ and $\bar{Q}$, respectively. ▮

† This definition is slightly different but equivalent to that provided in McCarthy (1984).

If the expression being circumscribed contains the equality predicate, or, if this predicate is allowed to vary in the process of minimization, we shall always assume that the theory under consideration includes its equality axioms.

There still remains the problem of specifying the set of formulae considered as consequences of formula circumscription. Following Lifschitz (1985b) we adopt the following semantic approach. In what follows, the symbol '$\models$' denotes the entailment relation of classical second-order logic.

Definition 6.29 We say that a formula A is a *consequence of formula circumscription of U in T with variable $\bar{Q}$* iff $\mathrm{CIRC_{FC}}(T; U; \bar{Q}) \models A$. If A is entailed by $\mathrm{CIRC_{FC}}(T; U; \bar{Q})$, we shall also say that *A follows from* $\mathrm{CIRC_{FC}}(T; U; \bar{Q})$. ▮

In view of Theorem 1.85 (Chapter 1), the following result holds:

$$\forall \Phi_1 \dots \Phi_n A(\Phi_1, \dots, \Phi_n) \models A(U_1, \dots, U_n)$$

where $A(U_1, \dots, U_n)$ obtains from $A(\Phi_1, \dots, \Phi_n)$ by the proper substitution of $U_1, \dots, U_n$ for $\Phi_1, \dots, \Phi_n$. We extensively use this fact in forthcoming examples.

Example 6.30 Let $T = \{Red(a) \wedge Green(b) \wedge Blue(c)\}$.
We circumscribe the predicate expression $U = \lambda x . E(Red, Green, x)$, where $E(Red, Green, x) = Red(x) \vee Green(x)$, in T with empty $\bar{Q}$.

$$\begin{aligned}\mathrm{CIRC_{FC}}(T; U; ()) = {} & [Red(a) \wedge Green(b) \wedge Blue(c)] \\ & \wedge \forall \Phi_1 \Phi_2 \{[[\Phi_1(a) \wedge \Phi_2(b) \wedge Blue(c)] \wedge \\ & \wedge [\forall x . \Phi_1(x) \vee \Phi_2(x) \supset Red(x) \vee Green(x)]] \supset \\ & \supset [\forall x . Red(x) \vee Green(x) \supset \Phi_1(x) \vee \Phi_2(x)]\}.\end{aligned}$$

Substituting $\{\Phi_1 \leftarrow \lambda x . x = a\}$ and $\{\Phi_2 \leftarrow \lambda x . x = b\}$, we obtain $\mathrm{CIRC_{FC}}(T; U; ()) \models F$, where

$$\begin{aligned}F = {} & [Red(a) \wedge Green(b) \wedge Blue(c)] \wedge [[a = a \wedge b = b \wedge Blue(c)] \wedge \\ & \wedge [\forall x . x = a \vee x = b \supset Red(x) \vee Green(x)]] \supset \\ & \supset [\forall x . Red(x) \vee Green(x) \supset x = a \vee x = b].\end{aligned}$$

Now, by straightforward verification, we infer $F \models G$, where

$$G = \forall x . Red(x) \vee Green(x) \supset x = a \vee x = b.$$

Thus, since $A \models B$ and $B \models C$ imply $A \models C$, we get

$$\mathrm{CIRC_{FC}}(T; U; ()) \models \forall x . Red(x) \vee Green(x) \supset x = a \vee x = b.$$

In conclusion, $\forall x . Red(x) \vee Green(x) \supset x = a \vee x = b$ is a consequence of circumscribing $\lambda x . Red(x) \vee Green(x)$ in T with empty $\bar{Q}$. ▮

As McCarthy (1984) observed and Etherington (1988) formally proved, the possibility of circumscribing predicate expressions, rather than predicate constants, does not strengthen the new formalism. Instead or circumscribing $\lambda \bar{x} . E(\bar{P}, \bar{x})$ in a theory T, one can always introduce a new predicate constant, say R, and circumscribe R in the theory $T \cup \{\forall \bar{x} . R(\bar{x}) \equiv E(\bar{P}, \bar{x})\}$. This works, provided that all predicate constants from $\bar{P}$ are allowed to vary. The details follow.

Theorem 6.31 (Etherington 1988) Let $T \subseteq L$ be a theory, where L is a fixed first- or second-order language over an alphabet AL . Let $E(\bar{P}, \bar{x}) \in L$ and suppose that $T' = T \cup \{\forall \bar{x} . R(\bar{x}) \equiv E(\bar{P}, \bar{x})\}$, where R is a predicate constant not in AL . Finally, let

$U = \lambda\bar{x}.E(\bar{P}, \bar{x})$. For any $A \in L$ and any tuple $\bar{Q}$ of predicate constants from AL

$$\text{CIRC}_{\text{FC}}(T; U; \bar{Q}) \models A \quad \text{iff} \quad \text{CIRC}_{\text{FC}}(T'; R; (\bar{Q}, \bar{P})) \models A.$$

∎

This result crucially depends on the fact that predicate constants occurring in the minimized expression are allowed to vary. Accordingly, a similar technique, i.e. the introduction of a new predicate constant and the appropriate definition, is generally useless to minimize arbitrary expressions in the framework of predicate circumscription (see Etherington 1988, for details).

As we remarked, formula circumscription is sufficiently strong to handle non-monotonic rules.

Example 6.32 Reconsider the theory from Example 6.23:

$$T = \{Bird(Tweety) \wedge [\forall x. Bird(x) \wedge \neg Ab(x) \supset Flies(x)]\}.$$

We circumscribe Ab in T. Since our intention is to derive $Flies(Tweety)$, the predicate constant $Flies$ should be taken as variable.

$$\begin{aligned} \text{CIRC}_{\text{FC}}(T; Ab; Flies) = T \wedge \forall\Phi\Psi\{&[Bird(Tweety) \wedge \\ &\wedge [\forall x. Bird(x) \wedge \neg\Phi(x) \supset \Psi(x)] \wedge \\ &\wedge [\forall x. \Phi(x) \supset Ab(x)]] \supset [\forall x. Ab(x) \supset \Phi(x)]\}. \end{aligned}$$

The next step is to make appropriate substitutions for Φ and Ψ. We want all objects to be normal. Thus, we put

$$\{\Phi \leftarrow \lambda x. False\}.$$

Similarly, since we want the fliers to be all birds, we put

$$\{\Psi \leftarrow \lambda x. Bird(x)\}.$$

Making these substitutions and simplifying, we easily obtain

$$\text{CIRC}_{\text{FC}}(T; Ab; Flies) \models \forall x \neg Ab(x)$$

and hence

$$\text{CIRC}_{\text{FC}}(T; Ab; Flies) \models \neg Ab(Tweety) \quad \text{and}$$
$$\text{CIRC}_{\text{FC}}(T; Ab; Flies) \models Flies(Tweety).$$

∎

Semantic characterization of formula circumscription is based on the following notions.

Definition 6.33 (Etherington 1988) Suppose that $T(\bar{P}, \bar{Q})$, $\bar{P}$, $\bar{Q}$, $E(\bar{P}, \bar{x})$ and U are as in Definition 6.28. Let M and N be models of T. We say that M is a $(U; \bar{Q})$-*submodel of* N, written $\text{M} \leq^{(U;\bar{Q})} \text{N}$, iff

(i) $|\text{M}| = |\text{N}|$;
(ii) $\text{M}|K| = \text{N}|K|$, for every constant K not in $(\bar{P}, \bar{Q})$;
(iii) $\text{M}|U| \subseteq \text{N}|U|$. ($\text{M}|U|$ (resp. $\text{N}|U|$) is the extension of U in M (resp. N).)

We write $\text{M} <^{(U;\bar{Q})} \text{N}$ iff $\text{M} \leq^{(U;\bar{Q})} \text{N}$ but not $\text{N} \leq^{(U;\bar{Q})} \text{M}$.

A model M of T is $(U; \bar{Q})$-*minimal* iff T has no model N such that $\text{N} <^{(U;\bar{Q})} \text{M}$. ∎

It may happen, if M and N differ only on how they interpret predicate constants in

$\bar{Q}$, that $M \leq^{(U;\bar{Q})} N$, $N \leq^{(U;\bar{Q})} M$ and $M \neq N$. Therefore, $\leq^{(U;\bar{Q})}$ need not be anti-symmetric and hence it is not necessarily a partial order. However, $\leq^{(U;\bar{Q})}$ is a *pre-order* (transitive and reflexive) and thus it makes sense to speak about minimality with respect to $\leq^{(U;\bar{Q})}$, as indicated in Definition 6.33.

For any theory T, we denote by $\text{MOD}(T)$ the class of all models of T. We denote by $\text{MOD}^{(U;\bar{Q})}(T)$ the class of all $(U;\bar{Q})$-minimal models of T. The following result is easy to verify:

Theorem 6.34 $\text{MOD}(\text{CIRC}_{\text{FC}}(T; U; \bar{Q})) = \text{MOD}^{(U;\bar{Q})}(T)$. ∎

Corollary 6.35 $\text{CIRC}_{\text{FC}}(T; U; \bar{Q}) \models A$ iff A is true in every $(U;\bar{Q})$-minimal model of T. ∎

Formula circumscription inherits general limitations of its predecessor as regards the equality predicate. In particular:

Theorem 6.36 For any $T, \bar{Q}$ and A,

$$\text{CIRC}_{\text{FC}}(T; \lambda xy.x = y; \bar{Q}) \models A \qquad \text{iff } T \models A.$$

Proof Notice that each model of T is $(\lambda xy.x = y; \bar{Q})$-minimal and apply Corollary 6.35. ∎

In view of Theorem 6.36, it is clear that formula circumscription offers no direct solution to the problem of formalizing the unique names assumption. McCarthy (1984) suggests dealing with this task by employing a pair of equality predicates. Apart from the usual equality, restricted to arguments denoting names of objects, he introduces another equality predicate, e, with the following interpretation: $e(x, y)$ iff the names x and y denote the same object. The trick is that while axiomatizing e, some of the substitutivity axioms normally required from the standard equality, are omitted. This prevents Theorem 6.36 from applying to e and, consequently, allows to formalize the unique names assumption by circumscribing $e(x, y)$ in the considered theory. Unfortunately, as McCarthy points out, his proposal is not free of its own drawbacks (see McCarthy 1984 for details).

A number of properties of formula circumscription will implicitly follow from results stated in the next section.

6.5 SECOND-ORDER CIRCUMSCRIPTION

From among various versions of circumscription, the most widely studied is perhaps that introduced by Lifschitz (1985b, 1986). Except for minor changes, Lifschitz's proposal, henceforth *second-order circumscription*, is a notational reformulation of formula circumscription.

6.5.1 Preliminaries

There are two differences between formula circumscription and second-order circumscription:

(i) Second-order circumscription restricts formula circumscription in that it is directed at circumscribing predicate constants, rather than arbitrary predicate expressions. As we know, this restriction is inessential (Theorem 6.31).

(ii) The new feature of second-order circumscription is that functions, apart from predicates, may be allowed to vary in the process of minimization. As we shall see, this generalization has interesting consequences.

In the following, we employ some notational conventions introduced in section 6.3. Recall that if U and V are predicate expressions of the same arity, then $U \leq V$ stands for $\forall \bar{x}. U(\bar{x}) \supset V(\bar{x})$. Similarly, if $\bar{U} = (U_1, \ldots, U_n)$ and $\bar{V} = (V_1, \ldots, V_n)$ are similar tuples of predicate expressions, i.e. U_i and V_i have the same arity, $1 \leq i \leq n$, then $\bar{U} \leq \bar{V}$ is an abbreviation for $\bigwedge_{i=1}^{n} [U_i \leq V_i]$. We write $\bar{U} = \bar{V}$ for $\bar{U} \leq \bar{V} \wedge \bar{V} \leq \bar{U}$, and $\bar{U} < \bar{V}$ for $(\bar{U} \leq \bar{V}) \wedge \neg(\bar{V} \leq \bar{U})$.

In this section, the term *theory* refers to a finite set of first- or second-order sentences; as usual, we do not distinguish between a theory and the conjunction of all its members.

Definition 6.37 (Lifschitz 1985b) Let $\bar{P}$ be a tuple of distinct predicate constants, $\bar{S}$ be a tuple of distinct function and/or predicate constants disjoint with $\bar{P}$, and let $T(\bar{P}, \bar{S})$ be a theory. The *second-order circumscription of $\bar{P}$ in $T(\bar{P}, \bar{S})$ with variable $\bar{S}$*, written $\mathrm{CIRC}_{SO}(T; \bar{P}; \bar{S})$, is the sentence

$$T(\bar{P}, \bar{S}) \wedge \forall \bar{\Phi} \bar{\Psi} \neg [T(\bar{\Phi}, \bar{\Psi}) \wedge \bar{\Phi} < \bar{P}] \tag{6.5.1}$$

where $\bar{\Phi}$ and $\bar{\Psi}$ are tuples of variables similar to $\bar{P}$ and $\bar{S}$, respectively.† ∎

Observe that (6.5.1) can be rewritten as

$$T(\bar{P}, \bar{S}) \wedge \forall \bar{\Phi} \bar{\Psi} . [T(\bar{\Phi}, \bar{\Psi}) \wedge [\bar{\Phi} \leq \bar{P}] \supset [\bar{P} \leq \bar{\Phi}]]$$

which, in turn, is an abbreviation for

$$T(\bar{P}, \bar{S}) \wedge \forall \bar{\Phi} \bar{\Psi} [T(\bar{\Phi}, \bar{\Psi}) \wedge \bigwedge_{i=1}^{n} [\forall \bar{x} . \Phi_i(\bar{x}) \supset P_i(\bar{x})] \supset \bigwedge_{i=1}^{n} [\forall \bar{x} . P_i(\bar{x}) \supset \Phi_i(\bar{x})]]$$

Definition 6.38 A formula A is said to be a *consequence of second-order circumscription of $\bar{P}$ in $T(\bar{P}, \bar{S})$ with variable $\bar{S}$* iff $\mathrm{CIRC}_{SO}(T; \bar{P}; \bar{S}) \models A$. ∎

Example 6.39 (Reiter 1980a) Assume that the following facts are true:

A person normally lives in the same city as his wife.
Bill's wife lives in Vancouver.

This can be represented by the theory T:

$$\forall x . \neg Ab(x) \supset city(x) = city(wife(x))$$
$$city(wife(Bill)) = Vancouver.$$

Let $\bar{P} = (Ab)$ and $\bar{S} = (city)$.

$$\begin{aligned} \mathrm{CIRC}_{SO}(T; \bar{P}; \bar{S}) = T(\bar{P}, \bar{S}) \wedge \\ \wedge \forall \Phi \, \forall \psi \{ & [[\forall x . \neg \Phi(x) \supset \psi(x) = \psi(wife(x))] \wedge \\ & \wedge [\psi(wife(Bill)) = Vancouver] \wedge \\ & \wedge [\forall x . \Phi(x) \supset Ab(x)]] \supset \\ & \supset [\forall x . Ab(x) \supset \Phi(x)]\} \end{aligned}$$

† As usual, if the equality predicate is contained in $(\bar{P}, \bar{Q})$, then T is assumed to include its equality axioms.

Substituting $\{\Phi \leftarrow \lambda x . False\}$ and simplifying, we get

$$\mathrm{CIRC}_{\mathrm{SO}}(T; \bar{P}; \bar{S}) \models A \tag{6.5.2}$$

where

$$A = \forall\psi\{[\forall x . \psi(x) = \psi(wife(x))] \wedge [\psi(wife(Bill)) = Vancouver] \supset [\forall x \neg Ab(x)]\}.$$

Substituting $\{\psi \leftarrow \lambda x . Vancouver\}$ and applying Theorem 1.90 (Chapter 1), we obtain

$$A \models \forall x \neg Ab(x).$$

Thus, by (6.5.2)

$$\mathrm{CIRC}_{\mathrm{SO}}(T; \bar{P}; \bar{S}) \models \forall x \neg Ab(x)$$

and so

$$\mathrm{CIRC}_{\mathrm{SO}}(T; \bar{P}; \bar{S}) \models city(Bill) = Vancouver.$$

∎

Semantic characterization of second-order circumscription is similar to that of formula circumscription.

Definition 6.40 (Lifschitz 1985b) Let $\bar{P}$, $\bar{S}$ and $T(\bar{P}, \bar{S})$ be as in Definition 6.37. Let M and N be models of T. We say that M is a $(\bar{P}; \bar{S})$-*submodel of* N, written $\mathrm{M} \leq^{(\bar{P};\bar{S})} \mathrm{N}$, iff

(i) $|\mathrm{M}| = |\mathrm{N}|$;
(ii) $\mathrm{M}|K| = \mathrm{N}|K|$, for every constant K not in $\bar{P}, \bar{S}$;
(iii) $\mathrm{M}|P_i| \subseteq \mathrm{N}|P_i|$, for every P_i in $\bar{P}$.

We write $\mathrm{M} <^{(\bar{P};\bar{S})} \mathrm{N}$ iff $\mathrm{M} \leq^{(\bar{P};\bar{S})} \mathrm{N}$ but not $\mathrm{N} \leq^{(\bar{P};\bar{S})} \mathrm{M}$.

A model of T is $(\bar{P}; \bar{S})$-minimal iff T has no model N such that $\mathrm{N} <^{(\bar{P};\bar{S})} \mathrm{M}$. ∎

We write $\mathrm{MOD}^{(\bar{P};\bar{S})}(T)$ to denote the class of all $(\bar{P}; \bar{S})$-minimal models of T. Recall that the class of all models of T is denoted by $\mathrm{MOD}(T)$.

Theorem 6.41 (Lifschitz 1985b) For any T, $\bar{P}$ and $\bar{S}$,

$$\mathrm{MOD}(\mathrm{CIRC}_{\mathrm{SO}}(T; \bar{P}; \bar{S})) = \mathrm{MOD}^{(\bar{P};\bar{S})}(T).$$

∎

Example 6.42 Let T consist of:

$$\forall x . R(x) \wedge \neg Ab_1(x) \supset \neg P(x)$$
$$\forall x . Q(x) \wedge \neg Ab_2(x) \supset P(x)$$
$$R(n) \wedge Q(n).$$

This is the 'Pacifist' theory with R, P, Q, n standing for *Republican*, *Pacifist*, *Quaker* and *Nixon*, respectively.

Let M and N be models of T such that $|\mathrm{M}| = |\mathrm{N}| = \{\mathrm{NIXON}\}$, $\mathrm{M}|n| = \mathrm{N}|n| = \mathrm{NIXON}$, $\mathrm{M}|R| = \mathrm{N}|R| = \{\mathrm{NIXON}\}$, $\mathrm{M}|Q| = \mathrm{N}|Q| = \{\mathrm{NIXON}\}$ and:

$$\mathrm{M}|P| = \{\mathrm{NIXON}\} \qquad \mathrm{N}|P| = \{\ \}$$
$$\mathrm{M}|Ab_1| = \{\mathrm{NIXON}\} \qquad \mathrm{N}|Ab_1| = \{\ \}$$
$$\mathrm{M}|Ab_2| = \{\ \} \qquad \mathrm{N}|Ab_2| = \{\mathrm{NIXON}\}.$$

It is immediately seen that for any $\bar{S}$, M and N are both $(\overline{AB}; \bar{S})$-minimal models of T, where $\overline{AB} = (Ab_1, Ab_2)$. Furthermore, $M \models P(n)$ and $N \models \neg P(n)$. It follows, therefore, that when we circumscribe $\overline{AB}$ in T, we shall not be able to infer whether Nixon is a pacifist or not. The best we may obtain is the disjunction $\neg Ab_1(n) \vee \neg Ab_2(n)$, stating that Nixon is either normal as a republican or as a quaker. The reader is asked to perform appropriate calculations. ▮

6.5.2 Satisfiability of second-order circumscription

We now turn our attention to the problem of satisfiability of second-order circumscription. We speak about satisfiability, rather than consistency, because the set of formulae obtainable by performing second-order circumscription is defined semantically. Furthermore, due to the lack of a complete deduction system, second-order logic lacks the notion of consistency which would be equivalent to that of satisfiability.

It is clear that any formula derivable by predicate circumscription can be obtained by performing second-order circumscription. More specifically, for any first-order theory T, any tuple of predicate constants $\bar{P}$ and any formula A, $\mathrm{CIRC}_{\mathrm{PR}}(T; \bar{P}) \vdash A$ implies $\mathrm{CIRC}_{\mathrm{SO}}(T; \bar{P}; ()) \models A$. Thus, by Example 6.14, we immediately have:

Theorem 6.43 Second-order circumscription need not preserve satisfiability. ▮

As we saw, predicate circumscription preserves consistency (and hence satisfiability), for well-founded theories.† This result carries over second-order circumscription, provided that the notion of well-foundedness is slightly reformulated.

Definition 6.44 (Lifschitz 1986; Etherington 1988) A theory T is *well-founded with respect to* $(\bar{P}; \bar{S})$ iff, for every $M \in \mathrm{MOD}(T)$, there is $N \in \mathrm{MOD}^{(\bar{P};\bar{S})}(T)$ such that $N \leq^{(\bar{P};\bar{S})} M$. ▮

Theorem 6.45 (Lifschitz 1986) If T is satisfiable and well-founded with respect to $(\bar{P}; \bar{S})$, then $\mathrm{CIRC}_{\mathrm{SO}}(T; \bar{P}; \bar{S})$ is satisfiable. ▮

Well-foundedness is not necessary for satisfiability of second-order circumscription:

Example 6.46 (Lifschitz 1986) Let $T_1 = T \vee P(c)$, where T is the theory from Example 6.14. It is easily checked that any frame M such that $M|P| = \{M|c|\}$ is a model of $\mathrm{CIRC}_{\mathrm{SO}}(T_1; P; ())$. On the other hand, any model N of T such that $N|c| \notin N|P|$ is a counterexample to the well-foundedness of T_1 with respect to $(P; ())$. ▮

If no constants are allowed to vary, then an analogon of Theorem 6.20 holds:

Theorem 6.47 (Lifschitz 1986) If T is almost universal with respect to $\bar{P}$, then T is well-founded with respect to $(\bar{P}; ())$. ▮

Corollary 6.48 If T is satisfiable and almost universal with respect to $\bar{P}$, then $\mathrm{CIRC}_{\mathrm{SO}}(T; \bar{P}; ())$ is satisfiable. ▮

Since every universal theory is almost universal with respect to any $\bar{P}$, we immediately have:

Corollary 6.49 If T is universal, then T is well-founded with respect to any $(\bar{P}; ())$. ▮

† Recall that predicate circumscription is based on first-order logic, for which the notions of satisfiability and consistency are equivalent.

Corollary 6.50 For any tuple of predicate constants $\bar{P}$ and any satisfiable universal theory T, $\mathrm{CIRC_{SO}}(T; \bar{P}; ())$ is satisfiable. ∎

A striking result is that second-order circumscription need not preserve satisfiability for universal theories if function constants are allowed to vary:

Example 6.51 (Lifschitz 1986) Let T consist of:

$$P(c) \wedge \forall y[P(y) \supset c \neq s(y)]$$
$$\forall x . P(x) \supset P(s(x))$$
$$\forall xy . s(x) = s(y) \supset x = y.$$

It is clear that T is satisfiable (to show this, consider the frame M from Example 6.14 and put $\mathrm{M}|c| = 0$).

$$\begin{aligned}\mathrm{CIRC_{SO}}(T; P; c) = T(P, c) &\wedge \forall\Phi\, \forall\psi\{[\Phi(\psi) \wedge \\ &\wedge [\forall y . \Phi(y) \supset \psi \neq s(y)] \wedge [\forall x . \Phi(x) \supset \Phi(s(x))] \wedge \\ &\wedge [\forall xy . s(x) = s(y) \supset x = y] \wedge [\forall x . \Phi(x) \supset P(x)]] \supset \\ &\supset [\forall x . P(x) \supset \Phi(x)]\}.\end{aligned}$$

Substituting $\{\Phi \leftarrow \lambda x[P(x) \wedge \exists z . P(z) \wedge x = s(z)]\}$ and $\{\psi \leftarrow \lambda x . s(c)\}$, it is readily verified that

$$\mathrm{CIRC_{SO}}(T; P; c) \models \exists z . P(z) \wedge c = s(z).$$

This contradicts the first axiom of T and hence shows that $\mathrm{CIRC_{SO}}(T; P; c)$ is unsatisfiable. ∎

In view of this example, we have:

Theorem 6.52 Universal theories are not necessarily well-founded if function constants are allowed to vary. ∎

The situation is different if varying constants are restricted to predicates:

Theorem 6.53 (Lifschitz 1986) For any disjoint tuples $\bar{P}$ and $\bar{S}$ of predicate constants, every universal theory is well-founded with respect to $(\bar{P}; \bar{S})$. ∎

Corollary 6.54 For any disjoint tuples $\bar{P}$ and $\bar{S}$ of predicate constants and any satisfiable universal theory T, $\mathrm{CIRC_{SO}}(T; \bar{P}; \bar{S})$ is satisfiable. ∎

6.5.3 Reducing second-order circumscription to first-order logic

Frequently, the second-order circumscription axiom can be replaced by an equivalent first-order sentence. The obvious advantage of such a replacement is the possibility of avoiding second-order logic and, consequently, the elimination of the problem of finding appropriate substitutions for second-order variables. The subsequent discussion is based on Lifschitz (1985b).

Throughout this subsection we employ the following terminology. We say that two formulae are *equivalent* if they have the same models. Since any first-order formula can be viewed as a formula of second-order logic, it makes sense to say that a first- and a second-order formulae are equivalent. The term *predicate expression* denotes a predicate expression without parameters, i.e. an expression of the form $\lambda x_1 \ldots x_n\, A(x_1, \ldots, x_n)$, where *all* free individual variables of $A(x_1, \ldots, x_n)$ are among $x_1, \ldots, x_n$. We say that a predicate constant P *occurs positively in a formula A* iff normal conjunctive form of A contains a subformula of the form $P(\bar{\alpha})$.

Definition 6.55 (Lifschitz 1985b) Let $\bar{P} = (P_1, \ldots, P_n)$ be a tuple of predicate constants. A theory T is called *separable with respect to* $\bar{P}$ iff T is equivalent to a formula of the form

$$\bigvee_{i=1}^{m} [B_i(\bar{P}) \wedge (\bar{U}_i \leq \bar{P})] \tag{6.5.3}$$

where $B_i(\bar{P})$ is a formula containing no positive occurrences of $P_1, \ldots, P_n$ and each $\bar{U}_i$ is an n-tuple of predicate expressions not containg $P_1, \ldots, P_n$ ∎

Example 6.56 The following theories are separable with respect to $\bar{P} = (P)$:

$\neg P(a)$	equivalent to	$\neg P(a) \wedge [(\lambda x\,.\,False) \leq P]$
$P(a)$	equivalent to	$True \wedge [(\lambda x\,.\,x = a) \leq P]$
$P(a) \vee P(b)$	equivalent to	$[True \wedge [(\lambda x\,.\,x = a) \leq P]] \vee$ $\vee\ [True \wedge [(\lambda x\,.\,x = b) \leq P]]$
$P(a) \wedge P(b)$	equivalent to	$True \wedge [(\lambda x\,.\,x = a \vee x = b) \leq P]$
$\forall x\,.\,Q(x) \supset P(x)$	equivalent to	$True \wedge Q \leq P$.

The theory

$P(a) \wedge Q(b)$	equivalent to	$True \wedge [(\lambda x\,.\,x = a) \leq P] \wedge$ $\wedge\ [(\lambda x\,.\,x = b) \leq Q]$

is separable with respect to (P, Q).

The theory $\exists x P(x)$ is not separable with respect to P.

∎

The crucial result is the following:

Theorem 6.57 (Lifschitz 1985b) If $T(\bar{P})$ is equivalent to (6.5.3), then $\mathrm{CIRC_{SO}}(T; \bar{P}; ())$ is equivalent to

$$\bigvee_{i=1}^{m} [C_i \wedge (\bar{U}_i = \bar{P})]$$

where C_i is

$$B_i(\bar{U}_i) \wedge \bigwedge_{j \neq i} \neg[B_j(\bar{U}_j) \wedge (\bar{U}_j < \bar{U}_i)].$$

∎

In view of this theorem, the result of second-order circumscription (without variable constants) in a separable first-order theory is equivalent to a first-order sentence.

Example 6.56 (continued)

$$\mathrm{CIRC_{SO}}(\neg P(a); P; ()) \Leftrightarrow \forall x \neg P(x)$$
$$\mathrm{CIRC_{SO}}(P(a); P; ()) \Leftrightarrow [\forall x\,.\,P(x) \equiv x = a]$$
$$\mathrm{CIRC_{SO}}(P(a) \vee P(b); P; ()) \Leftrightarrow [\forall x\,.\,P(x) \equiv x = a] \vee [\forall x\,.\,P(b) \equiv x = b]$$
$$\mathrm{CIRC_{SO}}(P(a) \wedge P(b); P; ()) \Leftrightarrow [\forall x\,.\,P(x) \equiv (x = a \vee x = b)]$$
$$\mathrm{CIRC_{SO}}(\forall x\,.\,Q(x) \supset P(x); P, Q; ()) \Leftrightarrow [\forall x\,.\,Q(x) \equiv P(x)]$$
$$\mathrm{CIRC_{SO}}(P(a) \wedge Q(b); P, Q; ()) \Leftrightarrow [(\forall x\,.\,P(x) \equiv x = a) \wedge (\forall x\,.\,Q(x) \equiv x = b)].$$

∎

There are non-separable theories for which the result of second-order circumscription can be replaced by a first-order sentence:

Example 6.58 The theory $\exists x P(x)$ is not separable with respect to P. However, as the reader may easily verify,

$$CIRC_{SO}(\exists x P(x); P; ()) \Leftrightarrow [\exists x P(x) \wedge \forall xy(P(x) \wedge P(y) \supset x = y)].$$

∎

Generally, the result of second-order circumscription is not reducible to a first-order sentence:

Example 6.59 (Lifschitz 1985b) Let T be

$$[\forall xy . Q(x, y) \supset P(x, y)] \wedge [\forall xyz . P(x, y) \wedge P(y, z) \supset P(x, z)].$$

$CIRC_{SO}(T; P; ())$ states that P is the transitive closure of Q. More precisely, the models of $CIRC_{SO}(T; P; ())$ are exactly those in which P is interpreted as the transitive closure of the interpretation of Q. It can be shown, but we omit a formal proof here, that this class of frames is not finitely axiomatizable in first-order logic. That is, there is no first-order sentence A such that M is a model of A iff $M|P|$ is the transitive closure of $M|Q|$. Therefore, $CIRC_{SO}(T; P; ())$ cannot be replaced by an equivalent first-order sentence.† ∎

Theorem 6.57 is inapplicable in the case when constants, different from those being circumscribed, are allowed to vary. This limitation can be often avoided by employing the following results.

Theorem 6.60 (Lifschitz 1985b) $CIRC_{SO}(T(\bar{P}, \bar{S}); \bar{P}; \bar{S})$ is equivalent to $T(\bar{P}, \bar{S}) \wedge CIRC_{SO}(\exists \bar{\Phi} . T(\bar{P}, \bar{\Phi}); \bar{P}; ())$. ∎

Example 6.61 Let T consist of:

$(A1)$ $\forall x . Flier(x) \wedge \neg Ab(x) \supset Winged(x)$
$(A2)$ $\forall x . Rocket(x) \supset Flier(x)$
$(A3)$ $\forall x . Rocket(x) \supset \neg Winged(x)$.

$CIRC_{SO}(T; Ab; Winged) \Leftrightarrow T(Ab, Winged) \wedge CIRC_{SO}(\exists \Phi[A1(\Phi) \wedge A2 \wedge A3(\Phi)]; Ab; ())$ where

$$A1(\Phi) = \forall x . Flier(x) \wedge \neg Ab(x) \supset \Phi(x)$$
$$A3(\Phi) = \forall x . Rocket(x) \supset \neg \Phi(x).$$

∎

In view of Theorem 6.60, any second-order circumscription can be transformed into a circumscription without variable constants. The problem, however, is that this transformation introduces new second-order variables. Fortunately, such variables can be often eliminated.

Definition 6.62 A theory T is *separable with respect to tuple of predicate variables*, $\bar{\Phi} = (\Phi_1, \ldots, \Phi_n)$, iff T is equivalent to a formula of the form

$$\bigvee_{i=1}^{m} [B_i(\bar{\Phi}) \wedge (\bar{U}_i \leq \bar{\Phi})] \tag{6.5.4}$$

† Consult Barwise (1977, Chapters 1 and 3) for various techniques used in proving axiomatizability results.

where $B_i(\bar{\Phi})$ and $\bar{U}_i$ are specified just as in Definition 6.55 with $\bar{P}$ replaced by $\bar{\Phi}$. ∎

Theorem 6.63 (Lifschitz 1985b) If $T(\bar{\Phi})$ is equivalent to (6.5.4), then $\exists\bar{\Phi}T(\bar{\Phi})$ is equivalent to $\bigvee_{i=1}^{m} B_i(\bar{U}_i)$. ∎

Example 6.61 (continued) Consider the formula

$$A(\Phi) = A1(\Phi) \wedge A2 \wedge A3(\Phi).$$

Since the only positive occurrence of Φ is in $A1(\Phi)$, we write $A(\Phi)$ as

$$A2 \wedge A3(\Phi) \wedge [(\lambda x . Flier(x) \wedge \neg Ab(x)) \leq \Phi].$$

By Theorem 6.63, $\exists\Phi A(\Phi)$ is equivalent to

$$A2 \wedge [\forall x . Rocket(x) \supset \neg(Flier(x) \wedge \neg Ab(x))]$$

which, in turn, is equivalent in T to

$$A2 \wedge [\forall x . Rocket(x) \supset Ab(x)].$$

Thus,

$$CIRC_{SO}(T; Ab; Winged) \Leftrightarrow$$
$$\Leftrightarrow T(Ab, Winged) \wedge CIRC_{SO}(A2 \wedge [\forall x . Rocket(x) \supset Ab(x)]; Ab; ()).$$

It remains to compute the last circumscription. The formula $A2 \wedge [\forall x . Rocket(x) \supset Ab(x)]$ can be written in the form

$$A2 \wedge [(\lambda x . Rocket(x)) \leq Ab].$$

Therefore, by Theorem 6.57,

$$CIRC_{SO}(A2 \wedge [\forall x . Rocket(x) \supset Ab(x)]; Ab; ()) \Leftrightarrow$$
$$\Leftrightarrow [\forall x . Rocket(x) \supset Flier(x)] \wedge [\forall x . Rocket(x) \equiv Ab(x)].$$

Since the first conjunct is already in T, we finally conclude

$$CIRC_{SO}(T; Ab; Winged) \Leftrightarrow T \wedge [\forall x . Rocket(x) \equiv Ab(x)].$$

∎

Although the transformations resulting from Theorems 6.60 and 6.63 need not preserve separability, so that the outlined method is not always applicable, many of practically occurring circumscriptions can be handled in this way.

A few other results concerning reducibility of second-order circumscription into first-order logic can be found in Kolaitis & Papadimitriou (1988). In particular, as these authors show, $CIRC_{SO}(T; \bar{P}; ())$ is equivalent to a first-order sentence, provided that T is a first-order existential theory, i.e. T is equivalent to $\exists\bar{x}T_1$, where T_1 is quantifier free.

Another case when the result of second-order circumscription can be expressed in first-order logic will be presented in section 6.8 (Theorem 6.110 and Corollary 6.111).

6.5.4 Expressive power of second-order circumscription

We now provide a number of results concerning the expressive power of second-order circumscription with respect to well-founded theories. The first such result, stated in a slightly different form in Etherington (1988), corresponds to Theorem 6.22:

Theorem 6.64 If $T(\bar{P}, \bar{S})$ is well-founded with respect to $(\bar{P}; \bar{S})$, $P \in \bar{P}$ is an n-ary predicate constant, $\bar{S}$ is a tuple of predicate constants disjoint with $\bar{P}$, and $\bar{\alpha}$ is an n-tuple of ground terms, then

$$\mathrm{CIRC}_{\mathrm{SO}}(T; \bar{P}; \bar{S}) \models P(\bar{\alpha}) \quad \text{iff} \quad T \models P(\bar{\alpha}).$$

Proof ($\Leftarrow$) Obvious.
($\Rightarrow$) Assume to the contrary that $\mathrm{CIRC}_{\mathrm{SO}}(T; \bar{P}; \bar{S}) \models P(\bar{\alpha})$ and T does not entail $P(\bar{\alpha})$. Then, there is a model M of T in which $\neg P(\bar{\alpha})$ is true. Since T is well-founded with respect to $(\bar{P}; \bar{S})$, there is $\mathrm{N} \in \mathrm{MOD}^{(\bar{P};\bar{S})}(T)$ such that $\mathrm{N} \leq^{(\bar{P};\bar{S})} \mathrm{M}$. Thus, since $\bar{S}$ includes no function constants and $\neg P(\bar{\alpha})$ is true in M, $\neg P(\bar{\alpha})$ must be also true in N. This implies, by Theorem 6.41, that $P(\bar{\alpha})$ is not entailed by $\mathrm{CIRC}_{\mathrm{SO}}(T; \bar{P}; \bar{S})$. A contradiction. ∎

The next result is a version of Theorem 6.24:

Theorem 6.65 (Etherington 1988) If $T(\bar{P}, \bar{S})$ is well-founded with respect to $(\bar{P}; \bar{S})$, $\bar{P} = (P_1, \ldots, P_n)$ and $\bar{S} = (S_1, \ldots, S_m)$ are disjoint tuples of predicate constants, R is a k-ary predicate constant, different from $P_1, \ldots, P_n, S_1, \ldots, S_m$, and $\bar{\alpha}$ is a k-tuple of ground terms, then

(i) $\mathrm{CIRC}_{\mathrm{SO}}(T; \bar{P}; \bar{S}) \models R(\bar{\alpha})$ iff $T \models R(\bar{\alpha})$
(ii) $\mathrm{CIRC}_{\mathrm{SO}}(T; \bar{P}; \bar{S}) \models \neg R(\bar{\alpha})$ iff $T \models \neg R(\bar{\alpha})$.
∎

Theorems 6.64 and 6.65 say that the only new ground literals that one may hope to obtain from well-founded theories by second-order circumscription (without varying function constants) are negative instances of circumscribed predicates and instances, both negative and positive, of variable predicates. The next example shows that this need not be true if function constants are allowed to vary. In such a case, both positive literals of circumscribed predicates and new instances of non-variable predicates may be obtainable.

Example 6.66 Let $T = \{P(a) \wedge P(b) \wedge Q(b) \wedge [Q(a) \supset P(c)]\}$.

$$\mathrm{CIRC}_{\mathrm{SO}}(T; P; (a, c)) = T \wedge \forall \Phi\, \forall yz\{[\Phi(y) \wedge \Phi(b) \wedge Q(b) \wedge \\ \wedge [Q(y) \supset \Phi(z)] \wedge [\forall x\,.\,\Phi(x) \supset P(x)]] \supset [\forall x\,.\,P(x) \supset \Phi(x)]\}.$$

Substituting $\{\Phi \leftarrow \lambda x\,.\,x = b\}$;$\{y \leftarrow \lambda x\,.\,b\}$; $\{z \leftarrow \lambda x\,.\,b\}$ and simplifying, we have

$$\mathrm{CIRC}_{\mathrm{SO}}(T; P; (a, c)) \models \forall x\,.\,P(x) \supset x = b$$

from which we get

$$\mathrm{CIRC}_{\mathrm{SO}}(T; P; (a, c)) \models a = b$$
$$\mathrm{CIRC}_{\mathrm{SO}}(T; P; (a, c)) \models Q(a)$$
$$\mathrm{CIRC}_{\mathrm{SO}}(T; P; (a, c)) \models P(c).$$

This example illustrates another important property of second-order circumscription with varying function constants: its ability in reaching new ground equality statements (here $a = b$). ∎

Even if function constants are allowed to vary, no new formulae can be obtained by circumscribing the equality predicate:

Theorem 6.67 For any T, $\bar{S}$ and A:

$$\mathrm{CIRC}_{\mathrm{SO}}(T;\ =;\bar{S}) \models A \qquad \text{iff } T \models A.$$

Proof Notice that each model of T is $(=;\bar{S})$-minimal and apply Theorem 6.41. ▮

Example 6.66 shows that new ground equality statements can be obtained by second-order circumscription with varying functions. The same is true for inequalities:

Example 6.68 Let $T = \{P(a) \wedge P(b) \wedge Q(b) \wedge \neg Q(c)\}$.

$$\mathrm{CIRC}_{\mathrm{SO}}(T; P; a) = T \wedge \forall\Phi\, \forall z\{[\Phi(z) \wedge \Phi(b) \wedge Q(b) \wedge \neg Q(c) \wedge \\ \wedge [\forall x.\Phi(x) \supset P(x)]] \supset [\forall x.P(x) \supset \Phi(x)]\}.$$

Letting $\{\Phi \leftarrow \lambda x.x = b\}$; $\{z \leftarrow \lambda x.b\}$ and simplifying, we obtain

$$\mathrm{CIRC}_{\mathrm{SO}}(T; P; a) \models \forall x.P(x) \supset x = b.$$

From this one easily gets $\mathrm{CIRC}_{\mathrm{SO}}(T; P; a) \models a \neq c$. ▮

We do not know whether second-order circumscription may yield new ground equalities or inequalities, provided that only predicate constants are allowed to vary. We suspect, but we have no proof, that this is impossible for at least well-founded theories. (Compare Theorem 6.26.)

Since the notion of $(\bar{P};\bar{S})$-*submodel* is defined for a pair of frames with identical domains, one may suspect that second-order circumscription cannot be used to obtain the domain closure axioms. This is easily proved for well-founded theories, provided that no function constants are allowed to vary:

Theorem 6.69 If $T(\bar{P};\bar{S})$ is well-founded with respect to $(\bar{P};\bar{S})$, $\bar{S}$ contains no function constants, and $\alpha_1, \ldots, \alpha_n$ are ground terms, then

$$\mathrm{CIRC}_{\mathrm{SO}}(T;\bar{P};\bar{S}) \models \forall x.x = \alpha_1 \vee \cdots \vee x = \alpha_n \\ \text{iff } T \models \forall x.x = \alpha_1 \vee \cdots \vee x = \alpha_n.$$

Proof ($\Leftarrow$) Immediate.

($\Rightarrow$) Assume on the contrary that $\mathrm{CIRC}_{\mathrm{SO}}(T;\bar{P};\bar{S}) \models \forall x.x = \alpha_1 \vee \cdots \vee x = \alpha_n$ and T does not entail $\forall x.x = \alpha_1 \vee \cdots \vee x = \alpha_n$. Thus, there is a model M of T in which $\forall x.x = \alpha_1 \vee \cdots \vee x = \alpha_n$ is false. Since T is well-founded with respect to $(\bar{P};\bar{S})$, M has a $(\bar{P};\bar{S})$-minimal submodel, say N. Clearly, since $|\mathrm{M}| = |\mathrm{N}|$ and no function constants are allowed to vary, $\forall x.x = \alpha_1 \vee \cdots \vee x = \alpha_n$ is false in N. Thus, in view of Theorem 6.41, $\mathrm{CIRC}_{\mathrm{SO}}(T;\bar{P};\bar{S})$ does not entail $\forall x.x = \alpha_1 \vee \cdots \vee x = \alpha_n$. A contradiction. ▮

6.5.5 Prioritized second-order circumscription

Suppose we are given a theory T consisting of the following axioms:

$$\forall x.Adult(x) \wedge \neg Ab_1(x) \supset Employed(x)$$
$$\forall x.High\text{-}School\text{-}Dropout(x) \wedge \neg Ab_2(x) \supset \neg Employed(x)$$
$$\forall x.High\text{-}School\text{-}Dropout(x) \supset Adult(x)$$
$$High\text{-}School\text{-}Dropout(Mary).$$

Given these axioms, Mary may be considered normal as a high-school dropout or as an adult, but not both. Accordingly, there are two conflicting minimizations of (Ab_1, Ab_2) *in* T, say m_1 and m_2, leading to

$$\neg Ab_1(Mary) \wedge Employed(Mary) \text{ and } \neg Ab_2(Mary) \wedge \neg Employed(Mary)$$

respectively. In consequence, all we can get by circumscribing Ab_1, Ab_2 in T is the disjunction

$$\neg Ab_1(Mary) \vee \neg Ab_2(Mary). \tag{6.5.5}$$

Obviously, (6.5.5) is too weak. Given that Mary is a high-school dropout, we do not want to remain agnostic about her employment status. Rather, we are prepared to assume that she is unemployed. In other words, we intuitively feel that there is no reason to view both the conflicting minimizations as equally plausible.

One way of avoiding an unintuitive minimization is to add a new piece of information to the original representation. In our example, it is sufficient to supply the theory T with

$$\forall x . High\text{-}School\text{-}Dropout(x) \supset Ab_1(x).$$

The obvious drawback of this solution is that in practical applications we may have a great number of unwanted minimizations, so that their elimination will require many additional axioms.

Lifschitz (1985b) suggests another way of avoiding undesirable minimizations. He generalizes second-order circumscription by introducing a priority ordering on predicates to be minimized. The intention is that any conflict arising from the minimization of two predicates is resolved in favour of that with higher priority. Lifschitz's generalization, which essentially may be based on any version of circumscription, is called *prioritized second-order circumscription.*[†]

Suppose we want to minimize a pair of predicate constants, say P_1 and P_2, in a theory T. Assume for simplicity that no additional constants are allowed to vary during the minimization. In standard second-order circumscription this is expressed by the sentence

$$T(P_1, P_2) \wedge \forall \Phi_1 \Phi_2 \{[T(\Phi_1, \Phi_2) \wedge [(\Phi_1, \Phi_2) \le (P_1, P_2)]] \supset \\ \supset [(P_1, P_2) \le (\Phi_1, \Phi_2)]\}$$

where, for arbitrary pairs of similar predicate expressions, (U_1, U_2) and (V_1, V_2), $(U_1, U_2) \le (V_1, V_2)$ is defined by

$$(U_1, U_2) \le (V_1, V_2) \quad \text{iff} \quad (U_1 \le V_1) \wedge (U_2 \le V_2).$$

Assume now that we want to minimize P_1 and P_2 in T, the former at higher priority than the latter. To express this, we may retain the original circumscription axiom with one exception: instead of minimizing (P_1, P_2) with respect to '$\le$', we employ the relation '$\lesssim$' specified by

$$(U_1, U_2) \lesssim (V_1, V_2) \quad \text{iff} \quad U_1 \le V_1 \wedge (U_1 = V_1 \supset U_2 \le V_2).$$

Notice that $(U_1, U_2) \lesssim (V_1, V_2)$ does not imply $U_2 \le V_2$. If $U_1 < V_1$, then $(U_1, U_2) \lesssim (V_1, V_2)$, for any U_2, V_2.

The relation '$\lesssim$' can be naturally extended into similar tuples of predicate

[†] The idea of prioritized circumscription can be also found in McCarthy (1984).

expressions:

$$(U_1, \ldots, U_n) \leqslant (V_1, \ldots, V_n) \quad \text{iff} \quad U_1 \le V_1 \wedge \bigwedge_{i=2}^{n} \left(\left(\bigwedge_{j=1}^{i-1} U_j = V_j \right) \supset U_i \le V_i \right)$$

and further, into similar lists of tuples consisting of predicate expressions:

$$(\bar{U}_1, \ldots, \bar{U}_n) \leqslant (\bar{V}_1, \ldots, \bar{V}_n) \quad \text{iff} \quad U_1 \le \ll_1 \wedge \bigwedge_{i=2}^{n} \left(\left(\bigwedge_{j=1}^{i-1} \bar{U}_j = \bar{V}_j \right) \supset \bar{U}_i \le \bar{V}_i \right).$$

We write $(\bar{U}_1, \ldots, \bar{U}_n) \ll (\bar{V}_1, \ldots, \bar{V}_n)$ for

$$[(\bar{U}_1, \ldots, \bar{U}_n) \leqslant (\bar{V}_1, \ldots, \bar{V}_n)] \wedge \neg[(\bar{V}_1, \ldots, \bar{V}_n) \leqslant (\bar{U}_1, \ldots, \bar{U}_n)].$$

We are now ready to provide a formal definition of prioritized circumscription. To minimize a tuple $\bar{P}$ of predicate constants, we begin by breaking $\bar{P}$ into disjoint sublists $\bar{P}^1, \bar{P}^2 \ldots \bar{P}^n$. The intention is that the elements of $\bar{P}^1$ are minimized at the highest priority, those of $\bar{P}^2$ at the second priority, etc. We express this by writing $\bar{P}^1 > \cdots > \bar{P}^n$.

Definition 6.70 (Lifschitz 1985) Let $\bar{P}$, $\bar{S}$ and $T(\bar{P}, \bar{S})$ be as in Definition 6.37. The *prioritized second-order circumscription of* $\bar{P}$ *in* $T(\bar{P}, \bar{S})$ *with variable* $\bar{S}$ *with respect to priorities* $\bar{P}^1 > \cdots > \bar{P}^n$, written $\mathrm{CIRC}_{\mathrm{SO}}(T; \bar{P}^1 > \cdots > \bar{P}^n; \bar{S})$, is the sentence

$$T(\bar{P}, \bar{S}) \wedge \forall \bar{\Phi} \bar{\Psi} \neg [T(\bar{\Phi}, \bar{\Psi}) \wedge \bar{\Phi} \ll \bar{P}]. \tag{6.5.6}$$

Here $\bar{\Phi} \ll \bar{P}$ is $(\bar{\Phi}^1, \ldots, \bar{\Phi}^n) \ll (\bar{P}^1, \ldots, \bar{P}^n)$, where each $\bar{\Phi}^i$ is a tuple of predicate variables similar to $\bar{P}^i$. ∎

Notice that (6.5.6) may be equivalently written as

$$T(\bar{P}, \bar{S}) \wedge \forall \bar{\Phi} \bar{\Psi} [T(\bar{\Phi}, \bar{\Psi}) \wedge [\bar{\Phi} \leqslant \bar{P}] \supset [\bar{P} \leqslant \bar{\Phi}]].$$

As usual, the set of consequences of prioritized circumscription is identified with the set of all formulae entailed by $\mathrm{CIRC}_{\mathrm{SO}}(T; \bar{P}^1 > \cdots > \bar{P}^n; \bar{S})$.

Example 6.71 Let T consist of:

$$\begin{aligned} &\forall x . A(x) \wedge \neg Ab_1(x) \supset E(x) \\ &\forall x . D(x) \wedge \neg Ab_2(x) \supset \neg E(x) \\ &\forall x . D(x) \supset A(x) \\ &D(m). \end{aligned}$$

This is the 'High-School Dropout' theory with A, D, E and m standing for *Adult*, *High-School-Dropout*, *Employed* and *Mary*, respectively. We circumscribe Ab_1, Ab_2, in T with variable E. Since minimization of Ab_2 is to be preferred over that of Ab_1, Ab_2 will be given higher priority than Ab_1.

$$\begin{aligned} &\mathrm{CIRC}_{\mathrm{SO}}(T; Ab_2 > Ab_1; E) = T \wedge \\ &\quad \wedge \forall \Phi_1 \Phi_2 \Psi \{ [[\forall x . A(x) \wedge \neg \Phi_1(x) \supset \Psi(x)] \wedge [\forall x . D(x) \supset A(x)] \wedge \\ &\qquad \wedge D(m) \wedge [\forall x . D(x) \wedge \neg \Phi_2(x) \supset \neg \Psi(x)] \wedge \\ &\qquad \wedge [\forall x . \Phi_2(x) \supset Ab_2(x)] \wedge \\ &\qquad \wedge [(\forall x . \Phi_2(x) \equiv Ab_2(x)) \supset (\forall x . \Phi_1(x) \supset Ab_1(x))]] \supset \\ &\qquad \supset [[\forall x . Ab_2(x) \supset \Phi_2(x)] \wedge \\ &\qquad \wedge [(\forall x . Ab_2(x) \equiv \Phi_2(x)) \supset (\forall x . Ab_1(x) \supset \Phi_1(x))]] \}. \end{aligned}$$

Putting $\{\Phi_1 \leftarrow \lambda x.D(x)\}$; $\{\Phi_2 \leftarrow \lambda x.\mathit{False}\}$; $\{\Psi \leftarrow \lambda x.A(x) \wedge \neg D(x)\}$, and making appropriate calculations, one easily obtains

$$\mathrm{CIRC}_{\mathrm{SO}}(T; Ab_2 > Ab_1; E) \models [\forall x.Ab_2(x) \supset \mathit{False}] \wedge \wedge [[\forall x.Ab_2(x) \equiv \mathit{False}] \supset [\forall x.Ab_1(x) \supset D(x)]].$$

From this, it is possible to get

$$\mathrm{CIRC}_{\mathrm{SO}}(T; Ab_2 > Ab_1; E) \models A_1 \wedge A_2 \wedge A_3, \text{ where}$$

$$A_1 = \forall x.\neg Ab_2(x)$$
$$A_2 = [\forall x.Ab_1(x) \equiv D(x)]$$
$$A_3 = \neg E(m).$$

▮

Prioritized circumscription can be given the following semantic characterization.

Definition 6.72 (Lifschitz 1986) Let $\bar{P}^1, \ldots, \bar{P}^n$ be disjoint sublists of all predicate constants from $\bar{P}$. Let $T(\bar{P}, \bar{S})$ be a theory, where $\bar{S}$ is a tuple (disjoint with $\bar{P}$) of function and/or predicate constants. Suppose that M and N are models of T. M is said to be a $(\bar{P}^1 > \cdots > \bar{P}^n; \bar{S})$*-submodel of* N, written $\mathrm{M} \leqslant^{(\bar{P}1 > \cdots > \bar{P}n; \bar{S})} \mathrm{N}$, iff

(i) $|\mathrm{M}| = |\mathrm{N}|$;
(ii) $\mathrm{M}|K| = \mathrm{N}|K|$, for every constant K not in $(\bar{P}, \bar{S})$;
(iii) For every $\mathrm{j} = 1, \ldots, \mathrm{n}$, if

$$\mathrm{M}|P_1| = \mathrm{N}|P_1|, \text{ for every } P_1 \in (\bar{P}^1, \ldots, \bar{P}^{\mathrm{j}-1}),$$

then

$$\mathrm{M}|P_1| \subseteq \mathrm{N}|P_1|, \text{ for every } P_1 \in \bar{P}^{\mathrm{j}}.$$

We write $\mathrm{M}^{(\bar{P}1 > \cdots > \bar{P}n; \bar{S})} \ll \mathrm{N}$ iff $\mathrm{M} \leqslant^{(\bar{P}1 > \cdots > \bar{P}n; \bar{S})} \mathrm{N}$ but not $\mathrm{N} \leqslant^{(\bar{P}1 > \cdots > \bar{P}n; \bar{S})} \mathrm{M}$.

A model of T is $(\bar{P}^1 > \cdots > \bar{P}^n; \bar{S})$*-minimal* iff T has no model N such that $\mathrm{N} \ll^{(\bar{P}1 > \cdots > \bar{P}n; \bar{S})} \mathrm{M}$. ▮

The set of all $(\bar{P}^1 > \cdots > \bar{P}^n; \bar{S})$-minimal models of T will be denoted by $\mathrm{MOD}^{(\bar{P}1 > \cdots > \bar{P}n; \bar{S})}(T)$.

Theorem 6.73 (Lifschitz 1986)

$$\mathrm{MOD}(\mathrm{CIRC}_{\mathrm{SO}}(T; \bar{P}^1 > \cdots > \bar{P}^n; \bar{S})) = \mathrm{MOD}^{(\bar{P}1 > \cdots > \bar{P}n; \bar{S})}(T).$$

▮

The notion of well-foundedness easily generalizes into prioritized circumscription:

Definition 6.74 (Lifschitz 1986) A theory T is *well-founded* with respect to $(\bar{P}^1 > \cdots > \bar{P}^n; \bar{S})$ iff for every $\mathrm{M} \in \mathrm{MOD}(T)$, there is $\mathrm{N} \in \mathrm{MOD}^{(\bar{P}1 > \cdots > \bar{P}n; \bar{S})}(T)$ such that $\mathrm{N} \leqslant^{(\bar{P}1 > \cdots > \bar{P}n; \bar{S})} \mathrm{M}$. ▮

The following results hold:

Theorem 6.75 (Lifschitz 1986) If T is satisfiable and well-founded with respect to $(\bar{P}^1 > \cdots > \bar{P}^n; \bar{S})$, then $\mathrm{CIRC}_{\mathrm{SO}}(T; \bar{P}^1 > \cdots > \bar{P}^n; \bar{S})$ is satisfiable. ▮

Theorem 6.76 (Lifschitz 1986) For any disjoint tuples $\bar{P}^1, \ldots, \bar{P}^n, \bar{S}$ of distinct predicate constants (i.e. $\bar{S}$ must not include function constants), every universal theory is well-founded with respect to $(\bar{P}^1 > \cdots > \bar{P}^n; \bar{S})$. ▮

Corollary 6.77 Under the premisses of Theorem 6.76, if T is a satisfiable universal theory, then $\mathrm{CIRC}_{SO}(T; \bar{P}^1 > \cdots > \bar{P}^n; \bar{S})$ is satisfiable. ▮

Like standard second-order circumscription, its prioritized version is expressible in first-order logic, provided that no constants are allowed to vary and the theories under consideration are separable. More specifically, we have the following analogon of Theorem 6.57:

Theorem 6.78 (Lifschitz 1985b) If $T(P)$ is equivalent to (6.5.3), where $\bar{P} = (\bar{P}^1, \ldots, \bar{P}^n$ then $\mathrm{CIRC}_{SO}(T; \bar{P}^1 > \cdots > \bar{P}^n; ())$ is equivalent to

$$\bigvee_{i=1}^{m} [C_i \wedge (\bar{U}_i = \bar{P})]$$

where C_i is

$$B_i(\bar{U}_i) \wedge \bigwedge_{j \neq i} \neg[B_j(\bar{U}_j) \wedge (\bar{U}_j \ll \bar{U}_i)].$$

▮

Example 6.79 Let $T = \{[\neg P(a) \wedge Q(b)] \vee [P(a) \wedge \neg Q(b)]\}$.

We circumscribe P and Q in T with $P > Q$. We first write T in the form

$$[\neg P(a) \wedge [(\lambda x . False) \leq P] \wedge [(\lambda x . x = b) \leq Q]] \vee \\ \vee [\neg Q(b) \wedge [(\lambda x . x = a) \leq P] \wedge [(\lambda x . False) \leq Q]]$$

$$\mathrm{CIRC}_{SO}(T; P > Q; ()) = \\ = [C_1 \wedge (\forall x . P(x) \equiv False) \wedge (\forall x . Q(x) \equiv x = b)] \vee \\ \vee [C_2 \wedge (\forall x . P(x) \equiv x = a) \wedge (\forall x . Q(x) \equiv False)]$$

where C_1 and C_2 simplify to *True* and *False*, respectively. Thus

$$\mathrm{CIRC}_{SO}(T; P > Q; ()) \Leftrightarrow \forall x \neg P(x) \wedge [\forall x . Q(x) \equiv x = b].$$

Performing similar calculations, the reader may verify that

$$\mathrm{CIRC}_{SO}(T; Q > P; ()) \Leftrightarrow \forall x \neg Q(x) \wedge [\forall x . P(x) \equiv x = a].$$

▮

Theorem 6.60 also generalizes into the prioritized form of circumscription:

Theorem 6.80 (Lifschitz 1985b) $\mathrm{CIRC}_{SO}(T; \bar{P}^1 > \cdots > \bar{P}^n; \bar{S})$ is equivalent to

$$T(\bar{P}, \bar{S}) \wedge \mathrm{CIRC}_{SO}(\exists \Phi\, T(\bar{P}, \bar{\Phi}); \bar{P}^1 > \cdots > \bar{P}^n; ()).$$

▮

By virtue of Theorems 6.78, 6.80 and 6.63, prioritized circumscription can be computed by the method outlined in subsection 6.5.3. However, as Lifschitz (1985b) points out, there exists a better technique. It is based on the observation that any prioritized circumscription is equivalent to a conjunction of standard circumscriptions. The details are given in the following theorem:

Theorem 6.81 (Lifschitz 1985b) $\mathrm{CIRC}_{SO}(T; \bar{P}^1 > \cdots > \bar{P}^n; \bar{S})$ is equivalent to

$$\bigwedge_{i=1}^{n} \mathrm{CIRC}_{SO}(T; \bar{P}^i; (\bar{P}^{i+1}, \ldots, \bar{P}^n, \bar{S})).$$

▮

Example 6.82 Let T be the 'High-School Dropout' theory from Example 6.71:

$$A_1 = \forall x . A(x) \wedge \neg Ab_1(x) \supset E(x)$$
$$A_2 = \forall x . D(x) \wedge \neg Ab_2(x) \supset \neg E(x)$$
$$A_3 = \forall x . D(x) \supset A(x)$$
$$A_4 = D(m)$$

$$\mathrm{CIRC}_{SO}(T; Ab_2 > Ab_1; E) = \mathrm{CIRC}_{SO}(T; Ab_2; (Ab_1, E)) \wedge \mathrm{CIRC}_{SO}(T; Ab_1; E).$$

We evaluate both the circumscriptions.

$$\mathrm{CIRC}_{SO}(T; Ab_2; (Ab_1, E)) \Leftrightarrow \text{(in view of Theorem 6.60)}$$
$$\Leftrightarrow T(Ab_2, Ab_1, E) \wedge \mathrm{CIRC}_{SO}(\exists \Phi_1 \Phi_2 T(Ab_2, \Phi_1, \Phi_2); Ab_2; ()) \Leftrightarrow$$
$$\Leftrightarrow T(Ab_2, Ab_1, E) \wedge \mathrm{CIRC}_{SO}(\exists \Phi_1 \Phi_2 . A_1(\Phi_1, \Phi_2) \wedge A_2(\Phi_2) \wedge$$
$$\wedge A_3 \wedge A_4; Ab_2; ()).$$

Consider the formula $B = A_1(\Phi_1, \Phi_2) \wedge A_2(\Phi_2) \wedge A_3 \wedge A_4$. We first write this conjunction in the form

$$A_2(\Phi_2) \wedge A_3 \wedge A_4 \wedge \lambda x . [A(x) \wedge \neg \Phi_1(x)] \leq \Phi_2.$$

Now applying Theorem 6.63, we get

$$\exists \Phi_2 B \Leftrightarrow A_3 \wedge A_4 \wedge [\forall x . D(x) \wedge \neg Ab_2(x) \supset \neg A(x) \vee \Phi_1(x)] \Leftrightarrow$$
$$\Leftrightarrow A_3 \wedge A_4 \wedge [(\lambda x . D(x) \wedge \neg Ab_2(x) \wedge A(x)) \leq \Phi_1].$$

Again, applying Theorem 6.63, we have

$$\exists \Phi_1 \Phi_2 B \Leftrightarrow A_3 \wedge A_4.$$

Therefore, $\mathrm{CIRC}_{SO}(T; Ab_2; (Ab_1, E)) \Leftrightarrow A_1 \wedge A_2 \wedge A_3 \wedge A_4 \wedge$
$\wedge \mathrm{CIRC}_{SO}(A_3 \wedge A_4; Ab_2; ()) \Leftrightarrow T \wedge [Ab_2(x) \equiv False]$.

Applying the same method, the reader may check that

$$\mathrm{CIRC}_{SO}(T; Ab_1; E) \Leftrightarrow A_1 \wedge A_2 \wedge A_3 \wedge A_4 \wedge$$
$$\wedge [\forall x . Ab_1(x) \equiv D(x) \wedge A(x) \wedge \neg Ab_2(x)].$$

Therefore, $\mathrm{CIRC}_{SO}(T; Ab_2 > Ab_1; E)$ is equivalent to

$$T \wedge [\forall x \neg Ab_2(x)] \wedge [\forall x . Ab_1(x) \equiv D(x)].$$

∎

There is a close connection between prioritized second-order circumscription and logic programs with negation. This subject will not be discussed here. The interested reader may consult Przymusinski (1988) and Gelfond & Lifschitz (1989).

This completes our exposition of second-order circumscription. It is perhaps the most interesting of all circumscriptive logics. Also, it is the most widely studied. However, the full potential of this formalism is still far from being realized. In particular, it is not quite clear how variable functions influence the minimization process. We saw that their presence may lead to rather unexpected results (Examples 6.51, 6.66 and 6.68). On the other hand, there are natural inference patterns which cannot be properly formalized (in the framework of circumscription) unless functions are allowed to vary. Reconsider the theory from Example 6.39:

$$\forall x . \neg Ab(x) \supset city(x) = city(wife(x))$$
$$city(wife(Bill)) = Vancouver.$$

To derive that Bill lives in Vancouver, the function *city* must be taken as variable.

Krishnaprasad (1988) showed various undecidability results concerning second-order circumscription. In particular, he demonstrated that the following problems are generally undecidable:

(i) Determine whether or not $\mathrm{CIRC}_{\mathrm{SO}}(T; \bar{P}; \bar{S})$ is satisfiable;
(ii) Determine whether or not $\mathrm{CIRC}_{\mathrm{SO}}(T; \bar{P}; \bar{S})$ is expressible in first-order logic;
(iii) Find first-order equivalent of $\mathrm{CIRC}_{\mathrm{SO}}(T; \bar{P}; \bar{S})$, provided that it exists.

6.6 NON-RECURSIVE CIRCUMSCRIPTION

To increase the power of predicate circumscription, Perlis & Minker (1986) introduced another circumscriptive logic. Their system, called *variable circumscription*, does not employ any second-order axiom. Rather, it redefines McCarthy's (1980) circumscription schema by admitting variable predicates. In this section, we briefly present a refinement of variable circumscription, introduced by Mott (1987). We shall refer to this variant as *non-recursive circumscription*. A nice property of Mott's formalism is that it always preserves consistency.

In this section, the term *theory* refers to a finite set of first-order sentences; as usual, we do not distinguish between a theory and the conjunction of all its members.

Definition 6.83 Let $T(\bar{P}, \bar{Q})$ be a theory, where $\bar{P} = (P_1, \ldots, P_n)$ and $\bar{Q} = (Q_1, \ldots, Q_m)$ are disjoint tuples of predicate constants. The *circumscription schema of $\bar{P}$ in T with variable $\bar{Q}$*, written $\mathrm{CS}(T; \bar{P}; \bar{Q})$, is the following second-order formula

$$[T(\bar{\Phi}, \bar{\Psi}) \wedge \bigwedge_{i=1}^{n} [\forall \bar{x} . \Phi_i(\bar{x}) \supset P_i(\bar{x})]] \supset \bigwedge_{i=1}^{n} [\forall \bar{x} . P_i(\bar{x}) \supset \Phi_i(\bar{x})] \qquad (6.6.1)$$

where $\bar{\Phi} = (\Phi_1, \ldots, \Phi_n)$ and $\bar{\Psi} = (\Psi_1, \ldots, \Psi_m)$ are tuples of predicate variables similar to $\bar{P}$ and $\bar{Q}$, respectively. ∎

We now proceed just as in the case of predicate circumscription. We view (6.6.1) as a set whose members are first-order formulae resulting from (6.6.1) by substituting first-order predicate expressions for $\Phi_1, \ldots, \Phi_n, \Psi_1, \ldots, \Psi_m$. Imposing no restrictions on these substitutions, we get Perlis & Minker's *variable circumscription*. In Mott's *non-recursive circumscription*, the substitutions are subject to the following constraints:

(1) Their applications to (6.6.1) are proper;
(2) If A obtains from (6.6.1) by substituting $U_1, \ldots, U_n, V_1, \ldots, V_m$ for $\Phi_1, \ldots, \Phi_n, \Psi_1, \ldots, \Psi_m$, then:
    (i) $U_1, \ldots, U_n, V_1, \ldots, V_m$ are first-order predicate expressions without parameters
    (ii) All predicate constants contained in $U_1, \ldots, U_n, V_1, \ldots, V_m$ are different from $P_1, \ldots, P_n, Q_1, \ldots, Q_m$. (This explains the term 'non-recursive circumscription'.)

Any substitution satisfying the above restrictions will be called *strongly proper with respect to $P_1, \ldots, P_n, Q_1, \ldots, Q_m$*.

Definition 6.84 (Mott 1987) Let $T(\bar{P}, \bar{Q})$ be a theory, where $\bar{P} = (P_1, \ldots, P_n)$ and $\bar{Q} = (Q_1, \ldots, Q_m)$ are disjoint tuples of predicate constants. Let $\overline{\mathrm{CS}}(T; \bar{P}; \bar{Q})$ be the set of all first-order sentences obtainable from $CS(T; \bar{P}; \bar{Q})$ by strongly proper (with respect to $\bar{P}$, $\bar{Q}$) substitutions of first-order predicate expressions for $\bar{\Phi}$, $\bar{\Psi}$.[†] The *non-recursive circumscription of* $\bar{P}$ *in* T *with variable* $\bar{Q}$, written $CIRC_{NR}(T; \bar{P}; \bar{Q})$, is the set $T \cup \overline{CS}(T; \bar{P}; \bar{Q})$. ∎

We say that a formula A is derivable by non-recursively circumscribing $\bar{P}$ in T with variable $\bar{Q}$ iff

$$CIRC_{NR}(T; \bar{P}; \bar{Q}) \vdash A$$

where '$\vdash$' is the provability relation of classical first-order logic. As usual, if $\bar{P}$ or $\bar{Q}$ contain '$=$', we assume that T includes its equality axioms.

Example 6.85 Let T consist of the following axioms:

$$\forall x. \neg Ab_1(x) \supset \neg Flies(x)$$
$$\forall x. Bird(x) \supset Ab_1(x)$$
$$\forall x. Bird(x) \wedge \neg Ab_2(x) \supset Flies(x).$$

We circumscribe (Ab_1, Ab_2) in T with the variable $Flies$.

$$\begin{aligned} CS(T; Ab_1, Ab_2; Flies) = [[&\forall x. \neg\Phi_1(x) \supset \neg\Psi(x)] \wedge \\ &\wedge [\forall x. Bird(x) \supset \Phi_1(x)] \wedge \\ &\wedge [\forall x. Bird(x) \wedge \neg\Phi_2(x) \supset \Psi(x)] \wedge \\ &\wedge [\forall x. \Phi_1(x) \supset Ab_1(x)] \wedge \\ &\wedge [\forall x. \Phi_2(x) \supset Ab_2(x)]] \supset \\ &\supset [[\forall x. Ab_1(x) \supset \Phi_1(x)] \wedge \\ &\quad \wedge [\forall x. Ab_2(x) \supset \Phi_2(x)]]. \end{aligned}$$

We put: $\{\Phi_1 \leftarrow \lambda x. Bird(x)\}$; $\{\Phi_2 \leftarrow \lambda x. False\}$; $\{\Psi \leftarrow \lambda x. Bird(x)\}$. (Notice that the substitution of $\lambda x. Bird(x)$, $\lambda x. False$, $\lambda x. Bird(x)$ for Φ_1, Φ_2, Ψ in $CS(T; Ab_1, Ab_2; Flies)$ is strongly proper with respect to $Ab_1, Ab_2, Flies$.) After straightforward simplifications, left to the reader, one easily obtains

$$CIRC_{NR}(T; Ab_1, Ab_2; Flies) \vdash [\forall x. Ab_1(x) \equiv Bird(x)] \wedge [\forall x \neg Ab_2(x)]$$

and thus

$$CIRC_{NR}(T; Ab_1, Ab_2; Flies) \vdash \forall x. Bird(x) \supset Flies(x).$$

∎

Reconsider the theory from Example 6.14:

$$\exists x. P(x) \wedge [\forall y. P(y) \supset x \neq s(y)]$$
$$\forall x. P(x) \supset P(s(x))$$
$$\forall xy. s(x) = s(y) \supset x = y.$$

As we saw, using predicate circumscription to circumscribe P in T, and letting $\{\Phi \leftarrow \lambda x[P(x) \wedge \exists y. x = s(y) \wedge P(y)]\}$, leads to inconsistency. This substitution is forbidden in non-recursive circumscription because it is not strongly proper ($\lambda x[P(x) \wedge \exists y. x = s(y) \wedge P(y)]$ involves P). It turns out that the restriction to strongly proper substitutions solves the consistency problem:

Theorem 6.86 (Mott 1987) If T is consistent, then $CIRC_{NR}(T; \bar{P}; \bar{Q})$ is consistent for any disjoint tuples, $\bar{P}$, $\bar{Q}$, of predicate constants. ∎

[†] Note that strongly proper substitutions never lead to open formulae, when applied to schema (6.6.1).

The standard semantics for non-recursive circumscription is based on the following notion.

Definition 6.87 (Mott 1987) Let $T(\bar{P}, \bar{Q})$ be a theory, where $\bar{P}$ and $\bar{Q}$ are as usual. A model M of T is a $(\bar{P}; \bar{Q})$-*submodel* of a model N of T, written $M \leq^{(\bar{P};\bar{Q})} N$, iff

(i) $|M| = |N|$;
(ii) $M|K| \subseteq N|K|$, for every predicate constant K in $\bar{P}$;
(iii) $M|K| = N|K|$, for every constant K not in $\bar{P}, \bar{Q}$.

$M <^{(\bar{P};\bar{Q})} N$ is an abbreviation for $M \leq^{(\bar{P};\bar{Q})} N$ and not $N \leq^{(\bar{P};\bar{Q})} M$.

A model M of T is a $(\bar{P}; \bar{Q})$-*minimal* model of T iff T has no model N such that $N <^{(\bar{P};\bar{Q})} M$. ∎

Theorem 6.88 (Soundness Theorem; Mott 1987) If $CIRC_{NR}(T; \bar{P}; \bar{Q}) \vdash A$, then A is true in every $(\bar{P}; \bar{Q})$-minimal model of T. ∎

Since non-recursive circumscription without varying predicates restricts predicate circumscription, it is clear that the above semantics is incomplete. To specify a complete semantics for Mott's formalism, we need the following notion:

Definition 6.89 Let M be a frame for a first-order language L and suppose that $\bar{P}$ and $\bar{Q}$ are disjoint tuples of predicate constants. A subset S of $|M|^n$ is *non-recursively definable in* M *wrt* $(\bar{P}; \bar{Q})$ iff there is a formula $A(x_1, \ldots, x_n) \in L$, whose free variables are precisely $x_1, \ldots, x_n$, such that

(i) A includes no predicate constants from $\bar{P}, \bar{Q}$;
(ii) $(d_1, \ldots, d_n) \in S$ iff $V^M_{a(x_1/d_1, \ldots, x_n/d_n)}(A) = 1$, for some $a \in As(M)$.†

A tuple $S_1, \ldots, S_k$ of subsets of $|M|^{n(1)}, \ldots, |M|^{n(k)}$, respectively, is *non-recursively definable in* M *wrt* $(\bar{P}; \bar{Q})$ iff every S_i is non-recursively definable in M with respect to $(\bar{P}; \bar{Q})$. ∎

Definition 6.90 Let $T(\bar{P}, \bar{Q})$ be a theory, where $\bar{P} = (P_1, \ldots, P_n)$ and $\bar{Q} = (Q_1, \ldots, Q_m)$ are as usual. A model M of T is a *weakly* $(\bar{P}; \bar{Q})$-*minimal model of* T iff there is no model N of T such that $N <^{(\bar{P};\bar{Q})} M$ and the tuple $N|P_1|, \ldots, N|P_n|, N|Q_1|, N|Q_m|$ is non-recursively definable in M with respect to $(\bar{P}, \bar{Q})$. ∎

Theorem 6.91 (Besnard *et al.* 1989) $CIRC_{NR}(T; \bar{P}; \bar{Q}) \vdash A$ iff A is true in every weakly $(\bar{P}; \bar{Q})$-minimal model of T.

Proof Similar to the proof of Theorem 6.9. ∎

In conclusion, non-recursive circumscription is one of the most attractive circumscriptive logics. Preserving consistency, it can be safely used for non-universal theories. By admitting variable predicates, it is strong enough to handle non-monotonic rules. Of course, it is weaker than the logics studied in the previous two sections and hence inherits their limitations concerning the equality predicate.

6.7 DOMAIN CIRCUMSCRIPTION

Domain circumscription is historically the earliest of all circumscriptive logics. It was originally introduced in McCarthy (1977), studied in Davis (1980), and substantially

† Notice that non-recursive definability does not depend on the assignment 'a' used in (ii).

improved by Etherington & Mercer (1987). The intention of domain circumscription is to syntactically formalize the domain closure assumption. As we saw, this assumption cannot be properly handled by the circumscriptive logics we have studied so far.

In this section the term *theory* refers to a finite set of first-order sentences; as usual, we do not distinguish between a theory and the conjunction of all its members.

Definition 6.92 (Etherington & Mercer 1987) The *domain circumscription schema for a theory* T, denoted by $\mathrm{DCS}(T)$, is the following formula of second-order logic:

$$\exists x\Phi(x) \wedge \mathrm{Axiom}(\Phi) \wedge T^{\Phi} \supset \forall x\Phi(x). \tag{6.7.1}$$

Here Φ is a one-place predicate variable. $\mathrm{Axiom}(\Phi)$ stands for the conjunction of $\Phi(a)$, for each object constant a included in T, and $\forall x_1 \ldots x_n[\Phi(x_1) \wedge \cdots \wedge \Phi(x_n) \supset \Phi(f(x_1, \ldots, x_n))]$, for each n-ary ($n \geq 1$) function constant f included in T. T^{Φ} is the result of rewriting T, replacing each occurrence of $\forall x$ and $\exists x$ in T with '$\forall x . \Phi(x) \supset$' and '$\exists x . \Phi(x) \wedge$', respectively. ∎

Since (6.7.1) is to be thought of as implicitly universally quantified, by $\forall\Phi$, we may view it as asserting that the domain of discourse is minimal with respect to T. The schema states that this domain can be identified with the extension of any predicate Φ, provided that the extension of Φ satisfies the following conditions:

(i) It is non-empty ($\exists x . \Phi(x)$);
(ii) It includes all individuals whose existence is assured either by object constants or by the applications of functions ($\mathrm{Axiom}(\Phi)$);
(iii) Its identification with the domain preserves all the axioms of T (T^{Φ}).

Example 6.93 Let $T = \{Bird(Tweety) \wedge \exists x Flies(x)\}$.

$$\begin{aligned}
&\mathrm{Axiom}(\Phi) = \Phi(Tweety)\\
&T^{\Phi} = Bird(Tweety) \wedge \exists x . \Phi(x) \wedge Flies(x)\\
&\mathrm{DCS}(T) = [\exists x\Phi(x) \wedge \Phi(Tweety) \wedge Bird(Tweety) \wedge\\
&\qquad \wedge [\exists x . \Phi(x) \wedge Flies(x)]] \supset \forall x\Phi(x).
\end{aligned}$$

∎

Definition 6.94 Let $\overline{\mathrm{DCS}}(T)$ be the set of all formulae obtainable from $\mathrm{DCS}(T)$ by proper substitutions of unary first-order predicate expressions (possibly with parameters) for Φ. The *domain circumscription of* T, denoted by $\mathrm{CIRC_D}(T)$, is the set $T \cup \overline{\mathrm{DCS}}(T)$. The set of theorems derivable by the domain circumscription of T is identified with the set of formulae classically derivable from $\mathrm{CIRC_D}(T)$.[†] ∎

Example 6.93 (continued) Putting $\{\Phi \leftarrow \lambda x[x = Tweety \vee x = z]\}$ and performing straightforward calculations, we obtain

$$\mathrm{CIRC_D}(T) \vdash [\exists x . [x = Tweety \vee x = z] \wedge Flies(x)] \supset \forall x . x = Tweety \vee x = z.$$

From this, using the equivalences

$$\begin{aligned}
&(A \vee B) \wedge C \equiv (A \wedge C) \vee (B \wedge C)\\
&\exists x(A \vee B) \equiv \exists x A \vee \exists x B
\end{aligned}$$

one easily gets

$$\begin{aligned}
\mathrm{CIRC_D}(T) \vdash [\exists x[x = Tweety \wedge Flies(x)] \vee \exists x[x = z \wedge Flies(x)]] \supset\\
\supset [\forall x . x = Tweety \vee x = z]
\end{aligned}$$

[†] Recall that A is classically derivable from a set of formulae S iff A is classically derivable from $\{\forall B \colon B \in S\}$.

and hence

$$\mathrm{CIRC_D}(T) \vdash [\exists x . x = z \wedge Flies(x)] \supset [\forall x . x = Tweety \vee x = z].$$

Therefore

$$\mathrm{CIRC_D}(T) \vdash \forall z[[\exists x . x = z \wedge Flies(x)] \supset [\forall x . x = Tweety \vee x = z]]$$

and so, since $\vdash \forall z(A \supset B) \supset (\exists z A \supset \exists z B)$

$$\mathrm{CIRC_D}(T) \vdash \exists xz[x = z \wedge Flies(x)] \supset \exists z \forall x[x = Tweety \vee x = z].$$

Thus, since $T \vdash \exists xz[x = z \wedge Flies(x)]$, we finally get

$$\mathrm{CIRC_D}(T) \vdash \exists z \forall x[x = Tweety \vee x = z].$$

The last sentence states that there exist at most two individuals and one of them is '*Tweety*'. ▮

Example 6.95 Let T consist of the following axioms:

$$Bird(Tweety) \wedge Ostrich(Joe)$$
$$\forall x . Ostrich(x) \supset Bird(x).$$

$$\mathrm{DCS}(T) = [\exists x\Phi(x) \wedge \Phi(Tweety) \wedge \Phi(Joe) \wedge Bird(Tweety) \wedge \wedge Ostrich(Joe) \wedge \forall x[\Phi(x) \supset (Ostrich(x) \supset Bird(x))]] \supset \forall x\Phi(x).$$

Letting $\{\Phi \leftarrow \lambda x . x = Tweety \vee x = Joe\}$, we get the domain closure axiom for T:

$$\mathrm{CIRC_D}(T) \vdash \forall x . x = Tweety \vee x = Joe.$$

▮

The next example shows that domain circumscription may not preserve consistency:

Example 6.96 (Davis 1980) Let T consist of the axioms:

(A_1) $\forall x \exists y S(x, y)$
(A_2) $\exists y \forall x \neg S(x, y)$
(A_3) $\forall xyz . S(x, y) \wedge S(x, z) \supset y = z$
(A_4) $\forall xyz . S(y, x) \wedge S(z, x) \supset y = z.$

T is consistent, for we obtain a model interpreting $S(x, y)$ as 'y is the successor of x' in the set of natural numbers.

$$\mathrm{DCS}(T) = [\exists x\Phi(x) \wedge B_1 \wedge B_2 \wedge B_3 \wedge B_4] \supset \forall x\Phi(x) \tag{6.7.2}$$

where

$$B_1 = \forall x . \Phi(x) \supset \exists y[\Phi(y) \wedge S(x, y)]$$
$$B_2 = \exists y . \Phi(y) \wedge \forall x[\Phi(x) \supset \neg S(x, y)]$$
$$B_3 = \forall x . \Phi(x) \supset [\forall y . \Phi(y) \supset \supset [\forall z . \Phi(z) \supset (S(x, y) \wedge S(x, z) \supset y = z)]]$$
$$B_4 = \forall x . \Phi(x) \supset [\forall y . \Phi(y) \supset \supset [\forall z . \Phi(z) \supset (S(y, x) \wedge S(z, x) \supset y = z)]].$$

It is easily verified that the substitution of $\lambda x[\exists u S(u, x)]$ for Φ in (6.7.2) makes all the conjuncts of the antecedent of (6.7.2) derivable from T. Thus, $\mathrm{CIRC_D}(T) \vdash \forall x \exists u S(u, x)$. This contradicts (A_2). ▮

The standard semantics of domain circumscription is based on the following concept:

Definition 6.97 A model M of T is a *submodel* of a model N of T, written $M \leq N$, iff

(i) $|M| \subseteq |N|$;
(ii) The interpretation of each (predicate or function) constant in M is the restriction of the corresponding interpretation in N to $|M|$.

A model is *minimal* if it has no proper submodel. ▮

$M < N$ stands for $M \leq N$ and $M \neq N$.

Employing a result of Davis (1980), Etherington & Mercer (1987) showed that the result of a proper substitution of any unary (first-order) predicate expression for Φ in (6.7.1) is true in all minimal models of the circumscribed theory. From this, we immediately have:

Theorem 6.98 (Soundness Theorem) If $CIRC_D(T) \vdash A$, then A is true in every minimal model of T. ▮

As Davis (1980) showed, the converse of this theorem is false. However:

Theorem 6.99 (Etherington & Mercer 1987) If all models of $CIRC_D(T)$ are finite and A is true in every minimal model of T, then $CIRC_D(T) \vdash A$. ▮

The complete semantics for domain circumscription can be obtained along the same lines as in the case of predicate and non-recursive circumscriptions. To this end, we introduce the following concept of definability:

Definition 6.100 Let M be a frame for a first-order language L. A subset S of $|M|$ is *definable in* M iff there is a formula $A(x) \in L$ such that

$$d \in S \quad \text{iff} \quad V^{M}_{a(x/d)}(A) = 1, \text{ for some } a \in As(M).$$

(Recall that $A(x)$ neither presupposes that x occurs free in A nor that A excludes other free variables.) ▮

Definition 6.101 A model M of T is *weakly minimal* iff there is no model N of T such that $N < M$ and $|N|$ is definable in M. ▮

Weakly minimal models precisely characterize domain circumscription:

Theorem 6.102 $CIRC_D(T) \vdash A$ iff A is true in every weakly minimal model of T.

Proof It suffices to show the following: a model M of T is a model of $\overline{DCS}(T)$ iff M is a weakly minimal model of T.

($\Rightarrow$) Assume to the contrary that M is a model of $\overline{DCS}(T)$ and M is not weakly minimal. Thus, there is a model N of T such that

$$N < M \tag{6.7.3}$$

and $|N|$ is definable in M, i.e. for some formula $A(x)$ and some $a \in As(M)$,

$$d \in |N| \quad \text{iff} \quad V^{M}_{a(x/d)}(A(x)) = 1. \tag{6.7.4}$$

Consider the substitution of $\lambda x A(x)$ for Φ in $DCS(T)$. We may assume that this is a proper substitution since, otherwise, we may always make it proper by renaming bound variables and eventually changing the assignment 'a'. Thus, since M is a model of $\overline{DCS}(T)$,

$$V_a^M([\exists x A(x) \wedge \text{Axiom}(\lambda x A(x)) \wedge T^{\lambda x A(x)}] \supset \forall x A(x)) = 1. \tag{6.7.5}$$

We claim that:

$$V_a^M(\exists x A(x)) = 1 \tag{6.7.6}$$

$$V_a^M(\text{Axiom}(\lambda x A(x))) = 1 \tag{6.7.7}$$

$$V_a^M(T^{\lambda x A(x)}) = 1. \tag{6.7.8}$$

(6.7.6) follows immediately from (6.7.4) and the fact that $|N|$ is non-empty. To show (6.7.7), it suffices to prove that $V_a^M(A(\alpha)) = 1$, for each object constant α in T, and $V_a^M(\forall x_1 \ldots x_n[A(x_1) \wedge \cdots \wedge A(x_n) \supset A(f(x_1, \ldots, x_n))]) = 1$, for each n-ary ($n \geq 1$) function constant f in T. Both these facts follow from (6.7.4) and the definition of a submodel. Finally, (6.7.8) follows from (6.7.4) and the fact that N is a model of T.

In view of (6.7.6)–(6.7.8), (6.7.5) reduces to $V_a^M(\forall x A(x)) = 1$ which, together with (6.7.4), implies that $|M| = |N|$. A contradiction with (6.7.3).

($\Leftarrow$) Let M be a weakly minimal model of T and suppose to the contrary that M is not a model of $\overline{\text{DCS}}(T)$. Thus, there is a proper substitution of $\lambda x . A(x)$ for Φ in DCS(T) such that

$$V_a^M(\exists x A(x) \wedge \text{Axiom}(\lambda x A(x)) \wedge T^{\lambda x A(x)}) = 1 \tag{6.7.9}$$

$$V_a^M(\forall x A(x)) = 0 \tag{6.7.10}$$

for some assignment $a \in As(M)$.

Consider a set $S \subseteq |M|$ given by

$$d \in S \quad \text{iff } V_{a(x/d)}^M(A(x)) = 1. \tag{6.7.11}$$

In view of (6.7.10), S is a proper subset of $|M|$. Moreover, since $V_a^M(\exists x A(x)) = 1$, S is non-empty. We define a frame N such that $|N| = S$ and the interpretation of each constant in N is the restriction of the corresponding interpretation in M to $|N|$. Using (6.7.9), one easily checks that N is a model of T. Furthermore, by (6.7.11), $|N|$ is definable in M. Thus, since $|N| < |M|$, M is not a weakly minimal model of T. A contradiction. ∎

For domain circumscription, the notion of well-foundedness is specified as follows:

Definition 6.103 A theory T *is well-founded for domain circumscription* iff each model of T has a minimal submodel. ∎

In view of Theorem 6.98, we immediately obtain:

Theorem 6.104 If T is consistent and well-founded for domain circumscription, then $\text{CIRC}_D(T)$ is consistent. ∎

We also have the following counterpart of Theorem 6.17:

Theorem 6.105 (Etherington & Mercer 1987) Universal theories are well-founded for domain circumscription. ∎

The next theorem shows that domain circumscription, at least when applied to well-founded theories, never produces new ground equality or inequality statements:

Theorem 6.106 (Etherington & Mercer 1987) If T is well-founded for domain circumscription and α, β are ground terms, then

(i) $T \vdash \alpha = \beta$ iff $\mathrm{CIRC_D}(T) \vdash \alpha = \beta$
(ii) $T \vdash \alpha \neq \beta$ iff $\mathrm{CIRC_D}(T) \vdash \alpha \neq \beta$.

∎

In view of Theorem 6.106 (ii), it is clear that domain circumscription is incapable to formalize the unique names assumption.

We conclude by remarking that the version of domain circumscription presented here, due to Etherington & Mercer (1987), is slightly stronger than that originally developed by McCarthy (1977). He defined the domain circumscription schema for a theory T as the formula

$$\mathrm{Axiom}(\Phi) \wedge T^{\Phi} \supset \forall x \Phi(x) \tag{6.7.12}$$

where Φ, Axiom(Φ) and T^{Φ} are specified as in Definition 6.92. The lack of the conjunct $\exists x \Phi(x)$, in the antecedent of (6.7.12), has the repercussion that the empty domain is not ruled out from considerations. This may easily result in inconsistency. Consider, for example, the theory $T = \{\forall x P(x)\}$. According to McCarthy's original definition, the domain circumscription schema for T is

$$[\forall x . \Phi(x) \supset P(x)] \supset \forall x \Phi(x).$$

Letting $\{\Phi \leftarrow \lambda x False\}$, we immediately obtain $\mathrm{CIRC_D}(T) \vdash$ *False*.

6.8 POINTWISE CIRCUMSCRIPTION

The interpretation of an n-ary predicate constant in a frame M can be represented in two, conceptually different, ways: either by a subset of $|\mathrm{M}|^n$, or by a function from $|\mathrm{M}|^n \rightarrow \{True, False\}$. If the former of these representations is chosen, i.e. if predicate constants are identified with their extensions, then it is natural to view minimality of a predicate as minimality with respect to set inclusion. This concept of minimality leads to the usual specification of circumscription: to circumscribe a predicate P in a theory T is to assume that the extension of P is minimal in the sense that it could not be made smaller without violating T. The interpretation of predicate constants as boolean-valued functions offers an additional possibility. We may think of making a predicate 'smaller' at point $x \in |\mathrm{M}|^n$ as changing its value at this point from *True* to *False*. The predicate is then viewed as minimal with respect to a theory T if it cannot be made smaller (in this sense) without violating T. It is this understanding of minimality that underlies *pointwise circumscription* (Lifschitz 1988b).

In this section, the term *theory* refers to a finite set of first- or second-order sentences; as usual, we do not distinguish between a theory and the conjunction of all its members.

6.8.1 The basic case

We begin with the simplest case of minimizing one predicate P in a theory $T(P, \bar{S})$ with predicate and/or function constants $\bar{S}$ allowed to vary. We want to express that it is impossible to change the value of P at any one point from *True* to *False* without violating T, even if the values of elements of $\bar{S}$ are arbitrarily changed.

Consider the formula

$$A = \exists \bar{x} \exists \bar{\Psi}[P(\bar{x}) \wedge T(\lambda \bar{y}(P(\bar{y}) \wedge \bar{y} \neq \bar{x}), \bar{\Psi})]$$

where $\bar{\Psi}$ is a tuple of predicate and/or function variables corresponding to $\bar{S}$. It is not difficult to see that A represents the following fact: there is a point, namely $\bar{x}$, and a tuple of predicate and/or function variables, namely $\bar{\Psi}$, such that the value of P at $\bar{x}$ can be changed from *True* to *False* without violating T, provided that the elements of $\bar{S}$ are replaced by those of $\bar{\Psi}$. Obviously, what we need is just the negation of A.

Definition 6.107 (Lifschitz 1988b) Let $T(P, \bar{S})$ be a theory, where P is a predicate constant and $\bar{S}$ is a tuple of predicate and/or function constants not containing P. The *pointwise circumscription of P in* $T(P, \bar{S})$ *with variable* $\bar{S}$, denoted by $\mathrm{CIRC_{PW}}(T; P; \bar{S})$, is the sentence,

$$T(P, \bar{S}) \wedge \forall \bar{x} \forall \bar{\Psi} \neg [P(\bar{x}) \wedge T(\lambda \bar{y}(P(\bar{y}) \wedge \bar{y} \neq \bar{x}), \bar{\Psi})]. \tag{6.8.1}$$

▮

As usual, if P is the equality predicate, or, if this predicate is contained in $\bar{S}$, we assume that T includes its equality axioms.

The set of theorems derivable by pointwise circumscription of P in T with variable $\bar{S}$ is identified with the set of formulae entailed by $\mathrm{CIRC_{PW}}(T; P; \bar{S})$.

As usual, two formulae are considered as equivalent if they have the same models.

Notice that $\mathrm{CIRC_{PW}}(T; P; ())$ is a first-order sentence, provided that T is a first-order theory.

Example 6.108 (Lifschitz 1988b) Let $T = \{P(a) \equiv P(b)\}$.

$$\begin{aligned}\mathrm{CIRC_{PW}}(T; P; ()) &= T \wedge \forall x \neg [P(x) \wedge [(P(a) \wedge x \neq a) \equiv (P(b) \wedge x \neq b)]] \Leftrightarrow \\ &\Leftrightarrow T \wedge \forall x . P(x) \supset [(P(a) \wedge x \neq a \wedge x = b) \vee (P(b) \wedge x = a \\ &\wedge x \neq b)]\end{aligned} \tag{6.8.2}$$

It is interesting to compare (6.8.2) with the result of the corresponding second-order circumscription. Using the methods of subsection 6.5.3, the reader may easily verify that

$$\mathrm{CIRC_{SO}}(T; P; ()) \Leftrightarrow [[P(a) \equiv P(b)] \wedge \forall x \neg P(x)] \Leftrightarrow \forall x \neg P(x). \tag{6.8.3}$$

Notice that any frame with P interpreted as universally false is a model of both (6.8.2) and (6.8.3). However, (6.8.2) has additional models, namely those in which P is interpreted as true at precisely two points: a and b. ▮

An important observation is that pointwise circumscription of P in T with variable $\bar{S}$ can be obtained from the corresponding second-order circumscription

$$T(P, \bar{S}) \wedge \forall \Phi \bar{\Psi} \neg [T(\Phi, \bar{\Psi}) \wedge \Phi < P]$$

by letting $\{\Phi \leftarrow \lambda y . (P(y) \wedge y \neq x)\}$ and employing the rule of generalization. Therefore we have:

Theorem 6.109 (Lifschitz 1988b)

$\mathrm{CIRC_{SO}}(T; P; \bar{S})$ entails $\mathrm{CIRC_{PW}}(T; P; \bar{S})$.

▮

As Example 6.108 shows, the converse of this theorem is not generally true. However:

Theorem 6.110 (Lifschitz 1988b) If all occurrences of P in T are positive, then $\text{CIRC}_{\text{PW}}(T; P; \bar{S})$ is equivalent to $\text{CIRC}_{\text{SO}}(T; P; \bar{S})$.† ▮

In view of this theorem, we obtain the following new result concerning reducibility of second-order circumscription into first-order logic:

Corollary 6.111 (Lifschitz 1988b) If all occurrences of P in a first-order theory T are positive, then $\text{CIRC}_{\text{PW}}(T; P; ())$ is equivalent to a first-order sentence.‡ ▮

Example 6.112 Let $T = \{\exists xyP(x, y)\}$. We compute $\text{CIRC}_{\text{SO}}(T; P; ())$. Since T is not separable, Theorem 6.57 does not work here. However, since P occurs positively in T, we may employ Theorem 6.110:

$$\begin{aligned}\text{CIRC}_{\text{SO}}(T; P; ()) \Leftrightarrow &\text{CIRC}_{\text{PW}}(T; P; ()) \Leftrightarrow \\ &\Leftrightarrow [\exists xyP(x, y) \wedge \forall xy \neg [P(x, y) \wedge \exists uv(P(u, v) \wedge \\ &\quad \wedge (x \neq u \vee y \neq v))]] \Leftrightarrow \\ &\Leftrightarrow [\exists xyP(x, y) \wedge \forall xyuv[P(x, y) \wedge \\ &\quad \wedge P(u, v) \supset x = u \wedge y = v]].\end{aligned}$$

▮

Since pointwise circumscription is entailed by second-order circumscription, but not necessarily vice versa, it might seem that the former of these formalisms is less powerful than the latter. This is, however, not the case. Instead of using second-order circumscription to minimize an n-ary predicate constant P in T with variable $\bar{S}$ we may even get a stronger result by introducing a new n-ary predicate constant R and employing pointwise circumscription to minimize R in $T \cup \{\forall \bar{x}.P(\bar{x}) \supset R(\bar{x})\}$ with variable $P, \bar{S}$. This is formally stated below.

Theorem 6.113 (Lifschitz 1988b) Let R be a new predicate constant of the same arity as P. Then

$$\text{CIRC}_{\text{PW}}(T \cup \{\forall \bar{x}.P(\bar{x}) \supset R(\bar{x})\}; R; (P, \bar{S}))$$

is equivalent to

$$\text{CIRC}_{\text{SO}}(T; P; \bar{S}) \wedge [\forall \bar{x}.P(\bar{x}) \equiv R(\bar{x})].$$

▮

6.8.2 Minimizing several predicates

We now generalize pointwise circumscription to the case when several predicates are jointly minimized. Considerations similar to those of the previous section suggest the following definition:

Definition 6.114 Let $\bar{P} = (P_1, \ldots, P_n)$ be a tuple of predicate constants and $\bar{S}$ be a tuple of predicate and/or function constants disjoint with $\bar{P}$. The *pointwise circumscription of $\bar{P}$ in $T(\bar{P}, \bar{S})$ with variable $\bar{S}$*, written $\text{CIRC}_{\text{PW}}(T; \bar{P}; \bar{S})$, is the sentence

$$T(\bar{P}, \bar{S}) \wedge \bigwedge_{i=1}^{n} [\forall \bar{x}\, \forall \bar{\Psi} \neg [P_i(\bar{x}) \wedge T(\lambda \bar{y}(P_i(\bar{y}) \wedge \bar{y} \neq \bar{x}), \bar{\Psi})]]. \tag{6.8.4}$$

▮

† Recall that all the occurrences of a predicate constant P are positive in a formula A iff the normal conjunctive form of A does not contain a subformula of the form $\neg P(\bar{\alpha})$. Therefore, not all occurrences of P are positive in the theory T from Example 6.108. (Note that the normal conjunctive form of T is $[\neg P(a) \vee P(b)] \wedge [\neg P(b) \vee P(a)]$.)

‡ The 'reducibility' results provided by Theorems 6.57, 6.110 and Corollary 6.111 have been further generalized by Rabinov (1989).

Notice that (6.8.4) states that it is impossible to change the value of any of the predicates $P_1, \ldots, P_n$ at any point from *True* to *False* without violating T, even if the values of elements of $\bar{S}$ are changed in arbitrary way.

Comparing Definitions 6.107 and 6.114, we immediately have:

Theorem 6.115 $\mathrm{CIRC_{PW}}(T; \bar{P}; \bar{S})$ is equivalent to

$$\bigwedge_{i=1}^{n} \mathrm{CIRC_{PW}}(T; P_i; \bar{S}). \tag{6.8.5}$$

▮

Theorem 6.115 shows that there is no need to provide a special definition for pointwise circumscription of several predicates since this notion can be directly introduced by the conjunction (6.8.5).

It is easy to notice that pointwise circumscription of $\bar{P} = (P_1, \ldots, P_n)$ in $T(\bar{P}, \bar{S})$ with variable $\bar{S}$ can be obtained from the corresponding second-order circumscription

$$T(\bar{P}, \bar{S}) \wedge \forall \bar{\Phi}\bar{\Psi} \neg [T(\bar{\Phi}, \bar{\Psi}) \wedge \bar{\Phi} < P]$$

by letting $\{\Phi_i \leftarrow \lambda \bar{y}(P_i(\bar{y}) \wedge \bar{x} \neq \bar{y})\}$, $1 \leq i \leq n$, and employing the rule of universal generalization. Therefore, we have:

Theorem 6.116 $\mathrm{CIRC_{SO}}(T; \bar{P}; \bar{S})$ entails $\mathrm{CIRC_{PW}}(T; \bar{P}; \bar{S})$. ▮

We also have an analogon of Theorem 6.110:

Theorem 6.117 (Lifschitz 1988b) Let $\bar{P} = (P_1, \ldots, P_n)$. If all occurrences of $P_1, \ldots, P_n$ in T are positive, then $\mathrm{CIRC_{SO}}(T; \bar{P}; \bar{S})$ and $\mathrm{CIRC_{PW}}(T; \bar{P}; \bar{S})$ are equivalent. ▮

We now proceed to the prioritized version of pointwise circumscription. Suppose we want to circumscribe a tuple $\bar{P}$ of predicate constants in $T(\bar{P}, \bar{S})$ with variable $\bar{S}$ with respect to priorities $\bar{P}^1 > \cdots > \bar{P}^n$. Recall that for second-order circumscription we have (Theorem 6.81):

$$\mathrm{CIRC_{SO}}(T; \bar{P}^1 > \cdots > \bar{P}^n; \bar{S}) \Leftrightarrow \bigwedge_{i=1}^{n} \mathrm{CIRC_{SO}}(T; \bar{P}^i; (\bar{P}^{i+1}, \ldots, \bar{P}^n, \bar{S})).$$

An obvious modification of this equivalence leads to the following definition:

Definition 6.118 (Lifschitz 1988b) The *prioritized pointwise circumscription of* $\bar{P}$ *in* $T(\bar{P}, \bar{S})$ *with variable* $\bar{S}$ *with respect to priorities* $\bar{P}^1 > \cdots > \bar{P}^n$ written $\mathrm{CIRC_{PW}}(T; \bar{P}^1 > \cdots > \bar{P}^n; \bar{S})$, is

$$\bigwedge_{i=1}^{n} \mathrm{CIRC_{PW}}(T; \bar{P}^i; (\bar{P}^{i+1}, \ldots, \bar{P}^n, \bar{S})).$$

▮

By virtue of Theorems 6.81, 6.116 and 6.117, we get the following results:

Theorem 6.119

$$\mathrm{CIRC_{SO}}(T; \bar{P}^1 > \cdots > \bar{P}^n; \bar{S}) \text{ entails } \mathrm{CIRC_{PW}}(T; \bar{P}^1 > \cdots > \bar{P}^n; \bar{S}).$$

▮

Theorem 6.120 Let $\bar{P}^1, \ldots, \bar{P}^n$ be disjoint sublists of all predicate constants from $\bar{P} = (P_1, \ldots, P_m)$. If all occurrences of $P_1, \ldots, P_m$ in T are positive, then $\mathrm{CIRC_{SO}}(T; \bar{P}^1 > \cdots > \bar{P}^n; \bar{S})$ and $\mathrm{CIRC_{PW}}(T; \bar{P}^1 > \cdots > \bar{P}^n; \bar{S})$ are equivalent. ▮

6.8.3 General pointwise circumscription

We now proceed to provide a general form of pointwise circumscription. This generalization allows us to formalize many common-sense settings inexpressible in the framework of other circumscriptive logics.

We employ the following notation (Lifschitz 1988b). If U, V and W are predicate expressions of the same arity, then $EQ_V(U, W)$, read 'U and W are equal outside V', stands for

$$\forall\bar{x}.\neg V(\bar{x}) \supset [U(\bar{x}) \equiv W(\bar{x})].$$

If f and g are function symbols of the same arity as V, then $EQ_V(f, g)$ is an abbreviation for

$$\forall\bar{x}.\neg V(\bar{x}) \supset [f(\bar{x}) = g(\bar{x})].$$

The pointwise approach to circumscription offers interesting possibilities. For instance, minimizing P at a point $\bar{x}$, we may admit that P is allowed to change its values, from *True* to *False* and vice versa (!), at some other points. This may result in an important effect: different points are assigned different priorities in the task of minimizing P. To formalize this idea, the following intuition will be useful.

Let V be a predicate expression of the form $\lambda\bar{x}A(\bar{x})$. V may be naturally viewed as the set of all values of $\bar{x}$ satisfying $A(\bar{x})$. For example, the expression $\lambda x Bird(x)$ may be regarded as the set of all birds. Similarly, $\lambda x Likes(y, x)$ may be considered as the set of those x that are liked by y, i.e. the set $\{x: Likes(y, x)\}$. Suppose now that V is the predicate expression of the form $\lambda\bar{x}\bar{y}A(\bar{x}, \bar{y})$. We may regard V as the function which assigns to each value of $\bar{x}$ the set of those $\bar{y}$ that satisfy $A(\bar{x}, \bar{y})$. Accordingly, we shall write $V(\bar{x})$ for $\lambda\bar{y}A(\bar{x}, \bar{y})$. For example, if V is $\lambda xy Loves(x, y)$, then $V(x)$ is $\lambda y Loves(x, y)$, i.e. the set $\{y: Loves(x, y)\}$.

Let $T(P)$ be a theory, where P is an n-ary predicate constant, and suppose that V is a predicate expression of the form $\lambda\bar{x}\bar{y}A(\bar{x}, \bar{y})$, where $\bar{x}$ and $\bar{y}$ are n-tuples of individual variables. It is assumed that V has no parameters and does not contain P. We want to minimize P in T at every point with the additional assumption: when P is minimized at $\bar{x}$, its values can be arbitrarily changed on $V(\bar{x})$, i.e. on the set $\{\bar{y}: A(\bar{x}, \bar{y})\}$. To express this minimization in the case when no other constants are allowed to vary, Lifschitz (1988b) suggests employing the following sentence:

$$T(P) \wedge \forall\bar{x}\, \forall\Phi \neg[P(\bar{x}) \wedge \neg\Phi(\bar{x}) \wedge EQ_{V(\bar{x})}(P, \Phi) \wedge T(\Phi)] \quad (6.8.6)$$

where Φ is an n-ary predicate variable. The second conjunct of (6.8.6) states that it is impossible to vary the value of P at any point $\bar{x}$ from *True* to *False* without violating T, even if the values of P are arbitrarily changed on $V(\bar{x})$. We denote (6.8.6) by $CIRC_{PW}(T; P/V)$. If V is $\lambda\bar{x}\bar{y}\bar{x} = \bar{y}$, then (6.8.6) reduces to $CIRC_{PW}(T; P; ())$ (the reader is asked to perform appropriate calculations).

To illustrate the new form of pointwise circumscription, we formalize a variant of common-sense reasoning from Chapter 2.

Example 6.121 Suppose that there are two shopping centres, c_1 and c_2, in the small town in which I live and assume that c_1 is nearer my house than c_2. I know that one of the centres, but I do not know which, is closed for some unspecified reason. Given this, if I want to go shopping, the best guess to make is to assume that it is c_1 which is open.

To formalize this the 'Best-guess' reasoning, we introduce the following axioms:

$$Closed(c_1) \vee Closed(c_2) \tag{6.8.7}$$

$$Nearer(c_1, c_2) \tag{6.8.8}$$

$$c_1 \neq c_2. \tag{6.8.9}$$

Let T be the theory consisting of (6.8.7)–(6.8.9). Our intention is to minimize *Closed* in T. Applying the standard form of second-order circumscription, all we can obtain is the disjunction

$$[\forall x.Closed(x) \equiv x = c_1] \vee [\forall x.Closed(x) \equiv x = c_2].$$

The new form of pointwise circumscription allows us to eliminate the first disjunct by preferring c_1 to c_2 in the process of minimizing *Closed*. Actually, we shall formalize a more general preference criterion: x is preferred to y, provided that x is nearer than y.

We apply (6.8.6), letting P to be *Closed* and $V(x)$ to be the predicate expression

$$\lambda y.y = x \vee Nearer(x, y). \tag{6.8.10}$$

(6.8.10) says that *Closed* may be varied on $\{y: y = x \vee Nearer(x, y)\}$ when minimized at x.

$$\begin{aligned} CIRC_{PW}(T; Closed/V) = T \wedge \forall x\, \forall \Phi \neg\{&Closed(x) \wedge \neg\Phi(x) \wedge \\ &\wedge \forall y[y \neq x \wedge \neg Nearer(x, y) \supset [Closed(y) \equiv \Phi(y)]] \wedge T(\Phi)\}. \end{aligned}$$

We show that $CIRC_{PW}(T; Closed/V) \models \forall x.Closed(x) \equiv x = c_2$. To this end, suppose that M is a model of $CIRC_{PW}(T; Closed/V)$ and consider two cases.

Case 1 There is $d \in |M|$ such that $d \in M|Closed|$, $d \neq M|c_1|$ and $d \neq M|c_2|$.

Let a be an assignment of variables such that $a(x) = d$ and $a(\Phi) = M|Closed| - \{d\}$. Let A be the formula

$$\begin{aligned} &Closed(x) \wedge \neg\Phi(x) \wedge \\ &\quad \wedge \forall y[y \neq x \wedge \neg Nearer(x, y) \supset [Closed(y) \equiv \Phi(y)]] \wedge T(\Phi). \end{aligned}$$

It is easily verified that $V_a^M(A) = 1$, and so

$$V_a^M(CIRC_{PW}(T; Closed/V)) = 0.$$

This contradicts that M is a model of $CIRC_{PW}(T; Closed/V)$ and thus shows that Case 1 is impossible.

Case 2 $M|c_1| \in M|Closed|$.

This case is also impossible: apply the same argument, letting $a(x) = M|c_1|$ and $a(\Phi) = \{M|Closed| - \{M|c_1|\}\} \cup \{M|c_2|\}$.

It follows, therefore, that $d \in M|Closed|$ implies $d = M|c_2|$. Thus, since M is a model of T and $(6.8.7) \in T$, we have $M|Closed| = \{M|c_2|\}$, and so, the sentence $\forall x.Closed(x) \equiv x = c_2$ is true in M. Since M was an arbitrary model of $CIRC_{PW}(T; Closed/V)$, we conclude that $CIRC_{PW}(T; Closed/V) \models \forall x.Closed(x) \equiv x = c_2$. ▮

The circumscription axiom (6.8.6) can be further generalized to the case when some function and/or predicate constants, are allowed to vary. For simplicity, we assume first that there is one such a constant S.

If S can be arbitrarily varied in the process of minimizing P in T, it suffices to replace (6.8.6) by

$$T(P, S) \wedge \forall \bar{x}\, \forall \Phi \Psi \neg [P(\bar{x}) \wedge \neg \Phi(\bar{x}) \wedge EQ_{V(\bar{x})}(P, \Phi) \wedge T(\Phi, \Psi)] \quad (6.8.11)$$

where Ψ is a (function or predicate) variable of the same arity as S. Notice that (6.8.11) reduces to (6.8.1), if $V = \lambda \bar{x}\bar{y}\bar{x} = \bar{y}$. The sentence (6.8.11) will be denoted by $\mathrm{CIRC_{PW}}(T; P/V; S)$.

Another possibility is to specify a part of the domain of S on which S may be varied in the task of minimizing P. As Lifschitz (1988b) points out, this idea can be essentially expressed in second-order circumscription. However, the pointwise approach allows for additional flexibility: $\bar{x}$ may affect the specification of the domain of S on which S may be varied when P is minimized on $\bar{x}$. To formalize this intuition, suppose that the arities of P and S are n and m, respectively, and consider a predicate expression, U, of the form $\lambda \bar{x}\bar{y} A(\bar{x}, \bar{y})$, where $\bar{x} = (x_1, \ldots, x_n)$ and $\bar{y} = (y_1, \ldots, y_m)$. Assume that U has no parameters and contains neither P nor S. The intention is that $U(\bar{x})$, i.e. $\lambda \bar{y} A(\bar{x}, \bar{y})$, represents the set of m-tuples of objects on which S may be changed when P is minimized on $\bar{x}$. Assuming further that minimizing P at $\bar{x}$, we are allowed to change the values of P on $V(\bar{x})$, Lifschitz (1988b) proposes the following generalization of (6.8.11):

$$T(P, S) \wedge \forall \bar{x}\, \forall \Phi \Psi \neg [P(\bar{x}) \wedge \neg \Phi(\bar{x}) \wedge EQ_{V(\bar{x})}(P, \Phi) \wedge \\ \wedge EQ_{U(\bar{x})}(S, \Psi) \wedge T(\Phi, \Psi)]. \quad (6.8.12)$$

It is interesting to notice that (6.8.12) reduces to (6.8.11), if $U(\bar{x})$ is identically *True*.

We are now ready to provide the most general form of pointwise circumscription.

Definition 6.122 (Lifschitz 1988b) Let $T(P, \bar{S})$ be a theory, where P is an n-ary predicate constant and $\bar{S} = (S_1, \ldots, S_m)$ is a tuple of function and/or predicate constants, each S_i different from P. Let V be a 2*n-ary predicate expression and suppose that $\bar{U} = (U_1, \ldots, U_m)$, where each U_i $(1 \leq i \leq m)$ is a predicate expression whose arity is the arity of S_i plus n. It is assumed that $V, U_1, \ldots, U_m$ have no parameters and contain none of $P, S_1, \ldots, S_m$. The *pointwise circumscription of P in T with P allowed to vary on* $V(\bar{x})$, *and* S_i *allowed to vary on* $U_i(\bar{x})$ $(1 \leq i \leq m)$, written $\mathrm{CIRC_{PW}}(T; P/V; \bar{S}/\bar{U})$, is the sentence

$$T(P, \bar{S}) \wedge \forall \bar{x}\, \forall \Phi \bar{\Psi} \neg \left\{ P(\bar{x}) \wedge \neg \Phi(\bar{x}) \wedge EQ_{V(\bar{x})}(P, \Phi) \wedge \right. \\ \left. \wedge \bigwedge_{i=1}^{m} [EQ_{U_i(\bar{x})}(\Psi_i, S_i)] \wedge T(\Phi, \bar{\Psi}) \right\} \quad (6.8.13)$$

where Φ and $\bar{\Psi}$ correspond to P and $\bar{S}$, respectively. ∎

We now turn to semantics of circumscription (6.8.13). In the following, we employ the following notation: if M is a frame and V is any predicate expression, without parameters, of the form $\lambda \bar{x} A(\bar{x})$, then $\mathrm{M}|V|$ is the set of those tuples $\bar{x}$ of elements of $|\mathrm{M}|$ which satisfy $A(\bar{x})$.

Definition 6.123 (Lifschitz 1988b) Let $T(P, \bar{S})$, V and $\bar{U}$ be as in Definition 6.122. Recall that the arity of P is n. Let D be a non-empty set, $\bar{x} \in \mathrm{D}^n$, and suppose that M and N are models of T with the domain D. We say that M is an $(\bar{x}; P/V; \bar{S}/\bar{U})$-*submodel* of N, written $\mathrm{M} \leq^{(\bar{x};P/V;\bar{S}/\bar{U})} \mathrm{N}$, iff

(i) $\mathrm{M}|K| = \mathrm{N}|K|$, for every constant K not in $(P, \bar{S})$;

(ii) M|P| and N|P| coincide on $\{\bar{y}: (\bar{x}, \bar{y}) \notin M|V|\}$;
(iii) M|S_i| and N|S_i| coincide on $\{\bar{y}: (\bar{x}, \bar{y}) \notin M|U_i|\}$ $(1 \leq i \leq m)$;
(iv) M|P|($\bar{x}$) $\leq$ N|P|($\bar{x}$), where $\leq$ is the usual ordering of Boolean values (*False* < *True*).

M $<^{(\bar{x};P/V;\bar{S}/\bar{U})}$ N is an abbreviation for M $\leq^{(\bar{x};P/V;\bar{S}/\bar{U})}$ N but not N $\leq^{(\bar{x};P/V;\bar{S}/\bar{U})}$ M.

M is an ($\bar{x}$; P/V; $\bar{S}/\bar{U}$)-*minimal model of T with respect to* D, iff T has no model with the domain D such that N $<^{(\bar{x};P/V;\bar{S}/\bar{U})}$ M. ▮

Theorem 6.124 (Lifschitz 1988b) A model M of T with the domain D is a model of $\mathrm{CIRC}_{PW}(T; P/V; \bar{S}/\bar{U})$ iff for each $\bar{x} \in D^n$, M is an ($\bar{x}$; P/V; $\bar{S}/\bar{U}$)-minimal model of T with respect to D. ▮

We conclude this section by presenting a famous example, known in the AI literature as the 'Yale shooting problem' (Hanks & McDermott 1987). To make our discussion self-contained, we must first say a little about *situation calculus*. It was introduced by McCarthy & Hayes (1969) to formalize reasoning about action. Here we focus on a specific non-monotonic version of this formalism, used by Hanks and McDermott.

The situation calculus is based on many-sorted first-order logic with variables ranging over four kinds of individuals: ordinary individuals, *situations*, *facts* and *actions*. Situations are abstract entities viewed as states of a world at moments of time. An object constant S_0 refers to a distinguished *initial situation*. Facts are assertions about the world and they are always relativized to situations. To state that a fact f holds in a situation s, we shall write *Holds*(f, s), where *Holds* is a special predicate constant and f, s are terms denoting a fact and a situation, respectively. For example, *Holds*(*On*(b, c), S_0) asserts that b is on c in the initial situation. Actions may be thought of as transformations from situations into situations. The situation resulting from performing an action a in a situation s is denoted by *result*(a, s), where *result* is a distinguished function constant. Thus,

$$Holds(On(b, c), result(put(b, top(c)), S_0))$$

states that b is on c in the situation being the result of putting b on the top of c in S_0.

To deal with the frame problem (see Chapter 2), we introduce a three-place predicate constant, *Ab*, which takes an action, a fact and a situation as its arguments. *Ab*(a, f, s) is to be read: 'a is abnormal with respect to preserving f in s'. The intention, of course, is that: (1) *Ab* will be minimized, i.e. any action will be considered normal with respect to preserving any fact in any situation unless the contrary is known, and (2) If a is normal with respect to preserving f in s, and f holds in s, then f remains to hold in *result*(a, s). Under this assumption, a natural solution to the frame problem is to employ the following *frame axiom*:

$$\forall afs.\, Holds(f, s) \wedge \neg Ab(a, f, s) \supset Holds(f, result(a, s))$$

where a, f and s are individual variables ranging over actions, facts and situations, respectively.

The idea of approaching the frame problem using circumscription is due to McCarthy (1980; 1984). Unfortunately, as Hanks & McDermott (1987) showed, this proposal is problematic with respect to the following *temporal projection task*: Given a description of an initial situation, a description of effects of possible actions, and a sequence of actions to be performed, determine the description of the resulting situation.† To support their claim, Hanks and McDermott consider the following example:

Example 6.125 Let T consist of the following axioms:‡

$$(A_1)\ Holds(alive, S_0) \wedge Holds(loaded, S_0)$$
$$(A_2)\ \forall s.Holds(loaded, s) \supset Holds(dead, result(shoot, s))$$
$$(A_3)\ \forall s.Holds(loaded, s) \supset Ab(shoot, alive, s)$$
$$(A_4)\ \forall afs.Holds(f, s) \wedge \neg Ab(a, f, s) \supset Holds(f, result(a, s)).$$

This theory refers to a person and a gun, both indefinite. In any situation the person is either alive or dead; the gun is either loaded or unloaded. Initially, the person is alive and the gun is loaded (A_1). When the loaded gun shoots, the person becomes dead (A_2) and, furthermore, shooting is abnormal with respect to staying alive in any situation when the gun is loaded (A_3). Finally, (A_4) is the frame axiom.

We additionally assume that there is an object constant, *wait*, denoting an action which normally does not cause any specific effects in the world.

Consider the following sequence of situations:

$$S_0; \qquad S_1 = result(wait, S_0); \qquad S_2 = result(shoot, S_1).$$

The question we are interested in is whether the person is dead in S_2.

Intuitively, we expect that waiting does not change the world, so that the gun is loaded in S_1 and, consequently, the person is dead in S_2. Unfortunately, as a careful analysis shows, the sentence $Holds(dead, S_2)$ cannot be derived by applying second-order circumscription. The reason is that there are two conflicting minimizations of Ab in T. In the intended one, abnormality is minimized in chronological order. We start by assuming $\neg Ab(wait, alive, S_0)$ and $\neg Ab(wait, loaded, S_0)$, apply (A_4) twice to derive $Holds(alive, S_1)$ and $Holds(loaded, S_1)$, and then infer $Ab(shoot, alive, S_1)$, by (A_3), and $Holds(dead, S_2)$, by (A_2). Somewhat surprisingly, there is another way to minimize Ab in T, corresponding to the scenario in which the gun is mysteriously unloaded at waiting stage. The key point is that as long as $\neg Ab(wait, loaded, S_0)$ is not assumed, we cannot infer $Holds(loaded, S_1)$ and the lack of this conclusion allows us to assume $\neg Ab(shoot, alive, S_1)$. The reader may easily check that starting by assuming $\neg Ab(shoot, alive, S_1)$, we get a quite different picture of the world, in which the person is alive in S_2. In conclusion, all we can get by applying second-order circumscription is $Holds(dead, S_2) \vee Holds(alive, S_2)$.

As our discussion shows, non-monotonic approach to the temporal projection task requires *chronological minimization of abnormality:* if there is a conflict between minimizing abnormality in two situations, the minimization in the temporarily earlier one should be preferred. Unfortunately, second-order circumscription cannot capture this type of minimization and so it offers no easy solution to the temporal projection task. We parenthetically remark that the formalisms studied in the previous chapters share the same difficulty. For instance, in default logic, the shooting setting can be naturally expressed by the default theory consisting of (A_1)–(A_4), together with the

† That circumscriptive logics are generally too weak to properly deal with this task has been already observed in McCarthy (1984).

‡ For simplicity, Hanks and McDermott's original example is slightly reformulated here.

default

$$\frac{:\neg Ab(a, f, s)}{\neg Ab(a, f, s)}.$$

It is easy to notice that applying the default to (*wait*, *loaded*, S_0) makes it inapplicable to (*shoot*, *alive*, S_1) and vice versa. Accordingly, apart from an extension containing $\neg Ab(wait, loaded, S_0)$, there is another extension including $\neg Ab(shoot, alive, S_1)$. The former of these extensions contains $Holds(dead, S_2)$; the latter contains $Holds(alive, S_2)$.

The idea of chronological minimization is easily formalized using the pointwise approach to circumscription. To this end, we supply T with the following axioms:

$$\begin{array}{ll} S_i \neq S_j & (0 \leq i < j \leq 2) \\ dead \neq loaded & \\ dead \neq alive & \\ alive \neq loaded & \\ wait \neq shoot & \\ \multicolumn{2}{l}{\forall s \forall s'.s < s' \equiv (s = S_0 \wedge s' = S_1) \vee (s = S_0 \wedge s' = S_2) \vee (s = S_1 \wedge s' = S_2)} \end{array}$$

We minimize Ab in (the extended) T with *Holds* allowed to vary. We use pointwise circumscription of the form (6.8.11), i.e. *Holds* may be varied in an arbitrary way. To express that chronologically earlier situations are to be preferred in the process of minimization, we let $V(a, f, s)$ be

$$\lambda a'f's'[(a, f, s) = (a', f', s') \vee s < s']$$

where $(a, f, s) = (a', f', s')$ stands for $a = a' \wedge f = f' \wedge s = s'$.

$$\begin{aligned} &\mathrm{CIRC}_{\mathrm{PW}}(T(Ab, Holds); Ab/V(a, f, s); Holds) = T(Ab, Holds) \wedge \\ &\quad \wedge \forall afs\bar{\Phi}\bar{\Psi}\neg[Ab(a, f, s) \wedge \neg\Phi(a, f, s) \wedge T(\Phi, \Psi) \wedge \\ &\qquad\qquad \wedge \forall a'f's'[\neg V(a, f, s)(a', f', s') \supset \\ &\qquad\qquad \supset (Ab(a', f', s') \equiv \Phi(a', f', s'))]]. \end{aligned}$$

Our purpose is to show that

$$\mathrm{CIRC}_{\mathrm{PW}}(T(Ab, Holds); Ab/V(a, f, s); Holds) \models Holds(dead, S_2).$$

Notice that we are working with many-sorted logic, so that the domain of any frame under consideration, M, consists of a tuple of disjoint subdomains. In our case, because there are no object individuals, there are three such subdomains, corresponding to actions, facts and situations. In what follows, we denote by $|M|_{AC}$ the first of these subdomains.

To show that $\mathrm{CIRC}_{\mathrm{PW}}(T(Ab, Holds); Ab/V(a, f, s); Holds)$ entails $Holds(dead, S_2)$, it is sufficient to demonstrate that $Holds(dead, S_2)$ is entailed by A, where A is an instance of $\mathrm{CIRC}_{\mathrm{PW}}(T(Ab, Holds); Ab/V(a, f, s); Holds)$ with (a, f, s) replaced by $(wait, loaded, S_0)$. That is

$$\begin{aligned} A = {} & T(Ab, Holds) \wedge \\ & \wedge \forall\Phi\Psi\neg[Ab(wait, loaded, S_0) \wedge \neg\Phi(wait, loaded, S_0) \wedge T(\Phi, \Psi) \wedge \\ &\qquad \wedge \forall a'f's'[\neg V(wait, loaded, S_0)(a', f', s') \supset \\ &\qquad \supset (Ab(a', f', s') \equiv \Phi(a', f', s'))]]. \end{aligned}$$

Suppose that M is a model of A and consider the formula

$$B = \neg[Ab(wait, loaded, S_0) \wedge \neg\Phi(wait, loaded, S_0) \wedge T(\Phi, \Psi) \wedge \\ \wedge \forall a'f's'[\neg V(wait, loaded, S_0)(a', f', s') \supset \\ \supset (Ab(a', f', s') \equiv \Phi(a', f', s'))]].$$

Since $A = T \wedge \forall\Phi\Psi B$ and M is a model of A, we conclude

$$V_a^M(B) = 1, \text{ for any assignment } a \in As(M). \qquad (6.8.14)$$

Let $a \in As(M)$ be an assignment satisfying:

$$a(\Phi) = \{M|Ab| - \{(M|wait|, M|loaded|, M|S_0|)\}\} \cup \\ \cup\{(M|shoot|, M|alive|, M|S_1|)\} \cup \\ \cup \{(d, M|dead|, M|S_2|): d \in |M|_{AC}\} \cup \\ \cup \{(d, M|loaded|, M|S_1|): d \in |M|_{AC}\}.$$

$$a(\Psi) = M|Holds| \cup \{(M|dead|, M|S_2|), (M|loaded|, M|S_1|)\}.$$

It is routine to verify that $V_a^M(C) = 1$, where

$$C = [\neg\Phi(wait, loaded, S_0) \wedge T(\Phi, \Psi) \wedge \\ \wedge \forall a'f, s'[\neg V(wait, loaded, S_0)(a', f', s') \supset \\ \supset (Ab(a', f', s') \equiv \Phi(a', f', s'))]].$$

Thus, since $B = \neg[Ab(wait, loaded, S_0) \wedge C]$, we have by (6.8.14),

$$V_a^M(\neg Ab(wait, loaded, S_0)) = 1.$$

Therefore, since M is a model of T, we get by (A_1) and (A_4), $V_a^M(Holds(loaded, S_1)) = 1$ and so, by (A_2), $V_a^M(Holds(dead, S_2)) = 1$. Since M was chosen arbitrarily, we finally conclude that A, and hence $CIRC_{PW}(T(Ab, Holds); Ab/V(a, f, s); Holds)$, entails $Holds(dead, S_2)$. ∎

It should be remarked that the employment of pointwise circumscription is only one of the possible solutions to the temporal projection task. For other proposals, see Kautz (1986), Lifschitz (1987), Łukaszewicz (1988), Morris (1988) and especially Shoham (1988).

I believe that the pointwise approach to circumscription offers interesting possibilities and is obviously worthy of further investigation. It has three important advantages. Firstly, the basic case of pointwise circumscription (without variable objects) is specified as a first-order sentence. Secondly, there is no need to minimize more than one predicate. Finally, in its general case, the pointwise approach is sufficiently powerful to cover inference patterns which are difficult to formalize by using other circumscriptive logics. The major drawback of pointwise circumscription is that its complex forms are not easy to compute.

Some connections between pointwise circumscription and logic programming with negation have been studied in Lifschitz (1988a).

6.9 CONCLUSIONS

Circumscription is the most controversial of all the formal approaches to non-monotonic reasoning. It has one major advantage and one major weakness when compared with other proposals.

The most important strength of circumscriptive logics is that they are entirely embedded in standard logical framework. When a circumscription axiom (schema) is constructed, all deductions proceed in monotonic logic. In fact, in circumscription, first-order non-monotonic inference reduces to monotonic inference in ordinary second-order logic. Accordingly, one may hope that circumscription can be computed by higher-order theorem provers. Unfortunately, this idea has not been realized so far, since no reasonable method of finding useful substitutions is currently known.

The major weakness of circumscriptive logics is that they are hard to use. There are two basic difficulties in applying any form of circumscription:

(1) How to select a circumscription axiom (schema)?
(2) How to compute the selected circumscription?

To answer the first of these questions, we should specify which predicates are minimized and which of the remaining ones, together with functions, are varied in the process of minimization. We may also wish to asign priorities to the circumscribed predicates and, in the case of pointwise circumscription, to define the variable parts of the minimized and/or varied objects. If circumscriptive logics are to be of practical importance, we need tools to make these decisions, depending on the goal at hand and the theory under consideration. Unfortunately, except for a paper of Papalaskaris & Bundy (1984), this subject has never been touched in the literature.

Having selected a particular circumscription axiom (schema) C, we are faced with the computational problem: How to determine whether a given sentence can be derived by performing the circumscription represented by C? Of course, this is an undecidable problem, so that no general algorithm is available. However, we need a better heuristic method than guessing correct substitutions. (We ignore here the cases when the result of circumscription can be expressed in first-order logic.) The problem of computing circumscription is now intensively studied in the context of its second-order version and several researchers have proposed methods covering various restricted classes of theories. For these proposals, often based on closed connections between circumscription and logic programming with negation, see Przymusinski (1986), Gelfond & Lifschitz (1989), Ginsberg (1989) and Przymusinski (1989).

Bossu & Siegel (1985) investigated a form of non-monotonic reasoning based on the concept of minimal models. Although their approach is purely semantic, so that they have nothing corresponding to a circumscription axiom, the system they actually developed is a special case of second-order circumscription. More precisely, they introduce a notion of *sub-implication* with the following interpretation: A formula A is sub-implied by a first-order universal theory T, written $T \succ\!\!- A$, iff A is true in all $(T; \bar{P}; ())$-minimal models of T, where $\bar{P}$ consists of all predicate constants occurring in T. (In other words, assuming that T is a finite theory, $T \succ\!\!- A$ iff $\mathrm{CIRC}_{\mathrm{SO}}(T; \bar{P}; ()) \models A$.) The most important result of Bossu & Siegel is a proof theory they provide. It turns out that by imposing certain reasonable restrictions on T and A, it is possible to construct a decidable resolution-based procedure for determining whether $T \succ\!\!- A$ (and hence $\mathrm{CIRC}_{\mathrm{SO}}(T; \bar{P}; ()) \models A$). For details, see Bossu & Siegel (1985).

There has been some work on translating from default logic into circumscription (Grosof 1984; Imielinski 1987), but the results of these proposals are not very encouraging. It seems that the existence of a reasonable translation is very problematic, due to fundamental differences between both the approaches (Etherington 1988):

(i) A default theory may give rise to many extensions, each viewed as an equally acceptable set of beliefs. In contrast, there is exactly one set of theorems derivable from a circumscriptive theory.
(ii) Default logic allows inferences to be made concerning equality and circumscription generally does not.
(iii) Circumscriptive conclusions apply to all individuals of the domain, whereas open defaults only apply to the individuals expressible in the language.
(iv) Default logic has no mechanism corresponding to varying predicates (functions) in circumscription.
(v) Default logic is a consistency-based formalism in the sense that a consistency test is needed to determine the applicability of a default; circumscription avoids this problem by employing second-order logic.

Lifschitz (1984) developed a very general circumscriptive logic which allows the predicates to be minimized according to arbitrary pre-orders (reflexive and transitive relations). More precisely, given a theory $T(\bar{P}, \bar{S})$, where $\bar{P}$ is a tuple of predicates to be minimized and $\bar{S}$ is a tuple of predicates (and/or functions) which may be varied, the *generalized circumscription of $\bar{P}$ in $T(\bar{P}, \bar{S})$ with variable $\bar{S}$ with respect to a pre-order $\leq_R$* is the sentence

$$T(\bar{P}, \bar{S}) \wedge \forall \bar{\Phi}\bar{\Psi}.\neg[T(\bar{\Phi}, \bar{\Psi}) \wedge \bar{\Phi} <_R \bar{P}] \tag{6.9.1}$$

where $\bar{\Phi}$ and $\bar{\Psi}$ are tuples of predicate (function) variables corresponding to $\bar{P}$ and $\bar{S}$, respectively, and $\bar{\Phi} <_R \bar{P}$ stands for $(\bar{\Phi} \leq_R \bar{P}) \wedge \neg(\bar{\Phi} = \bar{P})$. Clearly, both standard and prioritized versions of second-order circumscription are special cases of generalized circumscription. Specifically, if '$\leq_R$' is defined by

$$(\Phi_1, \ldots, \Phi_n) \leq_R (P_1, \ldots, P_n) \text{ iff } (\Phi_1, \ldots, \Phi_n) \leq (P_1, \ldots, P_n) \tag{6.9.2}$$

then (6.9.1) reduces to $\mathrm{CIRC_{SO}}(T; \bar{P}; \bar{S})$. On the other hand, if we divide $\bar{P}$ into disjoint sublists $\bar{P}^1, \ldots, \bar{P}^m$ and specify '$\leq_R$' by

$$(\Phi_1, \ldots, \Phi_n) \leq_R (P_1, \ldots, P_n) \text{ iff } (\bar{\Phi}^1, \ldots \bar{\Phi}^m) \lesssim (\bar{P}^1, \ldots, \bar{P}^m) \tag{6.9.3}$$

then (6.9.1) becomes equivalent to $\mathrm{CIRC_{SO}}(T; \bar{P}^1 > \cdots > \bar{P}^m; \bar{S})$. Lifschitz's generalized form of circumscription has not attracted much attention. The reason perhaps is that (6.9.2) and (6.9.3) appear to be the only pre-orders which are interesting from the standpoint of practical applications.

Minker & Perlis (1984) introduced a variant of predicate circumscription, called *protected circumscription*. Their formalism allows a predicate P to be minimized in a theory $T(P)$, under the additional assumption that all tuples of individuals satisfying a particular predicate R, of the same arity as P, are protected in the process of minimization. To express this idea, Minker and Perlis weaken McCarthy's (1980) circumscription schema to:

$$[T(\Phi) \wedge [\forall \bar{x}.\Phi(\bar{x}) \wedge \neg R(\bar{x}) \supset P(\bar{x})]] \supset [\forall \bar{x}.P(\bar{x}) \wedge \neg R(\bar{x}) \supset \Phi(\bar{x})]$$

where Φ is a predicate variable corresponding to P.

Obviously, if we wish to circumscribe P in T with protected R, then, *ipso facto*, we want to circumscribe the expression $\lambda\bar{x}.P(\bar{x}) \wedge \neg R(\bar{x})$ in T. This latter minimization can be directly formalized using formula circumscription, and indirectly, by means of any circumscriptive logic admitting variable predicates (see Theorem 6.31). Accordingly, the interest in protected circumscription seems now rather pointless.

For more exotic circumscriptive logics, the reader is referred to Perlis (1987a) and Perlis (1988). The former of these papers is devoted to a set-theoretic version of circumscription; the latter provides a circumscription-based formalization of the problem of negative introspection: How to determine that a given sentence is not among a reasoner's conclusions? The ideas of Perlis (1988) have been further generalized by Lifschitz (1989b), who introduces a version of circumscription closely related to autoepistemic logic.

7

Approaches to closed world assumption

7.1 INTRODUCTION

As we remarked earlier, the *closed world assumption* (CWA) is a non-monotonic rule, introduced by Reiter (1978) to efficiently represent completely specified worlds. The motivation for the rule stems from the observation that the number of negative facts about a given domain is typically much greater than the number of positive ones. What is worse, in many natural applications, the number of negative facts is so large that their explicit representation becomes practically impossible. Consider, for example, a simple data base representing a lending-library with 1000 readers and 10 000 books, and suppose that each reader is allowed to borrow up to 5 books. Obviously, we are not able to explicitly store 9 995 000–10 000 000 sentences to keep track of all readers and all the books they do not currently borrow. However, if we ignore this information, how can we infer that a given book is not lent to a given reader? In particular, how can we decide that the book is not lent at all?

The natural solution to this problem is to assume that all positive information has been specified, so that any positive fact which cannot be inferred from this information is false. This is precisely Reiter's CWA rule. It states that any atomic sentence which cannot be derived from a given collection of facts is assumed false. If the rule is in force, only positive facts are explicitly represented. Negative facts are inferred from the lack of proofs of their positive counterparts.

It should be stressed that the employment of the CWA rule (in its original form) is ill-motivated unless we assume the total knowledge about the world. Fortunately, this requirement is not so restrictive as it might appear. In particular, the rule is appropriate for most domains represented in typical data bases.†

† The CWA rule has been traditionally discussed from the standpoint of data bases. Here we adopt a slightly different course and all the results of this chapter will be stated in terms of pure logic. This shift in emphasis is inessential, since any data base, relational or deductive, can be always viewed as a first-order theory.

The CWA rule can be realized in the framework of the formalisms studied in the previous chapters. For instance, in default logic, we may express it by augmenting a given first-order theory T with the set of defaults

$$\left\{\frac{:\neg R(x_1, \ldots, x_n)}{\neg R(x_1, \ldots, x_n)} : R \in \mathbf{R}\right\}$$

where $\mathbf{R}$ is the set of all predicate constants occurring in T. In circumscriptive logics, the CWA naturally corresponds to the joint minimization of all predicates.

In this chapter, we present a number of logics specially constructed for the purpose of formalizing various versions of the CWA rule. We begin by discussing the earliest of these proposals, developed by Reiter (1978). We shall refer to this logic as *naive* CWA (NCWA, for short).[†] Limitations of Reiter's system led several researchers to formalize more sophisticated forms of the CWA rule. The first such attempt was made by Minker (1982). His logic, called *generalized* CWA (GCWA), is discussed in section 7.3. GCWA was further extended by Gelfond & Przymusinska (1986). Their proposal, referred to as *careful* CWA (CCWA), is examined in section 7.4. The new feature of this system is that it allows us to restrict the application of the CWA rule to a subset of freely chosen predicates. In section 7.5, we present the most general CWA logic, called *extended* CWA (ECWA). This formalism, introduced in Gelfond *et al.* (1989), subsumes NCWA, GCWA and CCWA. Finally, section 7.6 provides an introduction to *theory completion*, a highly original formalization of the CWA rule, developed by Clark (1978) in the context of logic programming.

Throughout this chapter we employ the following teminological conventions. Unless stated otherwise, the term 'theory' refers to a finite set of universal first-order sentences without equality. Recall that each such a theory has its equivalent in the clausal form (Theorem 1.51, Chapter 1). We shall often make use of this fact in the subsequent presentation. We always assume that the language of a theory T consists of the formulae constructable using individual, function and predicate constants occurring in T. The term 'function constant' will always refer to a function constant of a positive arity, whereas 0-ary function constants will be referred to as individual constants. The symbol '$\vdash$' (resp. '$\nvdash$') denotes the provability (resp. unprovability) relation of the classical first-order logic.

7.2 NAIVE CWA

We start by examining the earliest formalization of the CWA rule, introduced in Reiter (1978).

The set of all ground terms formed using the function and individual constants occurring in a theory T is called the *Herbrand universe* of T.[‡] By HB(T) we denote the *Herbrand base of* T, i.e. the set of all sentences of the form $P(\alpha_1, \ldots, \alpha_n)$, where P is a predicate constant occurring in T and $\alpha_1, \ldots, \alpha_n$ are elements of the Herbrand universe of T.

Reiter proposes the following syntactic formalization of the CWA rule.[§]

[†] The term 'naive' is borrowed from Etherington (1988), who called this formalism *naive closure*.

[‡] For simplicity, we assume that each theory has at least one individual constant.

[§] In his original formulation, Reiter considers finite universal theories without function constants. However, if the CWA rule is viewed from logical, rather than data base perspective, this restriction is unnecessary. On the other hand, Reiter bases his logic upon a many-sorted language, whereas the language used here is one-sorted. This limitation is inessential, since many-sorted first-order logic is a conservative extension of its one-sorted counterpart (see section 1.3.5).

Definition 7.1 (Reiter 1978) The *naive closure of a theory T*, denoted by NCWA(T), is the theory

$$T \cup \{\neg A\colon T \nvdash A \text{ and } A \in \mathrm{HB}(T)\}.$$

The set of theorems derivable from T by NCWA is identified with the set of all formulae classically derivable from NCWA(T). ▮

Example 7.2 Let T consist of:

$$\forall x . P(x) \supset Q(x)$$
$$P(a) \wedge R(b).$$

$$\mathrm{HB}(T) = \{P(a), Q(a), R(a), P(b), Q(b), R(b)\}$$
$$\mathrm{NCWA}(T) = T \cup \{\neg R(a), \neg P(b), \neg Q(b)\}.$$

▮

It is reasonable to ask whether NCWA preserves consistency. Unfortunately, the answer is negative:

Example 7.3 Let $T = \{Adult(Joe) \vee Adult(Bill)\}$. NCWA($T$), namely $T \cup \{\neg Adult(Joe), \neg Adult(Bill)\}$ is inconsistent. ▮

Although this result is pessimistic, it is fair to notice that the theory of the above example can be hardly accepted as a representation of a completely specified world.

For which theories does NCWA preserve consistency? While no complete syntactic characterization of such theories is currently known, Reiter provides the following partial result. A theory T (in the clausal form) is a Horn theory iff each clause of T contains at the most one positive literal.

Theorem 7.4 (Reiter 1978) If T is a consistent Horn theory, then NCWA(T) is consistent.

Proof Follows from Theorem 7.8 which will be proved later. ▮

It is worth noting that there are non-Horn theories for which NCWA preserves consistency. Consider, for instance, the theory $T = \{P(a) \vee P(b), \neg P(a)\}$. The naive closure of T, namely $T \cup \{\neg P(a)\}$, is clearly consistent.

Recall that a *ground sentence* is any sentence containing no variables. A ground sentence is called *positive*, iff it can be represented as a conjunction of disjunctions of ground atomic sentences.

Applying Definition 7.1, the reader may easily verify that the following result holds:

Theorem 7.5 Let T be a theory and suppose that NCWA(T) is consistent. If A is a ground positive sentence, then

(i) $\mathrm{NCWA}(T) \vdash A$ iff $T \vdash A$
(ii) $\mathrm{NCWA}(T) \vdash \neg A$ iff $T \nvdash A$.

▮

This theorem shows that NCWA, if consistent, does not allow us to prove any new ground positive sentence. Furthermore, if such a sentence cannot be derived from a given collection of facts, then its negation is derivable from the naive closure of these facts. This latter observation indicates that NCWA realizes the CWA rule with respect to arbitrary positive sentences rather than ground atoms.

We now proceed to provide a semantics for NCWA.

Definition 7.6 A *Herbrand frame of a theory T* is any frame M such that:

(i) |M| is the Herbrand universe for T;
(ii) For each individual constant c occurring in T, $\mathrm{M}|c| = c$;
(iii) For each n-ary function constant f occurring in T, $\mathrm{M}|f|$ is the function which assigns the ground term $f(\alpha_1, \ldots, \alpha_n)$ to a tuple $\alpha_1, \ldots, \alpha_n$ of ground terms.

∎

Since Herbrand frames of T differ only in how they interpret predicate constants, each such a frame can be identified with a subset (possibly empty) of the Herbrand base of T. More precisely, if M is a Herbrand frame of T, then it is identified with a subset S of HB(T), given by

$$P(\alpha_1, \ldots, \alpha_n) \in \mathrm{S} \quad \text{iff} \quad (\alpha_1, \ldots, \alpha_n) \in \mathrm{M}|P|.$$

For instance, the set $\{P(a), Q(a, f(a)), Q(b, a)\}$ corresponds to the Herbrand frame M with $\mathrm{M}|P| = \{a\}$ and $\mathrm{M}|Q| = \{(a, f(a)), (b, a)\}$.

A Herbrand frame for T in which all sentences of T are true is called a *Herbrand model of* T. It is well-known that each consistent universal theory without equality has a Herbrand model.

The one-to-one correspondence between Herbrand frames and subsets of Herbrand bases leads to a natural partial ordering in the class of Herbrand models of a given theory:

Definition 7.7 Let T be a theory and suppose that M and N are Herbrand models of T. We write $\mathrm{M} \leq \mathrm{N}$ iff $\mathrm{M}|P| \subseteq \mathrm{N}|P|$, for each predicate constant P occurring in T. We say that M is a *minimal Herbrand model of* T iff there is no Herbrand model N of T such that $\mathrm{N} \leq \mathrm{M}$ and $\mathrm{N} \neq \mathrm{M}$. M is the *least Herbrand model of* T iff $\mathrm{M} \leq \mathrm{N}$, for each Herbrand model N of T. ∎

The notion of the least Herbrand model provides a semantic characterization of the class of theories for which NCWA preserves consistency:

Theorem 7.8 For each theory T, NCWA (T) is consistent iff T has the least Herbrand model.

Proof (⇒) Assume that NCWA(T) is consistent. Since each consistent universal theory without equality has a Herbrand model, there is a Herbrand model, say M, for NCWA(T). Clearly, M is also a model of T. Take any n-ary predicate constant P, occurring in T, and consider $\mathrm{M}|P|$. Applying Theorem 7.5, we infer that

$$\mathrm{NCWA}(T) \vdash P(\alpha_1, \ldots, \alpha_n) \quad \text{iff} \quad T \vdash P(\alpha_1, \ldots, \alpha_n)$$

and

$$\mathrm{NCWA}(T) \vdash \neg P(\alpha_1, \ldots, \alpha_n) \quad \text{iff} \quad T \nvdash P(\alpha_1, \ldots, \alpha_n)$$

for any tuple $\alpha_1, \ldots, \alpha_n$ from the Herbrand universe of T. Thus, since M is a Herbrand model of NCWA(T), we have

$$\mathrm{M}|P| = \{(\alpha_1, \ldots, \alpha_n) : T \vdash P(\alpha_1, \ldots, \alpha_n)\}$$

and so, $\mathrm{M}|P| \subseteq \mathrm{N}|P|$, for each Herbrand model N of T. Thus, since P was chosen arbitrarily and M is a Herbrand model of T, we finally conclude that M is the least Herbrand model of T.

(⇐) We shall need the following lemma.

Lemma 7.8.1 For any (universal) theory T and any ground sentence A, $T \vdash A$ iff A is true in all Herbrand models of T.

Proof The proof is almost straightforward. It can be found in Gelfond & Przymusinska (1986, Lemma 3.3). ■

To prove the if part of the theorem, assume that M is the least Herbrand model of T. Take any n-ary predicate constant P, occurring in T, and consider $\mathrm{M}|P|$. Since $\mathrm{M}|P| \subseteq \mathrm{N}|P|$, for each Herbrand model N of T, we have

$$(\alpha_1, \ldots, \alpha_n) \in \mathrm{M}|P| \quad \text{iff} \quad P(\alpha_1, \ldots, \alpha_n) \text{ is true in all Herbrand models of } T$$

where $\alpha_1, \ldots, \alpha_n$ are elements of the Herbrand universe of T. Thus, by Lemma 7.8.1, $(\alpha_1, \ldots, \alpha_n) \in \mathrm{M}|P|$ iff $T \vdash P(\alpha_1, \ldots, \alpha_n)$. Applying Theorem 7.5, we therefore have

$$(\alpha_1, \ldots, \alpha_n) \in \mathrm{M}|P| \quad \text{iff } \mathrm{NCWA}(T) \vdash P(\alpha_1, \ldots, \alpha_n).$$

Thus, since P was chosen arbitrarily, we infer that M is a model of NCWA(T) and so NCWA(T) is consistent. ■

It is well-known (see, for example, van Emden & Kowalski 1976) that each consistent Horn theory has the least Herbrand model. Therefore, Theorem 7.8 implies Theorem 7.4.

Proving Theorem 7.8, we have shown the following facts:

(i) The least Herbrand model of T, if it exists, is a Herbrand model of NCWA(T).
(ii) If NCWA(T) is consistent, then NCWA(T) has a unique Herbrand model, namely the least Herbrand model of T.

Thus, in view of Lemma 7.8.1, we have:

Theorem 7.9 If NCWA(T) is consistent, then for any ground sentence A, $\mathrm{NCWA}(T) \vdash A$ iff A is true in the least Herbrand model of T. ■

Theorem 7.9 does not generalize into arbitrary sentences. Take, for instance, $T = \{\neg P(a)\}$. It is easy to see that the sentence $\forall x \neg P(x)$ is true in the least Herbrand model of T. However, $\mathrm{NCWA}(T) \nvdash \forall x \neg P(x)$.

Since NCWA corresponds roughly to circumscribing all predicates in a theory, one may wonder to which extent these approaches coincide. Following Lifschitz (1985a), we investigate this problem with respect to the second-order variant of circumscription.

In the rest of this section we limit ourselves to theories without function constants. Note that if T is such a theory, then NCWA(T) is finite and hence may be identified with the conjunction of all its members. We denote by $\mathrm{CIRC_{SO}}(T)$ the result of second-order circumscription of all predicate constants occurring in a theory T. Symbolically,

$$\mathrm{CIRC_{SO}}(T) = \mathrm{CIRC_{SO}}(T; \bar{P}; ())$$

where $\bar{P}$ is the tuple of all predicate constants from T.

As the next example shows, NCWA(T) and $\mathrm{CIRC_{SO}}(T)$ need not be equivalent.

Example 7.10 (Lifschitz 1985a) Let $T = \{P(a) \wedge Q(b)\}$.

$$\mathrm{NCWA}(T) \Leftrightarrow P(a) \wedge Q(b) \wedge \neg P(b) \wedge \neg Q(a)$$
$$\mathrm{CIRC_{SO}}(T) \Leftrightarrow \forall x(P(x) \equiv x = a) \wedge \forall x(Q(x) \equiv x = b).$$

None of these sentences entails the other. To infer $\mathrm{CIRC_{SO}}(T)$ from NCWA(T), we must assume that a and b are the only individuals in the domain: $\forall x . x = a \vee x = b$. To infer NCWA($T$) from $\mathrm{CIRC_{SO}}(T)$, we must assume that a and b denote different individuals: $a \neq b$. ∎

Let T be a theory (without function constants) all of whose individual constants are $c_1, \ldots, c_n$. In view of Example 7.10, one might suspect that NCWA(T) is equivalent to $\mathrm{CIRC_{SO}}(T)$ in those frames for T in which the *domain-closure axiom*

$$\forall x . \bigvee_{i=1}^{n} x = c_i \qquad \mathrm{D}(T)$$

and the *unique names axiom*

$$\bigwedge_{1 \leq i < j \leq n} c_i \neq c_j \qquad \mathrm{U}(T)$$

are both true. Lifschitz showed that this is indeed the case, provided that NCWA(T) is consistent.

Theorem 7.11 (Lifschitz 1985a) If NCWA(T) is consistent, then $\mathrm{D}(T), \mathrm{U}(T) \models \mathrm{NCWA}(T) \equiv \mathrm{CIRC_{SO}}(T)$.† ∎

Theorem 7.11 specifies a class of frames in which NCWA(T) and $\mathrm{CIRC_{SO}}(T)$ are equivalent. Another way of comparing between NCWA and circumscription is to isolate a class $\mathscr{T}$ of first-order theories for which these formalisms are equivalent in the following sense: For each $T \in \mathscr{T}$ and each formula A, $\mathrm{NCWA}(T) \vdash A$ iff $\mathrm{CIRC_{SO}}(T) \models A$.

Theorem 7.12 Let T be a finite (universal) theory without function constants. We say that T is a *fixed-domain theory* iff T contains its equality axioms, together with D(T) and U(T). ∎

Fixed-domain theories, which play a prominent role in the theory of deductive data bases (Reiter 1980b), explicitly state that their domains contain finitely many individuals, and that different individuals are denoted by different constants. It is worth noting that the domain-closure axiom allows us to eliminate quantifiers. More specifically, if T is a fixed-domain theory including the constants $c_1, \ldots, c_n$, then formulae of the form $\forall x A(x)$ and $\exists x A(x)$ are equivalent in T to $A(c_1) \wedge \cdots \wedge A(c_n)$ and $A(c_1) \vee \cdots \vee A(c_n)$, respectively. In consequence, when we speak about fixed-domain theories, we may restrict our attention to formulae being propositional combinations of ground atoms. One problem with fixed-domain theories is that they contain the equality predicate, whereas we have previously assumed that NCWA is applicable to theories without equality. There is a good reason to make this assumption, since consistent universal theories with equality may lack Herbrand models. In consequence, the semantics for NCWA provided in Theorem 7.9 is no longer valid if the equality is admitted. To see this, consider the theory T consisting of $a = b$, together with the appropriate set of equality axioms. It is clear that NCWA(T), which is equivalent to T, is consistent. However, there is no Herbrand model of NCWA(T).

It was the need to sacrify the elegant Herbrand model semantics for NCWA that prevented us from admitting theories with equality. Fortunately, this semantics is preserved for fixed-domain theories, because all their models are isomorphic to their

† NCWA(T) is to be viewed here as the conjunction of all its members.

Herbrand models. Furthermore, for each fixed-domain theory T, consistent with NCWA, NCWA(T) and $\mathrm{CIRC_{SO}}$ are equivalent. We conclude this section by showing these facts.

Definition 7.13 Let M and N be frames for a first-order language over an alphabet AL. A mapping $\phi: |M| \to |N|$ is said to be an *isomorphism* iff it is bijective and:

(i) $(d_1, \ldots, d_n) \in M|P|$ iff $(\phi(d_1), \ldots, \phi(d_n)) \in N|P|$, for each n-ary ($n > 0$) predicate constant $P \in AL$ and each $d_1, \ldots, d_n \in |M|$.
(ii) $M|p| = N|p|$, for each proposition constant $p \in AL$.
(iii) $\phi(M|f|(d_1, \ldots, d_n)) = N|f|(\phi\phi(d_1), \ldots, \phi(d_n))$, for each n-ary function constant $f \in AL$ and each $d_1, \ldots, d_n \in |M|$.
(iv) $\phi(M|c|) = N|c|$, for each individual constant $c \in AL$.

We say that M *is isomorphic to* N, and we write $M \cong N$, iff there is an isomorphism $\phi: |M| \to |N|$. ∎

The following result is well-known (see, for example, Shoenfield 1967):

Theorem 7.14 Let M and N be frames for a first-order language L. If $M \cong N$, then $M \models A$ iff $N \models A$, for each $A \in L$. ∎

The next theorem shows that dealing with fixed-domain theories, we may limit ourselves to the class of Herbrand models.

Theorem 7.15 Let M be a model for a fixed-domain theory T. Then there is a Herbrand model N for T such that $M \cong N$.

Proof Let $c_1, \ldots, c_n$ be all individual constants occurring in T and suppose that $M|c_i| = d_i$. Since D(T) and U(T) are true in M, we immediately infer that $|M| = \{d_1, \ldots, d_n\}$. We define a Herbrand frame N by:

$|N| = \{c_1, \ldots, c_n\}$;
$N|c_i| = c_i \quad (1 \le i \le n)$;
$N|P| = \{(c_{i1}, \ldots, c_{ik}): \ (d_{i1}, \ldots, d_{ik}) \in M|P|\}$, for each k-ary predicate constant P occurring in T.

Consider the mapping $\phi: |M| \to |N|$ such that $\phi(d_i) = c_i$ ($1 \le i \le n$). It is easily checked that ϕ is an isomorphism from |M| to |N|. Thus, since M is a model of T, N is also a model of T, by Theorem 7.14. ∎

It is immediately seen that Theorem 7.5 holds, provided that Definition 7.1 is made applicable to fixed-domain theories. We also have the following analogons of Theorems 7.8 and 7.9:

Theorem 7.16 If T is a fixed-domain theory, then:

(i) NCWA(T) is consistent iff T has the least Herbrand model;
(ii) If NCWA(T) is consistent, then for any formula A, NCWA(T) $\vdash A$ iff A is true in the least Herbrand model of T.

Proof (i)
($\Rightarrow$) Assume that NCWA(T) is consistent. Since T is a fixed-domain theory, NCWA(T) is also such a theory and so, by Theorem 7.15, there is a Herbrand model M of NCWA(T). Now the proof proceeds as in Theorem 7.8.
($\Leftarrow$) Similar to the proof of the if part of Theorem 7.8. The only difference is that Lemma 7.8.1 should be replaced by:

Lemma 7.16.1 For any fixed-domain theory T and any formula A, $T \vdash A$ iff A is true in all Herbrand models of T.

Proof By Theorem 7.15 and the fact that T contains its equality axioms. ■

(ii) Compare the discussion following Theorem 7.8. Notice that Lemma 7.16.1 applies not only to ground sentences, but to arbitrary formulae. This allows us to strengthen Theorem 7.9. ▌

We are now ready to prove the main theorem concerning fixed-domain theories:

Theorem 7.17 If T is a fixed-domain theory and NCWA(T) is consistent, then, for each formula A

$$\text{NCWA}(T) \vdash A \quad \text{iff} \quad \text{CIRC}_{\text{SO}}(T) \models A.$$

Proof Let $\bar{P}$ be the tuple of all predicate constants occurring in T. Comparing the concept of a minimal Herbrand model (as specified in this section) with the notion of a $(\bar{P}; \bar{S})$-minimal model (Definition 6.40 in Chapter 6), and applying Theorem 7.15 and Definition 7.13, one easily verifies that each $(\bar{P}; ())$-minimal model of T is isomorphic to some minimal Herbrand model of T. On the other hand, by Theorem 7.16 (i), we know that there is exactly one minimal Herbrand model of T, namely the least Herbrand model of T. It follows, therefore, that each $(\bar{P}; ())$-minimal model of T is isomorphic to the least Herbrand model of T. Thus, by Theorems 7.14, 7.16 (ii) and 6.41, we infer

$$\text{NCWA}(T) \vdash A \quad \text{iff} \quad \text{CIRC}_{\text{SO}}(T) \models A.$$

▌

7.3 GENERALIZED CWA

The use of NCWA requires that our knowledge of the actual state of affairs is complete. Otherwise, i.e. if we are in a state of partial ignorance, Reiter's formalism is both inappropriate and unsafe. This has led several researchers to formalize less restrictive versions of the CWA rule, safely applicable to partially specified worlds. In this section, we examine *generalized* CWA (GCWA), a consistency-preserving extension of NCWA, introduced by Minker (1982). We begin with a motivating example.

Example 7.18 Let T consist of the following axioms:

$$Course(c_1) \wedge Course(c_2)$$
$$Student(Bill) \vee Teacher(Bill).$$

Owing to the axiom $Student(Bill) \vee Teacher(Bill)$, T cannot be regarded as a representation of a completely specified world. Accordingly, the CWA rule is unjustified for T and, what is worse, its application leads to a contradiction. However, given T, it is still reasonable (and consistent) to assume that c_1 and c_2 are neither students nor teachers, and Bill is not a course. In other words, we may wish to apply the CWA rule in a restricted way. It is this observation that underlies Minker's proposal. ▌

Recall that the term 'theory' refers to any finite set of universal sentences without equality.†

† Minker restricts the application of GCWA to theories without function constants. This limitation is unnecessary.

To simplify the discussion in the next sections, we slightly change Minker's original presentation of GCWA. Our exposition is influenced by Gelfond & Przymusinska (1986).

Definition 7.19 Let T be a theory. A ground atom $A \in \mathrm{HB}(T)$ is *free for negation in T* iff there is no clause $C = C_1 \vee \cdots \vee C_n$ $(n \geq 0)$, where each $C_i \in \mathrm{HB}(T)$, such that

(i) $T \vdash A \vee C$
(ii) $T \nvdash C$.
∎

Notice that in the above definition the clause C may be empty.

We denote by NFREE(T) the set of all atoms from HB(T) which are free for negation in T.

Example 7.18 (continued) Inspecting the elements of HB(T), it is easily seen that

$$\mathrm{NFREE}(T) = \{Course(Bill), Student(c_1), Student(c_2), Teacher(c_1), Teacher(c_2)\}.$$
∎

We are now ready to provide a syntactic specification of GCWA:

Definition 7.20 (Minker 1982) The *generalized closure of a theory T*, written GCWA(T), is the theory

$$T \cup \{\neg A\colon A \in \mathrm{NFREE}(T)\}.$$

We say that a formula B is derivable by GCWA from T iff $\mathrm{GCWA}(T) \vdash B$. ∎

Example 7.18 (continued)

$$\mathrm{GCWA}(T) = T \cup \{\neg Course(Bill), \neg Student(c_1), \neg Student(c_2), \neg Teacher(c_1), \neg Teacher(c_2)\}.$$ ∎

The following theorem provides a partial relationship between GCWA and NCWA:

Theorem 7.21 For any theory T,

(i) $\mathrm{GCWA}(T) \subseteq \mathrm{NCWA}(T)$;
(ii) If NCWA(T) is consistent, then $\mathrm{GCWA}(T) = \mathrm{NCWA}(T)$.

Proof (i) If T in inconsistent, then (i) trivially holds. Assume, therefore; that T is consistent. Now, the proof immediately follows from the fact

If T is consistent and $A \in \mathrm{NFREE}(T)$, then $T \nvdash A$

which, in turn, is a simple consequence of Definition 7.19.

(ii) Suppose that NCWA(T) is consistent. In view of (i), it suffices to show the following: For any $A \in \mathrm{HB}(T)$, if $T \nvdash A$, then $A \in \mathrm{NFREE}(T)$. Assume to the contrary that this is not the case. Thus, $T \nvdash A$ and there is a clause C, whose elements are from HB(T), such that $T \vdash A \vee C$ and $T \nvdash C$. Given this, one easily shows (by Definition 7.1) that $A \vee C$ and $\neg(A \vee C)$ are both derivable from NCWA(T). This contradicts the assumption that NCWA(T) is consistent. ∎

Note that if T is inconsistent, then trivially $\text{GCWA}(T) = \text{NCWA}(T)$. Therefore, by Theorems 7.4 and 7.21 (ii), we immediately have:

Corollary 7.22 If T is a Horn theory, then $\text{GCWA}(T) = \text{NCWA}(T)$. ▮

The next theorem shows that no new positive ground sentence can be derived by applying GCWA.

Theorem 7.23 For each theory T and each positive ground sentence A, $\text{GCWA}(T) \vdash A$ iff $T \vdash A$.

Proof Since any positive ground sentence is a conjunction of disjunctions of ground atoms, and, for each theory T and each formulae $A_1, \ldots, A_n$,

$$T \vdash A_1 \wedge \cdots \wedge A_n \quad \text{iff} \quad T \vdash A_1 \text{ and } T \vdash A_2 \text{ and } \ldots\ T \vdash A_n$$

we may assume that A is a disjunction of ground atoms.
($\Rightarrow$) Let $\text{GCWA}(T) \vdash A$ and suppose that $B_1, \ldots, B_m$ are all ground atoms whose negations belong to $\text{GCWA}(T) - T$ and appear in the proof of A from $\text{GCWA}(T)$. If $m = 0$, then trivially $T \vdash A$. Otherwise, by the deduction theorem, we have

$$T \vdash B_1 \vee \cdots \vee B_m \vee A. \tag{7.3.1}$$

Consider B_1. Since $\neg B_1 \in \text{GCWA}(T) - T$, $B_1 \in \text{NFREE}(T)$. Moreover, A is a disjunction of ground atoms from $\text{HB}(T)$. Therefore, by Definition 7.19, (7.3.1) implies

$$T \vdash B_2 \vee \cdots \vee B_m \vee A.$$

Repeating this argument $(m - 1)$ times, we finally conclude that $T \vdash A$.
($\Leftarrow$) Immediate.
▮

As we remarked earlier, GCWA preserves consistency:

Theorem 7.24 If T is consistent, then $\text{GCWA}(T)$ is also consistent.

Proof Assume on the contrary that T is consistent and $\text{GCWA}(T)$ is not. Thus, there is an atom $A \in \text{HB}(T)$ such that $\text{GCWA}(T) \vdash A$ and $\text{GCWA}(T) \vdash \neg A$. By Theorem 7.23, $\text{GCWA}(T) \vdash A$ implies

$$T \vdash A. \tag{7.3.2}$$

On the other hand, $\text{GCWA}(T) \vdash \neg A$ implies

$$T \vdash \neg A \vee B_1 \vee \cdots \vee B_m \tag{7.3.3}$$

where $B_1, \ldots, B_m$ are ground atoms from $\text{NFREE}(T)$, specified as in the proof of Theorem 7.23. In view of (7.3.2) and (7.3.3),

$$T \vdash B_1 \vee \cdots \vee B_m.$$

Now, applying the same argument as in the proof of Theorem 7.23, one shows that $T \vdash \Box$ (the empty clause). This contradicts the consistency of T. ▮

The semantics for GCWA is based on minimal Herbrand models. Restricting his attention to theories without function constants, Minker (1982) showed that GCWA supplies a given theory T with the negations of all atoms from $\text{HB}(T)$ which are false in all minimal Herbrand models of T. This result carries over to theories with function constants:

Theorem 7.25 For each theory T and each $A \in \mathrm{HB}(T)$, $A \in \mathrm{NFREE}(T)$ iff $\neg A$ is true in each minimal Herbrand model of T.

Proof This theorem is a special case of Theorem 7.37 which will be proved in the next section. ∎

We shall write $T \models_m A$ to indicate that a formula A is true in all minimal Herbrand models of T.

Combining Theorems 7.23 and 7.25, one readily proves:

Theorem 7.26 For each theory T and each ground literal A, $\mathrm{GCWA}(T) \vdash A$ iff $T \models_m A$.

Proof If A is of the form $\neg P(\bar{\alpha})$, then the theorem follows from Theorem 7.25. (For the left to right direction, use the argument similar to that employed in the proof of Theorem 7.23.) Assume, therefore, that A is of the form $P(\bar{\alpha})$. In view of Theorem 7.23, it suffices to show

$$T \vdash P(\bar{\alpha}) \qquad \text{iff} \quad T \models_m P(\bar{\alpha}).$$

The left to right implication of this equivalence is straightforward. For the implication from right to left, observe that $T \models_m P(\bar{\alpha})$ implies that $P(\bar{\alpha})$ is true in each Herbrand model of T and apply Lemma 7.8.1. ∎

Theorem 7.26 does not generalize into arbitrary ground sentences:

Example 7.27 Let $T = \{Bird(Tweety) \vee Bird(Joe)\}$. This theory has three Herbrand models:

$$\begin{aligned} M_1 &= \{Bird(Tweety)\} \\ M_2 &= \{Bird(Joe)\} \\ M_3 &= \{Bird(Tweety), Bird(Joe)\} \end{aligned}$$

of which M_1 and M_2 are minimal.[†] Consider the ground sentence $A = \neg(Bird(Tweety) \wedge Bird(Joe))$. A is true in both the minimal Herbrand models of T. However, A cannot be derived using GCWA, since $\mathrm{NFREE}(T) = \{\ \}$ and hence $\mathrm{GCWA}(T) = T$. ∎

Yahya & Henschen (1985) extended GCWA in such a way that Theorem 7.26 becomes applicable to arbitrary ground sentences. Their system will not be discussed here, since it is a special case of a formalism presented in section 7.5.

In view of Example 7.27, it is not too surprising that the relationship between GCWA and circumscription is rather weak. In particular, the analogon of Theorem 7.11 does not hold:

Example 7.28 Let T be the theory from Example 7.27.

$$\begin{aligned} &\mathrm{GCWA}(T) \Leftrightarrow Bird(Tweety) \vee Bird(Joe) \\ &\mathrm{CIRC_{SO}}(T) \Leftrightarrow [\forall x . Bird(x) \equiv x = Tweety] \vee [\forall x . Bird(x) \equiv x = Joe] \\ &\mathrm{D}(T) = \forall x . x = Tweety \vee x = Joe \\ &\mathrm{U}(T) = Joe \neq Tweety. \end{aligned}$$

Clearly, $\mathrm{D}(T) \wedge \mathrm{U}(T)$ does not entail $\mathrm{GCWA}(T) \equiv \mathrm{CIRC_{SO}}(T)$. ∎

The analogon of Theorem 7.17 does not hold either. (To see this, extend the theory

[†] As usual, we identify Herbrand models of T with subsets of the Herbrand base of T.

from Example 7.27 by its equality axioms, together with D(T) and U(T), and show that the sentence $\neg$*Bird*(*Tweety*) $\vee$ $\neg$*Bird*(*Joe*) can be derived by circumscribing *Bird* in the extended theory, but not by applying GCWA to it.) However, we have the following weaker version of Theorem 7.17:

Theorem 7.29 If T is a fixed-domain theory and A is any ground literal, then GCWA(T) $\vdash A$ iff CIRC$_{SO}$(T) $\models A$.

Proof This theorem is a special case of Theorem 7.39 which will be proved in the next section. ∎

7.4 CAREFUL CWA

In this section, we present *careful* CWA (CCWA), an extension of GCWA developed by Gelfond & Przymusinska (1986). The new feature of CCWA is that it allows us to restrict the effects of closing the world by specifying the predicates which may be affected by the CWA rule. Furthermore, some other predicates, also indicated by the user, are permitted to vary in the process of closure. This generalization makes CCWA more powerful than the systems discussed in the previous sections. In particular, Gelfond & Przymusinska's proposal can be used to formalize general non-monotonic rules.

Given a theory T and a tuple $\bar{R}$ of predicate constants occurring in T, we denote by $\bar{R}^+_T$ and $\bar{R}^-_T$ the sets $\{P(\bar{\alpha})$: P is in $\bar{R}$ and $P(\bar{\alpha}) \in \mathrm{HB}(T)\}$ and $\{\neg P(\bar{\alpha})$: P is in $\bar{R}$ and $P(\bar{\alpha}) \in \mathrm{HB}(T)\}$, respectively. In words, $\bar{R}^+_T$ (resp. $\bar{R}^-_T$) is the set of all positive (resp. negative) ground literals constructable using predicate constants from $\bar{R}$ and function (individual) constants occurring in T. We omit the subscript T in $\bar{R}^+_T$ and $\bar{R}^-_T$ whenever its omission can cause no confusion.

In what follows, the set of all predicate constants occurring in a given theory will be always divided into three disjoint groups: $\bar{P}$, $\bar{Q}$ and $\bar{R}$. $\bar{P}$ represents those aspects of the world which are to be closed. $\bar{Q}$ refers to the predicates which may be arbitrarily varied in the process of closure. Finally, $\bar{R}$ includes the remaining predicate constants – those whose extensions must not be affected by the closure.

Definition 7.30 (Gelfond & Przymusinska 1986) Let T be a theory and suppose that $\bar{P}$, $\bar{Q}$ and $\bar{R}$ are disjoint tuples of all predicate constants occurring in T. A ground atom $A \in \mathrm{HB}(T)$ is *free for negation in T wrt $\bar{P}$, $\bar{Q}$ and $\bar{R}$* iff $A \in \bar{P}^+$ and there is no clause $C = C_1 \vee \cdots \vee C_n$ ($n \geq 0$), where each C_i is in $\bar{P}^+ \cup \bar{R}^+ \cup \bar{R}^-$, such that

(i) $T \vdash A \vee C$
(ii) $T \nvdash C$.

∎

We denote by NFREE(T; $\bar{P}$; $\bar{Q}$; $\bar{R}$) the set of all atoms from $\bar{P}^+$ which are free for negation in T wrt $\bar{P}$, $\bar{Q}$ and $\bar{R}$.

Example 7.31 Let $T = \{Bird(Tweety) \wedge (\forall x . Bird(x) \wedge \neg Ab(x) \supset Flies(x))\}$ and let $\bar{P} = (Ab)$, $\bar{Q} = (Flies)$ and $\bar{R} = (Bird)$.

$$\bar{P}^+ = \{Ab(Tweety)\}$$
$$\bar{P}^+ \cup \bar{R}^+ \cup \bar{R}^- = \{Ab(Tweety), Bird(Tweety), \neg Bird(Tweety)\}.$$

It is immediately seen that there is no clause C, whose literals are in $\bar{P}^+ \cup \bar{R}^+ \cup \bar{R}^-$, such that $T \vdash Ab(Tweety) \vee C$ and $T \nvdash C$. Therefore, *Ab*(*Tweety*) is free for negation in

T wrt $\bar{P}$, $\bar{Q}$ and $\bar{R}$. Since $Ab(Tweety)$ is the only element of $\bar{P}^+$, we conclude that $\text{NFREE}(T; \bar{P}; \bar{Q}; \bar{R}) = \{Ab(Tweety)\}$. ∎

Definition 7.32 (Gelfond & Przymusinska 1986) Let T, $\bar{P}$, $\bar{Q}$ and $\bar{R}$ be as in Definition 7.30. The *careful closure of T wrt* $\bar{P}$, $\bar{Q}$ *and* $\bar{R}$, written $\text{CCWA}(T; \bar{P}; \bar{Q}; \bar{R})$, is the theory

$$T \cup \{\neg A : A \in \text{NFREE}(T; \bar{P}; \bar{Q}; \bar{R})\}.$$

We say that a formula A is derivable by applying CCWA to a theory T wrt $\bar{P}$, $\bar{Q}$ and $\bar{R}$ iff $\text{CCWA}(T; \bar{P}; \bar{Q}; \bar{R}) \vdash A$. ∎

Example 7.31 (continued)

$$\text{CCWA}(T; \bar{P}; \bar{Q}; \bar{R}) = T \cup \{\neg Ab(Tweety)\}$$
$$\text{CCWA}(T; \bar{P}; \bar{Q}; \bar{R}) \vdash Flies(Tweety).$$

It is worth noting that GCWA does not allow us to derive $Flies(Tweety)$ from T (see Theorem 7.23). ∎

It is easy to see that CCWA reduces to GCWA if $\bar{P}$ contains all predicate constants occurring in a given theory:

Theorem 7.33 For each theory T,

$$\text{CCWA}(T; \bar{P}; (); ()) = \text{GCWA}(T)$$

where $\bar{P}$ is the tuple of all predicate constants from T.

Proof By Definitions 7.19, 7.20, 7.30 and 7.32. ∎

Let A be a sentence and assume that X is a set of literals. When we say that A contains no literal from X, we always assume that A is rewritten as a conjunction of disjunctions of literals.

The next theorem provides some clues towards the expressive power of CCWA:

Theorem 7.34 (Gelfond & Przymusinska 1986) Let T, $\bar{P}$, $\bar{Q}$ and $\bar{R}$ be as usual. If A is a ground sentence which contains no literals from $\bar{P}^- \cup \bar{Q}^+ \cup \bar{Q}^-$, then $\text{CCWA}(T; \bar{P}; \bar{Q}; \bar{R}) \vdash A$ iff $T \vdash A$.

Proof Applying the same argument as in the proof of Theorem 7.23, we may assume that A is a disjunction.

($\Rightarrow$) Let $\text{CCWA}(T; \bar{P}; \bar{Q}; \bar{R}) \vdash A$ and suppose that $B_1, \ldots, B_m$ are all ground atoms whose negations belong to $\text{CCWA}(T; \bar{P}; \bar{Q}; \bar{R}) - T$, and appear in the proof of A from $\text{CCWA}(T; \bar{P}; \bar{Q}; \bar{R})$. If $m = 0$, then trivially $T \vdash A$. Otherwise, by the deduction theorem,

$$T \vdash B_1 \vee \cdots \vee B_m \vee A. \tag{7.4.1}$$

Consider B_1. Since $\neg B_1 \in \text{CCWA}(T; \bar{P}; \bar{Q}; \bar{R}) - T$, $B_1 \in \text{NFREE}(T; \bar{P}; \bar{Q}; \bar{R})$. On the other hand, A is a disjunction of ground literals not in $\bar{P}^- \cup \bar{Q}^+ \cup \bar{Q}^-$ and hence each literal of A must be in $\bar{P}^+ \cup \bar{R}^+ \cup \bar{R}^-$. Thus, since each $B_i \in \bar{P}^+$, (7.4.1) implies

$$T \vdash B_2 \vee \cdots \vee B_m \vee A.$$

Repeating this argument $(m - 1)$ times, we conclude that $T \vdash A$.

($\Leftarrow$) Straightforward.

∎

Theorem 7.34 indicates that any new ground sentence that can be derived by CCWA includes either a negative instance of one of the predicates being closed or an instance (positive or negative) of a predicate allowed to vary. This fact shows that if we wish to use CCWA to derive a new ground atom $P(\bar{\alpha})$, then P must be contained in the tuple of varying predicate constants.

Inspecting the proof of Theorem 7.24, the reader will have no difficulty in proving that CCWA preserves consistency:

Theorem 7.35 (Gelfond & Przymusinska 1986) For each T, $\bar{P}$, $\bar{Q}$ and $\bar{R}$, CCWA$(T; \bar{P}; \bar{Q}; \bar{R})$ is consistent iff T is consistent. ▮

We now proceed to provide a semantics for CCWA.

Definition 7.36 Let $T, \bar{P}, \bar{Q}$ and $\bar{R}$ be as usual and suppose that M and N are Herbrand models of T. We say that M is a *Herbrand* $(\bar{P}; \bar{Q})$*-submodel of* N, and we write $\mathrm{M} \leq_{\mathrm{H}}^{(\bar{P};\bar{Q})} \mathrm{N}$ iff

(i) $\mathrm{M}|R| = \mathrm{N}|R|$, for each predicate constant R in $\bar{R}$;
(ii) $\mathrm{M}|P| \subseteq \mathrm{N}|P|$, for each P in $\bar{P}$.

We say that M is a $(\bar{P}; \bar{Q})$*-minimal Herbrand model of* T iff T has no Herbrand model N such that $\mathrm{N} \leq_{\mathrm{H}}^{(\bar{P};\bar{Q})} \mathrm{M}$ and not $\mathrm{M} \leq_{\mathrm{H}}^{(\bar{P};\bar{Q})} \mathrm{N}$. ▮

Example 7.31 (continued) The class of Herbrand models of T consists of:

$$\mathrm{M}_1 = \{Bird(Tweety), Flies(Tweety)\}$$
$$\mathrm{M}_2 = \{Bird(Tweety), Ab(Tweety)\}$$
$$M_3 = \{Bird(Tweety), Ab(Tweety), Flies(Tweety)\}.$$

M_1 is the only $(Ab; Flies)$-minimal Herbrand model of T. ▮

Gelfond & Przymusinska (1986) showed that a ground atom A from $\bar{P}^+$ is free for negation in T with respect to $\bar{\mathrm{P}}$, $\bar{\mathrm{Q}}$ and $\bar{R}$ iff $\neg A$ is true in all $(\bar{P}; \bar{Q})$-minimal Herbrand models of T. To prove this result, we need some preliminary terminology.

Let X be a countable set of formulae. We write DIS(X) to denote the disjunction (possibly infinite), in some standard order, of all members from X. We take DIS(X) to be *False* if X is empty. We say that DIS(X) is true in a frame M iff there is $A \in \mathrm{X}$ such that A is true in M. A *finite subdisjunction of* DIS(X) is any disjunction $A_1 \vee \cdots \vee A_n$ $(n \geq 0)$ such that each $A_i \in \mathrm{X}$.

Theorem 7.37 (Gelfond & Przymusinska 1986) Let T, $\bar{P}$, $\bar{Q}$ and $\bar{R}$ be as usual. A ground atom $A \in \bar{P}^+$ is a member of NFREE$(T; \bar{P}; \bar{Q}; \bar{R})$ iff for any $(\bar{P}; \bar{Q})$-minimal Herbrand model M of T, we have $\mathrm{M} \models \neg A$.

Proof We begin with preliminary lemmas.

Lemma 7.37.1 Suppose that X is a countable set of ground literals. If DIS(X) is true in all Herbrand models of T, then there is a finite subdisjunction $A_1 \vee \cdots \vee A_n$ of DIS(X) such that $T \vdash A_1 \vee \cdots \vee A_n$.

Proof Let $\neg$DIS(X) be the set $\{\neg B: B \in \mathrm{X}\}$ and consider the theory $T' = T \cup \neg$DIS(X). Since DIS(X) is true in all Herbrand models of T, and T' is universal, T' is unsatisfiable. Suppose that each finite subdisjunction of DIS(X) is false in some model of T. Then, all finite subsets of T' are satisfiable and so, by Compactness Theorem, T' is satisfiable. This leads to a contradiction and hence there is some finite subdisjunction $A_1 \vee \cdots \vee A_n$ of DIS(X) which is true in all models of T. Therefore, $T \vdash A_1 \vee \cdots \vee A_n$. ■

Lemma 7.37.2 If T is consistent, then there is a $(\bar{P}; \bar{Q})$-minimal Herbrand model of T.

Proof Since T is a consistent universal theory, there is a Herbrand model M of T. By Theorem 6.53, T is well-founded with respect to $\bar{P}$ and $\bar{Q}$. Therefore, there is a $(\bar{P}; \bar{Q})$-minimal model N of T (in the sense of Definition 6.40) such that $\mathrm{N} \leq^{(\bar{P};\bar{Q})} \mathrm{M}$. Since $\bar{Q}$ excludes function constants and M is a Herbrand model of T, N is a $(\bar{P}; \bar{Q})$-minimal Herbrand model of T (in the sense of Definition 7.36). This completes the proof of the lemma. ■

Lemma 7.37.3 If all elements of X are members of $\bar{R}^+ \cup \bar{R}^- \cup \bar{P}^+$, and DIS(X) is true in all $(\bar{P}; \bar{Q})$-minimal Herbrand models of T, then DIS(X) is true in all Herbrand models of T.

Proof By Lemma 7.37.2 and Definition 7.36. ■

Lemma 7.37.4 Let M be a $(\bar{P}; \bar{Q})$-minimal Herbrand model of T, A be a ground sentence not involving predicate constants from $\bar{Q}$, and suppose that $\mathrm{M} \models A$. For each Herbrand model N of T such that $\mathrm{N} \models \neg A$, there is a literal B_{N} from $\bar{R}^+ \cup \bar{R}^- \cup \bar{P}^+$ such that $\mathrm{N} \models B_{\mathrm{N}}$ and $\mathrm{M} \models \neg B_{\mathrm{N}}$.†

Proof Since $\mathrm{M} \models A$, $\mathrm{N} \models \neg A$ and A contains no predicate constants from $\bar{Q}$, we have

$$\mathrm{M}|K| \neq \mathrm{N}|K|, \text{ for some predicate constant } K \text{ in } (\bar{P}, \bar{R}). \tag{7.4.2}$$

If K is from $\bar{R}$, then the lemma obviously holds. Therefore, we may assume that all members of $\bar{R}$ have identical extensions in M and N, and K is from $\bar{P}$. To complete the proof, it suffices to show that there exists $B_{\mathrm{N}} \in \bar{P}^+$ such that $\mathrm{N} \models B_{\mathrm{N}}$ and $\mathrm{M} \models \neg B_{\mathrm{N}}$. Suppose that this is not the case. Then, $\mathrm{N} \leq_{\mathrm{H}}^{(\bar{P};\bar{Q})} \mathrm{M}$, and thus, since M is a $(\bar{P}; \bar{Q})$-minimal Herbrand model of T, each predicate constant from $(\bar{P}, \bar{R})$ has identical extensions in M and N. This contradicts (7.4.2) and hence proves the lemma. ■

We are now ready to prove the theorem.

($\Rightarrow$) Suppose that $A \in \mathrm{NFREE}(T; \bar{P}; \bar{Q}; \bar{R})$ and denote by ALL the class of all $(\bar{P}; \bar{Q})$-minimal Herbrand models of T. We divide ALL into two disjoint subclasses:

$$\mathbf{M} = \{\mathrm{M} \in \mathrm{ALL}: \mathrm{M} \models A\}$$
$$\mathbf{N} = \{\mathrm{N} \in \mathrm{ALL}: \mathrm{N} \models \neg A\}.$$

To prove the only-if part of the theorem, it suffices to show that $\mathbf{M}$ is empty. Suppose that this is not the case and let $\mathrm{M} \in \mathbf{M}$. By Lemma 7.37.4, for each $\mathrm{N} \in \mathbf{N}$, we may select a literal $B_{\mathrm{N}} \in \bar{R}^+ \cup \bar{R}^- \cup \bar{P}^+$ such that $\mathrm{N} \models B_{\mathrm{N}}$ and $\mathrm{M} \models \neg B_{\mathrm{N}}$. Consider DIS(X), where $\mathrm{X} = \{A\} \cup \{B_{\mathrm{N}}: \mathrm{N} \in \mathbf{N}\}$. Clearly, DIS(X) is true in all $(\bar{P}; \bar{Q})$-minimal Herbrand models of T and so, by Lemma 7.37.3, it is true in all Herbrand models of T. Thus, in view of Lemma 7.37.1, there is a finite subdisjunction of DIS(X), say $B_1 \vee \cdots \vee B_n$, such that $T \vdash B_1 \vee \cdots \vee B_n$. Since M is a model of T, we have $\mathrm{M} \models B_1 \vee \cdots \vee B_n$.

† We formulate this lemma in greater generality than is currently needed. This more general formulation is essential in proving Theorem 7.43.

On the other hand, for each $N \in \mathbf{N}$, $M \models \neg B_N$. Thus, one of the disjuncts $B_1, \ldots, B_n$ must be A. Given this, it is readily checked that $A \notin \mathrm{NFREE}(T; \bar{P}; \bar{Q}; \bar{R})$. A contradiction.

($\Leftarrow$) Assume on the contrary that $M \models \neg A$, for any $(\bar{P}; \bar{Q})$-minimal Herbrand model of T, and $A \notin \mathrm{NFREE}(T; \bar{P}; \bar{Q}; \bar{R})$. Then there is a clause $C = C_1 \vee \cdots \vee C_n$, where each $C_i \in \bar{R}^+ \cup \bar{R}^- \cup \bar{P}^+$, such that $T \vdash A \vee C$ and $T \nvdash C$. Let M be any $(\bar{P}; \bar{Q})$-minimal Herbrand model of T. $T \vdash A \vee C$ implies that $M \models A \vee C$. On the other hand, $M \models \neg A$. Therefore, $M \models C$. Since M was chosen arbitrarily, we conclude that C is true in all $(\bar{P}; \bar{Q})$-minimal Herbrand models of T and hence, by Lemma 7.37.3, C is true in all Herbrand models of T. Therefore, in view of Lemma 7.8.1, we conclude that $T \vdash C$. A contradiction. ▮

Notice that Theorem 7.37 implies Theorem 7.25.

We write $T \models_m^{(\bar{P};\bar{Q})} A$ to indicate that A is true in all $(\bar{P}; \bar{Q})$-minimal Herbrand models of T.

We have the following counterpart of Theorem 7.26:

Theorem 7.38 For each $T, \bar{P}, \bar{Q}, \bar{R}$ and each $A \in \bar{R}^+ \cup \bar{R}^- \cup \bar{P}^+ \cup \bar{P}^-$,

$$\mathrm{CCWA}(T; \bar{P}; \bar{Q}; \bar{R}) \vdash A \quad \text{iff} \quad T \models_m^{(\bar{P};\bar{Q})} A.$$

Proof We start with the following

Lemma 7.38.1 If $A \in \bar{P}^-$ and $\mathrm{CCWA}(T; \bar{P}; \bar{Q}; \bar{R}) \vdash A$, then $\neg A$ is a member of $\mathrm{NFREE}(T; \bar{P}; \bar{Q}; \bar{R})$.

Proof Suppose that the assumptions of the lemma hold and $\neg A \notin \mathrm{NFREE}(T; \bar{P}; \bar{Q}; \bar{R})$. Then there is a clause $C = C_1 \vee \cdots \vee C_n$, where each $C_i \in \bar{R}^+ \cup \bar{R}^- \cup \bar{P}^+$, such that $T \vdash \neg A \vee C$ and $T \nvdash C$. $T \vdash \neg A \vee C$ implies $\mathrm{CCWA}(T; \bar{P}; \bar{Q}; \bar{R}) \vdash \neg A \vee C$, and so, since $\mathrm{CCWA}(T; \bar{P}; \bar{Q}; \bar{R}) \vdash A$, we have $\mathrm{CCWA}(T; \bar{P}; \bar{Q}; \bar{R}) \vdash C$. But C is a ground sentence which contains no literals from $\bar{P}^- \cup \bar{Q}^+ \cup \bar{Q}^-$. Thus, by Theorem 7.34, $\mathrm{CCWA}(T; \bar{P}; \bar{Q}; \bar{R}) \vdash C$ implies $T \vdash C$. A contradiction. ■

To prove the theorem, consider two cases.

Case 1 $A \in \bar{P}^-$. Then the theorem immediately follows from Theorem 7.37 and Lemma 7.38.1.

Case 2 $A \in \bar{R}^+ \cup \bar{R}^- \cup \bar{P}^+$. By Theorem 7.34, it suffices to show

$$T \vdash A \quad \text{iff} \quad T \models_m^{(\bar{P};\bar{Q})} A.$$

The only-if part of this equivalence is obvious. For the implication from right to left, apply Lemmas 7.37.3 and 7.8.1 ▮

In view of Example 7.27, Theorem 7.38 does not generalize into arbitrary ground sentences. Furthermore, it cannot be even extended for literals from $\bar{Q}^+ \cup \bar{Q}^-$. (To see this, take the theory $T = \{P_1(a) \vee P_2(a), \neg P_1(a) \vee \neg P_2(a) \supset Q(a)\}$, put $\bar{P} = (P_1, P_2)$ and $\bar{Q} = (Q)$, and show that $Q(a)$ is true in each $(\bar{P}, \bar{Q})$-minimal Herbrand model of T, but $\mathrm{CCWA}(T; \bar{P}; \bar{Q}; \bar{R}) \nvdash Q(a)$.)

It is clear that CCWA attempts to capture the idea of minimizing a chosen tuple of predicates with some other ones treated as variables. Unfortunately, the relationship between CCWA and circumscription is very weak. In view of Example 7.28 and the discussion preceding Theorem 7.29, we may not hope for counterparts of Theorems

7.11 and 7.17. However, we have the following weaker version of this latter theorem (we assume here that Definitions 7.30 and 7.32 apply to fixed-domain theories):

Theorem 7.39 If T is a fixed-domain theory, then

$$\mathrm{CCWA}(T; \bar{P}; \bar{Q}; \bar{R}) \vdash A \qquad \text{iff } \mathrm{CIRC}_{\mathrm{SO}}(T; \bar{P}; \bar{Q}) \vdash A$$

for each $A \in \bar{R}^+ \cup \bar{R}^- \cup \bar{P}^+ \cup \bar{P}^-$.

Proof The crucial observation is the following lemma:

> **Lemma 7.39.1** If T is a fixed-domain theory, then for any formula B, B is true in all $(\bar{P}; \bar{Q})$-minimal Herbrand models of T iff B is true in all $(\bar{P}; \bar{Q})$-minimal models of T.
>
> **Proof** Apply Definitions 6.40, 7.36 and Theorems 7.14 and 7.15 ■

Inspecting the proofs of Theorems 7.34 and 7.37, and employing Theorem 7.15, the reader may easily check that Theorems 7.34 and 7.37, together with all the lemmas stated in their proofs, carry over to fixed-domain theories. Given this, there is no difficulty to show that Theorem 7.38 also holds, provided that T is a fixed-domain theory. Now, the proof of Theorem 7.39 follows immediately from Lemma 7.39.1 and Theorem 6.41. ■

Notice that Theorem 7.39 implies Theorem 7.29.

7.5 EXTENDED CWA

We now examine the most powerful of all of CWA logics, termed *extended* CWA (ECWA). It was developed by Gelfond *et al.* (1989) as a further generalization of CCWA. In contrast to this latter formalism, ECWA allows us to derive not only (some) ground literals which are true in all $(\bar{P}; \bar{Q})$-minimal Herbrand models, but all ground sentences with this property. In consequence, when applied to fixed-domain theories, ECWA is equivalent to second-order circumscription.

ECWA was originally developed for fixed-domain theories. Here we follow the course adopted in the previous sections. First, we discuss this formalism for arbitrary (finite universal) theories, and then we turn our attention to fixed-domain theories.

ECWA is very similar to CCWA with one crucial exception: the new formalism augments the theory under consideration with ground sentences, rather than ground atoms. The details follow.

Definition 7.40 (Gelfond *et al.* 1989) Let T, $\bar{P}$, $\bar{Q}$ and $\bar{R}$ be as in Definition 7.30 and suppose that A is arbitrary ground sentence not involving predicate constants from $\bar{Q}$. A is *free for negation in T wrt $\bar{P}$, $\bar{Q}$ and $\bar{R}$* iff there is no clause $C = C_1 \vee \cdots \vee C_n$ ($n \geq 0$), where each C_i is in $\bar{P}^+ \cup \bar{R}^+ \cup \bar{R}^-$, such that

(i) $T \vdash A \vee C$
(ii) $T \nvdash C$.
■

We denote by $\mathrm{NFREE}_{\mathrm{S}}(T; \bar{P}; \bar{Q}; \bar{R})$ the set of all sentences which are free for negation in T wrt $\bar{P}$, $\bar{Q}$ and $\bar{R}$.

Example 7.41 Consider the theory T from Example 7.27: $T = \{Bird(Tweety) \vee Bird(Joe)\}$, and suppose that $\bar{P} = (Bird)$; $\bar{Q} = \bar{R} = ()$. Consider the ground sentence $A = Bird(Tweety) \wedge Bird(Joe)$. Since neither $T \vdash A \vee Bird(Tweety)$ nor $T \vdash A \vee Bird(Joe)$, the only clause C such that $T \vdash A \vee C$ and all literals from C are in $\bar{P}^+ \cup \bar{R}^+ \cup \bar{R}^-$ is $Bird(Tweety) \vee Bird(Joe)$. Since this clause is derivable from T, we conclude that $A \in \mathrm{NFREE_S}(T; (Bird); (); ())$. The reader may easily check that neither $Bird(Tweety)$ nor $Bird(Joe)$ are members of $\mathrm{NFREE_S}(T; (Bird); (); ())$. ∎

Definition 7.42 (Gelfond *et al.* 1989) Let T, $\bar{P}$, $\bar{Q}$ and $\bar{R}$ be as usual. The *extended closure of T wrt $\bar{P}$, $\bar{Q}$ and $\bar{R}$*, written $\mathrm{ECWA}(T; \bar{P}; \bar{Q}; \bar{R})$, is the theory

$$T \cup \{\neg A \colon A \in \mathrm{NFREE_S}(T; \bar{P}; \bar{Q}; \bar{R})\}.$$

We say that a formula A is derivable by applying ECWA to a theory T wrt to $\bar{P}$, $\bar{Q}$ and $\bar{R}$ iff $\mathrm{ECWA}(T; \bar{P}; \bar{Q}; \bar{R}) \vdash A$. ∎

Example 7.41 (continued)

$$\mathrm{ECWA}(T; (Bird); (); ()) \vdash \neg Bird(Tweety) \vee \neg Bird(Joe)$$
$$\mathrm{ECWA}(T; (Bird); (); ()) \nvdash \neg Bird(Tweety)$$
$$\mathrm{ECWA}(T; (Bird); (); ()) \nvdash \neg Bird(Joe).$$

∎

The next theorem shows that the members of $\mathrm{NFREE_S}(T; \bar{P}; \bar{Q}; \bar{R})$ are precisely the ground sentences not involving predicate constants from $\bar{Q}$ which are false in all $(\bar{P}; \bar{Q})$-minimal Herbrand models of T.

Theorem 7.43 (Gelfond *et al.* 1989) Let A be a ground sentence not involving predicate constants from $\bar{Q}$. A belongs to $\mathrm{NFREE_S}(T; \bar{P}; \bar{Q}; \bar{R})$ iff $T \models_m^{(\bar{P};\bar{Q})} \neg A$.

Proof Almost identical as the proof of Theorem 7.37. ∎

The following result, which in a slightly different form can be found in Gelfond *et al.* (1989), provides a semantic characterization of ECWA:

Theorem 7.44 M is a Herbrand model of $\mathrm{ECWA}(T; \bar{P}; \bar{Q}; \bar{R})$ iff M is a $(\bar{P}; \bar{Q})$-minimal Herbrand model of T.

Proof We begin by proving two lemmas.

> **Lemma 7.44.1** Let X be a set (possibly infinite) of ground sentences not involving predicate constants from $\bar{Q}$. $X \subseteq \mathrm{NFREE_S}(T; \bar{P}; \bar{Q}; \bar{R})$ iff DIS(X) is false in all $(\bar{P}; \bar{Q})$-minimal Herbrand models of T.
>
> **Proof** By Theorem 7.43. ∎
>
> **Lemma 7.44.2** Let M be a Herbrand model of T which is not $(\bar{P}; \bar{Q})$-minimal. For each $(\bar{P}; \bar{Q})$-minimal Herbrand model N of T, there is a literal $B_N \in \bar{P}^+ \cup \bar{R}^+ \cup \bar{R}^-$ such that $N \models \neg B_N$ and $M \models B_N$.
>
> **Proof** Left to the reader (compare the proof of Lemma 7.37.4). ∎

We now proceed to prove the theorem.

(⇒) Suppose that M is a Herbrand model of $\mathrm{ECWA}(T; \bar{P}; \bar{Q}; \bar{R})$ and assume that M is not $(\bar{P}; \bar{Q})$-minimal. Let **N** be the class of all $(\bar{P}; \bar{Q})$-minimal Herbrand models of T. Since M is a model of $\mathrm{ECWA}(T; \bar{P}; \bar{Q}; \bar{R})$, it is a model of T. Thus, T is consistent, and so, by Lemma 7.37.2, **N** is non-empty. In view of Lemma 7.44.2, for each $N \in \mathbf{N}$, we may select a literal $B_N \in \bar{P}^+ \cup \bar{R}^+ \cup \bar{R}^-$ such that $N \models \neg B_N$ and $M \models B_N$. Let $X = \{B_N: N \in \mathbf{N}\}$ and consider DIS(X). Obviously, DIS(X) is false in all $(\bar{P}; \bar{Q})$-minimal Herbrand models of T and hence, by Lemma 7.44.1, $X \subseteq \mathrm{NFREE_S}(T; \bar{P}; \bar{Q}; \bar{R})$. Take any B_N from X. We know that $M \models B_N$. On the other hand, $B_N \in \mathrm{NFREE_S}(T; \bar{P}; \bar{Q}; \bar{R})$. Therefore, M is not a model of $\mathrm{ECWA}(T; \bar{P}; \bar{Q}; \bar{R})$. A contradiction.

($\Leftarrow$) Follows immediately from Theorem 7.43.

∎

Corollary 7.45 (Gelfond *et al.* 1989) For each ground sentence A, $\mathrm{ECWA}(T; \bar{P}; \bar{Q}; \bar{R}) \vdash A$ iff $T \models_m^{(\bar{P};\bar{Q})} A$.

Proof By Lemma 7.8.1. ∎

Corollary 7.45 implies two important results:

Corollary 7.46 (Gelfond *et al.* 1989) $\mathrm{ECWA}(T; \bar{P}; \bar{Q}; \bar{R})$ is consistent iff T is consistent.

Proof By Lemma 7.37.2. ∎

Corollary 7.47 For any ground sentence A containing neither predicate constants from $\bar{Q}$ nor negative occurrences of literals from $\bar{P}$, $\mathrm{ECWA}(T; \bar{P}; \bar{Q}; \bar{R}) \vdash A$ iff $T \vdash A$.

Proof It suffices to show the implication from left to right. Assume that $\mathrm{ECWA}(T; \bar{P}; \bar{Q}; \bar{R}) \vdash A$. Thus, by Corollary 7.45, $T \models_m^{(\bar{P};\bar{Q})} A$. Since A contains neither predicate constants from $\bar{Q}$ nor negative occurrences of literals from $\bar{P}$, $T \models_m^{(\bar{P};\bar{Q})} A$ implies that A is true in all Herbrand models of T. Therefore, by Lemma 7.8.1, $T \vdash A$. ∎

Inspecting the discussion following Theorem 7.9, the reader may easily verify that Corollary 7.45 does not generalize into arbitrary sentences. In view of this, one might attempt to strengthen the power of ECWA by dropping the assumption that the notion of freedom for negation is restricted to ground sentences. Unfortunately, if we adopted this generalization, ECWA would typically lead to inconsistency. For example, consider $T = \{P(a)\}$ and put $\bar{P} = (P)$ and $\bar{Q} = \bar{R} = ()$. If we admitted that arbitrary sentences, satisfying the conditions from Definition 7.40, were regarded as free for negation in T, then both $\exists x \neg P(x)$ and $\forall x P(x)$ would be the members of $\mathrm{NFREE_S}(T; \bar{P}; \bar{Q}; \bar{R})$. In consequence, $\mathrm{ECWA}(T; \bar{P}; \bar{Q}; \bar{R})$ would be inconsistent.

We now turn our attention to the relationship between ECWA and second-order circumscription.

For any sets of sentences, X, Y and Z, we write $X \models Y \Leftrightarrow Z$ to indicate that Y and Z have the same models, provided that these models are selected from the models of X.

We have the following counterpart of Theorem 7.11:

Theorem 7.48 Let T be any theory (without function constants). For each $\bar{P}$, $\bar{Q}$ and $\bar{R}$,

$$\mathrm{D}(T), \mathrm{U}(T) \models \mathrm{ECWA}(T; \bar{P}; \bar{Q}; \bar{R}) \Leftrightarrow \mathrm{CIRC_{SO}}(T; \bar{P}; \bar{Q}).$$

Proof Let M be any frame in which $\mathrm{D}(T)$ and $\mathrm{U}(T)$ hold. Applying the same argument as in the proof of Theorem 7.15, it is easily seen that M is isomorphic to a Herbrand model. Thus, by Theorem 7.14, we may assume that M is such a model. Now, the theorem is an immediate consequence of Theorem 7.44, Theorem 6.41 and the following fact: If $\bar{Q}$ contains no function constants and M is a Herbrand model of T, then any model N of T such that $N \leq^{(\bar{P};\bar{Q})} M$ is a Herbrand model. ▮

As regards fixed-domain theories, we have:

Theorem 7.49 (Gelfond *et al.* 1989) For any fixed-domain theory T and any formula A

$$\text{ECWA}(T; \bar{P}; \bar{Q}; \bar{R}) \vdash A \quad \text{iff} \quad \text{CIRC}_{SO}(T; \bar{P}; \bar{Q}) \models A.$$

Proof The careful reader will have no difficulty in showing that all the results stated in this section hold if the term 'theory' is replaced by 'fixed-domain theory'. Thus, by Corollary 7.45, the rule of generalization, and the fact that, in a fixed domain theory, any sentence is equivalent to a ground sentence, we immediately have:

$$\text{For any formula } A, \text{ECWA}(T; \bar{P}; \bar{Q}; \bar{R}) \vdash A \text{ iff } T \models_m^{(\bar{P};\bar{Q})} A.$$

Now, the theorem follows from Theorems 7.14, 7.15 and 6.41. ▮

7.6 THEORY COMPLETION

We conclude this chapter by briefly presenting an alternative CWA formalism, usually referred to as *theory completion* (COMP). It was developed by Clark (1978) to provide a theoretic basis for the treatment of negation in logic programming. A nice property of Clark's system is that it is semi-decidable, i.e. the set of theorems derivable by COMP is partially computable.†

Some preliminary terminology. Let L be the usual first-order language without equality, possibly admitting function constants. A *rule* is any formula of the form

$$B_1 \wedge \cdots \wedge B_n \supset A \tag{7.6.1}$$

where $B_1, \ldots, B_n, A$ ($n \geq 0$) are literals of L and A is positive. A is called the *head* of the rule; $B_1, \ldots, B_n$ form its *body*. If A is $P(\bar{\alpha})$, then the rule is said to be *about* P. If all $B_1, \ldots, B_n$ are positive, then the rule is *definite*; otherwise, it is *indefinite*. It is generally assumed that all free variables of the rule are implicitly universally quantified, so that we shall never distinguish between rules and their universal closures.‡

The rule of the form $B_1 \wedge \cdots \wedge B_n \supset A$ is logically equivalent to the clause $\neg B_1 \vee \cdots \neg B_n \vee A$. Conversely, there are k essentially different rules which are equivalent to a clause containing k positive literals, since each of these literals may be placed in the head position.

In this section, we shall limit ourselves to a specific class of theories, called *programs*. A program is a finite set of rules. A program is *definite* (resp. *indefinite*) iff each (resp. some) of its rules is definite (resp. indefinite). From a logical point of view, any program may be viewed as a finite universal theory which, in its clausal form,

---

† Strictly speaking, theory completion attempts to formalize not the CWA rule, but rather its weaker version, called the *negation as failure* (NAF) *rule* (Clark 1978). The NAF is used in most implementations of Prolog to handle negative information. Roughly, the rule states that the proof of a ground literal $\neg P(\alpha)$ succeeds if the attempt to prove $P(\alpha)$ fails finitely, i.e. if it fails having exhausted the space of all possible proofs. Neither implementational issues concerning the NAF nor its relationship to theory completion will be discussed in this book. The reader interested in the subject is referred to Lloyd (1984) and Apt *et al.* (1988).

‡ The term 'rule' is from Gelfond & Lifschitz (1989). In logic programming terminology, rules are called (generalized) program clauses and (7.6.1) is usually written as $A \leftarrow B_1, \ldots, B_n$.

consists of clauses with at least one positive literal. Definite programs are just Horn theories enjoying this property.

Example 7.50 Let T consist of:

$$Adult(Tom) \tag{7.6.2}$$

$$\forall x . Student(x) \supset Adult(x) \tag{7.6.3}$$

$$\forall x . Adult(x) \wedge \neg Student(x) \supset Employed(x). \tag{7.6.4}$$

Due to (7.6.4), T is an indefinite program. Notice that it is logically equivalent to the program T' in which (7.6.4) is replaced by

$$\forall x . Adult(x) \wedge \neg Employed(x) \supset Student(x).$$

∎

In passing, let us note the following important property of programs:

Theorem 7.51 Any program T is consistent.

Proof The Herbrand frame corresponding to HB(T) is a model of T. ∎

Theory completion is based on the observation that rules represent 'if' but not 'only-if' conditions on the predicates concerned. For instance, the rules (7.6.2)–(7.6.3) state that x is an adult if she/he is a student or Tom. However, they say nothing about whether students and Tom are the only adults. According to Clark, the CWA rule is the assumption that 'if' conditions, explicitly represented by rules, are to be viewed as 'if-and-only-if' conditions. To realize this idea, Clark provides an effective procedure which takes a program T, together with a predicate constant P occurring in T, and returns a single sentence stating that T represents 'if-and-only-if' conditions on P. Applying this procedure to all predicate constants appearing in T, and adding some auxiliary axioms, we obtain a new theory, COMP(T), called the *completion of* T. The intention, of course, is that reasoning from T under the CWA is just the ordinary monotonic reasoning from COMP(T). It should be remarked that unlike T, its completion involves the equality predicate.

To formally specify the completion of a program, we need the following notion:

Definition 7.52 For any program T, we denote by ID(T) the *identity axioms for* T. These are the equality axioms for T, together with:

(i) $c_i \neq c_j$, for any pair c_i, c_j of distinct individual constants occurring in T;
(ii) $f(x_1, \ldots, x_n) \neq g(x_1, \ldots, x_m)$, for any pair f, g of distinct function constants occurring in T;
(iii) $f(x_1, \ldots, x_n) = f(y_1, \ldots, y_n) \supset x_1 = y_1 \wedge \cdots \wedge x_n = y_n$, for any function constant f occurring in T;
(iv) $f(x_1, \ldots, x_n) \neq c$, for any function constant f in T and any individual constant c occurring in T;
(v) $\alpha(x) \neq x$, for any non-variable term $\alpha(x)$ containing x.

It is implicitly assumed that all variables appearing in (i)–(v) are universally quantified. ∎

The axioms (i)–(v) represent the unique names assumption. They guarantee that any pair of distinct ground terms denotes distinct individuals.

We are now ready to define the completion of a program:

Definition 7.53 (Clark 1978) Let T be a program involving the predicate constants $P_1, \ldots, P_n$. We first remove all universal quantifiers in T and add the rule

$$False \supset P_i(x_1, \ldots, x_m)$$

for each m-ary predicate constant P_i not appearing in the head of some rule occurring in T. Since the removal of universal quantifiers preserves validity and the added rules are valid, the resulting program is logically equivalent to T. Now, for $P_1, \ldots, P_n$, we successively perform the following steps:

Step 1. *Remove terms.* Consider all rules of the form

$$B_1 \wedge \cdots \wedge B_m \supset P_i(\alpha_1, \ldots, \alpha_k).$$

Employing the equivalence

$A \supset P_i(\alpha_1 \ldots \alpha_k) \Leftrightarrow A \wedge (x_j = \alpha_j) \supset P_i(\alpha_1, \ldots, x_j, \ldots, \alpha_k)$, where x_j does not appear in $A \supset P_i(\alpha_1, \ldots, \alpha_k)$

we eliminate all non-variable terms from $P_i(\alpha_1 \ldots \alpha_k)$. In particular, if none of $\alpha_1, \ldots, \alpha_k$ is a variable, then the rule $B_1 \wedge \cdots \wedge B_m \supset P_i(\alpha_1, \ldots, \alpha_k)$ is to be replaced by

$$B_1 \wedge \cdots \wedge B_m \wedge (x_1 = \alpha_1) \wedge \cdots \wedge (x_k = \alpha_k) \supset P_i(x_1, \ldots, x_k).$$

Step 2. *Unify consequents.* Let

$$C_1 \supset P_i(x_1^1, \ldots, x_k^1)$$
$$\vdots$$
$$C_p \supset P_i(x_1^p, \ldots, x_k^p)$$

be all formulae obtained in the previous step. By appropriate change of variables, transform these formulae into

$$C_1 \supset P_i(x_1, \ldots, x_k)$$
$$\vdots$$
$$C_p \supset P_i(x_1, \ldots, x_k).$$

Step 3. *Introduce existential quantifiers.* Transform each formula

$$C_j \supset P_i(x_1, \ldots, x_k)$$

obtained in Step 2 into

$$(\exists y_1 \ldots y_q C_j) \supset P_i(x_1, \ldots, x_k)$$

where $y_1, \ldots, y_q$ are all free variables in C_j, different from $x_1, \ldots, x_k$.

Step 4. *Construct IF definition.* Let

$$D_1 \supset P_i(x_1, \ldots, x_k)$$
$$\vdots$$
$$D_p \supset P_i(x_1, \ldots, x_k)$$

be all formulae obtained in the Step 3. Replace them by

$$\forall x_1 \ldots x_k[D_1 \vee \cdots \vee D_p \supset P_i(x_1, \ldots, x_k)].$$

This sentence, denoted by $IF(T, P_i)$, is called the IF *definition of* P_i *in* T.[†]

Step 5. *Construct IFF definition.* In $\mathrm{IF}(T, P_i)$, replace '$\supset$' by '$\equiv$'. The resulting sentence, denoted by $\mathrm{IFF}(T, P_i)$, is called the *IFF definition of* P_i *in* T.

Performing Steps 1–5, for $P_1, \ldots, P_n$, we obtain $\mathrm{IFF}(T, P_1), \ldots, \mathrm{IFF}(T, P_n)$. Denote by $\mathrm{IFF}(T)$ the theory $\{\mathrm{IFF}(T, P_1), \ldots, \mathrm{IFF}(T, P_n)\}$. The *completion of* T, written $\mathrm{COMP}(T)$, is given by

$$\mathrm{COMP}(T) = \mathrm{IFF}(T) \cup \mathrm{ID}(T).$$

In words, the completion of a program T is the collection of IFF definitions, for each predicate constant in T, together with the identity axioms for T. We say that A is derivable from T by completion iff $\mathrm{COMP}(T) \vdash A$. ∎

Example 7.50 (continued) We construct the completion of T. Removing universal quantifiers and adding the appropriate rule for *Student*, we have

$$\begin{aligned}&Adult(Tom)\\&Student(x) \supset Adult(x)\\&Adult(x) \wedge \neg Student(x) \supset Employed(x)\\&False \supset Student(x).\end{aligned}$$

Now, repeating Steps 1–5, for *Adult*, *Employed* and *Student*, respectively, we obtain

$$\begin{aligned}&\mathrm{IFF}(T, Adult) \Leftrightarrow [\forall x\,.\,Adult(x) \equiv Student(x) \vee (x = Tom)]\\&\mathrm{IFF}(T, Employed) \Leftrightarrow [\forall x\,.\,Employed(x) \equiv Adult(x) \wedge \neg Student(x)]\\&\mathrm{IFF}(T, Student) \Leftrightarrow [\forall x\,.\,False \equiv Student(x)] \Leftrightarrow [\forall x \neg Student(x)].\end{aligned}$$

These sentences, together with $\mathrm{ID}(T)$, form the completion of T. It is easy to see that $\mathrm{COMP}(T) \vdash Employed(Tom)$.

To evaluate the completion of T', we first write this program as

$$\begin{aligned}&Adult(Tom)\\&Student(x) \supset Adult(x)\\&Adult(x) \wedge \neg Employed(x) \supset Student(x)\\&False \supset Employed(x).\end{aligned}$$

Now, performing Steps 1–5, for *Adult*, *Student* and *Employed*, we have

$$\begin{aligned}&\mathrm{IFF}(T', Adult) \Leftrightarrow [\forall x\,.\,Adult(x) \equiv Student(x) \vee (x = Tom)]\\&\mathrm{IFF}(T', Student) \Leftrightarrow [\forall x\,.\,Student(x) \equiv Adult(x) \wedge \neg Employed(x)]\\&\mathrm{IFF}(T', Employed) \Leftrightarrow [\forall x \neg Employed(x)].\end{aligned}$$

Augmenting these sentences with $\mathrm{ID}(T')$, we obtain the completion of T'. It is easy to see that

$$\mathrm{COMP}(T') \vdash \neg Employed(\mathrm{Tom}).$$

Since both $\mathrm{COMP}(T)$ and $\mathrm{COMP}(T')$ are consistent, this example shows that **logically equivalent programs may have different completions!** ∎

If T is a program all of whose predicate constants are $P_1, \ldots, P_n$, then we denote by $\mathrm{IF}(T)$ the theory

$$\mathrm{IF}(T) = \{\mathrm{IF}(T, P_1), \ldots, \mathrm{IF}(T, P_n)\}.$$

[†] If $D_1 \vee \cdots \vee D_k$ is empty, it is to be identified with *True*.

Examining Definition 7.53, the reader may be convinced that all the transformations needed to construct IF(T) amount to replacing formulae by their equivalents, so that T and IF(T) have exactly the same models. Therefore, every model of COMP(T) is a model of T, and hence, since ID(T) includes the equality axioms for T, we immediately have:

Theorem 7.54 For any program T and any formula A,

$$T \vdash A \text{ implies } \mathrm{COMP}(T) \vdash A.$$

▮

Theory completion need not preserve consistency:

Example 7.55 Consider the program $T = \{\neg P(a) \supset P(a)\}$. Its completion, namely

$$\mathrm{ID}(T) \cup \{\forall x[P(x) \equiv x = a \wedge \neg P(a)]\}$$

is inconsistent. ▮

Although theory completion may lead to inconsistency, this never happens for definite programs. To prove this fact, we need the following concepts.

Definition 7.56 (Jaffar *et al.* 1983) A *pre-frame for a first-order language L* is a pair $\mathrm{J} = \langle \mathrm{D}, \mathrm{m} \rangle$, where

(i) D is a non-empty set, called the *domain* of J;
(ii) m is a function which assigns to each individual constant of L, an element of D, and to each n-ary (n > 0) function constant of L, a function from $\mathrm{D}^{\mathrm{n}} \to \mathrm{D}$.

▮

A pre-frame differs from a frame in that it provides no interpretation for predicate constants. We say that a frame M *is based on a pre-frame* J iff M obtains from J by specifying assignments to predicate constants. Obviously, for a given pre-frame J, there will in general be many frames based on J. Each such a frame may be uniquely identified with a subset of *generalized atoms*, i.e. objects of the form $P(\mathrm{d}_1, \ldots \mathrm{d}_\mathrm{n})$, where P is an n-ary predicate constant and $\mathrm{d}_1, \ldots \mathrm{d}_\mathrm{n}$ are elements of the domain of J. We shall employ this convention in the sequel.

If M is a frame, $P(\alpha_1, \ldots, \alpha_n)$ is an atom and 'a' is an assignment to variables in M, then we denote by $|P(\alpha_1, \ldots, \alpha_n)|^{\mathrm{M}}_{\mathrm{a}}$ the generalized atom $P(\mathrm{V}^{\mathrm{M}}_{\mathrm{a}}(\alpha_1), \ldots, \mathrm{V}^{\mathrm{M}}_{\mathrm{a}}(\alpha_n))$.

We write L_T to denote the language of T.

Definition 7.57 (Jaffar *et al.* 1983) Let T be a definite program, J be a pre-frame for L_T, and suppose that F(J) is the class of all frames based on J. We define a mapping, denoted by $\mathscr{T}^{\mathrm{J}}_{\mathrm{T}}$, from F(J) into itself as follows. For $\mathrm{M} \in \mathrm{F(J)}$

$$\mathscr{T}^{\mathrm{J}}_{\mathrm{T}}(\mathrm{M}) = \{P(\mathrm{d}_1, \ldots, \mathrm{d}_\mathrm{n})\colon B_1 \wedge \cdots \wedge B_m \supset B \text{ is a rule in } T \text{ and there is an assignment } \mathrm{a} \in \mathrm{As(M)} \text{ such that } |B|^{\mathrm{M}}_{\mathrm{a}} = P(\mathrm{d}_1, \ldots, \mathrm{d}_\mathrm{n}) \text{ and } \{|B_1|^{\mathrm{M}}_{\mathrm{a}}, \ldots, |B_m|^{\mathrm{M}}_{\mathrm{a}}\} \subseteq \mathrm{M}\}.$$

▮

The next theorem shows that fixpoints of $\mathscr{T}^{\mathrm{J}}_{\mathrm{T}}$ provide a semantic characterization of the completions of definite programs:

Theorem 7.58 (Jaffar *et al.* 1983) Let T be a definite program and let J be a pre-frame for L_T. Suppose further that M is a frame based on J. Then M is a model for COMP(T) iff M is a model for ID(T) and $\mathscr{T}^{\mathrm{J}}_{\mathrm{T}}(\mathrm{M}) = \mathrm{M}$.

Proof Since $\mathrm{ID}(T) \subseteq \mathrm{COMP}(T)$, it suffices to show that M is a model for $\mathrm{IFF}(T)$ iff $\mathcal{T}_T^J(\mathrm{M}) = \mathrm{M}$.
($\Rightarrow$) Assume that M is a model of $\mathrm{IFF}(T)$ and let P be any predicate constant occurring in T. Suppose that

$$\mathrm{IF}(T, P) = \forall \bar{x} . B \supset P(\bar{x})$$

and denote by ONLY-IF(T, P) the sentence $\forall \bar{x} . P(\bar{x}) \supset B$. Since M is a model of $\mathrm{IFF}(T)$, we have

$$\mathrm{M} \models \mathrm{IF}(T, P) \tag{7.6.5}$$

$$\mathrm{M} \models \text{ONLY-IF}(T, P). \tag{7.6.6}$$

Inspecting Definitions 7.53 and 7.57, one easily verifies that (7.6.5) implies $\mathcal{T}_T^J(\mathrm{M})|P| \subseteq \mathrm{M}|P|$ and (7.6.6) implies $\mathrm{M}|P| \subseteq \mathcal{T}_T^J(\mathrm{M})|P|$. Thus, since P was chosen arbitrarily, we infer that $\mathcal{T}_T^J(\mathrm{M}) = \mathrm{M}$.
($\Leftarrow$) Suppose that $\mathcal{T}_T^J(\mathrm{M}) = \mathrm{M}$ and let P be any predicate constant from T. Consider the IFF definition of P in T:

$$\mathrm{IFF}(T, P) = \forall x . P(\bar{x}) \equiv B.$$

Again, examining Definitions 7.53 and 7.57, the reader may easily check that $\mathcal{T}_T^J(\mathrm{M}) \subseteq \mathrm{M}$ implies $\mathrm{M} \models \mathrm{IF}(T, P)$, whereas $\mathrm{M} \subseteq \mathcal{T}_T^J(\mathrm{M})$ leads to $\mathrm{M} \models$ ONLY-IF(T, P). Thus, $\mathrm{M} \models \mathrm{IFF}(T, P)$, and hence, since P was chosen arbitrarily, M is a model for $\mathrm{IFF}(T)$. ▮

To each definite program T we may uniquely assign the *Herbrand pre-frame for* L_T, denoted by $\mathrm{HP}(T)$, i.e. the pair $\langle \mathrm{D}, \mathrm{m} \rangle$, where D is the Herbrand universe of T and m provides the usual Herbrand interpretation of individual and function constants from L_T. Notice that the class of all frames based on $\mathrm{HP}(T)$ is just the class of all Herbrand frames for T. In the sequel, we write $\mathcal{T}_T$ as an abbreviation for $\mathcal{T}_T^{\mathrm{HP}(T)}$.

By virtue of Theorem 7.58, we have:

Theorem 7.59 Let T be a definite program.

(i) A Herbrand frame M is a model of $\mathrm{COMP}(T)$ iff $\mathcal{T}_T(\mathrm{M}) = \mathrm{M}$;
(ii) $\mathrm{COMP}(T)$ has a Herbrand model which is the least Herbrand model for T.

Proof (i) Follows from Theorem 7.58 and the fact that each Herbrand frame of L_T is a model for $\mathrm{ID}(T)$.
(ii) As we already remarked (see the discussion following Theorem 7.8), each consistent Horn theory, and hence each definite program, has the least Herbrand model. Let M be the model for T. It is easily verified that $\mathcal{T}_T(\mathrm{M}) = \mathrm{M}$, and so, by (i), M is a Herbrand model for $\mathrm{COMP}(T)$. ▮

The next theorem illustrates two important properties of the completions of definite programs:

Theorem 7.60 Let T be a definite program.

(i) For any ground sentence A, $\mathrm{COMP}(T) \vdash A$ implies $\mathrm{NCWA}(T) \vdash A$;
(ii) If A is a ground positive sentence, then $\mathrm{COMP}(T) \vdash A$ iff $T \vdash A$.

Proof (i) Follows from Theorems 7.9 and 7.59 (ii).
(ii) Follows from (i), Theorem 7.5 and Theorem 7.54. ▮

Considering the program from Example 7.55, the reader may easily check that neither (i) nor (ii) hold for indefinite programs. The following example illustrates that the implication in Theorem 7.60 (i) cannot generally be strengthened into equivalence:

Example 7.61 (Lloyd 1984) Consider the definite program T:

$$\forall y.P(y) \supset P(f(y))$$
$$\forall y.P(y) \supset Q(a).$$

Since $T \not\vdash Q(a)$, $\text{NCWA}(T) \vdash \neg Q(a)$. The completion of T is given by

$$\text{COMP}(T) = \text{ID}(T) \cup \text{IFF}(T, P) \cup IFF(T, Q)$$

where

$$\text{IFF}(T, P) = (\forall x.P(x) \equiv \exists y.P(y) \wedge x = f(y))$$
$$\text{IFF}(T, Q) = (\forall x.Q(x) \equiv \exists y.P(y) \wedge x = a).$$

We show that $\text{COMP}(T) \not\vdash \neg Q(a)$. For this purpose, it suffices to find a model for $\text{COMP}(T) \cup \{Q(a)\}$. Denote by $\mathbf{Z}$ and $\mathbf{N}$ the sets $\{0, +1, -1, +2, -2, \ldots\}$ and $\{0', 1', 2', \ldots\}$, respectively, and consider the frame M such that

$$|\mathrm{M}| = \mathbf{Z} \cup \mathbf{N}; \qquad \mathrm{M}|a| = 0'; \qquad \mathrm{M}|P| = \mathbf{Z}; \qquad \mathrm{M}|Q| = \{0'\};$$
$$\mathrm{M}|f| = \text{the successor function in } \mathbf{Z} \text{ and } \mathbf{N}.$$

It is readily checked that M is a model for $\text{COMP}(T) \cup \{Q(a)\}$. ∎

It should be emphasized that in studying models of COMP(T) we must not limit our attention to Herbrand frames. To show this, reconsider the program T from the above example. As we have seen, the sentence $\neg Q(a)$ is not derivable from COMP(T). However, the reader may easily verify that $\neg Q(a)$ is true in every Herbrand model of COMP(T).

There is another important class of programs, called *stratified programs*, for which theory completion preserves consistency. This class was introduced by Apt *et al.* (1988) and, independently, by Van Gelder (1988). To specify the notion of a stratified program, we need the following notion.

Definition 7.62 Given a program T, its *dependency graph* is a pair $D_T = \langle \bar{P}, E \rangle$, where

(i) $\bar{P}$, called the *set of nodes of* D_T, consists of all predicate constants occurring in T;
(ii) E, called the *set of arcs of* D_T, is the set of all pairs (P, Q) such that P and Q are both in $\bar{P}$ and T contains a rule about P including Q in its body.

∎

We call an arc (P, Q) from E *positive* (resp. *negative*) iff there is a rule in T such that P appears in its head and Q appears in a positive (resp. negative) literal of its body. Note that an arc may be both positive and negative. A *cycle in* D_T is any sequence $(P_1, Q_1), \ldots, (P_n, Q_n)$ of arcs such that P_1 is Q_n and P_{i+1} is Q_i, for $1 \le i < n$.

Definition 7.63 A program is called *stratified* iff its dependency graph contains no cycle with a negative arc. ∎

Clearly, each definite program is stratified.

Example 7.64 The program

$$T = \{P(a), \forall x.P(x) \supset Q(x), \forall x.\neg Q(x) \supset R(x)\}$$

is stratified. Its dependency graph is

$$\langle\{P, Q, R\}, \{(Q, P), (R, Q)\}\rangle.$$

Consider now the program T' given by

$$\{P(a), \forall x . P(x) \wedge R(x) \supset Q(x), \forall x . \neg Q(x) \supset R(x)\}.$$

T' is not stratified since its dependency graph

$$\langle\{P, Q, R\}, \{(Q, P), (Q, R), (R, Q)\}\rangle$$

contains a cycle (Q, R), (R, Q) with a negative arc, namely (R, Q). ∎

The notion of a stratified program may be given an alternative formulation, which is frequently used in the literature.

Definition 7.65 (Apt *et al.* 1988) Let T be a program represented as a union of disjoint sets of rules

$$T = T_1 \cup T_2 \cup \cdots \cup T_n \tag{7.6.7}$$

with T_1 possibly empty. We say that (7.6.7) is a *stratification of* T iff the following conditions hold:

(i) If a predicate constant P occurs in T_i, then its definition is contained in $T_1 \cup \cdots \cup T_i$;[†]

(ii) If a predicate constant P occurs in T_i under negation, then its definition is contained in $T_1 \cup \cdots \cup T_{i-1}$.

∎

For a proof of the following fact, see Apt *et al.* (1988):

Theorem 7.66 (Apt *et al.* 1988) A program is stratified iff it has a stratification. ∎

Example 7.64 (continued) The program T has two stratifications:

$$\{P(a)\} \cup \{\forall x . P(x) \supset Q(x)\} \cup \{\forall x . \neg Q(x) \supset R(x)\} \qquad \text{and}$$
$$\{P(a), \forall x . P(x) \supset Q(x)\} \cup \{\forall x . \neg Q(x) \supset R(x)\}.$$

Due to Theorem 7.66, T' has no stratification. ∎

Apt *et al.* (1988) showed the following fact:

Theorem 7.67 (Apt *et al.* 1988) For any stratified program T, COMP(T) has a model which is a minimal Herbrand model of T. ∎

From Theorem 7.67, we immediately have:

Corollary 7.68 For any stratified program T,

(i) COMP(T) is consistent.

(ii) For any ground sentence A, COMP(T) $\vdash A$ implies NCWA(T) $\vdash A$.

Proof (i) Obvious. (ii) Follows easily from Theorem 7.9. ∎

It is worth noting that the counterpart of Theorem 7.60 (ii) does not hold for stratified programs. Consider, for example, the program $T = \{R(a), \forall x . \neg P(x) \supset Q(x)\}$. COMP($T$) = ID($T$) $\cup \{\forall x . R(x) \equiv x = a, \forall x . Q(x) \equiv \neg P(x), \forall x \neg P(x)\}$. It is easy to see that COMP(T) $\vdash Q(a)$ but $T \nvdash Q(a)$.

[†] The definition of P in a program T is the set of all rules in T about P.

Stratified programs are now given much attention in the logic programming literature. For semantic characterizations of their completions, see Apt *et al.* (1988) and Przymusinski (1988). Certain connections between the completions of stratified programs and pointwise circumscription can be found in Lifschitz (1988a).

Theory completion is obviously an interesting step towards formalizing the CWA rule. The major strength of Clark's system is its semi-decidability. Furthermore, the manipulations involved in constructing the completion of a program are simple and natural. A serious drawback of Clark's approach is that it lacks generality. It is defined only for programs and hence cannot be applied to theories containing negative sentences. Another shortcoming of the formalism is that it is syntax-sensitive: logically equivalent programs may have different completions (Example 7.50). What is worse, it may even happen that one of these completions is inconsistent. (To see this, note that the program T from Example 7.55 is equivalent to $T' = \{P(a)\}$; the completion of T' is consistent, whereas that of T is not.)[†]

[†] The fact that consistency of COMP(T) may depend on the syntactic form of T was first observed by Shepherdson (1984).

Bibliography

With a few exceptions the papers and books listed here are those mentioned in the text. The abbreviation AAAI stands for the conference organized in the United States by the American Association for Artificial Intelligence. ECAI (resp. IJCAI) refers to European (resp. International Joint) Conference on Artificial Intelligence.

Aiello, L., Levi, G. (1984) 'The Uses of Metaknowledge in AI Systems', in: *Proc. 6th ECAI*, Pisa, Italy, 705–717.

Aiello, L., Weyrauch, R. W. (1975) 'Checking Proofs in the Metamathematics of First-Order Logic', in: *Proc. 4th IJCAI*, Tbilisi, USSR, 1–8.

Anderson, A. R., Belnap, J. (1975) *Entailment: The Logic of Relevance and Necessity*, Princeton University Press, Princeton, NJ.

Appelt, D. E., Konolige, K. (1989) 'A Non-Monotonic Logic for Reasoning about Speech Acts and Belief Revision', in: *Proc. 2nd Int. Workshop on Non-Monotonic Reasoning*, Lecture Notes in Artificial Intelligence, 346, Springer-Verlag, Berlin, 164–175.

Apt, K. R., Blair, H. A., Walker, A. (1988) 'Towards a Theory of Declarative Knowledge', in: *Foundations of Deductive Databases and Logic Programming*, J. Minker (ed.), Morgan Kaufmann Publishers, Palo Alto, CA, 89–148.

Ascher, N. (1984) 'Linguistic Understanding and Non-Monotonic Reasoning', in: *Proc. AAAI Workshop on Non-Monotonic Reasoning*, New Paltz, NY, 1–20.

Attardi, G., Simi, M. (1981) 'Consistency and Completeness of Omega, a Logic for Knowledge Representation', in: *Proc. 7th IJCAI*, Vancouver, BC, 504–510.

Attardi, G., Simi, M. (1984) 'Metalanguage and Reasoning across Viewpoints', in: *Proc. 6th ECAI*, Pisa, Italy, 315–324.

Barwise, J. (1977) *Handbook of Mathematical Logic*, North-Holland, Amsterdam, J. Barwise (ed.).

Besnard, P. (1989) *Introduction to Default Logic*, Springer-Verlag, Berlin.

Besnard, P., Moinard, Y., Mercer, R. E. (1989) 'The Importance of Open and Recursive Circumscription', *Artificial Intelligence J.*, **40**, 251–262.

Bobrow, D. G., Winograd, T. (1977) 'An Overview of KRL, A Knowledge Representation Language', *Cognitive Science*, **1**, 3–46.

Bossu, G., Siegel, P. (1985) 'Saturation, Non-Monotonic Reasoning and the Closed-World Assumption', *Artificial Intelligence J.*, **25**, 13–63.

Bowen, K., Kowalski, R. (1982) 'Amalgamating Language and Metalanguage in Logic Programming', in: *Logic Programming*, K. L. Clark, S. A. Tarnlund (eds.), Academic Press, New York, 153–173.

Brachman, R. (1979) 'On the Epistemological Status of Semantic Networks', in: *Associative Networks: Representation and Use of Knowledge by Computers*, N. V. Findler (ed.), Academic Press, New York, 3–50.

Brown, A. L. (1985) 'Modal Propositional Semantics for Reason Maintenance', in: *Proc. 9th IJCAI*, Los Angeles, CA, 974–980.

Brown, A. L., Benanav, D., Gaucas, D. E. (1986) 'Reason Maintenance from a Lattice-Theoretic Point of View', in: *Proc. of Expert Systems Workshop*, Pacific Grove, CA, 83–87.

Brown, A. L., Benanav, D., Gaucas, D. E. (1987) 'An Algebraic Foundation for Truth Maintenance', in: *Proc. 10th IJCAI*, Milano, Italy, 973–980.

Brown, A. L., Shoham, Y. (1989). 'New Results on Semantical Non-Monotonic Reasoning', in: *Proc. 2nd Int. Workshop on Non-Monotonic Reasoning*, Lecture Notes in Artificial Intelligence, 346, Springer-Verlag, Berlin, 19–26.

Brown, F. M. (1987) *Proc. 1987 Workshop on the Frame Problem in Artificial Intelligence*, Lawrence, KS, F. M. Brown (ed.).

Chang, C. L., Lee, C. T. (1973) *Symbolic Logic and Mechanical Theorem Proving*, Academic Press, New York.

Cheeseman, P. (1985) 'In Defence of Probability', in: *Proc. 9th IJCAI*, Los Angeles, CA, 1002–1009.

Chellas, B. F. (1980) *Modal Logic: An Introduction*, Cambridge University Press, Cambridge, England.

Church, A. (1936) 'A Note on the Entscheidungsproblem', *Journal of Symbolic Logic*, **1**, 40–41. Correction, *ibid.*, 101–102.

Church, A. (1956) *Introduction to Mathematical Logic*, I, Princeton University Press, Princeton, NJ.

Clark, K. L. (1978) 'Negation as Failure', in: *Logic and Data Bases*, H. Gallaire, J. Minker (eds.), Plenum Press, New York, 293–322.

Clarke, M. R. B. (1988) 'Intuitionistic Non-Monotonic Reasoning – Further Results', in: *Proc. 8th ECAI*, München, West Germany, 525–527.

Cohen, P. R. (1987) 'Numeric and Symbolic Reasoning in Expert Systems', in: *Advances in Artificial Intelligence II*, B. du Boulay, D. Hogg, L. Steels (eds.), North-Holland, Amsterdam, 527–541.

Cottrell, G. W. (1985) 'Parallelism in Inheritance Hierarchies with Exceptions', in: *Proc. 9th IJCAI*, Los Angeles, CA, 194–202.

Davis, M. (1980) 'The Mathematics of Non-Monotonic Reasoning', *Artificial Intelligence J.*, **13**, 73–80.

de Kleer, J. (1986a) 'An Assumption Based TMS', *Artificial Intelligence J.*, **28**, 127–162.

de Kleer, J. (1986b) 'Extending the ATMS', *Artificial Intelligence J.*, **28**, 163–196.

de Kleer, J. (1986c) 'Problem Solving with the ATMS', *Artificial Intelligence J.*, **28**, 197–224.

Delgrande, J. P. (1988) 'An Approach to Default Reasoning Based on First-Order Conditional Logic: Revised Report', *Artificial Intelligence J.*, **36**, 63–90.

Dixon, M., de Kleer, J. (1989) 'Massively Parallel Assumption-Based Truth Maintenance', in: *Proc. 2nd Int. Workshop on Non-Monotonic Reasoning*, Lecture Notes in Artificial Intelligence, 346, Springer-Verlag, Berlin, 131–142.

Doyle, J. (1979) 'A Truth Maintenance System', *Artificial Intelligence J.*, **12**, 231–272.

Doyle, J. (1980) 'A Model for Deliberation, Action and Introspection', Ph.D. Thesis, Technical Report No. 581, MIT, AI Lab., Cambridge, MA.

Doyle, J. (1983a) 'The Ins and Outs of Reason Maintenance', in: *Proc. 8th IJCAI*, Karlsruhe, West Germany, 349–351.

Doyle, J. (1983b) 'Some Theories of Reasoned Assumptions: An Essay in Rational Psychology', Technical Report 83–125, Dept. of Computer Science, Carnegie-Mellon University, Pittsburgh, PA.

Doyle, J. (1985) 'Circumscription and Implicit Definability', *Journal of Automated Reasoning*, **1**, 391–405.

Dressler, O. (1989) 'An Extended ATMS', in: *Proc. 2nd Int. Workshop on Non-Monotonic Reasoning*, Lecture Notes in Artificial Intelligence, 346, Springer-Verlag, Berlin, 143–163.

Dummett, M. (1977) *Elements of Intuitionism*, Oxford University Press, Oxford.

Dunin-Kęplicz, B. (1984) 'Default Reasoning in Anaphora Resolution', in: *Proc. 6th ECAI*, Pisa, Italy, 157–166.

Dunin-Kęplicz, B., Łukaszewicz, W. (1986) 'Towards Discourse Oriented Non-Monotonic System', in: *Proc. 11th Conf. on Computational Linguistics*, Bonn, West Germany, 504–506.

Etherington, D. W. (1982) 'Finite Default Theories', M.Sc. Thesis, Dept. of Computer Science, University of British Columbia, Vancouver, BC.

Etherington, D. W. (1983) 'Formalizing Non-Monotonic Reasoning Systems', Technical Report 83-1, Dept. of Computer Science, University of British Columbia, Vancouver, BC. Also in: *Artificial Intelligence J.*, **31** (1987), 41–85.

Etherington, D. W. (1988) *Reasoning with Incomplete Information*, Pitman, London.

Etherington, D. W., Mercer, R. (1987) 'Domain Circumscription: A Revaluation', *Computational Intelligence*, **3**, 94–99.

Etherington, D. W., Mercer, R., Reiter, R. (1985) 'On the Adequacy of Predicate Circumscription for Closed-World Reasoning', *Computational Intelligence*, **1**, 11–15.

Etherington, D. W., Reiter, R. (1983) 'On Inheritance Hierarchies with Exceptions', in: *Proc. AAAI-83*, Seattle, WA, 104–108.

Fahlman, S. E. (1979) *NETL: A System for Representing and Using Real-World Knowledge*, MIT Press, Cambridge, MA.

Fahlman, S. E., Touretzky, D. S., van Roggen, W. (1981) 'Cancellation in a Parallel Semantic Network', in: *Proc. 7th IJCAI*, Vancouver, BC, 257–263.

Feferman, S. (1974) 'Applications of Many-Sorted Interpolation Theorem', in: *Proc. Tarski Symp. of American Mathematical Society*, Providence, RI, 102–148.

Fischler, M., Firschein, O. (1984) 'Computational Vision as a Non-Monotonic Reasoning Process', in: *Proc. AAAI Workshop on Non-Monotonic Reasoning*, New Paltz, NY, 89–92.

Fraenkel, A. A., Bar-Hillel, Y., Levy, A. (1973) *Foundations of Set Theory*, North Holland, Amsterdam.

Froidevaux, C. (1986) 'Taxonomic Default Theory', in: *Proc. 7th ECAI*, Brighton, England, 123–129.

Gabbay, D. (1982) 'Intuitionistic Basis for Non-Monotonic Logic', in: *Proc. 6th Conf. on Automated Deduction*, Lecture Notes in Computer Science, 138, Springer-Verlag, Berlin, 260–271.

Gabbay, D., Sergot, M. J. (1986) 'Negation as Inconsistency', *Journal of Logic Programming*, **3**, 1–35.

Gardenfors, P. (1978) 'Conditionals and Changes of Belief', *Acta Philosophica Fennica*, **30**, 381–404.

Geffner, H. (1989) 'Default Reasoning, Minimality and Coherence', in: *Proc. 1st Conf. on Principles of Knowledge Representation and Reasoning*, Morgan Kaufmann Publishers, Palo Alto, CA, 137–148.

Gelfond, M., Lifschitz, V. (1989) 'Compiling Circumscriptive Theories into Logic Programs', in: *Proc. 2nd Int. Workshop on Non-Monotonic Reasoning*, Lecture Notes in Artificial Intelligence, 346, Springer-Verlag, Berlin, 74–99.

Gelfond, M., Przymusinska, H. (1986) 'Negation as Failure: Careful Closure Procedure', *Artificial Intelligence J.*, **30**, 273–287.

Gelfond, M., Przymusinska, H., Przymusinski, T. (1989) 'On the Relationship between Circumscription and Negation as Failure', *Artificial Intelligence J.*, **38**, 75–94.

Ginsberg, M. L. (1985) 'Does Probability Have a Place in Non-Monotonic Reasoning?', in: *Proc. 9th IJCAI*, Los Angeles, CA, 107–110.

Ginsberg, M. L. (1988) 'Multivalued Logics: A Uniform Approach to Reasoning in Artificial Intelligence', *Computational Intelligence*, **4**, 265–316.

Ginsberg, M. L. (1989) 'A Circumscriptive Theorem Prover', in: *Proc. 2nd Int. Workshop on Non-Monotonic Reasoning*, Lecture Notes in Artificial Intelligence, 346, Springer-Verlag, Berlin, 100–115.

Ginsberg, M. L., Smith, D. E. (1988a) 'Reasoning about Action I: A Possible Worlds Approach', *Artificial Intelligence J.*, **35**, 165–195.

Ginsberg, M. L., Smith, D. E. (1988b) 'Reasoning about Action II: The Qualification Problem', *Artificial Intelligence J.*, **35**, 311–342.

Goldstein, I. P., Roberts, R. B. (1977) 'The FRL Primer', AI Memo No. 408, MIT, AI Lab., Cambridge, MA.

Goodwin, J. W. (1982) 'An Improved Algorithm for Non-Monotonic Dependency Update', Research Report 82-23, Linköping University, Linköping, Sweden.

Goodwin, J. W. (1987) 'A Theory and System for Non-Monotonic Reasoning', Ph.D. Thesis, Linköping University, Linköping, Sweden.

Grosof, B. (1984) 'Default Reasoning as Circumscription', in: *Proc. AAAI Workshop on Non-Monotonic Reasoning*, New Paltz, NY, 115–124.

Haack, S. (1974) *Deviant Logics*, Cambridge University Press, Cambridge.

Haack, S. (1978) *Philosophy of Logics*, Cambridge University Press, Cambridge.

Halpern, J. Y., Moses, Y. (1984) 'Towards a Theory of Knowledge and Ignorance: A Preliminary Report', in: *Proc. AAAI Workshop on Non-Monotonic Reasoning*, New Paltz, NY, 125–143.

Hanks, S., McDermott, D. (1987) 'Nonmonotonic Logic and Temporal Projection', *Artificial Intelligence J.*, **33**, 379–412.

Hayes, P. J. (1973) 'The Frame Problem and Related Problems in Artificial

Intelligence', in: *Artificial and Human Thinking*, A. Elithorn, D. Jones (eds.), Josey-Bass, Inc., San Francisco, 45–59.

Hayes, P. J. (1977) 'In Defence of Logic', in: *Proc. 5th IJCAI*, Cambridge, MA, 559–565.

Hayes, P. J. (1979) 'The Logic of Frames', in: *Frame Conceptions and Text Understanding*, D. Metzing (ed.), Walter de Gruyter and Co., Berlin, 46–61.

Hendrix, G. (1975) 'Expanding the Utility of Semantic Networks through Partitioning', in: *Proc. 4th IJCAI*, Tbilisi, USSR, 115–121.

Hewitt, C., Attardi, G., Simi, M. (1980) 'Knowledge Embedding with the Description System Omega', in: *Proc. AAAI-80*, Stanford, CA, 157–163.

Heyting, A. (1930) 'Die formale Regein der intuitionischen Logik', in: *Sitzungsberichte der Preussischen Akademie der Wissenschaften Phys.-Math. Klasse*, 42–56.

Heyting, A. (1956) *Intuitionism, An Introduction*, North-Holland, Amsterdam.

Hughes, G. E., Cresswell, M. J. (1972) *An Introduction to Modal Logic*, Methuen & Co. Ltd., London.

Imielinski, T. (1987) 'Results on Translating Defaults to Circumscription', *Artificial Intelligence J.*, **32**, 131–146.

Israel, D. J. (1980) 'What's Wrong with Non-Monotonic Logic', in: *Proc. AAAI-80*, Stanford, CA, 99–101.

Jaffar, J., Lassez, J. L., Lloyd, J. W. (1983) 'Completeness of the Negation as Failure Rule', in: *Proc. 8th IJCAI*, Karlsruhe, West Germany, 500–506.

Joshi, A., Webber, B., Weischedel, R. (1984) 'Default Reasoning in Interaction', in: *Proc. AAAI Workshop on Non-Monotonic Reasoning*, New Paltz, NY, 144–150.

Kautz, H. (1986) 'The Logic of Persistence', in: *Proc. AAAI-86*, Philadelphia, PA, 401–405.

Kautz, H., Selman, B. (1989) 'Hard Problems for Simple Default Logics', in: *Proc. 1st Int. Conf. on Principles of Knowledge Representation and Reasoning*, Morgan Kaufmann Publishers, Palo Alto, CA, 189–197.

Kleene, S. (1952) *Introduction to Metamathematics*, Van Nostrand, New Jersey.

Kolaitis, P., Papadimitriou, C. (1988) 'Some Computational Aspects of Circumscription', in: *Proc. AAAI-88*, St Paul, MN, 465–469.

Konolige, K. (1988) 'On the Relation between Default and Autoepistemic Logic', *Artificial Intelligence J.*, **35**, 343–382.

Konolige, K. (1989) 'Hierarchic Autoepistemic Theories for Non-Monotonic Reasoning', in: *Proc. 2nd Int. Workshop on Non-Monotonic Reasoning*, Lecture Notes in Artificial Intelligence, 346, Springer-Verlag, Berlin, 42–59.

Kowalski, R. (1979) *Logic for Problem Solving*, North-Holland, Amsterdam.

Kramosil, I. (1975) 'A Note on Deduction Rules with Negative Premisses', in: *Proc. 4th IJCAI*, Tbilisi, USSR, 53–56.

Kreisel, G., Krivine, J. L. (1967) *Elements of Mathematical Logic*, North-Holland, Amsterdam.

Kripke, S. (1965) 'Semantical Analysis of Intuitionistic Logic', in: *Formal Systems and Recursive Function Theory*, J. N. Crossley, M. Dummett (eds.), North-Holland, Amsterdam, 92–129.

Krishnaprasad, T. (1988) 'On the Computability of Circumscription', *Information Processing Letters*, **27**, 237–243.

Levesque, H. J. (1982) 'A Formal Treatment of Incomplete Knowledge', Technical Report 3, Fairchild Laboratory for AI Research, Menlo Park, CA.

Lewis, D. (1973) *Counterfactuals*, Oxford University Press, Oxford.

Lifschitz, V. (1984) 'Some Results on Circumscription', in: *Proc. AAAI Workshop on Non-Monotonic Reasoning*, New Paltz, NY, 151–164.

Lifschitz, V. (1985a) 'Closed-World Databases and Circumscription', *Artificial Intelligence J.*, **27**, 229–235.

Lifschitz, V. (1985b) 'Computing Circumscription', in: *Proc. 9th IJCAI*, Los Angeles, CA, 121–127.

Lifschitz, V. (1986) 'On the Satisfiability of Circumscription', *Artificial Intelligence J.*, **28**, 17–27.

Lifschitz, V. (1987) 'Formal Theories of Action', in: *Proc. 10th IJCAI*, Milan, Italy, 966–972.

Lifschitz, V. (1988a) 'On the Declarative Semantics of Logic Programs with Negation', in: *Readings in Nonmonotonic Reasoning*, M. Ginsberg (ed.), Morgan Kaufmann Publishers, Palo Alto, CA, 337–350.

Lifschitz, V. (1988b) 'Pointwise Circumscription', in: *Readings in Nonmonotonic Reasoning*, M. Ginsberg (ed.), Morgan Kaufmann Publishers, Palo Alto, CA, 179–193.

Lifschitz, V. (1989a) 'Benchmark Problems for Formal Non-Monotonic Reasoning, Version 2.00', in: *Proc. 2nd Int. Workshop on Non-Monotonic Reasoning*, Lecture Notes in Artificial Intelligence, 346, Springer-Verlag, Berlin, 202–218.

Lifschitz, V. (1989b) 'Between Circumscription and Autoepistemic Logic', in: *Proc. 1st Conf. on Principles of Knowledge Representation and Reasoning*, Morgan Kaufmann Publishers, Palo Alto, CA, 235–244.

Lin, F., Shoham, Y. (1989) 'Argument Systems: A Uniform Basis for Nonmonotonic Reasoning', in: *Proc. 1st Conf. on Principles of Knowledge Representation and Reasoning*, Morgan Kaufmann Publishers, Palo Alto, CA, 245–255.

Lloyd, J. W. (1984) *Foundations of Logic Programming*, Springer-Verlag, Berlin.

London, P. (1978) 'Dependency Networks as Representation for Modelling in General Problem Solvers', Ph.D. Thesis, Technical Report 698, Dept. Computer Science, University of Maryland, College Park, MD.

Loveland, D. W. (1970) 'A Linear Format for Resolution', in: *Proc. IRIA Symp. on Automatic Demonstration*, Springer-Verlag, Berlin, 147–162.

Loveland, D. W. (1978) *Automated Theorem Proving: A Logical Basis*, North-Holland, Amsterdam.

Luckham, D. (1970) 'Refinements in Resolution Theory', in: *Proc. IRIA Symp. on Automatic Demonstration*, Springer-Verlag, Berlin, 163–190.

Łukaszewicz, W. (1984a) 'Nonmonotonic Logic for Default Theories', in: *Proc. 6th ECAI*, Pisa, Italy, 305–314.

Łukaszewicz, W. (1984b) 'Considerations on Default Logic', in: *Proc. AAAI Workshop on Non-Monotonic Reasoning*, New Paltz, NY, 165–193. Also in: *Computational Intelligence*, **4**, 1–16 (1988).

Łukaszewicz, W. (1985) 'Two Results on Default Logic', in: *Proc. 9th IJCAI*, Los Angeles, CA, 459–461. Also in: *Computers and Artificial Intelligence*, **6**, 329–343 (1987).

Łukaszewicz, W. (1987) 'Minimization of Abnormality: A Simple System for Default Reasoning', in: *Advances in Artificial Intelligence*, B. Du Boulay, D. Hogg, L. Steels (eds.), North-Holland, Amsterdam, 175–182.

Łukaszewicz, W. (1988) 'Chronological Minimization of Abnormality: Simple

Theories of Action', in: *Proc. 8th ECAI*, München, West Germany, 574–576.

Makinson, D. (1989) 'General Theory of Cumulative Inference', In: *Proc. 2nd Int. Workshop on Non-Monotonic Reasoning'*, Lecture Notes in Artificial Intelligence, 346, Springer-Verlag, Berlin, 1–18.

Marek, W. (1985) 'Stable Theories in Autoepistemic Logic', Unpublished Note, Dept. of Computer Science, University of Kentucky, Lexington, KY. To appear in *Fundamenta Informaticae*.

Marek, W., Truszczynski, M. (1988) 'Autoepistemic Logic', Technical Report 115-88, Dept. of Computer Science, University of Kentucky, Lexington, KY.

Marek, W., Truszczynski, M. (1989) 'Relating Autoepistemic and Default Logics', in: *Proc. 1st Conf. on Principles of Knowledge Representation and Reasoning*, Morgan Kaufmann Publishers, Palo Alto, CA, 276–288.

Martins, J. (1983) 'Reasoning in Multiple Belief Spaces', Ph.D. Thesis, Technical Report 203, Dept. of Computer Science, State University of New York, Buffalo, NY.

Martins, J., Shapiro, S. C. (1984) 'A Model for Belief Revision', in: *Proc. AAAI Workshop on Non-Monotonic Reasoning*, New Paltz, NY, 241–294.

McAllester, D. A. (1980) 'An Outlook on Truth-Maintenance', AI Memo 551, MIT, AI Lab., Cambridge, MA.

McCarthy, J. (1977) 'Epistemological Problems of Artificial Intelligence', in: *Proc. 5th IJCAI*, Cambridge, MA, 1038–1044.

McCarthy, J. (1980) 'Circumscription – A Form of Non-Monotonic Reasoning', *Artificial Intelligence J.*, **13**, 27–39.

McCarthy, J. (1984) 'Applications of Circumscription to Formalizing Commonsense Knowledge', in: *Proc. AAAI Workshop on Non-Monotonic Reasoning*, New Paltz, NY, 295–324. Also in: *Artificial Intelligence J.*, **28**, 1986, 89–116.

McCarthy, J., Hayes, P. J. (1969) 'Some Philosophical Problems from the Standpoint of Artificial Intelligence', in: *Machine Intelligence 4*, B. Meltzer, D. Michie (eds.), American Elsevier, New York, 463–502.

McDermott, D. (1982) 'Non-Monotonic Logic II: Non-Monotonic Modal Theories', *Journal of ACM*, **29**, 33–57.

McDermott, D. (1983) 'Data Dependencies on Inequalities', in: *Proc. AAAI-83*, Washington, DC, 266–269.

McDermott, D., Doyle, J. (1980) Non-Monotonic Logic I', *Artificial Intelligence J.*, **13**, 41–72.

Mendelson, E. (1979) *An Introduction to Mathematical Logic*, Van Nostrand, New Jersey.

Mercer, R. E., Reiter, R. (1982) 'The Representation of Presupposition Using Defaults', Technical Report 82-1, Dept. of Computer Science, University of British Columbia, Vancouver, BC.

Minker, J. (1982) 'On Indefinite Databases and the Closed World Assumption', in: *Proc. 6th Conf. on Automated Deduction*, Lecture Notes in Computer Science, 138, Springer-Verlag, Berlin, 292–308.

Minker, J., Perlis, D. (1984) 'Protected Circumscription', in: *Proc. AAAI Workshop on Non-Monotonic Reasoning*, New Paltz, NY, 337–343.

Minsky, M. (1975) 'A Framework for Representing Knowledge', in: *Mind Design*, J. Haugeland (ed.), MIT Press, Cambridge, MA, 95–128.

Moore, R. (1983) 'Semantical Considerations on Non-Monotonic Logic', in: *Proc. 8th*

IJCAI, Karlsruhe, West Germany, 272–279. Also in: *Artificial Intelligence J.*, **25**, 75–94 (1985).

Moore, R. (1984) 'Possible-World Semantics for Autoepistemic Logic', in: *Proc. AAAI Workshop on Non-Monotonic Reasoning*, New Paltz, NY, 344–354.

Morgan, C. G. (1976) 'Methods for Automated Theorem Proving in Nonclassical Logics', *IEEE Transactions on Computers*, **8**, 852–862.

Morris, P. H. (1988) 'The Anomalous Extension Problem in Default Reasoning', *Artificial Intelligence J.*, **35**, 383–399.

Morris, P. H. (1989) 'Autoepistemic Stable Closures and Contradiction Resolution', in: *Proc. 2nd Int. Workshop on Non-Monotonic Reasoning*, Lecture Notes in Artificial Intelligence, 346, Springer-Verlag, Berlin, 60–73.

Mott, P. L. (1987) 'A Theorem on the Consistency of Circumscription', *Artificial Intelligence J.*, **31**, 87–98.

Niemelä, I. (1988) 'Decision Procedure for Autoepistemic Logic', in: *Proc. 9th Conf. on Automated Deduction*, Lecture Notes in Computer Science, 310, Springer-Verlag, Berlin, 676–684.

Papalaskaris, M. A., Bundy, A. (1984) 'Topics for Circumscription', in: *Proc. AAAI Workshop on Non-Monotonic Reasoning*, New Paltz, NY, 355–362.

Perlis, D. (1987a) 'Circumscribing with Sets', *Artificial Intelligence J.*, **31**, 201–211.

Perlis, D. (1987b) 'On the Consistency of Common-Sense Reasoning', *Computational Intelligence*, **2**, 180–190.

Perlis, D. (1988) 'Autocircumscription', *Artificial Intelligence J.*, **36**, 223–236.

Perlis, D., Minker, J. (1986) 'Completeness Results for Circumscription', *Artificial Intelligence J.*, **28**, 29–42.

Perrault, C. R. (1986) 'An Application of Default Logic to Speech Act Theory', in: *Proc. Conf. on Structure of Multimodal Dialogues Including Voice*, Venaco, France, 45–62.

Poole, D. (1984) 'A Logical System for Default Reasoning', in: *Proc. AAAI Workshop on Non-Monotonic Reasoning*, New Paltz, NY, 373–384.

Poole, D. (1985) 'On the Comparison of Theories: Preferring the Most Specific Explanation', in: *Proc. 9th IJCAI*, Los Angeles, CA, 144–147.

Poole, D. (1986) 'Default Reasoning and Diagnosis as Theory Formation', Technical Report, CS-86-08, Dept. of Computer Science, University of Waterloo, Waterloo, Canada.

Poole, D. (1987) 'Variables in Hypotheses', in: *Proc. 10th IJCAI*, Milan, Italy, 905–908.

Poole, D. (1988) 'A Logical Framework for Default Reasoning', *Artificial Intelligence J.*, **36**, 27–48.

Prade, H. (1988) 'A Quantitative Approach to Approximate Reasoning in Rule-Based Expert Systems', in: *Expert System Applications*, L. Bolc, M. J. Coombs (eds.), Springer-Verlag, Berlin, 199–256.

Priest, G., Routley, R. (1984) 'Introduction: Paraconsistent Logics', *Studia Logica*, **XLIII, 1/2**, 3–16.

Przymusinski, T. (1986) 'Query Answering in Circumscription and Closed-World Theories', in: *Proc. AAAI-86*, Philadelphia, PA, 186–190.

Przymusinski, T. (1988) 'On the Declarative Semantics of Deductive Databases and Logic Programs', in: *Foundations on Deductive Databases and Logic Programming*, J. Minker (ed.), Morgan Kaufmann Publishers, Palo Alto, CA, 193–216.

Przymusinski, T. (1989) 'An Algorithm to Compute Circumscription', *Artificial Intelligence J.*, **38**, 49–73.

Quillian, M. R. (1968) 'Semantic Memory', in: *Semantic. Information Processing*, M. Minsky (ed.), MIT Press, Cambridge, MA, 227–270.

Rabinov, A. (1989) 'A Generalization of Collapsible Cases of Circumscription', *Artificial Intelligence J.*, **38**, 111–117.

Rasiowa, H., Sikorski, R. (1970) *The Mathematics of Metamathematics*, Polish Scientific Publishers, Warsaw, Poland.

Reinfrank, M. (1985) 'An Introduction to Non-Monotonic Reasoning', Memo-Seki, 85-02, Fb Informatik, Universitaet Kaiserlautern, West Germany.

Reiter, R. (1978) 'On Closed-World Data Bases', in *Logic and Data Bases*, H. Gallaire, J. Minker (eds.), Plenum Press, New York, 55–76.

Reiter, R. (1980a) 'A Logic for Default Reasoning', *Artificial Intelligence J.*, **13**, 81–132.

Reiter, R. (1980b) 'Equality and Domain Closure in First-Order Data Bases', *Journal of ACM*, **27**, 235–249.

Reiter, R. (1987a) 'A Theory of Diagnosis from First Principles', *Artificial Intelligence J.*, **32**, 57–95.

Reiter, R. (1987b) 'Nonmonotonic Reasoning', *Annual Review of Computer Science*, **2**, 147–186.

Reiter, R., Criscuolo, G. (1983) 'Some Representational Issues in Default Reasoning', *Int. J. Computers and Mathematics*, **9**, 1–13.

Rescher, N. (1964) *Hypothetical Reasoning*, North-Holland, Amsterdam.

Rescher, N. (1976) *Plausible Inference*, Van Gorcum, Assen, The Netherlands.

Robinson, R. (1965) 'A Machine Oriented Logic Based on the Resolution Principle', *Journal of ACM*, **12**, 23–41.

Rogers, R. (1971) *Mathematical Logic and Formalized Theories*, North-Holland, Amsterdam.

Rumelhart, D. E., Norman, D. A. (1973) 'Active Semantic Networks as a Model of Human Memory', in: *Proc. 3rd IJCAI*, Palo Alto, CA, 470–476.

Saint-Dizier, P. (1988) 'Default Logic, Natural Language, and Generalized Quantifiers', in: *Proc. 12th Conf. on Computational Linguistics*, Budapest, Hungary, 555–560.

Sandewall, E. (1972) 'An Approach to the Frame Problem and Its Implementation', in: *Machine Intelligence 7*, B. Meltzer, D. Michie (eds.), Edinburgh University Press, Edinburgh, 195–204.

Sandewall, E. (1985) 'A Functional Approach to Non-Monotonic Logic', *Computational Intelligence*, **1**, 80–87.

Sandewall, E. (1989) 'The Semantics of Non-Monotonic Entailment Using Partial Interpretations', in: *Proc. 2nd Int. Workshop on Non-Monotonic Reasoning*, Lecture Notes in Artificial Intelligence, 346, Springer-Verlag, Berlin, 27–41.

Shastri, L., Feldman, J. A. (1985) 'Evidential Reasoning, in Semantic Networks: A Formal Theory', in: *Proc. 9th IJCAI*, Los Angeles, CA, 465–474.

Shepherdson, J. C. (1984) 'Negation as Failure: A Comparison of Clark's Completed Data Base and Reiter's Closed World Assumption', *Journal of Logic Programming*, **1**, 51–79.

Shoenfield, J. R. (1967) *Mathematical Logic*, Addison-Wesley, Reading, MA.

Shoham, Y. (1988) *Reasoning about Change: Time and Causation from the Standpoint of Artificial Inteligence*, MIT Press, Cambridge, MA.

Silver, B. (1986) *Meta-Level Inference, Studies in Computer Science and Artificial Intelligence*, North-Holland, Amsterdam.

Stalnaker, R. C. (1980) 'A Note on Non-Monotonic Modal Logic', Unpublished Note, Dept. of Philosophy, Cornell University, Ithaca, NY.

Studia Logica (1984) *Studia Logica* **XLIII, 1/2**, Special Issue on Paraconsistent Logics, G. Priest, R. Routley (eds.).

Sussman, G. J., Winograd, T., Charniak, E. (1971) 'Micro-Planner Reference Manual', Technical Report, 203A, MIT, AI Lab., Cambridge, MA.

Thomason, R. H., Horty, J. F. (1989) 'Logic for Inheritance Theory', in: *Proc. 2nd Int. Workshop on Non-Monotonic Reasoning*, Lecture Notes in Artificial Intelligence, 346, Springer-Verlag, Berlin, 220–237.

Thompson, A. (1979) 'Network Truth Maintenance for Deduction and Modelling', in: *Proc. 6th IJCAI*, Tokyo, Japan, 877–879.

Touretzky, D. S. (1982) 'Exceptions in an Inheritance Hierarchy', Unpublished Manuscript, Dept. of Computer Science, Carnegie-Mellon University, Pittsburgh, PA.

Touretzky, D. S. (1984) 'Implicit Ordering of Defaults in Inheritance Systems', in: *Proc. AAAI-84*, Austin, TX, 322–325.

Touretzky, D. S. (1986) *The Mathematics of Inheritance Systems*, Morgan Kaufmann Publishers, Palo Alto, CA.

Touretzky, D. S., Horty, J. F., Thomason, R. H. (1987) 'A Clash of Intuitions: The Current State of Nonmonotonic Multiple Inheritance Systems', in: *Proc. 10th IJCAI*, Milan, Italy, 476–482.

Turner, R. (1984) *Logics for Artificial Intelligence*, Ellis Horwood, Chichester, England.

van Dalen, D. (1980) *Logic and Structure*, Springer-Verlag, Berlin.

van Emden, M., Kowalski, R. (1976) 'The Semantics of Predicate Logic as a Programming Language', *Journal of ACM*, **23**, 733–742.

Van Gelder, A. (1988) 'Negation as Failure Using Tight Derivations for General Logic Programs', in: *Foundations on Deductive Databases and Logic Programming*, J. Minker (ed.), Morgan Kaufmann Publishers, Palo Alto, CA, 149–176.

van Marcke, K. (1986) 'A Parallel Algorithm for Consistency Maintenance in Knowledge Representation', in: *Proc. 7th ECAI*, Brighton, England, 278–290.

Vaught, R. L. (1985) *Set Theory: An Introduction*, Birkhauser Boston Inc., Boston.

Weyrauch, R. W. (1980) 'Prolegomena to a Theory of Mechanized Formal Reasoning', *Artificial Intelligence J.*, **13**, 133–170.

Weyrauch, R. W. (1982) 'An Example of FOL Using Metatheory: Formalizing Reasoning Systems and Introducing Derived Inference Rules', in: *Proc. 6th Conf. on Automated Deduction*, Lecture Notes in Computer Science, 138, Springer-Verlag, Berlin, 151-158.

Williams, C. (1984) 'ART The Advanced Reasoning Tool – Conceptual Overview', Inference Corporation.

Winograd, T. (1980) 'Extended Inference Modes in Reasoning', *Artificial Intelligence J.*, **13**, 5–26.

Woods, W. A. (1975) 'What's in a Link: Foundations for Semantic Networks', in: *Representation and Understanding: Studies in Cognitive Science*, D. G. Bobrow, A. Collins (eds.), Academic Press, New York, 35–82.

Yahya, A., Henschen, L. (1985) 'Deduction in Non-Horn Databases', *Journal of Automated Reasoning*, **1**, 141–160.

Index